CRIMINAL PROCEDURE TODAY

ISSUES AND CASES

CLIFF ROBERSON L.L.M, PH.D.

Prentice Hall, Upper Saddle River, New Jersey 07458

Library of Congress Cataloging-in-Publication Data
Roberson, Cliff
 Criminal procedure today : issues and cases / Cliff Roberson.
   p.   cm.
 Includes bibliographical references and index.
 ISBN 0-13-080520-3
 1. Criminal procedure—United States.   2. Criminal procedure—
United States Cases.   I. Title.
KF9619.3.R59 2000
347.73'05—dc21   99-14676
                                                                       CIP

$\mathcal{D}$EDICATED TO $\mathcal{L}$YNNE

Acquisitions editor: *Neil Marquardt*
Assistant editor: *Cheryl Adam*
Production editor: *Mary Jo Gregory*
Production liaison: *Barbara Marttine Cappuccio*
Director of manufacturing and production: *Bruce Johnson*
Managing editor: *Mary Carnis*
Manufacturing buyer: *Ed O'Dougherty*
Creative director: *Marianne Frasco*
Interior design: *York Production Services*
Cover design: *Miguel Ortiz*
Cover illustration: *Lois Sehlowsky*
Marketing manager: *Shannon Simonsen*
Marketing assistant: *Adam Kloza*
Formatting / page make-up: *York Production Services*
Printer/Binder: *Courier/Westford*

Printed in the United States of America

10 9 8 7 6 5 4 3 2 1

ISBN 0-13-080520-3

Prentice-Hall International (UK) Limited, *London*
Prentice-Hall of Australia Pty. Limited, *Sydney*
Prentice-Hall Canada Inc., *Toronto*
Prentice-Hall Hispanoamericana, S.A., *Mexico*
Prentice-Hall of India Private Limited, *New Delhi*
Prentice-Hall of Japan, Inc., *Tokyo*
Pearson Education Asia Pte. Ltd., *Singapore*
Editora Prentice-Hall do Brasil, Ltda., *Rio de Janeiro*

CONTENTS

CHAPTER 2   THE COURTS   28

CHAPTER 3   OVERVIEW OF THE JUSTICE PROCESS   58

CHAPTER 4   THE FOURTH AMENDMENT   89

CHAPTER 6   INTERROGATION, CONFESSIONS, AND ADMISSIONS   201

PREFACE

This book has been designed to assist professors in teaching a course in criminal procedure—my purpose being to provide a combination textbook and casebook that will be easily understood by the students, thus enabling instructors to focus on selected criminal procedure issues and topics during class time. Too often textbooks are written at a level that can only be understood by instructors, and thus valuable class time must be used to explain the meaning of the concepts. To overcome this problem, I have followed the example of Ernest Hemingway and used familiar, concrete words and short sentences whenever possible.

One decision that most professors struggle with when deciding how to teach a criminal procedure course is whether to use a casebook or a regular-type textbook—referred to as "black letter" law, "hornbook," or treatise by attorneys. There are significant advantages to using either approach. Accordingly, in this book I have used the black letter law approach and the case approach. Each chapter begins with a discussion of the law followed by significant cases in that area. Deciding which cases to include and which to exclude was no easy task. As a long-time student of criminal procedure, there are certain cases which I excluded only reluctantly. To include all relevant cases would have made the text size unmanageable. The cases included have been significantly edited and abridged. For a more in-depth coverage of any case, the reader should refer to the unedited version contained in one of the "reporters." In addition, since this is an introductory text, I have limited the case citations to a minimum.

For instructors teaching in programs that have a criminal courts course, I recommend that Chapters 1 and 2 be omitted and the course begun with Chapter 3.

Chapter 4 is designed as an overview chapter on the Fourth Amendment. The approach used in this chapter is different from that used in other criminal procedure textbooks and was developed by a former mentor, Justice Charles E. Moylan, Jr. of the Maryland Court of Special Appeals. I found this approach to be very

useful in providing students with foundational concepts of the Fourth Amendment. The following three questions are asked of readers:

1. Is the Fourth Amendment applicable? [open fields, consent, plain view, etc.—(if not evidence not excluded by reason of the Fourth)]
2. If the Fourth Amendment is applicable, has it been complied with? [if so not excluded by Fourth]
3. If the Fourth Amendment is applicable and has not been complied with, what sanctions will the court impose? [exclusionary rule and its exceptions]

Included in the instructor's manual is a scenario for a moot court case that instructors may want to use with student role players. The case will contain fact statements for each witness, a police report, and instructions for each role player. Students taking part in the moot court will gain an appreciation for the problems involved in trying or defending a criminal case.

While I am listed as the sole author of this text, it could not have been published without the assistance of many persons, including General William K. Suter, former Judge Advocate General, U.S. Army and presently Clerk, U.S. Supreme Court; Franz Jantzen of the Curator's Office, U.S. Supreme Court; Professors Robert Perez and Harvey Wallace, California State University, Fresno. A special thanks to the manuscript reviewers: Dr. Charles E. Chukwudolue, Northern Kentucky University; Dr. Rudolph De La Torre, Los Angeles Mission College; Dr. George Knox, Chicago State University and Dr. Wayne L. Wolf, South Suburban College. The text would not have been completed without the continual encouragement and persistence of my editor, Neil Marquardt. I want to thank others who have helped in the production of the work including Mary Jo Gregory and Susan Free of York Production Services.

I would be glad to hear from readers of the book about any suggestions, improvements, or errors noted.

Cliff Roberson, L.L.M., Ph.D.
Professor of Criminal Justice
Washburn University
Topeka, Kansas
e-mail: crimlawy@aol.com

1

INTRODUCTION

OVERVIEW

Definition and Sources

The study of our system of criminal law and procedure should be viewed not as a set of rules for memorization, but a cluster of ideas, principles, and values about which reasonable persons can and do disagree. The system is not fixed in stone; it is changing and flexible. Understanding our concept of justice requires a thoughtful comprehension of the historical background, social values, moral standards, and political realities that give direction to our system. The key elements are discussed in this book.

Criminal procedure refers to those laws and rules that govern the criminal justice process. Substantive criminal law defines those acts that are crimes. Criminal procedure describes those laws and rules by which crimes are investigated and prosecuted. Conduct that constitutes a crime is covered in substantive criminal law. The rules and regulations by which a crime is investigated and the accused prosecuted are covered in the study of criminal procedure. This text will focus on criminal procedure.

The sources of criminal procedure laws, rules and regulations include:

1. *Constitutions*—both state and federal.

2. *Statutes*—Both the state and federal governments have enacted statutes to regulate the administration of the criminal justice system. The primary state regulatory statute is the state code of criminal procedure which regulates procedure in state courts. The primary federal statute that governs the trial of criminal cases in

federal court is Title 18, U.S. Code. Except for constitutional issues, federal procedural rules apply only to federal criminal cases. State procedural rules apply only to state trials.

3. *Judicial opinions*—Judicial opinions construe the constitutionality, meaning, and effect of constitutional and statutory provisions. [The Capstone Cases included in each chapter provide examples of the importance of judicial opinions in criminal procedures.]

4. *Court rules*—Court rules consist of the various standard procedures used by the courts which were developed as the result of a court's inherent supervisory power over the administration of the criminal justice system. Court rules regulate the guilt-determining process in the courts in the areas not regulated by other rules. Most students of criminal procedure fail to consider the importance of court rules in the trial of criminal cases.

Examples of court rules which impact on the criminal justice system follow:

> *Los Angeles County Municipal Court Rule 532.6 provides:*
> Each judge is required to list [report] all causes [cases] under submission for more than 30 days, with an indication of the length of time each has been pending (30 through 60 days, 61 through 90 days; or over 90 days).
> *California Supreme Court Rule 22 [regarding oral arguments before the court] states:*
> Unless otherwise ordered: (1) counsel for each party shall be allowed 30 minutes for oral argument, except in a case in which a sentence of death has been imposed each party shall be allowed 45 minutes. . . .
> *U.S. District Court (EDCA) Rule 5a*
> (1) The trial of a defendant held in custody solely for purposes of trial on a federal charge shall commence within 90 days following the beginning of continuous custody.

Goals of the Justice System

Most experts on the justice system agree that the most basic goal of the criminal justice system is to protect society from crime. Beyond that, there is little agreement regarding the goals of the justice system. There are several competing philosophies on the purposes of the justice system, each with their own specific goals for the system. As Donald Newman stated: "The multiplicity of purposes, and of hopes, not only makes the system controversial, but often adds a dimension of confusion to any attempt to assess or evaluate it."[1] To help understand some of the more commonly accepted goals of the justice system, the goals are classified as orientation goals, pragmatic goals, abstract goals, or standards.

Orientation Goals Criminal justice professionals generally are oriented toward one of two opposite directions—"law and order" or "individual rights." The "law and order" orientation stresses the need to solve the crime problem. The "individual rights" orientation stresses the need to protect an individual's rights and considers this need greater than the need to punish offenders. Too great an emphasis on individual rights will restrict law enforcement and allow offenders to escape punishment. Arbitrary police practices that may occur under the "law and order" orientation may infringe on human and constitutional rights. As Chief Justice Earl Warren stated in *Miranda* v. *Arizona*:[2]

> The quality of a nation's civilization can be largely measured by the methods it uses in the enforcement of the criminal law. . . . All of these policies point to one overriding

thought: the constitutional foundation underlying the privilege is the respect a government—state or federal—must accord the dignity and integrity of its citizens. To maintain a fair state–individual balance, the government must shoulder the entire load.

Pragmatic Goals   The pragmatic goals of the justice system include:

Preventing crime. This goal includes providing potential criminals with conventional opportunities for success before they start a career of crime, building stronger social control units such as the family, providing guidance and counseling in our schools, and developing better environmental conditions in the neighborhoods that foster law-abiding behavior.

Diverting offenders. This goal refers to the efforts to take offenders out of the system and place them in non-punitive treatment programs. The purpose of this effort is to correct the offender without placing the stigma of a criminal conviction on the offender.

Deterring crime. The justice system attempts to deter crime by making potential criminals believe that the punishments received for criminal behavior outweigh any potential benefit (i.e., crime does not pay).

Controlling criminals. By this goal, the system attempts to control the behavior of known criminals by incarcerating the more serious offenders and placing the less serious ones in community correction programs.

Rehabilitating offenders. An objective of the system is to provide rehabilitation treatment to offenders in order to reduce the likelihood of future involvement in criminal behavior. The goal of rehabilitation was very popular in the 1960s. During the 1980s it has been discounted because of the popular belief that present rehabilitation programs are not effective.[3]

Abstract Goals   Abstract goals are the underlying principles upon which our justice system is based. The most common abstract goals include:

Fairness. The justice system should seek to ensure that all persons involved in the criminal justice system are treated fairly and humanely. More specifically, socio-economic status, ethnicity, etc., should not determine the type of treatment or form of punishment one receives from various criminal justice agencies.

Efficiency. The system should be organized and managed in a manner to ensure maximum utilization of personnel and resources.

Effectiveness. The goal of effectiveness is that the justice system should operate in an effective and efficient manner.

Justice. Justice is considered as the "ideal" of all government and the disposition of a criminal matter in a manner that the best interest of society is served. It is not measured solely by its application to the accused. Justice is the broad concept of reward and punishment currently accepted as proper by a society.[4] A state court judge in an early Texas case defined "justice" as follows:

> Justice is the dictate of right, according to the common consent of mankind generally, or of that portion of mankind who may be associated in one government, or who may be governed by the same principles and morals.[5]

Standards

Organizations such as the American Bar Association and the American Correctional Association have developed detailed goals to improve the justice system. These goals are called *standards*. For the most part, standards are designed to protect individual rights and promote the efficiency of the justice process. *Note*: Standards are goals, not binding rules. Selected standards on criminal justice are listed below:

AMERICAN BAR ASSOCIATION STANDARDS RELATING TO THE PROSECUTION FUNCTION

1.4 Duty to Improve the Law

It is an important function of the prosecutor to seek to reform and improve the administration of criminal justice. When inadequacies or injustices in the substantive or procedural law come to his or her attention, he or she should stimulate efforts for remedial action.

2.7 Relations with the Police

a. The prosecutor should provide legal advice to the police concerning police functions and duties in criminal matters.

b. The prosecutor should cooperate with police in providing the services of his or her staff to aid in training police in the performance of their function in accordance with the law.

NATIONAL ADVISORY COMMISSION ON CRIMINAL JUSTICE STANDARDS AND GOALS

4.11 Priority Case Scheduling

Cases should be given priority for trial where one or more of the following factors are present:

a. The defendant is in pretrial custody;

b. The defendant constitutes a significant threat of violent injury to others;

c. The defendant is a recidivist;

d. The defendant is a professional criminal;

e. The defendant is a public official.

6.5 Further Review

After a reviewing court has affirmed a trial court conviction and sentence, or after the expiration of a fair opportunity for a defendant to obtain a review with the aid of counsel, the conviction and the sentence generally should be final and not subject to further review in any state or federal court. Further review should be available only in unusual circumstances.

JUSTICE SYSTEM STRUCTURE AND PROCESS

We refer to the justice system as a "system," as if it were a system. It would be more accurate to refer to it as a non-system. The term *system* refers only to the interrelationship among all those agencies concerned with the prevention of crime in society. The systems approach to criminal justice sees a change in one part of the system affecting change in all the others. It implies that a closely knit, coordinated structure of organizations exists among the various components of the system.

The system, however, is not a close-knit, coordinated structure of organizations. The criminal justice system is actually three separate elements: police, courts, and corrections. Each operates almost independently of the other. In many cases the goal orientation of the various elements within a local jurisdiction are in conflict with each other as to the main functions of the criminal justice system. Thus the system can best be described as "fragmented" or "divided." Accordingly, the criminal justice system is a group of agencies organized around various functions that each is assigned.

EVOLUTION OF CRIMINAL PROCEDURE

Our system of criminal justice is based on English common law. The colonists brought English traditions and concepts with them when they settled our country. Included was the English concept of justice, on which our system is based. To this foundation, a bit of Spanish and French influence was added as the system was developed and changed to meet the requirements of our growing nation.[6]

LAW IN PRACTICE

FOUNDATIONAL CONCEPTS IN CRIMINAL PROCEDURE

As an introduction to the study of criminal procedure, the foundational concepts in criminal procedure below should be considered. These concepts will be explained in the text and are listed below in order to create an awareness of their existence.

- The guarantees of the Bill of Rights in the U.S. Constitution apply directly only to the federal government.

- The Due Process Clause of the Fourteenth Amendment by selective incorporation applies most of the rights contained in the Bill of Rights to the states.

- State constitutions may provide additional rights to citizens than those provided for in the U.S. Constitution but may not restrict the rights granted by the federal constitution.

- The two questions regarding the burdens of proof in criminal proceeding are: (1) Who has the burden of proving an issue? and (2) What is the magnitude of the burden? The magnitude may be (1) proof beyond a reasonable doubt, (2) clear and convincing evidence, or (3) preponderance of evidence.

- Formal charges in a criminal trial must first be formalized by either an indictment returned by a grand jury or by information prepared by a prosecutor.

- Prior to trial both the prosecutor and the defense may submit pretrial motions, and both have discovery rights imposed on them.

- Our system of criminal procedure is based on the adversarial process.

- Two famous quotes from Oliver Wendell Holmes should be noted:

  - Whatever disagreement there may be as to the scope of the phrase "due process of law," there can be no doubt that it embraces the fundamental conception of a fair trial, with opportunity to be heard. [*Frank* v. *Mangum*, 237 N.S. 309, 347 (1914)]

  - The life of the law has not been logic, it has been experience. [*The Common Law* (1881) 1.]

History of Criminal Codes

Our present criminal codes grew out of custom, tradition, and actual written codes. The first known criminal code was the Code of Hammurabi about 2100 B.C. The Code was a comprehensive series of laws covering not only crime but property rights, family law, and other civil matters. The Code of Hammurabi also contained rules protecting victims of crimes. The concept of "an eye for an eye and a tooth for a tooth" was first introduced by King Hammurabi with his *lex talionis* (punishment by retaliation). (*Note*: The above concept was based on the premise that the punishment should fit the crime.)

Development of the Trial System

Prior to the invasion by William the Conqueror and the Normans, England first used blood feuds and later a system called *compurgation* to keep law and order. Under compurgation, when an individual was accused of crime or the wrongful withholding of property, he could take an oath that he was innocent of any wrongdoing. He then called other witnesses (oath-helpers) to swear, not to the facts of the case, but that they believed the accused told the truth. If the accused gained the support of a sufficient number of "oath-helpers," he was acquitted. The system was based on the widespread fear of divine retribution for false swearing. It was from this practice that the present-day requirement for the witnesses to present their testimony under oath originated.

If the accused was unable to obtain sufficient oath-helpers, the judges had the alternative of leaving the case undecided or referring the case to a trial by ordeal. There were several forms of trial by ordeal. One test required the accused to put his hand in a kettle of boiling water. When the hand was withdrawn, it was bound with cloth for three days. At the end of three days when the cloth was removed, if the hand was unscathed, the accused was acquitted. Another ordeal required the accused to carry in his bare hands a red-hot bar of iron. If the accused was unable to carry the iron for a given distance without dropping it, he was considered guilty. Another ordeal consisted of walking barefooted across a number of heated plowshares placed side by side.

Still another popular method of trial by ordeal was to lower the accused with his hands tied behind his back into a body of cold water. If he floated, it meant that he was possessed by the devil and thus was guilty. This was based on the concept that when Satan invaded a person's body, his specific gravity was less than that of the water. If he sank, he was considered innocent. One problem with this ordeal was that often the "innocent" person drowned before he could be rescued. In most cases, the ordeals by hot irons were used for the nobility and ordeals by water for the commoners.

As the Normans gained power, they re-introduced the old feudal concept of "Trial by Duel." Under this system, in the case of a dispute a duel would be fought, and the winner of the duel became the winner of the case. Later, "Champions" could be hired by those involved to fight a duel.

Trial by jury emerged in the twelfth century to replace trial by ordeal and trial by duel. The county sheriff selected members of the jury. It was a common practice to select members who were favorable to the Crown. The sheriff also had the power to withhold food from the jury until they reached a decision. If the jurors made a "wrong decision," they could also be punished. The power to punish jury members was considered necessary to prevent the jury from siding with the accused against the Crown. The determination that a jury had made a wrong decision was based upon a retrial of the case before a jury of Knights.

In 1166, the King ordered that twelve family heads of each hundred be placed under oath and report to the King all individuals accused or known to be robbers, murderers, or thieves. This order was known as the *Assize of Clarendon*. *Assize* refered to an order of the King. Henry II provided that certain questions regarding conduct of an accused were resolved by a jury of twelve men selected from those who lived nearby. The procedure used to comply with the assize was similar to the process now used by grand juries. (*Note*: A grand jury is presently used as an investigative body that investigates and indicts persons suspected of committing criminal behavior. This also appears to be the origination for the size of a trial jury being twelve in number.)

By 1240, the use of trial juries was common. Persons accused of crime by a grand jury were given the option of banishment or trial by a jury. To discourage some persons accused of serious crime from choosing the option of banishment, many were tortured until they accepted the trial by jury alternative. The most common form of torture used was "pressing to death." The accused was first placed in solitary confinement, then stripped naked, and starved. His body was subjected to increasing weights of iron until he pleaded to the indictment and accepted a jury trial or died. Pressing to death lasted until the 1800s and was finally replaced with the automatic entry of a "not guilty" plea when the accused refused to plea.

Magna Carta

One of the greatest documents in English legal history was the *Magna Carta*, also known as the *Great Charter*. It was signed in 1215 at Runnymede by King John. The King was forced to sign the charter by the barons. The Charter greatly influenced the later drafting of our federal constitution. Under the charter, certain rights and privileges were guaranteed to "freemen." (*Note*: The term freemen did not include ordinary English citizens. King John and later kings, however, had a habit of ignoring the guarantees.)

The Magna Carta introduced the concept that people governed by a government should have a voice in establishing the government. Included is the concept that people who live under a system of law should have a voice in deciding the principles of law.

SELECTED PROVISIONS OF THE MAGNA CARTA

Article 38: No bailiff shall henceforth put any one to his law by merely suit without trustworthy witnesses presented for this purpose. [From this article evolved the right of the accused to confront the witnesses against him.]

Article 39: No freeman shall be captured or imprisoned or disseised (dispossessed of property) or outlawed or exiled or in any way destroyed, nor will we go against him or send against him, except by the lawful judgment of his peers or by the law of the land. [From this article evolved the right to a trial by jury of one's peers.]

Article 40: To no one will we sell, to no one will we deny or delay right or justice. [The right to a speedy and just trial evolved from this article.]

Adversarial System

Early English criminal procedure was based on two fundamental premises. First, the responsibility for accusing an individual of a crime rested with the victim or the victim's family. If no private accuser came forward, there was no prosecution. The second premise was the adversarial nature of criminal procedure. (Our system of justice today is still based on the adversarial concept.) The role of the judge was that of an impartial referee between two contending parties. In criminal cases, the adversaries were the accused and the private accuser. The private accuser was later replaced by a public prosecutor.

TYPES OF LAW

Law can be divided into several different classifications. The most common ones include crimes and torts, and common law and statutory law.

Crimes and Torts Distinguished

A *crime* is a wrong involving the violation of the peace and dignity of the State. In theory, it is committed against the interest of all of the people of the State.[7] Accordingly, crimes are prosecuted by the prosecutor in the name of the "State," "People," or "Commonwealth."

A *tort* is a wrong that is a violation of a private interest and thus gives rise to civil liability. The same conduct, however, may be both a crime and a tort. For example, a woman is forcibly raped by a neighbor. The criminal aspect of the conduct is a violation of the peace and dignity of the State and therefore a crime against all the people in the State. It also is a violation of the private interest of the victim, and she may file a civil suit to obtain civil damages against the offender. (*Note*: The offender may be acquitted at the criminal trial where proof of his or her guilt is required to be established beyond a reasonable doubt and yet held accountable at the civil trial where the degree of proof required to hold the offender accountable is much less.)

Common Law

Most of our criminal law principles are traceable to the common law of England. This is especially true of the underlying philosophy of criminal law. Common law crimes have not existed in most states since the adoptions of state penal codes.[8] There also are no federal common law crimes.[9] Accordingly, for conduct to be criminal under either state or federal law, there must be a statute, ordinance, or regulation denouncing it.[10] Even though common law crimes have been abolished, common law principles with regard to criminal procedure and construction of corresponding statutory crimes still apply.[11] As stated in *People* v. *Giles*,[12] with respect to criminal procedure, the common law has the force of law in absence of statutory provisions at variance with it.

> *California Civil Code 22.2 Common Law—When Rule of Decision*
> The common law of England, so far as it is not repugnant to or inconsistent with the Constitution of the United States or the Constitution or laws of this State, is the rule of decision in all courts of this State.

California Penal Code 6
No act or omission, commenced after twelve o'clock noon of the day on which this code takes effect as a law, is criminal or punishable, except as prescribed or authorized by this code, or by some statutes ... or by some ordinance, municipal, county, or township regulation. ... (*Note*: Since Penal Code 6 applies only to acts or omissions, it appears that the civil code provision also applies to criminal proceeding.)[13]

To understand the common law, we must understand the English customs and traditions that evolved into what is now known as *common law*. Medieval England was divided into tribal areas known as *shires*. The King's justice was administered by "shire-reeves," who presided over the shire courts. A sheriff is the modern counterpart of the shire-reeve. The law was based on ancient custom and varied with each tribal area.

Common law was the earliest source of criminal laws. It originated during the period of time that William the Conqueror was the King of England. At the time of the Conquest in 1066, there was no uniform criminal law in England. Individual courts were dominated by sheriffs who enforced the village rules as they saw fit. In order to reduce the arbitrary aspects of the law, William decreed that all prosecutions would be conducted in the name of the King. (*Note*: A similar practice exists today where all cases are prosecuted in the name of the People, the State, or the Commonwealth.)

The first known English code was written in the seventh century by King Aethelbert. The proclamations of the code were called *dooms*. The dooms were social class orientated. For example, theft was punishable by fines which ranged widely in magnitude according to the status of the victim. Stealing from the King was punishable by a fine equal to nine times the value of the property stolen. Theft from a person of the holy order was punishable by a fine three times the value of the property stolen. Crimes committed in the presence of the King were considered a violation of the "king's peace" and increased the punishment for the crime. In the ninth and eleventh centuries, the code was rewritten, but little new was added.

Most historians trace the common law of England to William the Conqueror who invaded England in 1066. At the time of the invasion, each county was controlled by a Sheriff (shire-reeve), who also controlled the courts in that county. Accordingly, there was no uniform English system. William took over the courts and made them royal courts, i.e., under the control of the King. He sent representatives to the many courts in England to record the decisions of the judges. William distributed selected decisions of the judges to all the judges. The judges then utilized the selected decisions in making their own decisions. As the routine of these courts became firmly established, it was possible to forecast their decisions in terms of similar cases decided by them in past cases. From this the doctrine of *stare decisis* developed.

William also complied the law of crimes that were common in most areas of the kingdom. These crimes became the Common Law Crimes of England. Later new statutory crimes were added by the King and Parliament. (*Note*: The concept of common law crimes was so ingrained in England that the traditional crimes such as burglary, larceny, and murder were not defined by statute in England until the 1960s.)

During William's time, very few people could read or write. The King, the judges, and the church authorities determined the elements and the scope of criminal offenses. In some cases they even created new crimes. As William unified England as a nation rather than isolated villages, the judges developed familiarity with the general customs, usages, and moral concepts of the people. Judicial decisions began to be based on these general customs, usages, and moral concepts.

By the 1600s, the primary criminal law of England was based on the mandatory rules of conduct laid down by the judges. These rules became the common law of England. Prior decisions were accepted as authoritative precepts and were applied to future cases. When the English settlers came to America in the 1600s, they brought with them the English common law. Except for few modifications, English common law became the common law of the colonies. During the American Revolution, there was a great deal of hostility toward the English in America. This hostility extended to the common law system. Accordingly, most of the new states enacted new statutes defining criminal acts and establishing criminal procedures. The statutes, however, basically enacted into statutory law what was formerly English common law.

As noted earlier, many aspects of our present-day criminal law system are based upon English common law. All states except Louisiana can trace their legal systems to the English common law system. In 1805, Louisiana, whose system was originally based on the French and Spanish codal law concept, officially adopted the common law of England as the basis for their system.

Statutory Law

Statutory law is law that originates with specifically designated lawmaking bodies. It is enacted by legislative bodies of government. The primary statutory laws dealing with crimes and criminal procedure are the state penal codes.

Case Law

"Case law" is the phrase used to indicate appellate court interpretations of the law. A substantial majority of "law" is case law, i.e., court opinions which interpret the meaning of constitutions and statutes. Case law also helps clarify and narrow statutory law. For example, the U.S. Constitution (Amendment XIV) provides that no state shall deprive any person of life, liberty, or property without due process of law. What constitutes "due process of law" is decided almost daily in the courts. There are hundreds of published opinions issued by federal and state appellate and supreme courts each year.

Court decisions interpret the relationship of one code provision to another, the meaning of words used in the code provision, the legislative intent in enacting the code provision, the scope and effect of the code provision, and whether or not the provision violates any constitutional restrictions.

The term *precedent* is used when a legal principle has been decided by a court. The court decision is then a precedent (guide) for similar situations. There are two basic types of precedent: mandatory and persuasive. Under mandatory precedent, when a higher appellate court renders a decision on an issue, the lower courts under the supervision of that court must follow the ruling or face reversal on appeal. For example, if the Arizona Supreme Court decides an issue, state appellate courts in Arizona must follow that precedent. Persuasive precedent indicates a court decision that is not binding on a second court but is persuasive to the second court. For example, a court in New Mexico is faced with an issue that has never been decided by a New Mexico court. There is, however, a court in Nevada that has considered the same issue. The Nevada court decision is not binding on the New Mexico court but is of some persuasive authority. Precedent is based on the principle of *stare decisis* which is discussed below.

Stare Decisis

Stare decisis is a Latin word meaning "to abide by, or adhere to, decided cases." The doctrine provides that when a court has once laid down a principle of law as applicable to a certain state of facts, it will adhere to that principle and apply it to all future cases where the facts are substantially the same.[14] *Stare decisis* is a policy founded on the theory that security and certainty require that accepted and established legal principles, under which rights may accrue, be recognized and followed.[15]

CRIMINAL LAW ADMINISTRATION

The primary state agency involved in criminal law administration in most states is the State Department of Justice or Office of Attorney General (Criminal Division). This department is usually composed of the State Attorney General and the Division of Law Enforcement. The typical goals of the department are to seek to control and eliminate organized crime in the State, to publish and distribute a compilation of the state laws relating to crimes and criminal law enforcement that are of general interest to peace officers, to operate the state's teletype and law enforcement telecommunications systems, and to promote training and professionalism of peace officers.

State Attorney General

The chief law officer of most states is the Attorney General. It is the Attorney General's duty to see that all laws of the State are uniformly and adequately enforced. The Attorney General, however, does not have direct supervision of district attorneys, sheriffs, and other law enforcement officers as may be designated by law, in all matters pertaining to the duties of their respective offices. In most states, however, the attorney general may require any of the officers to make reports concerning the investigation, detection, prosecution, and punishment of crime within their jurisdiction.

The attorney general in most states may prosecute any violations of law of which a superior or district court has jurisdiction when he or she is of the opinion that the law is not being adequately enforced in any county. Also, when directed by the Governor, the Attorney General shall assist any district attorney in the discharge of the duties of the district attorney. If a district attorney is disqualified to conduct a criminal prosecution, the Attorney General may appoint a special prosecutor.[16]

Regarding the broad authority given the Attorney General by the state constitution, one court opinion noted that the authority has been tempered by judicial construction. The court stated:

> These officials are public officers, as distinguished from mere employees, with public duties delegated and entrusted to them, as agents, the performance of which is an

exercise of a part of the governmental functions of the particular political unit for which they, as agents, are active. . . . [I]t is at once evident that 'supervision' does not contemplate control, and that sheriffs and district attorneys cannot avoid or evade the duties and responsibilities of the respective offices by permitting a substitution of judgment.[17]

District or State's Attorneys

District attorneys are elected county or judicial district officers in most states. In a few states, they are appointed. They also are officers of the state.[18] The district attorney is, in most cases, the public prosecutor. Duties of a district attorney in criminal matters normally include:

1. institution of proceeding before magistrates for the arrest of persons charged with or reasonably suspected of public offenses,
2. presents cases to the grand jury in those states that use grand juries for indictments, and
3. conducts all prosecution for public offenses.

In a few states (Florida and Rhode Island, for example), there are state attorneys who are appointed rather than elected that perform those duties normally performed by the district attorney. In a few states, they are called *county attorneys*. In other states there are both county attorneys and district attorneys, with the county attorneys involved mostly in misdemeanors cases.

CRIMINAL PROCEDURE'S CONTROVERSIES

In this section, three of the leading controversies in criminal procedure are examined. Those controversies are (1) competing models of criminal procedure, (2) the role of truth in criminal procedure, and (3) rule formulation in criminal procedure.[19]

Competing Models

The two competing models of criminal procedure are the crime control model and the due process model. Advocates of the crime control model contend that crime control is the most important goal of the criminal justice system. Included within the crime control model are the sub-goals of efficiency, uniformity, and presumption of factual guilt. According to the advocates of crime control, increasing the efficiency of the system will foster crime prevention and to be efficient, the system must be routinized.

The competing due process model stresses the importance of individual rights and the presumption of innocence. The advocates of this model contend that the role of the criminal justice system is more than just preventing crime. Its primary purpose should be to protect human rights. These advocates lack trust in informal police procedures and have a preference for formality. They believe that the best way to reduce abuses of individual rights is by the early intervention of judges and lawyers in the process. The due process advocates also are concerned with the effects of economic inequality on the judicial system.

The role of the judiciary varies according to the competing models. The crime control model sees less of a need for an active judiciary. On the other hand, due process advocates contend that the courts must take an active role to reduce the inequalities in the criminal justice system. A comparison of the decision of the Supreme Court of today with those of the Earl Warren Court of the 1960s is an excellent example of the two competing models, with the present-day court more inclined to follow the crime control model while the Warren Court tended to follow the due process model.

The Role of Truth

The rules of criminal procedure are designed to further the truth-finding process. The system does this by promoting the introduction of reliable evidence and the exclusion of unreliable evidence. Are erroneous acquittals of equal importance to erroneous convictions? Under the widely accepted view of American jurisprudence, it is far worse to convict an innocent person than to allow a guilty person to go free.

Rule Formulation

Should the courts adopt "bright-line rules" or use a case-by-case adjudication? A bright-line rule is a rule that is clear and definite. Advocates of bright-line rules contend that police officers must make instant decisions, and to do their jobs they need clear rules. Advocates of the case-by-case approach contend that we desire rules that lead to the right result as often as possible—that the world is not clear and definite; that the development of bright-line rules for all situations makes the law illogical in many situations. Both types of approaches will be noted in the cases studied in this text.

A similar concept involves whether the propriety of police officers' conduct should be judged from the subjective or objective states of mind of the officers. The subjective approach requires that the officer's conduct be motivated by constitutionally appropriate motives. The objective approach disregards the officer's motives and measures the officer's conduct based on objective standards. While the Supreme Court has adopted both subjective and objective rules, the present tendency is to use the objective approach.[20]

LEGAL RESEARCH AND METHODOLOGY

Researching legal issues and cases is different from standard literature research. Once the student has mastered the concepts and methodology, legal issues, case law, and statutes can be located quickly and efficiently.

In conducting legal research, the researcher should:

1. Research the subject systematically, going sequentially from one source (e.g., statutes, court decisions, or law reviews) to the next.

2. Check to insure that the latest available information has been consulted. For example, use only the latest copy of the penal code. Using only the latest references is essential because legal information and points of authority change frequently due to results of statutory modifications and new court decisions.

3. Be patient and thorough when researching legal questions. To many questions, the law frequently does not yield easy "yes" or "no" answers. At times, the answers will be considered as ambiguous and conflicting.

Legal Citations

Legal citations are a form of shorthand used to assist in locating legal sources. Appellate court decisions are published in case law books, more popularly known as *reporters*. The basic rules of legal citation are as follows:

1. In most citation formats, the volume or title number is presented first.
2. Following is the standardized abbreviation for the legal reference source.
3. In the case of court cases, the page number of the first page of the decision is listed last. In the case of statutory references, it is the section number of the statute.

For example, the citation 107 U.S. 468 refers to the case starting on page 468 of volume 107 of United States Reports. A citation of 18 U.S.C. 347, refers to title 18 U.S. Code, section 347.

National Reporter System

West Publishing Company's National Reporter System is the standard for researching court reports. The system includes, in bound volumes and advance sheets, decisions of all state and federal appellate courts and selected trial court opinions. Included in the bound volumes are the table of cases, table of cited statutes, criminal and appellate procedure tables, words and phrases, and a key number digest.

The Reporter system was started 1876 by two brothers doing business under the name of John B. West and Company. The brothers reported the decisions of courts in Minnesota in a series of pamphlets known as *The Syllabi*. In 1879, the name of the series was changed to *North Western Reporter*. By 1887, the venture had expanded to a total of seven regional reporters covering all the states. The seven regional reporters are still being published with only slight modifications in state coverage. The present day coverage is as follows:

Atlantic Reporter: Me., N.H., Conn., Vt., Pa., Del., Md., and N.J.

North Eastern Reporter: Mass., N.Y., Ohio, Ind., and Ill.

North Western Reporter: N.Dak., S.Dak., Nebr., Minn., Iowa, Wis., and Mich.

Pacific Reporter: Kan., Ok., N.M., Col., Wyo., Mont., Id., Utah, Ariz., Nev., Or., Wash., Ca., Alaska, and Ha.

South Eastern Reporter: Ga., S.Car., N.Car., Va., and W. Va.

South Western Reporter: Tex., Ark., Tenn., Ky., and Mo.

Southern Reporter: La., Miss., Ala., and Fla.

In addition to the regional reporters, West publishes the *Supreme Court Reporter*, which reports only decisions of the U.S. Supreme Court; The *Federal Reporter*, which reports decisions of the U.S. Courts of Appeal; and the *Federal Supplement*, which reports selected U.S. District Court decisions, decisions of federal judicial panels, and other special federal courts. The *New York Supplement*, which also reports New York state appellate cases, was started in 1887, and the *California Reporter*, which reports current decisions of the California Supreme

Court, District Courts of Appeal and Superior Court (Appellate Department) decisions, was started in 1960.

Official Reporters

As noted above, West's National Reporter System is the standard case reporter. In most cases they are not considered as the official reporter. Each high court designates a publisher as its official reporter. For example, the official reporter of the U.S. Supreme Court is the U.S. Reports (U.S.) whereas the reporter is the Supreme Court Reporter (S. Ct.). Contained in each case reported in the West reporter is the official reporter citation.

Legal Digests

Legal digests are not legal authorities but can be used as research tools. Legal digests identify and consolidate similar issues by topical arrangement. Most legal digests, using West's standard format, divide the body of law into seven main divisions that encompass thirty-two subheadings and approximately four hundred topics. West also publishes a digest for each series of case reporters. Each topic is assigned a digest "key" number. For example, Crim Law 625 is the key number for the legal issue of "exclusion from criminal trial."

The key number is the same for each digest published. Legal points from court decisions are published with a brief statement of the legal point involved and the case citation for the court decision being digested. If, for example, a point being researched is located in a digest under Crim Law 625, then reference to other digests using the same key number (Crim Law 625) will help locate other court decisions on the same or similar issues.

Shepard's Citations

Shepard's Citations, started in 1873 by Frank Shepard, are widely used to ascertain the current status of a statute or court decision. *Shepard's Citations*, more popularly known as *citators*, analyze each appellate court decision as to the history of the case, other decisions where that decision has been cited, and whether or not the rule of the case has been modified, overruled, or approved by other cases. A similar analysis is used for statutes. For a detailed explanation of how to use *Shepard's Citations*, read the first pages of any citator volume.

Legal Dictionaries and Encyclopedias

Like *Shepard's Citations* and legal digests, legal dictionaries and encyclopedias are not legal authorities but research tools. The most popular legal dictionary is *Black's Law Dictionary*.

Legal encyclopedias provide discussions on various legal points in encyclopedic form based on court decisions and statutes. They are arranged by broad legal topics and subdivided by individual areas. Most state legal encyclopedias provide detailed discussions on state legal issues. For example, the citation "17 Tex Jur 3d (Rev) 125" refers to volume 17 of Texas Jurisprudence, Third Edition (Revised), section 125. The cited section provides a detailed discussion on robbery.

Law Reviews

The major law schools publish law reviews. In general, law reviews contain scholarly articles on various aspects of law. They are not legal authority but are often cited as persuasive authorities. Law reviews are cited similarly to court cases. For example, an article in volume 50 of the *Texas Law Review* which begins on page 192 would be cited as 50 Tex. L. Rev. 192.

Standard Jury Instructions—Criminal

Standard Jury Instructions—Criminal are collections of standard jury instructions that a judge may use to instruct the jury regarding elements of crimes, defenses, and other matters relating to the trial. They also are used by non-judges as references, since the instructions contain explanations of crimes and criminal procedural matters.

CAPSTONE CASES

Do we have a "right of privacy" that is assumed in the Constitution? If the right of privacy is so important, why is the Constitution silent regarding it? The case below looks at those issues.

GRISWOLD V. CONNECTICUT
381 U.S. 479, 85 S.Ct. 1678 (1965)

Griswold, a medical doctor, provided information, instruction, and medical advice to a married couple for the purposes of preventing conception. He was prosecuted for being an accessory to a crime for this action. At the time, Connecticut had a statute that made it a misdemeanor to use any drug, medicinal article, or instrument for the purposes of preventing conception.

MR. JUSTICE DOUGLAS delivered the opinion of the Court.

. . . We do not sit as a super-legislature to determine the wisdom, need, and propriety of laws that touch economic problems, business affairs, or social conditions. This law, however, operates directly on an intimate relation of husband and wife and their physician's role in one aspect of that relation.

The association of people is not mentioned in the Constitution nor in the Bill of Rights. The right to educate a child in a school of the parents' choice—whether public or private or parochial—is also not mentioned. Nor is the right to study any particular subject or any foreign language. Yet the First Amendment has been construed to include certain of those rights.

By *Pierce* v. *Society of Sisters*, 268 U.S. 510 (1925), the right to educate one's children as one chooses is made applicable to the States by the force of the First and Fourteenth Amendments. . . .

In *NAACP* v. *Alabama*, 357 U.S. 449 (1958), we protected the "freedom to associate and privacy in one's associations," noting that the freedom of association

Justice William O. Douglas was appointed to the Supreme Court by President Franklin Roosevelt and served from 1939 to 1975. (Photograph by Harris & Ewing. Collection of the Supreme Court of the United States.)

was a peripheral First Amendment right . . . required disclosure of membership lists of a constitutionally valid association, we held, was invalid "as entailing the likelihood of a substantial restraint upon the exercise by petitioner's members of their right to freedom of association. . . ."

We deal with a right of privacy older than the Bill of Rights—older than our political parties, older than our school system. Marriage is a coming together for better or worse, hopefully enduring, and intimate to the degree of being sacred. It is an association that promotes a way of life, not causes; a harmony in living, not political faiths; a bilateral loyalty, not commercial or social projects. Yet it is an association for a noble a purpose as any involved in our prior decisions.

Reversed.

[Justice Stewart and Justice Black joined in a dissenting opinion and Justice Goldberg wrote a concurring opinion, which Chief Justice Warren and Justice Brennan joined.]

WHAT DO *YOU* THINK?

1. The court, in holding that the Connecticut statute was unconstitutional, used prior decisions to justify their conclusion that there is a constitutional right of privacy. Since the "right of privacy" is not specifically stated in the Constitution, is this an example of judge-made law?

2. Why is it necessary for the court to use precedent in their opinion?

3. Does this case hold that Congress passed a valid but unwise statute?

Can a state make it a crime for a person to be addicted to the use of narcotics? The following case looks at that issue.

ROBINSON V. CALIFORNIA
370 U.S. 660 (1962)

MR. JUSTICE STEWART delivered the opinion of the Court.

A California statute makes it a criminal offense for a person to "be addicted to the use of narcotics." This appeal draws into question the constitutionality of that provision of the state law, as construed by the California courts in the present case.

The appellant was convicted after a jury trial in the Municipal Court of Los Angeles. The evidence against him was given by two Los Angeles police officers. Officer Brown testified that he had occasion to examine the appellant's arms one evening on a street in Los Angeles some four months before the trial. The officer testified that at that time he had observed "scar tissue and discoloration on the inside" of the appellant's right arm, and "what appeared to be numerous needle marks and a scab which was approximately three inches below the crook of the elbow" on the appellant's left arm. The officer also testified that the appellant under questioning had admitted to the occasional use of narcotics.

Officer Lindquist testified that he had examined the appellant the following morning in the Central Jail in Los Angeles. The officer stated that at that time he had observed discolorations and scabs on the appellant's arms, and he identified photographs which had been taken of the appellant's arms shortly after his arrest the night before. Based upon more than ten years of experience as a member of the Narcotic Division of the Los Angeles Police Department, the witness gave his opinion that "these marks and the discoloration were the result of the injection of hypodermic needles into the tissue into the vein that was not sterile." He stated that the scabs were several days old at the time of his examination and that the appellant was neither under the influence of narcotics nor suffering withdrawal symptoms at the time he saw him. This witness also testified that the appellant had admitted using narcotics in the past.

The appellant testified on his own behalf, denying the alleged conversations with the police officers and denying that he had ever used narcotics or been addicted to their use. He explained the marks on his arms as resulting from an allergic condition contracted during his military service. His testimony was corroborated by two witnesses.

The trial judge instructed the jury that the statute made it a misdemeanor for a person "either to use narcotics, or to be addicted to the use of narcotics. . . . That portion of the statute referring to the 'use' of narcotics is based upon the 'act' of using. That portion of the statute referring to 'addicted to the use' of narcotics is based upon a condition or status. They are not identical. . . . To be addicted to the use of narcotics is said to be a status or condition and not an act. It is a continuing offense and differs from most other offenses in the fact that [it] is chronic rather than acute; that it continues after it is complete and subjects the offender to arrest at any time before he reforms. The existence of such a chronic condition may be ascertained from a single examination, if the characteristic reactions of that condition be found present."

The judge further instructed the jury that the appellant could be convicted under a general verdict if the jury agreed either that he was of the "status" or had committed the "act" denounced by the statute. "All that the People must show is either that the defendant did use a narcotic in Los Angeles County, or that while in the City of Los Angeles he was addicted to the use of narcotics. . . ."

Under these instructions the jury returned a verdict finding the appellant "guilty of the offense charged.". . . Although expressing some doubt as to the constitutionality of "the crime of being a narcotic addict," the reviewing court in an unreported opinion affirmed the judgment of conviction, citing two of its own previous unreported decisions which had upheld the constitutionality of the statute. We noted probable jurisdiction of this appeal because it squarely presents the issue whether the statute as construed by the California courts in this case is repugnant to the Fourteenth Amendment of the Constitution.

The broad power of a State to regulate the narcotic drugs traffic within its borders is not here in issue. More than forty years ago, in *Whipple* v. *Martinson*, 256 U.S. 41, this Court explicitly recognized the validity of that power: "There can be no question of the authority of the State in the exercise of its police power to regulate the administration, sale, prescription and use of dangerous and habit-forming drugs. . . . The right to exercise this power is so manifest in the interest of the public health and welfare, that it is unnecessary to enter upon a discussion of it beyond saying that it is too firmly established to be successfully called in question." 256 U.S., at 45.

Such regulation, it can be assumed, could take a variety of valid forms. A State might impose criminal sanctions, for example, against the unauthorized manufacture, prescription, sale, purchase, or possession of narcotics within its borders. In the interest of discouraging the violation of such laws, or in the interest of the general health or welfare of its inhabitants, a State might establish a program of compulsory treatment for those addicted to narcotics. Such a program of treatment might require periods of involuntary confinement. And penal sanctions might be imposed for failure to comply with established compulsory treatment procedures. Cf. *Jacobson* v. *Massachusetts*, 197 U.S. 11. Or a State might choose to attack the evils of narcotics traffic on broader fronts also—through public health education, for example, or by efforts to ameliorate the economic and social conditions under which those evils might be thought to flourish. In short, the range of valid choice which a State might make in this area is undoubtedly a wide one, and the wisdom of any particular choice within the allowable spectrum is not for us to decide. Upon that premise we turn to the California law in issue here.

It would be possible to construe the statute under which the appellant was convicted as one which is operative only upon proof of the actual use of narcotics within the State's jurisdiction. But the California courts have not so construed this law. Although there was evidence in the present case that the appellant had used narcotics in Los Angeles, the jury were instructed that they could convict him even if they disbelieved that evidence. The appellant could be convicted, they were told, if they found simply that the appellant's "status" or "chronic condition" was that of being "addicted to the use of narcotics." And it is impossible to know from the jury's verdict that the defendant was not convicted upon precisely such a finding.

The instructions of the trial court, implicitly approved on appeal, amounted to "a ruling on a question of state law that is as binding on us as though the precise words had been written" into the statute. *Terminiello* v. *Chicago*, 337 U.S. 1, 4. "We can only take the statute as the state courts read it." *Id.*, at 6. Indeed, in their

brief in this Court counsel for the State have emphasized that it is "the proof of addiction by circumstantial evidence . . . by the tell-tale track of needle marks and scabs over the veins of his arms, that remains the gist of the section."

This statute, therefore, is not one which punishes a person for the use of narcotics, for their purchase, sale or possession, or for antisocial or disorderly behavior resulting from their administration. It is not a law which even purports to provide or require medical treatment. Rather, we deal with a statute which makes the "status" of narcotic addiction a criminal offense, for which the offender may be prosecuted "at any time before he reforms." California has said that a person can be continuously guilty of this offense, whether or not he has ever used or possessed any narcotics within the State, and whether or not he has been guilty of any antisocial behavior there.

It is unlikely that any State at this moment in history would attempt to make it a criminal offense for a person to be mentally ill, or a leper, or to be afflicted with a venereal disease. A State might determine that the general health and welfare require that the victims of these and other human afflictions be dealt with by compulsory treatment, involving quarantine, confinement, or sequestration. But, in the light of contemporary human knowledge, a law which made a criminal offense of such a disease would doubtless be universally thought to be an infliction of cruel and unusual punishment in violation of the Eighth and Fourteenth Amendments.

We cannot but consider the statute before us as of the same category. In this Court counsel for the State recognized that narcotic addiction is an illness. Indeed, it is apparently an illness which may be contracted innocently or involuntarily. We hold that a state law which imprisons a person thus afflicted as a criminal, even though he has never touched any narcotic drug within the State or been guilty of any irregular behavior there, inflicts a cruel and unusual punishment in violation of the Fourteenth Amendment. To be sure, imprisonment for ninety days is not, in the abstract, a punishment which is either cruel or unusual. But the question cannot be considered in the abstract. Even one day in prison would be a cruel and unusual punishment for the "crime" of having a common cold.

We are not unmindful that the vicious evils of the narcotics traffic have occasioned the grave concern of government. There are, as we have said, countless fronts on which those evils may be legitimately attacked. We deal in this case only with an individual provision of a particularized local law as it has so far been interpreted by the California courts.

Reversed.

MR. JUSTICE FRANKFURTER took no part in the consideration or decision of this case.

MR. JUSTICE DOUGLAS, concurring.

While I join the Court's opinion, I wish to make more explicit the reasons why I think it is "cruel and unusual" punishment in the sense of the Eighth Amendment to treat as a criminal a person who is a drug addict.

In Sixteenth Century England one prescription for insanity was to beat the subject "until he had regained his reason." Deutsch, *The Mentally Ill in America* (1937), p. 13. In America "the violently insane went to the whipping post and into prison dungeons or, as sometimes happened, were burned at the stake or hanged"; and "the pauper insane often roamed the countryside as wild men and from time to time were pilloried, whipped, and jailed." *Action for Mental Health* (1961), p. 26, as cited by Justice Douglas.

As stated by Dr. Isaac Ray many years ago:

Nothing can more strongly illustrate the popular ignorance respecting insanity than the proposition, equally objectionable in its humanity and its logic, that the insane should be punished for criminal acts, in order to deter other insane persons from doing the same thing. *Treatise on the Medical Jurisprudence of Insanity* (5th ed. 1871), p. 56.

Today we have our differences over the legal definition of insanity. But however insanity is defined, it is in end effect treated as a disease. While afflicted people may be confined either for treatment or for the protection of society, they are not branded as criminals.

Yet terror and punishment linger on as means of dealing with some diseases. As recently stated:

... the idea of basing treatment for disease on purgatorial acts and ordeals is an ancient one in medicine. It may trace back to the Old Testament belief that disease of any kind, whether mental or physical, represented punishment for sin; and thus relief could take the form of a final heroic act of atonement. This superstition appears to have given support to fallacious medical rationales for such procedures as purging, bleeding, induced vomiting, and blistering, as well as an entire chamber of horrors constituting the early treatment of mental illness. The latter included a wide assortment of shock techniques, such as the "water cures" (dousing, ducking, and near-drowning), spinning in a chair, centrifugal swinging, and an early form of electric shock. All, it would appear, were planned as means of driving from the body some evil spirit or toxic vapor. *Action for Mental Health* (1961), pp. 27–28.

That approach continues as respects drug addicts. Drug addiction is more prevalent in this country than in any other nation of the western world. 1 S. Rep. No. 1440, 84th Cong., 2d Sess., p. 2. It is sometimes referred to as "a contagious disease." *Id.*, at p. 3. But those living in a world of black and white put the addict in the category of those who could, if they would, forsake their evil ways.

The first step toward addiction may be as innocent as a boy's puff on a cigarette in an alleyway. It may come from medical prescriptions. Addiction may even be present at birth. Earl Ubell recently wrote:

In Bellevue Hospital's nurseries, Dr. Saul Krugman, head of pediatrics, has been discovering babies minutes old who are heroin addicts.

More than 100 such infants have turned up in the last two years, and they show all the signs of drug withdrawal: irritability, jitters, loss of appetite, vomiting, diarrhea, sometimes convulsions and death.

"Of course, they get the drug while in the womb from their mothers who are addicts," Dr. Krugman said yesterday when the situation came to light. "We control the symptoms with Thorazine, a tranquilizing drug."

"You should see some of these children. They have a high-pitched cry. They appear hungry but they won't eat when offered food. They move around so much in the crib that their noses and toes become red and excoriated."

Dr. Lewis Thomas, professor of medicine at New York University–Bellevue, brought up the problem of the babies Monday night at a symposium on narcotics addiction sponsored by the New York County Medical Society. He saw in the way the babies respond to treatment a clue to the low rate of cure of addiction.

"Unlike the adult addict who gets over his symptoms of withdrawal in a matter of days, in most cases," Dr. Thomas explained later, "the infant has to be treated for weeks and months. The baby continues to show physical signs of the action of the drugs."

Perhaps in adults the drugs continue to have physical effects for a much longer time after withdrawal than we have been accustomed to recognize. That would mean that these people have a physical need for the drug for a long period, and this may be the clue to recidivism much more than the social or psychological pressures we've been talking about. *N.Y. Herald Tribune*, Apr. 25, 1962, p. 25, cols. 3–4.

The addict is under compulsions not capable of management without outside help. As stated by the Council on Mental Health:

> Physical dependence is defined as the development of an altered physiological state which is brought about by the repeated administration of the drug and which necessitates continued administration of the drug to prevent the appearance of the characteristic illness which is termed an abstinence syndrome. When an addict says that he has a habit, he means that he is physically dependent on a drug. When he says that one drug is habit-forming and another is not, he means that the first drug is one on which physical dependence can be developed and that the second is a drug on which physical dependence cannot be developed. Physical dependence is a real physiological disturbance. It is associated with the development of hyperexcitability in reflexes mediated through multi-neurone arcs. It can be induced in animals, it has been shown to occur in the paralyzed hind limbs of addicted chronic spinal dogs, and also has been produced in dogs whose cerebral cortex has been removed." Report on Narcotic Addiction, 165 A. M. A. J. 1707, 1713.

[Justice Harlan's concurring opinion and Justices Clark's and White's dissenting opinions are omitted.]

WHAT DO YOU THINK?

1. Do you agree with the decision of the court? Why?
2. Should it be a crime to be addicted to drugs or alcohol?

A California statute required that an individual provide "credible and reliable" identification when requested by an officer who has reasonable suspicion of criminal activity. Is such a statute susceptible to arbitrary enforcement? Does it give fair and adequate notice of the type of conduct prohibited? These issues are discussed in the next case.

KOLENDER V. LAWSON
461 U.S. 352 (1983)

O'CONNOR, J., delivered the opinion of the Court, in which BURGER, C. J., and BRENNAN, MARSHALL, BLACKMUN, POWELL, and STEVENS, JJ., joined. BRENNAN, J., filed a concurring opinion, WHITE, J., filed a dissenting opinion, in which REHNQUIST, J., joined. [Concurring and dissenting opinions are omitted.]

JUSTICE O'CONNOR delivered the opinion of the Court.

This appeal presents a facial challenge to a criminal statute that requires persons who loiter or wander on the streets to provide a "credible and reliable" identification and to account for their presence when requested by a peace officer under circumstances that would justify a stop under the standards of *Terry* v. *Ohio*, 392 U.S. 1 (1968). We conclude that the statute as it has been construed is unconstitutionally vague within the meaning of the Due Process Clause of the Fourteenth Amendment by failing to clarify what is contemplated by the requirement that a

suspect provide a "credible and reliable" identification. Accordingly, we affirm the judgment of the court below.

I

Appellee Edward Lawson was detained or arrested on approximately 15 occasions between March 1975 and January 1977 pursuant to Cal. Penal Code Ann. 647(e) (West 1970). Lawson was prosecuted only twice, and was convicted once. The second charge was dismissed.

Lawson then brought a civil action in the District Court for the Southern District of California seeking a declaratory judgment that 647(e) is unconstitutional, a mandatory injunction to restrain enforcement of the statute, and compensatory and punitive damages against the various officers who detained him. The District Court found that 647(e) was overbroad because "a person who is stopped on less than probable cause cannot be punished for failing to identify himself." . . . The District Court enjoined enforcement of the statute, but held that Lawson could not recover damages because the officers involved acted in the good-faith belief that each detention or arrest was lawful.

Appellant H. A. Porazzo, Deputy Chief Commander of the California Highway Patrol, appealed the District Court decision to the Court of Appeals for the Ninth Circuit. . . . The Court of Appeals affirmed the District Court determination as to the unconstitutionality of 647(e). . . . The appellate court determined that the statute was unconstitutional in that it violates the Fourth Amendment's proscription against unreasonable searches and seizures, it contains a vague enforcement standard that is susceptible to arbitrary enforcement, and it fails to give fair and adequate notice of the type of conduct prohibited. . . .

The officers appealed to this Court from that portion of the judgment of the Court of Appeals which declared 647(e) unconstitutional and which enjoined its enforcement. . . .

II

In the courts below, Lawson mounted an attack on the facial validity of 647(e). "In evaluating a facial challenge to a state law, a federal court must, of course, consider any limiting construction that a state court or enforcement agency has proffered." . . . As construed by the California Court of Appeal, 647(e) requires that an individual provide "credible and reliable" identification when requested by a police officer who has reasonable suspicion of criminal activity sufficient to justify a Terry detention. *People* v. *Solomon*, 33 Cal. App. 3d 429, 108 Cal. Rptr. 867 (1973). "Credible and reliable" identification is defined by the State Court of Appeal as identification "carrying reasonable assurance that the identification is authentic and providing means for later getting in touch with the person who has identified himself." . . . In addition, a suspect may be required to "account for his presence . . . to the extent that it assists in producing credible and reliable identification. . . ." . . . Under the terms of the statute, failure of the individual to provide "credible and reliable" identification permits the arrest.

III

Our Constitution is designed to maximize individual freedoms within a framework of ordered liberty. Statutory limitations on those freedoms are examined for substantive authority and content as well as for definiteness or certainty of expression. . .

As generally stated, the void-for-vagueness doctrine requires that a penal statute define the criminal offense with sufficient definiteness that ordinary people can understand what conduct is prohibited and in a manner that does not encourage arbitrary and discriminatory enforcement.... *Papachristou* v. *City of Jacksonville*, 405 U.S. 156 (1972); *Connally* v. *General Construction Co.*, 269 U.S. 385 (1926). Although the doctrine focuses both on actual notice to citizens and arbitrary enforcement, we have recognized recently that the more important aspect of the vagueness doctrine "is not actual notice, but the other principal element of the doctrine—the requirement that a legislature establish minimal guidelines to govern law enforcement." ... Where the legislature fails to provide such minimal guidelines, a criminal statute may permit "a standardless sweep [that] allows policemen, prosecutors, and juries to pursue their personal predilections."

Section 647(e), as presently drafted and as construed by the state courts, contains no standard for determining what a suspect has to do in order to satisfy the requirement to provide a "credible and reliable" identification. As such, the statute vests virtually complete discretion in the hands of the police to determine whether the suspect has satisfied the statute and must be permitted to go on his way in the absence of probable cause to arrest. An individual, whom police may think is suspicious but do not have probable cause to believe has committed a crime, is entitled to continue to walk the public streets "only at the whim of any police officer" who happens to stop that individual under 647(e).... Our concern here is based upon the "potential for arbitrarily suppressing First Amendment liberties...." In addition, 647(e) implicates consideration of the constitutional right to freedom of movement. See *Kent* v. *Dulles*, 357 U.S. 116, 126 (1958)....

Section 647(e) is not simply a "stop-and-identify" statute. Rather, the statute requires that the individual provide a "credible and reliable" identification that carries a "reasonable assurance" of its authenticity, and that provides "means for later getting in touch with the person who has identified himself." ... In addition, the suspect may also have to account for his presence "to the extent it assists in producing credible and reliable identification."

At oral argument, the appellants confirmed that a suspect violates 647(e) unless "the officer [is] satisfied that the identification is reliable." In giving examples of how suspects would satisfy the requirement, appellants explained that a jogger, who was not carrying identification, could, depending on the particular officer, be required to answer a series of questions concerning the route that he followed to arrive at the place where the officers detained him, or could satisfy the identification requirement simply by reciting his name and address.

It is clear that the full discretion accorded to the police to determine whether the suspect has provided a "credible and reliable" identification necessarily "entrust lawmaking 'to the moment-to-moment judgment of the policeman on his beat.' " ... Section 647(e) "furnishes a convenient tool for 'harsh and discriminatory enforcement by local prosecuting officials, against particular groups deemed to merit their displeasure,' " *Papachristou*, 405 U.S., at 170 ... And "confers on police a virtually unrestrained power to arrest and charge persons with a violation." *Lewis* v. *City of New Orleans*, 415 U.S. 130, 135 (1974) (POWELL, J., concurring in result). In providing that a detention under 647(e) may occur only where there is the level of suspicion sufficient to justify a Terry stop, the State ensures the existence of "neutral limitations on the conduct of individual officers." *Brown* v. *Texas*, 443 Page 361 U.S., at 51. Although the initial detention is justified, the State fails to establish standards by which the officers may determine whether the suspect has complied with the subsequent identification requirement.

Appellants stress the need for strengthened law enforcement tools to combat the epidemic of crime that plagues our Nation. The concern of our citizens with curbing criminal activity is certainly a matter requiring the attention of all branches of government. As weighty as this concern is, however, it cannot justify legislation that would otherwise fail to meet constitutional standards for definiteness and clarity. See *Lanzetta* v. *New Jersey*, 306 U.S. 451 (1939). Section 647(e), as presently construed, requires that "suspicious" persons satisfy some undefined identification requirement, or face criminal punishment. Although due process does not require "impossible standards" of clarity . . . this is not a case where further precision in the statutory language is either impossible or impractical.

IV

We conclude 647(e) is unconstitutionally vague on its face because it encourages arbitrary enforcement by failing to describe with sufficient particularity what a suspect must do in order to satisfy the statute. Accordingly, the judgment of the Court of Appeals is affirmed, and the case is remanded for further proceedings consistent with this opinion.

WHAT DO YOU THINK?

1. Lawson has been nicknamed as the "California walkman" because he walks in his spare time. He is a large imposing person who wears his hair in dreadlocks. Do you agree with the majority?
2. Lawson had a habit of walking in the "upper class" neighborhoods. Does he, a person of relatively modest means, have a right to walk in those neighborhoods?
3. Would the police have bothered him had he walked on the "other side of the track?"

SUMMARY

- Criminal procedure refers to the laws and rules that govern the criminal justice process. Substantive criminal law defines those acts that are crimes. Criminal procedure describes the laws and rules by which crimes are investigated and prosecuted.

- What conduct constitutes a crime is covered in substantive criminal law. The rules and regulations by which a crime is investigated and the accused prosecuted are covered in the study of criminal procedure. The sources of criminal procedure include constitutions, statutes, court rules, and judicial opinions.

- Both the state and federal governments have enacted statutes to regulate the administration of the criminal justice system. The primary federal statute that governs the trial of criminal cases in federal court is Title 18, U.S. Code. Except for constitutional issues, federal procedural rules apply only to federal trials, and state procedural rules apply only to state trials.

- Judicial opinions construe the constitutionality, meaning, and effect of constitutional and statutory provisions. Court rules consist of the various standard procedures used by the courts.

- Most experts on the justice system agree that the most basic goal of the criminal justice system should be to protect society from crime. Beyond that, there is little agreement regarding the goals of the justice system. Criminal justice professionals generally are oriented toward one of two opposite directions—"law and order" or "individual rights."

- The pragmatic goals of the justice system include preventing and deterring crime, diverting offenders, and controlling criminals. Abstract goals are the underlying principles upon which our justice system is based. The most common abstract goals include fairness, efficiency, effectiveness, and justice.

- We refer to the justice system as a "system," as if it were a system. It would be more accurate to refer to it as a non-system.

- Our system of criminal justice is based on English common law. Our present criminal codes grew out of custom, tradition, and actual written codes. The first known criminal code was the Code of Hammurabi, dated about 2100 B.C. One of the greatest documents in English legal history was the Magna Carta, also known as the great charter.

- Our system of justice today is based on the adversarial concept. The role of the judge was that of an impartial referee between two contending parties.

- Law can be divided into several different classifications. The most common ones include: (1) crimes and torts, and (2) common law and statutory law. Common law crimes have not existed in most states since the adoption of state penal codes. The primary statutory laws dealing with crimes and criminal procedure are the state penal codes. The primary state agency involved in criminal law administration in most states is the State Department of Justice or Office of Attorney General (Criminal Division).

- The district attorney is, in most cases, the public prosecutor.

- "Case law" is the phrase used to indicate appellate court interpretations of the law. A substantial majority of "law" is case law (i.e., court opinions which interpret the meaning of constitutions and statutes). Precedent is used when a legal principle has been decided by a court. Precedent is based on the principle of *stare decisis*.

- Common law comprises the body of principles and rules of action which are derived from usages and customs of immemorial antiquity. Most of our criminal law principles are traceable to the common law of England. Most historians trace the common law of England to William the Conqueror who invaded England in 1066.

- Researching legal issues and cases is different from standard literature research. Legal citations are a form of shorthand to assist in locating the legal sources.

- Attorney General opinions are considered as "quasi-judicial" in character.

DISCUSSION QUESTIONS

1. Is a state statute that defines the crime of criminal homicide a procedural or substantive law?
2. Explain the role of the defense counsel in an adversarial system. How does his or her role differ from that of the prosecuting attorney?
3. Explain the difference between common law and statutory law.

4. Explain the difference between precedent and *stare decisis*.
5. Only selected parts of *Griswold* opinion are set in the Capstone Cases. In what reporter would you find the entire opinion? On what page does the decision commence?
6. Why is case law considered by many as necessary in our system of jurisprudence?
7. How does the *Griswold* v. *Connecticut* case illustrate that state laws may not regulate certain aspects of our life?

ENDNOTES

1. Donald Newman, *Introduction to Criminal Justice* (New York: Lippincott, 1975:22).
2. 384 U.S. 436 (1966).
3. Joseph J. Senna and Larry Siegel, *Introduction to Criminal Justice*, 4th ed. (St. Paul: West, 1988:132).
4. John Jay Douglass, *The Prosecutor in America* (Houston: National College of District Attorneys, 1976).
5. *Duncan* v. *Magette*, 25 Tex. 245, 253.
6. Herbert A. Johnson, *History of Criminal Justice* (Cincinnati: Anderson, 1988).
7. *People* v. *Morrison*, 54 CA 469, 202 P 348 (1921).
8. Cal. Jur. 3d. (Rev), Part 1, page 27.
9. *United States* v. *Eaton*, 144 U.S. 677 (1892).
10. *People* v. *Talbott*, 65 CA2d 654; 151 P2d 317(1944).
11. *Lorenson* v. *Superior Court of Los Angeles County*, 35 C2d 49, 216 P2d 859 (1950).
12. (1945) 70 CA2d Supp 872, 161 P2d 623.
13. See 17 Cal Jur 3d (Rev) Part 1, page 57.
14. *Moore* v. *City of Albany*, 98 N.Y. 396.
15. *Otter Tail Power Co.* v. *Von Bank*, 72 N.D. 497.
16. *Sloane* v. *Hammond*, 81 CA 590; 254 P. 648 (1927).
17. *People* v. *Brophy*, 49 CA2d 15, 28; 120 P2d 946 (1942).
18. 80 ALR2d 1067.
19. See Joshua Dressler, *Understanding Criminal Procedure* (Boston: Matthew Bender, 1997).
20. See *Whren* v. *United States*, 135 L. Ed 2d 89 (1996).

2

THE COURTS

The principles of jurisdiction, venue, and the structure of American criminal court systems are discussed in this chapter. Other important topics discussed include the effect of court decisions and the writ of habeas corpus. As discussed later in this chapter, there are differences in the various state systems. Accordingly, there are instances where the terminology may differ from state to state.

Jurisdiction refers to the power of a court to try a case and the power the court has over the person. *Venue* refers to the geographic location of the court. Accordingly, before discussing the various court systems, the concepts of jurisdiction and venue are explored.

CHOOSING THE CORRECT COURT

Jurisdiction

Jurisdiction is the authority by which courts and judicial officers take cognizance of and decide cases. There are two types of jurisdiction: (1) over the subject matter and (2) over the person. A court must have jurisdiction over both the subject matter and the person before the court may decide the case. For example, a family court in Utah normally would not have jurisdiction over a criminal matter (subject matter jurisdiction).

Jurisdiction over the person in criminal cases normally is obtained by forcing the defendant to appear before the court. For example, Larry robs a bank in Texas. The state district court or criminal district court would have subject matter

Activity	Time
Start of Term	First Monday in October
Oral Argument Cycle	October–April: Mondays, Tuesdays, Wednesdays in seven two-week sessions
Recess Cycle	October–April: two or more consecutive weeks after two weeks of oral argument: Christmas, Easter holidays
Conferences	Wednesday afternoon following Monday oral arguments (discussion of four Monday cases)
	Friday following Tuesday, Wednesday oral arguments (discussion of eight Tuesday–Wednesday cases; *certiorari* petitions)
	Friday before two-week oral argument period
Majority Opinion Assignment	Following oral arguments/conferences
Opinion Announcement	Throughout term with bulk coming in spring/summer
Summer Recess	Late June/early July until first Monday in October
Initial Conference	Late September (resolve old business, consider *certiorari* petitions from the summer)

jurisdiction. The district court obtains jurisdiction over Larry (over the person) when he is brought before the court. If after the robbery Larry moves to South America, the district court would still have jurisdiction over the subject matter. The court, however, would lack jurisdiction over Larry until he is caught and taken before the court to answer the charges against him.

Jurisdiction over the subject matter cannot be conferred by consent or the failure to object. For example, Robert commits murder in Texas in violation of Texas penal statutes. He cannot be tried for that crime in an Iowa court because the Iowa court has no subject matter jurisdiction over a Texas crime. If Robert pleads guilty in the Iowa court and is convicted, the conviction will be set aside. Despite his guilty plea, he cannot waive the court's lack of jurisdiction. Accordingly, the Iowa proceedings would be null and void.

Venue

Venue refers to the geographical location of the trial; the judicial district or county in which the trial should be conducted. A change of venue from a court of one county to the same court in another county does not affect the latter court's jurisdiction over the subject matter of the case.

Unlike jurisdiction, the parties to a trial may consent to venue. For example, by pleading guilty to the sale of a controlled substance without objecting as to the proper venue, the accused admits or consents to the venue of the court. As a general rule, proper venue is in the county where the crime was committed. Since venue represents a question of fact, it must be alleged in the pleadings. This is normally accomplished by alleging that the offense occurred in *X* county or at *X* location.

U.S. CONSTITUTION, SIXTH AMENDMENT

In all criminal prosecutions, the accused shall enjoy the right to a speedy and public trial, by an impartial jury of the State and district wherein the crime shall have been committed. . . .

The defendant has a right to be tried in the county (in state prosecutions) or the district (in federal cases) where the crime occurred. The accused may, however, request a change of venue. Appropriate grounds must be established before a judge will approve a request for change of venue. For example, Rule 21, Federal Rules of Criminal Procedure provides that the defendant must establish: (1) that there exists in the place where the prosecution is pending so great a prejudice against the defendant that he cannot obtain a fair and impartial trial there; or (2) another location is more convenient for the parties and witnesses than the intended place of trial, and the interest of justice requires a transfer of location. The prosecution has no right to a change of venue.

In many states rather than granting a change of venue, the judge may try the case in the county in which the crime was committed, with the jury being selected in a different county and transported to the location of the trial.[1]

Venue may take place in more than one county. For example, John kidnaps his daughter in violation of a court child custody order. John takes custody of his daughter in Fairfax County, Virginia, and takes her to Prince William County, Virginia. In this situation, the crime occurs in both counties. The prosecutors may therefore elect which county to bring charges against John. If John is unhappy with the selection of the prosecutors, his only recourse is to file a motion for a change of venue.[2]

While venue is a fact that must be proven by the prosecutor in criminal cases, in the federal courts and many state courts the burden of proving that the crime occurred in the district or county is not invariably required to meet the "beyond a reasonable doubt" standard of proof. Generally, the courts take the view that the prosecution need only show "by a preponderance of evidence" that the trial is in the same district or county in which the crime occurred.[3] Venue can be established by circumstantial evidence.

Territorial Principle

In addition to the constitutional requirements regarding venue, states also are guided by the territorial principle. This principle is based on the concept that state constitutions and statutes provide that persons are liable to prosecution for crimes committed in whole or in part within the boundaries of the prosecuting state.

In order for an individual to be tried by a state court for a criminal offense, the defendant must be charged with a violation of that state's criminal code. Often the same conduct constitutes crimes in more than one state. For example, the defendant standing in the state of South Carolina shot and killed the victim who was standing in Georgia. He was prosecuted and convicted in a Georgia criminal court. The Georgia Supreme Court held that a crime is committed where the criminal act takes effect.[4] Since the act causing the death was committed in South Carolina, the defendant's conduct also constituted a violation of the South Carolina criminal statutes. South Carolina also could try him for murder.

Federal or State Issue

Federal courts have jurisdiction on federal issues and state courts have jurisdiction on state issues. The general rules on whether the offense will be tried in federal or state courts are as follows:

If the act is a violation of federal law, it will be tried in federal court. For example, the criminal violation of an individual's civil rights under federal law will normally be tried in federal court.

If the act is a violation of state law, it will be tried in a state court. For example, the murder of a person in New York would be a violation of the New York Criminal Code and thus the trial should be in a New York state court.

If the act violates both state and federal law, the case may be tried in both. For example, if a police officer uses excessive force in the arrest of a suspect, the officer may be charged with assault and battery in state court as a violation of that state's criminal code. The officer also may be tried in federal court if the officer's conduct also violates the federal civil rights of the suspect.

Federal courts may not decide issues originally tried in state courts unless there is a federal question involved, e.g., the state criminal court conviction infringed a right protected by the U.S. Constitution or a federal statute. For example, the police officer discussed above is tried in state court for assault and battery. During the trial, a statement made by the officer is used in evidence against her. After conviction, the officer files a writ in federal court alleging that the statement was taken in violation of her federal constitutional rights under the Fourth and Fourteenth Amendments to the U.S. Constitution. Whether or not the statement was taken in violation of her federal constitutional rights is a federal question and may be decided by the federal courts.

State courts are required to protect an individual's federal rights and those rights guaranteed by the state constitution or state statutes. Accordingly, while state courts are responsible for protecting a person's federal civil rights, the court normally has no jurisdiction to try and punish a person for violations of U.S. criminal laws. If exclusive federal jurisdiction exists or the offense is only a federal crime, then a state court has no jurisdiction.

The State Supreme Court or Court of Criminal Appeals is the highest court of appeal for state criminal cases that do not involve federal issues. The decision of a state supreme court that a particular practice violates the state constitution is not subject to review by the U.S. Supreme Court.[5]

In most states, death penalty cases are reviewed automatically by the State Supreme Court. The State Supreme Court generally has original jurisdiction (along with Court of Appeals and superior courts) in habeas corpus proceedings. In other criminal cases, the State Supreme Court accepts only those cases decided by the Court of Appeals. Except in death penalty cases, an accused generally has no absolute right to have the State Supreme Court decide his or her appeal of a criminal conviction.

The State Supreme Court may in most states, before a decision is entered, order a case transferred from a court of appeal to the State Supreme Court. The Supreme Court generally also may review any decision of a court of appeals.

State supreme courts generally do not have the jurisdiction to render advisory opinions.[6] Accordingly, there must be an actual case or controversy pending in the court before an opinion will be issued. For example, New Jersey enacts a new statute making it unconstitutional for a citizen to move from one county in the state to another county in the same state. In most instances, the New Jersey Supreme Court would not issue an opinion as to the validity of the statute until there is an actual case involving the statute before the court.

Court of appeals hear and decide appeals from superior or district courts and have original jurisdiction in habeas corpus proceedings. In most cases, an accused has a right to have his or her appeal of a criminal conviction in superior or district court decided by the court of appeals.

Superior or district courts are considered as courts of general jurisdiction and have original jurisdiction in all cases except those given by statutes to other trial courts. Superior or district courts have jurisdiction to try misdemeanors not otherwise provided for and felonies (criminal offenses punishable by death or by imprisonment in the state prison). Generally, a superior or district court has no jurisdiction over a case charging only a misdemeanor in a county with a county, municipal, or justice court. Superior or district courts in most cases have appellate jurisdiction in criminal cases that are tried in county, municipal, and justice courts.

Municipal, county, and justice courts usually have jurisdiction in criminal matters as follows:

1. to hear and decide cases involving misdemeanors and infractions;
2. to conduct the follow procedures in felony cases:
   a. arraignment,
   b. bail setting and reduction,
   c. accept pleas, and
   d. preliminary hearings; and
3. to issue search and arrest warrants.

THE DUAL COURT SYSTEM

There are two basic criminal court systems in the United States—federal and state. The term *dual federalism* often is used to describe the concept of two complete court systems. Over 95 percent of the criminal cases, however, are tried in state courts. There are some counties whose state courts prosecute more criminal cases each year than are prosecuted annually in the entire federal system. Los Angeles County, California, Harris County, Texas, and Cook County, Illinois, are three of those counties.

THE FEDERAL SYSTEM

U.S. Supreme Court (USSC)

The judicial power of the United States shall be invested in one Supreme Court. . . . (U.S. Constitution, Art. III, sec. 1)

The U.S. Supreme Court is the highest court in the federal system. The court is composed of one chief justice and eight associate justices. Justices are appointed by the president with the "advice and consent" of the U.S. Senate. Justices may be removed only by impeachment. The court always decides cases as one body. Except in unusual situations, the court acts as an appellate court and decides cases based on trial briefs, records of trial from the trial courts, and arguments of counsel. The Supreme Court also acts as a supervising authority over other federal courts.

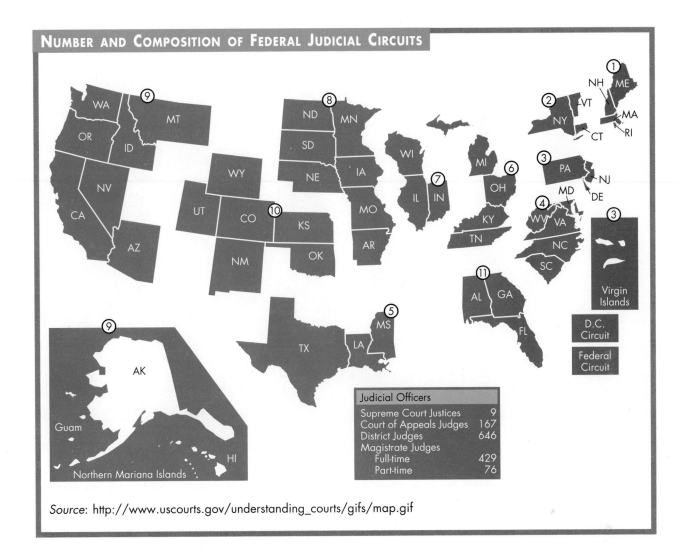

NUMBER AND COMPOSITION OF FEDERAL JUDICIAL CIRCUITS

Judicial Officers	
Supreme Court Justices	9
Court of Appeals Judges	167
District Judges	646
Magistrate Judges	
Full-time	429
Part-time	76

Source: http://www.uscourts.gov/understanding_courts/gifs/map.gif

U.S. Court of Appeals (USCA)

The United States is divided geographically into twelve judicial circuits (including the District of Columbia which has its own circuit and is the only one not numerically designated). A U.S. Court of Appeals is located in each judicial circuit. Like Supreme Court justices, Court of Appeals justices are appointed by the president with the "advice and consent" of the Senate. The Court of Appeals differs in the number of justices appointed to each. For example, the U.S. Court of Appeals for the 9th Circuit has 23 judges. The Court of Appeals normally hears cases in panels of three or five judges. In rare cases, a Court of Appeals will decide a case *en banc*, i.e., as a whole court.

U.S. District Courts (USDC)

The basic trial court in the federal system is the U.S. District Court (USDC). There is at least one district court in each state. Most states have more than one district court. In those states, the state is divided geographically into federal judicial districts.

The Supreme Court of the United States Official Photograph (1994–   ). Seated, front row: Associate Justices Antonin Scalia and John Paul Stevens, Chief Justice William H. Rehnquist, and Associate Justices Sandra Day O'Connor and Anthony Kennedy. Standing, back row: Associate Justices Ruth Bader Ginsburg, David Souter, Clarence Thomas, and Stephen Breyer. (Photograph by Richard Strauss, Smithsonian Institution, Courtesy by the Supreme Court of the United States.)

For example, Iowa is divided into two federal districts, northern and southern. In Texas there are four federal judicial districts:

1. U.S. District Court for the Southern District of Texas,
2. U.S. District Court for the Eastern District of Texas,
3. U.S. District Court for the Western District of Texas, and
4. U.S. District Court for the Northern District of Texas.

Federal district court judges are appointed by the president with "advice and consent" of the Senate. District judges are appointed for life. In most judicial districts, there is more than one judge sitting as the district court. For example, the U.S. District Court for the Southern District of New York (New York city) has over 100 judges, each sitting as the USDC for the Southern District.

In special cases (rarely) the USDC can sit and decide a case as a "three-judge" district court. The vast majority of cases are, however, presided over by a single judge. In all criminal cases heard in the USDC, the accused has a right to a jury trial.

U.S. Magistrates

U.S. magistrates are part of the federal judicial system but are not considered as separate courts. The federal magistrates are required to be attorneys and are appointed by the presiding judge of the judicial district for a specific term. Magistrates try minor offenses, perform pretrial matters, and perform other similar duties. They are considered as judicial officers and therefore can issue search and arrest warrants.

STATE COURT SYSTEMS

The judicial power of the State is vested in the Supreme Court, court of appeals, superior courts, municipal courts, and justice courts. All are courts of record except municipal and justice courts.

(California Constitution, Article VI, section 1)

Courts of Last Resort

In most states, the state supreme court is the court of last resort for the state. In Oklahoma and Texas, however, the state supreme court does not handle criminal cases. In Oklahoma and Texas, there are separate appellate criminal courts, e.g., the Texas Court of Criminal Appeals. The number of justices on the state high court for criminal appeals varies. In most cases, there are either seven or nine justices.

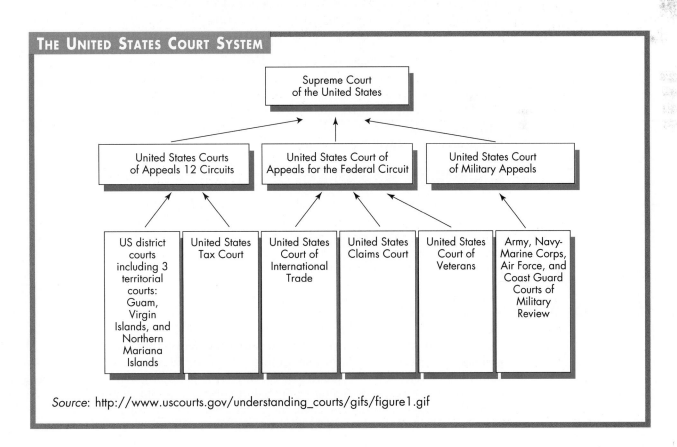

THE UNITED STATES COURT SYSTEM

Supreme Court of the United States

United States Courts of Appeals 12 Circuits

United States Court of Appeals for the Federal Circuit

United States Court of Military Appeals

US district courts including 3 territorial courts: Guam, Virgin Islands, and Northern Mariana Islands

United States Tax Court

United States Court of International Trade

United States Claims Court

United States Court of Veterans

Army, Navy-Marine Corps, Air Force, and Coast Guard Courts of Military Review

Source: http://www.uscourts.gov/understanding_courts/gifs/figure1.gif

The state constitutions establish the appointment procedure for state supreme court or court of criminal appeals judges. Most are elected. For example, in many states the justices of the Supreme Court are elected at large (statewide) for terms of four to twelve years. Most governors have the authority to appoint justices when vacancies occur. In cases where a justice is appointed by the governor, generally the justice stands for confirmation or election at the next general election.

Intermediate Courts of Appeals

Most state legislatures have divided their states into appellate districts, each containing a court of appeals with one or more divisions. Each division normally has a presiding justice and at least two associate justices. Justices are elected or appointed. Many of the appointed justices are subject to voter confirmation after a specified period of time. Court of appeals are appellate courts and do not try cases. Their decisions are based on record of trial in the trial court, appellate briefs submitted by the parties, and oral argument (in any) before the appellate court. A few states, like Nebraska, are not divided into appellate divisions. In those states, the court of appeals operates statewide.

Courts of General Jurisdiction

Normally, each county or judicial district has at least court of general jurisdiction. In most states it is a superior or district court consisting of one or more judges. The more populated counties may have several superior or district courts. The county clerk is ex-officio clerk of the superior or district court. Superior or district court judges normally serve four- or six-year terms. In most states they are elected.

Courts of Limited Jurisdiction

In most states, each county is divided into courts of limited jurisdiction generally called *municipal court districts* and/or *justice court districts* as provided by statutes. Usually if the judicial district has more than the specified number of residents, it will have at least one municipal court. If the district has less than the specified number of residents, it will have a justice court.

Subordinate Judicial Officers

The state legislatures are permitted by state constitutions to provide for the appointment of officers such as commissioners and referees to perform subordinate judicial duties. Commissioners of municipal or justice courts usually may adjudicate infractions. For example, in many counties a traffic court commissioner is appointed to adjudicate traffic infractions.

EFFECT OF JUDICIAL DECISIONS

Most state constitutions provide that no judgment shall be set aside, or new trial granted, in any cause, on the ground of misdirection of the jury, or of the improper admission or rejection of evidence, or for any error as to any matter of pleading, or for any error as to any matter of procedure, unless, after an examination of the entire cause, including the evidence, the court shall be of the opinion that the error complained of has resulted in a miscarriage of justice.[7]

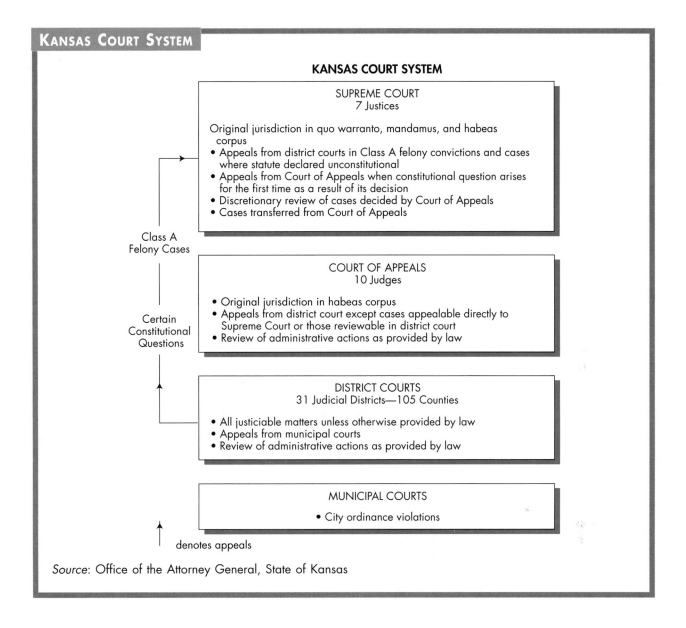

KANSAS COURT SYSTEM

SUPREME COURT
7 Justices

Original jurisdiction in quo warranto, mandamus, and habeas
corpus
• Appeals from district courts in Class A felony convictions and cases
  where statute declared unconstitutional
• Appeals from Court of Appeals when constitutional question arises
  for the first time as a result of its decision
• Discretionary review of cases decided by Court of Appeals
• Cases transferred from Court of Appeals

Class A
Felony Cases

COURT OF APPEALS
10 Judges

• Original jurisdiction in habeas corpus
• Appeals from district court except cases appealable directly to
  Supreme Court or those reviewable in district court
• Review of administrative actions as provided by law

Certain
Constitutional
Questions

DISTRICT COURTS
31 Judicial Districts—105 Counties

• All justiciable matters unless otherwise provided by law
• Appeals from municipal courts
• Review of administrative actions as provided by law

MUNICIPAL COURTS

• City ordinance violations

↑ denotes appeals

Source: Office of the Attorney General, State of Kansas

In our system of justice, an accused is not guaranteed a perfect trial, only one
that is substantially correct. A miscarriage of justice occurs only if, based on the
entire record, the appellate court concludes that it is probable that a result more
favorable to the defendant would have been reached in the absence of the error.[8]
Errors of trial, however, that deprive a defendant of the opportunity to present his
or her version of the case are ordinarily reversible, since there is no method to evaluate whether or not a missing defense resulted in a miscarriage of justice.[9]

Appeals

The accused may normally appeal a court's decision in the following situations:

1. a final conviction,
2. a sentence,

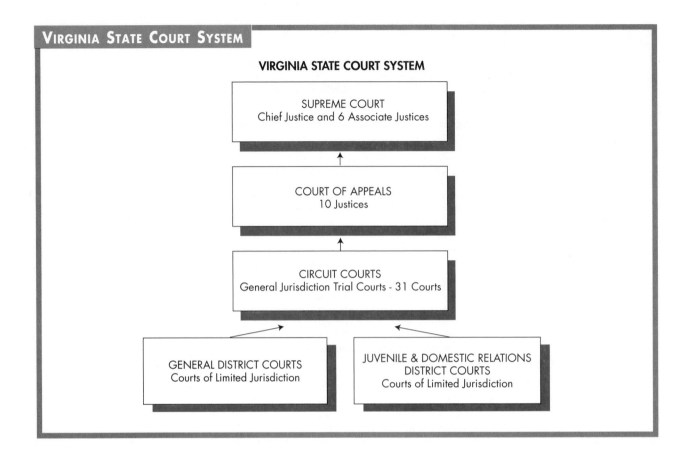

VIRGINIA STATE COURT SYSTEM

SUPREME COURT
Chief Justice and 6 Associate Justices

COURT OF APPEALS
10 Justices

CIRCUIT COURTS
General Jurisdiction Trial Courts - 31 Courts

GENERAL DISTRICT COURTS
Courts of Limited Jurisdiction

JUVENILE & DOMESTIC RELATIONS
DISTRICT COURTS
Courts of Limited Jurisdiction

3. an order which commits the defendant for insanity or for controlled substance addiction, and

4. an order granting or denying probation.

The state (People) may not appeal an acquittal. Generally, the prosecution may appeal the rulings listed below:

1. an order dismissing the case before the defendant has been placed in jeopardy,

2. a judgment for the defendant upon the sustaining of a demurrer (objection to pleadings),

3. an order granting a new trial,

4. an order arresting judgment, and

5. any order made after judgment affecting the substantial rights of the people.

When an appellate court reverses a conviction of a lower court, the case is returned to the original court for a determination by the trial court as to whether or not the case will be retried or dismissed. Exceptions to this general rule occur when the appellate court rules as a "matter of law" that there was insufficient evidence to sustain the conviction, or the appellate court rules that the original court lacked jurisdiction to try the case.

In determining whether a state court of appeals used the state constitution or the federal constitution in deciding an issue involving procedural rights, the Supreme Court presumes that the state court decided the case on federal constitutional grounds and hence that the Court can review the state court's decision. If there is no clear statement and the Supreme Court holds that the state court gave the defendant too much protection, the Supreme Court will remand the case to the state appellate court. Thus the state court may have the last word on remanded cases. (*Note*: The states may give a defendant additional rights not provided by the federal constitution but cannot restrict the rights afforded to a defendant by the U.S. Constitution.[10])

WRIT OF HABEAS CORPUS

Constitution of the United States
Article I, Section 9
The Privilege of the Writ of Habeas Corpus shall not be suspended, unless when in Cases of Rebellion or Invasion the public safety may require it.

The writ of habeas corpus is literally a request for the court to order the warden or jailor to produce the prisoner and justify why he or she is being detained in prison or other confinement. The writ is normally used by prisoners to attack their prison sentences. Many legal scholars have called this writ the most important human right in the U.S. Constitution. In 1769, Samuel Johnson wrote about the greatness of the British form of government, stating: "The Habeas Corpus is the single advantage our government has over other countries."

Scholars have traced the origins of the writ of habeas corpus as a protection against illegal imprisonment back to at least the New Testament time when Festus the Roman sought justice for Paul's imprisonment in Palestine. Festus is reported to have stated: "For it seemeth to me unreasonable to send a prisoner, and not withal to signify the crimes against him."

The writ of habeas corpus was adopted in England by the Habeas Corpus Act of 1679 as a weapon against tyranny. That act passed by the House of Lords provided: "No man may be accused, arrested, or detained except in cases fixed by the law. . . ."

THE FOLKLORE OF HABEAS CORPUS

At the time that the Habeas Corpus Act of 1679 was being debated in the English House of Lords, the act received strong support from an exceedingly portly member of the house. When the lords lineup to be counted, the parliamentary monitor (person who records the votes), as folklore has it, jokingly counted the portly lord's vote as ten votes. The monitor allowed the vote to stand when no one noticed his joke. The act passed by two votes.

The first federal habeas corpus act was passed by the United States in 1789. That act stated that judges "shall have power to grant writs of habeas corpus for the purpose of an inquiry into the cause of commitment." All fifty states have enacted similar provisions in either the state constitution or by statutes.

The writ must be filed in a court with jurisdiction over the person holding the prisoner or detainee. For example, if a prison sentence is given by a federal court, the writ may only be filed in a federal court, since the prisoner would be held in a federal prison or under the direction of a federal official. If the conviction is in a state court, the individual may appeal to a state court or to a federal court (if a violation of a federally protected right is concerned). There is no limit to the number of writs that a prisoner may file as long as each pertains to a different subject or issue. For example, a prisoner may appeal to a state court of appeals contending that his or her state court conviction was in violation of the state's constitutional protections against unreasonable searches. He or she also can file in federal court a writ contending that the state court conviction was in violation of the U.S. Constitution's protections against unreasonable searches.

If a prisoner or detainee submits a writ to a federal district court contending that his or her state court conviction was in violation of the rights guaranteed by the federal constitution and the federal district court denies his or her writ, then he or she may appeal the denial of the writ to a federal court of appeals. Many decisions of the U.S. Supreme Court regarding state convictions reach the Supreme Court via the writ. The U.S. Supreme Court in *Stone* v. *Powell*[11] attempted to limit federal habeas corpus petitions of state court convictions if the accused had a full and fair review in state court. This limitation has had only limited effect on the number of writs filed.

A writ is started by the prisoner (petitioner) filing a petition for habeas corpus with the appropriate court, naming the warden or head of the penal institution as the defendant. If the court orders a hearing after reviewing the petition, the defendant (warden) may be called to provide evidence in resistance to the petition. Habeas corpus also may be used in limited non-criminal situations and where the accused is in custody prior to trial.

The courts have used many grounds for granting habeas corpus relief. Some of the more popular grounds are listed below:

- The denial of counsel at various stages of trial proceedings.
- The failure of the state to disclose evidence favorable to the defendant.
- Prejudicial pretrial publicity prevented the defendant from obtaining a fair trial.
- Insanity of defendant at time that he entered a guilty plea.
- The use of evidence seized in violation of the defendant's constitutional rights.
- Questions regarding the use of confessions or admission by the defendant.

Most writs involving state cases are filed in state courts. The federal courts sit to ensure that individuals are not imprisoned in violation of their federal constitutional rights.[12] As a general rule, a federal court will not grant the writ in cases originally tried in state courts unless it is established that (1) state remedies have been exhausted, and (2) the prisoner or detainee makes a claim that his or her state trial or appeal involved a denial of federal constitutional rights.[13] The U.S. Supreme Court held in the *Rose* v. *Lundy* case that a petition containing both exhausted and unexhausted claims must be dismissed. ("Exhausted" refers to the fact that the petitioner has no further state remedies to redress a specific claim.) The Court reasoned that since there were claims that had not been exhausted, the petitioner had not exhausted all his state remedies.

CAPSTONE CASES

The case of Ex Parte Merryman *discusses the suspension of the Writ of Habeas Corpus. The writ is normally issued to determine if a person held in custody is being unlawfully detained or imprisoned. As noted earlier, it has been termed the* great writ *because its purpose is to obtain the immediate release of someone being unlawfully detained. The Constitution places limits on when the writ may be suspended. This case provides a look at how the Supreme Court can interfere with presidential actions.*

EX PARTE MERRYMAN
(U.S. Circuit Court, 1861; 17 Fed. Cases 145)

On May 25, 1861, Union troops entered the home of petitioner John Merryman, located outside of Baltimore, Maryland. The petitioner was a prominent local citizen and a state legislator. He also was noted for his strong Confederate sympathies. He was taken into custody by the military and detained at Fort McHenry. His attorney filed a writ of habeas corpus with the U.S. Circuit Court (then the name of the federal trial court). The presiding judge Roger Taney (also a Supreme Court justice who "rode circuit") issued the writ ordering the Commanding General of Fort McHenry to appear and justify the detention. The general did not appear; instead he sent a letter explaining that the petitioner was guilty of treason and that the President had authorized the general to suspend the writ of habeas corpus.

Chief Justice Taney delivered the opinion of the Court.

As the case comes before me . . . I understand that the President not only claims the right to suspend the writ of habeas corpus himself, at his discretion, but to delegate that discretionary power to a military officer. . . . Congress is, of necessity, the [only] judge of whether the public safety does or does not require it [suspension of writ]; and their judgment is conclusive. . . . The introduction of these words [Article I, Section 9] is a standing admonition to the legislative body of the danger of suspending it, and of the extreme caution they should exercise, before they give the government of the United States such power over the liberty of a citizen.

WHAT DO *YOU* THINK?

1. Article I of the U.S. Constitution provides, *inter alia*, that "the privilege of the Writ of Habeas Corpus shall not be suspended unless when in Cases of Rebellion or Invasion the public Safety may require it." How important to our justice system is the writ of habeas corpus?

2. In August 1861, Congress gave President Lincoln retrospective approval to suspend the writ of habeas corpus. Were Lincoln's actions in delegating this authority now legal?

[*Note*: A grand jury indicted Merryman for conspiracy to commit treason. He was released on bail. He was never tried. For more background on this case, see Carl Swisher, *The Taney Period, 1836–1864* (New York, Macmillan, 1974).]

Should a prisoner be allowed to delay his execution by the late filing of a writ of habeas corpus? The following case discusses that issue. Presently, the writ is used in many cases to attack state criminal convictions. Note: *The Federal Civil Rights of Institutional Persons Act of 1980 requires that state prisoners exhaust all state remedies before going to the federal courts on a civil rights issue. The 1996 Anti-Terrorism and Effective Death Penalty Act has placed time limits on the filing of habeas corpus petitions.[14] In most cases, prisoners now have only one year from the time their state convictions are final to file their writs.*

LONCHAR V. THOMAS
U.S. Supreme Court
517 U.S. 314 (1996)

Lonchar was sentenced to death in 1987 for capital murder. He refused to pursue post-conviction and habeas corpus relief after his state conviction became final. In addition, he opposed efforts by his family to file writs on his behalf. He was scheduled to be executed on June 30, 1995. On that day, June 30, 1995, he filed his first federal habeas corpus petition. In that petition he raised 22 claims regarding the legality of his conviction. Lonchar stated that the only reason that he was filing the petition was to delay his execution, with hope that the state would change its execution method to lethal injection so he could donate his organs.

A federal district judge granted a stay of execution and rejected the state's argument that the petition should be dismissed because of Lonchar's "inequitable conduct" in waiting nearly six years and until the last minute to file the petition. The district judge concluded that habeas rules, not some generalized equitable authority to dismiss, governed the case.

The next day, the state obtained a ruling from the Court of Appeals, 11th Circuit to vacate the stay (canceling the judge's stay). The appellate court held that the equitable doctrines required dismissal of the petition. The dismissal of the stay was appealed to the U.S. Supreme Court.

The U.S. Supreme Court ruled in favor of the petitioner (Lonchar) and directed the lower court to hold a hearing on his petition. The Court in an opinion written by Justice Breyer said that the history of the "Great Writ of habeas corpus" reveals the gradual evolution of more formal judicial, statutory, or rules-based doctrines of law. Justice Breyer concluded that arguments against departing from settled rules are particularly strong when a dismissal of a first petition is at issue and that "a dismissal of writ denies the petitioner the protections of the Great Writ." In addition, Justice Breyer stated that a long delay does not generally constitute an abuse

of the system. Justices Rehnquist, Kennedy, Scalia, and Thomas wrote a concurring opinion in which they agreed with the holding but not the rationale contained in the majority opinion.

What Do You Think?

1. Does it appear that the Supreme Court contends that the first federal habeas petition is very important and that the court should look beyond the mere facts of delay in deciding whether to hold a hearing on the petition?
2. Does the decision in this case mean that a defendant facing the death penalty would get an automatic stay of execution by waiting to the last day before filing his or her first petition with the federal courts?

Should a defendant be allowed to submit multiple writs to attack his conviction? The following two cases look at this issue.

IN RE ANTONIO CORDERO, JR.
208 Cal. 3d. 993 (Cal., 1988)

Mr. Justice Mosk delivered the opinion of the Court.

Petitioner Antonio Cordero, Jr. was convicted of murder in the first degree (Penal Code, Section 187) with the use of a firearm. . . . He was sentenced to a term of 25 years to life for the murder. Petitioner now seeks habeas corpus on allegations of ineffective assistance of counsel. We appointed the Honorable Harry T. Shafer, Judge of the Los Angeles Superior Court, retired, as referee to receive evidence and make findings of fact and conclusions of law. After conducting an evidentiary hearing, Judge Shafer concluded that the petitioner's trial counsel had performed deficiently in several respects . . . and that the petitioner received ineffective assistance of counsel. Accordingly, we reverse the judgment of the Court of Appeals with directions to grant the petition for habeas corpus.

Facts of the Case: At approximately 2 A.M. on April 17, 1982, petitioner was pumping gas into his car at a service station . . . in the City of Torrance. Petitioner's younger brother, Joe, and two of his friends, Vincent and Ronald, were inside a store on the premises. A truck drove into the station and parked at the pumps parallel to those where the petitioner stood. . . . Petitioner approached the truck (driven by Marceal Barajas) and asked for directions to Hollywood. An exchange of insults resulted. Marceal got out of the truck and approached the petitioner. The petitioner reached into the trunk of his car, lifted a handgun from a leather case and shot Marceal once in the chest at point-blank range. Marceal died shortly thereafter.

The day after the incident, the petitioner denied possessing a handgun and shooting the victim. He claimed that at the time of the shooting, he was 75 feet away. He also stated that at the time of the shooting, he was "high." At the trial, the People called 11 witnesses, 2 of whom testified that they saw the petitioner kill Marceal. Two others placed him at the scene of the crime and testified that he had argued with the deceased.

The public defender appointed to defend the petitioner made no opening statement and introduced no evidence to support a defense theory or to impeach the prosecution's case. The defense counsel also did not object to the admission of the statements made by the accused on the day after the shooting, and did not probe the differences between accounts of various eyewitnesses for the prosecution.

In January, 1985, the petitioner submitted a petition for writ of habeas corpus to the Court of Appeals. This writ was denied. . . . He submitted a second writ which was also denied by the Court of Appeals. . . . On February 20, 1986, we granted review of the Court of Appeals' denial of the second petition for habeas corpus. . . .

To the extent that we have sustained the referee's findings and upheld his conclusions, we adopt them as our own. The judgment of the Court of appeals is reversed with directions to grant the petition for habeas corpus, vacate the judgment of conviction, remand the petition to the superior court for filing. . . .

WHAT DO *YOU* THINK?

1. Note that the accused appealed his case and the conviction was upheld, at which time he submitted two writs or petitions for habeas corpus. Should an accused have the right for multiple attacks on his conviction or should he be limited to one appeal?

2. Does it make any difference that the grounds for his second petition was that he was denied effective assistance of counsel?

IN RE MCDONALD
489 U.S. 180 (1989)

The petitioner McDonald had filed 73 separate writs with the court since his conviction in 1972. The issue presented in present petition, by way of a habeas petition, had been raised unsuccessfully on four prior occasions. [*Note:* In each petition, he had filed in *forma pauperis* (without the payment of fees because of poverty).]

Opinion of the Court was issued *per curiam* (opinion written as a group action with no lead writer). The Court held that the petitioner has abused the writ process once too often and directed the clerk of the court not to accept any further petitions unless the petitioner pays the required fees (i.e., the Court will not accept any more writs filed in *forma pauperis*). The Court then indicated that other avenues of relief would be eliminated if he "similarly abused that privilege." The Court noted that the Court's resources are limited and a part of the Court's responsibility is to see that resources are allocated in a way that promotes the interests of justice, and that the continual processing of the petitioner's frivolous requests for writs do not promote that end.

[Justices Brennan, in a dissenting opinion joined by Justices Marshall, Blackmun, and Stevens, argued that the Court had no authority to prospectively refuse the petitions (writs) of a particular litigant.]

WHAT DO *YOU* THINK?

1. By refusing to accept writs from the petitioner, isn't the Court suspending the writ of habeas corpus in his case? Is this constitutional?

2. Does this mean that the petitioner may file as many writs as he desires as long as he pays the necessary fee?

What measures can be used to prevent the abuse of the right to submit a writ of habeas corpus? (In the following case, the petitioner had submitted 22 petitions attacking his conviction within a three year period.)

WRENN V. BENSON
490 U.S. 89 (1989)

PER CURIAM.

On March 27, 1989, we denied pro se petitioner Curtis Wrenn's request to proceed in *forma pauperis* (without paying court costs) under this Court's Rule 46.1 in filing petitions for certiorari in *Wrenn v. Benson* and *Wrenn v. Ohio Dept. of Mental Health*, 489 U.S. 1095. Since October Term 1986, petitioner has filed 22 petitions for certiorari with the Court. We denied him leave to proceed in *forma pauperis* with respect to 19 of those petitions, and he paid the docketing fee required by this Court's Rule 45(a) on one occasion. He also filed one petition for rehearing.

Our decision to deny a petitioner leave to proceed in *forma pauperis* is based on our review of the information contained in the supporting affidavit of indigency. In petitioner's case, a review of the affidavits he has filed with his last nine petitions for *certiorari* indicates that his financial condition has remained substantially unchanged. The Court denied him leave to proceed in *forma pauperis* with respect to each petition. Petitioner has nonetheless continued to file for leave to proceed in *forma pauperis.*

In *In re McDonald*, 489 U.S. 180, 184 (1989), we said: "Every paper filed with the Clerk of this Court, no matter how repetitious or frivolous, requires some portion of the institution's limited resources. A part of the Court's responsibility is to see that these resources are allocated in a way that promotes the interests of justice." We do not think that justice is served if the Court continues to process petitioner's requests to proceed in *forma pauperis* when his financial condition has not changed from that reflected in a previous filing in which he was denied leave to proceed in *forma pauperis.*

We direct the Clerk of the Court not to accept any further filings from petitioner in which he seeks leave to proceed in *forma pauperis* under this Court's Rule 46.1, unless the affidavit submitted with the filing indicates that petitioner's financial condition has substantially changed from that reflected in the affidavits submitted by him in *Wrenn v. Benson* and *Wrenn v. Ohio Dept. of Mental Health*, 489 U.S. 1095 (1989).

It is so ordered.

JUSTICE BRENNAN, with whom JUSTICE MARSHALL joins, dissenting.

I dissent from this order for the reasons stated in *In re McDonald*, 489 U.S. 180, 185 (BRENNAN, J., dissenting), and in *Brown v. Herald Co.*, 464 U.S. 928 (1983) (BRENNAN, J., dissenting).

JUSTICE STEVENS, dissenting.

Because I believe the preparation and enforcement of orders of this kind consume more of the Court's valuable time than is consumed by the routine denial of frivolous motions and petitions, see *In re McDonald*, 489 U.S. 180, 185 (1989) (BRENNAN, J., dissenting); *Brown v. Herald Co.*, 464 U.S. 928 (1983) (BRENNAN, J., dissenting); *id.*, at 931 (STEVENS, J., dissenting), I respectfully dissent.

WHAT DO *YOU* THINK?

1. Is this an effective method of reducing abuses to the system by inmates?

2. Does this mean that a rich defendant may continue to file writs while his or her indigent counterpart may not? The Prison Litigation Reform Act of 1995 (Pub. L. No. 104–134, 110 Stat. 1321, 1366–77) has attempted to address this problem.

Does the defendant have a right to a fair and impartial trial in a misdemeanor case? The following case discusses that issue.

GROPPI V. WISCONSIN
400 U.S. 505 (1971)

MR. JUSTICE STEWART delivered the opinion of the Court.

On August 31, 1967, during a period of civil disturbances in Milwaukee, Wisconsin, the appellant, a Roman Catholic priest, was arrested in that city on a charge of resisting arrest. Under Wisconsin law that offense is a misdemeanor, punishable by a fine of not more than $500 or imprisonment in the county jail for not more than one year, or both. After a series of continuances, the appellant was brought to trial before a jury in a Milwaukee County court on February 8, 1968. The first morning of the trial was occupied with qualifying the jurors, during the course of which the appellant exhausted all of his peremptory challenges. The trial then proceeded, and at its conclusion the jury convicted the appellant as charged.

Prior to the trial, counsel for the appellant filed a motion for a change of venue from Milwaukee County "to a county where community prejudice against this defendant does not exist and where an impartial jury trial can be had." The motion asked the court to take judicial notice of "the massive coverage by all news media in this community of the activities of this defendant," or, in the alternative, that "the defendant be permitted to offer proof of the nature and extent thereof, its effect upon this community and on the right of defendant to an impartial jury trial." The trial judge denied the motion, making clear that his ruling was based exclusively on his view that Wisconsin law did not permit a change of venue in misdemeanor cases.

On appeal, the Supreme Court of Wisconsin affirmed the conviction. 41 Wis. 2d 312, 164 N. W. 2d 266. It held that the trial judge had been correct in his understanding that a Wisconsin statute foreclosed the possibility of a change of venue in a misdemeanor prosecution. It further held that this state law was constitutionally valid, pointing out that "it would be extremely unusual for a community as a whole to prejudge the guilt of any person charged with a misdemeanor." 41 Wis.

Justice Potter Stewart was appointed to the Supreme Court by President Eisenhower and served from 1959 to 1985. (Photograph by Ken Rarich. Collection of the Supreme Court of the United States.)

2d, at 317, 164 N. W. 2d, at 268. The court also noted that a defendant in a Wisconsin misdemeanor prosecution has a right to ask for continuances and to challenge prospective jurors on *voir dire*, and if "these measures are still not sufficient to provide an impartial jury, the verdict can be set aside after trial based on the denial of a fair and impartial trial.". . .

This appeal followed, and we noted probable jurisdiction. 398 U.S. 957. As the case reaches us we must, of course, accept the construction that the Supreme Court of Wisconsin has put upon the state statute. . . . The question before us, therefore, goes to the constitutionality of a state law that categorically prevents a change of venue for a criminal jury trial, regardless of the extent of local prejudice against the defendant, on the sole ground that the charge against him is labeled a misdemeanor. We hold that this question was answered correctly by the dissenting justices in the Supreme Court of Wisconsin. [Two judges had dissented.]

The issue in this case is not whether the Fourteenth Amendment requires a State to accord a jury trial to a defendant on a charge such as the appellant faced here. The issue concerns, rather, the nature of the jury trial that the Fourteenth Amendment commands, when trial by jury is what the State has purported to accord. We had occasion to consider this precise question almost 10 years ago in *Irvin* v. *Dowd*, 366 U.S. 717. There we found that an Indiana conviction could not constitutionally stand because the jury had been infected by community prejudice

before the trial had commenced. What the Court said in that case is wholly relevant here:

> "In essence, the right to jury trial guarantees to the criminally accused a fair trial by a panel of impartial, 'indifferent' jurors. The failure to accord an accused a fair hearing violates even the minimal standards of due process. *In re Oliver*, 333 U.S. 257; *Tumey* v. *Ohio*, 273 U.S. 510. 'A fair trial in a fair tribunal is a basic requirement of due process.' *In re Murchison*, 349 U.S. 133, 136. In the ultimate analysis, only the jury can strip a man of his liberty or his life. In the language of Lord Coke, a juror must be as 'indifferent as he stands unsworne.' Co. Litt. 155b. His verdict must be based upon the evidence developed at the trial. Cf. *Thompson* v. *City of Louisville*, 362 U.S. 199. This is true, regardless of the heinousness of the crime charged, the apparent guilt of the offender or the station in life which he occupies. It was so written into our law as early as 1807 by Chief Justice Marshall in 1 Burr's Trial 416. . . ." 366 U.S., at 722.

There are many ways to try to assure the kind of impartial jury that the Fourteenth Amendment guarantees. In *Sheppard* v. *Maxwell*, 384 U.S. 333, the Court enumerated many of the procedures available, particularly in the context of a jury threatened by the poisonous influence of prejudicial publicity during the course of the trial itself. 384 U.S., at 357–363. Here we are concerned with the methods available to assure an impartial jury in a situation where, because of prejudicial publicity or for some other reason, the community from which the jury is to be drawn may already be permeated with hostility toward the defendant. The problem is an ancient one. Mr. Justice Holmes stated no more than a common-place when, two generations ago, he noted that "[a]ny judge who has sat with juries knows that in spite of forms they are extremely likely to be impregnated by the environing atmosphere." *Frank* v. *Mangum*, 237 U.S. 309, 349 (dissenting opinion).

One way to try to meet the problem is to grant a continuance of the trial in the hope that in the course of time the fires of prejudice will cool. But this hope may not be realized, and continuances, particularly if they are repeated, work against the important values implicit in the constitutional guarantee of a speedy trial. Another way is to provide a method of jury qualification that will promote, through the exercise of challenges to the venire—peremptory and for cause—the exclusion of prospective jurors infected with the prejudice of the community from which they come. But this protection, as *Irvin* v. *Dowd*, supra, shows, is not always adequate to effectuate the constitutional guarantee.

On at least one occasion this Court has explicitly held that only a change of venue was constitutionally sufficient to assure the kind of impartial jury that is guaranteed by the Fourteenth Amendment. That was in the case of *Rideau* v. *Louisiana*, 373 U.S. 723. We held that "it was a denial of due process of law to refuse the request for a change of venue, after the people of Calcasieu Parish had been exposed repeatedly and in depth" to the prejudicial pretrial publicity there involved. 373 U.S., at 726. *Rideau* was not decided until 1963, but its message echoes more than 200 years of human experience in the endless quest for the fair administration of criminal justice.

It is doubtless true, as the Supreme Court of Wisconsin said, that community prejudice is not often aroused against a man accused only of a misdemeanor. But under the Constitution a defendant must be given an opportunity to show that a change of venue is required in his case. The Wisconsin statute wholly denied that opportunity to the appellant.

Accordingly, the judgment is vacated, and the case is remanded to the Supreme Court of Wisconsin for further proceedings not inconsistent with this opinion.

It is so ordered.

MR. JUSTICE BLACKMUN, whom THE CHIEF JUSTICE joins, concurring. [omitted]

MR. JUSTICE BLACK, dissenting. [omitted]

WHAT DO YOU THINK?

1. Do you agree that the defendant has a right to move the location of his trial if he can establish that it is impossible to get a fair trial in the district in which the crime was committed?

2. In view of the added expense of moving a trial to a distant location, should this right be available only for felonies?

Should the burden be on the defendant to establish his or her incompetence to stand trial? May a state assume that the defendant is competent to stand trial and require the defendant to establish his or her incompetence by clear and convincing evidence?

COOPER V. OKLAHOMA
517 U.S. 348 (1996)

Justice Stevens delivered the opinion of the Court.

In Oklahoma the defendant in a criminal prosecution is presumed to be competent to stand trial unless he proves his incompetence by clear and convincing evidence. Okla. Stat., Tit. 22, §1175.4(B) (1991). Under that standard a defendant may be put to trial even though it is more likely than not that he is incompetent. The question we address in this case is whether the application of that standard to petitioner violated his right to due process under the Fourteenth Amendment.

In 1989 petitioner was charged with the brutal killing of an 86-year-old man in the course of a burglary. After an Oklahoma jury found him guilty of first-degree murder and recommended punishment by death, the trial court imposed the death penalty. The Oklahoma Court of Criminal Appeals affirmed the conviction and sentence.

Petitioner's competence was the focus of significant attention both before and during his trial. On five separate occasions a judge considered whether petitioner had the ability to understand the charges against him and to assist defense counsel. On the first occasion, a pretrial judge relied on the opinion of a clinical psychologist employed by the State to find petitioner incompetent. Based on that determination, he committed petitioner to a state mental health facility for treatment.

Upon petitioner's release from the hospital some three months later, the trial judge heard testimony concerning petitioner's competence from two state-employed psychologists. These experts expressed conflicting opinions regarding petitioner's ability to participate in his defense. The judge resolved the dispute against petitioner, ordering him to proceed to trial.

At the close of a pretrial hearing held one week before the trial was scheduled to begin, the lead defense attorney raised the issue of petitioner's competence for a third time. Counsel advised the court that petitioner was behaving oddly and refusing to communicate with him. Defense counsel opined that it would be a serious matter "if he's not faking." After listening to counsel's concerns, however, the judge declined to revisit his earlier determination that petitioner was competent to stand trial.

Petitioner's competence was addressed a fourth time on the first day of trial, when petitioner's bizarre behavior prompted the court to conduct a further competency hearing at which the judge observed petitioner and heard testimony from several lay witnesses, a third psychologist, and petitioner himself. The expert concluded that petitioner was presently incompetent and unable to communicate effectively with counsel, but that he could probably achieve competence within six weeks if treated aggressively. While stating that he did not dispute the psychologist's diagnosis, the trial judge ruled against petitioner. In so holding, however, the court voiced uncertainty:

> "Well, I think I've used the expression . . . in the past that normal is like us. Anybody that's not like us is not normal, so I don't think normal is a proper definition that we are to use with incompetence. My shirtsleeve opinion of Mr. Cooper is that he's not normal. Now, to say he's not competent is something else.
>
> * * * * *
>
> "But you know, all things considered, I suppose it's possible for a client to be in such a predicament that he can't help his defense and still not be incompetent. I suppose that's a possibility, too.
>
> "I think it's going to take smarter people than me to make a decision here. I'm going to say that I don't believe he has carried the burden by clear and convincing evidence of his incompetency and I'm going to say we're going to go to trial." Incidents that occurred during the trial, as well as the sordid history of petitioner's childhood that was recounted during the sentencing phase of the proceeding, were consistent with the conclusions expressed by the expert. In a final effort to protect his client's interests, defense counsel moved for a mistrial or a renewed investigation into petitioner's competence. After the court summarily denied these motions, petitioner was convicted and sentenced to death.

In the Court of Criminal Appeals, petitioner contended that Oklahoma's presumption of competence, combined with its statutory requirement that a criminal defendant establish incompetence by clear and convincing evidence, Okla. Stat., Tit. 22, §1175.4(B), placed such an onerous burden on him as to violate his right to due process of law. The appellate court rejected this argument. After noting that it can be difficult to determine whether a defendant is malingering, given "the inexactness and uncertainty attached to [competency] proceedings," the court held that the standard was justified because the "State has great interest in assuring its citizens a thorough and speedy judicial process," and because a "truly incompetent criminal defendant, through his attorneys and experts, can prove incompetency with relative ease." We granted *certiorari* to review the Court of Criminal Appeals' conclusion that application of the clear and convincing evidence standard does not violate due process.

No one questions the existence of the fundamental right that petitioner invokes. We have repeatedly and consistently recognized that "the criminal trial of an incompetent defendant violates due process." . . . Nor is the significance of this right open to dispute. As JUSTICE KENNEDY recently emphasized:

> Competence to stand trial is rudimentary, for upon it depends the main part of those rights deemed essential to a fair trial, including the right to effective assistance of counsel, the rights to summon, to confront, and to cross-examine witnesses, and the

right to testify on one's own behalf or to remain silent without penalty for doing so. . . . The test for incompetence is also well-settled. A defendant may not be put to trial unless he "has sufficient present ability to consult with his lawyer with a reasonable degree of rational understanding . . . [and] a rational as well as factual understanding of the proceedings against him."

Our recent decision in *Medina* v. *California*, 505 U.S. 437 (1992), establishes that a State may presume that the defendant is competent and require him to shoulder the burden of proving his incompetence by a preponderance of the evidence. In reaching that conclusion we held that the relevant inquiry was whether the presumption offends some principle of justice so rooted in the traditions and conscience of our people as to be ranked as fundamental. We contrasted the "deep roots in our common-law heritage" underlying the prohibition against trying the incompetent with the absence of any settled tradition concerning the allocation of the burden of proof in a competency proceeding. Our conclusion that the presumption of competence offends no recognized principle of "fundamental fairness" rested in part on the fact that the procedural rule affects the outcome "only in a narrow class of cases where the evidence is in equipoise; that is, where the evidence that a defendant is competent is just as strong as the evidence that he is incompetent."

The question we address today is quite different from the question posed in *Medina*. Petitioner's claim requires us to consider whether a State may proceed with a criminal trial after the defendant has demonstrated that he is more likely than not incompetent. Oklahoma does not contend that it may require the defendant to prove incompetence beyond a reasonable doubt. The State maintains, however, that the clear and convincing standard provides a reasonable accommodation of the opposing interests of the State and the defendant. We are persuaded, by both traditional and modern practice and the importance of the constitutional interest at stake, that the State's argument must be rejected.

"Historical practice is probative of whether a procedural rule can be characterized as fundamental," *Medina*, 505 U.S., at 446. In this case, unlike in *Medina*, there is no indication that the rule Oklahoma seeks to defend has any roots in prior practice. Indeed, it appears that a rule significantly more favorable to the defendant has had a long and consistent application.

We turn first to an examination of the relevant common-law traditions of England and this country. The prohibition against trying the incompetent defendant was well-established by the time Hale and Blackstone wrote their famous commentaries. 4 W. Blackstone, Commentaries *24 ("[I]f a man in his sound memory commits a capital offence . . . [a]nd if, after he has pleaded, the prisoner becomes mad, he shall not be tried: for how can he make his defence?"); 1 M. Hale, Pleas of the Crown *34–*35 (same). The English cases which predate our Constitution provide no guidance, however, concerning the applicable standard of proof in competency determinations. See *Trial of Charles Bateman* (1685), reported in 11 How. St. Tr. 464, 467 (1816), and Hawles, *Remarks on the Trial of Mr. Charles Bateman*, 11 How. St. Tr. 474, 476 (1816) (noting that the court in the 1685 trial incurred "censure" for proceeding to trial with a doubt as to the defendant's competence); *Kinloch's Case* (1746), 18 How. St. Tr. 395, 411 (1813); *King* v. *Steel*, 1 Leach 452, 168 Eng. Rep. 328 (1787).

Beginning in the late eighteenth century, cases appear which provide an inkling of the proper standard. In *King* v. *Frith*, 22 How. St. Tr. 307 (1790), for example, the court instructed the jury to "diligently inquire . . . whether John Frith, the now prisoner at the bar . . . be of sound mind and understanding or not. . . ." *Id.*, at 311. Some 50 years later the jurors received a nearly identical admonition in *Queen*

v. *Goode*, 7 Ad. & E. 536, 112 Eng. Rep. 572 (K. B. 1837): "You shall diligently inquire and true presentment make . . . whether John Goode . . . be insane or not. . . ." *Id.*, at 536, n. *(a)*, 112 Eng. Rep., at 572–573, n. (a). Similarly, in *King* v. *Pritchard*, 7 Car. & P. 303, 173 Eng. Rep. 135 (1836), the court empaneled a jury to consider "whether the prisoner is mute of malice or not; secondly, whether he can plead to the indictment or not; thirdly, whether he is of sufficient intellect to comprehend the course of proceedings on the trial. . . ." *Ibid.*

These authorities, while still speaking less clearly than we might wish, are instructive. By phrasing the inquiry in a simple disjunctive, *Frith*, *Goode*, and *Pritchard* suggest that traditional practice required the jury to determine whether the defendant was "more likely than not" incompetent. Nothing in the jury instructions of these cases will bear the interpretation of a clear and convincing standard. What is more, the cases contain no indication that the use of a preponderance standard represented a departure from earlier (pre-Constitution) practice.

Modern English authority confirms our interpretation of these early cases as applying a preponderance standard. Relying on "principles . . . laid down in a number of cases," including *Pritchard* and *King* v. *Dyson*, 7 Car. & P. 305, n. *(a)*, 173 Eng. Rep. 135, n. *(a)* (1831), the court in *Queen* v. *Podola*, 43 Crim. App. 220, 3 All E. R. 418 (1959), ruled:

> If the contention that the accused is insane is put forward by the defence and contested by the prosecution, there is, in our judgment, a burden upon the defence of satisfying the jury of the accused's insanity. In such a case, as in other criminal cases in which the onus of proof rests upon the defence, the onus is discharged if the jury are satisfied on the balance of probabilities that the accused's insanity has been made out." *Id.*, at 235, 3 All E. R., at 429.

Likewise, we are aware of no decisional law from this country suggesting that any State employed Oklahoma's heightened standard until quite recently. Rather, the earliest available sources typically refer to English authorities, see, *e.g.*, *Freeman* v. *People*, 47 Am. Dec. 216, 223–225 (N.Y. 1847), *State* v. *Harris*, 78 Am. Dec. 272, 272–275 (N.C. 1860) (adopting procedures outlined in *King* v. *Dyson*, 7 Car. & P. 305, n. *(a)*, 173 Eng. Rep. 135, n. *(a)* (1831) and *King* v. *Pritchard*, 7 Car. & P. 303, 173 Eng. Rep. 135 (1836), and employ the disjunctive language used by the English courts, see, *e.g.*, *Commonwealth* v. *Hathaway*, 13 Mass. 299, 299 (1816); *People* v. *Kleim*, 1 N.Y. 13, 15 (1845); *Harris*, 78 Am. Dec., at 275; *United States* v. *Chisolm*, 149 F. 284, 290 (SD Ala. 1906). By the turn of the twentieth century, however, American courts were explicitly applying a preponderance standard. In 1896, Ohio juries were instructed that "[t]he burden is upon the prisoner to show by a preponderance of the proof that he is insane." *State* v. *O'Grady*, 5 Ohio Dec. 654, 655 (1896). Some 15 years later, the Tennessee Supreme Court described the competency determination as "controlled by the preponderance of the proof," *Jordan* v. *State*, 124 Tenn. 81, 89, 135 S. W. 327, 329 (1911), and the highest court of Pennsylvania held that competence is "decided by a preponderance of the evidence," *Commonwealth* v. *Simanowicz*, 242 Pa. 402, 405, 89 A. 562, 563 (1913). These early authorities are bereft of language susceptible of supporting a clear and convincing evidence standard.

Contemporary practice demonstrates that the vast majority of jurisdictions remain persuaded that the heightened standard of proof imposed on the accused in Oklahoma is not necessary to vindicate the State's interest in prompt and orderly disposition of criminal cases. Only 4 of the 50 States presently require the criminal defendant to prove his incompetence by clear and convincing evidence. None

of the remaining 46 jurisdictions imposes such a heavy burden on the defendant. Indeed, a number of States place no burden on the defendant at all, but rather require the prosecutor to prove the defendant's competence to stand trial once a question about competency has been credibly raised. The situation is no different in federal court. Congress has directed that the accused in a federal prosecution must prove incompetence by a preponderance of the evidence. 18 U. S. C. §4241.

The near-uniform application of a standard that is more protective of the defendant's rights than Oklahoma's clear and convincing evidence rule supports our conclusion that the heightened standard offends a principle of justice that is deeply "rooted in the traditions and conscience of our people." *Medina* v. *California*, 505 U.S., at 445 (internal quotation marks omitted). We turn next to a consideration of whether the rule exhibits " 'fundamental fairness' in operation." *Id.*, at 448 (quoting *Dowling* v. *United States*, 493 U.S. 342, 352 [1990]).

Contemporary and historical procedures are fully consistent with our evaluation of the risks inherent in Oklahoma's practice of requiring the defendant to prove incompetence by clear and convincing evidence. In *Addington* v. *Texas* we explained that:

> The function of a standard of proof, as that concept is embodied in the Due Process Clause and in the realm of factfinding, is "to instruct the factfinder concerning the degree of confidence our society thinks he should have in the correctness of factual conclusions for a particular type of adjudication. *In re Winship*, 397 U.S. 358, 370 (1970) (Harlan, J., concurring)." 441 U.S. 418, 423 (1979). The "more stringent the burden of proof a party must bear, the more that party bears the risk of an erroneous decision." See *Cruzan* v. *Director, Mo. Dept. of Health*, 497 U.S. 261, 283 (1990). For that reason, we have held that due process places a heightened burden of proof on the State in civil proceedings in which the "individual interests at stake . . . are both 'particularly important' and 'more substantial than mere loss of money.' " *Santosky* v. *Kramer*, 455 U.S. 745, 756 (1982) (termination of parental rights) (quoting *Addington*, 441 U.S., at 424).

Far from "jealously guard[ing]," *Jacob* v. *New York City*, 315 U.S. 752, 752–753 (1942), an incompetent criminal defendant's fundamental right not to stand trial, Oklahoma's practice of requiring the defendant to prove incompetence by clear and convincing evidence imposes a significant risk of an erroneous determination that the defendant is competent. In *Medina* we found no comparable risk because the presumption would affect only the narrow class of cases in which the evidence on either side was equally balanced. "Once a State provides a defendant access to procedures for making a competency evaluation," we stated, there is "no basis for holding that due process further requires the State to assume the burden of vindicating the defendant's constitutional right by persuading the trier of fact that the defendant is competent to stand trial." *Medina* v. *California*, 505 U.S., at 449. Unlike the presumption at issue in *Medina*, however, Oklahoma's clear and convincing evidence standard affects a class of cases in which the defendant has already demonstrated that he is more likely than not incompetent.

For the defendant, the consequences of an erroneous determination of competence are dire. Because he lacks the ability to communicate effectively with counsel, he may be unable to exercise other "rights deemed essential to a fair trial." *Riggins* v. *Nevada*, 504 U.S., at 139 (KENNEDY, J., concurring in judgment). After making the "profound" choice whether to plead guilty, *Godinez* v. *Moran*, 509 U.S. 389, 398 (1993), the defendant who proceeds to trial

> ". . . will ordinarily have to decide whether to waive his 'privilege against compulsory self-incrimination,' *Boykin* v. *Alabama*, 395 U.S. 238, 243 (1969), by taking the

witness stand; if the option is available, he may have to decide whether to waive his 'right to trial by jury,' *ibid.*; and, in consultation with counsel, he may have to decide whether to waive his 'right to confront [his] accusers,' *ibid.*, by declining to cross-examine witnesses for the prosecution." *Ibid.* With the assistance of counsel, the defendant also is called upon to make myriad smaller decisions concerning the course of his defense. The importance of these rights and decisions demonstrates that an erroneous determination of competence threatens a "fundamental component of our criminal justice system"—the basic fairness of the trial itself.

By comparison to the defendant's interest, the injury to the State of the opposite error—a conclusion that the defendant is incompetent when he is in fact malingering—is modest. To be sure, such an error imposes an expense on the state treasury and frustrates the State's interest in the prompt disposition of criminal charges. But the error is subject to correction in a subsequent proceeding and the State may detain the incompetent defendant for "the reasonable period of time necessary to determine whether there is a substantial probability that he will attain [competence] in the foreseeable future." *Jackson* v. *Indiana*, 406 U.S. 715, 738 (1972).

The Oklahoma Court of Criminal Appeals correctly observed that the "inexactness and uncertainty" that characterize competency proceedings may make it difficult to determine whether a defendant is incompetent or malingering. 889 P. 2d 293, 303 (1995). We presume, however, that it is unusual for even the most artful malingerer to feign incompetence successfully for a period of time while under professional care. In this regard it is worth reiterating that only four jurisdictions currently consider it necessary to impose on the criminal defendant the burden of proving incompetence by clear and convincing evidence. Moreover, there is no reason to believe that the art of dissimulation is new. Eighteenth and nineteenth century courts, for example, warned jurors charged with making competency determinations that "there may be great fraud in this matter," *King* v. *Dyson*, 7 Car. & P. 305, n. *(a)*, 173 Eng. Rep., at 136, n. *(a)* (quoting 1 Hale, Pleas of the Crown, at *35), and that "[i]t would be a reproach to justice if a guilty man . . . postponed his trial upon a feigned condition of mind, as to his inability to aid in his defense," *United States* v. *Chisolm*, 149 F., at 288. Although they recognized this risk, the early authorities did not resort to a heightened burden of proof in competency proceedings. See Part III, *supra*.

More fundamentally, while the difficulty of ascertaining where the truth lies may make it appropriate to place the burden of proof on the proponent of an issue, it does not justify the additional onus of an especially high standard of proof. As the *Chisolm* Court continued,

> [I]t would be likewise a reproach to justice and our institutions, if a human being . . . were compelled to go to trial at a time when he is not sufficiently in possession of his mental faculties to enable him to make a rational and proper defense. The latter would be a more grievous error than the former; since in the one case an individual would go unwhipped of justice, while in the other the great safeguards which the law adopts in the punishment of crime and the upholding of justice would be rudely invaded by the tribunal whose sacred duty it is to uphold the law in all its integrity. 149 F., at 288

A heightened standard does not decrease the risk of error, but simply reallocates that risk between the parties. See *Cruzan* v. *Director, Mo. Dept. of Health*, 497 U.S., at 283. In cases in which competence is at issue, we perceive no sound basis for allocating to the criminal defendant the large share of the risk which accompanies a clear and convincing evidence standard. We assume that questions of competence will arise in a range of cases including not only those in which one side will prevail with relative ease, but also those in which it is more likely than not that the defendant is incompetent but the evidence is insufficiently strong to satisfy a clear and convincing standard. While important state interests are unquestionably at stake, in these latter cases the defendant's fundamental right to be tried only while competent outweighs the State's interest in the efficient operation of its criminal justice system.

. . . More importantly, our decision today is in complete accord with the basis for our ruling in *Addington*. Both cases concern the proper protection of fundamental rights in circumstances in which the State proposes to take drastic action against an individual. The requirement that the grounds for civil commitment be shown by clear and convincing evidence protects the individual's fundamental interest in liberty. The *prohibition* against requiring the criminal defendant to demonstrate incompetence by clear and convincing evidence safeguards the fundamental right not to stand trial while incompetent. Because Oklahoma's procedural rule allows the State to put to trial a defendant who is more likely than not incompetent, the rule is incompatible with the dictates of due process.

For the foregoing reasons, the judgment is reversed and the case is remanded to the Oklahoma Court of Criminal Appeals for further proceedings not inconsistent with this opinion.

It is so ordered.

WHAT DO *YOU* THINK?

1. Do you agree with the decision of the court that the initial burden of producing evidence on the issue of competency is properly placed on the defendant?
2. Is this a "due process" issue?

SUMMARY

- There are two types of jurisdiction: (1) over the subject matter and (2) over the person. A court must have jurisdiction over the accused and the subject matter before the court may decide a criminal case. Federal courts have jurisdiction over federal issues, and state courts have jurisdiction over state issues.

- *Venue* refers to the geographical location of the trial. *Jurisdiction* refers to the power of a court to try a case. Normal venue of a criminal case is in the county or the judicial district in which the crime occurred.

- There are two basic criminal court systems in the United States—federal and state. The U.S. Supreme Court is the highest court in the federal system. The basic trial court in the federal system is the U.S. District Court (USDC). There is at least one federal district court in each state. Federal justices and judges are appointed by the president with "advice and consent" of the Senate. Except for special legislative courts, federal judges and justices are appointed for life. In most judicial districts there is more than one judge.

- State supreme courts are common in most states, which act as the final state authority on criminal appeals. In Oklahoma and Texas, the state supreme court does not handle criminal cases. In these states there are separate courts of criminal appeals as the court of last resort for criminal matters.

- The state constitutions generally establish the procedure for the appointments to state supreme courts or courts of criminal appeals. Most state legislatures have divided their states into appellate districts, each containing a court of appeals with one or more divisions. The general trial court in most states is the superior or district court.

- County, municipal (urban), and justice (rural) courts normally handle cases involving misdemeanors.

- Normally each county or judicial district has at least one superior or district court with one or more judges. The state legislatures are permitted by state constitutions to provide for the appointment of officers such as commissioners and referees to perform subordinate judicial duties.

- Appellate courts reverse criminal cases only when the court considers that there has been a miscarriage of justice. A miscarriage of justice occurs only if, based on the entire record, the appellate court concludes that it is probable that a result more favorable to the defendant would have been reached in the absence of the error.

- In most cases, the accused has a right to appeal a felony conviction to a state court of appeal. The state (People) may not appeal an acquittal.

- The writ of habeas corpus is literally a request for the court to order the warden or jailor to produce the prisoner or detainee and justify why he or she is being detained in prison or other confinement. The writ is normally used by prisoners or detainees to attack their sentences to confinement.

DISCUSSION QUESTIONS

1. Joe Boren is arrested for robbing a fast food restaurant. He is convicted in state court for *robbery*. How can he appeal his conviction to a federal court?
2. Mary Born is arrested in Oregon for a crime she committed in another state. Her ex-husband lives in the other state, and she does not wish to return to that state. Can she waive her right to be tried in the judicial district in which the crime occurred? Can she be tried with her permission in an Oregon state court for a crime that is a violation of the other state's laws?
3. At Jerry Johnson's criminal trial, the prosecution made several errors in presenting the evidence to the jury. What does Jerry's attorney need to establish to have the case reversed on appeal?
4. Dennis X commits the crime of murder in Florida. He moves to Hawaii. Florida has the death penalty, Hawaii does not. Dennis requests a Hawaii district attorney charge him for the murder committed in Florida. He does not want to be subject to the death penalty. He is tried in Hawaii and receives a life sentence based on his guilty plea. Is the trial in the Hawaiian court a valid exercise of that court's jurisdiction? *Note*: As will be discussed in chapter 13, the defense of double jeopardy would not be available to Dennis if a Florida court attempts to try him for the same offense.
5. Ms. Botkin mailed a box of poisoned candy from San Francisco to her victim in Dover, Delaware. The victim died as a result of eating the poisoned

candy. Can Ms. Botkin be tried for murder in California? [*People* v. *Botkin*, 64 P. 286 (Cal.1901).]

6. Draw a diagram of the hierarchy of your state criminal court system.

ENDNOTES

1. Rule 19.2, Georgia Unified Superior Court Rules.
2. *Moor* v. *Commonwealth*, 523 S.W. 2d 635 (Ky. 1975).
3. *United States* v. *Davis*, 666 F. 2d 195 (5th Cir. 1982).
4. *Simpson* v. *State*, 17 S.E. 984 (Ga. 1983).
5. *Payton* v. *New York*, 445 U.S. 573 (1980).
6. *Younger* v. *Superior Court*, 21 Cal. 3d 102 (Cal. 1978).
7. This statement was taken from the Texas Constitution.
8. *People* v. *Foster* 169 Cal. App. 3d 519 (1st Dist. Cal. 1985).
9. *People* v. *Fisher*, 153 Cal. App. 3d 826 (2nd Dist. Cal. 1984).
10. *People* v. *P.J. Video*, 68 N.Y. 2d 296 (1986).
11. (1976) 428 U.S. 465,
12. *Herrera* v. *Collins*, 113 S.Ct. 853 (1993).
13. *Rose* v. *Lundy*, 102 S.Ct. 1198 (1982).
14. Pub.L. No. 104–132, 110 Stat. 1218 (1995).

3

*O*VERVIEW OF THE *J*USTICE *P*ROCESS

LEGAL AUTHORIZATION FOR THE SYSTEM

This chapter presents an overview of the justice process. The rules governing criminal proceedings conducted by the federal and state governments are based on three basic sources of power: constitutions (state and federal), statutes, and court rules. The constitutions of the various states and the federal government contain important rights that are available to an accused in a criminal prosecution. The second major source of law is the state and federal codes of criminal procedure. (*Note*: The state code of criminal procedure applies to state criminal prosecutions within that state and the federal applies only to federal trials.) The third major source is the court rules which are issued under the court's inherent supervisory power over the administration of justice. (*Note*: Federal courts have inherent supervisory power over federal criminal cases, and state courts have the same power over state criminal cases.) Court rules are discussed in Chapter 1.

THE DUE PROCESS CONCEPT

The Bill of Rights, the first eight amendments to the U.S. Constitution, contains twenty-three separate rights, twelve of them concern procedural rights for persons accused of criminal conduct.[1] In 1798 the U.S. Supreme Court ruled that the prohibitions against government action contained in those amendments were restrictions only on the federal government and not on state governments. *Calder* v. *Bull*[2] involved a statute passed by the legislature of Connecticut which set aside a probate court judgment and directed the probate judge to refuse the recording of a will (an *ex posto* law). The justices noted that the Bill of Rights was designed to prevent the federal abuse of power, not state abuse.

The Fourteenth Amendment, one of the anti-slavery amendments enacted in 1868, however, has been used by the courts to place *due process* requirements on the states in criminal prosecutions.

U.S. CONSTITUTION, AMENDMENT XIV

Section 1. All persons born or naturalized in the United States, and subject to the jurisdiction thereof, are citizens of the United States and of the State wherein they reside. No State shall make or enforce any law which shall abridge the privileges or immunities of citizens of the United States; nor shall any State deprive any person of life, liberty, or property, without due process; nor deny to any person within its jurisdiction the equal protection of the laws.

The clause *without due process* of the Fourteenth Amendment has been interpreted by the U.S. Supreme Court as "incorporating" most of the provisions of the Bill of Rights. Accordingly, those rights which are incorporated under that clause apply to state as well as federal criminal proceedings. In 1897 the Court using the due process clause of the Fourteenth Amendment applied the Fifth Amendment's requirement of payment of "just compensation" for the taking of private property for public use to the states. Later in 1925, in *Gitlow* v. *New York*,[3] the Court held that the First Amendment's protection on free speech restricted the state's right to control free speech. The Sixth Amendment's right to counsel was imposed on the states by *Powell* v. *Alabama*,[4] and the requirement of a trial by "an impartial jury" in jury cases was imposed by *Duncan* v. *Louisiana*.[5]

The Incorporation Controversy

For many years there was a controversy over whether all of the rights contained in the Bill of Rights were incorporated into the due process clause of the Fourteenth Amendment and thus applied to the states or only those that were considered as fundamental to due process. While it was always clear that the Fourteenth Amendment's Due Process Clause imposes limitations on the criminal procedure in state criminal courts, the exact limitation was not as clear.

The *total incorporation* approach holds that the Fourteenth Amendment incorporates the entire Bill of Rights and makes all the Bill of Rights protections applicable to the states. Justice Hugo Black, in his many years on the court, contended that not only should there be total incorporation of the Bill of Rights but also some other "fundamental" rights not included in the Bill of Rights. Critics of the total incorporation approach contend that there is little in the legislative history of the Fourteenth Amendment, which indicates that the drafters intended to incorporate all Bill of Rights protections. While the Court never adopted Black's "total incorporation" concept, it has adopted his concept that the Due Process Clause includes other "fundamental" rights not contained in the Bill of Rights.

Until the 1960s the *fundamental rights* approach was predominantly used by the Supreme Court. This approach held that the Fourteenth Amendment prohibits only those practices inconsistent with the concept of "ordered liberty."[6] Under this approach, the Due Process Clause required a case-by-case approach to determine if a particular right so shocks the conscience that it is unacceptable in our system of justice.[7] Critics of this approach contend that the test imposed few meaningful limitations on the states.

The Modern Approach

Presently the Court is using the *selective incorporation* approach. The Court has accepted the concept that not all rights enumerated in the Bill of Rights are necessarily fundamental, and that other rights may be fundamental even though not contained in the Bill of Rights. To determine if a right is fundamental, the Court looks at whether the procedural safeguard is "fundamental to the American scheme of Justice" or "necessary" in the context of the criminal process maintained by the various states.

The following Bill of Rights guarantees that have been selectively incorporated and thus are held enforceable against the states to the same standards that the rights protect against federal encroachment include:

First Amendment

- free speech[8]
- freedom of press[9]
- freedom of assembly[10]

Fourth Amendment

- general right to privacy[11]
- protection against unreasonable searches and seizures[12]
- exclusionary rule[13]
- requirement of probable cause to arrest[14]

Fifth Amendment

- protection against self-incrimination[15]
- protection against double jeopardy[16]

Sixth Amendment

- right to trial by jury in serious cases[17]
- right to speedy trial[18]
- right to be informed of nature of charges[19]
- right to confront and cross-examine adverse witnesses[20]
- right to subpoena witnesses in a criminal case[21]

Eighth Amendment

- protection against "cruel and unusual" punishment[22]

The following rights, although required in federal criminal proceedings, have not been imposed on the states:

Fifth Amendment

- right to grand jury indictment[23]

Sixth Amendment

- right to jury trial in minor criminal cases[24]

Eighth Amendment

- prohibition against excessive bail[25]

CONSTITUTION AND STATE CODES

> **CALIFORNIA CONSTITUTION, ARTICLE 7**
>
> (a) A person may not be deprived of life, liberty, or property without due process of law or denied equal protection of the laws. . . .

The above provision from the California Constitution is similar to that contained in most state constitutions. (*Note*: It is almost a restatement of the due process clause of the Fourteenth Amendment to the U.S. Constitution. Rarely are these state due process clauses invoked in criminal proceeding because of the Fourteenth Amendment requirements.)

CONTINUITY OF PROCEDURES

Once the police are aware of possible criminal conduct, they must determine if (1) a crime actually occurred and (2) if so, who committed the crime. Once the police have answered these questions, the case is forwarded to the prosecutor.

Arrest

The term *arrest* has various meanings. For the purpose of this study, the common statutory definition will be used. An arrest is the taking of a person into custody so that he or she may be held to answer for the commission of an offense. (*Note*: While all arrests involve restraint of a person's liberty, not all restraints are considered as arrests.) The four essential elements of an arrest are:

1. An intention to arrest,
2. The authority to arrest,
3. A seizure and detention of the person, and
4. An understanding by the person that he or she is being arrested.

Charging

Felonies are normally prosecuted either by indictment or, after examination and commitment by a magistrate, by information. In a minority of states, a grand jury indictment is required before a person may be prosecuted for a felony. In other states that require an indictment, the accused, after consulting with an attorney, may waive the indictment requirement. The process of bringing an accused to trial is discussed in Chapters 11 and 12.

In states like California and Kansas, where a person may be prosecuted based only on information, a complaint (information) is sworn to by a citizen (normally the police officer) under penalty of perjury and filed by the district attorney in a court in the county where the felony is triable. The accused is then required to be taken without unnecessary delay before a magistrate of that court. The magistrate is required to give the defendant a copy of the complaint, inform the defendant of the defendant's right to counsel, allow the defendant a reasonable time to send for counsel, and on the defendant's request the magistrate shall require a peace officer to transmit within the county where the court is located a message to counsel named by the defendant.

A person unable to understand English who is charged with a crime has a right to an interpreter throughout the proceedings.

In most states every public offense must be prosecuted by indictment or information, except where:

1. The proceedings are had for the removal of civil officers of the State;
2. There are offenses arising in the militia when in actual service, and in the land and naval forces in the time of war;
3. Offenses are tried in municipal and justice courts;
4. All misdemeanors of which jurisdiction has been conferred upon superior or district courts are sitting as juvenile courts (juvenile court cases);
5. There has been a felony to which the defendant has pleaded guilty to the complaint before a magistrate, where permitted by law.

No person can be punished for a public offense, except upon a legal conviction in a court having jurisdiction thereof. The criminal justice system can be divided into three basic parts: pretrial procedures, trial phases, and posttrial proceedings.

Sentencing

In most states once guilt is ascertained, the judge determines the appropriate sentence subject to statutory limits. Often, the judge will have the ability to choose between probation and imprisonment. Normally, felony sentencing is not undertaken until the judge receives a presentence report (PSI) that is prepared by a probation or presentence officer. This report is designed to provide the judge with sufficient information upon which to base his or her sentencing decision. The defendant, through his or her attorney, also may present information to the judge for use in making the decision. (*Note*: Witnesses are not normally presented during the sentencing process, and often the information considered by the judge would not be admissable during the guilt phase of the trial.)

Appeal

The right to appeal only exists by law generally in capital cases and otherwise only if error is alleged. An accused normally has the right to appeal his or her conviction and sentence to the court of appeals. The function of an appellate court is to provide a legal review of rulings made by the trial court. If the appellate court finds no substantial error, the conviction is affirmed (upheld); if the court finds error and concludes that the error may have prevented the accused from obtaining a fair trial, the court may reverse (set aside) the conviction and return the case to the original trial court for proceeding not inconsistent with the appellate court's decision. In most cases, the accused or the state may petition to the high court (state supreme court) for a review of the appellate court decision. The petition, except in death penalty cases, does not have to be accepted by the high court. If the high court does accept the petition, then the court will render an opinion as to the validity of the procedures. Only a limited number of petitions to the state high courts are accepted.

What Happens to Felony Arrests

Status	Violent Crimes	Property Crimes
Prosecution declined by prosecutor or dismissed by Court	36%	22%
Diversion	2%	2%
Guilty Pleas	52%	72%
Trials	8%	4%
Acquittal	2%	1%
Jail or Prison	76% of those convicted	63% of those convicted

Source: Bureau of Justice Statistics, 1998.

PARTICIPANTS IN THE PROCEEDINGS

The three chief participants in any criminal trial are the prosecutor, defense counsel, and the judiciary.

Prosecutor

At common law in England, the victim or complainant hired private counsel to prosecute the case against the accused. In America, however, the practice of using a public prosecutor was present even before the American Revolution. At first, the public prosecutor was supplemental to the private prosecutors. As the offices of public prosecutor grew in status, they replaced private prosecution—then viewed as impractical and subject to abuse. As the result of the Jacksonian reform movement, most public prosecutors became elected officials and were given a virtual monopoly over criminal prosecution. Today, the prosecutor has extensive discretion over the filing and selection of criminal charges.

Similar to police agencies, the authority of public prosecutors has not been centralized by the federal government or in most states. While the Attorney General of the United States is the chief federal prosecutor, federal prosecutorial authority has long been a function of the U.S. Attorneys. Presently there are 94 U.S. Attorneys, one for each federal judicial district. U.S. Attorneys are appointed by the president and confirmed by the Senate. The U.S. Attorney offices range in size from a single prosecutor to over 60 in the large urban districts like the Southern District of New York.

The primary responsibility for the prosecution of state criminal cases is, in most states, the local prosecutor (district attorney, county attorney, or state's attorney). In most states, the local prosecutor (chief prosecutor) is elected by the voters of the local judicial district or county. There are over 2,500 prosecutor offices in the United States. They range in size from the part-time public prosecutor in many rural areas to the largest office, located in Los Angeles County, with almost 900 attorneys. In large offices, cases are prosecuted by the assistant prosecutors.

Standard problems faced by local prosecutors include the high turnover rate for assistant prosecutors, heavy case loads, police–prosecutor relationships and less compensation than that enjoyed by attorneys in private practice.

About 90 percent of defendants plea guilty. Many of these pleas are induced by a plea bargain or arrangement with the prosecutor. Prosecutors plea bargain with the defense in order to expedite the processing of criminal cases. The Supreme Court in *Brady* v. *United States*,[26] upheld the constitutionality of plea bargaining. The Court recognized its importance in disposing of criminal cases, facilitating rehabilitation of the accused, and giving the accused some voice in determining the appropriate punishment. In most cases, the defendant agrees to enter his or her plea of guilty in return for the agreement of leniency to dismiss other pending charges or to plea guilty to a lesser offense, thereby dismissing the more serious charges.

In addition to the prosecution of the case, general duties of the prosecutor include:

- The duty to disclose exculpatory evidence to the accused's counsel[27]
- The duty to reveal information necessary to correct any misleading impressions created by prosecution witnesses[28]
- The duty to disclose without request any evidence that creates reasonable doubt as to the defendant's guilt.[29]

The above duties are part of the prosecutor's duty to insure justice. In most jurisdictions, a prosecutor is ethically bound not to prosecute a case when the prosecutor has reasonable doubt as to the guilt of the defendant.

The prosecutor must depend on the police to investigate and arrest criminals. Often there are conflicts between police and the prosecutor's office because of their different functions. Although both are interested in effective law enforcement, their immediate goals and interests may differ. Whereas the police see the crime as it is committed in the streets, the prosecutor sees the crime in the context of the need to keep the court process moving. The police tend to focus on their role of keeping the streets safe, whereas the prosecutor focuses on his or her role as the legal representative of the state and as a member of the courtroom "work group" of prosecutor, defense counsel, and judge. In addition, the prosecutor is more often influenced by the accused's subsequent reaction to his or her criminal behavior than the police officer. (*Note*: After an arrest, the police are not normally involved in the criminal proceedings except as witnesses.)

Defense Counsel

Chapter 10 contains an in-depth study of the right to counsel for indigent accused. As noted in that chapter, in all criminal cases the accused has the right to the "assistance of counsel." The two major issues in this regard are the right of an indigent accused to have counsel provided by the state and the issue of what constitutes adequate assistance of counsel.

The Judiciary

The discussion in this section is limited to trial court judges. The staffing and structure of the courts differ considerably from state to state. In some states, the judges are elected in a non-partisan manner; in other states, the judges run as members of a political party. In still other states, the judges are initially appointed. After a specified term in office, they are then required to stand at a general election on the question of whether or not they should be retained in office (Missouri Plan). For many years, the lower court judges were not required to have legal

1998 SALARY RATES OF JUSTICES AND JUDGES OF THE UNITED STATES

Office	Rate
Chief Justice of the United States	$175,400
Associate Justices of the Supreme Court of the United States	$167,900
Judges, United States Courts of Appeals	$145,000
Judges, United States District Courts	$136,700
Judges, United States Court of International Trade	$136,700
Judges, United States Court of Federal Claims	$136,700
United States Bankruptcy Judges	$125,764
United States Magistrate Judges (Full-Time)	$125,764
United States Magistrate Judges (Part-Time)	
Level 1	$58,065
Level 2	$52,787
Level 3	$42,229
Level 4	$31,672
Level 5	$21,115
Level 6	$10,557
Level 7	$5,279
Level 8	$3,167

training. The modern trend, however, is to require judges to be members of the bar of the state (an attorney). Most trial court judges are either former prosecutors or public defenders.

EXTRADITION

Generally, a state criminal court has no jurisdiction to try violations of other states' law. In addition, a state court has no jurisdiction over the courts or police agencies of other states. What happens when a person commits a crime in one state and then is found in a different state? In such instances most states have commonly adopted the Uniform Criminal Extradition Act. Under this act, if a wanted person is found in a different state, the governor of the state can forward a request to the governor of the state where the person is located in order to take custody of the person and turn him or her over to the requesting state. This procedure is known as *extradition*. The general rules of extradition are as follows:

- The request for extradition must be in writing by a person performing the function of governor.
- The request must be supported by an indictment or information supported by an affidavit stating the offense and date, place, and time of commission of the crime.
- The governor of the state receiving the demand may investigate the case to determine the situation and circumstances surrounding the crime.

- If the governor decides to comply with the demand, the governor shall sign a warrant of arrest.

- The person arrested shall have a right to a hearing before a judge of a court of record (District or Superior Court).

- If the court orders the extradition, the requesting state is notified and the person is turned over to peace officers of the requesting state. (*Note*: The accused has a right to file a writ of habeas corpus to test the legality of his or her arrest.)

CAPSTONE CASES

The following case looks at the issue of due process. This case also stands for the proposition that the concept of due process includes more than those rights protected by the Bill of Rights.

ROCHIN V. CALIFORNIA
342 U.S. 165, 72 S.Ct. 205 (1952)

MR. JUSTICE FRANKFURTER delivered the opinion of the Court.

On the early morning of July 1, 1949, three Los Angeles County deputy sheriffs entered the two-story house in which Rochin lived with his mother, common-law wife, brothers, and sisters. Finding the outside door open, they entered and then forced open the door to Rochin's room on the second floor. Inside they found Rochin sitting partly dressed on the side of the bed, upon which his wife was lying. On the night stand beside the bed the deputies spied two capsules. When asked, "Whose stuff is this?" Rochin seized the capsules and put them in his mouth. A struggle ensued, in the course of which the three officers "jumped upon him" and attempted to extract the capsules. [Evidence indicates that the attempted extraction was by kicking and punching the defendant in the stomach and sticking their fingers down his throat to try to make him vomit.] The force they applied proved unavailing against Rochin's resistance. He was handcuffed and taken to a hospital. At the direction of one of the officers, a doctor forced an emetic solution through a tube into Rochin's stomach against his will. This "stomach pumping" produced vomiting. In the vomited matter were found two capsules which proved to contain morphine.

. . . Rochin was convicted and sentenced to sixty days' imprisonment. The chief evidence against him was the two capsules. They were admitted over the petitioner's objection.

. . . The District Court of Appeals affirmed the conviction despite the finding that the officers "were guilty of unlawfully breaking into and entering defendant's room and were guilty of unlawfully assaulting, battering, torturing, and falsely imprisoning the defendant. . . . One of the three judges, while finding that "the records in this case reveals a shocking series of violations of constitutional rights," concurred only because he felt bound by decisions of his Supreme Court. The California Supreme Court denied without opinion Rochin's petition for a hearing. [Note: This

case was prior to *Mapp* v. *Ohio* and therefore states were not required at that time to exclude illegally seized evidence.]

... In our federal system the administration of criminal justice is predominately committed to the care of the States. ...

Regard for the requirements of the Due Process Clause "inescapably imposes upon this Court an excise of judgment upon the whole course of the proceedings [resulting in a conviction] in order to ascertain whether they offend those cannons of decency and fairness which express the notions of justice of English-speaking peoples even toward those charged with the most heinous offenses. (cites omitted.) These standards of justice are not authoritatively formulated anywhere as though they were specifics. Due process of law is a summarized constitutional guarantee of respect for those personal immunities which, as Justice Cardozo twice wrote for the Court, are "so rooted in the traditions and conscience of our people as to be ranked as fundamental," or are "implicit in the concept of ordered liberty."

The Court's function in the observation of this settled conception of the Due Process Clause does not leave us without adequate guides in subjecting State criminal procedures to constitutional judgment. In dealing not with the machinery of government but with human rights, the absence of formal exactitude, or want of fixity of meaning, is not an unusual or even regrettable attribute of constitutional provisions. Words being symbols do not speak without a gloss. On the one hand the gloss may be the deposit of history, whereby a term gains technical content. Thus the requirements of the Sixth and Seventh Amendments for trial by jury in the federal courts have a rigid meaning. No changes or chances can alter the content of the verbal symbol of "jury"—a body of twelve men and women who must reach a unanimous conclusion if the verdict is to go against the defendant. On the other hand, the gloss of some of the verbal symbols of the Constitution does not give them a fixed technical content. It exacts a continuing process of application.

When the gloss has thus not been fixed but is a function of the process of judgment, the judgment is bound to fall differently at different times and differently at the same time through different judges. Even more specific provisions, such as the guaranty of freedom of speech and the detailed protection against unreasonable searches and seizures, have inevitably evoked as sharp divisions in this Court as the least specific and most comprehensive protection of liberties, the Due Process Clause.

The vague contours of the Due Process Clause do not leave judges at large. We may not draw on our merely personal and private notions and disregard the limits that bind judges in their judicial function. Even though the concepts of due process of law are not final and fixed, these limits are derived from considerations that are fused in the whole nature of our judicial process. ... These are considerations deeply rooted in reason and in the compelling traditions of the legal profession. ...

Restraints on our jurisdiction are self-imposed only in the sense that there is from our decision no immediate appeal short of impeachment or constitutional amendment. But that does not make due process of law a matter of judicial caprice. ... In each case "due process of law" requires an evaluation based on a disinterested inquiry pursued in the spirit of science, on a balanced order of facts exactly and fairly stated on the detached consideration of conflicting claims.

Applying these general considerations to the circumstances of the present case, we are compelled to conclude that the proceedings by which this conviction was obtained do more than offend some fastidious squeamishness or private sentimentalism about combatting crime too energetically. This is conduct that shocks the conscience. ... This course of proceeding by agents of government to obtain

evidence is bound to offend even hardened sensibilities. They are methods too close to the rack and the screw to permit constitutional differentiation.

[Conviction was reversed. Justices Black and Douglas wrote concurring opinions.]

WHAT DO YOU THINK?

1. Based on the Rochin opinion, explain the meaning of *due process*.
2. Before it is a violation of due process, must the police conduct shock the conscience?

The following case was decided almost 170 years ago. It discusses the relationship between the states and the federal government. The Court under the leadership of John Marshall held that the due process rights contained in the Bill of Rights were restrictions only on the federal government.

BARRON V. CITY OF BALTIMORE
32 U.S. 243 (1833)

MARSHALL, Ch. J., delivered the opinion of the court.

The judgment brought up by this writ of error having been rendered by the court of a state, this tribunal can exercise no jurisdiction over it, unless it be shown to come within the provisions of the 25th section of the judiciary act. The plaintiff in error contends, that it comes within that clause in the fifth amendment to the constitution, which inhibits the taking of private property for public use, without just compensation. He insists, that this amendment being in favor of the liberty of the citizen, ought to be so construed as to restrain the legislative power of a state, as well as that of the United States. If this proposition be untrue, the court can take no jurisdiction of the cause.

The question thus presented is, we think, of great importance, but not of much difficulty. The constitution was ordained and established by the people of the United States for themselves, for their own government, and not for the government of the individual states. Each state established a constitution for itself, and in that constitution, provided such limitations and restrictions on the powers of its particular government, as its judgment dictated. The people of the United States framed such a government for the United States as they supposed best adapted to their situation and best calculated to promote their interests. The powers they conferred on this government were to be exercised by itself; and the limitations on power, if expressed in general terms, are naturally, and, we think, necessarily, applicable to the government created by the instrument. They are limitations of power granted in the instrument itself; not of distinct governments, framed by different persons and for different purposes.

If these propositions be correct, the fifth amendment must be understood as restraining the power of the general government, not as applicable to the states. In their several constitutions, they have imposed such restrictions on their respective governments, as their own wisdom suggested; such as they deemed most proper for

Chief Justice John Marshall was appointed to the Supreme Court by President John Adams and served from 1801 to 1835. (Engraving by Alonzo Chappell. Collection of the Supreme Court of the United States.)

themselves. It is a subject on which they judge exclusively, and with which others interfere no further than they are supposed to have a common interest.

The counsel for the plaintiff in error insists that the constitution was intended to secure the people of the several states against the undue exercise of power by their respective state governments; as well as against that which might be attempted by their general government. In support of this argument he relies on the

inhibitions contained in the tenth section of the first article. We think that section affords a strong, if not a conclusive, argument in support of the opinion already indicated by the court. The preceding section contains restrictions which are obviously intended for the exclusive purpose of restraining the exercise of power by the departments of the general government. Some of them use language applicable only to congress; others are expressed in general terms. The third clause, for example, declares that "no bill of attainder or *ex post facto* law shall be passed." No language can be more general; yet the demonstration is complete, that it applies solely to the government of the United States. In addition to the general arguments furnished by the instrument itself, some of which have been already suggested, the succeeding section, the avowed purpose of which is to restrain state legislation, contains in terms the very prohibition. It declares that "no state shall pass any bill of attainder or *ex post facto* law." This provision, then, of the ninth section, however comprehensive its language, contains no restriction on state legislation.

The ninth section having enumerated, in the nature of a bill of rights, the limitations intended to be imposed on the powers of the general government, the tenth proceeds to enumerate those which were to operate on the state legislatures. These restrictions are brought together in the same section, and are by express words applied to the states. "No state shall enter into any treaty." Perceiving, that in a constitution framed by the people of the United States, for the government of all, no limitation of the action of government on the people would apply to the state government, unless expressed in terms, the restrictions contained in the tenth section are in direct words so applied to the states.

It is worthy of remark, too, that these inhibitions generally restrain state legislation on subjects intrusted to the general government, or in which the people of all the states feel an interest. A state is forbidden to enter into any treaty, alliance, or confederation. If these compacts are with foreign nations, they interfere with the treaty-making power, which is conferred entirely on the general government; if with each other, for political purposes, they can scarcely fail to interfere with the general purpose and intent of the constitution. To grant letters of marque and reprisal, would lead directly to war; the power of declaring which is expressly given to congress. To coin money is also the exercise of a power conferred on congress. It would be tedious to recapitulate the several limitations on the powers of the states which are contained in this section. They will be found, generally, to restrain state legislation on subjects intrusted to the government of the Union, in which the citizens of all the states are interested. In these alone, were the whole people concerned. The question of their application to states is not left to construction. It is averred in positive words.

If the original constitution, in the ninth and tenth sections of the first article, draws this plain and marked line of discrimination between the limitations it imposes on the powers of the general government, and on those of the state; if, in every inhibition intended to act on state power, words are employed, which directly express that intent; some strong reason must be assigned for departing from this safe and judicious course, in framing the amendments, before that departure can be assumed. We search in vain for that reason.

Had the people of the several states, or any of them, required changes in their constitutions; had they required additional safe-guards to liberty from the apprehended encroachments of their particular governments; the remedy was in their own hands, and could have been applied by themselves. A convention could have been assembled by the discontented state, and the required improvements could have been made by itself. The unwieldy and cumbrous machinery of procuring a rec-

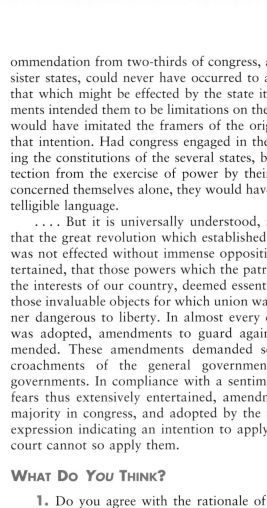

ommendation from two-thirds of congress, and the assent of three-fourths of their sister states, could never have occurred to any human being, as a mode of doing that which might be effected by the state itself. Had the framers of these amendments intended them to be limitations on the powers of the state governments, they would have imitated the framers of the original constitution, and have expressed that intention. Had congress engaged in the extraordinary occupation of improving the constitutions of the several states, by affording the people additional protection from the exercise of power by their own governments, in matters which concerned themselves alone, they would have declared this purpose in plain and intelligible language.

. . . . But it is universally understood, it is a part of the history of the day, that the great revolution which established the constitution of the United States, was not effected without immense opposition. Serious fears were extensively entertained, that those powers which the patriot statesmen, who then watched over the interests of our country, deemed essential to union, and to the attainment of those invaluable objects for which union was sought, might be exercised in a manner dangerous to liberty. In almost every convention by which the constitution was adopted, amendments to guard against the abuse of power were recommended. These amendments demanded security against the apprehended encroachments of the general government—not against those of the local governments. In compliance with a sentiment thus generally expressed, to quiet fears thus extensively entertained, amendments were proposed by the required majority in congress, and adopted by the states. These amendments contain no expression indicating an intention to apply them to the state governments. This court cannot so apply them.

WHAT DO YOU THINK?

1. Do you agree with the rationale of the Court regarding the fact that the Fifth Amendment was meant to apply only to the federal government?

2. Justice Oliver Wendell Homes once stated that "due process is more a matter of experience than logic." After reading the above case and the following cases on the meaning of due process, do you agree with his statement?

Is a trial by jury a fundamental part of American due process? If it is fundamental, are the states required to provide for juries in criminal cases? The following case looks at the issue of what constitutes due process and the right to trial by jury.

DUNCAN V. LOUISIANA
391 U.S. 145, 88 S.Ct. 1444 (1968)

Duncan was convicted of simple battery which under state law is a misdemeanor punishable by two years' imprisonment and a $300 fine. At his trial, Duncan requested trial by jury. His request was denied by the judge based on Louisiana law which allowed trial by jury only in capital cases (death penalty) or cases where

imprisonment at hard labor [under Louisiana law the imprisonment of hard labor had a minimum one year sentence] may be imposed. Duncan was convicted and sentenced to serve 60 days in the parish jail [similar to a county jail], and ordered to pay a fine of $150.

JUSTICE WHITE delivered the opinion of the Court.

. . . Because we believe that trial by jury in criminal cases is fundamental to the American scheme of justice, we hold that the Fourteenth Amendment guarantees a right of jury trial in all criminal cases which—were they to be tried in a federal court—would come within the Sixth Amendment's guarantee.

Since we consider the appeal before us to be such a case, we hold that the constitution was violated when appellant's demand for jury trial was refused.

. . . By the time our Constitution was written, jury trial in criminal cases had been in existence in England for several centuries and carried impressive credentials traced by many to the Magna Carta. Its preservation and proper operation as a protection against arbitrary rule were among the major objectives of the revolutionary settlement which was expressed in the Declaration and Bill of Rights of 1689.

Jury trial came to America with English colonists, and received strong support from them. Royal interference with the jury trial was deeply resented. Among the resolutions adopted by the First Congress of the American Colonies (Stamp Act Congress) on October 19, 1765—resolutions deemed by their authors to state "the most essential rights and liberties of the colonists"—was the declaration: "That trial by jury is the inherent and invaluable right of every British subject in these colonies."

. . . The constitutions adopted by the original States guaranteed jury trial. Also, the constitution of every State entering the Union thereafter in one form or another protected the right to jury trial in criminal cases. . . .

. . . Jury trial continues to receive strong support. The laws of every state guarantee a right to jury trial in serious criminal cases; no state has dispensed with it; nor are there significant movements underway to do so. . . .

The state of Louisiana urges that holding that the Fourteenth Amendment assures a right to jury trial will cast doubt on the integrity of every trial conducted without a jury. Plainly this is not the import of our holding. . . .

We would not assert that every criminal trial—or any particular trial held before a judge alone—is unfair or that a defendant may never be as fairly treated by a judge as he would be by jury. Thus we hold no constitutional doubts about the practices, common in both federal and state courts, of accepting waivers of jury trial and prosecuting petty crimes without extending a right to jury trial. However, the fact is that in most places more trials for serious crimes are to juries than to a court alone; a great many defendants prefer the judgment of a jury to that of a court. Even where defendants are satisfied with bench trials, the right to a jury trial very likely serves its intended purpose of making judicial or prosecutorial unfairness less likely.

Louisiana's final contention is that even if it must grant jury trial in serious criminal cases, the conviction before us is valid and constitutional because here the petitioner was tried for simple battery and was sentenced to only 60 days in the parish prison. We are not persuaded. It is doubtless true that there is a category of petty crimes or offenses which is not subject to the Sixth Amendment jury trial provision and should not be subject to the Fourteenth Amendment jury trial requirement here applied to the States. But the penalty authorized for a particular crime is of major relevance in determining whether it is serious or not and may in itself, if severe enough, subject the trial to the mandates of the Sixth Amendment. . . .

[Justice Black, with whom Justice Douglas joined, wrote a concurring opinion that contended that in all criminal cases, the accused should have the right to a jury trial. Justice Harlan wrote a dissenting opinion, which Justice Stewart joined.]

WHAT DO YOU THINK?

1. The majority opinion used common law to establish the right to a jury trial. Why was this necessary since there are specific constitutional provisions protecting the right to a jury trial?
2. Is the use of common law concepts necessary to ascertain the meaning of the right to a jury trial?
3. Why do you think that the Court elected to use the maximum punishment Duncan could have received in determining whether he had a right to a jury trial? (*Note*: He only received 60 days confinement.)

Does the concept of due process include the right of the defendant to have the jury instructed on the presumption of innocence? The following case looks at that issue.

TAYLOR V. KENTUCKY
436 U.S. 478 (1978)

JUSTICE POWELL delivered the opinion of the Court.

Only two Terms ago, this Court observed that the "presumption of innocence," although not articulated in the Constitution, is a basic component of a fair trial under our system of criminal justice. . . . In this felony case, the trial court instructed the jury as to the prosecution's burden of proof beyond a reasonable doubt, but refused petitioner's (accused) timely request for instructions on the presumption of innocence and the indictment's lack of evidentiary value. We are asked to decide whether the Due Process Clause of the Fourteenth Amendment requires either or both instructions.

The petitioner was tried for robbery in 1976, allegedly having forced his way into the home of James Maddox and stolen a house key and a billfold containing $10 to $15. . . . The Commonwealth's only witness was Maddox. He testified that he had known the petitioner for several years and had entertained petitioner at his home on several occasions. According to Maddox, petitioner and a friend knocked on his door on the evening of February 16, 1976, asking to be admitted. Maddox refused, saying he had to go to bed. The two left, but returned 15 minutes later. They forced their way in, hit Maddox over the head, and fled with his billfold and house key, which were never recovered.

Petitioner then took the stand as the only witness for the defense. He admitted having been at Maddox's home on other occasions but denied going there on February 16 or participating in the robbery. . . . Defense counsel requested that the Court instruct the jury that "the law presumes a defendant to be innocent of the

Justice Lewis F. Powell, Jr., was appointed to the Supreme Court by President Nixon and served from 1971 to 1987. (Photograph by Ken Heinen. Collection of the Supreme Court of the United States.)

crime." The Court declined to give the instruction and instructed the jury that the Commonwealth had the burden of proving the accused's guilt beyond a reasonable doubt. The petitioner was found guilty and sentenced to five years in prison. . . .

This Court has declared that one accused of a crime is entitled to have his guilt or innocence determined solely on the basis of evidence introduced at trial. . . . And it long has been recognized that an instruction on the presumption is one way of impressing upon the jury the importance of that right. . . .

We hold that on the facts of this case the trial judge's refusal to give the requested instruction resulted in a violation of his right to a fair trial as guaranteed by the Due Process Clause of the Fourteenth Amendment. The judgment of conviction is reversed, and the case is remanded for further proceedings not inconsistent with this opinion. [Justice Brennan wrote a concurring opinion and Justices Stevens and Rehnquist wrote dissenting opinions.]

WHAT DO YOU THINK?

1. Since the majority of people are aware that the accused is presumed innocent of the charge until his or her guilt is established beyond a reasonable doubt, should it make any difference in the case if the jury was aware of this requirement without being so instructed by the judge?

2. Why did the Court remand the case to the original court for further proceedings not inconsistent with its opinion? What does this mean?

The case of Duncan *v.* Louisiana *involves the question of substantive due process. Also important is the concept of procedural due process. The following civil case discusses what procedural due process means.*

GOLDBERG V. KELLY
397 U.S. 254 (1970)

MR. JUSTICE BRENNAN delivered the opinion of the Court.

The question for decision is whether a State that terminates public assistance payments to a particular recipient without affording him the opportunity for an evidentiary hearing prior to termination denies the recipient procedural due process in violation of the Due Process Clause of the Fourteenth Amendment.

This action was brought in the District Court for the Southern District of New York by residents of New York City receiving financial aid under the federally assisted program of Aid to Families with Dependent Children (AFDC) or under New York State's general Home Relief program. Their complaint alleged that the New York State and New York City officials administering these programs terminated, or were about to terminate, such aid without prior notice and hearing, thereby denying them due process of law. At the time the suits were filed there was no requirement of prior notice or hearing of any kind before termination of financial aid. However, the State and city adopted procedures for notice and hearing after the suits were brought, and the plaintiffs, appellees here, then challenged the constitutional adequacy of those procedures.

The State Commissioner of Social Services amended the State Department of Social Services' Official Regulations to require that local social services officials proposing to discontinue or suspend a recipient's financial aid do so according to a procedure that conforms to either subdivision (a) or subdivision (b) of 351.26 of the regulations as amended. The City of New York elected to promulgate a local procedure according to subdivision (b). That subdivision, so far as here pertinent, provides that the local procedure must include the giving of notice to the recipient of the reasons for a proposed discontinuance or suspension at least seven days prior to its effective date, with notice also that upon request the recipient may have the proposal reviewed by a local welfare official holding a position superior to that of the supervisor who approved the proposed discontinuance or suspension, and, further, that the recipient may submit, for purposes of the review, a written statement to demonstrate why his grant should not be discontinued or suspended. The decision by the reviewing official whether to discontinue or suspend aid must be made expeditiously, with written notice of the decision to the recipient. The section further expressly provides that "[a]ssistance shall not be discontinued or suspended prior to the date such notice of decision is sent to the recipient and his representative, if any, or prior to the proposed effective date of discontinuance or suspension, whichever occurs later."

Pursuant to subdivision (b), the New York City Department of Social Services promulgated Procedure No. 68–18. A caseworker who has doubts about the recipient's continued eligibility must first discuss them with the recipient. If the caseworker concludes that the recipient is no longer eligible, he recommends termination of aid to a unit supervisor. If the latter concurs, he sends the recipient a letter stating the reasons for proposing to terminate aid and notifying him that within seven days he may request that a higher official review the record, and may support the request with a written statement prepared personally or with the aid of an attorney or other person. If the reviewing official affirms the determination of ineligibility, aid is stopped immediately and the recipient is informed by letter of the reasons for the action. Appellees' challenge to this procedure emphasizes the absence of any provisions for the personal appearance of the recipient before the reviewing official, for oral presentation of evidence, and for confrontation and cross-examination of adverse witnesses. However, the letter does inform the recipient that he may request a post-termination "fair hearing." This is a proceeding before an independent state hearing officer at which the recipient may appear personally, offer oral evidence, confront and cross-examine the witnesses against him, and have a record made of the hearing. If the recipient prevails at the "fair hearing" he is paid all funds erroneously withheld. HEW Handbook, pt. IV, 6200–6500; 18 NYCRR 84.2–84.23. A recipient whose aid is not restored by a "fair hearing" decision may have judicial review. N.Y. Civil Practice Law and Rules, Art. 78 (1963). The recipient is so notified, 18 NYCRR 84.16.

I

The constitutional issue to be decided, therefore, is the narrow one whether the Due Process Clause requires that the recipient be afforded an evidentiary hearing before the termination of benefits. The District Court held that only a pre-termination evidentiary hearing would satisfy the constitutional command, and rejected the argument of the state and city officials that the combination of the post-termination "fair hearing" with the informal pre-termination review disposed of all due process claims. The court said: "While post-termination review is relevant, there is one overpowering fact which controls here. By hypothesis, a welfare recipient is destitute, without funds or assets. . . . Suffice it to say that to cut off a welfare recipient in the face of . . . 'brutal need' without a prior hearing of some sort is unconscionable, unless overwhelming considerations justify it." *Kelly* v. *Wyman*, 294 F. Supp. 893, 899, 900 (1968). The court rejected the argument that the need to protect the public's tax revenues supplied the requisite "overwhelming consideration." "Against the justified desire to protect public funds must be weighed the individual's over-powering need in this unique situation not to be wrongfully deprived of assistance. . . . While the problem of additional expense must be kept in mind, it does not justify denying a hearing meeting the ordinary standards of due process. Under all the circumstances, we hold that due process requires an adequate hearing before termination of welfare benefits, and the fact that there is a later constitutionally fair proceeding does not alter the result." *Id.*, at 901. Although state officials were party defendants in the action, only the Commissioner of Social Services of the City of New York appealed. We noted probable jurisdiction, 394 U.S. 971 (1969), to decide important issues that have been the subject of disagreement in principle between the three-judge court in the present case and that convened in *Wheeler* v. *Montgomery*, No. 14, post, p. 280, also decided today. We affirm.

Appellant does not contend that procedural due process is not applicable to the termination of welfare benefits. Such benefits are a matter of statutory entitlement for persons qualified to receive them. Their termination involves state action that adjudicates important rights. The constitutional challenge cannot be answered by an argument that public assistance benefits are "a 'privilege' and not a 'right.' "

Shapiro v. *Thompson*, 394 U.S. 618, 627 n. 6 (1969). Relevant constitutional restraints apply as much to the withdrawal of public assistance benefits as to disqualification for unemployment compensation, *Sherbert* v. *Verner*, 374 U.S. 398 (1963); or to denial of a tax exemption, *Speiser* v. *Randall*, 357 U.S. 513 (1958); or to discharge from public employment, *Slochower* v. *Board of Higher Education*, 350 U.S. 551 (1956). The extent to which procedural due process must be afforded the recipient is influenced by the extent to which he may be "condemned to suffer grievous loss," *Joint Anti-Fascist Refugee Committee* v. *McGrath*, 341 U.S. 123, 168 (1951) (Frankfurter, J., concurring), and depends upon whether the recipient's interest in avoiding that loss outweighs the governmental interest in summary adjudication. Accordingly, as we said in *Cafeteria & Restaurant Workers Union* v. *McElroy*, 367 U.S. 886, 895 (1961), "consideration of what procedures due process may require under any given set of circumstances must begin with a determination of the precise nature of the government function involved as well as of the private interest that has been affected by governmental action." See also *Hannah* v. *Larche*, 363 U.S. 420, 440, 442 (1960). . . .

"The fundamental requisite of due process of law is the opportunity to be heard." *Grannis* v. *Ordean*, 234 U.S. 385, 394 (1914). The hearing must be "at a meaningful time and in a meaningful manner." *Armstrong* v. *Manzo*, 380 U.S. 545, 552 (1965). In the present context these principles require that a recipient have timely and adequate notice detailing the reasons for a proposed termination, and an effective opportunity to defend by confronting any adverse witnesses and by presenting his own arguments and evidence orally. These rights are important in cases such as those before us, where recipients have challenged proposed terminations as resting on incorrect or misleading factual premises or on misapplication of rules or policies to the facts of particular cases. . . .

In almost every setting where important decisions turn on questions of fact, due process requires an opportunity to confront and cross-examine adverse witnesses. e.g., *ICC* v. *Louisville & N. R. Co.*, 227 U.S. 88, 93–94 (1913); *Willner* v. *Committee on Character & Fitness*, 373 U.S. 96, 103–104 (1963). What we said in *Greene* v. *McElroy*, 360 U.S. 474, 496–497 (1959), is particularly pertinent here:

> "Certain principles have remained relatively immutable in our jurisprudence. One of these is that where governmental action seriously injures an individual, and the reasonableness of the action depends on fact findings, the evidence used to prove the Government's case must be disclosed to the individual so that he has an opportunity to show that it is untrue. While this is important in the case of documentary evidence, it is even more important where the evidence consists of the testimony of individuals whose memory might be faulty or who, in fact, might be perjurers or persons motivated by malice, vindictiveness, intolerance, prejudice, or jealousy. We have formalized these protections in the requirements of confrontation and cross-examination. They have ancient roots. They find expression in the Sixth Amendment. . . . This Court has been zealous to protect these rights from erosion. It has spoken out not only in criminal cases, . . . but also in all types of cases where administrative . . . actions were under scrutiny."

Affirmed.

[Chief Justice Burger and Justice Steward wrote dissenting opinions.]

WHAT DO YOU THINK?

1. What constitutes procedural due process?
2. How is procedural due process different from substantive due process?

Is it a violation of due process to allow warrants to be issued by municipal court clerks? Is it necessary that the individual issuing a warrant be an attorney or have legal training?

SHADWICK V. CITY OF TAMPA
407 U.S. 345 (1972)

MR. JUSTICE POWELL delivered the opinion of the Court.

The charter of Tampa, Florida, authorizes the issuance of certain arrest warrants by clerks of the Tampa Municipal Court. The sole question in this case is whether these clerks qualify as neutral and detached magistrates for purposes of the Fourth Amendment. We hold that they do.

Appellant was arrested for impaired driving on a warrant issued by a clerk of the municipal court. He moved the court to quash the warrant on the ground that it was issued by a nonjudicial officer in violation of the Fourth and Fourteenth Amendments. When the motion was denied, he initiated proceedings in the Florida courts by means of that State's writ of common-law *certiorari*. The state proceedings culminated in the holding of the Florida Supreme Court that "[t]he clerk and deputy clerks of the municipal court of the City of Tampa are neutral and detached 'magistrates' . . . for the purpose of issuing arrest warrants within the requirements of the United States Constitution. . . ." 250 So.2d 4, 5 (1971).

I

A clerk of the municipal court is appointed by the city clerk from a classified list of civil servants and assigned to work in the municipal court. The statute does not specify the qualifications necessary for this job, but no law degree or special legal training is required. The clerk's duties are to receive traffic fines, prepare the court's dockets and records, fill out commitment papers, and perform other routine clerical tasks. Apparently he may issue subpoenas. He may not, however, sit as a judge, and he may not issue a search warrant or even a felony or misdemeanor arrest warrant for violations of state laws. The only warrants he may issue are for the arrest of those charged with having breached municipal ordinances of the city of Tampa.

Appellant, contending that the Fourth Amendment requires that warrants be issued by "judicial officers," argues that even this limited warrant authority is constitutionally invalid. He reasons that warrant applications of whatever nature cannot be assured the discerning, independent review compelled by the Fourth Amendment when the review is performed by less than a judicial officer. It is less than clear, however, as to who would qualify as a "judicial officer" under appellant's theory. There is some suggestion in appellant's brief that a judicial officer must be a lawyer or the municipal court judge himself. A more complete portrayal of appellant's position would be that the Tampa clerks are disqualified as judicial officers not merely because they are not lawyers or judges, but because they lack the institutional independence associated with the judiciary in that they are members of the civil service, appointed by the city clerk, "an executive official," and enjoy no statutorily specified tenure in office.

Past decisions of the Court have mentioned review by a "judicial officer" prior to issuance of a warrant, *Whiteley* v. *Warden*, 401 U.S. 560, 564 (1971); *Katz* v. *United States*, 389 U.S. 347, 356 (1967); *Wong Sun* v. *United States*, 371 U.S. 471, 481–482 (1963); *Jones* v. *United States*, 362 U.S. 257, 270 (1960); *Johnson* v. *United States*, 333 U.S. 10, 14 (1948). In some cases the term "judicial officer" appears to have been used interchangeably with that of "magistrate." *Katz* v. *United States*, *supra*, and *Johnson* v. *United States*, *supra*. In others, it was intended simply to underscore the now accepted fact that someone independent of the police and prosecution must determine probable cause. *Jones* v. *United States*, *supra*; *Wong Sun* v. *United States*, *supra*. The very term "judicial officer" implies, of course, some connection with the judicial branch. But it has never been held that only a lawyer or judge could grant a warrant, regardless of the court system or the type of warrant involved. In *Jones*, *supra*, at 270–271, the Court implied that United States Commissioners, many of whom were not lawyers or judges, were nonetheless "independent judicial officers."

The Court frequently has employed the term "magistrate" to denote those who may issue warrants. *Coolidge* v. *New Hampshire*, 403 U.S. 443, 449–453 (1971); *Whiteley* v. *Warden*, *supra*, at 566; *Katz* v. *United States*, *supra*, at 356–357; *United States* v. *Ventresca*, 380 U.S. 102, 108 (1965); *Giordenello* v. *United States*, 357 U.S. 480, 486 (1958); *Johnson* v. *United States*, *supra*, at 13–14; *United States* v. *Lefkowitz*, 285 U.S. 452, 464 (1932). Historically, a magistrate has been defined broadly as "a public civil officer, possessing such power, legislative, executive or judicial, as the government appointing him may ordain," *Compton* v. *Alabama*, 214 U.S. 1, 7 (1909), or, in a narrower sense "an inferior judicial officer, such as a justice of the peace." *Ibid.* More recent definitions have not much changed.

An examination of the Court's decisions reveals that the terms "magistrate" and "judicial officer" have been used interchangeably. Little attempt was made to define either term, to distinguish the one from the other, or to advance one as the definitive Fourth Amendment requirement. We find no commandment in either term, however, that all warrant authority must reside exclusively in a lawyer or judge. Such a requirement would have been incongruous when even within the federal system warrants were until recently widely issued by nonlawyers.

To attempt to extract further significance from the above terminology would be both unnecessary and futile. The substance of the Constitution's warrant requirements does not turn on the labeling of the issuing party. The warrant traditionally has represented an independent assurance that a search and arrest will not proceed without probable cause to believe that a crime has been committed and that the person or place named in the warrant is involved in the crime. Thus, an issuing magistrate must meet two tests. He must be neutral and detached, and he must be capable of determining whether probable cause exists for the requested arrest or search. This Court long has insisted that inferences of probable cause be drawn by "a neutral and detached magistrate instead of being judged by the officer engaged in the often competitive enterprise of ferreting out crime." *Johnson* v. *United States*, *supra*, at 14; *Giordenello* v. *United States*, *supra*, at 486. In *Coolidge* v. *New Hampshire*, *supra*, the Court last Term voided a search warrant issued by the state attorney general "who was actively in charge of the investigation and later was to be chief prosecutor at the trial." *Id.*, at 450. If, on the other hand, detachment and capacity do conjoin, the magistrate has satisfied the Fourth Amendment's purpose.

The requisite detachment is present in the case at hand. Whatever else neutrality and detachment might entail, it is clear that they require severance and disengagement from activities of law enforcement. There has been no showing whatever here of partiality, or affiliation of these clerks with prosecutors or police. The record shows no connection with any law enforcement activity or authority which would distort the independent judgment the Fourth Amendment requires. Appellant himself expressly refused to allege anything to that effect. The municipal court clerk is assigned not to the police or prosecutor but to the municipal court judge for whom he does much of his work. In this sense, he may well be termed a "judicial officer." While a statutorily specified term of office and appointment by someone other than "an executive authority" might be desirable, the absence of such features is hardly disqualifying. Judges themselves take office under differing circumstances. Some are appointed, but many are elected by legislative bodies or by the people. Many enjoy but limited terms and are subject to re-appointment or re-election. Most depend for their salary level upon the legislative branch. We will not elevate requirements for the independence of a municipal clerk to a level higher than that prevailing with respect to many judges. The clerk's neutrality has not been impeached: he is removed from prosecutor or police and works within the judicial branch subject to the supervision of the municipal court judge.

Appellant likewise has failed to demonstrate that these clerks lack capacity to determine probable cause. The clerk's authority extends only to the issuance of arrest warrants for breach of municipal ordinances. We presume from the nature of the clerk's position that he would be able to deduce from the facts on an affidavit before him whether there was probable cause to believe a citizen guilty of impaired driving, breach of peace, drunkenness, trespass, or the multiple other common offenses covered by a municipal code. There has been no showing that this is too difficult a task for a clerk to accomplish. Our legal system has long entrusted non-lawyers to evaluate more complex and significant factual data than that in the case at hand. Grand juries daily determine probable cause prior to rendering indictments, and trial juries assess whether guilt is proved beyond a reasonable doubt. The significance and responsibility of these lay judgments betray any belief that the Tampa clerks could not determine probable cause for arrest.

We decide today only that clerks of the municipal court may constitutionally issue the warrants in question. We have not considered whether the actual issuance was based upon an adequate showing of probable cause. *Aguilar* v. *Texas*, 378 U.S. 108 (1964). Appellant did not submit this question to the courts below, 237 So.2d 231 (1970), 250 So.2d 4 (1971), and we will not decide it here initially. The single question is whether power has been lawfully vested, not whether it has been constitutionally exercised.

Nor need we determine whether a State may lodge warrant authority in someone entirely outside the sphere of the judicial branch. Many persons may not qualify as the kind of "public civil officers" we have come to associate with the term "magistrate." Had the Tampa clerk been entirely divorced from a judicial position, this case would have presented different considerations. Here, however, the clerk is an employee of the judicial branch of the city of Tampa, disassociated from the role of law enforcement. On the record in this case, the independent status of the clerk cannot be questioned.

What we do reject today is any per se invalidation of a state or local warrant system on the ground that the issuing magistrate is not a lawyer or judge.

Communities may have sound reasons for delegating the responsibility of issuing warrants to competent personnel other than judges or lawyers. Many municipal courts face stiff and unrelenting caseloads. A judge pressured with the docket before him may give warrant applications more brisk and summary treatment than would a clerk. All this is not to imply that a judge or lawyer would not normally provide the most desirable review of warrant requests. But our federal system warns of converting desirable practice into constitutional commandment. It recognizes in plural and diverse state activities one key to national innovation and vitality. States are entitled to some flexibility and leeway in their designation of magistrates, so long as all are neutral and detached and capable of the probable-cause determination required of them.

We affirm the judgment of the Florida Supreme Court.

Affirmed.

WHAT DO YOU THINK?

1. Should we entrust the decision to issue a warrant to a non-legally trained person?
2. Is the clerk a "judicial" officer?

Should the prosecutor open his or her files to the defense? What are the duties of the prosecutor to disclose evidence that may be favorable to the defense? The next case looks at those questions.

UNITED STATES V. AGURS
427 U.S. 97 (1976)

MR. JUSTICE STEVENS delivered the opinion of the Court.

After a brief interlude in an inexpensive motel room, respondent repeatedly stabbed James Sewell, causing his death. She was convicted of second-degree murder. The question before us is whether the prosecutor's failure to provide defense counsel with certain background information about Sewell, which would have tended to support the argument that respondent acted in self-defense, deprived her of a fair trial under the rule of *Brady* v. *Maryland*, 373 U.S. 83.

The answer to the question depends on (1) a review of the facts, (2) the significance of the failure of defense counsel to request the material, and (3) the standard by which the prosecution's failure to volunteer exculpatory material should be judged.

I

At about 4:30 p.m. on September 24, 1971, respondent, who had been there before, and Sewell, registered in a motel as man and wife. They were assigned a room without a bath. Sewell was wearing a bowie knife in a sheath, and carried another knife in his pocket. Less than two hours earlier, according to the testimony of his estranged wife, he had had $360 in cash on his person.

About 15 minutes later three motel employees heard respondent screaming for help. A forced entry into their room disclosed Sewell on top of respondent

struggling for possession of the bowie knife. She was holding the knife; his bleeding hand grasped the blade; according to one witness he was trying to jam the blade into her chest. The employees separated the two and summoned the authorities. Respondent departed without comment before they arrived. Sewell was dead on arrival at the hospital.

Circumstantial evidence indicated that the parties had completed an act of intercourse, that Sewell had then gone to the bathroom down the hall, and that the struggle occurred upon his return. The contents of his pockets were in disarray on the dresser and no money was found; the jury may have inferred that respondent took Sewell's money and that the fight started when Sewell re-entered the room and saw what she was doing.

On the following morning respondent surrendered to the police. She was given a physical examination which revealed no cuts or bruises of any kind, except needle marks on her upper arm. An autopsy of Sewell disclosed that he had several deep stab wounds in his chest and abdomen, and a number of slashes on his arms and hands, characterized by the pathologist as "defensive wounds."

Respondent offered no evidence. Her sole defense was the argument made by her attorney that Sewell had initially attacked her with the knife, and that her actions had all been directed toward saving her own life. The support for this self-defense theory was based on the fact that she had screamed for help. Sewell was on top of her when help arrived, and his possession of two knives indicated that he was a violence-prone person. It took the jury about 25 minutes to elect a foreman and return a verdict.

Three months later defense counsel filed a motion for a new trial asserting that he had discovered (1) that Sewell had a prior criminal record that would have further evidenced his violent character; (2) that the prosecutor had failed to disclose this information to the defense; and (3) that a recent opinion of the United States Court of Appeals for the District of Columbia Circuit made it clear that such evidence was admissible even if not known to the defendant. Sewell's prior record included a plea of guilty to a charge of assault and carrying a deadly weapon in 1963, and another guilty plea to a charge of carrying a deadly weapon in 1971. Apparently both weapons were knives.

The Government opposed the motion, arguing that there was no duty to tender Sewell's prior record to the defense in the absence of an appropriate request; that the evidence was readily discoverable in advance of trial and hence was not the kind of "newly discovered" evidence justifying a new trial; and that, in all events, it was not material.

The District Court denied the motion. It rejected the Government's argument that there was no duty to disclose material evidence unless requested to do so. The court assumed that the evidence was admissible, but held that it was not sufficiently material. The District Court expressed the opinion that the prior conviction shed no light on Sewell's character that was not already apparent from the uncontradicted evidence, particularly the fact that he carried two knives; the court stressed the inconsistency between the claim of self-defense and the fact that Sewell had been stabbed repeatedly while respondent was unscathed.

The Court of Appeals reversed. The court found no lack of diligence on the part of the defense and no misconduct by the prosecutor in this case. It held, however, that the evidence was material, and that its nondisclosure required a new trial because the jury might have returned a different verdict if the evidence had been received.

The decision of the Court of Appeals represents a significant departure from this Court's prior holding; because we believe that that court has incorrectly interpreted the constitutional requirement of due process, we reverse.

II

The rule of *Brady* v. *Maryland*, 373 U.S. 83, arguably applies in three quite different situations. Each involves the discovery, after trial, of information which had been known to the prosecution but unknown to the defense.

In the first situation, typified by *Mooney* v. *Holohan*, 294 U.S. 103, the undisclosed evidence demonstrates that the prosecution's case includes perjured testimony and that the prosecution knew, or should have known, of the perjury. In a series of subsequent cases, the Court has consistently held that a conviction obtained by the knowing use of perjured testimony is fundamentally unfair, and must be set aside if there is any reasonable likelihood that the false testimony could have affected the judgment of the jury. It is this line of cases on which the Court of Appeals placed primary reliance. In those cases the Court has applied a strict standard of materiality, not just because they involve prosecutorial misconduct, but more importantly because they involve a corruption of the truth-seeking function of the trial process. Since this case involves no misconduct, and since there is no reason to question the veracity of any of the prosecution witnesses, the test of materiality followed in the Mooney line of cases is not necessarily applicable to this case.

The second situation, illustrated by the Brady case itself, is characterized by a pretrial request for specific evidence. In that case defense counsel had requested the extrajudicial statements made by Brady's accomplice, one Boblit. This Court held that the suppression of one of Boblit's statements deprived Brady of due process, noting specifically that the statement had been requested and that it was "material." A fair analysis of the holding in Brady indicates that implicit in the requirement of materiality is a concern that the suppressed evidence might have affected the outcome of the trial.

Brady was found guilty of murder in the first degree. Since the jury did not add the words "without capital punishment" to the verdict, he was sentenced to death. At his trial Brady did not deny his involvement in the deliberate killing, but testified that it was his accomplice, Boblit, rather than he, who had actually strangled the decedent. This version of the event was corroborated by one of several confessions made by Boblit but not given to Brady's counsel despite an admittedly adequate request.

After his conviction and sentence had been affirmed on appeal, Brady filed a motion to set aside the judgment, and later a post-conviction proceeding, in which he alleged that the State had violated his constitutional rights by suppressing the Boblit confession. The trial judge denied relief largely because he felt that Boblit's confession would have been inadmissible at Brady's trial. The Maryland Court of Appeals disagreed; it ordered a new trial on the issue of punishment. It held that the withholding of material evidence, even "without guile," was a denial of due process and that there were valid theories on which the confession might have been admissible in Brady's defense.

This Court granted *certiorari* to consider Brady's contention that the violation of his constitutional right to a fair trial vitiated the entire proceeding. The holding that the suppression of exculpatory evidence violated Brady's right to due process was affirmed, as was the separate holding that he should receive a new trial on the

issue of punishment but not on the issue of guilt or innocence. The Court interpreted the Maryland Court of Appeals opinion as ruling that the confession was inadmissible on that issue. For that reason, the confession could not have affected the outcome on the issue of guilt but could have affected Brady's punishment. It was material on the latter issue but not the former. And since it was not material on the issue of guilt, the entire trial was not lacking in due process.

The test of materiality in a case like Brady in which specific information has been requested by the defense is not necessarily the same as in a case in which no such request has been made. Indeed, this Court has not yet decided whether the prosecutor has any obligation to provide defense counsel with exculpatory information when no request has been made. Before addressing that question, a brief comment on the function of the request is appropriate.

In Brady the request was specific. It gave the prosecutor notice of exactly what the defense desired. Although there is, of course, no duty to provide defense counsel with unlimited discovery of everything known by the prosecutor, if the subject matter of such a request is material, or indeed if a substantial basis for claiming materiality exists, it is reasonable to require the prosecutor to respond either by furnishing the information or by submitting the problem to the trial judge. When the prosecutor receives a specific and relevant request, the failure to make any response is seldom, if ever, excusable.

In many cases, however, exculpatory information in the possession of the prosecutor may be unknown to defense counsel. In such a situation he may make no request at all, or possibly ask for "all Brady material" or for "anything exculpatory." Such a request really gives the prosecutor no better notice than if no request is made. If there is a duty to respond to a general request of that kind, it must derive from the obviously exculpatory character of certain evidence in the hands of the prosecutor. But if the evidence is so clearly supportive of a claim of innocence that it gives the prosecution notice of a duty to produce, that duty should equally arise even if no request is made. Whether we focus on the desirability of a precise definition of the prosecutor's duty or on the potential harm to the defendant, we conclude that there is no significant difference between cases in which there has been merely a general request for exculpatory matter and cases, like the one we must now decide, in which there has been no request at all. The third situation in which the Brady rule arguably applies, typified by this case, therefore embraces the case in which only a general request for "Brady material" has been made.

We now consider whether the prosecutor has any constitutional duty to volunteer exculpatory matter to the defense, and if so, what standard of materiality gives rise to that duty.

III

We are not considering the scope of discovery authorized by the Federal Rules of Criminal Procedure, or the wisdom of amending those Rules to enlarge the defendant's discovery rights. We are dealing with the defendant's right to a fair trial mandated by the Due Process Clause of the Fifth Amendment to the Constitution. Our construction of that Clause will apply equally to the comparable clause in the Fourteenth Amendment applicable to trials in state courts.

The problem arises in two principal contexts. First, in advance of trial, and perhaps during the course of a trial as well, the prosecutor must decide what, if anything, he should voluntarily submit to defense counsel. Second, after trial a judge may be required to decide whether a nondisclosure deprived the defendant of his

right to due process. Logically the same standard must apply at both times. For unless the omission deprived the defendant of a fair trial, there was no constitutional violation requiring that the verdict be set aside; and absent a constitutional violation, there was no breach of the prosecutor's constitutional duty to disclose.

Nevertheless, there is a significant practical difference between the pretrial decision of the prosecutor and the post-trial decision of the judge. Because we are dealing with an inevitably imprecise standard, and because the significance of an item of evidence can seldom be predicted accurately until the entire record is complete, the prudent prosecutor will resolve doubtful questions in favor of disclosure. But to reiterate a critical point, the prosecutor will not have violated his constitutional duty of disclosure unless his omission is of sufficient significance to result in the denial of the defendant's right to a fair trial.

The Court of Appeals appears to have assumed that the prosecutor has a constitutional obligation to disclose any information that might affect the jury's verdict. That statement of a constitutional standard of materiality approaches the "sporting theory of justice" which the Court expressly rejected in Brady. For a jury's appraisal of a case "might" be affected by an improper or trivial consideration as well as by evidence giving rise to a legitimate doubt on the issue of guilt. If everything that might influence a jury must be disclosed, the only way a prosecutor could discharge his constitutional duty would be to allow complete discovery of his files as a matter of routine practice.

Whether or not procedural rules authorizing such broad discovery might be desirable, the Constitution surely does not demand that much. While expressing the opinion that representatives of the State may not "suppress substantial material evidence," former Chief Justice Traynor of the California Supreme Court has pointed out that "they are under no duty to report *sua sponte* to the defendant all that they learn about the case and about their witnesses." *In re Imbler*, 60 Cal. 2d 554, 569, 387 P.2d 6, 14 (1963). And this Court recently noted that there is "no constitutional requirement that the prosecution make a complete and detailed accounting to the defense of all police investigatory work on a case." *Moore v. Illinois*, 408 U.S. 786, 795. The mere possibility that an item of undisclosed information might have helped the defense, or might have affected the outcome of the trial, does not establish "materiality" in the constitutional sense.

Nor do we believe the constitutional obligation is measured by the moral culpability, or the willfulness, of the prosecutor. If evidence highly probative of innocence is in his file, he should be presumed to recognize its significance even if he has actually overlooked it. Cf. *Giglio v. United States*, 405 U.S. 150, 154. Conversely, if evidence actually has no probative significance at all, no purpose would be served by requiring a new trial simply because an inept prosecutor incorrectly believed he was suppressing a fact that would be vital to the defense. If the suppression of evidence results in constitutional error, it is because of the character of the evidence, not the character of the prosecutor.

As the District Court recognized in this case, there are situations in which evidence is obviously of such substantial value to the defense that elementary fairness requires it to be disclosed even without a specific request. For though the attorney for the sovereign must prosecute the accused with earnestness and vigor, he must always be faithful to his client's overriding interest that "justice shall be done." He is the "servant of the law, the twofold aim of which is that guilt shall not escape or innocence suffer." *Berger v. United States*, 295 U.S. 78, 88. This description of the prosecutor's duty illuminates the standard of materiality that governs his obligation to disclose exculpatory evidence.

On the one hand, the fact that such evidence was available to the prosecutor and not submitted to the defense places it in a different category than if it had simply been discovered from a neutral source after trial. For that reason the defendant should not have to satisfy the severe burden of demonstrating that newly discovered evidence probably would have resulted in acquittal. If the standard applied to the usual motion for a new trial based on newly discovered evidence were the same when the evidence was in the State's possession as when it was found in a neutral source, there would be no special significance to the prosecutor's obligation to serve the cause of justice.

On the other hand, since we have rejected the suggestion that the prosecutor has a constitutional duty routinely to deliver his entire file to defense counsel, we cannot consistently treat every nondisclosure as though it were error. It necessarily follows that the judge should not order a new trial every time he is unable to characterize a nondisclosure as harmless under the customary harmless-error standard. Under that standard when error is present in the record, the reviewing judge must set aside the verdict and judgment unless his "conviction is sure that the error did not influence the jury, or had but very slight effect." *Kotteakos* v. *United States*, 328 U.S. 750, 764. Unless every nondisclosure is regarded as automatic error, the constitutional standard of materiality must impose a higher burden on the defendant.

The proper standard of materiality must reflect our overriding concern with the justice of the finding of guilt. Such a finding is permissible only if supported by evidence establishing guilt beyond a reasonable doubt. It necessarily follows that if the omitted evidence creates a reasonable doubt that did not otherwise exist, constitutional error has been committed. This means that the omission must be evaluated in the context of the entire record. If there is no reasonable doubt about guilt whether or not the additional evidence is considered, there is no justification for a new trial. On the other hand, if the verdict is already of questionable validity, additional evidence of relatively minor importance might be sufficient to create a reasonable doubt.

This statement of the standard of materiality describes the test which courts appear to have applied in actual cases although the standard has been phrased in different language. It is also the standard which the trial judge applied in this case. He evaluated the significance of Sewell's prior criminal record in the context of the full trial which he recalled in detail. Stressing in particular the incongruity of a claim that Sewell was the aggressor with the evidence of his multiple wounds and respondent's unscathed condition, the trial judge indicated his unqualified opinion that respondent was guilty. He noted that Sewell's prior record did not contradict any evidence offered by the prosecutor, and was largely cumulative of the evidence that Sewell was wearing a bowie knife in a sheath and carrying a second knife in his pocket when he registered at the motel.

Since the arrest record was not requested and did not even arguably give rise to any inference of perjury, since after considering it in the context of the entire record the trial judge remained convinced of respondent's guilt beyond a reasonable doubt, and since we are satisfied that his firsthand appraisal of the record was thorough and entirely reasonable, we hold that the prosecutor's failure to tender Sewell's record to the defense did not deprive respondent of a fair trial as guaranteed by the Due Process Clause of the Fifth Amendment. Accordingly, the judgment of the Court of Appeals is Reversed.

Mr. Justice Marshall, with whom Mr. Justice Brennant joins, dissenting. [Omitted.]

WHAT DO *YOU* THINK?

1. If the prosecutor's first duty is to promote "justice," what obligations does she have to turn over favorable information to the defense?

2. Why is it important to require the prosecutor to provide the defense with copies of witness statements that are material to the case?

3. What obligations should the defense have to turn over information to the prosecutor?

SUMMARY

- The rules governing criminal proceedings are based on three basic sources of power: constitutions (state and federal), statutes, and court rules. Higher federal courts have inherent supervisory power over lower federal courts, and state high courts have the same power over state courts.

- The Bill of Rights, the first eight amendments to the U.S. Constitution, contains procedural rights for persons accused of criminal conduct. The Fourteenth Amendment has been used by the U.S. Supreme Court to place "due process" requirements on the states in criminal prosecutions. The clause "without due process" of the Fourteenth Amendment has been interpreted by the U.S. Supreme Court as "incorporating" most of the provisions of the Bill of Rights.

- An *arrest* is the taking of a person into custody so that he or she may be held to answer for the commission of an offense. Felonies are normally prosecuted either by indictment or, after examination and commitment by a magistrate, by information. No person can be punished for a public offense, except upon a legal conviction in a court having jurisdiction thereof.

- In most states, once guilt is determined, the judge determines the appropriate sentence subject to statutory limits. An accused normally has the right to appeal his or her conviction and sentence to the court of appeals. The function of an appellate court is to provide a legal review of rulings made by the trial court.

- The three chief participants in any criminal trial are the prosecutor, defense counsel, and the judiciary. In most states the local prosecutor (district attorney, county attorney or state's attorney) carries the primary responsibility for the prosecution of state criminal cases.

- In most states, the local prosecutor (chief prosecutor) is elected by the voters of the local judicial district or county. There are over 2,500 prosecutor offices in the United States. Standard problems faced by local prosecutors include the high turnover rate for assistant prosecutors, heavy case loads, police–prosecutor relationships, and less compensation than that received by attorneys in private practice.

DISCUSSION QUESTIONS

1. Distinguish between the "total incorporation" and the "selective incorporation" approaches to the due process clause.

2. What are the practical results of the Court's use of "selective incorporation"?

3. What is required in order to extradite a person from another state? Does the *Duncan* v. *Louisiana* case stand for the proposition that the terms "privileges and immunities" and "due process" are convenient shorthand for an entire restatement of the Bill of Rights?
4. Why should a defendant have a right to a jury trial in minor criminal cases in the federal system, but not in minor state criminal proceedings?
5. Is this due process?

ENDNOTES

1. While there are ten amendments in the Bill of Rights, only the first eight contain rights for individuals in the criminal justice system.
2. 3 U.S. 386 (1798).
3. 268 U.S. 652 (1925).
4. 287 U.S. 45 (1932).
5. 391 U.S. 145 (1968).
6. *Palko* v. *Connecticut*, 302 U.S. 319 (1937).
7. *Betts* v. *Brady*, 316 U.S. 455 (1942).
8. *Gitlow* v. *New York*
9. *Near* v. *Minnesota*
10. *Dejonge* v. *Oregon*
11. *Griswold* v. *Connecticut*
12. *Wolf* v. *Colorado*, 338 U.S. 25 (1949).
13. *Mapp* v. *Ohio*, 367 U.S. 643 (1961).
14. *Terry* v. *Ohio*, 392 U.S. 1 (1961).
15. *Malloy* v. *Hogan*, 378 U.S. 1 (1968).
16. *Benton* v. *Maryland*, 395 U.S. 784 (1969).
17. *Duncan* v. *Louisiana*, 391 U.S. 145 (1968).
18. *Klopfer* v. *North Carolina*, 386 U.S. 213 (1967).
19. *Connally* v. *General Construction Co.*
20. *Pointer* v. *Texas*, 380 U.S. 400 (1965).
21. *Washington* v. *Texas*, 388 U.S. 14 (1967).
22. *Robinson* v. *California*, 370 U.S. 660 (1962).
23. *Hurtado* v. *California*, 110 U.S. 516 (1984).
24. *Duncan* v. *Louisiana*, 391 U.S. 145 (1968).
25. The Court has never decided this issue, but indicated in *Schilb* v. *Kuebel*, 404 U.S. 357 (1971), that it would apply to the states.
26. 397 U.S. 742 (1970).
27. *Miller* v. *Pate*, 386 U.S. 1 (1967).
28. *United States* v. *Agurs*, 427 U.S. 97 (1972).
29. *United States* v. *Agurs*, 427 U.S. 97 (1972).

4

THE FOURTH AMENDMENT

INTRODUCTION

The Fourth Amendment to the U.S. Constitution is one long complex sentence with two clauses. It is a type of sentence that is frowned on by English grammar teachers. The first clause is considered the "reasonableness clause" because it provides the general standard that all searches and seizures be reasonable. The second clause describes the requirements for obtaining a valid warrant. Researchers argue over which clause predominates. From a historical point of view, the warrant clause should dominate. It was the British officials' use of general warrants that the Fourth Amendment was designed to prevent. A main proponent of the historical approach is Supreme Court Justice Anthony Scalia.[1] The Supreme Court still considers the warrant clause as the first reference point for deciding the legality of a search or seizure. As often stated: "you should get a warrant unless you can't." While the warrant clause has been influential with the Supreme Court, only one case, *California* v. *Hodari D.*[2] has been decided on that view. Currently, the Supreme Court has moved to the point that most search and seizure issues are decided based on the reasonableness of the search or seizure.

As noted later in this chapter, the Fourth Amendment is applicable to the states through the due process clause of the Fourteenth Amendment. It is important to note that the Fourth Amendment only governs conduct of federal and state agents (including local police and other local government employees). It does not govern the conduct of private individuals who are not acting as government agents. For example, an ex-girlfriend may conduct an illegal search of the defendant's apartment and turn the evidence over to the police. As long as she was not working as a government agent, the evidence is admissible in court. Evidence obtained by a security guard who illegally searched a car will probably be admissible in court. If, however, the security guard is an off-duty police officer the evidence probably will not be admissible because of his status as a police officer.

The Fourth Amendment covers only our "national community." Accordingly, it is inapplicable to the search of a person's Mexican residence.[3] The same standards of reasonableness and probable cause are applicable to state and federal cases. Evidence taken in violation of the Fourth Amendment is subjected to exclusion in court as discussed in Chapter 7.

Since an arrest is a seizure, the Fourth Amendment also covers arrests. The amendment is, however, more often thought of as a limitation on the power of the police to search and seize evidence. One reason for this is that when a person is illegally arrested, he or she may still be prosecuted for the crime. Whereas when evidence is illegally discovered or seized, the evidence generally is excluded from the trial. Note even the abduction of a defendant in lieu of resort to extradition proceedings does not prevent trial of that defendant.[4]

A seizure may occur without a search and a search may occur without a seizure. There may be situations where the search was legal and the seizure was illegal.

The major issues involved in Fourth Amendment questions include the meaning of *probable cause*, what constitutes a search, when is a warrant required, and the coverage of the amendment. As noted in the Preface, a recommended approach to studying Fourth Amendment issues is to ask the following three questions:

1. Is the Fourth Amendment applicable? (If the amendment is not applicable, then there is no Fourth Amendment issue. Instances of inapplicablity include open fields, consent, and plain view.)

2. If the Fourth Amendment is applicable, has it been complied with? (If so, evidence will not be excluded. If not go to question 3.)

3. If the Fourth Amendment is applicable and it has not been complied with, what sanctions will the court impose? (See discussion in Chapter 7 on the exclusionary rule and its exceptions.)

LAW IN PRACTICE

Fourth Amendment Diagrammed

I. The right of the people to be secure in their

    A. persons

    B. houses

    C. papers

    D. and effects

    against unreasonable searches and seizures, shall not be violated, and

II. no warrants shall issue, but

    A. upon probable cause

    B. supported by oath or affirmation,

and

III. particularly describing the

    A. place to be searched

    B. and the persons or things to be seized.

    [U.S. Constitution, Fourth Amendment (Designations added.)]

COVERAGE OF THE FOURTH AMENDMENT

What Constitutes a Search?

Prior to *Katz* v. *United States* in 1967, the property approach was the traditional method used in deciding what constitutes a search.[5] This approach was rejected in *Katz* in favor of a "privacy approach." In *Katz*, federal agents intercepted Katz's telephone conversations by the use of an electronic listening device attached to the outside of a public telephone booth. The prosecution argued that there was no search of a person, house, papers, or effects, and therefore no coverage by the Fourth Amendment. The government also contended that there was no seizure since the voice is an intangible item. The Court rejected the arguments of the government and stated that the Fourth Amendment protects people, not places. The Court also stated: "What a person knowingly exposes to the public, even in his own home or office, is not a subject of Fourth Amendment protection . . . But what he seeks to preserve as private, even in an area accessible to the public, may be constitutionally protected. Under the *Katz* rationale, a search is considered as a governmental intrusion into area or interest where a person has a reasonable expectation of privacy. The expectation of privacy must be reasonable. Reasonableness includes the requirement that it must be an expectation that the people (society) is willing to accept. As noted under the discussion involving "open fields," there are some expectations of privacy that society is not willing to accept.

Does the Fourth Amendment protect only reasonable and legitimate interests in privacy? The Court has noted on several occasions that there is no legitimate privacy interest in illegal activity.[6] If that is true, then why should Katz receive Fourth Amendment protection? Katz's protection and others in similar situations are protected because it is not possible to know in advance of the search that their activities are illegal. The amendment is designed to protect innocent people with legitimate privacy expectations from false assumptions by governmental agents. Accordingly, certain interests are presumed to be legal and thus protected before the intrusion takes place. To hold otherwise would allow the police to justify a search based on the results of the search and thus render the protections of the amendment void.

The courts have required that individuals be protective of their privacy interests. For example, had an undercover police agent dressed as a bum been standing near the telephone while Katz was making his telephone calls, the agent could testify as to what he or she heard. Under this fact situation, Katz would have willfully exposed the contents of his conversation by talking within the hearing distance of someone else.

Home and Its Curtilage

The tradition of protecting the home and the surrounding "living space" existed long before the U.S. Constitution was adopted. William Pitt's address to the English House of Commons in 1763 stated:

> The poorest man may in his cottage bid defiance to all the forces of the Crown. It may be frail; its roof may shake; the wind may blow through it; the storm may enter; but the King of England cannot enter—all his force dares not cross the threshold of the ruined tenement.[7]

The U.S. Supreme Court has interpreted the Fourth Amendment's protection of the home to include that area immediately surrounding the home, the curtilage. The area outside of the curtilage which is often referred to as the *open fields area* and is not protected, however, by the amendment. The Supreme Court has described the curtilage as "the area to which extends the intimate activity associated with the sanctity of a person's home and the privacies of life."[8] In *United States* v. *Dunn*,[9] the Supreme Court set four factors to be used in deciding whether an area is within the curtilage of the home: 1) what is the proximity of the area to the home; 2) is the area within the same enclosure as the home; 3) what is the nature of the use to which the area is put; and 4) what steps have been taken by the resident to protect the area from the view of passersby? The court, in that case, ruled that a barn was not within the curtilage of the house. It was located on a 198-acre ranch, and the barn was 60 yards from the house and 50 yards from a second fence surrounding the house. There was no indication that the barn was being used for those intimate activities normally associated with the home, and the defendant had not taken sufficient steps to protect the barn area from those standing in the open field. The fence around the barn was of the type to corral cattle and not that normally used to block the view of the public. Officers from the Houston Police Department had crossed a perimeter fence that surrounded two barns and the house. The officers smelled the odor of precursor chemicals used in the illegal manufacture of drugs coming from one of the barns. Based on the smell and other evidence, the officers obtained a search warrant and found sufficient evidence in the barn to convict the defendant of manufacturing illegal drugs. The court admitted the evidence.

PROBABLE CAUSE

As required by the Fourth Amendment, probable cause is needed before a warrant may be issued to search a place, etc., or seize a person (arrest). Probable cause is a difficult and complex concept to explain. The probable cause standard is designed to strike a balance between the rights of the individual to privacy and security and the interest of the government in investigating and prosecuting crime. The probable cause standard requires only a fair probability that the officers are correct in their assessment of the facts. Accordingly, in some cases where probable cause exists to search, the police may be mistaken and arrest an innocent person or uncover no incriminating evidence during the search. As the Court once stated: "sufficient probability, not certainty, is the touchstone of reasonableness under the Fourth Amendment."[10]

The Supreme Court in *Draper* v. *United States* faced the task of defining *probable cause*. Set forth below is their explanation of the concept:

> In dealing with probable cause, . . . as the very name implies, we deal with probabilities. These are not technical; they are the factual and practical considerations of every-

day life on which reasonable and prudent men, not legal technicians, act. Probable cause exists where the facts and circumstances with [the arresting officers'] knowledge and of which they had reasonably trustworthy information [are] sufficient in themselves to warrant a man of reasonable caution in the belief that an offense has been or is being committed.[11]

The Fourth Amendment states only that probable cause is needed before a warrant may be issued. The Supreme Court generally has applied the same standards of probable cause for arrests without a warrant. As indicated in *Beck* v. *Ohio*[12] in a closed case, the Court may uphold an arrest with a warrant where they would not uphold an arrest without a warrant. The *Beck* case is cited by many as indicating that presence of a warrant creates the assumption that the arrest was legal and that the probable cause standard is relaxed in warrant cases. Note that in issuing a warrant a judicial officer has made the decision that probable cause exists and the courts are less likely to reverse that finding.

The basic test for probable cause to search is the same as that for arrest with the added requirement of a reasonable belief that the *property to be seized* will be found in a particular place or on a particular person.

The following general rules regarding probable cause apply to both searches and arrests:

- Probable cause may be based on hearsay information.
- The phrase "person of reasonable caution" or "ordinary prudent and cautious person" does not refer to a person with special legal training. It refers to the average person "on the street" who, under the circumstances, would believe that the individual being arrested had committed the offense or that items to be seized would be found in a particular place.
- The experience of the police officer may be considered in determining whether the officer had probable cause. Accordingly, what may be insufficient to establish probable cause to an untrained person may be sufficient to establish for a specially trained officer.
- "Reasonable ground" and "probable cause" are used interchangeably in many courts.
- Probable cause requires an "honest and reasonable" belief.
- Proof beyond a reasonable doubt is not required—only that it is more probable than not, i.e., more than 50 percent certainty that the person has committed a crime or that the items to be seized will be found in a certain place.
- Probable cause must exist before the search or the arrest. A search or arrest cannot be justified by the facts which are discovered during the search or arrest. For example, you cannot justify a search of a person by the fact that during the search drugs were discovered on her.
- Probable cause may be established by (1) the officer's own knowledge of certain facts and circumstances, (2) information given by informants, or (3) information plus corroboration.
- If the information on which probable cause is based is provided by an informant, additional corroboration is normally required. This is based on the questionable status of informants. The informant's information may be corroborated by a showing that the informant has been reliable in the past or gives a precise description of the alleged wrongdoing. The Court applies the "totality of the circumstances analysis" in informant cases to determine if

there is sufficient corroboration to constitute probable cause, *Illinois* v. *Gates*.[13] Under this analysis, the Court looks at all the facts to determine if sufficient corroboration is present to establish probable cause.

■ Probable cause may be required in the following four basic situations: arrests with warrant, arrests without warrant, searches and seizures with warrant, and searches and seizures without warrant.

SEARCH WARRANTS

As noted earlier, the Fourth Amendment requires that no warrants shall be issued but upon probable cause supported by oath or affirmation, and particularly describing the place to be searched and the persons or things to be seized. A *warrant* is a judicial document issued by a judicial officer authorizing a law enforcement official to make a search or seizure. Generally the judicial officer is a magistrate. The magistrate must be neutral and detached.

Neutral and Detached Magistrate

The rationale for a warrant issued by a neutral and detached judicial officer is to put a buffer between the citizen and the police agent. The police officer is in the competitive practice of ferreting out crime and in the process may become over zealous and reach wrong conclusions about the existence of probable cause.

The judicial officer must be neutral. In *Connelly* v. *Georgia*,[14] the Supreme Court held that a magistrate who received $5 for every warrant he issued, but nothing when the application for a warrant is refused, was not a neutral magistrate. Since his salary was based partially upon issuing warrants, such pecuniary interest could impermissibly affect his "impartial" judgment.

A state attorney general cannot issue a warrant because he or she is the highest law enforcement official under state law and thus not detached nor neutral. In the *Collidge* v. *New Hampshire*[15] case, the Court invalidated warrants issued by the attorney general who was in fact participating in the investigation. In *Lo-Ji Sales, Inc.* v. *New York*,[16] after the magistrate issued the warrant he accompanied the law enforcement officers and actively participated in the search. The magistrate examined the items in question to determine if they could be seized. The Court held that his actions destroyed his neutrality and thus resulted in an illegal search and seizure.

The Supreme Court in *Shadwick* v. *City of Tampa*[17] held that the judicial officer who issues the warrant does not need to be an attorney nor have special legal training. The U.S. Court of Appeals, Eighth Circuit, invalidated a warrant where the magistrate was a "rubber stamp" and did not read the supporting application for a warrant. The Court of Appeals held that the magistrate loses his neutral and detached status when he fails to read a warrant affidavit.[18] There appears to be no requirement that the magistrate give reasons for his or her decision to issue or deny the issuance of a warrant.

Determination of Probable Cause

The determination of the presence of probable cause is the responsibility of the magistrate. Accordingly, probable cause must be based only on the facts presented in the affidavit to the magistrate. Facts known to the police, but not presented to the magistrate, may not be used to support the decision to issue a warrant.

In most cases, the officer requesting a warrant will submit an application for a warrant to the magistrate with supporting documents. An affidavit containing all the facts necessary to support a finding of probable cause must be submitted under oath or affirmation. In some states, an officer may give sworn oral testimony to supplement the application. In other states, all the facts to support the finding must be contained within the affidavit.

A warrant is issued at an exparte hearing. The defendant does not have the right to be present at any hearing on a warrant application.

Some states and the federal government permit the use of telephonic warrants under certain circumstances. Generally in these cases the officer must prepare a formal application for a warrant and then read the information over the telephone to the magistrate. A record must be made of the telephone conversation. Any testimony received over the telephone must be under oath.

Warrants Based on False Information A facially valid warrant may be attacked on the ground that the affiant knowingly and intentionally or with reckless disregard for the truth made a false statement in the affidavit and that without the false statement the warrant would not have been issued.[19] The defense may request a "Franks hearing" to have any such statements struck from the affidavit. The burden is on the defense to establish by a preponderance of evidence his or her allegations regarding the misstatements. If the court concludes that the statements should be struck, then the court will next consider if probable cause still exists after the statements are struck. If not, the warrant will be invalidated. If probable cause does still exist, the challenge to the warrant on this issue will be denied. The defense must show not only that the statements are false but also that the police knew or should have known that they were false. Mere negligence on the part of the police will not entitle the defendant to relief. The *Franks* case holds that only material statements that affect the determination of the existence of probable cause may be attacked.

Particularity The requirement that the location to be searched must be described with reasonable particularity is based on the Colonial experience with the general warrants used by the British. The warrant is invalid if the place to be searched is not specifically described. The degree of particularity required depends on the nature of the place or property to be searched. Variances between the actual address and the specified address is not necessarily fatal to the warrant. The warrant will be upheld if there is sufficient information contained in the warrant to guide the officers to the correct address. Things to be seized also must be described with particularity. The degree of precision will depend on the facts and circumstances of the case.

The use of catch-all clauses in the warrant may cause problems. For example, a clause allowing the seizure of specified property and "any other evidence of the crime" may result in the exclusion of items not named in the warrant. If, however, the catch-all clause is qualified by the previously described property, the seizure of other property is generally upheld. For example, the statement contained in a warrant authorizing the seizure of certain specified cocaine substitutes that the officers were authorized to seize "other cocaine substances" was considered as valid.[20]

Execution of Warrants

There are no restrictions in the Fourth Amendment regarding the correct procedure for executing a warrant. Most jurisdictions, however, have statutes on executing warrants. Generally a search warrant must be executed within a specified time period. In addition, probable cause may no longer exist since the information upon which the warrant was issued may become stale. Approximately half of the states restrict the ability of the officers to execute a warrant at night unless exigent circumstances exist.

Anticipatory Warrants Anticipatory search warrants have been upheld. The warrants are based on the magistrate's determination that if certain things happen in the future, then probable cause will exist to execute the warrant. For example, in *United States* v. *Becerra*[21] a U.S. Court of Appeals upheld a warrant based on the future delivery of a package of contraband to a specific location. The Court noted that the warrant contained explicit conditions under which probable cause would exist and thus limited the discretion of the officers involved.

Occupants of Searched Premises While the Supreme Court has never ruled on the issue, they have indicated in dictum that a search is permissible in the absence of the occupants.[22] An individual who is present in the premises where a search is being executed may not, by virtue of that fact alone, be searched. If there is some basis for suspecting that the individual may be armed, he or she may be frisked under *Terry* v. *Ohio*.[23] The warrant, however, could authorize the search of the residents if probable cause exists to support their search. In addition, residents of premises where a search for contraband is being executed may be detained during the warrant execution. The Court in *Michigan* v. *Summers*[24] indicated that detaining the residents during the execution of the warrant served three government interests: preventing flight in the event incriminating evidence was discovered, minimizing the risk of harm to the police, and facilitating the orderly completion of the search.

Covert Searches A court of appeals in *United States* v. *Freitas*[25] held that a warrant which authorized covert and surreptitious entries without any provisions for post-search notification to the residents was unconstitutional. The Court stated that surreptitious entry should not be authorized except under highly unusual circumstances because searches of residences are unusually intrusive. The Court in *Freitas* stated that the "mere thought of strangers walking though and visually examining the center of our privacy interest, our home, arouses our passion for freedom as does nothing else." In that case, the warrant had allowed surreptitious entry to scrutinize the operation of a drug lab.

Notice In most cases, notice is required before entering a private premise. The Supreme Court has concluded that the common law rule of "knock and announce" forms a part of the reasonableness of the amendment. In *Wilson* v. *Arkansas*,[26] the Supreme Court stated that the entry of a home without satisfying the knock and announce rule constituted an unreasonable search even though the police had a valid warrant. The Supreme Court has acknowledged the right of the police to enter without notice in three situations: (1) where notice would present a threat of physical violence, (2) in hot-pursuit cases, and (3) where the officers have probable cause to believe that evidence would likely be destroyed if they gave notice before entering. The Supreme Court in *Richards* v. *Wisconsin*[27] held that to justify a no-knock entry, the police must have a reasonable suspicion that knocking and announcing their presence, under the particular circumstances, would be dangerous or futile, or that it would inhibit the effective investigation of the crime by, for example, allowing the destruction of evidence. The Court also concluded that it was the duty of a court confronted with the question to determine whether the facts and circumstances of the particular entry justified dispensing with the knock and announce requirements. In *Richards*, the magistrate who signed the warrant to search a hotel room deleted the portions of the warrant that would have given the officers permission to execute a no-knock entry. The Court stated that the act of the magistrate in deleting the no-knock provisions "does not alter the reasonableness of the officers' decision, which must be evaluated as of the time they entered the hotel room." The Supreme Court in *Richards* stated that the "reasonable suspicion" standard for a no-knock entry is not high and implied that it was less than the "probable cause" standard needed to issue the warrant.

In *United States* v. *Nabors*,[28] a court of appeals held that the officers were excused from knock and announcement when they reasonably believed that notice would put themselves in danger of bodily harm. In *Nabors*, the officers believed that a large-scale drug trafficking operation was being carried on and that the defendant owned an array of firearms and habitually wore a bulletproof vest.

In *Richards*, the Court rejected a Wisconsin Supreme Court rule that police officers are never required to knock and announce their presence when executing a search warrant in a felony drug investigation. The Supreme Court in *Richards* indicated that the decision as to a no-knock entry must be made on a case-by-case basis.

Once the officers knock and announce their presence and intention, they are required to wait a reasonable time for voluntary admittance. The courts have tended to defer to the police as to what constitutes a reasonable time. In some cases, a delay of only 10 seconds was considered as adequate, especially where the officers hear clicking sounds that may reasonably assumed to be the occupants locking the front door.[29]

If the announcement would be a useless gesture, the police may forego it. In *United States* v. *James*,[30] the police heard sounds of running feet immediately after announcing their presence. The Court of Appeals stated that the officers were justified in forgoing the rest of the announcement and breaking in.

Use of Extraordinary Force   In *United States* v. *Stewart*,[31] a court of appeals held that the use of a steel battering ram was unreasonable. The California Supreme Court in *Langford* v. *Superior Court*[32] enjoined the Los Angeles Police Department from using a motorized battering ram, concluding that it posed a serious risk of physical injury and excessive property damage. In *Langford*, the court upheld the use of low-impact explosive devices (flashbangs) to gain entrance to "fortress-like" buildings. The court noted that the police department guidelines were sufficient to control the discretion of the officers employing flashbangs. The court also concluded that the flashbangs caused suspects only momentary disorientation and a minimal risk of physical injury.

Scope of Search   The scope and duration of the search must relate directly to the magistrate's previous determination of probable cause. A warrant authorizing the search of a house generally allows the search not only of the house but the surrounding curtilage, which includes backyards and associated buildings. A warrant that authorizes search of a premises will permit the search of any vehicles located on the premises as long as there is probable cause to believe that the items listed in the warrant may be in the vehicles.

A warrant that authorizes the search of a premises authorizes the search of any area in the premises that may contain items listed in the warrant. Enclosed areas within the premises may be searched and the search is not limited by the fact that acts of entry are required. If the items listed in the warrant are large, however, then small areas where those items could not possibly be may not be searched. The scope of the search is limited to only those places where the items described in the warrant may be located. Accordingly, it would be unreasonable to search a small notebook when looking for a handgun with a nine-inch barrel.[33]

Seizure of Items Not Listed in the Warrant   The Supreme Court stated in *Coolidge* v. *New Hampshire*,[34] that "Where, once an otherwise lawful search is in progress, the police inadvertently come upon a piece of evidence, it would often be a needless inconvenience, and sometimes dangerous—to the evidence or to the police themselves—to require them to ignore it until they have obtained a warrant particularly describing it. Later in *Arizona* v. *Hicks*[35] the Supreme Court held that the observed object may be seized only if there is probable cause to believe it constitutes the fruits, instrumentalities, or evidence of a crime. That reasonable suspicion is not a sufficient reason to conduct a closer examination of the item not otherwise permissible in executing the present warrant.

The type of procedure used to conduct a search is generally left to the officers' discretion. Officers should remain on the premises only as long as necessary and refrain from committing unnecessary property damage. If officers flagrantly disregard warrant limitations, any evidence discovered as the results of the limitation violations may be excluded.

EAVESDROPPING

In 1928 the U.S. Supreme Court in *Olmstead* v. *United States*[36] held that wiretapping was not a search for two reasons; first, at no time did the police trespass on the defendant's premises, so that nothing was searched, and second, only conversations were obtained, so that no things were seized. The Court has later rejected both of the grounds, and wiretaps are now considered as a search. The Federal Communication Act of 1934 made it a crime to wiretap without the approval of at least one of the parties or a court order. Accordingly, wiretapping and electronic surveillance are subject to the limitations of the Fourth Amendment.

LAW OF ARREST

An *arrest* (seizure of a person) is the taking of a person into custody so that the person may be held to answer for the commission of a crime. The four essential elements required for an arrest are as follows:

1. Intention to arrest,
2. Authority to arrest,
3. Seizure and detention, and
4. An understanding by the arrestee that he or she is being arrested.

Elements of An Arrest

Intent to Arrest   There must be an intent to arrest the person. The police cannot accidentally arrest an individual. Since this is a subjective requirement, it is often difficult to establish in court unless the police officer's actions clearly indicate that the officer intended to arrest the individual.

Authority to Arrest The individual making the arrest must have the authority to arrest. Authority to arrest distinguishes an arrest from a false imprisonment or kidnapping. There are two types of legal arrests—those with a warrant and those without a warrant. Like searches, the courts have demonstrated a bias toward arrests with warrants. An arrest with a warrant is presumed to be legal unless the contrary is established. An arrest without a warrant is presumed illegal. Accordingly, the prosecution has the duty to establish the legality of an arrest without a warrant.

Seizure and Detention There must be a seizure and detention of the person. The seizure and detention may be an actual seizure such as handcuffing a person, or constructive when the individual submits without the use of force. (*Note*: Mere words do not constitute an arrest. Merely telling a person that "you are under arrest" is not an arrest unless it is accompanied by an actual seizure or by submission of the individual to the officer's will and control. The submission may be implied by the individual merely going with the police officer.)

The seizure and detention may under certain circumstances be a "constructive restraint." For example, in *People* v. *Logue*,[37] the accused and several others were seriously injured in an automobile accident allegedly caused by the accused's driving under the influence of alcohol. The police officer at the scene informed the accused that he was under arrest. The defendant lapsed into unconsciousness. He was taken by ambulance and given a blood test while unconscious. The officer then proceeded to assist other injured persons and did not accompany the accused to the hospital. Several days thereafter, the accused was released from the hospital with a notice to appear in court. The accused contended that he was never arrested and therefore pursuant to state law there was no authority to take a blood sample from him without his permission or a court order. (*Note*: The state statute permitted the taking of a blood sample from an individual arrested for driving under the influence.) The appeals court stated that "We deem it wholly unreasonable under the circumstances . . . to require the officer to closely attend that person to the exclusion of the officer's duty to obtain aid for the accident victims, and to prevent further traffic pileups and injuries."

Understanding The person detained must understand that he or she is being arrested. Normally the understanding is conveyed through words such as "you are under arrest." Sometimes the understanding is conveyed by actions of the police, such as handcuffing of an individual. If the accused is too drunk, drugged, insane, or unconscious to understand that he or she is being arrested, then the understanding element is excused. The test used by the courts in these situations is: Would an individual with normal facilities understand that he or she is being arrested?

Arrest Authority

An arrest may be made by a peace officer pursuant to authorization by state law. Private persons may under certain circumstances have the authority to arrest an individual (often referred to as *citizen's arrest*). (*Note*: In most states there are special rules regarding the arrest of individuals for motor vehicle offenses.)

The validity of an arrest is determined by the law of the jurisdiction within which the arrest occurred.[38] Since an arrest also is a seizure of the person, it must comply with Fourth Amendment standards to be legal.[39] A state cannot avoid the Fourth Amendment requirements by classifying the arrest as only a "detention."[40]

An officer may arrest a person without a warrant whenever he or she has reasonable cause to believe that the person to be arrested has committed a felony, whether or not a felony has been committed by the defendant or anyone. A felony need not have been committed within the presence of the officer. An officer may arrest a person without a warrant if the officer has probable cause to believe that the person has committed a misdemeanor in the officer's presence. Absent of statutory authority, an officer may not arrest without a warrant for a misdemeanor not committed in the officer's presence. States traditionally give officers statutory authority to arrest for traffic offenses that occurred out of the presence of the officer. For example, an officer arrives at the scene of a traffic accident where one of the drivers is under the influence. Since this may be a misdemeanor and the driving occurred out of the presence of the officer, he or she needs statutory authority to arrest the drunk driver. Most states' traffic codes provide such authority. Other common exceptions include misdemeanors committed on school property and crimes committed by juveniles.

Arrest Warrant

An arrest with a warrant is valid if the magistrate (judicial officer) who issued the warrant had sufficient facts before him or her to establish probable cause. (*Note*: An arrest with a warrant may still be illegal if the arrest is conducted in a manner not authorized by the warrant.)

For a warrant to be valid, it must be issued by a magistrate (judicial officer) based on facts presented to the officer establishing the existence of probable cause. The magistrate must be "neutral and detached." In some states, the warrant may be issued by a court clerk if empowered to do so by state law. Since an arrest is the seizure of a person, most of the rules discussed earlier in this chapter regarding a search warrant are applicable to arrest warrants.

General rules regarding an arrest warrant are as follows:

- The warrant must describe the offense charged and contain the name of the accused, or if name is unknown, a description of the accused.
- The warrant also must indicate the time of issuance, the city or county and state where it is issued, and the duty of the arresting officer to bring the defendant before the magistrate.
- It is directed to, and thus may be acted on, by any peace officer in the jurisdiction. (*Note*: A warrant issued by a state court is directed to any peace officer in the state.)
- Arrest warrants, unlike search warrants, are valid until they are recalled by the court.
- The arrest warrant can specify the amount of bail needed by the accused to be released.
- The officer making the arrest pursuant to a warrant need not have the warrant in his or her presence, as long as the officer is aware of its contents. If the officer has the warrant, he or she must display it if requested. If the officer does not have the warrant in his or her presence, the officer must explain to the defendant the reason for the arrest.

Place of Arrest

Suspects may be arrested in a public place at any time providing there is authority to arrest. Traditionally, a person's home is that person's castle. Accordingly, absent exigent circumstances, an arrest warrant is necessary in order to arrest someone inside his or her home.[41] A home or dwelling includes any place the suspect resides, i.e., a tent, boat, mobile home, van, or hotel room. To arrest someone in a third person's home—absent exigent circumstances, consent, or other exceptions—a search warrant is needed (to search for the suspect). Exigent circumstances are emergency situations requiring immediate action to prevent imminent danger to life or serious damage to property, or to prevent the escape of a felon.

The rules regarding consent to enter the home to arrest a suspect are similar to the rules regarding consent to search. For example, a police officer asked permission to enter a home. When permission was granted, he entered and arrested the suspect. The consent was valid, since he did not misrepresent the purpose of the entry,[42] however, the entry was illegal where the police officer asked permission to enter "to talk to" a suspect. Immediately after entering, he arrested the suspect. The court stated that the officer lied about the reason for entering and therefore the entry was "coerced." (The court determined that the officer never intended to talk to the suspect, only to arrest him.)

A federal arrest warrant is valid in all states. A state arrest warrant is valid only within the jurisdiction of the state. There is a "hot pursuit" exception whereby officers may cross state lines to arrest an individual if in "hot pursuit."

Search Incident to Arrest

With a lawful arrest comes the authority to search the arrested person and limited areas within his or her reach. Accordingly, it is sometimes necessary to determine if an individual was actually arrested in order to justify the search or seizure that occurred. Searches incident to arrest are discussed in Chapter 5.

CAPSTONE CASES

What constitutes probable cause? The following case discusses that issue.

DRAPER V. UNITED STATES
358 U.S. 307, 79 S.Ct. 329 (1959)

MR. JUSTICE WHITTAKER delivered the opinion of the Court.

Petitioner was convicted of knowingly concealing and transporting narcotic drugs in Denver, Colorado, in violation of 35 Stat. 614, as amended, 21 U.S.C. 174. His conviction was based in part on the use in evidence against him of two "envelopes containing [865 grains of] heroin" and a hypodermic syringe that had been taken from his person, following his arrest, by the arresting officer. Before the trial, he moved to suppress that evidence as having been secured through an unlawful search and seizure. After hearing, the District Court found that the arresting officer had probable cause to arrest petitioner without a warrant and that the subsequent search and seizure were therefore incident to a lawful arrest, and overruled the motion to suppress. 146 F. Supp. 689. At the subsequent trial, that evidence was offered and, over petitioner's renewed objection, was received in evidence, and the trial resulted, as we have said, in

petitioner's conviction. The Court of Appeals affirmed the conviction, 248 F.2d 295, and *certiorari* was sought on the sole ground that the search and seizure violated the Fourth Amendment and therefore the use of the heroin in evidence vitiated the conviction. We granted the writ to determine that question. 357 U.S. 935.

The evidence offered at the hearing on the motion to suppress was not substantially disputed. It established that one Marsh, a federal narcotic agent with 29 years' experience, was stationed at Denver; that one Hereford had been engaged as a "special employee" of the Bureau of Narcotics at Denver for about six months, and from time to time gave information to Marsh regarding violations of the narcotic laws, for which Hereford was paid small sums of money, and that Marsh had always found the information given by Hereford to be accurate and reliable. On September 3, 1956, Hereford told Marsh that James Draper (petitioner) recently had taken up abode at a stated address in Denver and "was peddling narcotics to several addicts" in that city. Four days later, on September 7, Hereford told Marsh "that Draper had gone to Chicago the day before [September 6] by train [and] that he was going to bring back three ounces of heroin [and] that he would return to Denver either on the morning of the 8th of September or the morning of the 9th of September also by train." Hereford also gave Marsh a detailed physical description of Draper and of the clothing he was wearing, and said that he would be carrying "a tan zipper bag," and that he habitually "walked real fast."

On the morning of September 8, Marsh and a Denver police officer went to the Denver Union Station and kept watch over all incoming trains from Chicago, but they did not see anyone fitting the description that Hereford had given. Repeating the process on the morning of September 9, they saw a person, having the exact physical attributes and wearing the precise clothing described by Hereford, alight from an incoming Chicago train and start walking "fast" toward the exit. He was carrying a tan zipper bag in his right hand and the left was thrust in his raincoat pocket. Marsh, accompanied by the police officer, overtook, stopped and arrested him. They then searched him and found the two "envelopes containing heroin" clutched in his left hand in his raincoat pocket, and found the syringe in the tan zipper bag. Marsh then took him (petitioner) into custody. Hereford died four days after the arrest and therefore did not testify at the hearing on the motion.

26 U.S.C. (Supp. V) 7607, added by 104 (a) of the Narcotic Control Act of 1956, 70 Stat. 570, provides, in pertinent part:

> "The Commissioner . . . and agents, of the Bureau of Narcotics . . . may (2) make arrests without warrant for violations of any law of the United States relating to narcotic drugs . . . where the violation is committed in the presence of the person making the arrest or where such person has reasonable grounds to believe that the person to be arrested has committed or is committing such violation."

The crucial question for us then is whether knowledge of the related facts and circumstances gave Marsh "probable cause" within the meaning of the Fourth Amendment, and "reasonable grounds" within the meaning of 104 (a), *supra*, to believe that petitioner had committed or was committing a violation of the narcotic laws.[1] If it did, the arrest, though without a warrant, was lawful and the subsequent search of petitioner's person and the seizure of the found heroin were validly

---

[1][Court's Footnote 3] The terms "probable cause" as used in the Fourth Amendment and "reasonable grounds" as used in 104 (a) of the Narcotic Control Act, 70 Stat. 570, are substantial equivalents of the same meaning. *United States* v. *Walker*, 246 F.2d 519, 526 (C. A. 7th Cir.); *cf. United States* v. *Bianco*, 189 F.2d 716, 720 (C. A. 3d Cir.).

made incident to a lawful arrest, and therefore the motion to suppress was properly overruled and the heroin was competently received in evidence at the trial. . . .

Petitioner does not dispute this analysis of the question for decision. Rather, he contends (1) that the information given by Hereford to Marsh was "hearsay" and, because hearsay is not legally competent evidence in a criminal trial, could not legally have been considered, but should have been put out of mind, by Marsh in assessing whether he had "probable cause" and "reasonable grounds" to arrest petitioner without a warrant, and (2) that, even if hearsay could lawfully have been considered, Marsh's information should be held insufficient to show "probable cause" and "reasonable grounds" to believe that petitioner had violated or was violating the narcotic laws and to justify his arrest without a warrant.

Considering the first contention, we find petitioner entirely in error. *Brinegar* v. *United States*, 338 U.S. 160, 172–173, has settled the question the other way. There, in a similar situation, the convict contended "that the factors relating to inadmissibility of the evidence [for] purposes of proving guilt at the trial, deprived the evidence as a whole of sufficiency to show probable cause for the search. . . ." *Id.*, at 172. But this Court, rejecting that contention, said: "[T]he so-called distinction places a wholly unwarranted emphasis upon the criterion of admissibility in evidence, to prove the accused's guilt, of the facts relied upon to show probable cause. That emphasis, we think, goes much too far in confusing and disregarding the difference between what is required to prove guilt in a criminal case and what is required to show probable cause for arrest or search.[2] It approaches requiring (if it does not in practical effect require) proof sufficient to establish guilt in order to substantiate the existence of probable cause. There is a large difference between the two things to be proved [guilt and probable cause], as well as between the tribunals which determine them, and therefore a like difference in the quanta and modes of proof required to establish them." 338 U.S., at 172–173.

Nor can we agree with petitioner's second contention that Marsh's information was insufficient to show probable cause and reasonable grounds to believe that petitioner had violated or was violating the narcotic laws and to justify his arrest without a warrant. The information given to narcotic agent Marsh by "special employee" Hereford may have been hearsay to Marsh, but coming from one employed for that purpose and whose information had always been found accurate and reliable, it is clear that Marsh would have been derelict in his duties had he not pursued it. And when, in pursuing that information, he saw a man, having the exact physical attributes and wearing the precise clothing and carrying the tan zipper bag that Hereford had described, alight from one of the very trains from the very place stated by Hereford and start to walk at a "fast" pace toward the station exit, Marsh had personally verified every facet of the information given him by Hereford except whether petitioner had accomplished his mission and had the three ounces of heroin on his person or in his bag. And surely, with every other bit of Hereford's information being thus personally verified, Marsh had "reasonable grounds" to believe that the remaining unverified bit of Hereford's information—that Draper would have the heroin with him—was likewise true.

---

[2][Court's Footnote 4] In *United States* v. *Heitner*, 149 F.2d 105, 106 (C. A. 2d Cir.), Judge Learned Hand said "It is well settled that an arrest may be made upon hearsay evidence; and indeed, the 'reasonable cause' necessary to support an arrest cannot demand the same strictness of proof as the accused's guilt upon a trial, unless the powers of peace officers are to be so cut down that they cannot possibly perform their duties."

"In dealing with probable cause, . . . as the very name implies, we deal with probabilities. These are not technical; they are the factual and practical considerations of everyday life on which reasonable and prudent men, not legal technicians, act." *Brinegar* v. *United States, supra*, at 175. Probable cause exists where "the facts and circumstances within [the arresting officers'] knowledge and of which they had reasonably trustworthy information [are] sufficient in themselves to warrant a man of reasonable caution in the belief that" an offense has been or is being committed. *Carroll* v. *United States*, 267 U.S. 132, 162.5

We believe that, under the facts and circumstances here, Marsh had probable cause and reasonable grounds to believe that petitioner was committing a violation of the laws of the United States relating to narcotic drugs at the time he arrested him. The arrest was therefore lawful, and the subsequent search and seizure, having been made incident to that lawful arrest, were likewise valid. It follows that petitioner's motion to suppress was properly denied and that the seized heroin was competent evidence lawfully received at the trial.

Affirmed.

THE CHIEF JUSTICE and MR. JUSTICE FRANKFURTER took no part in the consideration or decision of this case.

MR. JUSTICE DOUGLAS, dissenting

Decisions under the Fourth Amendment, taken in the long view, have not given the protection to the citizen which the letter and spirit of the Amendment would seem to require. One reason, I think, is that wherever a culprit is caught red-handed, as in leading Fourth Amendment cases, it is difficult to adopt and enforce a rule that would turn him loose. A rule protective of law-abiding citizens is not apt to flourish where its advocates are usually criminals. Yet the rule we fashion is for the innocent and guilty alike. If the word of the informer on which the present arrest was made is sufficient to make the arrest legal, his word would also protect the police who, acting on it, hauled the innocent citizen off to jail.

Of course, the education we receive from mystery stories and television shows teaches that what happened in this case is efficient police work. The police are tipped off that a man carrying narcotics will step off the morning train. A man meeting the precise description does alight from the train. No warrant for his arrest has been—or, as I see it, could then be—obtained. Yet he is arrested; and narcotics are found in his pocket and a syringe in the bag he carried. This is the familiar pattern of crime detection which has been dinned into public consciousness as the correct and efficient one. It is, however, a distorted reflection of the constitutional system under which we are supposed to live.

With all due deference, the arrest made here on the mere word of an informer violated the spirit of the Fourth Amendment and the requirement of the law, 26 U.S.C. (Supp. V) 7607, governing arrests in narcotics cases. If an arrest is made without a warrant, the offense must be committed in the presence of the officer or the officer must have "reasonable grounds to believe that the person to be arrested has committed or is committing" a violation of the narcotics law. The arresting officers did not have a bit of evidence, known to them and as to which they could take an oath had they gone to a magistrate for a warrant, that petitioner had committed any crime. The arresting officers did not know the grounds on which the informer based his conclusion; nor did they seek to find out what they were. They acted solely on the informer's word. In my view that was not enough.

The rule which permits arrest for felonies, as distinguished from misdemeanors, if there are reasonable grounds for believing a crime has been or is being commit-

ted (*Carroll* v. *United States*, 267 U.S. 132, 157), grew out of the need to protect the public safety by making prompt arrests. *Id.* Yet, apart from those cases where the crime is committed in the presence of the officer, arrests without warrants, like searches without warrants, are the exception, not the rule in our society. Lord Chief Justice Pratt in *Wilkes* v. *Wood*, 19 How. St. Tr. 1153, condemned not only the odious general warrant, in which the name of the citizen to be arrested was left blank, but the whole scheme of seizures and searches under "a discretionary power" of law officers to act "wherever their suspicions may chance to fall"—a practice which he denounced as "totally subversive of the liberty of the subject." *Id.*, at 1167. See III May, *Constitutional History of England*, c. XI. Wilkes had written in 1762, "To take any man into custody, and deprive him of his liberty, without having some seeming foundation at least, on which to justify such a step, is inconsistent with wisdom and sound policy." *The Life and Political Writings of John Wilkes*, p. 372.

George III in 1777 pressed for a bill which would allow arrests on suspicion of treason committed in America. The words were "suspected of" treason and it was to these words that Wilkes addressed himself in Parliament. "There is not a syllable in the Bill of the degree of probability attending the suspicion. . . . Is it possible, Sir, to give more despotic powers to a bashaw of the Turkish empire? What security is left for the devoted objects of this Bill against the malice of a prejudiced individual, a wicked magistrate . . . ?" *The Speeches of Mr. Wilkes*, p. 102.

These words and the complaints against which they were directed were well known on this side of the water. Hamilton wrote about "the practice of arbitrary imprisonments" which he denounced as "the favorite and most formidable instruments of tyranny." *The Federalist* No. 84. The writs of assistance, against which James Otis proclaimed, were vicious in the same way as the general warrants, since they required no showing of "probable cause" before a magistrate, and since they allowed the police to search on suspicion and without "reasonable grounds" for believing that a crime had been or was being committed. Otis' protest was eloquent; but he lost the case. His speech, however, rallied public opinion. "Then and there," wrote John Adams, "the child Independence was born." 10 *Life and Works of John Adams* (1856), p. 248.

The attitude of Americans to arrests and searches on suspicion was also greatly influenced by the *lettres de cachet* extensively used in France. This was an order emanating from the King and countersigned by a minister directing the seizure of a person for purposes of immediate imprisonment or exile. The ministers issued the lettres in an arbitrary manner, often at the request of the head of a noble family to punish a deviant son or relative. See Mirabeau, *A Victim of the Lettres de Cachet*, 3 Am. Hist. Rev. 19. One who was so arrested might remain incarcerated indefinitely, as no legal process was available by which he could seek release. "Since the action of the government was secret, his friends might not know whither he had vanished, and he might even be ignorant of the cause of his arrest." The Camb. Mod. Hist. 50. In the Eighteenth Century the practice arose of issuing the lettres in blank, the name to be filled in by the local mandatory. Thus the King could be told in 1770 "that no citizen of your realm is guaranteed against having his liberty sacrificed to revenge. For no one is great enough to be beyond the hate of some minister, nor small enough to be beyond the hate of some clerk." III Encyc. Soc. Sci. 138. As Blackstone wrote, ". . . if once it were left in the power of any, the highest, magistrate to imprison arbitrarily whomever he or his officers thought proper, (as in France it is daily practiced by the crown,) there would soon be an end of all other rights and immunities." I Commentaries (4th ed. Cooley).

The Virginia Declaration of Rights, adopted June 12, 1776, included the fore-runner of the Fourth Amendment:

> That general warrants, whereby an officer or messenger may be commanded to search suspected places without evidence of a fact committed, or to seizure any person or persons not named, or whose offence is not particularly described and supported by evidence, are grievous and oppressive, and ought not to be granted."

The requirement that a warrant of arrest be "supported by evidence" was by then deeply rooted in history. And it is inconceivable that in those days, when the right of privacy was so greatly cherished, the mere word of an informer—such as we have in the present case—would be enough. For whispered charges and accusations, used in lieu of evidence of unlawful acts, were the main complaint of the age. *Frisbie* v. *Butler*, Kirby's Rep. (Conn.) 1785–1788, p. 213, decided in 1787, illustrates, I think, the mood of the day in the matter of arrests on suspicion. A warrant of arrest and search was issued by a justice of the peace on the oath of a citizen who had lost some pork from a cellar, the warrant stating, "said Butler suspects one Benjamin Frisbie, of Harwinton, to be the person that hath taken said pork." The court on appeal reversed the judgment of conviction, holding *inter alia* that the complaint "contained no direct charge of the theft, but only an averment that the defendant was suspected to be guilty." *Id.*, at 215. Nothing but suspicion is shown in the instant case—suspicion of an informer, not that of the arresting officers. Nor did they seek to obtain from the informer any information on which he based his belief. The arresting officers did not have a bit of evidence that the petitioner had committed or was committing a crime before the arrest. The only evidence of guilt was provided by the arrest itself.

When the Constitution was up for adoption, objections were made that it contained no Bill of Rights. And Patrick Henry was one who complained in particular that it contained no provision against arbitrary searches and seizures:

> . . . general warrants, by which an officer may search suspected places, without evidence of the commission of a fact, or seize any person without evidence of his crime, ought to be prohibited. As these are admitted, any man may be seized, any property may be taken, in the most arbitrary manner, without any evidence or reason. Every thing the most sacred may be searched and ransacked by the strong hand of power. We have infinitely more reason to dread general warrants here than they have in England, because there, if a person be confined, liberty may be quickly obtained by the writ of habeas corpus. But here a man living many hundred miles from the judges may get in prison before he can get that writ. *I Elliot's Debates* 588.

The determination that arrests and searches on mere suspicion would find no place in American law enforcement did not abate following the adoption of a Bill of Rights applicable to the Federal Government. In *Conner* v. *Commonwealth*, 3 Binn. (Pa.) 38, an arrest warrant issued by a magistrate stating his "strong reason to suspect" that the accused had committed a crime because of "common rumor and report" was held illegal under a constitutional provision identical in relevant part to the Fourth Amendment. "It is true, that by insisting on an oath, felons may sometimes escape. This must have been very well known to the framers of our constitution; but they thought it better that the guilty should sometimes escape, than that every individual should be subject to vexation and oppression." *Id.*, at 43–44. In *Grumon* v. *Raymond*, 1 Conn. 40, the warrant stated that "several persons are suspected" of stealing some flour which is concealed in Hyatt's house or somewhere else, and ordered the constable to search Hyatt's house or other places and arrest the suspected persons if found with the flour. The court held the warrant void, stating it knew of "no such process as one to arrest all suspected persons, and bring

them before a court for trial. It is an idea not to be endured for a moment." *Id.*, at 44. See also *Fisher* v. *McGirr*, 1 Gray (Mass.) 1; *Lippman* v. *People*, 175 Ill. 101, 51 N. E. 872; *Somerville* v. *Richards*, 37 Mich. 299; *Commonwealth* v. *Dana*, 2 Metc. (Mass.) 329, 335–336. [358 U.S. 307, 321]

It was against this long background that Professors Hogan and Snee of Georgetown University recently wrote:

> . . . it must be borne in mind that any arrest based on suspicion alone is illegal. This indisputable rule of law has grave implications for a number of traditional police investigative practices. The round-up or dragnet arrest, the arrest on suspicion, for questioning, for investigation or on an open charge all are prohibited by the law. It is undeniable that if those arrests were sanctioned by law, the police would be in a position to investigate a crime and to detect the real culprit much more easily, much more efficiently, much more economically, and with much more dispatch. It is equally true, however, that society cannot confer such power on the police without ripping away much of the fabric of a way of life which seeks to give the maximum of liberty to the individual citizen. The finger of suspicion is a long one. In an individual case it may point to all of a certain race, age group or locale. Commonly it extends to any who have committed similar crimes in the past. Arrest on mere suspicion collides violently with the basic human right of liberty. It can be tolerated only in a society which is willing to concede to its government powers which history and experience teach are the inevitable accoutrements of tyranny. 47 Geo. L. J. 1, 22.

Down to this day our decisions have closely heeded that warning. So far as I can ascertain the mere word of an informer, not bolstered by some evidence that a crime had been or was being committed, has never been approved by this Court as "reasonable grounds" for making an arrest without a warrant. Whether the act complained of be seizure of goods, search of premises, or the arrest of the citizen, the judicial inquiry has been directed toward the reasonableness of inferences to be drawn from suspicious circumstances attending the action thought to be unlawful. Evidence required to prove guilt is not necessary. But the attendant circumstances must be sufficient to give rise in the mind of the arresting officer at least to inferences of guilt. *Locke* v. *United States*, 7 Cranch 339; *The Thompson*, 3 Wall. 155; *Stacey* v. *Emery*, 97 U.S. 642; *Director General* v. *Kastenbaum*, 263 U.S. 25; *Carroll* v. *United States*, 267 U.S. 132, 159–162; *United States* v. *Di Re*, 332 U.S. 581, 591–592; *Brinegar* v. *United States*, 338 U.S. 160, 165–171.

The requirement that the arresting officer know some facts suggestive of guilt has been variously stated:

> If the facts and circumstances before the officer are such as to warrant a man of prudence and caution in believing that the offense has been committed, it is sufficient. *Stacey* v. *Emery, supra*, at 645.

> . . . good faith is not enough to constitute probable cause. That faith must be grounded on facts within knowledge of the . . . agent, which in the judgment of the court would make his faith reasonable. *Director General* v. *Kastenbaum, supra*, at 28.

Even when officers had information far more suggestive of guilt than the word of the informer used here, we have not sustained arrests without a warrant. In *Johnson* v. *United States*, 333 U.S. 10, 16, the arresting officer not only had an informer's tip but he actually smelled opium coming out of a room; and on breaking in found the accused. That arrest was held unlawful. Yet the smell of opium is far more tangible direct evidence than an unverified report that someone is going to commit a crime. And in *United States* v. *Di Re, supra*, an arrest without a warrant of a man sitting in a car, where counterfeit coupons had been found passing

between two men, was not justified in absence of any shred of evidence implicating the defendant, a third person. And see *Giacona* v. *State*, 164 Tex. Cr. R. 325, 298 S. W. 2d 587. Yet the evidence before those officers was more potent than the mere word of the informer involved in the present case.

The Court is quite correct in saying that proof of "reasonable grounds" for believing a crime was being committed need not be proof admissible at the trial. It could be inferences from suspicious acts, e.g., consort with known peddlers, the surreptitious passing of a package, an intercepted message suggesting criminal activities, or any number of such events coming to the knowledge of the officer. See *People* v. *Rios*, 46 Cal. 2d 297, 294 P.2d 39. But, if he takes the law into his own hands and does not seek the protection of a warrant, he must act on some evidence known to him. The law goes for to protect the citizen. Even suspicious acts observed by the officers may be as consistent with innocence as with guilt. That is not enough, for even the guilty may not be implicated on suspicion alone. *Baumboy* v. *United States*, 24 F.2d 512. The reason is, as I have said, that the standard set by the Constitution and by the statute is one that will protect both the officer and the citizen. For if the officer acts with "probable cause" or on "reasonable grounds," he is protected even though the citizen is innocent. This important requirement should be strictly enforced, lest the whole process of arrest revert once more to whispered accusations by people. When we lower the guards as we do today, we risk making the role of the informer—odious in our history—once more supreme. I think the correct rule was stated in *Poldo* v. *United States*, 55 F.2d 866, 869. "Mere suspicion is not enough; there must be circumstances represented to the officers through the testimony of their senses sufficient to justify them in a good-faith belief that the defendant had violated the law.". . .

WHAT DO YOU THINK?

1. What are Justice Douglas's problems with the majority opinion?
2. Do you agree with the majority opinion or the dissenting opinion of Justice Douglas?
3. Should someone be searched on probable cause which is based entirely on inadmissible evidence?

Does a factual mistake invalidate a warrant that undoubtedly would have been valid if it had reflected a completely accurate understanding of the building's floor plan? The next case discusses this issue.

MARYLAND V. GARRISON
480 U.S. 79 (1987)

JUSTICE STEVENS delivered the opinion of the Court.

Baltimore police officers obtained and executed a warrant to search the person of Lawrence McWebb and "the premises known as 2036 Park Avenue third floor apartment." When the police applied for the warrant and when they conducted the search pursuant to the warrant, they reasonably believed that there was only one apartment on the premises described in the warrant. In fact, the third floor was divided into two apartments, one occupied by McWebb and one by respondent

Garrison. Before the officers executing the warrant became aware that they were in a separate apartment occupied by respondent, they had discovered the contraband that provided the basis for respondent's conviction for violating Maryland's Controlled Substances Act. The question presented is whether the seizure of that contraband was prohibited by the Fourth Amendment.

The trial court denied respondent's motion to suppress the evidence seized from his apartment . . . and the Maryland Court of Special Appeals affirmed. . . . The Court of Appeals of Maryland reversed and remanded with instructions to remand the case for a new trial. . . .

There is no question that the warrant was valid and was supported by probable cause. . . . The trial court found, and the two appellate courts did not dispute, that after making a reasonable investigation, including a verification of information obtained from a reliable informant, an exterior examination of the three-story building at 2036 Park Avenue, and an inquiry of the utility company, the officer who obtained the warrant reasonably concluded that there was only one apartment on the third floor and that it was occupied by McWebb. . . . When six Baltimore police officers executed the warrant, they fortuitously encountered McWebb in front of the building and used his key to gain admittance to the first-floor hallway and to the locked door at the top of the stairs to the third floor. As they entered the vestibule on the third floor, they encountered respondent, who was standing in the hallway area. The police could see into the interior of both McWebb's apartment to the left and respondent's to the right, for the doors to both were open. Only after respondent's apartment had been entered and heroin, cash, and drug paraphernalia had been found did any of the officers realize that the third floor contained two apartments. As soon as they became aware of that fact, the search was discontinued. All of the officers reasonably believed that they were searching McWebb's apartment. No further search of respondent's apartment was made.

The matter on which there is a difference of opinion concerns the proper interpretation of the warrant. A literal reading of its plain language, as well as the language used in the application for the warrant, indicates that it was intended to authorize a search of the entire third floor. This is the construction adopted by the intermediate appellate court and it also appears to be the construction adopted by the trial judge. One sentence in the trial judge's oral opinion, however, lends support to the construction adopted by the Court of Appeals, namely, that the warrant authorized a search of McWebb's apartment only. Under that interpretation, the Court of Appeals concluded that the warrant did not authorize the search of respondent's apartment and the police had no justification for making a warrantless entry into his premises.

The opinion of the Maryland Court of Appeals relies on Article 26 of the Maryland Declaration of Rights and Maryland cases as well as the Fourth Amendment to the Federal Constitution and federal cases. . . . We reverse.

In our view, the case presents two separate constitutional issues, one concerning the validity of the warrant and the other concerning the reasonableness of the manner in which it was executed. See *Dalia* v. *United States*, 441 U.S. 238, 258 (1979). We shall discuss the questions separately.

I

The Warrant Clause of the Fourth Amendment categorically prohibits the issuance of any warrant except one "particularly describing the place to be searched and the persons or things to be seized." The manifest purpose of this particularity requirement was to prevent general searches. By limiting the authorization to search to the

specific areas and things for which there is probable cause to search, the requirement ensures that the search will be carefully tailored to its justifications, and will not take on the character of the wide-ranging exploratory searches the Framers intended to prohibit. Thus, the scope of a lawful search is "defined by the object of the search and the places in which there is probable cause to believe that it may be found. Just as probable cause to believe that a stolen lawnmower may be found in a garage will not support a warrant to search an upstairs bedroom, probable cause to believe that undocumented aliens are being transported in a van will not justify a warrantless search of a suitcase." *United States* v. *Ross*, 456 U.S. 798, 824 (1982).

In this case there is no claim that the "persons or things to be seized" were inadequately described or that there was no probable cause to believe that those things might be found in "the place to be searched" as it was described in the warrant. With the benefit of hindsight, however, we now know that the description of that place was broader than appropriate because it was based on the mistaken belief that there was only one apartment on the third floor of the building at 2036 Park Avenue. The question is whether that factual mistake invalidated a warrant that undoubtedly would have been valid if it had reflected a completely accurate understanding of the building's floor plan.

Plainly, if the officers had known, or even if they should have known, that there were two separate dwelling units on the third floor of 2036 Park Avenue, they would have been obligated to exclude respondent's apartment from the scope of the requested warrant. But we must judge the constitutionality of their conduct in light of the information available to them at the time they acted. Those items of evidence that emerge after the warrant is issued have no bearing on whether or not a warrant was validly issued. Just as the discovery of contraband cannot validate a warrant invalid when issued, so is it equally clear that the discovery of facts demonstrating that a valid warrant was unnecessarily broad does not retroactively invalidate the warrant. The validity of the warrant must be assessed on the basis of the information that the officers disclosed, or had a duty to discover and to disclose, to the issuing Magistrate. On the basis of that information, we agree with the conclusion of all three Maryland courts that the warrant, insofar as it authorized a search that turned out to be ambiguous in scope, was valid when it was issued.

II

The question whether the execution of the warrant violated respondent's constitutional right to be secure in his home is somewhat less clear. We have no difficulty concluding that the officers' entry into the third-floor common area was legal; they carried a warrant for those premises, and they were accompanied by McWebb, who provided the key that they used to open the door giving access to the third-floor common area. If the officers had known, or should have known, that the third floor contained two apartments before they entered the living quarters on the third floor, and thus had been aware of the error in the warrant, they would have been obligated to limit their search to McWebb's apartment. Moreover, as the officers recognized, they were required to discontinue the search of respondent's apartment as soon as they discovered that there were two separate units on the third floor and therefore were put on notice of the risk that they might be in a unit erroneously included within the terms of the warrant. The officers' conduct and the limits of the search were based on the information available as the search proceeded. While the purposes justifying a police search strictly limit the permissible extent of the search, the Court has also recognized the need to allow some latitude for honest mistakes that are made by officers in the dangerous and difficult process of making arrests and executing search warrants. In *Hill v. California*, 401 U.S. 797 (1971), we considered the validity of the arrest of a man named Miller based on the mistaken belief that he was Hill. The police had probable cause to arrest Hill and they in good faith believed that Miller was Hill when they found him in Hill's apartment. As we explained:

> The upshot was that the officers in good faith believed Miller was Hill and arrested him. They were quite wrong as it turned out, and subjective good-faith belief would not in itself justify either the arrest or the subsequent search. But sufficient probability, not certainty, is the touchstone of reasonableness under the Fourth Amendment and on the record before us the officers' mistake was understandable and the arrest a reasonable response to the situation facing them at the time. *Id.*, at 803–804

While Hill involved an arrest without a warrant, its underlying rationale that an officer's reasonable misidentification of a person does not invalidate a valid arrest is equally applicable to an officer's reasonable failure to appreciate that a valid warrant describes too broadly the premises to be searched. Under the reasoning in Hill, the validity of the search of respondent's apartment pursuant to a warrant authorizing the search of the entire third floor depends on whether the officers' failure to realize the overbreadth of the warrant was objectively understandable and reasonable. Here it unquestionably was. The objective facts available to the officers at the time suggested no distinction between McWebb's apartment and the third-floor premises.

For that reason, the officers properly responded to the command contained in a valid warrant even if the warrant is interpreted as authorizing a search limited to McWebb's apartment rather than the entire third floor. Prior to the officers' discovery of the factual mistake, they perceived McWebb's apartment and the third-floor premises as one and the same; therefore their execution of the warrant reasonably included the entire third floor. Under either interpretation of the warrant, the officers' conduct was consistent with a reasonable effort to ascertain and identify the place intended to be searched within the meaning of the Fourth Amendment.

The judgment of the Court of Appeals is reversed, and the case is remanded for further proceedings not inconsistent with this opinion.

It is so ordered.

JUSTICE BLACKMUN, with whom JUSTICE BRENNAN and JUSTICE MARSHALL join, dissenting. [Omitted.]

WHAT DO YOU THINK?

1. Should the evidence be admissible?
2. What should the police do when they discover an error in a warrant?

What test should be used to determine the credability of informants? The next case discusses this issue.

ILLINOIS V. GATES
462 U.S. 213 (1983)

JUSTICE REHNQUIST delivered the opinion of the Court.

Respondents Lance and Susan Gates were indicted for violation of state drug laws after police officers, executing a search warrant, discovered marijuana and

William H. Rehnquist was appointed to the Supreme Court by President Nixon. He served as an Associate Justice from 1971 to 1986. In 1986 President Ronald Reagan elevated him to Chief Justice and he has served in that capacity since then. (Photograph by Dane Penland, Smithsonian Institution. Courtesy the Supreme Court of the United States.)

other contraband in their automobile and home. Prior to trial the Gateses moved to suppress evidence seized during this search. The Illinois Supreme Court affirmed the decisions of lower state courts granting the motion. . . . It held that the affidavit submitted in support of the State's application for a warrant to search the Gateses' property was inadequate under this Court's decisions in *Aguilar* v. *Texas*, 378 U.S. 108 (1964), and *Spinelli* v. *United States*, 393 U.S. 410 (1969). . . .

We now turn to the question presented in the State's original petition for *certiorari*, which requires us to decide whether respondents' rights under the Fourth and Fourteenth Amendments were violated by the search of their car and house. A chronological statement of events usefully introduces the issues at stake. Bloomingdale, Ill., is a suburb of Chicago located in Du Page County. On May 3, 1978, the Bloomingdale Police Department received by mail an anonymous hand-written letter which read as follows:

> "This letter is to inform you that you have a couple in your town who strictly make their living on selling drugs. They are Sue and Lance Gates, they live on Greenway, off Bloomingdale Rd. in the condominiums. Most of their buys are done in Florida. Sue his wife drives their car to Florida, where she leaves it to be loaded up with drugs, then Lance flys down and drives it back. Sue flys back after she drops the car off in Florida. May 3 she is driving down there again and Lance will be flying down in a few days to drive it back. At the time Lance drives the car back he has the trunk loaded with over $100,000.00 in drugs. Presently they have over $100,000.00 worth of drugs in their basement.

"They brag about the fact they never have to work, and make their entire living on pushers.

"I guarantee if you watch them carefully you will make a big catch. They are friends with some big drugs dealers, who visit their house often.

"Lance & Susan Gates

"Greenway

"in Condominiums"

The letter was referred by the Chief of Police of the Bloomingdale Police Department to Detective Mader, who decided to pursue the tip. Mader learned, from the office of the Illinois Secretary of State, that an Illinois driver's license had been issued to one Lance Gates, residing at a stated address in Bloomingdale. He contacted a confidential informant, whose examination of certain financial records revealed a more recent address for the Gateses, and he also learned from a police officer assigned to O'Hare Airport that "L. Gates" had made a reservation on Eastern Airlines Flight 245 to West Palm Beach, Fla., scheduled to depart from Chicago on May 5 at 4:15 p.m.

Mader then made arrangements with an agent of the Drug Enforcement Administration for surveillance of the May 5 Eastern Airlines flight. The agent later reported to Mader that Gates had boarded the flight, and that federal agents in Florida had observed him arrive in West Palm Beach and take a taxi to the nearby Holiday Inn. They also reported that Gates went to a room registered to one Susan Gates and that, at 7 o'clock the next morning, Gates and an unidentified woman left the motel in a Mercury bearing Illinois license plates and drove northbound on an interstate highway frequently used by travelers to the Chicago area. In addition, the DEA agent informed Mader that the license plate number on the Mercury was registered to a Hornet station wagon owned by Gates. The agent also advised Mader that the driving time between West Palm Beach and Bloomingdale was approximately 22 to 24 hours.

Mader signed an affidavit setting forth the foregoing facts, and submitted it to a judge of the Circuit Court of Du Page County, together with a copy of the anonymous letter. The judge of that court thereupon issued a search warrant for the Gateses' residence and for their automobile. The judge, in deciding to issue the warrant, could have determined that the *modus operandi* of the Gateses had been substantially corroborated. As the anonymous letter predicted, Lance Gates had flown from Chicago to West Palm Beach late in the afternoon of May 5th, had checked into a hotel room registered in the name of his wife, and, at 7 o'clock the following morning, had headed north, accompanied by an unidentified woman, out of West Palm Beach on an interstate highway used by travelers from South Florida to Chicago in an automobile bearing a license plate issued to him.

At 5:15 a.m. on March 7, only 36 hours after he had flown out of Chicago, Lance Gates, and his wife, returned to their home in Bloomingdale, driving the car in which they had left West Palm Beach some 22 hours earlier. The Bloomingdale police were awaiting them, searched the truck of the Mercury, and uncovered approximately 350 pounds of marihuana. A search of the Gateses' home revealed marihuana, weapons, and other contraband. The Illinois Circuit court ordered suppression of all these items, on the ground that the affidavit submitted to the Circuit Judge failed to support the necessary determination of probable cause to believe that the Gateses' automobile and home contained the contraband in question. This decision was affirmed in turn by the Illinois Appellate Court . . . and by a divided vote of the Supreme court of Illinois. . . .

The Illinois Supreme Court concluded—and we are inclined to agree—that, standing alone, the anonymous letter sent to the Bloomingdale Police Department would

not provide the basis for a magistrate's determination that there was probable cause to believe contraband would be found in the Gateses' car and home. The letter provides virtually nothing from which one might conclude that its author is either honest or his information reliable; likewise, the letter gives absolutely no indication of the basis for the writer's predictions regarding the Gateses' criminal activities. Something more was required, then, before a magistrate could conclude that there was probable cause to believe that contraband would be found in the Gateses' home and car. . . .

The Illinois Supreme Court also properly recognized that Detective Mader's affidavit might be capable of supplementing the anonymous letter with information sufficient to permit a determination of probable cause. . . . In holding that the affidavit in fact did not contain sufficient additional information to sustain a determination of probable cause, the Illinois court applied a "two-pronged test," derived from our decision in *Spinelli* v. *United States*, 393 U.S. 410 (1969). The Illinois Supreme Court, like some others, apparently understood Spinelli as requiring that the anonymous letter satisfy each of two independent requirements before it could be relied on. 85 Ill. 2d, at 383, 423 N. E. 2d, at 890. According to this view, the letter, as supplemented by Mader's affidavit, first had to adequately reveal the "basis of knowledge" of the letterwriter—the particular means by which he came by the information given in his report. Second, it had to provide facts sufficiently establishing either the "veracity" of the affiant's informant, or, alternatively, the "reliability" of the informant's report in this particular case.

The Illinois court, alluding to an elaborate set of legal rules that have developed among various lower courts to enforce the "two-pronged test," found that the test had not been satisfied. First, the "veracity" prong was not satisfied because, "[t]here was simply no basis [for] conclud[ing] that the anonymous person [who wrote the letter to the Bloomingdale Police Department] was credible." *Id.*, at 385, 423 N. E. 2d, at 891. The court indicated that corroboration by police of details contained in the letter might never satisfy the "veracity" prong, and in any event, could not do so if, as in the present case, only "innocent" details are corroborated. *Id.*, at 390, 423 N. E. 2d, at 893. In addition, the letter gave no indication of the basis of its writer's knowledge of the Gateses' activities. The Illinois court understood Spinelli as permitting the detail contained in a tip to be used to infer that the informant had a reliable basis for his statements, but it thought that the anonymous letter failed to provide sufficient detail to permit such an inference. Thus, it concluded that no showing of probable cause had been made.

We agree with the Illinois Supreme Court that an informant's "veracity," "reliability," and "basis of knowledge" are all highly relevant in determining the value of his report. We do not agree, however, that these elements should be understood as entirely separate and independent requirements to be rigidly exacted in every case, which the opinion of the Supreme Court of Illinois would imply. Rather, as detailed below, they should be understood simply as closely intertwined issues that may usefully illuminate the common-sense, practical question whether there is "probable cause" to believe that contraband or evidence is located in a particular place.

III

This totality-of-the-circumstances approach is far more consistent with our prior treatment of probable cause than is any rigid demand that specific "tests" be satisfied by every informant's tip. Perhaps the central teaching of our decisions bearing on the probable-cause standard is that it is a "practical, nontechnical conception." . . . "In dealing with probable cause, . . . as the very name implies, we deal with probabilities. These are not technical; they are the factual and practical considerations of everyday life on which reasonable and prudent men, not legal technicians, act." *Id.*, at 175. Our observation in *United States* v. *Cortez*, 449 U.S. 411, 418 (1981), regarding "particularized suspicion," is also applicable to the probable-cause standard:

> The process does not deal with hard certainties, but with probabilities. Long before the law of probabilities was articulated as such, practical people formulated certain common-sense conclusions about human behavior; jurors as factfinders are permitted to do the same—and so are law enforcement officers. Finally, the evidence thus collected must be seen and weighed not in terms of library analysis by scholars, but as understood by those versed in the field of law enforcement.

As these comments illustrate, probable cause is a fluid concept—turning on the assessment of probabilities in particular factual contexts—not readily, or even usefully, reduced to a neat set of legal rules. Informants' tips doubtless come in many shapes and sizes from many different types of persons. As we said in *Adams* v. *Williams*, 407 U.S. 143, 147 (1972): "Informants' tips, like all other clues and evidence coming to a policeman on the scene, may vary greatly in their value and reliability." Rigid legal rules are ill-suited to an area of such diversity. "One simple rule will not cover every situation." *Ibid.*

Moreover, the "two-pronged test" directs analysis into two largely independent channels—the informant's "veracity" or "reliability" and his "basis of knowledge." . . . There are persuasive arguments against according these two elements such independent status. Instead, they are better understood as relevant considerations in the totality-of-the-circumstances analysis that traditionally has guided probable-cause determinations: a deficiency in one may be compensated for, in determining the overall reliability of a tip, by a strong showing as to the other, or by some other indicia of reliability. . . .

For all these reasons, we conclude that it is wiser to abandon the "two-pronged test" established by our decisions in *Aguilar* and *Spinelli*. In its place we reaffirm the totality-of-the-circumstances analysis that traditionally has informed probable-cause determinations. . . . The task of the issuing magistrate is simply to make a practical, common-sense decision whether, given all the circumstances set forth in the affidavit before him, including the "veracity" and "basis of knowledge" of persons supplying hearsay information, there is a fair probability that contraband or evidence of a crime will be found in a particular place. And the duty of a reviewing court is simply to ensure that the magistrate had a "substantial basis for . . . conclud[ing]" that probable cause existed. . . . We are convinced that this flexible, easily applied standard will better achieve the accommodation of public and private interests that the Fourth Amendment requires than does the approach that has developed from *Aguilar* and *Spinelli*. . . .

. . . The judgment of the Supreme Court of Illinois therefore must be
Reversed.
JUSTICE WHITE, concurring in the judgment. [Omitted.]
JUSTICE STEVENS, with whom JUSTICE BRENNAN joins, dissenting. [Omitted.]

WHAT DO *YOU* THINK?

1. Did the total circumstances in this case add up to probable cause?
2. What actions would you have taken if you were the police chief when the letter was received?

Should an individual have a right to privacy in his hotel room? Do the police need a search warrant to search a hotel when the hotel manager gives them permission? The following case looks at those decisions.

STONER V. CALIFORNIA
376 U.S. 483 (1964)

Mr. Justice Stewart delivered the opinion of the Court.

The petitioner was convicted of armed robbery after a jury trial in the Superior Court of Los Angeles County, California. At the trial several articles which had been found by police officers in a search of the petitioner's hotel room during his absence were admitted into evidence over his objection. A District Court of Appeal of California affirmed the conviction, and the Supreme Court of California denied further review. We granted *certiorari*, limiting review "to the question of whether evidence was admitted which had been obtained by an unlawful search and seizure." For the reasons which follow, we conclude that the petitioner's conviction must be set aside.

The essential facts are not in dispute. On the night of October 25, 1960, the Budget Town Food Market in Monrovia, California, was robbed by two men, one of whom was described by eyewitnesses as carrying a gun and wearing horn-rimmed glasses and a grey jacket. Soon after the robbery a checkbook belonging to the petitioner was found in an adjacent parking lot and turned over to the police. Two of the stubs in the checkbook indicated that checks had been drawn to the order of the Mayfair Hotel in Pomona, California. Pursuing this lead, the officers learned from the Police Department of Pomona that the petitioner had a previous criminal record, and they obtained from the Pomona police a photograph of the petitioner. They showed the photograph to the two eyewitnesses to the robbery, who both stated that the picture looked like the man who had carried the gun. On the basis of this information the officers went to the Mayfair Hotel in Pomona at about 10 o'clock on the night of October 27. They had neither search nor arrest warrants. There then transpired the following events, as later recounted by one of the officers:

> "We approached the desk, the night clerk, and asked him if there was a party by the name of Joey L. Stoner living at the hotel. He checked his records and stated 'Yes, there is.' And we asked him what room he was in. He stated he was in Room 404 but he was out at this time.
>
> "We asked him how he knew that he was out. He stated that the hotel regulations required that the key to the room would be placed in the mail box each time they left the hotel. The key was in the mail box, that he therefore knew he was out of the room.
>
> "We asked him if he would give us permission to enter the room, explaining our reasons for this.
>
> Q. What reasons did you explain to the clerk?
>
> A. We explained that we were there to make an arrest of a man who had possibly committed a robbery in the City of Monrovia, and that we were concerned about the fact that he had a weapon. He stated 'In this case, I will be more than happy to give you permission and I will take you directly to the room.'
>
> Q. Is that what the clerk told you?
>
> A. Yes, sir.

Q. What else happened?

A. We left one detective in the lobby, and Detective Oliver, Officer Collins, and myself, along with the night clerk, got on the elevator and proceeded to the fourth floor, and went to Room 404. The night clerk placed a key in the lock, unlocked the door, and says, 'Be my guest.' "

The officers entered and made a thorough search of the room and its contents. They found a pair of horn-rimmed glasses and a grey jacket in the room, and a .45-caliber automatic pistol with a clip and several cartridges in the bottom of a bureau drawer. The petitioner was arrested two days later in Las Vegas, Nevada. He waived extradition and was returned to California for trial on the charge of armed robbery. The gun, the cartridges and clip, the horn-rimmed glasses, and the grey jacket were all used as evidence against him at his trial.

The search of the petitioner's room by the police officers was conducted without a warrant of any kind, and it therefore "can survive constitutional inhibition only upon a showing that the surrounding facts brought it within one of the exceptions to the rule that a search must rest upon a search warrant. . . . The District Court of Appeal thought the search was justified as an incident to a lawful arrest. But a search can be incident to an arrest only if it is substantially contemporaneous with the arrest and is confined to the immediate vicinity of the arrest. . . . Whatever room for leeway there may be in these concepts, it is clear that the search of the petitioner's hotel room in Pomona, California, on October 27 was not incident to his arrest in Las Vegas, Nevada, on October 29. The search was completely unrelated to the arrest, both as to time and as to place. . . .

In this Court the respondent has recognized that the reasoning of the California District Court of Appeal cannot be reconciled with our decision in *Agnello*, nor, indeed, with the most recent California decisions. Accordingly, the respondent has made no argument that the search can be justified as an incident to the petitioner's arrest. Instead, the argument is made that the search of the hotel room, although conducted without the petitioner's consent, was lawful because it was conducted with the consent of the hotel clerk. We find this argument unpersuasive.

Even if it be assumed that a state law which gave a hotel proprietor blanket authority to authorize the police to search the rooms of the hotel's guests could survive constitutional challenge, there is no intimation in the California cases cited by the respondent that California has any such law. Nor is there any substance to the claim that the search was reasonable because the police, relying upon the night clerk's expressions of consent, had a reasonable basis for the belief that the clerk had authority to consent to the search. Our decisions make clear that the rights protected by the Fourth Amendment are not to be eroded by strained applications of the law of agency or by unrealistic doctrines of "apparent authority." As this Court has said,

> . . . it is unnecessary and ill-advised to import into the law surrounding the constitutional right to be free from unreasonable searches and seizures subtle distinctions, developed and refined by the common law in evolving the body of private property law which, more than almost any other branch of law, has been shaped by distinctions whose validity is largely historical. . . . [W]e ought not to bow to them in the fair administration of the criminal law. To do so would not comport with our justly proud claim of the procedural protections accorded to those charged with crime. *Jones* v. *United States*, 362 U.S. 257, 266–267.

It is important to bear in mind that it was the petitioner's constitutional right which was at stake here, and not the night clerk's nor the hotel's. It was a right, therefore, which only the petitioner could waive by word or deed, either directly

or through an agent. It is true that the night clerk clearly and unambiguously consented to the search. But there is nothing in the record to indicate that the police had any basis whatsoever to believe that the night clerk had been authorized by the petitioner to permit the police to search the petitioner's room.

At least twice this Court has explicitly refused to permit an otherwise unlawful police search of a hotel room to rest upon consent of the hotel proprietor. . . . *Lustig* v. *United States*, 338 U.S. 74; *United States* v. *Jeffers*, 342 U.S. 48. In *Lustig* the manager of a hotel allowed police to enter and search a room without a warrant in the occupant's absence, and the search was held unconstitutional. In *Jeffers* the assistant manager allowed a similar search, and that search was likewise held unconstitutional.

It is true, as was said in Jeffers, that when a person engages a hotel room he undoubtedly gives "implied or express permission" to "such persons as maids, janitors or repairmen" to enter his room "in the performance of their duties." But the conduct of the night clerk and the police in the present case was of an entirely different order. In a closely analogous situation the Court has held that a search by police officers of a house occupied by a tenant invaded the tenant's constitutional right, even though the search was authorized by the owner of the house, who presumably had not only apparent but actual authority to enter the house for some purposes, such as to "view waste." *Chapman* v. *United States*, 365 U.S. 610. The Court pointed out that the officers' purpose in entering was not to view waste but to search for distilling equipment, and concluded that to uphold such a search without a warrant would leave tenants' homes secure only in the discretion of their landlords.

No less than a tenant of a house, or the occupant of a room in a boarding house, *McDonald* v. *United States*, 335 U.S. 451, a guest in a hotel room is entitled to constitutional protection against unreasonable searches and seizures. *Johnson* v. *United States*, 333 U.S. 10. That protection would disappear if it were left to depend upon the unfettered discretion of an employee of the hotel. It follows that this search without a warrant was unlawful. Since evidence obtained through the search was admitted at the trial, the judgment must be reversed. . . .

Mr. Justice Harlan, concurring in part and dissenting in part.

I entirely agree with the Court's opinion, except as to its disposition of the case. I would remand the case to the California District Court of Appeal so that it may consider whether or not admission of the illegally seized evidence was harmless error. . . .

WHAT DO *YOU* THINK?

1. Do you agree that the police needed a warrant to search the hotel room?
2. Did the defendant have a reasonable expectation of privacy in his hotel room, in view of the fact that the maid had a key to the room and was expected to enter the room to clean it up?

The next case looks at the definition of curtilage.

UNITED STATES V. JENKINS
124 F.3d. 768 (6ᵗʰ Cir, 1987)

Alice M. Batchelder, Circuit Judge.

In July 1992, members of the Governor's Marijuana Strike/Task Force of Kentucky seized approximately 862 marijuana plants and other incriminating evi-

dence from the rural property of defendants Noel and Linda Jenkins. A jury subsequently convicted defendants of conspiring to manufacture marijuana, manufacturing marijuana, and possessing marijuana with intent to distribute, in violation of 21 U.S.C.[o] 841 and 846. The jury also forfeited Noel Jenkins's interest in the property. Defendants appeal their convictions and sentences. Noel Jenkins also appeals the forfeiture of his interest in the property. For the following reasons, we AFFIRM.

I. BACKGROUND

On July 23, 1992, Sargent Ron West, a twenty-eight year veteran of the Kentucky State Police, directed members of the Governor's Marijuana Strike/Task Force to perform an aerial inspection for marijuana in the southwest portion of Monroe County, Kentucky. West ordered the inspection because he had previously received information that defendants were cultivating marijuana in that locality. Consistent with this information, the helicopter crew observed marijuana growing in a wooded field located directly behind defendants' residence.

Defendants live on a multi-acre plot of farmland, some of which is heavily wooded. This land lies on both sides of a public road; defendants' house is on one side of the road, set well back from it. A wire fence separates defendants' house and yard from the remainder of the property on that side of the road. A gravel driveway leads from the road to a "car-port" located on one side of the house. Defendants' backyard, much of which is shielded from the road by the house, consists of a neatly trimmed lawn, numerous small trees and flower arrangements, and a shed. Behind the backyard is a wooded field, accessible from the backyard through a gate.

Based on the aerial observations, West decided to perform a ground search of defendants' property, although he had not obtained a search warrant. Upon arrival at the property, West and his "team," which consisted of two Kentucky National Guard oversized jeep-like vehicles ("humvees") manned by ten to fifteen Kentucky State Police troopers and National Guardsmen, observed Linda Jenkins standing in the backyard outside her home. West introduced himself, advised Linda that marijuana was growing on her property, and asked her how his team could best access the wooded field behind her house. Linda told West to drive down the road toward a barn and enter through a gate located in that general vicinity. Linda then left the premises.

Instead of following Linda Jenkins's directions, West and his team parked the humvees in defendants' driveway and members of the team began wandering around defendants' backyard, where they discovered the gate leading into the wooded field. Various team members and at least one humvee used this gate to access the wooded field. West searched defendants' backyard before entering the field. He noticed a can of green spray paint and containers of hog-rings, hog-ring pliers, and tin snips lying near the shed. He also observed an empty naphthalene mothball box in a bucket that was resting against the back of defendants' house.

Proceeding into the field, West discovered a flotation growing device located approximately 85 feet behind the wire fence that separated defendants' backyard from the wooded field and 238 feet from defendants' house. The device contained 570 "young" marijuana plants growing in styrofoam trays. The growing device was surrounded by a loosely-run strand of poultry wire and was covered by three wooden boards and green-painted utility wire. This cover, however, did not obstruct West's view into the device. Two connected hoses formed a water line leading from the

flotation device to the wire fence enclosing defendants' backyard. West seized the marijuana, the wire cover, and the hoses.

Other team members discovered patches of marijuana growing in the woods approximately 100 feet behind defendants' backyard and just inside the woods across the road from defendants' house. Like the growing device, the patches were surrounded by poultry wire, some of which was hog-ringed together. A number of the patches contained naphthalene mothballs. The team seized the marijuana and the poultry wire. A further search of the woods behind defendants' house revealed an old refrigerator containing styrofoam cups full of plant food and a plastic camouflage tarpaulin. Only the tarpaulin was seized.

Realizing that "this was a pretty good sized case," West suspended the search until one of the team members could obtain a video camera. The search did not resume for approximately two hours, at which point West again searched defendants' backyard. He noticed a hose coiled up next to a faucet attached to defendants' house, and uncoiled it to see if it would reach the back fence, where the hoses from the growing device led. It did. West recoiled the hose and placed it back were he found it. He then seized the can of green spray paint, the hog-rings and hog-ring pliers, and the tin snips that were located near the shed, along with the empty mothball box from the bucket next to defendants' house.

Eventually, Noel Jenkins, who apparently had been away from home during the search, returned home and went into his house. West knocked on the door, stepped inside the foyer, and called to him. When Noel answered, West stepped back outside and waited for Noel to come out of the house. Informing Noel that the team had found marijuana growing in the field behind his house, West advised Noel of his rights, but explained that he was not under arrest and did not handcuff him. West then asked Noel for permission to search the shed, with the understanding that any incriminating evidence that West found would be used against him. Noel consented to the search, stating that he had nothing to hide. West seized two boxes of naphthalene mothballs, a styrofoam tray, and a light from the shed. West informed Noel that he was free to go and Noel went to his barn and tended to his livestock.

On July 21, 1993, a federal grand jury returned a three-count indictment against defendants, charging them with conspiring to manufacture marijuana, manufacturing marijuana, and possessing marijuana with intent to distribute, in violation of 21 U.S.C. 841 and 846. Defendants moved to suppress the evidence seized from their property. This motion was referred to a magistrate judge, who, after conducting a lengthy suppression hearing, recommended that the motion be denied. The magistrate judge reasoned that the evidence West seized from the shed was admissible because Noel Jenkins freely and voluntarily consented to a search of that area. The magistrate judge concluded that the remaining evidence was admissible because defendants' land, including the backyard, is an open field not entitled to Fourth Amendment protection. See *Oliver* v. *United States*, 466 U.S. 170 (1984). The magistrate judge rejected defendants' contention that the backyard is part of their home's curtilage. The district court, over defendants' objections, adopted the magistrate judge's recommendation in full.

On August 8, 1995, the grand jury returned a superceding indictment, adding a fourth count seeking criminal forfeiture of defendants' property. Defendants filed additional defensive motions, including another motion to suppress, which the district court denied.

On October 31, 1995, a jury found defendants guilty of counts one through three and forfeited Noel Jenkins's interest in the property. The jury did not, how-

ever, forfeit Linda Jenkins's interest. The district court issued a preliminary order of forfeiture of Noel Jenkins's interest in the property and sentenced defendants to sixty months imprisonment on each of the three counts, to be served concurrently. Defendants timely appealed, raising a scatter-shot of issues attacking their convictions and sentences. Noel Jenkins also appeals the forfeiture of his interest in the property. Only one issue, however, merits further discussion—whether the district court erroneously admitted the items seized from defendants' backyard.

II. DISCUSSION

Defendants assert that the district court erred in admitting the items that the team seized from their backyard. Defendants argue that their backyard is part of the "curtilage" of their house, and that West and his team violated the Fourth Amendment when they physically invaded and seized items from that area. We agree.

When reviewing the denial of a motion to suppress evidence, we review the district court's findings of fact for clear error and its conclusions of law *de novo*. *United States* v. *Williams*, 962 F.2d 1218, 1221 (6th Cir. 1992). We must review the evidence "in the light most likely to support the district court's decision." *Id.* (quoting *United States* v. *Gomez*, 846 F.2d 557, 560 [9th Cir. 1988]).

The Fourth Amendment provides for "people to be secure in their persons, houses, papers, and effects, against unreasonable searches and seizures . . . and [that] no Warrants shall issue, but upon probable cause. . . ." U.S. CONST. amend. IV. It is well established that the protection provided by the Fourth Amendment extends to the "curtilage" area of a house. . . . Indeed, the curtilage is considered part of the house itself for Fourth Amendment purposes. *Oliver*, 466 U.S. at 180. As we explained in *Dow Chemical Co.* v. *United States*, 749 F.2d 307, 314 (6th Cir. 1984), aff'd, 476 U.S. 227 (1986), the protection afforded to curtilage is grounded in the peculiarly strong concepts of intimacy, personal autonomy and privacy associated with the home. The home is fundamentally a sanctuary, where personal concepts of self and family are forged, where relationships are nurtured and where people normally feel free to express themselves in intimate ways. The potent individual privacy interests that inhere in living within a home expand into the areas that enclose the home as well. The backyard and area immediately surrounding the home are really extensions of the dwelling itself. This is not true simply in a mechanical sense because the areas are geographically proximate. It is true because people have both actual and reasonable expectations that many of the private experiences of home life often occur outside the house. Personal interactions, daily routines and intimate relationships revolve around the entire home place. There are compelling reasons, then, for applying Fourth Amendment protection to the entire dwelling area. See also *Ciraolo*, 476 U.S. at 212–13 ("The protection afforded the curtilage is essentially a protection of families and personal privacy in an area intimately linked to the home, both physically and psychologically, where privacy expectations are most heightened.").

The concept of curtilage, unfortunately, evades precise definition. In *Oliver*, 466 U.S. at 180 (quoting *Boyd* v. *United States*, 116 U.S. 616, 630 [1886]), the Supreme Court explained that at common law curtilage was defined to include those areas "to which extends the intimate activity associated with the 'sanctity of a man's home and the privacies of life.'" Therefore, the federal courts have historically defined curtilage "by reference to the factors that determine whether an individual reasonably may expect that an area immediately adjacent to the home will remain

private." *Id.* (citations omitted). In *United States* v. *Dunn*, 480 U.S. 294, 301 (1987), the Court elaborated upon these articulations and explained that curtilage questions should be resolved with reference to four factors: (1) "the proximity of the area claimed to be curtilage to the home"; (2) "whether the area is included within an enclosure surrounding the home"; (3) "the nature of the uses to which the area is put"; and (4) "the steps taken by the resident to protect the area from observation by people passing by." The Court cautioned, however, that it was not announcing a rigid test. "Rather, these factors are useful analytical tools only to the degree that, in any given case, they bear upon the centrally relevant consideration—whether the area in question is so intimately tied to the home itself that it should be placed under the home's 'umbrella' of Fourth Amendment protection." *Id.*

Applying the factors delineated in *Dunn* to defendants' backyard, we conclude that it is within the curtilage of defendants' house. First, defendants' backyard is in close proximity to their house. The yard is not large and is immediately accessible from a sliding glass door located in the back of the house. The second *Dunn* factor also supports a finding that the backyard is curtilage. Defendants' yard is enclosed on three sides by a wire fence, making it impossible for someone to enter the yard from the fields without using the gate or climbing over the fence. Entry from the remaining side, although not completely barred, is partially obstructed by the house. The fact that the yard and the house lie within the same fenced-off area is particularly significant. *Id.* at 302; see also *United States* v. *Reilly*, 76 F.3d 1271, 1277–78 (2d Cir.) (finding of curtilage where defendant's property was enclosed by three-sided wire fence and woods), aff'd on reh'g, 91 F.3d 331 (2d Cir. 1996); *United States* v. *Swepston*, 987 F.2d 1510, 1515 (10th Cir. 1993) (finding of curtilage where "chicken shed" and defendant's house were partially enclosed by wire fence). As the Supreme Court stated in *Oliver*, 466 U.S. at 182 n.12, "for most homes, the boundaries of the curtilage will be clearly marked; and the conception defining the curtilage—as the area around the home to which the activity of home life extends—is a familiar one easily understood from our daily experience." Defendants' backyard is clearly demarked as a continuation of the home itself. No one could mistake the yard, and its neatly mowed lawn and garden arrangements, for the unkept open fields composing the remaining portion of defendants' rural property. See *Reilly*, 76 F.3d at 1279 ("The park-like appearance of the area made it readily apparent to observers that the area was private.").

The third *Dunn* factor also weighs in defendants' favor. Defendants used the backyard as an area to garden, planting numerous small trees and flowers. Defendants also used this area for such things as hanging their wet laundry on a clothesline to dry. Such activities are related to the intimate activities normally associated with the home. Although not dispositive, it is certainly worth mentioning that West and his team possessed objective data indicating that the defendants put their backyard to such uses. See *Dunn*, 480 U.S. at 301–02 (holding that defendant's barn is not curtilage and observing that "[i]t is especially significant that the law enforcement officials possessed objective data indicating that the barn was not being used for intimate activities of the home"). Indeed, as the team entered the backyard, the gardens were in plain view and, according to the Government's brief, defendant Linda Jenkins was "attending to a clothesline" there.

This leaves the fourth *Dunn* factor, the steps defendants took to protect their backyard from observation by passing individuals. Defendants' backyard is a good distance from the road and is located, quite obviously, behind the house. The yard is therefore well shielded from the view of people passing by on the only public thoroughfare near defendants' property. Moreover, the wooded field behind defendants' house helps protect against undesired public viewing of the backyard. It is also important to remember that defendants live in a remote and sparsely populated rural area where they would have had no particular reason to believe that they needed to construct a high impenetrable fence around the backyard in order to ensure their privacy.

Taken together, as they must be, the *Dunn* factors militate in favor of the conclusion that defendants' backyard "is so intimately tied to [their] home itself that it should be placed under the home's 'umbrella' of Fourth Amendment protection." *Dunn*, 480 U.S. at 301. Defendants had a reasonable expectation that their backyard would remain private and free from physical invasion.

We do not mean to suggest that because defendants' backyard is within the curtilage of the house, it receives protection from all police observation. The protection extended to a house by the Fourth Amendment does not require police officers to shield their eyes when passing on a public concourse. *California* v. *Ciraolo*, 476 U.S. 207, 213 (1986); see also *Florida* v. *Riley*, 488 U.S. 445, 449–50 (1989) (plurality opinion). "What a person knowingly exposes to the public, even in his own home or office, is not a subject of Fourth Amendment protection." *Katz* v. *United States*, 389 U.S. 347, 351 (1967) (citations omitted). Visual inspection from a lawful vantage point, however, is quite different from the physical assault on defendants' backyard that occurred in this case. See *Riley*, 488 U.S. at 449, 452 (plurality opinion) (distinguishing lawful visual inspection of curtilage from physical invasion).

The government argues that even if defendants' backyard is curtilage, the items seized therefrom are admissible under the "plain view" doctrine. This contention is wholly without merit. Four conditions must be present before police may seize an item pursuant to the plain view doctrine: (1) the item must be in plain view; (2) the item's incriminating nature must be immediately apparent; (3) the item must be viewed by an officer lawfully located in a place from which the object can be seen; and (4) the item must be seized by an officer who has a lawful right of access to the object itself. *Horton* v. *California*, 496 U.S. 128, 136–37 (1990); *United States* v. *Calloway*, 116 F.3d 1129, 1133 (6th Cir. 1997); *United States* v. *Roark*, 36 F.3d 14, 18 (6th Cir. 1994). West seized a can of green spray paint, an empty naphthalene mothball box, hog-rings, hog-ring pliers, and tin snips from defendants' backyard. Even if we assume that these items were in plain view and that West immediately associated these items with criminal activity, the plain view doctrine does not save this unlawful seizure. West first took notice of these objects when he began searching the backyard, an area we have determined to be part of the curtilage of defendants' house. He first searched the backyard before he ever entered the open fields to perform the lawful search of that area. Therefore, West did not observe these items from an area where he was lawfully entitled to be. Moreover, if we could assume that West did observe the items from a permissible vantage point, he still had to enter defendants' protected curtilage in order to seize them. For these reasons, we hold the plain view doctrine inapplicable. We therefore hold that the district court erred in denying defendants' motion to suppress the items seized from the backyard.

Despite the district court's error, defendants' convictions must stand. Given the vast amount of evidence lawfully seized from the open fields and defendants' shed, including approximately 862 marijuana plants and other drug cultivating paraphernalia, and in light of the incriminating testimony elicited at trial, we find the district court's admission of the tainted evidence to be harmless error. *Chapman* v. *California*, 386 U.S. 18, 23–24 (1967); United States v. Baro, 15 F.3d 563, 568 (6th Cir. 1994).

Defendants have raised a number of other issues, challenging their convictions, sentences, and the forfeiture of Noel Jenkins's interest in defendants' property. We have carefully considered the record, counsels' arguments, and the applicable law, and have determined these issues to be without merit and deserving of no further discussion.

III. CONCLUSION

For the preceding reasons, we AFFIRM defendants' convictions and sentences, and the forfeiture of Noel Jenkins's interest in defendants' property.

WHAT DO YOU THINK?

1. Does the defendant have a right to privacy in the "living area" of his or her residence?
2. What points did the court use to determine that there was no reasonable expectation of privacy?

In the next case, the court also looks at the issue of what constitutes the curtilage and whether government agents who are authorized to search for aliens also may search for drugs.

UNITED STATES V. SANTA MARIA
15 F.3d 879 (9th Cir. 1994)

RYMER, Circuit Judge:

Border Patrol agents, looking for aliens and drugs along a trail well traveled with both, came upon Gilbert Santa Maria's property and, without consent, searched a trailer near his mobile home for drugs. They discovered burlap bags of marijuana. The district court found that the trailer was outside the curtilage; held that the search was authorized under 8 U.S.C. 1357(a)(3), which permits access to private lands within twenty-five miles of the border to prevent the illegal entry of aliens into the United States; and denied Santa Maria's motion to suppress. Following his conviction for conspiracy to possess marijuana and possession of marijuana with intent to distribute, in violation of 21 U.S.C. 846 and 841(a) and (b), and conspiracy to import marijuana and importation of marijuana, in violation of 21 U.S.C. 963, 960(b), and 952(a), Santa Maria appeals.

We must decide whether 1357(a)(3) authorizes the Border Patrol to search a structure such as Santa Maria's trailer for drugs. We hold that while the agents had authority to enter Santa Maria's lands to search for aliens, 1357(a)(3) confers no authority to search the trailer for drugs. In the absence of a warrant, consent, or exigent circumstances, their search runs afoul of the Fourth Amendment. Therefore, marijuana from the trailer should have been suppressed. Because the agents had probable cause to search Santa Maria's mobile home only as a result of the marijuana in the trailer, the burlap bags (similar to those in the trailer) and rope seized in the mobile home should likewise have been suppressed. We have jurisdiction, 28 U.S.C. 1291, and we reverse.

On June 10, 1992, Border Patrol agents, inspecting a known narcotics smuggling trail about ten miles north of the border between Arizona and Mexico, found approximately eight fresh sets of tracks leading north. The agents examined the trail on which the tracks were found because they had recently made two marijuana seizures from that trail. They followed the tracks north for several miles and arrived at Gilbert Santa Maria's property.

The property is surrounded by widely-strung barbed wire. From the road, the agents could see a mobile home and a trailer near it. The agents then went onto Santa Maria's property without a warrant and followed the tracks to his RV trailer. At least some of the agents climbed over or under the wire. Other agents entered through a gate. From outside the trailer, they could neither see nor smell anything unusual.

Upon arriving at the trailer, Agent John France met and spoke with Gilbert Santa Maria. Shortly thereafter, Victor Santa Maria, Gilbert's brother, joined them. France asked Victor his citizenship. Angel Lopez-Molina and another defendant who was acquitted at trial were standing nearby.

France told Gilbert Santa Maria that he suspected there was marijuana in the trailer and either asked for his consent or told him to open the trailer "for the purpose of searching for those narcotics."

Santa Maria went to the mobile home, got the key, and opened the trailer. The district court found that the government failed to meet its burden of proving that Santa Maria freely and voluntarily consented to the search. Once the door was opened, France smelled marijuana and saw burlap sugar sacks. There were 357 pounds of marijuana in the sacks. The sacks were not visible from the small window in the back of the trailer because they were underneath some carpet.

After arresting all four men, the agents made a sweep of the mobile home. In it, they found burlap bags similar to those containing marijuana in the trailer and rope used for carrying bundles of marijuana.

II

We review the denial of a motion to suppress *de novo*. *United States* v. *Garcia*, 997 F.2d 1273, 1279 (9th Cir. 1993). The trial court's factual findings are reviewed for clear error. *Id.*

The district court found that the border patrol agents were lawfully on Santa Maria's property pursuant to 8 U.S.C. 1357(a)(3) and held that the agents were within their statutory authority when they entered the trailer. Section 1357(a)(3) provides:

> Any officer or employee of the Service authorized under regulations prescribed by the Attorney General shall have power without warrant . . . within a reasonable distance from any external boundary of the United States, to board and search for aliens any vessel within the territorial waters of the United States and any railway car, aircraft, conveyance, or vehicle, and within a distance of twenty-five miles from any such external boundary to have access to private lands, but not dwellings, for the purpose of patrolling the border to prevent the illegal entry of aliens into the United States.

Santa Maria argues that, based on the plain meaning of 1357(a)(3), agents are only authorized to have access to private lands to patrol the border to prevent the illegal entry of aliens. He contends that the agents here did not come onto Santa

Maria's property to prevent illegal immigration; instead they came to search for narcotics. In addition, he urges that the statute does not authorize agents to search buildings that are "dwellings."

The government argues that the agents were authorized to enter the property and search the trailer because the trailer was not a "dwelling." It also argues that since the agents were trying to prevent the illegal entry of aliens as well as to look for drugs, the search for drugs was within the statute.

The parties do not disagree that so long as no constitutional violation occurs, section 1357(a)(3) permits Border Patrol agents to enter private lands such as Santa Maria's. The dispute centers on whether, once there, the agents could look for anything other than aliens.

A

Section 1357(a)(3) only authorizes the Border Patrol to "have access to private lands, but not dwellings, for the purpose of patrolling the border to prevent the illegal entry of aliens into the United States." 8 U.S.C. 1357(a)(3). Border Patrol authority was extended to private lands within 25 miles of the border because "the activities of the border patrol [had] in certain areas been seriously impaired by the refusal of some property owners along the border to allow patrol officers access to extensive border areas in order to prevent such illegal entries." H.R.Rep. No. 1377, 82 Cong., 2d Sess. (1952), reprinted in 1952 U.S.C.C.A.N. 1358, 1360. Nothing in the statute or its history authorizes a search for drugs.

The district court found that the agents in this case were searching for both aliens and drugs, and the government seeks to justify its search on the footing that 90% of the backpackers carrying marijuana in the area of Santa Maria's property are illegal aliens. However, illegal aliens and illegal drugs are two different things. A lawful search for one is not a lawful search for the other.

Although neither the Supreme Court nor our court has considered the reach of 1357(a)(3) beyond automobile searches at the border or its functional equivalent, it is clear that we must construe statutes to be constitutional, if possible, and that "no Act of Congress can authorize a violation of the Constitution." *Almeida-Sanchez* v. *United States*, 413 U.S. 266, 272, 93 S.Ct. 2535, 2539 (1973). In *Almeida-Sanchez*, the Court held that a roving patrol stop more than 20 miles from the border and a warrantless vehicle search, without probable cause, that turned up marijuana were not justified under 1357(a)(3) and violated the Fourth Amendment right to be free of unreasonable searches and seizures. Even though the dissent would have upheld the search for aliens and discovery of marijuana under 1357(a)(3), Justice White acknowledged that:

> Section 1357(a)(3) authorizes only searches for aliens and only searches of conveyances and other property. No searches of the person or for contraband are authorized by the section. The authority extended by the statute is limited to that reasonably necessary for the officer to assure himself that the vehicle or other conveyance is not carrying an alien who is illegally within this country; and more extensive searches of automobiles without probable cause are not permitted by the section. *Id.* at 294, 93 S.Ct. at 2550. (White, J., dissenting).

In *United States* v. *Martinez-Fuerte*, 428 U.S. 543, 562, 96 S.Ct. 3074, 3085, 49 L.Ed.2d 1116 (1976), the Court approved stops at permanent border checkpoints in the absence of articulable individualized reasons for suspicion to ask about citizenship and immigration status. However, "[n]either the vehicle nor its occupants are searched, and visual inspection of the vehicle is limited to what can be seen without a search." *Id.* at *558*, 96 S.Ct. at 3083. Any further search requires consent or probable cause. *Id.* at *567*, 96 S.Ct. at 3087.

We recently revisited the issue of permanent border checkpoint stops in *United States* v. *Soyland*, 3 F.3d 1312 (9th Cir. 1993). There, Border Patrol agents asked for permission to search the car and when the hatchback door was opened, smelled methamphetamine. In holding there was no impropriety in the search, we noted that the parties did not argue and there was no evidence that the Border Patrol intended to search for illegal drugs. *Id.* at 1314.

In each of these cases, drugs were discovered only incidentally to a lawfully conducted stop or search for aliens. Here, the Border Patrol agents had a dual purpose for entering Santa Maria's property, but intended only to search for illegal drugs in the trailer. Section 1357(a)(3) does not authorize searches for drugs. As there is nothing in the record to indicate that the agents were looking for anything other than drugs in Santa Maria's trailer, there is no statutory basis for the search.

B

The government argues that even though the search was not authorized by section 1357(a)(3), it was valid under the Constitution because the trailer was neither a dwelling nor within the curtilage of a dwelling and therefore must be "open fields" to which no Fourth Amendment protection attaches. *Oliver* v. *United States*, 466 U.S. 170, 104 S.Ct. 1735, 80 L.Ed.2d 214 (1984); see also *United States* v. *Dunn*, 480 U.S. 294, 107 S.Ct. 1134, 94 L.Ed.2d 326 (1987). This argument fails. The Fourth Amendment protects structures other than dwellings. "[O]ne may have a legally sufficient interest in a place other than her own house so as to extend Fourth Amendment protection from unreasonable searches and seizures in that place." *United States* v. *Broadhurst*, 805 F.2d 849, 851 (9th Cir. 1986). "[A] structure need not be within the curtilage in order to have Fourth Amendment protection." *Id.* at 854 n. 7; see also *Dow Chemical Co.* v. *United States*, 476 U.S. 227, 236, 106 S.Ct. 1819, 1825, 90 L.Ed.2d 226 (1986) (reasonable expectation of privacy in interior of covered buildings); *United States* v. *Wright*, 991 F.2d 1182 (4th Cir. 1993) (barn); *United States* v. *Johns*, 851 F.2d 1131, 1135–36 (9th Cir. 1988) (per curiam) (storage locker), cert. denied, ___ U.S. ___, 112 S.Ct. 3046, 120 L.Ed.2d 913 (1992); *United States* v. *Trickey*, 711 F.2d 56 (6th Cir. 1983) (outbuilding outside curtilage located on residential property with boarded up windows); *United States* v. *Hoffman*, 677 F.Supp. 589, 596 (E.D.Wis. 1988) ("[A] person can have a protected expectation of privacy in buildings (i.e., barns, garages, boathouses, stables, etc.) that are located far outside the area of the curtilage of the home.").

The government submits that Santa Maria's trailer is analogous to a stand of trees, *United States* v. *Pruitt*, 464 F.2d 494 (9th Cir. 1972), or a covered man-made ditch, *Care* v. *United States*, 231 F.2d 22 (10th Cir.), cert. denied, 351 U.S. 932, 76 S.Ct. 788, 100 L.Ed. 1461 (1956), to which Fourth Amendment protection does not extend. We disagree. It was a locked unit which housed tools, a chainsaw, and an aquarium in addition to burlap sacks of marijuana. The government does not directly argue that Santa Maria had no expectation of privacy in the trailer, and we have no trouble concluding that the trailer is not an "open field."

Nor was the search consensual. While the government argues that Santa Maria did consent, the district court found to the contrary and there is no cross-appeal

from that ruling. Since the search of the trailer was unauthorized by 1357(a)(3) and the agents lacked consent, the search violated the Fourth Amendment. Therefore the marijuana seized is inadmissible.

IV

The agents had probable cause to search the mobile home only because of the marijuana found as a result of the illegal search of the trailer. Because the original search of the trailer was illegal, all the evidence subsequently derived from that search, including the evidence found as a result of the search of the mobile home, is inadmissible as "fruit of the poisonous tree." *Nardone* v. *United States*, 308 U.S. 338, 341, 60 S.Ct. 266, 267, 84 L.Ed. 307 (1939); see also *Segura* v. *United States*, 468 U.S. 796, 804, 104 S.Ct. 3380, 3385, 82 L.Ed.2d 599 (1984). Accordingly, the burlap bags and rope found in the mobile home are also inadmissible.

V

We conclude that 1357(a)(3) does not authorize the Border Patrol to search only for drugs. The Border Patrol is empowered by 1357(a)(3) to conduct administrative searches for aliens. To expand this power to include searches for narcotics is impermissible. Absent probable cause or consent, this search was both unauthorized and a violation of the Fourth Amendment. Therefore Gilbert Santa Maria's convictions must be reversed.
    REVERSED.

WHAT DO *YOU* THINK?

1. Should the evidence be excluded?
2. What if the officers were searching for aliens and discovered the drugs, would the drugs then be admissible?

The next case discusses the requirements of an employee to submit to a urine test. Does the Fourth Amendment apply to urine samples?

SKINNER V. RAILWAY LABOR EXECUTIVES' ASSN.
489 U.S. 602 (1989)

JUSTICE KENNEDY delivered the opinion of the Court.
    The Federal Railroad Safety Act of 1970 authorizes the Secretary of Transportation to "prescribe, as necessary, appropriate rules, regulations, orders, and standards for all areas of railroad safety." 84 Stat. 971, 45 U.S.C. 431(a). Finding that alcohol and drug abuse by railroad employees poses a serious threat to safety, the Federal Railroad Administration (FRA) has promulgated regulations that mandate blood and urine tests of employees who are involved in certain train accidents. The FRA also has adopted regulations that do not require, but do authorize, railroads to administer breath and urine tests to employees who violate certain safety rules. The question presented by this case is whether these regulations violate the Fourth Amendment.

I

A

The problem of alcohol use on American railroads is as old as the industry itself, and efforts to deter it by carrier rules began at least a century ago. For many years, railroads have prohibited operating employees from possessing alcohol or being intoxicated while on duty and from consuming alcoholic beverages while subject to being called for duty. More recently, these proscriptions have been expanded to forbid possession or use of certain drugs. These restrictions are embodied in "Rule G," an industry-wide operating rule promulgated by the Association of American Railroads, and are enforced, in various formulations, by virtually every railroad in the country. The customary sanction for Rule G violations is dismissal.

. . . After occurrence of an event which activates its duty to test, the railroad must transport all crew members and other covered employees directly involved in the accident or incident to an independent medical facility, where both blood and urine samples must be obtained from each employee. After the samples have been collected, the railroad is required to ship them by prepaid air freight to the FRA laboratory for analysis. 219.205(d). There, the samples are analyzed using "state-of-the-art equipment and techniques" to detect and measure alcohol and drugs. The FRA proposes to place primary reliance on analysis of blood samples, as blood is "the only available body fluid . . . that can provide a clear indication not only of the presence of alcohol and drugs but also their current impairment effects." 49 Fed. Reg. 24291 (1984). Urine samples are also necessary, however, because drug traces remain in the urine longer than in blood, and in some cases it will not be possible to transport employees to a medical facility before the time it takes for certain drugs to be eliminated from the bloodstream. In those instances, a "positive urine test, taken with specific information on the pattern of elimination for the particular drug and other information on the behavior of the employee and the circumstances of the accident, may be crucial to the determination of" the cause of an accident. *Ibid.*

The regulations require that the FRA notify employees of the results of the tests and afford them an opportunity to respond in writing before preparation of any final investigative report. See 219.211(a)(2). Employees who refuse to provide required blood or urine samples may not perform covered service for nine months, but they are entitled to a hearing concerning their refusal to take the test. 219.213.

Subpart D of the regulations, which is entitled "Authorization to Test for Cause," is permissive. It authorizes railroads to require covered employees to submit to breath or urine tests in certain circumstances not addressed by Subpart C. Breath or urine tests, or both, may be ordered (1) after a reportable accident or incident, where a supervisor has a "reasonable suspicion" that an employee's acts or omissions contributed to the occurrence or severity of the accident or incident, 219.301(b)(2); or (2) in the event of certain specific rule violations, including noncompliance with a signal and excessive speeding, 219.301(b)(3). A railroad also may require breath tests where a supervisor has a "reasonable suspicion" that an employee is under the influence of alcohol, based upon specific, personal observations concerning the appearance, behavior, speech, or body odors of the employee. 219.301(b)(1). Where impairment is suspected, a railroad, in addition, may require urine tests, but only if two supervisors make the appropriate determination, 219.301(c)(2)(i), and, where the supervisors suspect impairment due to a substance other than alcohol, at least one of those supervisors must have received specialized training in detecting the signs of drug intoxication, 219.301(c)(2)(ii).

Subpart D further provides that whenever the results of either breath or urine tests are intended for use in a disciplinary proceeding, the employee must be given the opportunity to provide a blood sample for analysis at an independent medical facility. 219.303(c). If an employee declines to give a blood sample, the railroad may presume impairment, absent persuasive evidence to the contrary, from a positive showing of controlled substance residues in the urine. The railroad must, however, provide detailed notice of this presumption to its employees, and advise them of their right to provide a contemporaneous blood sample. . . .

Respondents, the Railway Labor Executives' Association and various of its member labor organizations, brought the instant suit in the United States District Court for the Northern District of California, seeking to enjoin the FRA's regulations on various statutory and constitutional grounds. In a ruling from the bench, the District Court granted summary judgment in petitioners' favor. The court concluded that railroad employees "have a valid interest in the integrity of their own bodies" that deserved protection under the Fourth Amendment. App. to Pet. for Cert. 53a. The court held, however, that this interest was outweighed by the competing "public and governmental interest in the . . . promotion of . . . railway safety, safety for employees, and safety for the general public that is involved with the transportation." *Id.*, at 52a. The District Court found respondents' other constitutional and statutory arguments meritless.

A divided panel of the Court of Appeals for the Ninth Circuit reversed. *Railway Labor Executives' Assn. v. Burnley*, 839 F.2d 575 (1988). The court held, first, that tests mandated by a railroad in reliance on the authority conferred by Subpart D involve sufficient Government action to implicate the Fourth Amendment, and that the breath, blood, and urine tests contemplated by the FRA regulations are Fourth Amendment searches. The court also "agre[ed] that the exigencies of testing for the presence of alcohol and drugs in blood, urine or breath require prompt action which precludes obtaining a warrant." *Id.*, at 583. The court further held that "accommodation of railroad employees' privacy interest with the significant safety concerns of the government does not require adherence to a probable cause requirement," and, accordingly, that the legality of the searches contemplated by the FRA regulations depends on their reasonableness under all the circumstances. *Id.*, at 587.

The court concluded, however, that particularized suspicion is essential to a finding that toxicological testing of railroad employees is reasonable. *Ibid.* A requirement of individualized suspicion, the court stated, would impose "no insuperable burden on the government," *id.*, at 588, and would ensure that the tests are confined to the detection of current impairment, rather than to the discovery of "the metabolites of various drugs, which are not evidence of current intoxication and may remain in the body for days or weeks after the ingestion of the drug." *Id.*, at 588–589. Except for the provisions authorizing breath and urine tests on a "reasonable suspicion" of drug or alcohol impairment, 49 CFR 219.301(b)(1) and (c)(2) (1987), the FRA regulations did not require a showing of individualized suspicion, and, accordingly, the court invalidated them.

Judge Alarcon dissented. He criticized the majority for "fail[ing] to engage in [a] balancing of interests" and for focusing instead "solely on the degree of impairment of the workers' privacy interests." 839 F.2d, at 597. The dissent would have held that "the government's compelling need to assure railroad safety by controlling drug use among railway personnel outweighs the need to protect privacy interests." *Id.*, at 596.

We granted the federal parties' petition for a writ of *certiorari*, 486 U.S. 1042 (1988), to consider whether the regulations invalidated by the Court of Appeals violate the Fourth Amendment. We now reverse.

II

The Fourth Amendment provides that "[t]he right of the people to be secure in their persons, houses, papers, and effects, against unreasonable searches and seizures, shall not be violated. . . ." The Amendment guarantees the privacy, dignity, and security of persons against certain arbitrary and invasive acts by officers of the Government or those acting at their direction. *Camara* v. *Municipal Court of San Francisco*, 387 U.S. 523, 528 (1967). See also *Delaware* v. *Prouse*, 440 U.S. 648, 653–654 (1979); *United States* v. *Martinez-Fuerte*, 428 U.S. 543, 554 (1976). Before we consider whether the tests in question are reasonable under the Fourth Amendment, we must inquire whether the tests are attributable to the Government or its agents, and whether they amount to searches or seizures. We turn to those matters.

A

Although the Fourth Amendment does not apply to a search or seizure, even an arbitrary one, effected by a private party on his or her own initiative, the Amendment protects against such intrusions if the private party acted as an instrument or agent of the Government. See *United States* v. *Jacobsen*, 466 U.S. 109, 113–114 (1984); *Coolidge* v. *New Hampshire*, 403 U.S. 443, 487 (1971). See also *Burdeau* v. *McDowell*, 256 U.S. 465, 475 (1921). A railroad that complies with the provisions of Subpart C of the regulations does so by compulsion of sovereign authority, and the lawfulness of its acts is controlled by the Fourth Amendment. Petitioners contend, however, that the Fourth Amendment is not implicated by Subpart D of the regulations, as nothing in Subpart D compels any testing by private railroads.

We are unwilling to conclude, in the context of this facial challenge, that breath and urine tests required by private railroads in reliance on Subpart D will not implicate the Fourth Amendment. Whether a private party should be deemed an agent or instrument of the Government for Fourth Amendment purposes necessarily turns on the degree of the Government's participation in the private party's activities, *cf. Lustig* v. *United States*, 338 U.S. 74, 78–79 (1949) (plurality opinion); *Byars* v. *United States*, 273 U.S. 28, 32–33 (1927), a question that can only be resolved "in light of all the circumstances," *Coolidge* v. *New Hampshire*, *supra*, [489 U.S. 602, 615] at 487. The fact that the Government has not compelled a private party to perform a search does not, by itself, establish that the search is a private one. Here, specific features of the regulations combine to convince us that the Government did more than adopt a passive position toward the underlying private conduct.

. . . We are unwilling to accept petitioners' submission that tests conducted by private railroads in reliance on Subpart D will be primarily the result of private initiative. The Government has removed all legal barriers to the testing authorized by Subpart D, and indeed has made plain not only its strong preference for testing, but also its desire to share the fruits of such intrusions. In addition, it has mandated that the railroads not bargain away the authority to perform tests granted by Subpart D. These are clear indices of the Government's encouragement, endorsement, and participation, and suffice to implicate the Fourth Amendment.

Our precedents teach that where, as here, the Government seeks to obtain physical evidence from a person, the Fourth Amendment may be relevant at several levels. See, e.g., *United States* v. *Dionisio*, 410 U.S. 1, 8 (1973). The initial detention necessary to procure the evidence may be a seizure of the person, *Cupp* v. *Murphy*, 412 U.S. 291, 294–295 (1973); *Davis* v. *Mississippi*, 394 U.S. 721, 726–727 (1969), if the detention amounts to a meaningful interference with his freedom of movement. *INS* v. *Delgado*, 466 U.S. 210, 215 (1984); *United States* v. *Jacobsen, supra*, at 113, n. 5. Obtaining and examining the evidence may also be a search, see *Cupp* v. *Murphy, supra*, at 295; *United States* v. *Dionisio, supra*, at 8, 13–14, if doing so infringes an expectation of privacy that society is prepared to recognize as reasonable, see, e.g., *California* v. *Greenwood*, 486 U.S. 35, 43 (1988); *United States* v. *Jacobsen, supra*, at 113.

We have long recognized that a "compelled intrusio[n] into the body for blood to be analyzed for alcohol content" must be deemed a Fourth Amendment search. See *Schmerber* v. *California*, 384 U.S. 757, 767–768 (1966). See also *Winston* v. *Lee*, 470 U.S. 753, 760 (1985). In light of our society's concern for the security of one's person, see, e.g., *Terry* v. *Ohio*, 392 U.S. 1, 9 (1968), it is obvious that this physical intrusion, penetrating beneath the skin, infringes an expectation of privacy that society is prepared to recognize as reasonable. The ensuing chemical analysis of the sample to obtain physiological data is a further invasion of the tested employee's privacy interests. Cf. *Arizona* v. *Hicks*, 480 U.S. 321, 324–325 (1987). Much the same is true of the breath-testing procedures required under Subpart D of the regulations. Subjecting a person to a breathalyzer test, which generally requires the production of alveolar or "deep lung" breath for chemical analysis, see, e.g., *California* v. *Trombetta*, 467 U.S. 479, 481 (1984), implicates similar concerns about bodily integrity and, like the blood-alcohol test we considered in *Schmerber*, should also be deemed a search, see 1 W. LaFave, Search and Seizure 2.6(a), p. 463 (1987). See also *Burnett* v. *Anchorage*, 806 F.2d 1447, 1449 (CA9 1986); *Shoemaker* v. *Handel*, 795 F.2d 1136, 1141 (CA3), cert. denied, 479 U.S. 986 (1986).

Unlike the blood-testing procedure at issue in *Schmerber*, the procedures prescribed by the FRA regulations for collecting and testing urine samples do not entail a surgical intrusion into the body. It is not disputed, however, that chemical analysis of urine, like that of blood, can reveal a host of private medical facts about an employee, including whether he or she is epileptic, pregnant, or diabetic. Nor can it be disputed that the process of collecting the sample to be tested, which may in some cases involve visual or aural monitoring of the act of urination, itself implicates privacy interests. As the Court of Appeals for the Fifth Circuit has stated:

> There are few activities in our society more personal or private than the passing of urine. Most people describe it by euphemisms if they talk about it at all. It is a function traditionally performed without public observation; indeed, its performance in public is generally prohibited by law as well as social custom. *National Treasury Employees Union* v. *Von Raab*, 816 F.2d 170, 175 (1987).

Because it is clear that the collection and testing of urine intrudes upon expectations of privacy that society has long recognized as reasonable, the Federal Courts of Appeals have concluded unanimously, and we agree, that these intrusions must be deemed searches under the Fourth Amendment.

In view of our conclusion that the collection and subsequent analysis of the requisite biological samples must be deemed Fourth Amendment searches, we need

not characterize the employer's antecedent interference with the employee's freedom of movement as an independent Fourth Amendment seizure. As our precedents indicate, not every governmental interference with an individual's freedom of movement raises such constitutional concerns that there is a seizure of the person. See *United States* v. *Dionisio, supra,* at 9–11 (grand jury subpoena, though enforceable by contempt, does not effect a seizure of the person); *United States* v. *Mara,* 410 U.S. 19, 21 (1973) (same). For present purposes, it suffices to note that any limitation on an employee's freedom of movement that is necessary to obtain the blood, urine, or breath samples contemplated by the regulations must be considered in assessing the intrusiveness of the searches effected by the Government's testing program. Cf. *United States* v. *Place,* 462 U.S. 696, 707–709 (1983).

III

A

To hold that the Fourth Amendment is applicable to the drug and alcohol testing prescribed by the FRA regulations is only to begin the inquiry into the standards governing such intrusions. *O'Connor* v. *Ortega,* 480 U.S. 709, 719 (1987) (plurality opinion); *New Jersey* v. *T. L. O.,* 469 U.S. 325, 337 (1985). For the Fourth Amendment does not proscribe all searches and seizures, but only those that are unreasonable. *United States* v. *Sharpe,* 470 U.S. 675, 682 (1985); *Schmerber* v. *California,* 384 U.S., at 768. What is reasonable, of course, "depends on all of the circumstances surrounding the search or seizure and the nature of the search or seizure itself." *United States* v. *Montoya de Hernandez,* 473 U.S. 531, 537 (1985). Thus, the permissibility of a particular practice "is judged by balancing its intrusion on the individual's Fourth Amendment interests against its promotion of legitimate governmental interests." *Delaware* v. *Prouse,* 440 U.S., at 654; *United States* v. *Martinez-Fuerte,* 428 U.S. 543 (1976).

In most criminal cases, we strike this balance in favor of the procedures described by the Warrant Clause of the Fourth Amendment. See *United States* v. *Place, supra,* at 701, and n. 2; *United States* v. *United States District Court,* 407 U.S. 297, 315 (1972). Except in certain well-defined circumstances, a search or seizure in such a case is not reasonable unless it is accomplished pursuant to a judicial warrant issued upon probable cause. See, e.g., *Payton* v. *New York,* 445 U.S. 573, 586 (1980); *Mincey* v. *Arizona,* 437 U.S. 385, 390 (1978). We have recognized exceptions to this rule, however, "when 'special needs, beyond the normal need for law enforcement, make the warrant and probable-cause requirement impracticable.' " *Griffin* v. *Wisconsin,* 483 U.S. 868, 873 (1987), quoting *New Jersey* v. *T. L. O., supra,* at 351 (BLACKMUN, J., concurring in judgment). When faced with such special needs, we have not hesitated to balance the governmental and privacy interests to assess the practicality of the warrant and probable-cause requirements in the particular context. See, e.g., *Griffin* v. *Wisconsin, supra,* at 873 (search of probationer's home); *New York* v. *Burger,* 482 U.S. 691, 699–703 (1987) (search of premises of certain highly regulated businesses); *O'Connor* v. *Ortega, supra,* at 721–725 (work-related searches of employees' desks and offices); *New Jersey* v. *T. L. O., supra,* at 337–342 (search of student's property by school officials); *Bell* v. *Wolfish,* 441 U.S. 520, 558–560 (1979) (body cavity searches of prison inmates).

The Government's interest in regulating the conduct of railroad employees to ensure safety, like its supervision of probationers or regulated industries, or its operation of a government office, school, or prison, "likewise presents 'special needs' beyond normal law enforcement that may justify departures from the usual

warrant and probable-cause requirements." *Griffin* v. *Wisconsin, supra,* at 873–874. The hours of service employees covered by the FRA regulations include persons engaged in handling orders concerning train movements, operating crews, and those engaged in the maintenance and repair of signal systems. 50 Fed. Reg. 31511 (1985). It is undisputed that these and other covered employees are engaged in safety-sensitive tasks. The FRA so found, and respondents conceded the point at oral argument. Tr. of Oral Arg. 46–47. As we have recognized, the whole premise of the Hours of Service Act is that "[t]he length of hours of service has direct relation to the efficiency of the human agencies upon which protection [of] life and property necessarily depends." *Baltimore & Ohio R. Co.* v. *ICC,* 221 U.S. 612, 619 (1911). See also *Atchison, T. & S. F. R. Co.* v. *United States,* 244 U.S. 336, 342 (1917) ("[I]t must be remembered that the purpose of the act was to prevent the dangers which must necessarily arise to the employee and to the public from continuing men in a dangerous and hazardous business for periods so long as to render them unfit to give that service which is essential to the protection of themselves and those entrusted to their care").

The FRA has prescribed toxicological tests, not to assist in the prosecution of employees, but rather "to prevent accidents and casualties in railroad operations that result from impairment of employees by alcohol or drugs." 49 CFR 219.1(a) (1987). This governmental interest in ensuring the safety of the traveling public and of the employees themselves plainly justifies prohibiting covered employees from using alcohol or drugs on duty, or while subject to being called for duty. This interest also "require[s] and justif[ies] the exercise of supervision to assure that the restrictions are in fact observed." *Griffin* v. *Wisconsin, supra,* at 875. The question that remains, then, is whether the Government's need to monitor compliance with these restrictions justifies the privacy intrusions at issue absent a warrant or individualized suspicion.

B

An essential purpose of a warrant requirement is to protect privacy interests by assuring citizens subject to a search or seizure that such intrusions are not the random or arbitrary acts of government agents. A warrant assures the citizen that the intrusion is authorized by law, and that it is narrowly limited in its objectives and scope. See, e.g., *New York* v. *Burger, supra,* at 703; *United States* v. *Chadwick,* 433 U.S. 1, 9 (1977); *Camara* v. *Municipal Court of San Francisco,* 387 U.S., at 532. A warrant also provides the detached scrutiny of a neutral magistrate, and thus ensures an objective determination whether an intrusion is justified in any given case. See *United States* v. *Chadwick, supra,* at 9. In the present context, however, a warrant would do little to further these aims. Both the circumstances justifying toxicological testing and the permissible limits of such intrusions are defined narrowly and specifically in the regulations that authorize them, and doubtless are well known to covered employees. Cf. *United States* v. *Biswell,* 406 U.S. 311, 316 (1972). Indeed, in light of the standardized nature of the tests and the minimal discretion vested in those charged with administering the program, there are virtually no facts for a neutral magistrate to evaluate. Cf. *Colorado* v. *Bertine,* 479 U.S. 367, 376 (1987) (BLACKMUN, J., concurring).

We have recognized, moreover, that the government's interest in dispensing with the warrant requirement is at its strongest when, as here, "the burden of obtaining a warrant is likely to frustrate the governmental purpose behind the search." *Camara* v. *Municipal Court of San Francisco, supra,* at 533. See also *New Jersey*

v. *T. L. O.*, 469 U.S., at 340; *Donovan* v. *Dewey*, 452 U.S. 594, 603 (1981). As the FRA recognized, alcohol and other drugs are eliminated from the bloodstream at a constant rate, see 49 Fed. Reg. 24291 (1984), and blood and breath samples taken to measure whether these substances were in the bloodstream when a triggering event occurred must be obtained as soon as possible. See *Schmerber* v. *California*, 384 U.S., at 770–771. Although the metabolites of some drugs remain in the urine for longer periods of time and may enable the FRA to estimate whether the employee was impaired by those drugs at the time of a covered accident, incident, or rule violation, 49 Fed. Reg. 24291 (1984), the delay necessary to procure a warrant nevertheless may result in the destruction of valuable evidence.

The Government's need to rely on private railroads to set the testing process in motion also indicates that insistence on a warrant requirement would impede the achievement of the Government's objective. Railroad supervisors, like school officials, see *New Jersey* v. *T. L. O.*, *supra*, at 339–340, and hospital administrators, see *O'Connor* v. *Ortega*, 480 U.S., at 722, are not in the business of investigating violations of the criminal laws or enforcing administrative codes, and otherwise have little occasion to become familiar with the intricacies of this Court's Fourth Amendment jurisprudence. "Imposing unwieldy warrant procedures . . . upon supervisors, who would otherwise have no reason to be familiar with such procedures, is simply unreasonable." *Ibid.*

In sum, imposing a warrant requirement in the present context would add little to the assurances of certainty and regularity already afforded by the regulations, while significantly hindering, and in many cases frustrating, the objectives of the Government's testing program. We do not believe that a warrant is essential to render the intrusions here at issue reasonable under the Fourth Amendment.

C

Our cases indicate that even a search that may be performed without a warrant must be based, as a general matter, on probable cause to believe that the person to be searched has violated the law. See *New Jersey* v. *T. L. O.*, *supra*, at 340. When the balance of interests precludes insistence on a showing of probable cause, we have usually required "some quantum of individualized suspicion" before concluding that a search is reasonable. See, e.g., *United States* v. *Martinez-Fuerte*, 428 U.S., at 560. We made it clear, however, that a showing of individualized suspicion is not a constitutional floor, below which a search must be presumed unreasonable. *Id.*, at 561. In limited circumstances, where the privacy interests implicated by the search are minimal, and where an important governmental interest furthered by the intrusion would be placed in jeopardy by a requirement of individualized suspicion, a search may be reasonable despite the absence of such suspicion. We believe this is true of the intrusions in question here.

By and large, intrusions on privacy under the FRA regulations are limited. To the extent transportation and like restrictions are necessary to procure the requisite blood, breath, and urine samples for testing, this interference alone is minimal given the employment context in which it takes place. Ordinarily, an employee consents to significant restrictions in his freedom of movement where necessary for his employment, and few are free to come and go as they please during working hours. See, e.g., *INS* v. *Delgado*, 466 U.S., at 218. Any additional interference with a railroad employee's freedom of movement that occurs in the time it takes to procure a blood, breath, or urine sample for testing cannot, by itself, be said to infringe significant privacy interests. . . .

1. Do you agree with the court's opinion that blood and urine samples are protected by the Fourth Amendment?
2. Under the guidelines of this decision, what is required before the railroad company may obtain a urine sample from an employee?

SUMMARY

- The Fourth Amendment is applicable to the states through the due process clause of the Fourteenth Amendment. It only governs conduct of federal and state agents (including local police and other local government employees). It does not govern the conduct of private individuals who are not acting as government agents. The same standards of reasonableness and probable cause are applicable to both state and federal cases. Evidence taken in violation of the Fourth Amendment is subjected to exclusion in court

- Since an arrest is a seizure, the Fourth Amendment also covers arrests. The amendment is, however, more often thought of as a limitation on the power of the police to search and seize evidence. One reason for this is that when a person is illegally arrested, he or she may still be prosecuted for the crime. Whereas when evidence is illegally discovered or seized, the evidence generally is excluded from the trial.

- A search is considered as a governmental intrusion into an area or interest where a person has a reasonable expectation of privacy. Reasonableness includes the requirement that it must be an expectation that the people (society) is willing to accept.

- The U.S. Supreme Court has interpreted the Fourth Amendment's protection of the home to include the curtilage, that area immediately surrounding the home. The area outside of the curtilage is often referred to as the *open fields area* and is not protected.

- Probable cause is needed before a warrant may be issued to search a place, etc., or seize a person (arrest). Probable cause is a difficult and complex concept to explain. The probable cause standard is designed to strike a balance between the rights of the individual to privacy and security and the interest of the government in investigating and prosecuting crime. The probable cause standard requires only a fair probability that the officers are correct in their assessment of the facts.

- A warrant is a judicial document issued by a judicial officer that authorizes a law enforcement official to make a search or seizure. Generally the judicial officer is a magistrate. The magistrate must be neutral and detached.

- The determination of the presence of probable cause is the responsibility of the magistrate. Accordingly, probable cause must be based only on the facts presented in the affidavit to the magistrate. Facts known to the police, but not presented to the magistrate, may not be used to support the decision to issue a warrant.

- There are no restrictions in the Fourth Amendment regarding the correct procedure for executing a warrant. Most jurisdictions, however, have statutes on executing warrants. Generally a search warrant must be executed within a specified time period.

■ The Supreme Court has acknowledged the right of the police to enter without notice in three situations: (1) where notice would present a threat of physical violence, (2) in hot-pursuit cases, and (3) where the officers have probable cause to believe that evidence would likely be destroyed if they gave notice before entering.

■ The scope and duration of the search must relate directly to the magistrate's previous determination of probable cause. A warrant authorizing the search of a house generally allows the search not only of the house but the surrounding curtilage, which includes backyards and associated buildings.

■ An *arrest* (seizure of a person) is the taking of a person into custody so that the person may be held to answer for the commission of a crime. The four essential elements required for an arrest are intent to arrest, authority to arrest, seizure and detention, and an understanding by the arrestee that he or she is being arrested.

DISCUSSION QUESTIONS

1. Explain what areas the Fourth Amendment protects.
2. What is required before a search can take place or an arrest warrant may be issued?
3. Define *probable cause*.
4. What constitutes a search?
5. Under what conditions may an individual be arrested without a warrant?
6. Joe is illegally arrested. At the time of his arrest he had a stolen watch in his possession. What actions can the police take regarding the stolen watch?

ENDNOTES

1. *California* v. *Acevodo*, 500 U.S. 565 (1991).
2. 499 U.S. 621 (1991).
3. *United States* v. *Verdugo-Urquidez*, 494 U.S. 858 (1990).
4. *United States* v. *Alverez-Machain*, 112 S.Ct. 2188 (1992).
5. *Katz* v. *United States*, 389 U.S. 347 (1967).
6. *United States* v. *Place*, 462 U.S. 696 (1983).
7. Edward M. Hendrie, "Curtilage: The Expectation of Privacy in the Yard," *F.B.I. Law Enforcement Bulletin*, April 1998, pp. 25–28.
8. *Boyd* v. *United States*, 116 U.S. 616 (1886).
9. 480 U.S. 294 (1987)
10. *Hill* v. *California*, 401 U.S. 797 (1971).
11. *Draper* v. *United States*, 358 U.S. 307, 79 S.Ct. 329 (1959).
12. 379 U.S. 89 (1964).
13. 462 U.S. 213 (1983).
14. 429 U.S. 245 (1977).
15. 403 U.S. 443 (1971).
16. 442 U.S. 319 (1979).
17. 407 U.S. 345 (1972).

18. *United States* v. *Decker*, 958 F.2d 783 (8th Cir. 1992).

19. *Franks* v. *Delaware*, 438 U.S. 174 (1978).

20. *United States* v. *Storage Spaces*, 777 F.2d 1363 (9th Cir. 1985).

21. 97 F.3d. 669 (2d Cir. 1996).

22. *Alderman* v. *United States*, 394 U.S. 165 (1969).

23. 392 U.S. 1 (1968).

24. 452 U.S. 692 (1981).

25. 800 F.2d. 1451 (9th Cir. 1986).

26. 115 S.Ct. 1914 (1995).

27. 137 L.Ed. 2d 615 (1997).

28. 901 F.2d. 1351 (6th Cir. 1990).

29. *State* v. *Rusco*, 212 Conn. 223 (1989).

30. 764 F.2d. 885 (D.C. Cir. 1985).

31. 867 F.2d. 581 (5th Cir. 1989).

32. 43 Cal. 3d 21 (1987).

33. *Miles* v. *State*, 742 P.2d. 1150 (Okl. Crim. App. 1987).

34. 403 U.S. 443 (1978).

35. 480 U.S. 321 (1987).

36. 277 U.S. 438 (1928).

37. 35 C.A.3rd 1 (1973).

38. *United States* v. *DiRe*, 332 U.S. 581 (1948).

39. *Ker* v. *California*, 374 U.S. 23 (1963).

40. *United States* v. *Miller*, 452 F.2d 731 (10th Cir. 1972).

41. *Payton* v. *New York*, 445 U.S. 573 (1980).

42. *In re Timothy E.* 99 C.A.3d 349 (1979) and *In People* v. *Kenner*, 73 C.A.3d 65 (1977).

5

THE FOURTH AMENDMENT— EXCEPTIONS

INTRODUCTION

The exceptions to the Fourth Amendment will be examined in this chapter. Also considered are searches without warrants. As stated in Chapter 4, the Fourth Amendment is not applicable to open fields, abandoned property, and areas where there is no reasonable expectation of privacy. The material covered in this chapter should help answer the question: Is the Fourth Amendment applicable? If the governmental intrusion is considered a search, two additional issues should be considered—first, is a warrant needed? and second, is probable cause needed? Some searches do not need a warrant, but probable cause must be present, i.e., automobile searches. First, we examine those searches that need neither a warrant nor probable cause. Then we will examine those situations where probable cause is needed but for some reason the lack of a warrant is excused. Temporary detentions and "Terry-type" situations will be discussed in a separate section of this chapter.

SEARCHES WITHOUT PROBABLE CAUSE

Searches or government intrusions where probable cause is not needed include plain view, open fields, searches incident to arrest, consent searches, inventory searches, inspections and regulatory searches, and border searches.

Scope of the Fourth Amendment

What is the scope of the Fourth Amendment? Does it prohibit warrantless searches? Justice Anthony Scalia in his concurring opinion in *California* v. *Acevedo*[1] provides an excellent summary of the scope of the amendment:

> The Fourth Amendment does not, by its terms, require a prior warrant for searches and seizures; it merely prohibits searches and seizures that are "unreasonable." . . . Even before today's decision, the "warrant requirement" had become so riddled with exceptions that it was basically unrecognizable. In 1985, one commentator cataloged nearly 20 such exceptions, including "searches incident to arrest . . . automobile searches . . . border searches . . . administrative searches of regulated businesses . . . exigent circumstances . . . search[es] incident to nonarrest when there is probable cause to arrest . . . boat boarding for document checks . . . welfare searches . . . inventory searches . . . airport searches . . . school search[es]. . . ." Since then, we have added at least two more. *California* v. *Carney*, 471 U.S. 386 (1985) (searches of mobile homes); *O'Connor* v. *Ortega*, 480 U.S. 709 (1987) (searches of offices of government employees). Our intricate body of law regarding "reasonable expectation of privacy" has been developed largely as a means of creating these exceptions, enabling a search to be denominated not a Fourth Amendment "search," and therefore not subject to the general warrant requirement. . . .

Plain View

Plain view is not considered to be a search. If something can be observed from an area open to the public there has been no search. To be a search, there must be a violation of the reasonable expectation of privacy. Once contraband located in a private area is observed from a public area, the police may need a warrant to seize the property. Under the plain view doctrine, if the police are lawfully in a position from which they view an object, if its incriminating character is immediately apparent, and if the officers have a lawful right of access to the object, it may then be seized without a warrant.[2] The rationale of the plain view doctrine is that if contraband is left in open view and is observed by the police officer from a lawful vantage point, there has been no invasion of a legitimate expectation of privacy and thus no "search" has taken place within the meaning of the Fourth Amendment.

In *Arizona* v. *Hicks*[3] the Supreme Court held invalid the seizure of stolen stereo equipment found by the police while executing a valid search warrant for other evidence. The Court held that the plain view doctrine did not apply to this situation. Although the police were lawfully on the premises pursuant to a valid search warrant, they obtained probable cause to seize the stereo equipment only after they had moved the equipment in order to read the serial numbers. Accordingly, the incriminating character of the stereo equipment was not immediately apparent and the moving of it was not authorized by the warrant to search for other property.

In some cases, "plain touch" has been considered as analogous to plain view. Ordinarily, however, the touching will itself constitute a search activity that must be justified.

An item is still considered to be in plain view when the common means of enhancing the senses, such as a flashlight or binoculars, are used. If the devices in a particular circumstance are highly intrusive, however, it may be considered a search[4]—for example, using a high-powered telescope to determine what a person is reading in a high-rise apartment. The use of a drug dog to detect the odor of narcotics in a suitcase is not a search because it exposes only contraband and other items that remain hidden and unexposed.[5]

Open Fields

The U.S. Supreme Court has held that open fields are not protected by the Fourth Amendment. Accordingly, police officers may enter and search unoccupied or undeveloped areas.[6] The rationale for the open fields doctrine is that only "homes, persons, effects and papers" are protected by the Fourth Amendment and there is a lesser expectation of privacy in open fields. (*Note*: "Open fields" includes forests, fields, etc. Even if the field is "posted," the police may still search the field without probable cause or a warrant, except for the curtilage [the area immediately surrounding the dwelling].)

Border Searches

A *border search* is a superficial search or inspection conducted without a warrant or probable cause of persons, vehicles, and property entering the United States. The purpose of these searches is to combat smuggling and theft problems at international borders, airports, and seaports. The Supreme Court in *Martinez-Fuerte*[7] upheld border searches as inherently reasonable under the Constitution without the need for warrant or probable cause.

Any person entering the United States is subject to search, i.e., visitors, employees, transportation workers, and citizens re-entering the United States. The border area is any place that is the functional equivalent of the border, e.g., the first airport where the plane lands or established inspection stations near borders.

While searches without probable cause or warrants are permissible at the border or its functional equivalent, the courts have restricted customs/immigration searches at points away from the border. Established checkpoint stops for brief routine questioning sixty miles from the border without a particular reason are, however, permissible. (*Note*: Searches without a reasonable suspicion at checkpoints located a distance from the border are not permissible.[8] A roving patrol cannot justify detaining a vehicle near the border merely because the occupants "looked Mexican."[9])

Health and Safety and Other Administrative Inspections

Health and safety inspections are different from normal searches and seizures in that their primary purpose is for reasons other than to discover evidence of criminal activity. They are, however, subject to the limitations set forth in the Fourth Amendment.[10] Generally a warrant is required, except in emergency situations.

A showing of probable cause is *not* needed if the inspection is part of a general "neutral" enforcement plan. In certain businesses, because of the need for closer government supervision, a warrant may not be required, e.g., liquor sales.[11]

Generally a warrant is not required for administrative/code inspections when the business is closely regulated if the interest served by the regulations advance a substantial societal interest, i.e., to protect the health or safety of employees and the warrantless entries are necessary to enforce the regulations.

Public school administrators and teachers may search students without a warrant and such searches are generally based only on reasonable suspicion that the search will turn up information indicating that the student has violated or is violating either the law or rules of the school. The search, under these circumstances, should not be excessively intrusive taking into consideration the age and sex of the student.[12]

In *Vernonia School District 47J* v. *Acton*[13], the Supreme Court upheld the requirement for random urinalysis drug testing of students who wish to participate in the school district's athletic programs. They held that there was a legitimate need for the testing and that the testing was done in a manner that eliminated discretion on the part of the school district. The Court concluded that the district's interest in conducting the testing outweighed the relatively limited privacy interest that was invaded.

The warrantless, suspicionless testing of blood, breath, and urine of public employees for evidence of drug and or alcohol use was upheld by the Supreme Court in *Skinner* v. *Railway Labor Executives' Ass'n*.[14] To permit such tests, the employee must be working in a job already pervasively regulated by the government and there must be a significant link between the employee's on-the-job performance and the need to test for drug use or alcohol. Care is required to be taken to guard the personal dignity and privacy of the tested employee.

Parole and Probation Searches

A standard condition of parole release agreement is that the parolee is subject to being searched at any time without a warrant and with no requirement for probable cause. Generally for a search based on this condition to be admissable, the search must be directly and closely related to parole supervision purposes.[15] As stated by the California Supreme Court, "A parole search is reasonable under the Fourth Amendment if there is a reasonable nexus (a direct and close relationship) between the search and the parole process, and a reasonable suspicion, based on articulable facts, that the parolee has violated the terms of his parole or engaged in criminal activity."[16] In some states, even "reasonable suspicion is not needed to search a parolee. In a few states, the parole officer must be contacted prior to the search for authorization to search.

Not all probation agreements contain a search condition. If there are no search conditions, the normal rules of search and seizure apply. If there is a search condition, the terms of the condition must be followed to justify the search on the basis of the condition. For example, if the condition requires the probationer to submit to a search "on request" the officer must first ask permission to search. If the condition is limited to searching for drugs, then a search for any other reason cannot be justified under this condition. If the condition authorizes a search by any law enforcement officer, there is no requirement to first contact the probation officer.

Jail and Prison Searches

A person being jailed or already in confinement may be searched without a warrant if it is reasonably necessary to provide for the security of the institution and the public. As the U.S. Supreme Court noted in *Hudson* v. *Palmer*,[17] a prisoner has no reasonable expectation of privacy in his prison cell.

Airport Searches

The courts have upheld the reasonableness of subjecting anyone who travels on an airplane to a search by metal detector and x-rays before the person is allowed to board the airplane. The rationale for these type searches is that (1) it is necessary to prevent hijacking and bombing, (2) the passenger "consents" to the search as a condition to air travel, and (3) the intrusion is limited only to a search for weapons or explosives.[18]

Business Records

Federal rules do not recognize an expectation of privacy in business, financial, telephone, and post office box records. Accordingly, no warrant is required to search these records. Most states, like California and Texas, require a warrant or subpoena to search the above records unless (1) exigent circumstances exist, (2) consent is obtained, or (3) the search is part of a valid inventory.[19]

Consent Searches

A person may waive his or her constitutional rights and consent to a search. To constitute consent, there must be a voluntary, duress-free permission to search. The question of whether the consent is voluntary depends on all the surrounding circumstances.[20] There is no requirement that the police advise the person of his or her constitutional rights prior to obtaining permission to search.

An undercover police officer may deceive a person regarding his or her identity when obtaining consent to enter a home. The fact that the consent was given by mistake or as the direct result of police deception does not make the entry unlawful unless the deception is unreasonably fraudulent—"misplaced trust" doctrine.[21] Consent given based on the officer's false statement that he had a warrant was not a valid consent search.[22]

Effective consent may be given only by the suspect or someone who possesses common authority to the premises or effects in question (co-occupant).[23] Common authority involves the mutual use or control of the property. For example, a wife or live-in girlfriend could give permission to search the home of a suspected drug dealer.

In *Burton* v. *U.S.*[24], Burton was approached at a bus station by two officers. One of the officers asked permission to search his luggage and person for drugs. Burton consented. When the officer started to search Burton's jacket, Burton grabbed the jacket and put his hand in the jacket pocket. The officer told Burton to move his hand. He did, and the officer found drugs in the pocket of it. At a suppression hearing, Burton's counsel claimed that Burton had withdrawn his consent and thus the search was illegal since there was no probable cause to search. The court disagreed. The court held that to be an effective withdrawal of consent, there must be unequivocal conduct in the form of either an act, statement, or some combination of the two, that is inconsistent with the consent to the search previously given.

In *United States* v. *Hyppolite*[25], the police attempted to use Hyppolite's refusal to consent to a search to establish probable cause. The court of appeals held that a defendant's refusal to consent cannot establish probable cause to search. The court stated that to hold otherwise would vitiate the protections of the Fourth Amendment—that the amendment would mean little if officers could manufacture probable cause by asking questions until a suspect either consents or exercises constitutional rights.

In *United States* v. *Morning*[26], the defendant Morning and a person named Leon-Yanez shared the same house. A federal agent asked Morning to consent to a search of the house. She replied that she would prefer the agent get a warrant. The agent then obtained consent to search the house from Leon-Yanez. The court of appeals held that either Morning or Leon-Yanez could give permission to search the common area of the house. Since Leon-Yanez gave permission, the search was legal.

The Supreme Court held in *Schneckloth* v. *Bustamonte*[27] that the knowledge that a person may refuse to consent may be taken into account in determining whether the consent was voluntary based on the totality of the circumstances. There is no requirement to advise a person of his or her rights before asking for permission to search. The scope of a consent search is limited by the physical bounds by which the consent is granted.

A consent search given by a third party does not depend on whether the third party had the authority to give consent but depends on the third party's apparent authority. A consent search was held reasonable in *Illinois* v. *Rodriguez*[28] when the person actually giving consent to the search had no authority but told the police that she lived there and had a key to the premises. The Court held that the police's mistake in believing that she lived there was reasonable.

Technological Information Gathering and Surveillance

In the area of technological information gathering and surveillance, there are no clear general rules. Each activity must be examined separately to determine if the activities are protected by the Fourth Amendment.

Pen Registers   The police may install a pen register on a target's telephone without probable cause and without a warrant. A *pen register* is a device that records all numbers dialed from the monitored telephone, whether or not the call is completed. The rationale for holding that this is not a search is that a person has no legitimate expectation of privacy in information that he or she voluntarily conveys to another. The caller assumes the risk that when he or she calls a number that the other person or the telephone company will furnish the fact of the call to the government.

Beepers   The police may use an electronic beeper tracking device to monitor a person's movements while a person is in public places. The use of a beeper constitutes a search when it reveals information that is private, such as the movement within the house. In *United States* v. *Karo*[29], the police used a beeper to follow the movements of an ether drum as Karo tansported it to and through various houses. The Court held that the monitoring of property in public was legal, but when the property was withdrawn from public view (moved into the home) then there was a reasonable expectation of privacy, i.e., a search.

Aerial Surveillance   Aerial surveillance of activities by the government does not constitute a search if the surveillance occurs from public, navigable airspace; is conducted in a physically nonintrusive manner; and does not reveal intimate activities traditionally connected with the use of a home or curtilage.[30] In the Riley case the Supreme Court held that helicopter sighting of contraband was legal. In this case, the helicopter was flying at an altitude of 500 feet. The Court, however, hinted that it may have reached a different decision if the surveillance revealed "intimate details" connected with the home.

Standing to Object

The protections of the Fourth Amendment are personal. A defendant cannot raise the Fourth Amendment objection unless he or she demonstrates that his or her rights under the amendment were violated. For example, the police may violate Edward's rights and obtain evidence that may be used against Thomas as long as Thomas's rights were not violated. Suppose that Thomas was the target of the investigation and not Edward. In *Rakas* v. *Illinois*[31], the Supreme Court held that a person does not have standing to object to an unreasonable search or seizure merely because he was the target or focus of the police activity.

The Supreme Court decided in *Rakas* that the capacity of a person to contest a search—standing—depends on whether the person who claims the protection of the Fourth Amendment had a legitimate expectation of privacy in the area searched. As noted in Chapter 4, according to *Katz* a search occurs when someone has a reasonable expectation of privacy in the area searched. *Rakas* requires that the someone be the defendant who has a reasonable expectation of privacy. For example, in *Rawlings* v. *Kentucky*[32] the defendant placed a vial of drugs in a friend's purse, with the friend's permission. The defendant had known the friend only a few days and had not previously had access to the purse. Both the defendant and the friend were present when the police searched the purse and found the drug vial. The Court held that the defendant did not have sufficient legitimate expectation of privacy in the purse to contest the legality of the search. The Supreme Court has delineated factors to be considered in determining whether the defendant has a reasonable expectation of privacy—standing. They include the following:

- Did defendants have a possessory interest in the area or object searched or seized?
- Have the defendants taken measures to ensure their privacy?
- Was the item in plain view?
- Was the area searched in a private dwelling or within the curtilage?
- Was the defendant legitimately on the premises searched?
- Did the defendant have exclusive control over the area searched?

In the *Olson* case, the defendant was an overnight guest in the house that was searched. The Court held that because of his status as an overnight guest, he had a right to a reasonable expectation of privacy although he was not the sole occupant of the house at the time of the search. In *Alderman* v. *United States*[33], the Supreme Court concluded that a person does not have standing to raise a Fourth Amendment claim merely because the seized evidence was obtained unlawfully from a co-conspirator.

In December 1998, the U.S. Supreme Court decided the *Minnesota* v. *Carter* case, 98 C.D.O.S. 8754. In the case, the respondents and the lessee of an apartment were sitting in one of the apartment's rooms bagging cocaine. They were observed by a police officer who was looking through a drawn window blind. Prior to trial, the defendant Carter moved to suppress the evidence claiming that the officer's actions constituted an unlawful search. The trial court held that since Carter was not an overnight guest but a temporary visitor, he did not have "standing" to object to the constitutionality of the search. The Minnesota Court of Appeals agreed with the trial court. The Supreme Court of Minnesota, however, reversed and held that Carter did have "standing" to raise the Fourth Amendment claims.

The U.S. Supreme Court, with Chief Justice Rehnquist writing the opinion, reversed the decision of the state supreme court. The Court stated that the respondents were not overnight guests but were essentially present for a business transaction and were only in the home a matter of hours. There was no suggestion that they had a previous relationship with Thompson (lessee) or that there was any other purpose to their visit. Nor was there anything similar to the overnight guest relationship to suggest a degree of acceptance into the household. While the apartment was home for Thompson, for Carter it was simply a place to do business. The Court further stated that property used for commercial purposes is treated differently for Fourth Amendment purposes than for residential property. The "home" which Carter was in was not his home. Accordingly, the Court held, since Carter had no reasonable expectation of privacy in the apartment, his rights under the Fourth Amendment were not violated by the search. (*Note:* Since the apartment was Thompson's home, Thompson would have had standing to object to the search, but Thompson was not involved in this case.)

SEARCHES WITHOUT WARRANTS

The two most frequent situations in which the police are allowed to search without a warrant but with probable cause (unless the probable cause requirement is excused for another reason), are vehicles on public roads and searches under exigent circumstances. Vehicles on public roads may be searched without a warrant but on probable cause because of the lesser expectation of privacy associated with them. This exception is discussed in the next section.

The basis for the exigent circumstances exception is that for some reason it is impractical for the police to obtain a warrant. The general features of the exigency exception include:

- It would be impractical to obtain a search warrant.
- The emergency that justifies the warrantless search also defines the limits of the search.
- The probable cause requirement must still be examined. This does not mean that all exigency searches need probable cause, but that in addition to complying with the exigent circumstances the police must either meet the probable cause requirement or meet one of the exceptions to the requirement for probable cause.

The most frequently used exigency is the intrusion into a person's body. For example, the police need to take a blood sample for the presence of alcohol and, if they wait for a warrant, the alcohol in the bloodstream may be dissipated.[34] Since intrusions into the human body involve a "significantly heightened privacy," the police must be justified in believing that the intrusion will result in the discovery of evidence.[35] Generally intrusions into a person's body must be under acceptable medical standards.

Most external body searches are under the exigency exception. A warrantless search of a person incident to a lawful arrest may be accomplished without probable cause. A weapons pat down may generally be accomplished under the *Terry* rules discussed later in this chapter.

The warrantless physical entries into a home under exigent circumstances have been limited. Generally the only circumstances that would permit such entry are those in hot pursuit of a fleeing felon, to prevent the immediate destruction of evidence inside, to prevent harm to persons, and to prevent the escape of a felon.[36]

VEHICLE STOPS AND SEARCHES

The courts have upheld the warrantless searches of vehicles based on the premise that there is a lesser expectation of privacy in a vehicle than in a home or office and that the mobility of the vehicle makes the logistics of obtaining a warrant more difficult. In most situations, while the courts have excused the warrant requirements, the police must establish the existence of probable cause. As the Court stated in *Henry* v. *United States*[37]: "The fact that the suspects were in an automobile is not enough. *Carroll v. United States*[38] liberalized the rules governing searches when a moving vehicle is involved. However, that decision merely relaxed the requirements for a warrant on the grounds of practicality. It did not dispense with the need for probable cause."

Traffic Violation Stops

Traffic or vehicle code violations will provide sufficient basis to detain a vehicle, as demonstrated in *Baker*[39]. For example, in one case, *People v. Franklin*[40], the officer suspected that a vehicle had been involved in a robbery. The officer, while following the vehicle, noticed that the vehicle had a defective brake light and an expired registration. The officer stopped the vehicle. As the occupants of the vehicle got out, the officer recognized one of them as a "known burglar" and observed clothes on the back seat of the automobile similar to those worn in the robbery. The officer then made a cursory search of the vehicle (after backup officers had arrived). A sawed-off shotgun was discovered under the front seat. The court, in upholding the search, stated that the traffic stop was not an illegal pretext stop to search for evidence of an unrelated crime. Once the officer had identified one of the occupants and noticed the clothes, he had sufficient additional evidence to constitute probable cause to search the vehicle.

Normally a driver may be detained pursuant to a traffic stop only as long as is necessary to issue a citation or warn the driver regarding the traffic violation. If, upon stopping the vehicle, the officer discovers facts sufficient to constitute reasonable suspicion regarding criminal activity, the officer may then detain the vehicle and its occupants for investigation (investigative detention) for a reasonable period of time.

Unless prohibited by state law, if the officer has probable cause to search a vehicle, the officer may search any closed container found anywhere in the vehicle.

In *California* v. *Carney*[41], the U.S. Supreme Court applied the "automobile exception" to motor homes that are being used on the highways or are capable of such use. (*Note*: The Court indicated that if the motor home was on blocks on private land, it would be more of a home than a motor vehicle.)

When an arrest of occupants in a vehicle occurs, the officer may search the vehicle without probable cause. If the vehicle has been abandoned, the owner loses his or her reasonable expectation of privacy and the abandoned vehicle may be searched by the police without the requirement for probable cause. If a vehicle has been legally repossessed, an officer may search the vehicle with permission of the repossession agency. The police may not use the repossessor as an agent to obtain the car in order to search it.

In December 1998, the U.S. Supreme Court decided *Knowles* v. *Iowa*, 98 C.D.O.S. 8954. An Iowa police officer had stopped Knowles for speeding. The officer could have arrested Knowles but did not. After issuing a citation, the officer then searched Knowles's car and found a bag of marijuana under the driver's seat. Before trial, Knowles moved to suppress the marijuana, arguing that the search was without probable cause and was not a "search incident to arrest." At the pretrial hearing, the officer conceded that he had neither Knowles's consent nor probable cause and that he had not arrested him. The officer had relied on an Iowa statute that provided the issuance of a citation in lieu of an arrest "does not affect the officer's authority to conduct an otherwise lawful search." The Iowa Supreme Court upheld that the search was legal as a "search incident to citation." The U.S. Supreme Court reversed. The Court stated that the authority to conduct a full field search as incident to an arrest was a "bright-line-rule," based on the concern for officer safety and destruction or loss of evidence but which did not depend in every case upon the existence of either concern. The Court held that they were not ready to extend that "bright-line-rule" to a situation where the concern for officer safety is not present to the same extent and where the concern for the destruction or loss of evidence is not present at all.

Ordering Occupants Out of a Vehicle

There is a conflict of authority over whether a police officer can order the occupants to exit a vehicle that has been stopped for a routine traffic case. In many states the police may immediately order all occupants out of a stopped vehicle. The majority rule appears to be that for routine traffic stops, the officer needs additional justification to require occupants to vacate the vehicle. (*Note:* If there are any factors present that threaten the safety of the officer, all jurisdictions will allow the officer to order the occupants out of the vehicle. If any person in the vehicle is wanted for a felony, all persons may be ordered out.[42] The federal rule allows an officer to order the driver to step out of the vehicle in all traffic stops.[43])

Roadblocks

In most cases the officer must have at least a "reasonable suspicion" to stop a car on the public roads and detain its occupants. Accordingly, roadblocks which indiscriminately stop cars are normally improper. Exceptions to this general rule are those general roadblocks established for special purposes. For example, many states permit a "sobriety checkpoint" roadblock. In upholding these special purpose roadblocks, the courts generally make analogies to airport screening.[44]

In *Michigan Dep't of State Police* v. *Sitz*[45], the Supreme Court held that the police may briefly detain all cars on a public road in order to check drivers for intoxication, even though the police lack individualized suspicion that any particular driver is under the influence. The Court used the balancing approach—balancing the state's interest in curbing driving under the influence with the "slight" intrusion upon the drivers concerned.

Inventory Searches

An inventory search occurs when the officers search the contents of a vehicle for purposes other than the search for evidence of a crime. The police may make an inventory search of any vehicle that the police have lawfully impounded. The general rules regarding inventory searches are as follows:

- In conducting the inventory, the officer must follow standardized written procedures of his or her agency.
- The inventory must be in good faith and not a pretext to examine the personal belongings of an individual.
- The police may open any type of closed container while conducting the inventory search.
- The inventory may be conducted only after the vehicle is in police custody. (*Note*: This may be done at the scene where the vehicle is impounded or later at the police impound lot.)

A detention is more substantial than a single contract or consensual encounter. A *detention* occurs when a reasonable person believes that he or she is not free to leave or whenever an officer stops an individual because the officer suspects that the person may be personally involved in criminal activity, *Sokolow*.[46] The U.S. Supreme Court in *Brower*[47] stated that the "seizure of a person occurs only when there is a governmental terminated freedom of movement through means intentionally applied."

SEARCHES INCIDENT TO LAWFUL ARREST

It is reasonable for the police to make a full-body search of an individual incident to a lawful arrest. If the arrest is legal, probable cause is not needed to search the arrested individual. The officer may search any area within the immediate control of the accused at the time of the arrest. For example, if the police arrest an individual in his home, the police may search that portion of the home within the immediate control of the accused, i.e., the room in which the arrest occurs.[48] The rationale for the search of the nearby area is to keep the accused from obtaining a weapon or destroying evidence (lunge distance). It does not matter that the search of the area occurs after the accused is under control and cannot possibly reach those areas nearby. The fact that the accused was handcuffed and his or her reach was impaired was held not to limit the permissible area of search.[49]

If an individual is arrested in his car, the police may search the entire passenger compartment of the automobile. There is a conflict of authority as to whether the police can search the trunk of an automobile. Under the federal rule and in most states, the police may search any containers found in the automobile while conducting a search pursuant to a valid arrest.[50]

Contemporaneously Requirement

The search will be valid as an incident to arrest only if the search and arrest are carried out contemporaneously. Accordingly, the search and the arrest must occur at the same location and at approximately the same time, although either may slightly precede the other.[51] (*Note*: If the search precedes the arrest, it will not be valid as a search incident to an arrest unless probable cause to arrest existed at the time of the search.[52])

Pretext Searches

The courts in some states have invalidated searches pursuant to an arrest if the courts are convinced that the arrest was used as only a pretext to obtain the right to search—for example, stopping and arresting a driver for a traffic offense in order to search the car the person is driving. The U.S. Supreme Court refused to invalidate a search under similar circumstances in *United States* v. *Robinson*.[53]

STOP AND FRISK AND OTHER DETENTIONS

Not too long ago, a "search" was an all-or-nothing concept. It was either a search subject to the probable cause and warrant requirements or it was not a search. This often was referred to as the *bright-line approach*. In 1967 and 1968, the Supreme Court devised non-traditonal definitions of probable cause based on the concept of a floating reasonableness standard. The 1967 case involved administrative inspections[54]. The 1968 case was *Terry* v. *Ohio*,[55] discussed later in this chapter. *Terry* developed the concept of searches of differential intrusiveness and in those cases where the intrusiveness is minimal the standard of "reasonable suspicion" was deemed sufficent. The Supreme Court in *Terry* stated that: "there is no ready test for determining the reasonableness other than by balancing the need to search against the invasion which the search entails. The procedures used by the police in these situations must be governed by the exigencies which justify its initiation."

The *Terry* case developed the concept of stop and frisk. A stop and frisk is less than an arrest. The rules applying to temporary detention also apply to stop and frisk situations. It was a standard police practice to stop suspicious persons in public places for the purposes of questioning them or conducting an investigation. Until

---

HANDLING OF PERSONS QUESTIONED BY POLICE

Of Those Frisked by Police

(16% of the persons questioned as possible suspects were frisked by the police.)
30% were handcuffed
39% claimed that the police used force
31% were neither handcuffed nor claimed that the police used force

Of Those Not Frisked by Police

(84% of the persons questioned as possible suspects were not frisked by the police.)
4% were handcuffed
2% claimed that the police used force
94% were neither handcuffed nor claimed that the police used force

---

the *Terry* case, there was a question as to whether this procedure constituted a violation of the Fourth Amendment since the officers generally do not have probable cause to detain and question the individuals.

In *Terry* v. *Ohio*, an officer observed Terry and two other men walking back and forth in front of a store. The officer decided that the men were casing the store for a possible robbery. When he approached them and asked for identification, he received only mumbled replies. He then grabbed Terry, turned him around, and patted him down. The officer found a pistol in Terry's pocket. Terry, an ex-con, was arrested for carrying a concealed weapon. The Court upheld the search and found no Fourth Amendment violation.

The Court held that a police officer may temporarily detain a person for questioning if the officer has a reasonable suspicion that criminal activity may be involved. The officer may pat down for weapons only if the officer has the additional reasonable suspicion that the pat down is necessary for safety reasons.

Temporary Detention

Mere temporary detention for questioning is not considered to be an arrest.[56] If, however, police restraint goes beyond that which is reasonably necessary for questioning, an arrest may result. For example, handcuffing an alleged drug dealer and moving to another area of the airport for questioning is considered to be an arrest.[57]

A temporary detention of a vehicle is less of a full arrest and, accordingly, the level of probable cause necessary to support a temporary detention is less than that required for a full arrest. A detention starts the moment that the officer directs the vehicle to stop, e.g., when an officer turns on the red lights. It is not a detention if the vehicle is already parked and the officer asks the driver for his or her license or other identification, *People* v. *Gonzales*.[58]

Reasonable Suspicion

A detention requires at least reasonable suspicion. (*Note*: Reasonable suspicion is less than probable cause. The officer must have reasonable suspicion that criminal activity is occurring, is about to occur, or has recently occurred and that the vehicle or a person in the vehicle is connected with that criminal activity.) The reasonable suspicion must be based on specific facts that can be articulated to a court. If the suspicion relates to any person in the vehicle (including a passenger), the officer may stop the vehicle.

In one case[59], an appellate court upheld the stop of the vehicle based on the officer's reasonable suspicion. In this case the officer saw a van he did not recognize driving slowly in a residential neighborhood at 1:30 AM. The officer followed the van and noticed that it was traveling in a circle. He stopped the van. His stop was upheld based on the following articulable facts:

1. The van's speed and route were suggestive of a "casing" operation.
2. The officer was familiar with the neighborhood, its vehicles, and driving patterns.
3. He did not recognize the vehicle.
4. He knew that many residential burglaries occurred in the neighborhood.
5. He knew that vans were frequently used in such burglaries.

In one case, the court upheld a detention of the vehicle when the identities of the persons within the vehicle were unknown and a warrant existed for the registered owner.[60] The court indicated that if none of the people could be the registered owner, i.e., of a different race, then the legality of the detention would be questionable.

A stop based on a "wanted flyer" or a similar notice or bulletin issued by another jurisdiction and related to completed criminal activity is sufficient basis to detain a vehicle and its occupants if the other jurisdiction had a valid basis to issue the flyer, etc.[61]

Distinguishing an Arrest from a *Terry*-Type Detention

Often it is necessary to distinguish an arrest from a stop and frisk situation, especially if evidence is found during the detention. The leading Supreme Court decision on this question is *United States* v. *Sharp*.[62] In that case, the length of the detention was considered. The Court indicated that a *Terry* level stop will ordinarily be for a fairly short duration and the detention will be no longer than necessary to effectuate the purpose of the detention. Other factors considered include the following: Did the police pursue the investigation diligently? Was the method of investigation likely to confirm or dispel the officer's suspicions quickly?

A warrantless "protective sweep" of a residence by the police who are making a lawful arrest in the residence is considered to be legal if the police have a reasonable suspicion that the residence may contain an individual who poses a danger to the officers or to others.[63] The protective sweep should be a quick and limited search of the premises and narrowly confined to a cursory visual inspection of those places where an individual may be hiding.

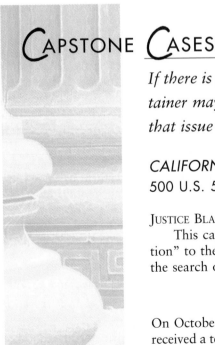

CAPSTONE CASES

If there is probable cause only as to a container in a car, may the container may searched without a warrant? The following case looks at that issue and the automobile exception to the warrant requirement.

CALIFORNIA V. ACEVEDO
500 U.S. 565 (1991)

JUSTICE BLACKMUN delivered the opinion of the Court.

This case requires us once again to consider the so-called "automobile exception" to the warrant requirement of the Fourth Amendment and its application to the search of a closed container in the trunk of a car.

I.

On October 28, 1987, Officer Coleman of the Santa Aba, Cal., Police Department received a telephone call from a federal drug enforcement agent in Hawaii. The agent informed Coleman that he had seized a package containing marijuana which was to

have been delivered to the Federal Express Office in Santa Aba and which was addressed to J.R. Daza at 805 West Stevens Avenue in that city. The agent arranged to send the package to Coleman instead. Coleman then was to take the package to the Federal Express office and arrest the person who arrived to claim it.

Coleman received the package on October 29, verified its contents, and took it to the Senior Operations Manager at the Federal Express office. At about 10:30 A.M. on October 30, a man, who identified himself as Jamie Daza, arrived to claim the package. He accepted it and drove to his apartment on West Stevens. He carried the package into the apartment.

At 11:45 a.m., officers observed Daza leave the apartment and drop the box and paper that had contained the marijuana into a trash bin. Coleman at that point left the scene to get a search warrant. About 12:05 p.m., the officers saw Richard St. George leave the apartment carrying a blue knapsack which appeared to be half full. The officers stopped him as he was driving off, searched the knapsack, and found 1-1/2 pounds of marijuana.

At 12:30 p.m., respondent Charles Steven Acevedo arrived. He entered Daza's apartment, left after about 10 minutes, and reappeared carrying a brown paper bag that looked full. The officers noticed that the bag was the size of one of the wrapped marijuana packages sent from Hawaii. Acevedo walked to a silver Honda in the parking lot. He placed the bag in the trunk of the car and started to drive away. Fearing the loss of evidence, officers in a marked police car stopped him. They opened the trunk and the bag, and found marijuana.

Respondent was charged in state court with possession of marijuana for sale, in violation of Cal. Health & Safety Code Ann. 11359 (West Supp. 1991). App. 2. He moved to suppress the marijuana found in the car. The motion was denied. He then pleaded guilty, but appealed the denial of the suppression motion.

The California Court of Appeal, Fourth District, concluded that the marijuana found in the paper bag in the carts trunk should have been suppressed. . . . The court concluded that the officers had probable cause to believe that the paper bag contained drugs, but lacked probable cause to suspect that Acevedo's car, itself, otherwise contained contraband. . . . Because the officers' probable cause was directed specifically at the bag, the court held that the case was controlled by *United States* v. *Chadwick*, 433 U.S. 1 (1977), rather than by *United States* v. *Ross*, 456 U.S. 798 (1982). Although the court agreed that the officers could seize the paper bag, it held that, under Chadwick, they could not open the bag without first obtaining a warrant for that purpose. The court then recognized "the anomalous nature" of the dichotomy between the rule in Chadwick and the rule in Ross. . . . That dichotomy dictates that, if there is probable cause to search a car, then the entire car—including any closed container found therein—may be searched without a warrant, but if there is probable cause only as to a container in the car, the container may be held, but not searched, until a warrant is obtained. . . .

We granted *certiorari*, 498 U.S. 807 (1990), to reexamine the law applicable to a closed container in an automobile, a subject that has troubled courts and law enforcement officers since it was first considered in Chadwick.

II.

The Fourth Amendment protects the "right of the people to be secure in their persons, houses, papers, and effects, against unreasonable searches and seizures." Contemporaneously with the adoption of the Fourth Amendment, the First Congress, and, later, the Second and Fourth Congresses, distinguished between the

need for a warrant to search for contraband concealed in "a dwelling house or similar place" and the need for a warrant to search for contraband concealed in a movable vessel. In Carroll, this Court established an exception to the warrant requirement for moving vehicles, for it recognized:

> . . . a necessary difference between a search of a store, dwelling house or other structure in respect of which a proper official warrant readily may be obtained, and a search of a ship, motor boat, wagon or automobile, for contraband goods, where it is not practicable to secure a warrant because the vehicle can be quickly moved out of the locality or jurisdiction in which the warrant must be sought. 267 U.S., at 153.

It therefore held that a warrantless search of an automobile based upon probable cause to believe that the vehicle contained evidence of crime in the light of an exigency arising out of the likely disappearance of the vehicle did not contravene the Warrant Clause of the Fourth Amendment. . . .

The Court refined the exigency requirement in *Chambers* v. *Maroney*, 399 U.S. 42 (1970), when it held that the existence of exigent circumstances was to be determined at the time the automobile is seized. The car search at issue in Chambers took place at the police station, where the vehicle was immobilized, some time after the driver had been arrested. Given probable cause and exigent circumstances at the time the vehicle was first stopped, the Court held that the later warrantless search at the station passed constitutional muster. The validity of the later search derived from the ruling in *Carroll* that an immediate search without a warrant at the moment of seizure would have been permissible. See *Chambers*, 399 U.S., at 51. The Court reasoned in *Chambers* that the police could search later whenever they could have searched earlier, had they so chosen. *Id.*, at 51–52.

Following *Chambers*, if the police have probable cause to justify a warrantless seizure of an automobile on a public roadway, they may conduct either an immediate or a delayed search of the vehicle.

In *United States* v. *Ross*, 456 U.S. 798, decided in 1982, we held that a warrantless search of an automobile under the Carroll doctrine could include a search of a container or package found inside the car when such a search was supported by probable cause. The warrantless search of Ross' car occurred after an informant told the police that he had seen Ross complete a drug transaction using drugs stored in the trunk of his car. The police stopped the car, searched it, and discovered in the trunk a brown paper bag containing drugs. We decided that the search of Ross' car was not unreasonable under the Fourth Amendment: "The scope of a warrantless search based on probable cause is no narrower—and no broader—than the scope of a search authorized by a warrant supported by probable cause." *Id.*, at 823. Thus, "[i]f probable cause justifies the search of a lawfully stopped vehicle, it justifies the search of every part of the vehicle and its contents that may conceal the object of the search." *Id.*, at 825. In *Ross*, therefore, we clarified the scope of the Carroll doctrine as properly including a "probing search" of compartments and containers within the automobile so long as the search is supported by probable cause. *Id.*, at 800.

In addition to this clarification, *Ross* distinguished the *Carroll* doctrine from the separate rule that governed the search of closed containers. See 456 U.S., at 817. The Court had announced this separate rule, unique to luggage and other closed packages, bags, and containers, in *United States* v. *Chadwick*, 433 U.S. 1 (1977). In *Chadwick*, federal narcotics agents had probable cause to believe that a 200-pound double-locked footlocker contained marijuana. The agents tracked the locker as the defendants removed it from a train and carried it through the station

to a waiting car. As soon as the defendants lifted the locker into the trunk of the car, the agents arrested them, seized the locker, and searched it. In this Court, the United States did not contend that the locker's brief contact with the automobile's trunk sufficed to make the *Carroll* doctrine applicable. Rather, the United States urged that the search of movable luggage could be considered analogous to the search of an automobile. 433 U.S., at 11–12.

The Court rejected this argument because, it reasoned, a person expects more privacy in his luggage and personal effects than he does in his automobile. *Id.*, at 13. Moreover, it concluded that, as "may often not be the case when automobiles are seized," secure storage facilities are usually available when the police seize luggage. *Id.*, at 13, n. 7.

In *Arkansas* v. *Sanders*, 442 U.S. 753 (1979), the Court extended Chadwick's rule to apply to a suitcase actually being transported in the trunk of a car. In *Sanders*, the police had probable cause to believe a suitcase contained marijuana. They watched as the defendant placed the suitcase in the trunk of a taxi and was driven away. The police pursued the taxi for several blocks, stopped it, found the suitcase in the trunk, and searched it. Although the Court had applied the *Carroll* doctrine to searches of integral parts of the automobile itself, (indeed, in *Carroll*, contraband whiskey was in the upholstery of the seats, see 267 U.S., at 136), it did not extend the doctrine to the warrantless search of personal luggage "merely because it was located in an automobile lawfully stopped by the police." 442 U.S., at 765. Again, the *Sanders* majority stressed the heightened privacy expectation in personal luggage, and concluded that the presence of luggage in an automobile did not diminish the owner's expectation of privacy in his personal items. *Id.*, at 764–765. Cf. *California* v. *Carney*, 471 U.S. 386 (1985).

In *Ross*, the Court endeavored to distinguish between *Carroll*, which governed the Ross automobile search, and *Chadwick*, which governed the Sanders automobile search. It held that the *Carroll* doctrine covered searches of automobiles when the police had probable cause to search an entire vehicle, but that the *Chadwick* doctrine governed searches of luggage when the officers had probable cause to search only a container within the vehicle. Thus, in a *Ross* situation, the police could conduct a reasonable search under the Fourth Amendment without obtaining a warrant, whereas in a *Sanders* situation, the police had to obtain a warrant before they searched.

JUSTICE STEVENS is correct, of course, that *Ross* involved the scope of an automobile search. . . . *Ross* held that closed containers encountered by the police during a warrantless search of a car pursuant to the automobile exception could also be searched. Thus, this Court in *Ross* took the critical step of saying that closed containers in cars could be searched without a warrant because of their presence within the automobile. Despite the protection that *Sanders* purported to extend to closed containers, the privacy interest in those closed containers yielded to the broad scope of an automobile search.

III.

The facts in this case closely resemble the facts in *Ross*. In *Ross*, the police had probable cause to believe that drugs were stored in the trunk of a particular car. See 456 U.S., at 800. Here, the California Court of Appeal concluded that the police had probable cause to believe that respondent was carrying marijuana in a bag in his car's trunk. . . . Furthermore, for what it is worth, in *Ross*, as here, the drugs in the trunk were contained in a brown paper bag.

This Court in *Ross* rejected *Chadwick's* distinction between containers and cars. It concluded that the expectation of privacy in one's vehicle is equal to one's expectation of privacy in the container, and noted that "the privacy interests in a car's trunk or glove compartment may be no less than those in a movable container." It also recognized that it was arguable that the same exigent circumstances that permit a warrantless search of an automobile would justify the warrantless search of a movable container. *Id.*, at 809. In deference to the rule of *Chadwick* and *Sanders*, however, the Court put that question to one side. *Id.*, at 809–810. It concluded that the time and expense of the warrant process would be misdirected if the police could search every cubic inch of an automobile until they discovered a paper sack, at which point the Fourth Amendment required them to take the sack to a magistrate for permission to look inside. We now must decide the question deferred in *Ross*: whether the Fourth Amendment requires the police to obtain a warrant to open the sack in a movable vehicle simply because they lack probable cause to search the entire car. We conclude that it does not.

IV.

Dissenters in *Ross* asked why the suitcase in *Sanders* was "more private, less difficult for police to seize and store, or in any other relevant respect more properly subject to the warrant requirement, than a container that police discover in a probable cause search of an entire automobile?" *Id.*, at 839–840. We now agree that a container found after a general search of the automobile and a container found in a car after a limited search for the container are equally easy for the police to store and for the suspect to hide or destroy. In fact, we see no principled distinction in terms of either the privacy expectation or the exigent circumstances between the paper bag found by the police in Ross and the paper bag found by the police here. Furthermore, by attempting to distinguish between a container for which the police are specifically searching and a container which they come across in a car, we have provided only minimal protection for privacy, and have impeded effective law enforcement.

The line between probable cause to search a vehicle and probable cause to search a package in that vehicle is not always clear, and separate rules that govern the two objects to be searched may enable the police to broaden their power to make warrantless searches and disserve privacy interests. We noted this in Ross in the context of a search of an entire vehicle. Recognizing under *Carroll*, that the "entire vehicle itself . . . could be searched without a warrant," we concluded that "prohibiting police from opening immediately a container in which the object of the search is most likely to be found, and instead forcing them first to comb the entire vehicle, would actually exacerbate the intrusion on privacy interests." 456 U.S., at 821, n. 28. At the moment when officers stop an automobile, it may be less than clear whether they suspect with a high degree of certainty that the vehicle contains drugs in a bag or simply contains drugs. If the police know that they may open a bag only if they are actually searching the entire car, they may search more extensively than they otherwise would in order to establish the general probable cause required by *Ross*.

Such a situation is not far-fetched. In *United States* v. *Johns*, 469 U.S. 478 (1985), Customs agents saw two trucks drive to a private airstrip and approach two small planes. The agents drew near the trucks, smelled marijuana, and then

saw in the backs of the trucks packages wrapped in a manner that marijuana smugglers customarily employed. The agents took the trucks to headquarters and searched the packages without a warrant. *Id.*, at 481. Relying on *Chadwick*, the defendants argued that the search was unlawful. *Id.*, at 482. The defendants contended that *Ross* was inapplicable because the agents lacked probable cause to search anything but the packages themselves, and supported this contention by noting that a search of the entire vehicle never occurred. *Id.*, at 483. We rejected that argument, and found *Chadwick* and *Sanders* inapposite because the agents had probable cause to search the entire body of each truck, although they had chosen not to do so. *Id.*, at 482–483. We cannot see the benefit of a rule that requires law enforcement officers to conduct a more intrusive search in order to justify a less intrusive one.

To the extent that the *Chadwick–Sanders* rule protects privacy, its protection is minimal. Law enforcement officers may seize a container and hold it until they obtain a search warrant. *Chadwick*, 433 U.S., at 13. "Since the police, by hypothesis, have probable cause to seize the property, we can assume that a warrant will be routinely forthcoming in the overwhelming majority of cases." *Sanders*, 442 U.S., at 770 (dissenting opinion). And the police often will be able to search containers without a warrant, despite the *Chadwick–Sanders* rule, as a search incident to a lawful arrest. In *New York* v. *Belton*, 453 U.S. 454 (1981), the Court said: "[W]e hold that, when a policeman has made a lawful custodial arrest of the occupant of an automobile, he may, as a contemporaneous incident of that arrest, search the passenger compartment of that automobile. "It follows from this conclusion that the police may also examine the contents of any containers found within the passenger compartment." *Id.*, at 460 (footnote omitted).

Under *Belton*, the same probable cause to believe that a container holds drugs will allow the police to arrest the person transporting the container and search it.

Finally, the search of a paper bag intrudes far less on individual privacy than does the incursion sanctioned long ago in *Carroll*. In that case, prohibition agents slashed the upholstery of the automobile. This Court nonetheless found their search to be reasonable under the Fourth Amendment. If destroying the interior of an automobile is not unreasonable, we cannot conclude that looking inside a closed container is. In light of the minimal protection to privacy afforded by the *Chadwick–Sanders* rule, and our serious doubt whether that rule substantially serves privacy interests, we now hold that the Fourth Amendment does not compel separate treatment for an automobile search that extends only to a container within the vehicle. . . .

Until today, this Court has drawn a curious line between the search of an automobile that coincidentally turns up a container and the search of a container that coincidentally turns up in an automobile. The protections of the Fourth Amendment must not turn on such coincidences. We therefore interpret *Carroll* as providing one rule to govern all automobile searches. The police may search an automobile and the containers within it where they have probable cause to believe contraband or evidence is contained. The judgment of the California Court of Appeal is reversed, and the case is remanded to that court for further proceedings not inconsistent with this opinion.

It is so ordered.

JUSTICE SCALIA, concurring in the judgment. [Omitted.]

JUSTICE WHITE, dissenting. [Omitted.]

JUSTICE STEVENS, with whom JUSTICE MARSHALL joins, dissenting. [Omitted.]

1. Do you agree with the majority opinion? Why?
2. Justice Scalia noted many exceptions to the warrant requirement. He concludes that we should really look only at the reasonableness of the search and not whether there is a warrant. What is your opinion?
3. State the rule of law that governs this case.

In the Greenwood *case, the Court discusses the privacy rights we have in relation to our garbage.*

CALIFORNIA V. GREENWOOD
486 U.S. 35 (1988)

JUSTICE WHITE delivered the opinion of the Court.

The issue here is whether the Fourth Amendment prohibits the warrantless search and seizure of garbage left for collection outside the curtilage of a home. We conclude, in accordance with the vast majority of lower courts that have addressed the issue, that it does not.

I.

In early 1984, Investigator Jenny Stracner of the Laguna Beach Police Department received information indicating that respondent Greenwood might be engaged in narcotics trafficking. Stracner learned that a criminal suspect had informed a federal drug enforcement agent in February 1984 that a truck filled with illegal drugs was en route to the Laguna Beach address at which Greenwood resided. In addition, a neighbor complained of heavy vehicular traffic late at night in front of Greenwood's single-family home. The neighbor reported that the vehicles remained at Greenwood's house for only a few minutes.

Stracner sought to investigate this information by conducting a surveillance of Greenwood's home. She observed several vehicles make brief stops at the house during the late-night and early morning hours, and she followed a truck from the house to a residence that had previously been under investigation as a narcotics-trafficking location.

On April 6, 1984, Stracner asked the neighborhood's regular trash collector to pick up the plastic garbage bags that Greenwood had left on the curb in front of his house and to turn the bags over to her without mixing their contents with garbage from other houses. The trash collector cleaned his truck bin of other refuse, collected the garbage bags from the street in front of Greenwood's house, and turned the bags over to Stracner. The officer searched through the rubbish and found items indicative of narcotics use. She recited the information that she had gleaned from the trash search in an affidavit in support of a warrant to search Greenwood's home.

Police officers encountered both respondents at the house later that day when they arrived to execute the warrant. The police discovered quantities of cocaine and hashish during their search of the house. Respondents were arrested on felony narcotics charges. They subsequently posted bail.

Justice Byron R. White was appointed to the Supreme Court by President Kennedy and served from 1962 to 1993. (Photograph by Joseph Bailey, National Geographic Society. Courtesy the Supreme Court of the United States.)

The police continued to receive reports of many late-night visitors to the Greenwood house. On May 4, Investigator Robert Rahaeuser obtained Greenwood's garbage from the regular trash collector in the same manner as had Stracner. The garbage again contained evidence of narcotics use.

Rahaeuser secured another search warrant for Greenwood's home based on the information from the second trash search. The police found more narcotics and evidence of narcotics trafficking when they executed the warrant. Greenwood was again arrested.

The Superior Court dismissed the charges against respondents on the authority of *People* v. *Krivda*, 5 Cal. 3d 357, 486 P.2d 1262 (1971), which held that warrantless trash searches violate the Fourth Amendment and the California Constitution. The court found that the police would not have had probable cause to search the Greenwood home without the evidence obtained from the trash searches.

The Court of Appeal affirmed. 182 Cal. App. 3d 729, 227 Cal. Rptr. 539 (1986). The court noted at the outset that the fruits of warrantless trash searches could no longer be suppressed if *Krivda* were based only on the California Constitution, because since 1982 the State has barred the suppression of evidence seized in violation of California law but not federal law. See Cal. Const., Art. I, 28(d); *In re Lance W.*, 37 Cal. 3d 873, 694 P.2d 744 (1985). But *Krivda*, a decision binding on the Court of Appeal, also held that the fruits of warrantless trash searches were to be excluded under federal law. Hence, the Superior Court was

correct in dismissing the charges against respondents. 182 Cal. App. 3d, at 735, 227 Cal. Rptr, at 542.

The California Supreme Court denied the State's petition for review of the Court of Appeal's decision. We granted *certiorari*, 483 U.S. 1019, and now reverse.

II.

The warrantless search and seizure of the garbage bags left at the curb outside the Greenwood house would violate the Fourth Amendment only if respondents manifested a subjective expectation of privacy in their garbage that society accepts as objectively reasonable. . . . Respondents do not disagree with this standard.

They assert, however, that they had, and exhibited, an expectation of privacy with respect to the trash that was searched by the police: The trash, which was placed on the street for collection at a fixed time, was contained in opaque plastic bags, which the garbage collector was expected to pick up, mingle with the trash of others, and deposit at the garbage dump. The trash was only temporarily on the street, and there was little likelihood that it would be inspected by anyone.

It may well be that respondents did not expect that the contents of their garbage bags would become known to the police or other members of the public. An expectation of privacy does not give rise to Fourth Amendment protection, however, unless society is prepared to accept that expectation as objectively reasonable.

Here, we conclude that respondents exposed their garbage to the public sufficiently to defeat their claim to Fourth Amendment protection. It is common knowledge that plastic garbage bags left on or at the side of a public street are readily accessible to animals, children, scavengers, snoops, and other members of the public. See *Krivda, supra*, at 367, 486 P.2d, at 1269. Moreover, respondents placed their refuse at the curb for the express purpose of conveying it to a third party, the trash collector, who might himself have sorted through respondents' trash or permitted others, such as the police, to do so. Accordingly, having deposited their garbage "in an area particularly suited for public inspection and, in a manner of speaking, public consumption, for the express purpose of having strangers take it," *United States* v. *Reicherter*, 647 F.2d 397, 399 (CA3 1981), respondents could have had no reasonable expectation of privacy in the inculpatory items that they discarded.

Furthermore, as we have held, the police cannot reasonably be expected to avert their eyes from evidence of criminal activity that could have been observed by any member of the public. Hence, "[w]hat a person knowingly exposes to the public, even in his own home or office, is not a subject of Fourth Amendment protection." *Katz* v. *United States, supra*, at 351. We held in *Smith* v. *Maryland*, 442 U.S. 735 (1979), for example, that the police did not violate the Fourth Amendment by causing a pen register to be installed at the telephone company's offices to record the telephone numbers dialed by a criminal suspect. An individual has no legitimate expectation of privacy in the numbers dialed on his telephone, we reasoned, because he voluntarily conveys those numbers to the telephone company when he uses the telephone. Again, we observed that "a person has no legitimate expectation of privacy in information he voluntarily turns over to third parties." *Id.*, at 743–744.

Similarly, we held in *California* v. *Ciraolo, supra*, that the police were not required by the Fourth Amendment to obtain a warrant before conducting surveillance of the respondent's fenced backyard from a private plane flying at an altitude of 1,000 feet. We concluded that the respondent's expectation that his yard was

protected from such surveillance was unreasonable because "[a]ny member of the public flying in this airspace who glanced down could have seen everything that these officers observed." *Id.*, at 213–214.

Our conclusion that society would not accept as reasonable respondents' claim to an expectation of privacy in trash left for collection in an area accessible to the public is reinforced by the unanimous rejection of similar claims by the Federal Courts of Appeals. . . .

III.

We reject respondent Greenwood's alternative argument for affirmance: that his expectation of privacy in his garbage should be deemed reasonable as a matter of federal constitutional law because the warrantless search and seizure of his garbage was impermissible as a matter of California law. He urges that the state-law right of Californians to privacy in their garbage, announced by the California Supreme Court in *Krivda, supra*, survived the subsequent state constitutional amendment eliminating the suppression remedy as a means of enforcing that right. . . . Hence, he argues that the Fourth Amendment should itself vindicate that right. . . .

The judgment of the California Court of Appeal is therefore reversed, and this case is remanded for further proceedings not inconsistent with this opinion.

It is so ordered.

JUSTICE KENNEDY took no part in the consideration or decision of this case.

JUSTICE BRENNAN, with whom JUSTICE MARSHALL joins, dissenting.

Every week for two months, and at least once more a month later, the Laguna Beach police clawed through the trash that respondent Greenwood left in opaque, sealed bags on the curb outside his home. Record 113. Complete strangers minutely scrutinized their bounty, undoubtedly dredging up intimate details of Greenwood's private life and habits. The intrusions proceeded without a warrant, and no court before or since has concluded that the police acted on probable cause to believe Greenwood was engaged in any criminal activity.

Scrutiny of another's trash is contrary to commonly accepted notions of civilized behavior. I suspect, therefore, that members of our society will be shocked to learn that the Court, the ultimate guarantor of liberty, deems unreasonable our expectation that the aspects of our private lives that are concealed safely in a trash bag will not become public. . . .

The Framers of the Fourth Amendment understood that "unreasonable searches" of "paper and effects"—no less than "unreasonable searches" of "person and houses"—infringe privacy. As early as 1878, this Court acknowledged that the contents of "[l]etters and sealed packages . . . in the mail are as fully guarded from examination and inspection . . . as if they were retained by the parties forwarding them in their own domiciles." *Ex parte Jackson*, 96 U.S. 727, 733. In short, so long as a package is "closed against inspection," the Fourth Amendment protects its contents, "wherever they may be," and the police must obtain a warrant to search it just "as is required when papers are subjected to search in one's own household." *Ibid.* Accord, *United States* v. *Van Leeuwen*, 397 U.S. 249 (1970).

With the emergence of the reasonable-expectation-of-privacy analysis, see *Katz* v. *United States*, 389 U.S. 347, 361 (1967) (Harlan, J., concurring); *Smith* v. *Maryland*, 442 U.S. 735, 740 (1979), we have reaffirmed this fundamental principle. In *Robbins* v. *California*, 453 U.S. 420 (1981), for example, Justice Stewart, writing for a plurality of four, pronounced that "unless the container is such that

its contents may be said to be in plain view, those contents are fully protected by the Fourth Amendment," *id.*, at 427, and soundly rejected any distinction for Fourth Amendment purposes among various opaque, sealed containers:

> [E]ven if one wished to import such a distinction into the Fourth Amendment, it is difficult if not impossible to perceive any objective criteria by which that task might be accomplished. What one person may put into a suitcase, another may put into a paper bag. . . . And . . . no court, no constable, no citizen, can sensibly be asked to distinguish the relative "privacy interests" in a closed suitcase, briefcase, portfolio, duffelbag, or box. *Id.*, at 426–427.

When a tabloid reporter examined then-Secretary of State Henry Kissinger's trash and published his findings, Kissinger was "really revolted" by the intrusion and his wife suffered "grave anguish." *N.Y. Times*, July 9, 1975, p. A1, col. 8. The public response roundly condemning the reporter demonstrates that society not only recognized those reactions as reasonable, but shared them as well. Commentators variously characterized his conduct as "a disgusting invasion of personal privacy," Flieger, Investigative Trash, *U.S. News & World Report*, July 28, 1975, p. 72 (editor's page); "indefensible . . . as civilized behavior," *Washington Post*, July 10, 1975, p. A18, col. 1 (editorial); and contrary to "the way decent people behave in relation to each other," *ibid.*

Beyond a generalized expectation of privacy, many municipalities, whether for reasons of privacy, sanitation, or both, reinforce confidence in the integrity of sealed trash containers by "prohibit[ing] anyone, except authorized employees of the Town . . . , to rummage into, pick up, collect, move or otherwise interfere with articles or materials placed on . . . any public street for collection." . . .

WHAT DO YOU THINK?

1. How would you feel if your nosey next door neighbor went through your garbage each day?
2. Do you have a reasonable expectation of privacy in your garbage until it becomes mingled with other people's garbage?
3. The California Supreme Court's decision in this case was the subject matter of a movie, *Star Chamber*, starring Michael Douglas. Could the U.S. Supreme Court's decision have been influenced by the movie?

May the police trick a person into consenting to a search? The next case looks at this issue.

BUMPER V. NORTH CAROLINA
391 U.S. 543 (1968)

MR. JUSTICE STEWART delivered the opinion of the Court.

The petitioner was brought to trial in a North Carolina court upon a charge of rape, an offense punishable in that state by death unless the jury recommends life imprisonment. Among the items of evidence introduced by the prosecution at the trial was a .22-caliber rifle allegedly used in the commission of the crime. The

jury found the petitioner guilty, but recommended a sentence of life imprisonment. The trial court imposed that sentence, and the Supreme Court of North Carolina affirmed the judgment. We granted *certiorari* to consider.... Secondly, the petitioner contends that the .22-caliber rifle introduced in evidence against him was obtained by the State in a search and seizure violative of the Fourth and Fourteenth Amendments....

The petitioner lived with his grandmother, Mrs. Hattie Leath, a 66-year-old Negro widow, in a house located in a rural area at the end of an isolated mile-long dirt road. Two days after the alleged offense but prior to the petitioner's arrest, four white law enforcement officers—the county sheriff, two of his deputies, and a state investigator—went to this house and found Mrs. Leath there with some young children. She met the officers at the front door. One of them announced, "I have a search warrant to search your house." Mrs. Leath responded, "Go ahead," and opened the door. In the kitchen the officers found the rifle that was later introduced in evidence at the petitioner's trial after a motion to suppress had been denied.

At the hearing on this motion, the prosecutor informed the court that he did not rely upon a warrant to justify the search, but upon the consent of Mrs. Leath. She testified at the hearing, stating, among other things:

> Four of them came. I was busy about my work, and they walked into the house and one of them walked up and said, "I have a search warrant to search your house," and I walked out and told them to come on in.... He just come on in and said he had a warrant to search the house, and he didn't read it to me or nothing. So, I just told him to come on in and go ahead and search, and I went on about my work. I wasn't concerned what he was about. I was just satisfied. He just told me he had a search warrant, but he didn't read it to me. He did tell me he had a search warrant.... He said he was the law and had a search warrant to search the house, why I thought he could go ahead. I believed he had a search warrant. I took him at his word.... I just seen them out there in the yard. They got through the door when I opened it. At that time, I did not know my grandson had been charged with crime. Nobody told me anything. They didn't tell me anything, just picked it up like that. They didn't tell me nothing about my grandson.

Upon the basis of Mrs. Leath's testimony, the trial court found that she had given her consent to the search, and denied the motion to suppress. The Supreme Court of North Carolina approved the admission of the evidence on the same basis.

The issue thus presented is whether a search can be justified as lawful on the basis of consent when that "consent" has been given only after the official conducting the search has asserted that he possesses a warrant. We hold that there can be no consent under such circumstances.

When a prosecutor seeks to rely upon consent to justify the lawfulness of a search, he has the burden of proving that the consent was, in fact, freely and voluntarily given. This burden cannot be discharged by showing no more than acquiescence to a claim of lawful authority. A search conducted in reliance upon a warrant cannot later be justified on the basis of consent if it turns out that the warrant was invalid. The result can be no different when it turns out that the State does not even attempt to rely upon the validity of the warrant, or fails to show that there was, in fact, any warrant at all.

When a law enforcement officer claims authority to search a home under a warrant, he announces in effect that the occupant has no right to resist the search. The situation is instinct with coercion—albeit colorably lawful coercion. Where there is coercion there cannot be consent.

We hold that Mrs. Leath did not consent to the search, and that it was constitutional error to admit the rifle in evidence against the petitioner. *Mapp* v. *Ohio*,

367 U.S. 643. Because the rifle was plainly damaging evidence against the petitioner with respect to all three of the charges against him, its admission at the trial was not harmless error. *Chapman* v. *California*, 386 U.S. 18.

The judgment of the Supreme Court of North Carolina is, accordingly, reversed, and the case is remanded for further proceedings not inconsistent with this opinion.

It is so ordered.

WHAT DO YOU THINK?

1. Do you agree that the consent to search was not willingly given?
2. To what extent should the police be allowed to mislead a person into giving consent for a search?

When may premises be searched pursuant to administrative inspection programs? The next case looks at this type of inspection.

CAMARA V. MUNICIPAL COURT
387 U.S. 523 (1967)

MR. JUSTICE WHITE delivered the opinion of the Court.

In *Frank* v. *Maryland*, 359 U.S. 360, this Court upheld, by a five-to-four vote, a state court conviction of a home-owner who refused to permit a municipal health inspector to enter and inspect his premises without a search warrant. In *Eaton* v. *Price*, 364 U.S. 263, a similar conviction was affirmed by an equally divided Court. Since those closely divided decisions, more intensive efforts at all levels of government to contain and eliminate urban blight have led to increasing use of such inspection techniques, while numerous decisions of this Court have more fully defined the Fourth Amendment's effect on state and municipal action. . . . In view of the growing nationwide importance of the problem, we noted probable jurisdiction in this case . . . to re-examine whether administrative inspection programs, as presently authorized and conducted, violate Fourth Amendment rights as those rights are enforced against the States through the Fourteenth Amendment.

Though there were no judicial findings of fact in this prohibition proceeding, we shall set forth the parties' factual allegations. On November 6, 1963, an inspector of the Division of Housing Inspection of the San Francisco Department of Public Health entered an apartment building to make a routine annual inspection for possible violations of the city's Housing Code. The building's manager informed the inspector that appellant, lessee of the ground floor, was using the rear of his leasehold as a personal residence. Claiming that the building's occupancy permit did not allow residential use of the ground floor, the inspector confronted appellant and demanded that he permit an inspection of the premises. Appellant refused to allow the inspection because the inspector lacked a search warrant.

The inspector returned on November 8, again without a warrant, and appellant again refused to allow an inspection. A citation was then mailed ordering appellant to appear at the district attorney's office. When appellant failed to appear, two inspectors returned to his apartment on November 22. They informed appellant that he was required by law to permit an inspection under 503 of the Housing Code. . . .

Appellant nevertheless refused the inspectors access to his apartment without a search warrant. Thereafter, a complaint was filed charging him with refusing to permit a lawful inspection in violation of 507 of the Code. Appellant was arrested on December 2 and released on bail. When his demurrer to the criminal complaint was denied, appellant filed this petition for a writ of prohibition.

Appellant has argued throughout this litigation that 503 is contrary to the Fourth and Fourteenth Amendments in that it authorizes municipal officials to enter a private dwelling without a search warrant and without probable cause to believe that a violation of the Housing Code exists therein. Consequently, appellant contends, he may not be prosecuted under 507 for refusing to permit an inspection unconstitutionally authorized by 503. Relying on *Frank* v. *Maryland*, *Eaton* v. *Price*, and decisions in other States, the District Court of Appeal held that 503 does not violate Fourth Amendment rights because it "is part of a regulatory scheme which is essentially civil rather than criminal in nature, inasmuch as that section creates a right of inspection which is limited in scope and may not be exercised under unreasonable conditions." Having concluded that *Frank* v. *Maryland*, to the extent that it sanctioned such warrantless inspections, must be overruled, we reverse.

I.

The Fourth Amendment provides that, "The right of the people to be secure in their persons, houses, papers, and effects, against unreasonable searches and seizures, shall not be violated, and no Warrants shall issue, but upon probable cause, supported by Oath or affirmation, and particularly describing the place to be searched, and the persons or things to be seized." The basic purpose of this Amendment, as recognized in countless decisions of this Court, is to safeguard the privacy and security of individuals against arbitrary invasions by governmental officials. The Fourth Amendment thus gives concrete expression to a right of the people which "is basic to a free society." *Wolf* v. *Colorado*, 338 U.S. 25, 27. As such, the Fourth Amendment is enforceable against the States through the Fourteenth Amendment. *Ker* v. *California*, 374 U.S. 23, 30.

Though there has been general agreement as to the fundamental purpose of the Fourth Amendment, translation of the abstract prohibition against "unreasonable searches and seizures" into workable guidelines for the decision of particular cases is a difficult task which has for many years divided the members of this Court. Nevertheless, one governing principle, justified by history and by current experience, has consistently been followed: except in certain carefully defined classes of cases, a search of private property without proper consent is "unreasonable" unless it has been authorized by a valid search warrant. . . . As the Court explained in *Johnson* v. *United States*, 333 U.S. 10, 14:

> The right of officers to thrust themselves into a home is also a grave concern, not only to the individual but to a society which chooses to dwell in reasonable security and freedom from surveillance. When the right of privacy must reasonably yield to the right of search is, as a rule, to be decided by a judicial officer, not by a policeman or government enforcement agent.

In *Frank* v. *Maryland*, this Court upheld the conviction of one who refused to permit a warrantless inspection of private premises for the purposes of locating and abating a suspected public nuisance. Although *Frank* can arguably be distinguished

from this case on its facts, the *Frank* opinion has generally been interpreted as carving out an additional exception to the rule that warrantless searches are unreasonable under the Fourth Amendment. See *Eaton* v. *Price*, *supra*. The District Court of Appeal so interpreted *Frank* in this case, and that ruling is the core of appellant's challenge here. We proceed to a re-examination of the factors which persuaded the *Frank* majority to adopt this construction of the Fourth Amendment's prohibition against unreasonable searches.

To the *Frank* majority, municipal fire, health, and housing inspection programs "touch at most upon the periphery of the important interests safeguarded by the Fourteenth Amendment's protection against official intrusion," 359 U.S., at 367, because the inspections are merely to determine whether physical conditions exist which do not comply with minimum standards prescribed in local regulatory ordinances. Since the inspector does not ask that the property owner open his doors to a search for "evidence of criminal action" which may be used to secure the owner's criminal conviction, historic interests of "self-protection" jointly protected by the Fourth and Fifth Amendments are said not to be involved, but only the less intense "right to be secure from intrusion into personal privacy." *Id.*, at 365.

We may agree that a routine inspection of the physical condition of private property is a less hostile intrusion than the typical policeman's search for the fruits and instrumentalities of crime. For this reason alone, *Frank* differed from the great bulk of Fourth Amendment cases which have been considered by this Court. But we cannot agree that the Fourth Amendment interests at stake in these inspection cases are merely "peripheral." It is surely anomalous to say that the individual and his private property are fully protected by the Fourth Amendment only when the individual is suspected of criminal behavior. For instance, even the most law-abiding citizen has a very tangible interest in limiting the circumstances under which the sanctity of his home may be broken by official authority, for the possibility of criminal entry under the guise of official sanction is a serious threat to personal and family security. And even accepting *Frank's* rather remarkable premise, inspections of the kind we are here considering do in fact jeopardize "self-protection" interests of the property owner. Like most regulatory laws, fire, health, and housing codes are enforced by criminal processes. In some cities, discovery of a violation by the inspector leads to a criminal complaint. Even in cities where discovery of a violation produces only an administrative compliance order, refusal to comply is a criminal offense, and the fact of compliance is verified by a second inspection, again without a warrant. Finally, as this case demonstrates, refusal to permit an inspection is itself a crime, punishable by fine or even by jail sentence.

The *Frank* majority suggested, and appellee reasserts, two other justifications for permitting administrative health and safety inspections without a warrant. First, it is argued that these inspections are "designed to make the least possible demand on the individual occupant." 359 U.S., at 367. The ordinances authorizing inspections are hedged with safeguards, and at any rate the inspector's particular decision to enter must comply with the constitutional standard of reasonableness even if he may enter without a warrant. In addition, the argument proceeds, the warrant process could not function effectively in this field. The decision to inspect an entire municipal area is based upon legislative or administrative assessment of broad factors such as the area's age and condition. Unless the magistrate is to review such policy matters, he must issue a "rubber stamp" warrant which provides no protection at all to the property owner.

In our opinion, these arguments unduly discount the purposes behind the warrant machinery contemplated by the Fourth Amendment. Under the present system, when the inspector demands entry, the occupant has no way of knowing whether enforcement of the municipal code involved requires inspection of his premises, no way of knowing the lawful limits of the inspector's power to search, and no way of knowing whether the inspector himself is acting under proper authorization. These are questions which may be reviewed by a neutral magistrate without any reassessment of the basic agency decision to canvass an area. Yet, only by refusing entry and risking a criminal conviction can the occupant at present challenge the inspector's decision to search. And even if the occupant possesses sufficient fortitude to take this risk, as appellant did here, he may never learn any more about the reason for the inspection than that the law generally allows housing inspectors to gain entry. The practical effect of this system is to leave the occupant subject to the discretion of the official in the field. This is precisely the discretion to invade private property which we have consistently circumscribed by a requirement that a disinterested party warrant the need to search. See cases cited, p. 529, *supra*. We simply cannot say that the protections provided by the warrant procedure are not needed in this context; broad statutory safeguards are no substitute for individualized review, particularly when those safeguards may only be invoked at the risk of a criminal penalty.

The final justification suggested for warrantless administrative searches is that the public interest demands such a rule: it is vigorously argued that the health and safety of entire urban populations is dependent upon enforcement of minimum fire, housing, and sanitation standards, and that the only effective means of enforcing such codes is by routine systematized inspection of all physical structures. Of course, in applying any reasonableness standard, including one of constitutional dimension, an argument that the public interest demands a particular rule must receive careful consideration. But we think this argument misses the mark. The question is not, at this stage at least, whether these inspections may be made, but whether they may be made without a warrant. For example, to say that gambling raids may not be made at the discretion of the police without a warrant is not necessarily to say that gambling raids may never be made. In assessing whether the public interest demands creation of a general exception to the Fourth Amendment's warrant requirement, the question is not whether the public interest justifies the type of search in question, but whether the authority to search should be evidenced by a warrant, which in turn depends in part upon whether the burden of obtaining a warrant is likely to frustrate the governmental purpose behind the search. See *Schmerber* v. *California*, 384 U.S. 757, 770–771. It has nowhere been urged that fire, health, and housing code inspection programs could not achieve their goals within the confines of a reasonable search warrant requirement. Thus, we do not find the public need argument dispositive.

In summary, we hold that administrative searches of the kind at issue here are significant intrusions upon the interests protected by the Fourth Amendment, that such searches when authorized and conducted without a warrant procedure lack the traditional safeguards which the Fourth Amendment guarantees to the individual, and that the reasons put forth in *Frank* v. *Maryland* and in other cases for upholding these warrantless searches are insufficient to justify so substantial a weakening of the Fourth Amendment's protections. Because of the nature of the municipal programs under consideration, however, these conclusions must be the beginning, not the end, of our inquiry. The *Frank* majority gave recognition to the unique character of these inspection programs by refusing to require search warrants; to reject that disposition does not justify ignoring the question whether some other accommodation between public need and individual rights is essential.

II.

The Fourth Amendment provides that, "no Warrants shall issue, but upon probable cause." Borrowing from more typical Fourth Amendment cases, appellant argues not only that code enforcement inspection programs must be circumscribed by a warrant procedure, but also that warrants should issue only when the inspector possesses probable cause to believe that a particular dwelling contains violations of the minimum standards prescribed by the code being enforced. We disagree.

In cases in which the Fourth Amendment requires that a warrant to search be obtained, "probable cause" is the standard by which a particular decision to search is tested against the constitutional mandate of reasonableness. To apply this standard, it is obviously necessary first to focus upon the governmental interest which allegedly justifies official intrusion upon the constitutionally protected interests of the private citizen. For example, in a criminal investigation, the police may undertake to recover specific stolen or contraband goods. But that public interest would hardly justify a sweeping search of an entire city conducted in the hope that these goods might be found. Consequently, a search for these goods, even with a warrant, is "reasonable" only when there is "probable cause" to believe that they will be uncovered in a particular dwelling.

Unlike the search pursuant to a criminal investigation, the inspection programs at issue here are aimed at securing city-wide compliance with minimum physical standards for private property. The primary governmental interest at stake is to prevent even the unintentional development of conditions which are hazardous to public health and safety. Because fires and epidemics may ravage large urban areas, because unsightly conditions adversely affect the economic values of neighboring structures, numerous courts have upheld the police power of municipalities to impose and enforce such minimum standards even upon existing structures. In determining whether a particular inspection is reasonable—and thus in determining whether there is probable cause to issue a warrant for that inspection—the need for the inspection must be weighed in terms of these reasonable goals of code enforcement.

There is unanimous agreement among those most familiar with this field that the only effective way to seek universal compliance with the minimum standards required by municipal codes is through routine periodic inspections of all structures. It is here that the probable cause debate is focused, for the agency's decision to conduct an area inspection is unavoidably based on its appraisal of conditions in the area as a whole, not on its knowledge of conditions in each particular building. Appellee contends that, if the probable cause standard urged by appellant is adopted, the area inspection will be eliminated as a means of seeking compliance with code standards and the reasonable goals of code enforcement will be dealt a crushing blow.

In meeting this contention, appellant argues first that his probable cause standard would not jeopardize area inspection programs because only a minute portion of the population will refuse to consent to such inspections, and second, that individual privacy in any event should be given preference to the public interest in conducting such inspections. The first argument, even if true, is irrelevant to the question whether the area inspection is reasonable within the meaning of the Fourth Amendment. The second argument is in effect an assertion that the area inspection is an unreasonable search. Unfortunately, there can be no ready test for determining reasonableness other than by balancing the need to search against the invasion

which the search entails. But we think that a number of persuasive factors combine to support the reasonableness of area code-enforcement inspections. First, such programs have a long history of judicial and public acceptance. See *Frank* v. *Maryland*, 359 U.S., at 367–371. Second, the public interest demands that all dangerous conditions be prevented or abated, yet it is doubtful that any other canvassing technique would achieve acceptable results. Many such conditions—faulty wiring is an obvious example—are not observable from outside the building and indeed may not be apparent to the inexpert occupant himself. Finally, because the inspections are neither personal in nature nor aimed at the discovery of evidence of crime, they involve a relatively limited invasion of the urban citizen's privacy. Both the majority and the dissent in Frank emphatically supported this conclusion:

> Time and experience have forcefully taught that the power to inspect dwelling places, either as a matter of systematic area-by-area search or, as here, to treat a specific problem, is of indispensable importance to the maintenance of community health; a power that would be greatly hobbled by the blanket requirement of the safeguards necessary for a search of evidence of criminal acts. The need for preventive action is great, and city after city has seen this need and granted the power of inspection to its health officials; and these inspections are apparently welcomed by all but an insignificant few. Certainly, the nature of our society has not vitiated the need for inspections first thought necessary 158 years ago, nor has experience revealed any abuse or inroad on freedom in meeting this need by means that history and dominant public opinion have sanctioned. 359 U.S., at 372
>
> . . . This is not to suggest that a health official need show the same kind of proof to a magistrate to obtain a warrant as one must who would search for the fruits or instrumentalities of crime. Where considerations of health and safety are involved, the facts that would justify an inference of "probable cause" to make an inspection are clearly different from those that would justify such an inference where a criminal investigation has been undertaken. Experience may show the need for periodic inspections of certain facilities without a further showing of cause to believe that substandard conditions dangerous to the public are being maintained. The passage of a certain period without inspection might of itself be sufficient in a given situation to justify the issuance of a warrant. The test of "probable cause" required by the Fourth Amendment can take into account the nature of the search that is being sought. 359 U.S., at 383 (MR. JUSTICE DOUGLAS, dissenting)

Having concluded that the area inspection is a "reasonable" search of private property within the meaning of the Fourth Amendment, it is obvious that "probable cause" to issue a warrant to inspect must exist if reasonable legislative or administrative standards for conducting an area inspection are satisfied with respect to a particular dwelling. Such standards, which will vary with the municipal program being enforced, may be based upon the passage of time, the nature of the building (e.g., a multi-family apartment house), or the condition of the entire area, but they will not necessarily depend upon specific knowledge of the condition of the particular dwelling. It has been suggested that to vary the probable cause test from the standard applied in criminal cases would be to authorize a "synthetic search warrant" and thereby to lessen the overall protections of the Fourth Amendment. *Frank* v. *Maryland*, 359 Page 539 U.S., at 373. But we do not agree. The warrant procedure is designed to guarantee that a decision to search private property is justified by a reasonable governmental interest. But reasonableness is still the ultimate standard. If a valid public interest justifies the intrusion contemplated, then there is probable cause to issue a suitably restricted search warrant. . . .

1. Should a warrant be required for administrative searches?
2. Does the Court establish a different standard of probable cause for administrative searches?

The next case examines the question of whether a prisoner has a reasonable expectation of privacy.

HUDSON V. PALMER
468 U.S. 517 (1984)

CHIEF JUSTICE BURGER delivered the opinion of the Court.

We granted *certiorari* in No. 82-1630 to decide whether a prison inmate has a reasonable expectation of privacy in his prison cell entitling him to the protection of the Fourth Amendment against unreasonable searches and seizures. . . . The facts underlying this dispute are relatively simple. Respondent Palmer is an inmate at the Bland Correctional Center in Bland, Va., serving sentences for forgery, uttering, grand larceny, and bank robbery convictions. On September 16, 1981, petitioner Hudson, an officer at the Correctional Center, with a fellow officer, conducted a "shakedown" search of respondent's prison locker and cell for contraband. During the "shakedown," the officers discovered a ripped pillowcase in a trash can near

Chief Justice Warren E. Burger was appointed to the Supreme Court by President Nixon and served from 1969 to 1986. (Photograph by Joseph Bailey, National Geographic Society. Courtesy the Supreme Court of the United States.)

respondent's cell bunk. Charges against Palmer were instituted under the prison disciplinary procedures for destroying state property. After a hearing, Palmer was found guilty on the charge and was ordered to reimburse the State for the cost of the material destroyed; in addition, a reprimand was entered on his prison record.

Palmer subsequently brought this *pro se* action [on his own behalf, without an attorney] in United States District Court under 42 U.S.C. § 1983. Respondent claimed that Hudson had conducted the shakedown search of his cell and had brought a false charge against him solely to harass him, and that, in violation of his Fourteenth Amendment right not to be deprived of property without due process of law. . . .

The first question we address is whether respondent has a right of privacy in his prison cell entitling him to the protection of the Fourth Amendment against unreasonable searches.

We have repeatedly held that prisons are not beyond the reach of the Constitution. No "iron curtain" separates one from the other. *Wolff* v. *McDonnell*, 418 U.S. 539, 555 (1974). Indeed, we have insisted that prisoners be accorded those rights not fundamentally inconsistent with imprisonment itself or incompatible with the objectives of incarceration. For example, we have held that invidious racial discrimination is as intolerable within a prison as outside, except as may be essential to "prison security and discipline." *Lee* v. *Washington*, 390 U.S. 333 (1968). Like others, prisoners have the constitutional right to petition the Government for redress of their grievances, which includes a reasonable right of access to the courts. *Johnson* v. *Avery*, 393 U.S. 483 (1969).

Prisoners must be provided "reasonable opportunities" to exercise their religious freedom guaranteed under the First Amendment. *Cruz* v. *Beto*, 405 U.S. 319 (1972). Similarly, they retain those First Amendment rights of speech "not inconsistent with [their] status as . . . prisoner[s] or with the legitimate penological objectives of the corrections system." *Pell* v. *Procunier*, 417 U.S. 817, 822 (1974). They enjoy the protection of due process. *Wolff* v. *McDonnell, supra*; *Haines* v. *Kerner*, 404 U.S. 519 (1972). And the Eighth Amendment ensures that they will not be subject to "cruel and unusual punishments." *Estelle* v. *Gamble*, 429 U.S. 97 (1976). The continuing guarantee of these substantial rights to prison inmates is testimony to a belief that the way a society treats those who have transgressed against it is evidence of the essential character of that society. . . . However, while persons imprisoned for crime enjoy many protections of the Constitution, it is also clear that imprisonment carries with it the circumscription or loss of many significant rights. See *Bell* v. *Wolfish*, 441 U.S. at 545. These constraints on inmates, and in some cases the complete withdrawal of certain rights, are "justified by the considerations underlying our penal system." . . . The curtailment of certain rights is necessary, as a practical matter, to accommodate a myriad of "institutional needs and objectives" of prison facilities, . . . chief among which is internal security. . . .

Of course, these restrictions or retractions also serve, incidentally, as reminders that, under our system of justice, deterrence and retribution are factors in addition to correction. We have not before been called upon to decide the specific question whether the Fourth Amendment applies within a prison cell, but the nature of our inquiry is well defined. We must determine here, as in other Fourth Amendment contexts, if a "justifiable" expectation of privacy is at stake. *Katz* v. *United States*, 389 U.S. 347 (1967). The applicability of the Fourth Amendment turns on whether the person invoking its protection can claim a "justifiable," a "reasonable," or a "legitimate expectation of privacy" that has been invaded by government action. *Smith* v. *Maryland*, 442 U.S. 735, 740 (1979), and cases cited. We must decide, in

Justice Harlan's words, whether a prisoner's expectation of privacy in his prison cell is the kind of expectation that "society is prepared to recognize as 'reasonable.' " *Katz, supra,* at 360, 361 (concurring opinion).

Notwithstanding our caution in approaching claims that the Fourth Amendment is inapplicable in a given context, we hold that society is not prepared to recognize as legitimate any subjective expectation of privacy that a prisoner might have in his prison cell and that, accordingly, the Fourth Amendment proscription against unreasonable searches does not apply within the confines of the prison cell. The recognition of privacy rights for prisoners in their individual cells simply cannot be reconciled with the concept of incarceration and the needs and objectives of penal institutions. Prisons, by definition, are places of involuntary confinement of persons who have a demonstrated proclivity for antisocial, criminal, and often violent, conduct. Inmates have necessarily shown a lapse in ability to control and conform their behavior to the legitimate standards of society by the normal impulses of self-restraint; they have shown an inability to regulate their conduct in a way that reflects either a respect for law or an appreciation of the rights of others.

Even a partial survey of the statistics on violent crime in our Nation's prisons illustrates the magnitude of the problem. During 1981 and the first half of 1982, there were over 120 prisoners murdered by fellow inmates in state and federal prisons. A number of prison personnel were murdered by prisoners during this period. Over 29 riots or similar disturbances were reported in these facilities for the same timeframe. And there were over 125 suicides in these institutions. See *Prison Violence,* 7 Corrections Compendium (Mar. 1983). Additionally, informal statistics from the United States Bureau of Prisons show that, in the federal system during 1983, there were 11 inmate homicides, 359 inmate assaults on other inmates, 227 inmate assaults on prison staff, and 10 suicides. There were in the same system in 1981 and 1982 over 750 inmate assaults on other inmates and over 570 inmate assaults on prison personnel. Within this volatile "community," prison administrators are to take all necessary steps to ensure the safety of not only the prison staffs and administrative personnel, but also visitors. They are under an obligation to take reasonable measures to guarantee the safety of the inmates themselves. They must be ever alert to attempts to introduce drugs and other contraband into the premises which, we can judicially notice, is one of the most perplexing problems of prisons today; they must prevent, so far as possible, the flow of illicit weapons into the prison; they must be vigilant to detect escape plots, in which drugs or weapons may be involved, before the schemes materialize. In addition to these monumental tasks, it is incumbent upon these officials at the same time to maintain as sanitary an environment for the inmates as feasible, given the difficulties of the circumstances.

The administration of a prison, we have said, is "at best an extraordinarily difficult undertaking." *Wolff* v. *McDonnell,* 418 U.S. at 566; *Hewitt* v. *Helms,* 459 U.S. 460, 467 (1983). But it would be literally impossible to accomplish the prison objectives identified above if inmates retained a right of privacy in their cells. Virtually the only place inmates can conceal weapons, drugs, and other contraband is in their cells. Unfettered access to these cells by prison officials, thus, is imperative if drugs and contraband are to be ferreted out and sanitary surroundings are to be maintained.

Determining whether an expectation of privacy is "legitimate" or "reasonable" necessarily entails a balancing of interests. The two interests here are the interest of society in the security of its penal institutions and the interest of the prisoner in privacy within his cell. The latter interest, of course, is already limited by the exi-

gencies of the circumstances: a prison "shares none of the attributes of privacy of a home, an automobile, an office, or a hotel room." *Lanza* v. *New York*, 370 U.S. 139, 143–144 (1962). We strike the balance in favor of institutional security, which we have noted is "central to all other corrections goals," *Pell* v. *Procunier*, 417 U.S. at 823. A right of privacy in traditional Fourth Amendment terms is fundamentally incompatible with the close and continual surveillance of inmates and their cells required to ensure institutional security and internal order. We are satisfied that society would insist that the prisoner's expectation of privacy always yield to what must be considered the paramount interest in institutional security. We believe that it is accepted by our society that "[l]oss of freedom of choice and privacy are inherent incidents of confinement." *Bell* v. *Wolfish*, 441 U.S. at 537. The Court of Appeals was troubled by the possibility of searches conducted solely to harass inmates; it reasoned that a requirement that searches be conducted only pursuant to an established policy or upon reasonable suspicion would prevent such searches to the maximum extent possible. Of course, there is a risk of maliciously motivated searches, and of course, intentional harassment of even the most hardened criminals cannot be tolerated by a civilized society. However, we disagree with the court's [Court of Appeals] proposed solution. The uncertainty that attends random searches of cells renders these searches perhaps the most effective weapon of the prison administrator in the constant fight against the proliferation of knives and guns, illicit drugs, and other contraband. The Court of Appeals candidly acknowledged that "the device [of random cell searches] is of . . . obvious utility in achieving the goal of prison security." 697 F.2d at 1224.

A requirement that even random searches be conducted pursuant to an established plan would seriously undermine the effectiveness of this weapon. It is simply naive to believe that prisoners would not eventually decipher any plan officials might devise for "planned random searches," and thus be able routinely to anticipate searches. The Supreme Court of Virginia identified the shortcomings of an approach such as that adopted by the Court of Appeals and the necessity of allowing prison administrators flexibility.

For one to advocate that prison searches must be conducted only pursuant to an enunciated general policy or when suspicion is directed at a particular inmate is to ignore the realities of prison operation. Random searches of inmates, individually or collectively, and their cells and lockers are valid and necessary to ensure the security of the institution and the safety of inmates and all others within its boundaries. This type of search allows prison officers flexibility and prevents inmates from anticipating, and thereby thwarting, a search for contraband. *Marrero* v. *Commonwealth*, 222 Va. 754, 757, 284 S.E.2d 809, 811 (1981). We share the concerns so well expressed by the Supreme Court and its view that wholly random searches are essential to the effective security of penal institutions. We, therefore, cannot accept even the concededly limited holding of the Court of Appeals.

Respondent acknowledges that routine shakedowns of prison cells are essential to the effective administration of prisons. . . . He contends, however, that he is constitutionally entitled not to be subjected to searches conducted only to harass. The crux of his claim is that, because searches and seizures to harass are unreasonable, a prisoner has a reasonable expectation of privacy not to have his cell, locker, personal effects, person invaded for such a purpose. *Id.* at 24. This argument, which assumes the answer to the predicate question whether a prisoner has a legitimate expectation of privacy in his prison cell at all, is merely a challenge to the reasonableness of the particular search of respondent's cell. Because we conclude that prisoners have no legitimate expectation of privacy, and that the Fourth

Amendment's prohibition on unreasonable searches does not apply in prison cells, we need not address this issue.

Our holding that respondent does not have a reasonable expectation of privacy enabling him to invoke the protections of the Fourth Amendment does not mean that he is without a remedy for calculated harassment unrelated to prison needs. Nor does it mean that prison attendants can ride roughshod over inmates' property rights with impunity. The Eighth Amendment always stands as a protection against "cruel and unusual punishments." By the same token, there are adequate state tort and common law remedies available to respondent to redress the alleged destruction of his personal property. . . .

WHAT DO YOU THINK?

1. Should a prisoner have a reasonable expectation of privacy in his or her cell?

2. What does the Court mean when it states that there are adequate tort and common law remedies available to the respondent?

3. Does the Court mean that under no circumstances does a prisoner have a reasonable expectation of privacy?

The open fields doctrine is discussed in the next case.

OLIVER V. UNITED STATES
466 U.S. 170 (1984)

JUSTICE POWELL delivered the opinion of the Court.

The "open fields" doctrine, first enunciated by this Court in *Hester* v. *United States*, 265 U.S. 57 (1924), permits police officers to enter and search a field without a warrant. We granted *certiorari* in these cases to clarify confusion that has arisen as to the continued vitality of the doctrine.

I.

Acting on reports that marijuana was being raised on the farm of petitioner Oliver, two narcotics agents of the Kentucky State Police went to the farm to investigate. Arriving at the farm, they drove past petitioner's house to a locked gate with a "No Trespassing" sign. A footpath led around one side of the gate. The agents walked around the gate and along the road for several hundred yards, passing a barn and a parked camper. At that point, someone standing in front of the camper shouted: "No hunting is allowed, come back up here." The officers shouted back that they were Kentucky State Police officers, but found no one when they returned to the camper. The officers resumed their investigation of the farm and found a field of marijuana over a mile from petitioner's home.

Petitioner was arrested and indicted for "manufactur[ing]" a "controlled substance." 21 U.S.C. 841(a)(1). After a pretrial hearing, the District Court suppressed evidence of the discovery of the marijuana field. Applying *Katz* v. *United States*, 389 U.S. 347, 357 (1967), the court found that petitioner had a reasonable expectation that the field would remain private because petitioner "had done all that could be expected of him to assert his privacy in the area of farm that was searched."

He had posted "No Trespassing" signs at regular intervals and had locked the gate at the entrance to the center of the farm. Further, the court noted that the field itself is highly secluded: it is bounded on all sides by woods, fences, and embankments and cannot be seen from any point of public access. The court concluded that this was not an "open" field that invited casual intrusion.

The Court of Appeals for the Sixth Circuit, sitting *en banc*, reversed the District Court. 686 F.2d 356 (1982). The court concluded that *Katz*, upon which the District Court relied, had not impaired the vitality of the open fields doctrine of *Hester*. Rather, the open fields doctrine was entirely compatible with *Katz'* emphasis on privacy. The court reasoned that the "human relations that create the need for privacy do not ordinarily take place" in open fields, and that the property owner's common-law right to exclude trespassers is insufficiently linked to privacy to warrant the Fourth Amendment's protection. We granted *certiorari*. After receiving an anonymous tip that marijuana was being grown in the woods behind respondent Thornton's residence, two police officers entered the woods by a path between this residence and a neighboring house. They followed a footpath through the woods until they reached two marijuana patches fenced with chicken wire. Later, the officers determined that the patches were on the property of respondent, obtained a warrant to search the property, and seized the marijuana. On the basis of this evidence, respondent was arrested and indicted. The trial court granted respondent's motion to suppress the fruits of the second search. The warrant for this search was premised on information that the police had obtained during their previous warrantless search, that the court found to be unreasonable. "No Trespassing" signs and the secluded location of the marijuana patches evinced a reasonable expectation of privacy. Therefore, the court held, the open fields doctrine did not apply.

The Maine Supreme Judicial Court affirmed. 453 A. 2d 489 (1982). It agreed with the trial court that the correct question was whether the search "is a violation of privacy on which the individual justifiably relied," *id.*, at 493, and that the search violated respondent's privacy. The court also agreed that the open fields doctrine did not justify the search. That doctrine applies, according to the court, only when officers are lawfully present on property and observe "open and patent" activity. *Id.*, at 495. In this case, the officers had trespassed upon defendant's property, and the respondent had made every effort to conceal his activity. We granted *certiorari*. 460 U.S. 1068 (1983).

The rule announced in *Hester* v. *United States* was founded upon the explicit language of the Fourth Amendment. That Amendment indicates with some precision the places and things encompassed by its protections. As Justice Holmes explained for the Court in his characteristically laconic style: "[T]he special protection accorded by the Fourth Amendment to the people in their 'persons, houses, papers, and effects, is not extended to the open fields. The distinction between the latter and the house is as old as the common law."

... Nor are the open fields "effects" within the meaning of the Fourth Amendment. In this respect, it is suggestive that James Madison's proposed draft of what became the Fourth Amendment preserves "[t]he rights of the people to be secured in their persons, their houses, their papers, and their other property, from all unreasonable searches and seizures. . . . Although Congress' revisions of Madison's proposal broadened the scope of the Amendment in some respects, *id.*, at 100–103, the term "effects" is less inclusive than "property" and cannot be said to encompass open fields. We conclude, as did the Court in deciding *Hester* v. *United States*, that the government's intrusion upon the open fields is not one of those "unreasonable searches" proscribed by the text of the Fourth Amendment.

III.

This interpretation of the Fourth Amendment's language is consistent with the understanding of the right to privacy expressed in our Fourth Amendment jurisprudence. Since *Katz* v. *United States*, 389 U.S. 347 (1967), the touchstone of Amendment analysis has been the question whether a person has a "constitutionally protected reasonable expectation of privacy." *Id.*, at 360 (Harlan, J., concurring). The Amendment does not protect the merely subjective expectation of privacy, but only those "expectation[s] that society is prepared to recognize as 'reasonable.' " *Id.*, at 361. . . .

A.

No single factor determines whether an individual legitimately may claim under the Fourth Amendment that a place should be free of government intrusion not authorized by warrant. . . . In assessing the degree to which a search infringes upon individual privacy, the Court has given weight to such factors as the intention of the Framers of the Fourth Amendment, e.g., *United States* v. *Chadwick*, 433 U.S. 1, 7–8 (1977), the uses to which the individual has put a location, e.g., *Jones* v. *United States*, 362 U.S. 257, 265 (1960), and our societal understanding that certain areas deserve the most scrupulous protection from government invasion, e.g., *Payton* v. *New York*, 445 U.S. 573 (1980). These factors are equally relevant to determining whether the government's intrusion upon open fields without a warrant or probable cause violates reasonable expectations of privacy and is therefore a search proscribed by the Amendment.

In this light, the rule of *Hester* v. *United States*, *supra*, that we reaffirm today may be understood as providing that an individual may not legitimately demand privacy for activities conducted out of doors in fields, except in the area immediately surrounding the home. See also *Air Pollution Variance Bd.* v. *Western Alfalfa Corp.*, 416 U.S. 861, 865 (1974). This rule is true to the conception of the right to privacy embodied in the Fourth Amendment. The Amendment reflects the recognition of the Framers that certain enclaves should be free from arbitrary government interference. For example, the Court since the enactment of the Fourth Amendment has stressed "the overriding respect for the sanctity of the home that has been embedded in our traditions since the origins of the Republic." *Payton* v. *New York*, *supra*, at 601.8 See also *Silverman* v. *United States*, 365 U.S. 505, 511 (1961); *United States* v. *United States District Court*, 407 U.S. 297, 313 (1972).

In contrast, open fields do not provide the setting for those intimate activities that the Amendment is intended to shelter from government interference or surveillance. There is no societal interest in protecting the privacy of those activities, such as the cultivation of crops, that occur in open fields. Moreover, as a practical matter these lands usually are accessible to the public and the police in ways that a home, an office, or commercial structure would not be. It is not generally true that fences or "No Trespassing" signs effectively bar the public from viewing open fields in rural areas. And both petitioner Oliver and respondent Thornton concede that the public and police lawfully may survey lands from the air. For these reasons, the asserted expectation of privacy in open fields is not an expectation that "society recognizes as reasonable."

The historical underpinnings of the open fields doctrine also demonstrate that the doctrine is consistent with respect for "reasonable expectations of privacy." As Justice Holmes, writing for the Court, observed in *Hester*, 265 U.S., at 59, the common law distinguished "open fields" from the "curtilage," the land immediately

surrounding and associated with the home. See 4 W. Blackstone, *Commentaries* *225. The distinction implies that only the curtilage, not the neighboring open fields, warrants the Fourth Amendment protections that attach to the home. At common law, the curtilage is the area to which extends the intimate activity associated with the "sanctity of a man's home and the privacies of life," *Boyd* v. *United States*, 116 U.S. 616, 630 (1886), and therefore has been considered part of the home itself for Fourth Amendment purposes. Thus, courts have extended Fourth Amendment protection to the curtilage; and they have defined the curtilage, as did the common law, by reference to the factors that determine whether an individual reasonably may expect that an area immediately adjacent to the home will remain private. . . . Conversely, the common law implies, as we reaffirm today, that no expectation of privacy legitimately attaches to open fields.

We conclude, from the text of the Fourth Amendment and from the historical and contemporary understanding of its purposes, that an individual has no legitimate expectation that open fields will remain free from warrantless intrusion by government officers.

B.

Petitioner Oliver and respondent Thornton contend, to the contrary, that the circumstances of a search sometimes may indicate that reasonable expectations of privacy were violated; and that courts therefore should analyze these circumstances on a case-by-case basis. The language of the Fourth Amendment itself answers their contention.

Nor would a case-by-case approach provide a workable accommodation between the needs of law enforcement and the interests protected by the Fourth Amendment. Under this approach, police officers would have to guess before every search whether landowners had erected fences sufficiently high, posted a sufficient number of warning signs, or located contraband in an area sufficiently secluded to establish a right of privacy. The lawfulness of a search would turn on " '[a] highly sophisticated set of rules, qualified by all sorts of ifs, ands, and buts and requiring the drawing of subtle nuances and hairline distinctions. . . .' " *New York* v. *Belton*, 453 U.S. 454, 458 (1981) (quoting LaFave, "Case-By-Case Adjudication" versus "Standardized Procedures": *The Robinson Dilemma*, 1974 S. Ct. Rev. 127, 142). This Court repeatedly has acknowledged the difficulties created for courts, police, and citizens by an ad hoc, case-by-case definition of Fourth Amendment standards to be applied in differing factual circumstances. See *Belton*, *supra*, at 458–460; *Robbins* v. *California*, 453 U.S. 420, 430 (1981) (POWELL, J., concurring in judgment); *Dunaway* v. *New York*, 442 U.S. 200, 213–214 (1979); *United States* v. *Robinson*, 414 U.S. 218, 235 (1973). The ad hoc approach not only makes it difficult for the policeman to discern the scope of his authority, *Belton*, *supra*, at 460; it also creates a danger that constitutional rights will be arbitrarily and inequitably enforced. . . .

IV.

In any event, while the factors that petitioner Oliver and respondent Thornton urge the courts to consider may be relevant to Fourth Amendment analysis in some contexts, these factors cannot be decisive on the question whether the search of an open field is subject to the Amendment. Initially, we reject the suggestion that steps taken to protect privacy establish that expectations of privacy in an open field are legitimate. It is true, of course, that petitioner Oliver and respondent Thornton, in

order to conceal their criminal activities, planted the marijuana upon secluded land and erected fences and "No Trespassing" signs around the property. And it may be that because of such precautions, few members of the public stumbled upon the marijuana crops seized by the police. Neither of these suppositions demonstrates, however, that the expectation of privacy was legitimate in the sense required by the Fourth Amendment. The test of legitimacy is not whether the individual chooses to conceal assertedly "private" activity. Rather, the correct inquiry is whether the government's intrusion infringes upon the personal and societal values protected by the Fourth Amendment. As we have explained, we find no basis for concluding that a police inspection of open fields accomplishes such an infringement.

Nor is the government's intrusion upon an open field a "search" in the constitutional sense because that intrusion is a trespass at common law. The existence of a property right is but one element in determining whether expectations of privacy are legitimate. The premise that property interests control the right of the Government to search and seize has been discredited. . . .

JUSTICE WHITE, concurring in part and concurring in the judgment.

I concur in the judgment and join Parts I and II of the Court's opinion. These Parts dispose of the issue before us; there is no need to go further and deal with the expectation of privacy matter. However reasonable a landowner's expectations of privacy may be, those expectations cannot convert a field into a "house" or an "effect."

JUSTICE MARSHALL, with whom JUSTICE BRENNAN and JUSTICE STEVENS join, dissenting.

In each of these consolidated cases, police officers, ignoring clearly visible "No Trespassing" signs, entered upon private land in search of evidence of a crime. At a spot that could not be seen from any vantage point accessible to the public, the police discovered contraband, which was subsequently used to incriminate the owner of the land. In neither case did the police have a warrant authorizing their activities.

The Court holds that police conduct of this sort does not constitute an "unreasonable search" within the meaning of the Fourth Amendment. The Court reaches that startling conclusion by two independent analytical routes. First, the Court argues that, because the Fourth Amendment by its terms renders people secure in their "persons, houses, papers, and effects," it is inapplicable to trespasses upon land not lying within the curtilage of a dwelling. *Ante*, at 176–177. Second, the Court contends that "an individual may not legitimately demand privacy for activities conducted out of doors in fields, except in the area immediately surrounding the home." *Ante*, at 178. Because I cannot agree with either of these propositions, I dissent.

I.

The first ground on which the Court rests its decision is that the Fourth Amendment "indicates with some precision the places and things encompassed by its protections," and that real property is not included in the list of protected spaces and possessions. *Ante*, at 176. This line of argument has several flaws. Most obviously, it is inconsistent with the results of many of our previous decisions, none of which the Court purports to overrule. For example, neither a public telephone booth nor a conversation conducted therein can fairly be described as a person, house, paper, or effect; yet we have held that the Fourth Amendment forbids the police without a warrant to eavesdrop on such a conversation. *Katz* v. *United States*, 389 U.S. 347 (1967). Nor can it plausibly be argued that an office or commercial establishment

is covered by the plain language of the Amendment; yet we have held that such premises are entitled to constitutional protection if they are marked in a fashion that alerts the public to the fact that they are private. . . .

WHAT DO YOU THINK?

1. Should we have a right to privacy in the "back forty acres?"
2. Why did the Supreme Court reject the trespass doctrine?
3. Explain the open fields doctrine.

What should be the test (standard) for traffic stops? Should the police be able to use traffic stops as a means of investigating other law violations? The Whren *case looks at these issues.*

WHREN ET AL. V. UNITED STATES
135 L. Ed. 2d 89 (1996)

On Writ of Certiorari to the United States Court of Appeals for the District of Columbia Circuit. JUSTICE SCALIA delivered the opinion of the Court. In this case we decide whether the temporary detention of a motorist who the police have probable cause to believe has committed a civil traffic violation is inconsistent with the Fourth Amendment's prohibition against unreasonable seizures unless a reasonable officer would have been motivated to stop the car by a desire to enforce the traffic laws.

I.

On the evening of June 10, 1993, plainclothes vice-squad officers of the District of Columbia Metropolitan Police Department were patrolling a "high drug area" of the city in an unmarked car. Their suspicions were aroused when they passed a dark Pathfinder truck with temporary license plates and youthful occupants waiting at a stop sign, the driver looking down into the lap of the passenger at his right. The truck remained stopped at the intersection for what seemed an unusually long time—more than 20 seconds. When the police car executed a U-turn in order to head back toward the truck, the Pathfinder turned suddenly to its right, without signalling, and sped off at an "unreasonable" speed. The policemen followed, and in a short while overtook the Pathfinder when it stopped behind other traffic at a red light. They pulled up alongside, and Officer Ephraim Soto stepped out and approached the driver's door, identifying himself as a police officer and directing the driver, petitioner Brown, to put the vehicle in park. When Soto drew up to the driver's window, he immediately observed two large plastic bags of what appeared to be crack cocaine in petitioner Whren's hands. Petitioners were arrested, and quantities of several types of illegal drugs were retrieved from the vehicle.

Petitioners were charged in a four-count indictment with violating various federal drug laws, including 21 U. S. C. Section(s) 844(a) and 860(a). At a pretrial suppression hearing, they challenged the legality of the stop and the resulting seizure of the drugs. They argued that the stop had not been justified by probable cause to believe, or even reasonable suspicion, that petitioners were engaged in illegal

drug-dealing activity; and that Officer Soto's asserted ground for approaching the vehicle—to give the driver a warning concerning traffic violations—was pretextual. The District Court denied the suppression motion, concluding that "the facts of the stop were not controverted," and "[t]here was nothing to really demonstrate that the actions of the officers were contrary to a normal traffic stop."

Petitioners were convicted of the counts at issue here. The Court of Appeals affirmed the convictions, holding with respect to the suppression issue that, "regardless of whether a police officer subjectively believes that the occupants of an automobile may be engaging in some other illegal behavior, a traffic stop is permissible as long as a reasonable officer in the same circumstances could have stopped the car for the suspected traffic violation." 53 F. 3d 371. . . .

<h2 style="text-align:center">II.</h2>

The Fourth Amendment guarantees "[t]he right of the people to be secure in their persons, houses, papers, and effects, against unreasonable searches and seizures." Temporary detention of individuals during the stop of an automobile by the police, even if only for a brief period and for a limited purpose, constitutes a "seizure" of "persons" within the meaning of this provision. See *Delaware* v. *Prouse*, 440 U.S. 648, 653 (1979); *United States* v. *Martinez-Fuerte*, 428 U.S. 543, 556 (1976); *United States* v. *Brignoni-Ponce*, 422 U.S. 873, 878 (1975). An automobile stop is thus subject to the constitutional imperative that it not be "unreasonable" under the circumstances. As a general matter, the decision to stop an automobile is reasonable where the police have probable cause to believe that a traffic violation has occurred. See *Prouse*, *supra*, at 659; *Pennsylvania* v. *Mimms*, 434 U.S. 106, 109 (1977) (*per curiam*).

Petitioners accept that Officer Soto had probable cause to believe that various provisions of the District of Columbia traffic code had been violated. See 18 D. C. Mun. Regs. Section(s) 2213.4 (1995) ("An operator shall . . . give full time and attention to the operation of the vehicle"); 2204.3 ("No person shall turn any vehicle . . . without giving an appropriate signal"); 2200.3 ("No person shall drive a vehicle . . . at a speed greater than is reasonable and prudent under the conditions"). They argue, however, that "in the unique context of civil traffic regulations" probable cause is not enough. Since, they contend, the use of automobiles is so heavily and minutely regulated that total compliance with traffic and safety rules is nearly impossible, a police officer will almost invariably be able to catch any given motorist in a technical violation. This creates the temptation to use traffic stops as a means of investigating other law violations, as to which no probable cause or even articulable suspicion exists. Petitioners, who are both black, further contend that police officers might decide which motorists to stop based on decidedly impermissible factors, such as the race of the car's occupants. To avoid this danger, they say, the Fourth Amendment test for traffic stops should be, not the normal one (applied by the Court of Appeals) of whether probable cause existed to justify the stop; but rather, whether a police officer, acting reasonably, would have made the stop for the reason given.

<h2 style="text-align:center">A.</h2>

Petitioners contend that the standard they propose is consistent with our past cases' disapproval of police attempts to use valid bases of action against citizens as pretexts for pursuing other investigatory agendas. We are reminded that in *Florida* v. *Wells*, 495 U.S. 1, 4 (1990), we stated that "an inventory search must not be used as a ruse for a general rummaging in order to discover incriminating evidence"; that in *Colorado* v. *Bertine*, 479 U.S. 367, 372 (1987), in approving an inventory search, we apparently thought it significant that there had been "no showing that the police, who were following standard procedures, acted in bad faith or for the sole purpose of investigation"; and that in *New York* v. *Burger*, 482 U.S. 691, 716–717, n. 27 (1987), we observed, in upholding the constitutionality of a warrantless administrative inspection, that the search did not appear to be "a 'pretext' for obtaining evidence of . . . violation of . . . penal laws." But only an undiscerning reader would regard these cases as endorsing the principle that ulterior motives can invalidate police conduct that is justifiable on the basis of probable cause to believe that a violation of law has occurred. In each case we were addressing the validity of a search conducted in the absence of probable cause. Our quoted statements simply explain that the exemption from the need for probable cause (and warrant), which is accorded to searches made for the purpose of inventory or administrative regulation, is not accorded to searches that are not made for those purposes. See *Bertine*, *supra*, at 371–372; *Burger*, *supra*, at 702–703.

Petitioners also rely upon *Colorado* v. *Bannister*, 449 U.S. 1 (1980) (*per curiam*), a case which, like this one, involved a traffic stop as the prelude to a plain-view sighting and arrest on charges wholly unrelated to the basis for the stop. Petitioners point to our statement that "there was no evidence whatsoever that the officer's presence to issue a traffic citation was a pretext to confirm any other previous suspicion about the occupants" of the car. *Id.*, at 4, n. 4. That dictum at most demonstrates that the Court in Bannister found no need to inquire into the question now under discussion; not that it was certain of the answer. And it may demonstrate even less than that: if by "pretext" the Court meant that the officer really had not seen the car speeding, the statement would mean only that there was no reason to doubt probable cause for the traffic stop. . . .

We think these cases foreclose any argument that the constitutional reasonableness of traffic stops depends on the actual motivations of the individual officers involved. We of course agree with petitioners that the Constitution prohibits selective enforcement of the law based on considerations such as race. But the constitutional basis for objecting to intentionally discriminatory application of laws is the Equal Protection Clause, not the Fourth Amendment. Subjective intentions play no role in ordinary, probable-cause Fourth Amendment analysis.

B.

Recognizing that we have been unwilling to entertain Fourth Amendment challenges based on the actual motivations of individual officers, petitioners disavow any intention to make the individual officer's subjective good faith the touchstone of "reasonableness." They insist that the standard they have put forward—whether the officer's conduct deviated materially from usual police practices, so that a reasonable officer in the same circumstances would not have made the stop for the reasons given—is an "objective" one.

But although framed in empirical terms, this approach is plainly and indisputably driven by subjective considerations. Its whole purpose is to prevent the police from doing under the guise of enforcing the traffic code what they would like to do for different reasons. Petitioners' proposed standard may not use the word "pretext," but it is designed to combat nothing other than the perceived "danger" of the pretextual stop, albeit only indirectly and over the run of cases. Instead of asking whether the individual officer had the proper state of mind, the petitioners would have us ask, in effect, whether (based on general police practices) it is plausible to believe that the officer had the proper state of mind.

Why one would frame a test designed to combat pretext in such fashion that the court cannot take into account actual and admitted pretext is a curiosity that can only be explained by the fact that our cases have foreclosed the more sensible option. If those cases were based only upon the evidentiary difficulty of establishing subjective intent, petitioners' attempt to root out subjective vices through objective means might make sense. But they were not based only upon that, or indeed even principally upon that. Their principal basis—which applies equally to attempts to reach subjective intent through ostensibly objective means—is simply that the Fourth Amendment's concern with "reasonableness" allows certain actions to be taken in certain circumstances, whatever the subjective intent. See, e.g., *Robinson, supra,* at 236 ("Since it is the fact of custodial arrest which gives rise to the authority to search, it is of no moment that [the officer] did not indicate any subjective fear of the [arrestee] or that he did not himself suspect that [the arrestee] was armed"); *Gustafson, supra,* at 266 (same). But even if our concern had been only an evidentiary one, petitioners' proposal would by no means assuage it. Indeed, it seems to us somewhat easier to figure out the intent of an individual officer than to plumb the collective consciousness of law enforcement in order to determine whether a "reasonable officer" would have been moved to act upon the traffic violation. While police manuals and standard procedures may sometimes provide objective assistance, ordinarily one would be reduced to speculating about the hypothetical reaction of a hypothetical constable—an exercise that might be called virtual subjectivity.

Moreover, police enforcement practices, even if they could be practically assessed by a judge, vary from place to place and from time to time. We cannot accept that the search and seizure protections of the Fourth Amendment are so variable, *cf. Gustafson, supra,* at 265; *United States* v. *Caceres,* 440 U.S. 741, 755–756 (1979), and can be made to turn upon such trivialities. The difficulty is illustrated by petitioners' arguments in this case. Their claim that a reasonable officer would not have made this stop is based largely on District of Columbia police regulations which permit plainclothes officers in unmarked vehicles to enforce traffic laws "only in the case of a violation that is so grave as to pose an immediate threat to the safety of others." Metropolitan Police Department-Washington, D.C., General Order 303.1, pt. 1, Objectives and Policies (A)(2)(4) (Apr. 30, 1992), reprinted as Addendum to Brief for Petitioners. This basis of invalidation would not apply in jurisdictions that had a different practice. And it would not have applied even in the District of Columbia, if Officer Soto had been wearing a uniform or patrolling in a marked police cruiser.

Petitioners argue that our cases support insistence upon police adherence to standard practices as an objective means of rooting out pretext. They cite no holding to that effect, and dicta in only two cases. In *Abel* v. *United States,* 362 U.S. 217 (1960), the petitioner had been arrested by the Immigration and Naturalization Service (INS), on the basis of an administrative warrant that, he claimed, had been issued on pretextual grounds in order to enable the Federal Bureau of Investigation (FBI) to search his room after his arrest. We regarded this as an allegation of "serious misconduct," but rejected Abel's claims on the ground that "[a] finding of bad faith is . . . not open to us on th[e] record" in light of the findings below, including the finding that "'the proceedings taken by the [INS] differed in no respect from what would have been done in the case of an individual concerning whom [there was no pending FBI investigation],'" *id.,* at 226–227. But it is a long leap from the proposition that following regular procedures is some evidence of lack of pretext to the proposition that failure to follow regular procedures proves (or is an operational substitute for) pretext. Abel, moreover, did not involve the assertion

that pretext could invalidate a search or seizure for which there was probable cause—and even what it said about pretext in other contexts is plainly inconsistent with the views we later stated in *Robinson, Gustafson, Scott*, and *Villamonte-Marquez*. In the other case claimed to contain supportive dicta, *United States* v. *Robinson*, 414 U.S. 218 (1973), in approving a search incident to an arrest for driving without a license, we noted that the arrest was "not a departure from established police department practice." *Id.*, at 221, n. 1. That was followed, however, by the statement that "[w]e leave for another day questions which would arise on facts different from these." *Ibid.* This is not even a dictum that purports to provide an answer, but merely one that leaves the question open.

III.

In what would appear to be an elaboration on the "reasonable officer" test, petitioners argue that the balancing inherent in any Fourth Amendment inquiry requires us to weigh the governmental and individual interests implicated in a traffic stop such as we have here. That balancing, petitioners claim, does not support investigation of minor traffic infractions by plainclothes police in unmarked vehicles; such investigation only minimally advances the government's interest in traffic safety, and may indeed retard it by producing motorist confusion and alarm—a view said to be supported by the Metropolitan Police Department's own regulations generally prohibiting this practice. And as for the Fourth Amendment interests of the individuals concerned, petitioners point out that our cases acknowledge that even ordinary traffic stops entail "a possibly unsettling show of authority"; that they at best "interfere with freedom of movement, are inconvenient, and consume time" and at worst "may create substantial anxiety," *Prouse*, 440 U.S., at 657. That anxiety is likely to be even more pronounced when the stop is conducted by plainclothes officers in unmarked cars.

It is of course true that in principle every Fourth Amendment case, since it turns upon a "reasonableness" determination, involves a balancing of all relevant factors. With rare exceptions not applicable here, however, the result of that balancing is not in doubt where the search or seizure is based upon probable cause. That is why petitioners must rely upon cases like *Prouse* to provide examples of actual "balancing" analysis. There, the police action in question was a random traffic stop for the purpose of checking a motorist's license and vehicle registration, a practice that—like the practices at issue in the inventory search and administrative inspection cases upon which petitioners rely in making their "pretext" claim—involves police intrusion without the probable cause that is its traditional justification. Our opinion in *Prouse* expressly distinguished the case from a stop based on precisely what is at issue here: "probable cause to believe that a driver is violating any one of the multitude of applicable traffic and equipment regulations." 440 U.S., at 661. It noted approvingly that "[t]he foremost method of enforcing traffic and vehicle safety regulations . . . is acting upon observed violations," *id.*, at 659, which afford the "'quantum of individualized suspicion' " necessary to ensure that police discretion is sufficiently constrained, *id.*, at 654–655 (quoting *United States* v. *Martinez-Fuerte*, 428 U.S., at 560). What is true of *Prouse* is also true of other cases that engaged in detailed "balancing" to decide the constitutionality of automobile stops, such as *Martinez-Fuerte, supra*, which upheld checkpoint stops, see 428 U.S., at 556–562, and *Brignoni-Ponce, supra*, which disallowed so-called "roving patrol" stops, see 422 U.S., at 882–884: the detailed "balancing" analysis was necessary because they involved seizures without probable cause.

Where probable cause has existed, the only cases in which we have found it necessary actually to perform the "balancing" analysis involved searches or seizures conducted in an extraordinary manner, unusually harmful to an individual's privacy or even physical interests—such as, for example, seizure by means of deadly force, see *Tennessee* v. *Garner*, 471 U.S. 1 (1985), unannounced entry into a home, see *Wilson* v. *Arkansas*, 514 U.S. ___ (1995), entry into a home without a warrant, see *Welsh* v. *Wisconsin*, 466 U.S. 740 (1984), or physical penetration of the body, see *Winston* v. *Lee*, 470 U.S. 753 (1985). The making of a traffic stop out-of-uniform does not remotely qualify as such an extreme practice, and so is governed by the usual rule that probable cause to believe the law has been broken "outbalances" private interest in avoiding police contact.

Petitioners urge as an extraordinary factor in this case that the "multitude of applicable traffic and equipment regulations" is so large and so difficult to obey perfectly that virtually everyone is guilty of violation, permitting the police to single out almost whomever they wish for a stop. But we are aware of no principle that would allow us to decide at what point a code of law becomes so expansive and so commonly violated that infraction itself can no longer be the ordinary measure of the lawfulness of enforcement. And even if we could identify such exorbitant codes, we do not know by what standard (or what right) we would decide, as petitioners would have us do, which particular provisions are sufficiently important to merit enforcement.

For the run-of-the-mine case, which this surely is, we think there is no realistic alternative to the traditional common-law rule that probable cause justifies a search and seizure.

Here the District Court found that the officers had probable cause to believe that petitioners had violated the traffic code. That rendered the stop reasonable under the Fourth Amendment, the evidence thereby discovered admissible, and the upholding of the convictions by the Court of Appeals for the District of Columbia Circuit correct.

Judgment affirmed.

WHAT DO *YOU* THINK?

1. What does the Court mean by the statement "Subjective intentions play no role in ordinary, probable-cause Fourth Amendment analysis?"

2. Why does the Court hold that there is no realistic alternative to the traditional common-law rule that probable cause justifies a search and seizure?

Is a temporary detention protected by the Fourth Amendment? The Terry *case looks at this issue and formulates the "stop and frisk" doctrine.*

TERRY V. OHIO
392 U.S. 1 (1968)

MR. CHIEF JUSTICE WARREN delivered the opinion of the Court.

This case presents serious questions concerning the role of the Fourth Amendment in the confrontation on the street between the citizen and the policeman investigating suspicious circumstances.

Chief Justice Earl Warren was appointed to the Supreme Court by President Eisenhower and served from 1954 to 1969. (Photograph by Harris & Ewing. Collection of the Supreme Court of the United States.)

Petitioner Terry was convicted of carrying a concealed weapon and sentenced to the statutorily prescribed term of one to three years in the penitentiary. Following the denial of a pretrial motion to suppress, the prosecution introduced in evidence two revolvers and a number of bullets seized from Terry and a codefendant, Richard Chilton, by Cleveland Police Detective Martin McFadden. At the hearing on the motion to suppress this evidence, Officer McFadden testified that while he was patrolling in plain clothes in downtown Cleveland at approximately 2:30 in the afternoon of October 31, 1963, his attention was attracted by two men, Chilton and Terry, standing on the corner of Huron Road and Euclid Avenue. He had never seen the two men before, and he was unable to say precisely what first drew his eye to them. However, he testified that he had been a policeman for 39 years and a detective for 35 and that he had been assigned to patrol this vicinity of downtown Cleveland for shoplifters and pickpockets for 30 years. He explained that he had developed routine habits of observation over the years and that he would "stand and watch people or walk and watch people at many intervals of the day." He added: "Now, in this case when I looked over they didn't look right to me at the time."

His interest aroused, Officer McFadden took up a post of observation in the entrance to a store 300 to 400 feet away from the two men. "I get more purpose to

watch them when I seen their movements," he testified. He saw one of the men leave the other one and walk southwest on Huron Road, past some stores. The man paused for a moment and looked in a store window, then walked on a short distance, turned around and walked back toward the corner, pausing once again to look in the same store window. He rejoined his companion at the corner, and the two conferred briefly. Then the second man went through the same series of motions, strolling down Huron Road, looking in the same window, walking on a short distance, turning back, peering in the store window again, and returning to confer with the first man at the corner. The two men repeated this ritual alternately between five and six times apiece—in all, roughly a dozen trips. At one point, while the two were standing together on the corner, a third man approached them and engaged them briefly in conversation. This man then left the two others and walked west on Euclid Avenue. Chilton and Terry resumed their measured pacing, peering, and conferring. After this had gone on for 10 to 12 minutes, the two men walked off together, heading west on Euclid Avenue, following the path taken earlier by the third man.

By this time Officer McFadden had become thoroughly suspicious. He testified that after observing their elaborately casual and oft-repeated reconnaissance of the store window on Huron Road, he suspected the two men of "casing a job, a stick-up," and that he considered it his duty as a police officer to investigate further. He added that he feared "they may have a gun." Thus, Officer McFadden followed Chilton and Terry and saw them stop in front of Zucker's store to talk to the same man who had conferred with them earlier on the street corner. Deciding that the situation was ripe for direct action. Officer McFadden approached the three men, identified himself as a police officer and asked for their names. At this point his knowledge was confined to what he had observed. He was not acquainted with any of the three men by name or by sight, and he had received no information concerning them from any other source. When the men "mumbled something" in response to his inquiries, Officer McFadden grabbed petitioner Terry, spun him around so that they were facing the other two, with Terry between McFadden and the others, and patted down the outside of his clothing. In the left breast pocket of Terry's overcoat Officer McFadden felt a pistol. He reached inside the overcoat pocket, but was unable to remove the gun. At this point, keeping Terry between himself and the others, the officer ordered all three men to enter Zucker's store. As they went in, he removed Terry's overcoat completely, removed a .38-caliber revolver from the pocket and ordered all three men to face the wall with their hands raised. Officer McFadden proceeded to pat down the outer clothing of Chilton and the third man, Katz. He discovered another revolver in the outer pocket of Chilton's overcoat, but no weapons were found on Katz. The officer testified that he only patted the men down to see whether they had weapons, and that he did not put his hands beneath the outer garments of either Terry or Chilton until he felt their guns. So far as appears from the record, he never placed his hands beneath Katz' outer garments. Officer McFadden seized Chilton's gun, asked the proprietor of the store to call a police wagon, and took all three men to the station, where Chilton and Terry were formally charged with carrying concealed weapons. . . .

I.

The Fourth Amendment provides that "the right of the people to be secure in their persons, houses, papers, and effects, against unreasonable searches and seizures, shall not be violated. . . ." This inestimable right of personal security belongs as much to the citizen on the streets of our cities as to the homeowner closeted in his

study to dispose of his secret affairs. For, as this Court has always recognized, "No right is held more sacred, or is more carefully guarded, by the common law, than the right of every individual to the possession and control of his own person, free from all restraint or interference of others, unless by clear and unquestionable authority of law."

We have recently held that "the Fourth Amendment protects people, not places," *Katz* v. *United States*, 389 U.S. 347, 351 (1967), and wherever an individual may harbor a reasonable "expectation of privacy," *id.*, at 361 (MR. JUSTICE HARLAN, concurring), he is entitled to be free from unreasonable governmental intrusion. Of course, the specific content and incidents of this right must be shaped by the context in which it is asserted. For "what the Constitution forbids is not all searches and seizures, but unreasonable searches and seizures." *Elkins* v. *United States*, 364 U.S. 206, 222 (1960). Unquestionably petitioner was entitled to the protection of the Fourth Amendment as he walked down the street in Cleveland. . . . The question is whether in all the circumstances of this on-the-street encounter, his right to personal security was violated by an unreasonable search and seizure.

We would be less than candid if we did not acknowledge that this question thrusts to the fore difficult and troublesome issues regarding a sensitive area of police activity—issues which have never before been squarely presented to this Court. Reflective of the tensions involved are the practical and constitutional arguments pressed with great vigor on both sides of the public debate over the power of the police to "stop and frisk"—as it is sometimes euphemistically termed—suspicious persons.

On the one hand, it is frequently argued that in dealing with the rapidly unfolding and often dangerous situations on city streets, the police are in need of an escalating set of flexible responses, graduated in relation to the amount of information they possess. For this purpose it is urged that distinctions should be made between a "stop" and an "arrest" (or a "seizure" of a person), and between a "frisk" and a "search." Thus, it is argued, the police should be allowed to "stop" a person and detain him briefly for questioning upon suspicion that he may be connected with criminal activity. Upon suspicion that the person may be armed, the police should have the power to "frisk" him for weapons. If the "stop" and the "frisk" give rise to probable cause to believe that the suspect has committed a crime, then the police should be empowered to make a formal "arrest," and a full incident "search" of the person. This scheme is justified in part upon the notion that a "stop" and a "frisk" amount to a mere "minor inconvenience and petty indignity," which can properly be imposed upon the citizen in the interest of effective law enforcement on the basis of a police officer's suspicion.

On the other side the argument is made that the authority of the police must be strictly circumscribed by the law of arrest and search as it has developed to date in the traditional jurisprudence of the Fourth Amendment. It is contended with some force that there is not—and cannot be—a variety of police activity which does not depend solely upon the voluntary cooperation of the citizen and yet which stops short of an arrest based upon probable cause to make such an arrest. The heart of the Fourth Amendment, the argument runs, is a severe requirement of specific justification for any intrusion upon protected personal security, coupled with a highly developed system of judicial controls to enforce upon the agents of the State the commands of the Constitution. Acquiescence by the courts in the compulsion inherent in the field interrogation practices at issue here, it is urged, would constitute an abdication of judicial control over, and indeed an encouragement of, substantial interference with liberty and personal security by police officers whose

judgment is necessarily colored by their primary involvement in "the often competitive enterprise of ferreting out crime." *Johnson* v. *United States*, 333 U.S. 10, 14 (1948). This, it is argued, can only serve to exacerbate police–community tensions in the crowded centers of our Nation's cities.

In this context, we approach the issues in this case mindful of the limitations of the judicial function in controlling the myriad daily situations in which policemen and citizens confront each other on the street. The State has characterized the issue here as "the right of a police officer . . . to make an on-the-street stop, interrogate and pat down for weapons (known in street vernacular as 'stop and frisk')." But this is only partly accurate. For the issue is not the abstract propriety of the police conduct, but the admissibility against petitioner of the evidence uncovered by the search and seizure. Ever since its inception, the rule excluding evidence seized in violation of the Fourth Amendment has been recognized as a principal mode of discouraging lawless police conduct. Thus its major thrust is a deterrent one and experience has taught that it is the only effective deterrent to police misconduct in the criminal context, and that without it the constitutional guarantee against unreasonable searches and seizures would be a mere "form of words." *Mapp* v. *Ohio*, 367 U.S. 643, 655 (1961). The rule also serves another vital function—"the imperative of judicial integrity." Courts which sit under our Constitution cannot and will not be made party to lawless invasions of the constitutional rights of citizens by permitting unhindered governmental use of the fruits of such invasions. Thus in our system evidentiary rulings provide the context in which the judicial process of inclusion and exclusion approves some conduct as comporting with constitutional guarantees and disapproves other actions by state agents. A ruling admitting evidence in a criminal trial, we recognize, has the necessary effect of legitimizing the conduct which produced the evidence, while an application of the exclusionary rule withholds the constitutional imprimatur.

The exclusionary rule has its limitations, however, as a tool of judicial control. It cannot properly be invoked to exclude the products of legitimate police investigative techniques on the ground that much conduct which is closely similar involves unwarranted intrusions upon constitutional protections. Moreover, in some contexts the rule is ineffective as a deterrent. Street encounters between citizens and police officers are incredibly rich in diversity. They range from wholly friendly exchanges of pleasantries or mutually useful information to hostile confrontations of armed men involving arrests, or injuries, or loss of life. Moreover, hostile confrontations are not all of a piece. Some of them begin in a friendly enough manner, only to take a different turn upon the injection of some unexpected element into the conversation. Encounters are initiated by the police for a wide variety of purposes, some of which are wholly unrelated to a desire to prosecute for crime. Doubtless some police "field interrogation" conduct violates the Fourth Amendment. But a stern refusal by this Court to condone such activity does not necessarily render it responsive to the exclusionary rule. Regardless of how effective the rule may be where obtaining convictions is an important objective of the police, it is powerless to deter invasions of constitutionally guaranteed rights where the police either have no interest in prosecuting or are willing to forgo successful prosecution in the interest of serving some other goal.

Proper adjudication of cases in which the exclusionary rule is invoked demands a constant awareness of these limitations. The wholesale harassment by certain elements of the police community, of which minority groups. . . . will not be stopped by the exclusion of any evidence from any criminal trial. Yet a rigid and unthinking application of the exclusionary rule, in futile protest against practices which it

can never be used effectively to control, may exact a high toll in human injury and frustration of efforts to prevent crime. No judicial opinion can comprehend the protean variety of the street encounter, and we can only judge the facts of the case before us. Nothing we say today is to be taken as indicating approval of police conduct outside the legitimate investigative sphere. Under our decision, courts still retain their traditional responsibility to guard against police conduct which is overbearing or harassing, or which trenches upon personal security without the objective evidentiary justification which the Constitution requires. When such conduct is identified, it must be condemned by the judiciary and its fruits must be excluded from evidence in criminal trials. And, of course, our approval of legitimate and restrained investigative conduct undertaken on the basis of ample factual justification should in no way discourage the employment of other remedies than the exclusionary rule to curtail abuses for which that sanction may prove inappropriate.

Having thus roughly sketched the perimeters of the constitutional debate over the limits on police investigative conduct in general and the background against which this case presents itself, we turn our attention to the quite narrow question posed by the facts before us: whether it is always unreasonable for a policeman to seize a person and subject him to a limited search for weapons unless there is probable cause for an arrest. Given the narrowness of this question, we have no occasion to canvass in detail the constitutional limitations upon the scope of a policeman's power when he confronts a citizen without probable cause to arrest him.

II.

Our first task is to establish at what point in this encounter the Fourth Amendment becomes relevant. That is, we must decide whether and when Officer McFadden "seized" Terry and whether and when he conducted a "search." There is some suggestion in the use of such terms as "stop" and "frisk" that such police conduct is outside the purview of the Fourth Amendment because neither action rises to the level of a "search" or "seizure" within the meaning of the Constitution. We emphatically reject this notion. It is quite plain that the Fourth Amendment governs "seizures" of the person which do not eventuate in a trip to the station house and prosecution for crime—"arrests" in traditional terminology. It must be recognized that whenever a police officer accosts an individual and restrains his freedom to walk away, he has "seized" that person. And it is nothing less than sheer torture of the English language to suggest that a careful exploration of the outer surfaces of a person's clothing all over his or her body in an attempt to find weapons is not a "search." Moreover, it is simply fantastic to urge that such a procedure performed in public by a policeman while the citizen stands helpless, perhaps facing a wall with his hands raised, is a "petty indignity." It is a serious intrusion upon the sanctity of the person, which may inflict great indignity and arouse strong resentment, and it is not to be undertaken lightly.

The danger in the logic which proceeds upon distinctions between a "stop" and an "arrest," or "seizure" of the person, and between a "frisk" and a "search" is twofold. It seeks to isolate from constitutional scrutiny the initial stages of the contact between the policeman and the citizen. And by suggesting a rigid all-or-nothing model of justification and regulation under the Amendment, it obscures the utility of limitations upon the scope, as well as the initiation, of police action as a means of constitutional regulation. This Court has held in the past that a search which is reasonable at its inception may violate the Fourth Amendment by virtue of its intolerable intensity and scope. The scope of the search must be "strictly tied to and justified by" the circumstances which rendered its initiation permissible.

The distinctions of classical "stop-and-frisk" theory thus serve to divert attention from the central inquiry under the Fourth Amendment—the reasonableness in all the circumstances of the particular governmental invasion of a citizen's personal security. "Search" and "seizure" are not talismans. We therefore reject the notions that the Fourth Amendment does not come into play at all as a limitation upon police conduct if the officers stop short of something called a "technical arrest" or a "full-blown search."

In this case there can be no question, then, that Officer McFadden "seized" petitioner and subjected him to a "search" when he took hold of him and patted down the outer surfaces of his clothing. We must decide whether at that point it was reasonable for Officer McFadden to have interfered with petitioner's personal security as he did. And in determining whether the seizure and search were "unreasonable" our inquiry is a dual one—whether the officer's action was justified at its inception, and whether it was reasonably related in scope to the circumstances which justified the interference in the first place.

III.

If this case involved police conduct subject to the Warrant Clause of the Fourth Amendment, we would have to ascertain whether "probable cause" existed to justify the search and seizure which took place. However, that is not the case. We do not retreat from our holdings that the police must, whenever practicable, obtain advance judicial approval of searches and seizures through the warrant procedure . . . or that in most instances failure to comply with the warrant requirement can only be excused by exigent circumstances. . . . But we deal here with an entire rubric of police conduct—necessarily swift action predicated upon the on-the-spot observations of the officer on the beat—which historically has not been, and as a practical matter could not be, subjected to the warrant procedure. Instead, the conduct involved in this case must be tested by the Fourth Amendment's general proscription against unreasonable searches and seizures.

Nonetheless, the notions which underlie both the warrant procedure and the requirement of probable cause remain fully relevant in this context. In order to assess the reasonableness of Officer McFadden's conduct as a general proposition, it is necessary "first to focus upon the governmental interest which allegedly justifies official intrusion upon the constitutionally protected interests of the private citizen," for there is "no ready test for determining reasonableness other than by balancing the need to search [or seize] against the invasion which the search [or seizure] entails." And in justifying the particular intrusion the police officer must be able to point to specific and articulable facts which, taken together with rational inferences from those facts, reasonably warrant that intrusion. The scheme of the Fourth Amendment becomes meaningful only when it is assured that at some point the conduct of those charged with enforcing the laws can be subjected to the more detached, neutral scrutiny of a judge who must evaluate the reasonableness of a particular search or seizure in light of the particular circumstances. And in making that assessment it is imperative that the facts be judged against an objective standard: would the facts available to the officer at the moment of the seizure or the search "warrant a man of reasonable caution in the belief" that the action taken was appropriate? Anything less would invite intrusions upon constitutionally guaranteed rights based on nothing more substantial than inarticulate hunches, a result this

Court has consistently refused to sanction. subjective good faith alone were the test, the protections of the Fourth Amendment would evaporate, and the people would be 'secure in their persons, houses, papers, and effects,' only in the discretion of the police." *Beck* v. *Ohio*, *supra*, at 97.

Applying these principles to this case, we consider first the nature and extent of the governmental interests involved. One general interest is of course that of effective crime prevention and detection; it is this interest which underlies the recognition that a police officer may in appropriate circumstances and in an appropriate manner approach a person for purposes of investigating possibly criminal behavior even though there is no probable cause to make an arrest. It was this legitimate investigative function Officer McFadden was discharging when he decided to approach petitioner and his companions. He had observed Terry, Chilton, and Katz go through a series of acts, each of them perhaps innocent in itself, but which taken together warranted further investigation. There is nothing unusual in two men standing together on a street corner, perhaps waiting for someone. Nor is there anything suspicious about people in such circumstances strolling up and down the street, singly or in pairs. Store windows, moreover, are made to be looked in. But the story in quite different where, as here, two men hover about a street corner for an extended period of time, at the end of which it becomes apparent that they are not waiting for anyone or anything; where these men pace alternately along an identical route, pausing to stare in the same store window roughly 24 times; where each completion of this route is followed immediately by a conference between the two men on the corner; where they are joined in one of these conferences by a third man who leaves swiftly; and where the two men finally follow the third and rejoin him a couple of blocks away. It would have been poor police work indeed for an officer of 30 years' experience in the detection of thievery from stores in this same neighborhood to have failed to investigate this behavior further.

The crux of this case, however, is not the propriety of Officer McFadden's taking steps to investigate petitioner's suspicious behavior, but rather, whether there was justification for McFadden's invasion of Terry's personal security by searching him for weapons in the course of that investigation. We are now concerned with more than the governmental interest in investigating crime; in addition, there is the more immediate interest of the police officer in taking steps to assure himself that the person with whom he is dealing is not armed with a weapon that could unexpectedly and fatally be used against him. Certainly it would be unreasonable to require that police officers take unnecessary risks in the performance of their duties. American criminals have a long tradition of armed violence, and every year in this country many law enforcement officers are killed in the line of duty, and thousands more are wounded. Virtually all of these deaths and a substantial portion of the injuries are inflicted with guns and knives.

In view of these facts, we cannot blind ourselves to the need for law enforcement officers to protect themselves and other prospective victims of violence in situations where they may lack probable cause for an arrest. When an officer is justified in believing that the individual whose suspicious behavior he is investigating at close range is armed and presently dangerous to the officer or to others, it would appear to be clearly unreasonable to deny the officer the power to take necessary measures to determine whether the person is in fact carrying a weapon and to neutralize the threat of physical harm.

We must still consider, however, the nature and quality of the intrusion on individual rights which must be accepted if police officers are to be conceded the right to search for weapons in situations where probable cause to arrest for crime

is lacking. Even a limited search of the outer clothing for weapons constitutes a severe, though brief, intrusion upon cherished personal security, and it must surely be an annoying, frightening, and perhaps humiliating experience. Petitioner contends that such an intrusion is permissible only incident to a lawful arrest, either for a crime involving the possession of weapons or for a crime the commission of which led the officer to investigate in the first place. However, this argument must be closely examined.

Petitioner does not argue that a police officer should refrain from making any investigation of suspicious circumstances until such time as he has probable cause to make an arrest; nor does he deny that police officers in properly discharging their investigative function may find themselves confronting persons who might well be armed and dangerous. Moreover, he does not say that an officer is always unjustified in searching a suspect to discover weapons. Rather, he says it is unreasonable for the policeman to take that step until such time as the situation evolves to a point where there is probable cause to make an arrest. When that point has been reached, petitioner would concede the officer's right to conduct a search of the suspect for weapons, fruits or instrumentalities of the crime, or "mere" evidence, incident to the arrest.

There are two weaknesses in this line of reasoning, however. First, it fails to take account of traditional limitations upon the scope of searches, and thus recognizes no distinction in purpose, character, and extent between a search incident to an arrest and a limited search for weapons. The former, although justified in part by the acknowledged necessity to protect the arresting officer from assault with a concealed weapon, *Preston* v. *United States*, 376 U.S. 364, 367 (1964), is also justified on other grounds, *ibid.*, and can therefore involve a relatively extensive exploration of the person. A search for weapons in the absence of probable cause to arrest, however, must, like any other search, be strictly circumscribed by the exigencies which justify its initiation. Thus it must be limited to that which is necessary for the discovery of weapons which might be used to harm the officer or others nearby, and may realistically be characterized as something less than a "full" search, even though it remains a serious intrusion. A second, and related, objection to petitioner's argument is that it assumes that the law of arrest has already worked out the balance between the particular interests involved here—the neutralization of danger to the policeman in the investigative circumstance and the sanctity of the individual. But this is not so. An arrest is a wholly different kind of intrusion upon individual freedom from a limited search for weapons, and the interests each is designed to serve are likewise quite different. An arrest is the initial stage of a criminal prosecution. It is intended to vindicate society's interest in having its laws obeyed, and it is inevitably accompanied by future interference with the individual's freedom of movement, whether or not trial or conviction ultimately follows. The protective search for weapons, on the other hand, constitutes a brief, though far from inconsiderable, intrusion upon the sanctity of the person. It does not follow that because an officer may lawfully arrest a person only when he is apprised of facts sufficient to warrant a belief that the person has committed or is committing a crime, the officer is equally unjustified, absent that kind of evidence, in making any intrusions short of an arrest. Moreover, a perfectly reasonable apprehension of danger may arise long before the officer is possessed of adequate information to justify taking a person into custody for the purpose of prosecuting him for a crime. Petitioner's reliance on cases which have worked out standards of reasonableness with regard to "seizures" constituting arrests and searches incident thereto is thus misplaced. It assumes that the interests sought to be vindicated and the invasions of personal security may be equated in the two cases, and thereby ignores a vital aspect of the analysis of the reasonableness of particular types of conduct under the Fourth Amendment.

Our evaluation of the proper balance that has to be struck in this type of case leads us to conclude that there must be a narrowly drawn authority to permit a reasonable search for weapons for the protection of the police officer, where he has reason to believe that he is dealing with an armed and dangerous individual, regardless of whether he has probable cause to arrest the individual for a crime. The officer need not be absolutely certain that the individual is armed; the issue is whether a reasonably prudent man in the circumstances would be warranted in the belief that his safety or that of others was in danger. And in determining whether the officer acted reasonably in such circumstances, due weight must be given, not to his inchoate and unparticularized suspicion or "hunch," but to the specific reasonable inferences which he is entitled to draw from the facts in light of his experience.

IV.

We must now examine the conduct of Officer McFadden in this case to determine whether his search and seizure of petitioner were reasonable, both at their inception and as conducted. He had observed Terry, together with Chilton and another man, acting in a manner he took to be preface to a "stick-up." We think that based on the facts and circumstances Officer McFadden detailed before the trial judge a reasonably prudent man would have been warranted in believing petitioner was armed and thus presented a threat to the officer's safety while he was investigating his suspicious behavior. The actions of Terry and Chilton were consistent with McFadden's hypothesis that these men were contemplating a daylight robbery—which, it is reasonable to assume, would be likely to involve the use of weapons—and nothing in their conduct from the time he first noticed them until the time he confronted them and identified himself as a police officer gave him sufficient reason to negate that hypothesis. Although the trio had departed the original scene, there was nothing to indicate abandonment of an intent to commit a robbery at some point. Thus, when Officer McFadden approached the three men gathered before the display window at Zucker's store he had observed enough to make it quite reasonable to fear that they were armed; and nothing in their response to his hailing them, identifying himself as a police officer, and asking their names served to dispel that reasonable belief. We cannot say his decision at that point to seize Terry and pat his clothing for weapons was the product of a volatile or inventive imagination, or was undertaken simply as an act of harassment; the record evidences the tempered act of a policeman who in the course of an investigation had to make a quick decision as to how to protect himself and others from possible danger, and took limited steps to do so.

The manner in which the seizure and search were conducted is, of course, as vital a part of the inquiry as whether they were warranted at all. The Fourth Amendment proceeds as much by limitations upon the scope of governmental action as by imposing preconditions upon its initiation. Compare *Katz* v. *United States*, 389 U.S. 347, 354–356 (1967). The entire deterrent purpose of the rule excluding evidence seized in violation of the Fourth Amendment rests on the assumption that "limitations upon the fruit to be gathered tend to limit the quest itself." . . . Thus, evidence may not be introduced if it was discovered by means of a seizure and search which were not reasonably related in scope to the justification for their initiation. We need not develop at length in this case, however, the limitations which the Fourth Amendment places upon a protective seizure and search for weapons. These limitations will have to be developed in the concrete factual circumstances of individual cases. See *Sibron* v. *New York*, post, p. 40, decided today. Suffice it to note that such a search, unlike a search without a warrant incident to a lawful arrest, is not justified by any need to prevent the disappearance or destruction of evidence of crime. See *Preston* v. *United States*, 376 U.S. 364, 367 (1964). The sole justification of the search in the present situation is the protection of the police officer and others nearby, and it must therefore be confined in scope to an intrusion reasonably designed to discover guns, knives, clubs, or other hidden instruments for the assault of the police officer. . . .

Affirmed.

[The concurring opinions of JUSTICES BLACK, HARLAN, and WHITE and the dissenting opinion of JUSTICE MARSHALL are omitted.]

WHAT DO *YOU* THINK?

1. Should the police have a right to pat down someone without probable cause?
2. When the officer grabbed Terry and turned him around, did this amount to a seizure?
3. What is required before you may stop and question a citizen?
4. What is required additionally before a citizen may be patted down?
5. What are the limits of the pat down?

Is it possible to articulate what "reasonable suspicion" and "probable cause" mean? The Supreme Court looks at this problem in the Ornelas case.

ORNELAS ET AL. V. UNITED STATES
134 L.Ed. 2d 911 (1996)

The facts are not disputed. In the early morning of a December day in 1992, Detective Michael Pautz, a 20-year veteran of the Milwaukee County Sheriff's Department with 2 years specializing in drug enforcement, was conducting drug-interdiction surveillance in downtown Milwaukee. Pautz noticed a 1981 two-door Oldsmobile with California license plates in a motel parking lot. The car attracted Pautz's attention for two reasons: because older model, two-door General Motors cars are a favorite with drug couriers because it is easy to hide things in them; and because California is a "source State" for drugs. Detective Pautz radioed his dispatcher to inquire about the car's registration. The dispatcher informed Pautz that the owner was either Miguel Ledesma Ornelas or Miguel Ornelas Ledesma from San Jose, California; Pautz was unsure which name the dispatcher gave. Detective Pautz checked the motel registry and learned that an Ismael Ornelas accompanied by a second man had registered at 4:00 a.m., without reservations.

Pautz called for his partner, Donald Hurrle, a detective with approximately 25 years of law enforcement experience, assigned for the past 6 years to the drug enforcement unit. When Hurrle arrived at the scene, the officers contacted the local

office of the Drug Enforcement Administration (DEA) and asked DEA personnel to run the names Miguel Ledesma Ornelas and Ismael Ornelas through the Narcotics and Dangerous Drugs Information System (NADDIS), a federal database of known and suspected drug traffickers. Both names appeared in NADDIS. The NADDIS report identified Miguel Ledesma Ornelas as a heroin dealer from El Centro, California, and Ismael Ornelas, Jr. as a cocaine dealer from Tucson, Arizona. The officers then summoned Deputy Luedke and the department's drug-sniffing dog, Merlin. Upon their arrival, Detective Pautz left for another assignment. Detective Hurrle informed Luedke of what they knew and together they waited.

Sometime later, petitioners emerged from the motel and got into the Oldsmobile. Detective Hurrle approached the car, identified himself as a police officer, and inquired whether they had any illegal drugs or contraband. Petitioners answered "No." Hurrle then asked for identification and was given two California driver's licenses bearing the names Saul Ornelas and Ismael Ornelas. Hurrle asked them if he could search the car and petitioners consented. The men appeared calm, but Ismael was shaking somewhat. Deputy Luedke, who over the past nine years had searched approximately 2,000 cars for narcotics, searched the Oldsmobile's interior. He noticed that a panel above the right rear passenger armrest felt somewhat loose and suspected that the panel might have been removed and contraband hidden inside. Luedke would testify later that a screw in the door jam adjacent to the loose panel was rusty, which to him meant that the screw had been removed at some time. Luedke dismantled the panel and discovered two kilograms of cocaine. Petitioners were arrested.

Petitioners filed pretrial motions to suppress, alleging that the police officers violated their Fourth Amendment rights when the officers detained them in the parking lot and when Deputy Luedke searched inside the panel without a warrant. The Government conceded in the court below that when the officers approached petitioners in the parking lot, a reasonable person would not have felt free to leave, so the encounter was an investigatory stop. See 16 F. 3d 714, 716 (CA7 1994). An investigatory stop is permissible under the Fourth Amendment if supported by reasonable suspicion, *Terry* v. *Ohio*, 392 U.S. 1 (1968), and a warrantless search of a car is valid if based on probable cause, *California* v. *Acevedo*, 500 U.S. 565, 569–570 (1991).

After conducting an evidentiary hearing, the Magistrate Judge concluded that the circumstances gave the officers reasonable suspicion, but not probable cause. The Magistrate found, as a finding of fact, that there was no rust on the screw and hence concluded that Deputy Luedke had an insufficient basis to conclude that drugs would be found within the panel. The Magistrate nonetheless recommended that the District Court deny the suppression motions because he thought, given the presence of the drug-sniffing dog, that the officers would have found the cocaine by lawful means eventually and therefore the drugs were admissible under the inevitable discovery doctrine. See *Nix* v. *Williams*, 467 U.S. 431 (1984).

The District Court adopted the Magistrate's recommendation with respect to reasonable suspicion, but not its reasoning as to probable cause. The District Court thought that the model, age, and source-State origin of the car, and the fact that two men traveling together checked into a motel at 4 o'clock in the morning without reservations, formed a drug-courier profile and that this profile together with the NADDIS reports gave rise to reasonable suspicion of drug-trafficking activity; in the court's view, reasonable suspicion became probable cause when Deputy Luedke found the loose panel. Accordingly, the court ruled that the cocaine need not be excluded.

On remand, the Magistrate Judge expressly found the testimony credible. The District Court accepted the finding, and once again ruled that probable cause supported the search. The Seventh Circuit held that determination not clearly erroneous. . . .

We granted *certiorari* to resolve the conflict among the Circuits over the applicable standard of appellate review. . . .

Articulating precisely what "reasonable suspicion" and "probable cause" mean is not possible. They are commonsense, nontechnical conceptions that deal with " 'the factual and practical considerations of everyday life on which reasonable and prudent men, not legal technicians, act.' " *Illinois* v. *Gates*, 462 U.S. 213, 231 (1983) (quoting *Brinegar* v. *United States*, 338 U.S. 160, 176 [1949]); see *United States* v. *Sokolow*, 490 U.S. 1, 7–8 (1989). As such, the standards are "not readily, or even usefully, reduced to a neat set of legal rules." *Gates, supra,* at 232. We have described reasonable suspicion simply as "a particularized and objective basis" for suspecting the person stopped of criminal activity, *United States* v. *Cortez*, 449 U.S. 411, 417–418 (1981), and probable cause to search as existing where the known facts and circumstances are sufficient to warrant a man of reasonable prudence in the belief that contraband or evidence of a crime will be found, see *Brinegar, supra,* at 175–176; *Gates, supra,* at 238. We have cautioned that these two legal principles are not "finely-tuned standards," comparable to the standards of proof beyond a reasonable doubt or of proof by a preponderance of the evidence. *Gates, supra,* at 235. They are instead fluid concepts that take their substantive content from the particular contexts in which the standards are being assessed. *Gates, supra,* at 232; *Brinegar, supra,* at 175 ("The standard of proof [for probable cause] is . . . correlative to what must be proved"); *Ker* v. *California,* 374 U.S. 23, 33 (1963) ("This Cour[t] [has a] long-established recognition that standards of reasonableness under the Fourth Amendment are not susceptible of Procrustean application"; "[e]ach case is to be decided on its own facts and circumstances" [internal quotation marks omitted]); *Terry* v. *Ohio, supra,* at 29 (the limitations imposed by the Fourth Amendment "will have to be developed in the concrete factual circumstances of individual cases").

The principal components of a determination of reasonable suspicion or probable cause will be the events which occurred leading up to the stop or search, and then the decision whether these historical facts, viewed from the standpoint of an objectively reasonable police officer, amount to reasonable suspicion or to probable cause. The first part of the analysis involves only a determination of historical facts, but the second is a mixed question of law and fact: "[T]he historical facts are admitted or established, the rule of law is undisputed, and the issue is whether the facts satisfy the [relevant] statutory [or constitutional] standard, or to put it another way, whether the rule of law as applied to the established facts is or is not violated." *Pullman-Standard* v. *Swint,* 456 U.S. 273, 289, n. 19 (1982).

We think independent appellate review of these ultimate determinations of reasonable suspicion and probable cause is consistent with the position we have taken in past cases. We have never, when reviewing a probable-cause or reasonable-suspicion determination ourselves, expressly deferred to the trial court's determination. See, e.g., *Brinegar, supra* (rejecting district court's conclusion that the police lacked probable cause); *Alabama* v. *White,* 496 U.S. 325 (1990) (conducting independent review and finding reasonable suspicion). A policy of sweeping deference would permit, "[i]n the absence of any significant difference in the facts," "the Fourth Amendment's incidence [to] tur[n] on whether different trial judges draw general conclusions that the facts are sufficient or insufficient to constitute probable cause." *Brinegar, supra,* at 171. Such varied results would be inconsistent with the idea of a unitary system of law. This, if a matter-of-course, would be unacceptable.

It is true that because the mosaic which is analyzed for a reasonable-suspicion or probable-cause inquiry is multi-faceted, "one determination will seldom be a useful 'precedent' for another," *Gates, supra,* at 238, n. 11. But there are exceptions. For instance, the circumstances in *Brinegar, supra,* and *Carroll v. United States,* 267 U. S. 132 (1925), were so alike that we concluded that reversing the Circuit Court's decision in *Brinegar* was necessary to be faithful to *Carroll. Brinegar, supra,* at 178 ("Nor . . . can we find in the present facts any substantial basis for distinguishing this case from the *Carroll* case"). We likewise recognized the similarity of facts in *United States v. Sokolow,* 490 U.S. 1 (1989) and *Florida v. Royer,* 460 U.S. 491 (1983) (in both cases, the defendant traveled under an assumed name; paid for an airline ticket in cash with a number of small bills; traveled from Miami, a source city for illicit drugs; and appeared nervous in the airport). The same was true both in *United States v. Ross,* 456 U.S. 798 (1982) and *California v. Acevedo,* 500 U.S. 565 (1991), see *id.,* at 572 ("The facts in this case closely resemble the facts in *Ross*"); and in *United States v. Mendenhall,* 446 U.S. 544 (1980), and *Reid v. Georgia,* 448 U.S. 438 (1980), see *id.,* at 443 (POWELL, J., concurring) ("facts [in *Mendenhall*] [are] remarkably similar to those in the present case"). And even where one case may not squarely control another one, the two decisions when viewed together may usefully add to the body of law on the subject.

. . . We . . . hold that as a general matter determinations of reasonable suspicion and probable cause should be reviewed *de novo* on appeal. Having said this, we hasten to point out that a reviewing court should take care both to review findings of historical fact only for clear error and to give due weight to inferences drawn from those facts by resident judges and local law enforcement officers.

A trial judge views the facts of a particular case in light of the distinctive features and events of the community; likewise a police officer views the facts through the lens of his police experience and expertise. The background facts provide a context for the historical facts, and when seen together yield inferences that deserve deference. For example, what may not amount to reasonable suspicion at a motel located alongside a transcontinental highway at the height of the summer tourist season may rise to that level in December in Milwaukee. That city is unlikely to have been an overnight stop selected at the last minute by a traveler coming from California to points east. The 85-mile width of Lake Michigan blocks any further eastward progress. And while the city's salubrious summer climate and seasonal attractions bring many tourists at that time of year, the same is not true in December. Milwaukee's average daily high temperature in that month is 31 degrees and its average daily low is 17 degrees; the percentage of possible sunshine is only 38 percent. It is a reasonable inference that a Californian stopping in Milwaukee in December is either there to transact business or to visit family or friends. The background facts, though rarely the subject of explicit findings, inform the judge's assessment of the historical facts.

In a similar vein, our cases have recognized that a police officer may draw inferences based on his own experience in deciding whether probable cause exists. See, e.g., *United States v. Ortiz,* 422 U.S. 891, 897 (1975). To a layman the sort of loose panel below the back seat arm rest in the automobile involved in this case may suggest only wear and tear, but to Officer Luedke, who had searched roughly 2,000 cars for narcotics, it suggested that drugs may be secreted inside the panel. An appeals court should give due weight to a trial court's finding that the officer was credible and the inference was reasonable.

We vacate the judgments and remand the case to the Court of Appeals to review *de novo* the District Court's determinations that the officer had reasonable suspicion and probable cause in this case.

It is so ordered.

JUSTICE SCALIA, dissenting. [Omitted]

WHAT DO YOU THINK?

1. Does the above case provide you with an understanding of the meaning of *reasonable suspicion* and *probable cause?*

2. Do you agree with the Court that the standards are not reducible to a neat set of legal rules?

3. In your opinion, what is the key difference between reasonable suspicion and probable cause?

SUMMARY

- If the governmental intrusion is considered a search, two additional issues should be considered—first, is a warrant needed? and second, is probable cause needed? Some searches do not need a warrant, but probable cause must be present, i.e., automobile searches.

- Plain view is not considered as a search. If something can be observed from an area opened to the public there has been no search. To be a search, there must be a violation of the reasonable expectation of privacy. Once contraband located in a private area is observed from a public area, the police may need a warrant to seize the property.

- The U.S. Supreme Court has held that "open fields" are not protected by the Fourth Amendment. Accordingly, police officers may enter and search unoccupied or undeveloped areas. The rationale for the open fields doctrine is that only "homes, persons, effects and papers" are protected by the Fourth Amendment and there is a lesser expectation of privacy in open fields.

- Any person entering the United States is subject to search, i.e., visitors, employees, transportation workers, and citizens re-entering the United States. The border area is any place that is the "functional equivalent" or the border, e.g., first airport where the plane lands or established inspection stations near borders.

- Health and safety inspections are different from normal searches and seizures in that their primary purpose is for reasons other than to discover evidence of criminal activity. They are, however, subject to the limitations set forth in the Fourth Amendment.

- Generally a warrant is not required for administrative/code inspections when the business is closely regulated if the interest served by the regulations advance a substantial societal interest, i.e., to protect the health or safety of employees or that the warrantless entries are necessary to enforce the regulations.

- A person may waive his or her constitutional rights and consent to a search. To constitute "consent," there must be a voluntary, duress-free permission to search. The question of whether the consent is voluntary depends on all the surrounding circumstances.

- The protections of the Fourth Amendment are personal. A defendant cannot raise the Fourth Amendment objection unless he or she demonstrates that his or her rights under the amendment were violated.

- The two most frequent situations in which the police are allowed to search without a warrant, but with probable cause (unless the probable cause requirement is excused for another reason), are vehicles on public roads and searches under exigent circumstances. Vehicles on public roads may be searched without a warrant but on probable cause because of the lesser expectation of privacy associated with them.

- The courts have upheld the warrantless searches of vehicles based on the premise that there is a lesser expectation of privacy in a vehicle than in a home or office, and the mobility of the vehicle makes the logistics of obtaining a warrant more difficulty.

- It is reasonable for the police to make a full body search of an individual incident to a lawful arrest. If the arrest is legal, you do not need probable cause to search the arrested individual. The officer may search any area within the immediate control of the accused at the time of the arrest.

- The *Terry* case developed the concept of *stop and frisk*. A stop and frisk is less than an arrest. The rules applying to temporary detention also apply to *stop and frisk* situations.

DISCUSSION QUESTIONS

1. What is the difference between probable cause and reasonable suspicion?
2. Identify the two-stage process in a stop and frisk.
3. Under what conditions may a police officer search a vehicle on a public road?
4. How does stop and frisk differ from an arrest?
5. Under what circumstances may the police establish a road-block to catch drunk drivers?
6. What is an inventory search? When may it be accomplished?
7. What is a consent search?
8. How did *California* v. *Acevedo* modify the rules regarding the search of closed containers found in automobiles?
9. Who may consent to the search of your apartment or home?
10. What are the exceptions to the search warrant requirements?

ENDNOTES

1. 111 S. Ct. 1982 (1991).
2. *Minnesota* v. *Dickerson*, 508 U.S. 366 (1993).
3. 480 U.S. 321 (1987).
4. *United States* v. *Dunn*, 480 U.S. 294 (1987).
5. *United States* v. *Place*, 462 U.S. 696 (1983).
6. *Oliver* v. *United States*, 466 U.S. 170 (1984).
7. 428 U.S. 543 (1976).
8. *Almeida-Sanchez* v. *United States*, 413 U.S. 413 (1975).

9. *United States* v. *Brignoni-Ponce*, 422 U.S. 873 (1975).
10. *Camara* v. *Municipal Court*, 387 U.S. 523 (1967).
11. *Colonnade Catering Corp.* v. *United States*, 397 U.S. 72 (1970).
12. *New Jersey* v. *T.L.O.*, 469 U.S. 325 (1985).
13. 115 S.Ct. 2386 (1995).
14. 489 U.S. 602 (1989).
15. *People* v. *Burgner*, 41 Cal.3d 505 (1986).
16. *People* v. *Johnson*, 47 Cal.3d 576 (1988).
17. 468 U.S. 517 (1984).
18. *Biswell*, 406 U.S. 311 (1972).
19. *People* v. *Chapman*, 36 Cal.3d 98 (1984).
20. *Schneckloth* v. *Bustamonte*, 412 U.S. 218 (1973).
21. *Lewis* v. *United States*, 385 U.S. 206 (1966).
22. *Bumper* v. *North Carolina*, 391 U.S. 543 (1968).
23. *United States* v. *Matlock*, 415 U.S. 164 (1974).
24. 657 A.2d. 741 (D.C. Cr.App. 1994).
25. 65 F.3d 1151 (4th Cir. 1995).
26. 64F.3d 531 (9th Cir. 1995).
27. 412 U.S. 218 (1973).
28. 497 U.S. 177 (1990).
29. 468 U.S. 705 (1984).
30. *Florida* v. *Riley*, 488 U.S. 445 (1989).
31. 439 U.S. 128 (1978).
32. 448 U.S. 98 (1980).
33. 394 U.S. 165 (1969).
34. *Schmerber* v. *California*, 384 U.S. 757 (1966).
35. *Winton* v. *Lee*, 470 U.S. 753 (1985).
36. *Minnesota* v. *Olson*, 495 U.S. 91 (1990).
37. 361 U.S. 98 (1951).
38. 267 U.S. 132 (1925).
39. 850 F.2d 1365 (1988).
40. 171 C.A.3d 627 (1985).
41. 471 U.S. 386 (1985).
42. *People* v. *Padilla*, 132 C.A.3d. 555 (1982).
43. *Mimms* v. *Pa.*, 434 U.S. 106 (1977).
44. *People* v. *Ingersoll*, 43 Cal.3d. 1321 (1987).
45. 496 U.S. 444 (1990).
46. 109 S.Ct. 1581 (1989).
47. 109 S.Ct. 1378 (1989).
48. *Chimel* v. *California*, 395 U.S. 752 (1969).
49. *State* v. *Cox*, 200 N.W. 2d 305 (Minn., 1972).
50. *New York* v. *Belton*, 453 U.S. 454 (1981).
51. *Rawlings* v. *Kentucky*, 448 U.S. 98 (1980).
52. *People* v. *Adams*, 175 C.A.3d. 855 (1985).
53. 441 U.S. 218 (1973).
54. *Camara* v. *Municipal Court of City and County of San Francisco*, 387 U.S. 523 (1967).
55. 392 U.S. 1 (1968).
56. 50 Cal. L. Rev. 99 and 5 Am. Jur. 2d, Arrest 1.
57. *People* v. *Campbell*, 118 C.A. 3d 588 (1981).
58. 164 C. A.3d. 1194 (1985).
59. *People* v. *Remiro*, 89 C.A.3d 809 (1979).
60. *People* v. *Dominguez*, 194 C.A.3d. 1315 (1985).
61. *U.S.* v. *Hemsley*, 105 S.Ct. 675 (1985).
62. 470 U.S. 675 (1990).
63. *Maryland* v. *Buie*, 494 U.S. 325 (1990).

6

INTERROGATION, CONFESSIONS, AND ADMISSIONS

INTRODUCTION

Consider this argument by a prosecutor to a jury:

> Ladies and gentlemen of the jury, you have heard several versions of what happened on the night Susan died. It is your duty to make a finding as to what happened. I do not know and apparently the witnesses can not agree as to what happened. There is one person in the courtroom who really knows what happened, the defendant. He has chosen to remain silent. His failure to testify must mean that his testimony would be unfavorable to his defense.

Should a prosecutor be allowed to make the above argument to a jury? What value would the privilege against self-incrimination be if a prosecutor could make such a statement to the jury?

The Fifth Amendment of the U.S. Constitution provides that no person "shall be compelled in any criminal case to be a witness against himself." A literal reading of the amendment indicates that the individual is protected only from being required to testify and not from unsworn statements obtained out of court by the police. In 1897, the Supreme Court held, however, that the prohibition against being a witness against him or herself also applies to out-of-court confessions and compelled admissions.[1] The Supreme Court concluded that there was a historical connection between the privilege against forced self-incrimination and the law of confessions. The Court's conclusion, however, that there was a historical connection between the privilege and the law of confessions, has been challenged by many commentators as incorrect.[2]

While the exact origin of right against compelled self-incrimination is unclear, it was a part of the common law of England in the seventeenth century.[3] The scope of the privilege includes four basic parts. First, the compulsion to testify must be by the government. Second, the compulsion to testify is prohibited only if it forces a person to be a witness against him or herself. Third, the privilege protects the person from being a witness against him or herself for criminal cases only. Fourth, only testimonial self-incrimination is protected from compulsion. Each of these basic parts must be present in order for a person to effectively claim the privilege against self-incrimination.

Should the defendant be compelled to testify? What is the purpose of the privilege against compulsory self-incrimination? The purpose of the Fourth Amendment is to promote the protection of privacy. The purpose of the protection against compulsory self-incrimination is not as clear. The Supreme Court's majority opinion in *Miranda* v. *Arizona*[4] stated that the privilege is needed to prevent the police from extracting false confessions through torture or threats. Another reason stated in the majority opinion is that it helps maintain a "fair state–individual balance" by requiring the government to "shoulder the entire load" of proving the defendant's guilt. How valid are those reasons? Professor Dolinko contends that those two reasons are not valid. For example, the court decisions in cases involving the prohibition against torture or threats are based on the "due process" clause, not the privilege against self-incrimination. Dolinko also contends that since the main purpose of a criminal trial should be to seek the truth, the fair state–individual balance should be irrelevant. He points out that we require the defendant to provide fingerprints, blood samples, handwriting exemplars, etc. What is so different about testimony? Parties to a civil case may not refuse to give testimony on the grounds that the testimony may cause them to lose the case. He also notes that it is illegal for a defendant to destroy evidence or to intimidate witnesses.[5]

Generally two questions arise when considering the admissibility of a defendant's out-of-court statement: First, was the statement voluntary? i.e., not the result of coercion and second, have the *Miranda* requirements, if applicable, been complied with? Each of these requirements will be examined later in this chapter.

WHEN THE PRIVILEGE APPLIES

Testimonial Evidence

Evidence is not protected by the privilege unless the evidence is testimonial in nature. A defendant may be forced to provide fingerprints, voice exemplars, blood tests, etc. The Fifth Amendment applies only to testimonial evidence. Testimonial evidence is evidence that only a witness provides. Any physical evidence is not included in the privilege. In *United States* v. *Dionisio*[6], the Supreme Court held that the compulsion of voice-prints does not violate the Fifth Amendment since they were physical not testimonial evidence. In *United States* v. *Wade*[7], the Supreme Court held that forced participation in a police line-up does not violate the privilege. In *Gilbert* v. *California*[8], the Supreme Court upheld the right to force a defendant to provide handwriting exemplars. While handwriting and voice are means of communication, as long as the compulsion is directed to the physical characteristics of the voice or handwriting and not the actual content of the written or oral statement, the Fifth Amendment does not apply.

One interesting case in this area is the *Pennsylvania* v. *Muniz* case[9]. In *Muniz,* police officers arrested the defendant for drunk driving. During custodial interrogation and without the required *Miranda* warning, he exhibited slurred speech, failed the sobriety test, and could not state the date of his sixth birthday. Accordingly, three pieces of evidence were offered to the trial court: (1) the evidence of slurred speech, (2) the failure of the sobriety test, and (3) the fact that he did not know the date of his sixth birthday. The Court assumed compulsion since the individual was not properly warned as required by *Miranda.* The slurred speech was considered as physical evidence and therefore admissible. The issue of the sobriety test was not appealed, but it appears that the court would have held that such evidence was offered to show only a physical impairment and thus was not testimonial and therefore admissible. The Court held that the fact that the defendant did not know the date of his sixth birthday was testimonial, not physical, and therefore should not have been admitted into evidence. The Court noted that the prosecutor was trying to show that the physiological functioning of the defendant was impaired by alcohol and was trying to do that by the use of testimonial evidence.

One test for whether the statement is testimonial is whether it is capable of being true or false. If it is not capable of being true or false, then it is non-testimonial. For example, requiring a person to sign a form authoring release of foreign bank records, if any, is non-testimonial. (*Note*: If the form had stated that "I authorize the bank to release my records" this would be testimonial evidence because it contains the implied statement that the defendant has bank records in that bank.[10])

LAW IN PRACTICE

*H*ANDWRITING *E*XEMPLARS

Timothy McVeigh was arrested for bombing the Oklahoma City federal building that caused many deaths. A federal grand jury issued a subpoena ordering him to furnish exemplars of his handwriting. He refused, contending that the subpoena was a violation of his Fifth Amendment privilege against self-incrimination. As judge, how would you rule? [*United States* v. *McVeigh*, 896 F. Supp. 1549 (W.D. Okla, 1995).

Documents

Would a subpoena compelling a defendant to turn over pre-existing documents be a violation of the Fifth Amendment? This question has been the subject of several Supreme Court decisions. In an early case, *Boyd* v. *United States*[11], the Supreme Court held that a subpoena given to obtain private records of an individual violates the Fifth Amendment. Later cases, however, appear to hold that if the documents were pre-existing at the time the subpoena was issued, it is not a violation of the Fifth Amendment. For example, in *Fisher* v. *United States*[12], the Supreme Court held that the contents of an existing document are not protected by the Fifth Amendment since the preparation of those documents were not compelled by the government. In the *Doe* case discussed earlier, the Supreme Court held that records voluntarily prepared by a taxpayer are not protected by the privilege, since the government did not compel the taxpayer to prepare the documents.

Does the act of producing pre-existing documents communicate the fact that the documents exist and are under the control of the defendant? For example, ordering the defendant to produce all records regarding the illegal sale of drugs would admit that the defendant has such records and therefore must be involved in selling drugs. If the existence of the documents is obvious and not incriminating, the act of producing them is not incriminating. If, however, the existence of the documents is not obvious and is incriminating, the courts will be reluctant to require the defendant to produce them.[13] A similar view is taken regarding admitting possession and control of the records. If there is nothing incriminating in having possession and control of the records, the courts will generally compel the production of such records. If, however, admitting possession and control of the documents is incriminating, generally the courts do not require their production. For example, admitting that the defendant has control of the drugs may establish that the defendant is involved with the criminal activity in question. In the latter case, the courts generally would not require their production.

If the documents are required by law or governmental regulation to be kept for legitimate administrative purposes, the Fifth Amendment does not protect the contents nor the act of production of these documents.[14] This rule applies only for those records required to be kept in accordance with a legitimate administrative recordkeeping purpose. For example, requiring businesses to keep certain records for tax purposes would be within the rule. A statute that required individuals to keep records of illegal gambling activities is not a legitimate administrative recordkeeping purpose and therefore the "required records exception" does not apply. The Court noted that the statute was addressed to a select group of individuals inherently involved in a criminal acitivity and thus the required recordkeeping was not for a legitimate administrative purpose.

In *California* v. *Byers*[15], the Supreme Court held that the "required records exception" applied to a California statute that required anyone involved in an accident to stop at the scene and leave his or her name and address. The court held that the statute was a legitimate recordkeeping requirement and was essentially regulatory since it was designed to make it more efficient to process insurance claims and accident suits. The Court also noted that the statute was addressed to the motoring public at large rather than to a selective group of individuals inherently suspected of criminal activities.

Agents of Business Entities

The Fifth Amendment protection against self-incrimination does not apply to business entities. In *Braswell* v. *United States*[16], the government issued a subpoena for Braswell, as a corporate officer, to provide certain records involving his solely owned corporation. Braswell contended that to produce the documents would incriminate him personally. He contended that producing the records which were pre-existing would be admitting that they existed and that he had control over them. The Supreme Court denied his claims and ruled that he had to produce them. The Court stated that it would be inconsistent to apply the personal privilege to an act that was really accomplished by a corporation. Accordingly, the production of the entity's documents would be an act of the entity (corporation) and not a personal act.

In *Curcio* v. *United States*[17], the Supreme Court held that the collective entity rule does not apply to oral testimony and that the corporate agent could refuse to give oral testimony if that testimony would incriminate the agent. In a similar case, a court of appeals noted that the government may compel the production of corporate or partnership records, but has no right to compel a person to provide oral testimony when to do so would incriminate that person.[18]

PROCEEDINGS IN WHICH THE PRIVILEGE APPLIES

While the privilege against self-incrimination applies only to criminal cases, it possesses a broader scope than the language applies. For example, a person may not be compelled to make a statement in an administrative hearing or in a civil case if the information could ultimately be used against him or her in a criminal case.[19] The Supreme Court, in *Lefkowitz* v. *Turley*[20], held that the privilege protects individuals from answering any questions in any proceedings if the answers might incriminate them in a future criminal proceeding.

In *United States* v. *Conte*[21], a court of appeals held that the state could force an individual to testify at a probation revocation proceeding on the grounds that it was not a criminal case and that there was no risk that the testimony could be used in a subsequent criminal case.

PROCEDURAL ASPECTS OF PRIVILEGE

The privilege against self-incrimination applies if there is any possibility of criminal sanctions. It does not matter that the offense is rarely prosecuted. But could the offense be prosecuted? The person who is protected by the privilege must assert it. If there is a possibility that the testimony would provide a link in the chain of evidence, the Fifth Amendment protects such testimony.[22] Testimony that is purely cumulative does not present a threat of incrimination and may in some circumstances be compelled.[23]

Failure to assert the privilege results in it being lost. For example, answering a question rather than claiming the privilege could result in the loss of the privilege. In addition, individuals may waive the privilege by giving testimony that is inconsistent with claiming the privilege. If a witness testifies or supplies information regarding an event, the witness cannot claim the privilege about a related subject matter. The witness, however, may testify regarding on subject matter and claim the privilege about an unrelated topic. In *Lesko* v. *Lehman*[24], an appeals court held that a defendant who testified at a capital sentencing hearing regarding his biographical information could still claim the privilege with respect to the circumstances surrounding the murder.

When Patty Hearst, in a famous case, testified that she was under duress at the time of a bank robbery, an appeals court held that she waived the privilege as to cross examination concerning a later period in which she allegedly lived with the Symbionese Liberation Army voluntarily. The court considered the conditions of the defendant's confinement at the two different times as really part of the same subject matter.[25]

Before a confession or admission of an accused may be entered into evidence, it must meet the test of voluntariness and then, if applicable, the requirements of *Miranda*. In *Brown* v. *Mississippi*[26], the defendant was tied to a tree and beaten until he confessed to the crime. Evidence also was presented that he was severely whipped while on the way to jail. His confession was used to help convict him. On appeal the Supreme Court held that convictions which rest upon confessions shown to have been extorted is a violation of the due process of law required by the Fourteenth Amendment and must be reversed.

The *Brown* case banned the use of confessions obtained by physical torture. The Supreme Court, in *Spano* v. *New York*, banned the use of confessions obtained by psychological coercion.[27] The courts generally consider the actions of the police, the characteristics of the defendant, and the circumstances surrounding the confession to determine if the confession was a violation of the due process rights of the defendant. If those factors strongly suggest the presence of psychological coercion, then the confession will not be admitted. Facts that the courts have considered include length of questioning, mental abilities of the defendant, whether or not the defendant was continuously interrogated, whether the defendant was denied contact with friends or family, and whether the defendant was questioned for long periods without being given food, water, or opportunity to sleep.

The Supreme Court in *Arizona* v. *Fulminate*[28] held that the threat of violence was sufficient to render a confession involuntary. In this case the defendant was a prison inmate who felt he was in danger of harm from other inmates since they considered him a child murderer. A government informant masqueraded as an organized crime figure and informed the defendant that he would offer protection to the defendant only if the defendant confessed. The defendant, fearful for his life, confessed. The court held the confession involuntary. Actual violence is not required, and the Court held that a "credible threat was sufficient." In this case, the Court held that if the government proves that the admission of the confession was harmless error beyond a reasonable doubt, a court could uphold the conviction. The Court cautioned, however, that the reviewing court must exercise extreme caution before upholding a conviction in which an involuntary confession has been received in evidence.

Some police coercion is required to make the confession inadmissible on this issue. In *Colorado* v. *Connelly*[29], the accused confessed because voices told him to. The Court held that the due process clause was not violated because there was no "coercive government misconduct."

Not all police tricks will invalidate a confession. For example, falsely telling a defendant that his fingerprints were found at the scene does not invalidate the confession. To determine if a confession is involuntary, the court uses the "totality of circumstances test."[30] The factors deemed most important to the Supreme Court are physical abuse, threats, extensive questioning, incommunicado detention, denial of the right to counsel, and the characteristics and status of the suspect. The test is imprecise and is decided on an ad hoc basis.

The Court in the *Brown* case indicated that the ban on involuntary confessions was derived from its concern regarding their reliability. The courts have, however, invalidated convictions involving involuntary confessions despite the availability of independent evidence which validated the confession.

As will be noted later, confessions which violate the *Miranda* rules may still be used for certain limited purposes, e.g, for impeachment when the defendant takes the stand in his or her own defense. An involuntary confession may not, however, be used by the government for any purposes.[31]

THE DUE PROCESS TEST

There are two types of due process violations, substantive and procedural. Substantive due process issues generally involve the constitutionality of statutes, regulations, and other laws. It concerns mainly the state's authority to pass a law regulating an issue or area. Procedural due process issues involve the processes or procedures used by the government. When looking at the due process limitations on interrogation, we are examining procedural due process issues.

The opinion in *Miranda* v. *Arizona* never expressly rejected the "due process" test. In addition, there can be a due process violation without violating the *Miranda* rules. As noted in Chapter 5, the due process test looks at the totality of the circumstances to determine if the defendant's confession is voluntary. For a statement to be admissible under this test, the statement must be the product of the defendant's free will and his or her rational choice. For example, a police officer could advise the defendant of her rights under *Miranda*. The officer then could tell the defendant that if she does not confess, he will beat her. Any confession received under these circumstances would not violate *Miranda*, but under the due process test would be inadmissible.

A California Supreme Court Justice once stated that there were two policies underlying the rule barring coerced confessions—first, to deter improper police interrogation methods, and second, to keep out unreliable confessions.[32] There is a lack of evidence that coerced confessions are unreliable, but most judges and attorneys have always assumed that fact.

There is no bright line as to what constitutes a violation of the due process test. As stated in several cases, the Supreme Court has not outlawed police interrogation. In addition, it is expected that the police will place some pressure on a suspect to confess. Generally if the police pressure is likely to produce a statement that is not the product of the suspect's free and rational choice, then the confession or admission violates the due process test. As one California court stated, "A confession is deemed involuntary and hence inadmissible if procured by an express or implied promise of benefit beyond that naturally flowing from a truthful statement."[33]

The due process requirement applies to confessions that are considered involuntary. As the Supreme Court noted in *Townsend* v. *Sain*[34], a confession is involuntary when it is not a product of a rational intellect and a free will. The Court also stated in *Sain* that a confession is involuntary whether coerced by physical intimidation or psychological pressure. Before a court will admit a confession for any purposes, the prosecution must establish by a preponderance of evidence that the confession is voluntary.[35] For example, a suspect was told that she "will not see her two-year-old child for a while" and that "she had a lot at stake" made her statement involuntary. She was also told that if she cooperated the officer would inform the prosecutor of this fact. If, however, she refused to talk, he would communicate to the prosecutor that she was "stubborn or hard-headed." The court held that it was clear that the purpose and the objective of the interrogation was to cause her to fear that if she failed to cooperate, she would not see her young child for a long time. The court held that her confession was not the product of a free will and that the police had exerted improper influence.[36]

LAW IN PRACTICE

USING PSYCHOLOGICAL ADVANTAGES IN INTERROGATION

The defendant Hawkins was arrested for rape and murder. While being interrogated by Officer LeFavers, he asked the police officer if he would be sentenced to death for his crime. The police officer stated: "Sam, to be honest with you, I would think that the courts in your situation would be very lenient. I really do. I think that they will observe the fact that you need help—you're trying to seek that help already, psychological, psychiatric help, and I think they would recommend a psychiatrist." The defendant was black and had professed a dislike for "honkies." The police used a black officer to interrogate him hoping to obtain a psychological advantage. Taken together, does the statement of the police officer and use of the black officer establish improper psychological techniques and thus result in a confession that is not the result of the free will and rational choice of the defendant?

The court held in the above factual situation that the confession was admissible. The court stated that the comments were not promises of leniency and that predictions about future events are not the same as a promise of leniency. The court also stated that there is nothing inherently wrong with the police's efforts to create a favorable climate for confession and that the use of the black police officer, even though designed to gain a psychological advantage, was not improper.[37]

Limitations on Interrogation

To determine whether a confession is voluntary the due process test looks at many factors, including the sophistication of the defendant and the methods used by the police. As discussed in Chapter 7, the due process test remains important because a confession taken in violation of *Miranda*, but not in violation of the due process test, may be used by the prosecution for impeachment purposes. A review of the court cases provides some guidance as to the actions that the police may take without tainting the confession. For example, it may be appropriate for a police officer to represent to a suspect that her cooperation would be made known to the prosecutor.[38]

Confessions taken after lengthy interrogations during incommunicado detention have been considered involuntary. While the courts generally approve of police using the "good guy–bad guy" approach, some confessions have been considered as involuntary where the police have used the device of assuming a non-adversarial role with the suspect to elicit information. In *Beckwith* v. *United States*[39], the Supreme Court looked at the issue of the interrogator adopting a sympathetic approach. The Court held in that case that adopting a sympathetic approach is not in itself enough to render a confession involuntary, but if other aspects of the interrogation strengthened the illusion that the interrogation was non-adversarial, the confession may be considered as involuntary because of psychological coercion.

In *Bram* v. *United States*[40], the Supreme Court held that for a confession to be voluntary, it must not have been extracted by any sort of threat or violence, nor obtained by any direct or implied promises, however slight. A later Supreme Court case which generally upheld the *Bram* rule stated that it does not matter that the suspect confessed after receiving a promise as long as the promise did not overbear his will.[41] In that case the Court indicated that promises should be considered as part of the totality of circumstances in assessing the voluntariness of the confession.

MIRANDA

The Supreme Court, in *Miranda* v. *Arizona*[42], held that custodial interrogation is inherently coercive. To offset this the Court established the rule that a confession, admission, or any statement made by a person during custodial interrogation is inadmissible in court unless the person receives the four warnings which describe his or her rights and the person makes a knowing, intelligent, and voluntary waiver of his or her rights. The Court also stated that the police must stop questioning when the person invokes his or her rights to remain silent or to speak to an attorney.

The court stated a two-fold purpose in establishing the *Miranda* rule—first, to insure that the suspect was "adequately and effectively" advised of his or her rights, and second, to insure that the "exercise of those rights" were "fully honored" by the police. The court stated that the warnings would help overcome the inherent pressures of the interrogation atmosphere. The warnings should indicate to the suspect that the police are ready to honor his or her rights. In addition, the warnings should make the suspect aware that he or she is not in the presence of persons acting solely in his or her interest.

The suspect must be apprised of the following rights:

- You have the right to remain silent.
- Anything you say can and will be used against you in court.
- You have a right to consult with a lawyer and to have the lawyer present during any questioning.
- If you cannot afford an attorney, one will be appointed for you.

When Miranda Applies

The Supreme Court held that *Miranda* warnings are required before any "custodial interrogation." Accordingly, two conditions must be present prior to issue of *Miranda* warnings. First, the suspect must be in custody and, second, there must be interrogation. If one of these conditions is missing, then no *Miranda* warnings are required.

Interrogation As noted earlier, *Miranda* warnings are required when an in-custody suspect is interrogated. The courts have broadened the meaning of interrogation to include the "functional equivalent" of interrogation. For example, interrogation includes any words or actions by the police that the police should know are reasonably likely to elicit an incriminating response from the suspect.[43]

In *Rhode Island* v. *Innis*[44], the Supreme Court held that the focus in determining if interrogation has occurred is on the suspect. The subjective intentions of the officer to elicit incriminating responses is not the key. The test is whether the officer should have known that his or her words or actions were likely to elicit an incriminating response from the suspect. Under this test, any peculiar susceptibilities of the suspect known to the police are relevant in determining what the officer should have foreseen as likely responses. For example in the *Brewer* case, the police knew that the suspect was deeply religious and that the officer's "Christian burial speech" would elicit an incriminating response from the suspect. In that case a small child was missing and the suspect was being transported by the police. Brewer had contacted an attorney and had invoked his *Miranda* rights. The officer made the comment that it would be nice to locate the body so that a good Christian burial would be conducted. The suspect told the police where the body could be found, and incriminating evidence was found there. The Supreme Court held that the comments of the officer were functionally equivalent to an interrogation.

In Custody   Under the *Miranda* definition, a person is in custody when the individual is otherwise deprived of his or her freedom of action in any significant way. In *Berkemer* v. *McCarty*[45], the Supreme Court established an objective test to determine whether the suspect was in custody. The Court stated that an officer's unarticulated plan to arrest the suspect has no bearing on the question of custody. The only relevant inquiry, according to the Court, is how a reasonable person in the suspect's situation would have understood his or her situation. The Court has made a distinction between "seizure" and "custody." To constitute custody under *Miranda*, the loss of freedom must be significant. For example, stopping a motorist on a public road to issue a traffic citation may constitute a temporary seizure but not custody for the purposes of *Miranda* requirements. In determining the custody question, the nature and seriousness of the crime in question is immaterial. Even a person arrested on a minor offense should be given the *Miranda* warnings prior to custodial interrogation. The location of the interrogation may have a bearing on the "in custody" issue, but it is not the key factor. In *Orozco* v. *Texas*[46], the defendant was determined to be in custody when he was interrogated in his bedroom, whereas in *Oregon* v. *Mathiason*[47] the accused was not considered in custody even though the questioning took place at the police station. In the latter case, the police had informed the suspect before the interrogation began that he was not in custody, and he was allowed to leave after the questioning was completed. In the *Orozco* case, the officers entered the accused's home at 4:00 AM. It was a forcible entry, and a reasonable person would have believed that the defendant was under arrest.

Exceptions to *Miranda*

At the time that *Miranda* was decided, most courts understood it to mean that statements obtained during custodial interrogation without *Miranda* warnings violated the Fifth Amendment and could not be used for any purposes. In *Michigan* v. *Tucker*[48], the Supreme Court stated, however, that a violation of *Miranda* was not by itself a violation of the Fifth Amendment. In *Tucker* the police failed to give the complete *Miranda* warning to a suspect. The interrogation occurred before the *Miranda* decision was announced, but the trial took place after *Miranda*. Since

Miranda had retroactive application, the statement obtained could not be used. The issue on appeal involved evidence discovered as the results of the statement. The question before the court was whether to use the "fruit of the poisonous-tree" doctrine. The Court noted that the police conduct did not directly violate the defendant's right against self-incrimination but only the prophylactic rules developed to protect that right. Later in *Oregon* v. *Elstad*[49] the Supreme Court noted that the *Miranda* exclusionary rule serves the Fifth Amendment and sweeps more broadly than the Fifth Amendment itself. Accordingly the rule may be triggered even in the absence of a Fifth Amendment violation.

Public Safety Exceptions In *New York* v. *Quarles*[50], the Supreme Court stated that *Miranda* warnings need not be given in a situation involving a threat to public safety. The Court held that if there is an objectively reasonable need to protect the police or the public from immediate danger that the police could forgo the warning. In *Quarles*, the victim informed the police that she had been raped by a man with a gun and that the man went into the store across the street. When the defendant was arrested, he did not have a gun on him. The police arrested him and then interrogated him, without giving a warning, regarding the location of the gun. The Court indicated that it did not matter that besides public safety, the officers also were motivated to obtain incriminating evidence, as long as there was a reasonable belief that an emergency situation existed.

Covert Interrogations The U.S. Supreme Court held in *Illinois* v. *Perkins*[51], that interrogations by an undercover agent did not require the *Miranda* warnings because the suspect is unaware that he or she is being interrogated and therefore the coerciveness generally present is missing. In *Perkins*, the police placed an undercover agent in the same jail cell with the defendant. The defendant did not realize that he was being interrogated.

The defendant cannot waive his rights during covert interrogations because it is impossible to waiver rights regarding interrogation if he or she does not know that he or she is being interrogated. Accordingly there may be a counsel problem if the defendant is represented by counsel. This issue is discussed later in this chapter.

GRANTS OF IMMUNITY

The government may compel the testimony of a witness if he or she has been granted immunity. When immunity is granted, the witness's testimony is not self-incriminating. There are two types of immunity: (1) transactional and (2) use and derivative use. If a person receives *transactional immunity*, he or she cannot be prosecuted for the transaction about which the witness was compelled to testify. It is the broadest type of immunity and gives the witnesses greater protection than is constitutionally required.[52]

Use and derivative use immunity restricts the government from using the testimony or any other information obtained directly or indirectly from the testimony. For example, the government may still prosecute a person who has use and derivative use immunity as long as the government establishes that the evidence it offers at trial was derived from a legitimate independent source. In *Kastigar*, the Supreme Court held that use and derivative use immunity was sufficient to compel a person to testify regarding an event. The Court noted that the burden was on the government to establish that the evidence used to convict the defendant was not obtained as a result of the compelled testimony. In *United States* v. *North*[53], a court of appeals held that the government did not fulfill its burden of showing that the evidence was free from the taint of immunized testimony where the government witnesses used at trial had seen Oliver North's immunized testimony on national television.

RIGHT TO COUNSEL DURING INTERROGATIONS

There are certain Sixth Amendment rights to counsel during interrogations. A confession may be obtained that does not violate the Fifth Amendment but may be excluded because the defendant's Sixth Amendment rights may have been violated. In *Massiah* v. *United States*[54], the defendant had been indicted for a narcotics offense. He was being represented by an attorney. At arraignment, he pled not guilty and was released to await trial. After indictment, the defendant met with a co-defendant. The co-defendant was acting as a government informer and questioned the defendant regarding the case. The informant was wired. The Court held that questioning the defendant after indictment and in the absence of his counsel violated his Sixth Amendment rights. The *Massiah* case occurred two years before *Miranda* and was the first case to hold that right to counsel attaches prior to trial. The Court indicated that the most critical phase of a trial was the period when proceedings begin (pre-trial) and that to deny him the right to counsel at this period was to deny him effective representation of counsel. Later, in *Brewer* v. *Williams*[55], the Supreme Court held that the Sixth Amendment right to counsel attaches when adversary judicial proceedings begin, whether by way of formal charges, preliminary hearing, indictment, or arraignment. The right to counsel will be discussed in Chapter 10. It is important to note that the Sixth Amendment right to counsel is not the same as the *Miranda* right to consult with an attorney. The *Miranda* requirements attach when conducting custodial interrogation, and the Sixth Amendment right to counsel attaches when adversarial proceedings begin.

WAIVER OF RIGHTS UNDER *MIRANDA*

The burden is on the government to establish an intentional relinquishment or abandonment of a known right or privilege.[56] To determine if a waiver is voluntary, the courts use the voluntariness test discussed earlier in this chapter. One of the leading cases on waiver of *Miranda* rights is *Patterson* v. *Illinois*[57]. Patterson was in custody. He had been indicted, and a copy of the indictment had been read to him. He was advised of his *Miranda* rights and was interrogated. The Court held that he had made a knowing and intelligent waiver of his *Miranda* rights and his right to counsel under the Sixth Amendment.

Patterson had not yet obtained an attorney. If the accused has obtained an attorney, either by retention or appointment, the government may not intentionally or knowingly create the opportunity to elicit incriminating statements from he or she outside the presence of the attorney.[58]

Once the accused invokes his or her *Miranda* rights or indicates that he or she wishes to remain silent or to consult with an attorney, the interrogation must stop. After that, the government must not deliberately elicit information from a defendant until he or she consults an attorney or until the suspect initiates communications or conversations with the government about the crime. The request for an attorney under *Miranda* must be made under circumstances that can reasonably be construed as a request for an attorney.

CAPSTONE CASES

MIRANDA V. ARIZONA
384 U.S. 436 (1966)

MR. CHIEF JUSTICE WARREN delivered the opinion of the Court.

On March 13, 1963, petitioner, Ernesto Miranda, was arrested at his home and taken in custody to a Phoenix police station. He was there identified by the complaining witness. The police then took him to "Interrogation Room No. 2" of the detective bureau. There he was questioned by two police officers. The officers admitted at trial that *Miranda* was not advised that he had a right to have an attorney present. Two hours later, the officers emerged from the interrogation room with a written confession signed by *Miranda*. At the top of the statement was a typed paragraph stating that the confession was made voluntarily, without threats or promises of immunity and "with full knowledge of my legal rights, understanding any statement I make may be used against me." . . .

The cases before us raise questions which go to the roots of our concepts of American criminal jurisprudence: the restraints society must observe consistent with the Federal Constitution in prosecuting individuals for crime. More specifically, we deal with the admissibility of statements obtained from an individual who is subjected to custodial police interrogation and the necessity for procedures which assure that the individual is accorded his privilege under the Fifth Amendment to the Constitution not to be compelled to incriminate himself.

We dealt with certain phases of this problem recently in *Escobedo* v. *Illinois*, 378 U.S. 478 (1964). There, as in the four cases before us, law enforcement officials took the defendant into custody and interrogated him in a police station for the purpose of obtaining a confession. The police did not effectively advise him of his right to remain silent or of his right to consult with his attorney. Rather, they confronted him with an alleged accomplice who accused him of having perpetrated a murder. When the defendant denied the accusation and said "I didn't shoot Manuel, you did it," they handcuffed him and took him to an interrogation room. There, while handcuffed and standing, he was questioned for four hours until he confessed. During this interrogation, the police denied his request to speak to his attorney, and they prevented his retained attorney, who had come to the police station, from consulting with him. At his trial, the State, over his objection, introduced the confession against him. We held that the statements thus made were constitutionally inadmissible.

This case has been the subject of judicial interpretation and spirited legal debate since it was decided two years ago. Both state and federal courts, in assessing its implications, have arrived at varying conclusions. A wealth of scholarly material has been written tracing its ramifications and underpinnings. Police and prosecutor have speculated on its range and desirability. We granted *certiorari* in these cases . . . in

order further to explore some facets of the problems, thus exposed, of applying the privilege against self-incrimination to in-custody interrogation, and to give concrete constitutional guidelines for law enforcement agencies and courts to follow.

We start here, as we did in *Escobedo*, with the premise that our holding is not an innovation in our jurisprudence, but is an application of principles long recognized and applied in other settings. We have undertaken a thorough re-examination of the *Escobedo* decision and the principles it announced, and we reaffirm it. That case was but an explication of basic rights that are enshrined in our Constitution—that "No person . . . shall be compelled in any criminal case to be a witness against himself," and that "the accused shall . . . have the Assistance of Counsel"—rights which were put in jeopardy in that case through official overbearing. These precious rights were fixed in our Constitution only after centuries of persecution and struggle. And in the words of Chief Justice Marshall, they were secured "for ages to come, and . . . designed to approach immortality as nearly as human institutions can approach it," *Cohens* v. *Virginia*, 6 Wheat. 264, 387 (1821).

Over 70 years ago, our predecessors on this Court eloquently stated:

"The maxim nemo tenetur seipsum accusare had its origin in a protest against the inquisitorial and manifestly unjust methods of interrogating accused persons, which [have] long obtained in the continental system, and, until the expulsion of the Stuarts from the British throne in 1688, and the erection of additional barriers for the protection of the people against the exercise of arbitrary power, [were] not uncommon even in England. While the admissions or confessions of the prisoner, when voluntarily and freely made, have always ranked high in the scale of incriminating evidence, if an accused person be asked to explain his apparent connection with a crime under investigation, the ease with which the questions put to him may assume an inquisitorial character, the temptation to press the witness unduly, to browbeat him if he be timid or reluctant, to push him into a corner, and to entrap him into fatal contradictions, which is so painfully evident in many of the earlier state trials, notably in those of Sir Nicholas Throckmorton, and Udal, the Puritan minister, made the system so odious as to give rise to a demand for its total abolition. The change in the English criminal procedure in that particular seems to be founded upon no statute and no judicial opinion, but upon a general and silent acquiescence of the courts in a popular demand. But, however adopted, it has become firmly embedded in English, as well as in American jurisprudence. So deeply did the iniquities of the ancient system impress themselves upon the minds of the American colonists that the States, with one accord, made a denial of the right to question an accused person a part of their fundamental law, so that a maxim, which in England was a mere rule of evidence, became clothed in this country with the impregnability of a constitutional enactment." *Brown* v. *Walker*, 161 U.S. 591, 596–597 (1896).

In stating the obligation of the judiciary to apply these constitutional rights, this Court declared in *Weems* v. *United States*, 217 U.S. 349, 373 (1910):

. . . our contemplation cannot be only of what has been but of what may be. Under any other rule a constitution would indeed be as easy of application as it would be deficient in efficacy and power. Its general principles would have little value and be converted by precedent into impotent and lifeless formulas. Rights declared in words might be lost in reality. And this has been recognized. The meaning and vitality of the Constitution have developed against narrow and restrictive construction.

This was the spirit in which we delineated, in meaningful language, the manner in which the constitutional rights of the individual could be enforced against overzealous police practices. It was necessary in *Escobedo*, as here, to insure that what was proclaimed in the Constitution had not become but a "form of words," *Silverthorne Lumber Co.* v. *United States*, 251 U.S. 385, 392 (1920), in the hands of government officials. And it is in this spirit, consistent with our role as judges, that we adhere to the principles of *Escobedo* today.

Our holding will be spelled out with some specificity in the pages which follow but briefly stated it is this: the prosecution may not use statements, whether exculpatory or inculpatory, stemming from custodial interrogation of the defendant unless it demonstrates the use of procedural safeguards effective to secure the privilege against self-incrimination. By custodial interrogation, we mean questioning initiated by law enforcement officers after a person has been taken into custody or otherwise deprived of his freedom of action in any significant way. As for the procedural safeguards to be employed, unless other fully effective means are devised to inform accused persons of their right of silence and to assure a continuous opportunity to exercise it, the following measures are required. Prior to any questioning, the person must be warned that he has a right to remain silent, that any statement he does make may be used as evidence against him, and that he has a right to the presence of an attorney, either retained or appointed. The defendant may waive effectuation of these rights, provided the waiver is made voluntarily, knowingly and intelligently. If, however, he indicates in any manner and at any stage of the process that he wishes to consult with an attorney before speaking there can be no questioning. Likewise, if the individual is alone and indicates in any manner that he does not wish to be interrogated, the police may not question him. The mere fact that he may have answered some questions or volunteered some statements on his own does not deprive him of the right to refrain from answering any further inquiries until he has consulted with an attorney and thereafter consents to be questioned.

. . . An understanding of the nature and setting of this in-custody interrogation is essential to our decisions today. The difficulty in depicting what transpires at such interrogations stems from the fact that in this country they have largely taken place incommunicado. From extensive factual studies undertaken in the early 1930's, including the famous Wickersham Report to Congress by a Presidential Commission, it is clear that police violence and the "third degree" flourished at that time. In a series of cases decided by this Court long after these studies, the police resorted to physical brutality—beating, hanging, whipping—and to sustained and protracted questioning incommunicado in order to extort confessions. The Commission on Civil Rights in 1961 found much evidence to indicate that "some policemen still resort to physical force to obtain confessions," 1961 Comm'n on Civil Rights Rep., Justice, pt. 5, 17. The use of physical brutality and violence is not, unfortunately, relegated to the past or to any part of the country. Only recently in Kings County, New York, the police brutally beat, kicked, and placed lighted cigarette butts on the back of a potential witness under interrogation for the purpose of securing a statement incriminating a third party. *People* v. *Portelli*, 15 N. Y. 2d 235, 205 N. E. 2d 857, 257 N. Y. S. 2d 931 (1965).

The examples given above are undoubtedly the exception now, but they are sufficiently widespread to be the object of concern. Unless a proper limitation upon custodial interrogation is achieved—such as these decisions will advance—there can be no assurance that practices of this nature will be eradicated in the foreseeable future. The conclusion of the Wickersham Commission Report, made over 30 years ago, is still pertinent:

> To the contention that the third degree is necessary to get the facts, the reporters aptly reply in the language of the present Lord Chancellor of England (Lord Sankey): "It is not admissible to do a great right by doing a little wrong. . . . It is not sufficient to do

justice by obtaining a proper result by irregular or improper means." Not only does the use of the third degree involve a flagrant violation of law by the officers of the law, but it involves also the dangers of false confessions, and it tends to make police and prosecutors less zealous in the search for objective evidence. As the New York prosecutor quoted in the report said, "It is a short cut and makes the police lazy and unenterprising." Or, as another official quoted remarked: "If you use your fists, you are not so likely to use your wits." We agree with the conclusion expressed in the report, that "The third degree brutalizes the police, hardens the prisoner against society, and lowers the esteem in which the administration of justice is held by the public." IV National Commission on Law Observance and Enforcement, Report on Lawlessness in Law Enforcement 5 (1931).

Again we stress that the modern practice of in-custody interrogation is psychologically rather than physically oriented. As we have stated before, "Since *Chambers* v. *Florida*, 309 U.S. 227, this Court has recognized that coercion can be mental as well as physical, and that the blood of the accused is not the only hallmark of an unconstitutional inquisition." *Blackburn* v. *Alabama*, 361 U.S. 199, 206 (1960). Interrogation still takes place in privacy. Privacy results in secrecy and this in turn results in a gap in our knowledge as to what in fact goes on in the interrogation rooms. A valuable source of information about present police practices, however, may be found in various police manuals and texts which document procedures employed with success in the past, and which recommend various other effective tactics. These texts are used by law enforcement agencies themselves as guides. It should be noted that these texts professedly present the most enlightened and effective means presently used to obtain statements through custodial interrogation. By considering these texts and other data, it is possible to describe procedures observed and noted around the country.

The officers are told by the manuals that the "principal psychological factor contributing to a successful interrogation is privacy—being alone with the person under interrogation." The efficacy of this tactic has been explained as follows:

> If at all practicable, the interrogation should take place in the investigator's office or at least in a room of his own choice. The subject should be deprived of every psychological advantage. In his own home he may be confident, indignant, or recalcitrant. He is more keenly aware of his rights and more reluctant to tell of his indiscretions or criminal behavior within the walls of his home. Moreover his family and other friends are nearby, their presence lending moral support. In his own office, the investigator possesses all the advantages. The atmosphere suggests the invincibility of the forces of the law.

To highlight the isolation and unfamiliar surroundings, the manuals instruct the police to display an air of confidence in the suspect's guilt and from outward appearance to maintain only an interest in confirming certain details. The guilt of the subject is to be posited as a fact. The interrogator should direct his comments toward the reasons why the subject committed the act, rather than court failure by asking the subject whether he did it. Like other men, perhaps the subject has had a bad family life, had an unhappy childhood, had too much to drink, had an unrequited desire for women. The officers are instructed to minimize the moral seriousness of the offense, to cast blame on the victim or on society. These tactics are designed to put the subject in a psychological state where his story is but an elaboration of what the police purport to know already—that he is guilty. Explanations to the contrary are dismissed and discouraged.

The texts thus stress that the major qualities an interrogator should possess are patience and perseverance. One writer describes the efficacy of these characteristics in this manner:

> In the preceding paragraphs emphasis has been placed on kindness and stratagems. The investigator will, however, encounter many situations where the sheer weight of his personality will be the deciding factor. Where emotional appeals and tricks are employed to no avail, he must rely on an oppressive atmosphere of dogged persistence. He must interrogate steadily and without relent, leaving the subject no prospect of surcease. He must dominate his subject and overwhelm him with his inexorable will to obtain the truth. He should interrogate for a spell of several hours pausing only for the subject's necessities in acknowledgment of the need to avoid a charge of duress that can be technically substantiated. In a serious case, the interrogation may continue for days, with the required intervals for food and sleep, but with no respite from the atmosphere of domination. It is possible in this way to induce the subject to talk without resorting to duress or coercion. The method should be used only when the guilt of the subject appears highly probable.

The manuals suggest that the suspect be offered legal excuses for his actions in order to obtain an initial admission of guilt. Where there is a suspected revenge-killing, for example, the interrogator may say:

> Joe, you probably didn't go out looking for this fellow with the purpose of shooting him. My guess is, however, that you expected something from him and that's why you carried a gun—for your own protection. You knew him for what he was, no good. Then when you met him he probably started using foul, abusive language and he gave some indication that he was about to pull a gun on you, and that's when you had to act to save your own life. That's about it, isn't it, Joe?

Having then obtained the admission of shooting, the interrogator is advised to refer to circumstantial evidence which negates the self-defense explanation. This should enable him to secure the entire story. One text notes that "Even if he fails to do so, the inconsistency between the subject's original denial of the shooting and his present admission of at least doing the shooting will serve to deprive him of a self-defense 'out' at the time of trial."

When the techniques described above prove unavailing, the texts recommend they be alternated with a show of some hostility. One ploy often used has been termed the "friendly-unfriendly" or the "Mutt and Jeff" act:

> . . . In this technique, two agents are employed. Mutt, the relentless investigator, who knows the subject is guilty and is not going to waste any time. He's sent a dozen men away for this crime and he's going to send the subject away for the full term. Jeff, on the other hand, is obviously a kindhearted man. He has a family himself. He has a brother who was involved in a little scrape like this. He disapproves of Mutt and his tactics and will arrange to get him off the case if the subject will cooperate. He can't hold Mutt off for very long. The subject would be wise to make a quick decision. The technique is applied by having both investigators present while Mutt acts out his role. Jeff may stand by quietly and demur at some of Mutt's tactics. When Jeff makes his plea for cooperation, Mutt is not present in the room.

The interrogators sometimes are instructed to induce a confession out of trickery. The technique here is quite effective in crimes which require identification or which run in series. In the identification situation, the interrogator may take a break in his questioning to place the subject among a group of men in a line-up. "The witness or complainant (previously coached, if necessary) studies the line-up and

confidently points out the subject as the guilty party." Then the questioning resumes "as though there were now no doubt about the guilt of the subject." A variation on this technique is called the "reverse line-up":

> The accused is placed in a line-up, but this time he is identified by several fictitious witnesses or victims who associated him with different offenses. It is expected that the subject will become desperate and confess to the offense under investigation in order to escape from the false accusations.

The manuals also contain instructions for police on how to handle the individual who refuses to discuss the matter entirely, or who asks for an attorney or relatives. The examiner is to concede him the right to remain silent. "This usually has a very undermining effect. First of all, he is disappointed in his expectation of an unfavorable reaction on the part of the interrogator. Secondly, a concession of this right to remain silent impresses the subject with the apparent fairness of his interrogator." After this psychological conditioning, however, the officer is told to point out the incriminating significance of the suspect's refusal to talk:

> "Joe, you have a right to remain silent. That's your privilege and I'm the last person in the world who'll try to take it away from you. If that's the way you want to leave this, O.K. But let me ask you this. Suppose you were in my shoes and I were in yours and you called me in to ask me about this and I told you, 'I don't want to answer any of your questions.' You'd think I had something to hide, and you'd probably be right in thinking that. That's exactly what I'll have to think about you, and so will everybody else. So let's sit here and talk this whole thing over."

Few will persist in their initial refusal to talk, it is said, if this monologue is employed correctly.

In the event that the subject wishes to speak to a relative or an attorney, the following advice is tendered:

> [T]he interrogator should respond by suggesting that the subject first tell the truth to the interrogator himself rather than get anyone else involved in the matter. If the request is for an attorney, the interrogator may suggest that the subject save himself or his family the expense of any such professional service, particularly if he is innocent of the offense under investigation. The interrogator may also add, "Joe, I'm only looking for the truth, and if you're telling the truth, that's it. You can handle this by yourself."

From these representative samples of interrogation techniques, the setting prescribed by the manuals and observed in practice becomes clear. In essence, it is this: To be alone with the subject is essential to prevent distraction and to deprive him of any outside support. The aura of confidence in his guilt undermines his will to resist. He merely confirms the preconceived story the police seek to have him describe. Patience and persistence, at times relentless questioning, are employed. To obtain a confession, the interrogator must "patiently maneuver himself or his quarry into a position from which the desired objective may be attained." When normal procedures fail to produce the needed result, the police may resort to deceptive stratagems such as giving false legal advice. It is important to keep the subject off balance, for example, by trading on his insecurity about himself or his surroundings. The police then persuade, trick, or cajole him out of exercising his constitutional rights.

Even without employing brutality, the "third degree" or the specific stratagems described above, the very fact of custodial interrogation exacts a heavy toll on individual liberty and trades on the weakness of individuals. . . .

. . . From the foregoing, we can readily perceive an intimate connection between the privilege against self-incrimination and police custodial questioning. It is fitting

to turn to history and precedent underlying the Self-Incrimination Clause to determine its applicability in this situation.

II.

We sometimes forget how long it has taken to establish the privilege against self-incrimination, the sources from which it came and the fervor with which it was defended. Its roots go back into ancient times. Perhaps the critical historical event shedding light on its origins and evolution was the trial of one John Lilburn, a vocal anti-Stuart Leveller, who was made to take the Star Chamber Oath in 1637. The oath would have bound him to answer to all questions posed to him on any subject. The Trial of John Lilburn and John Wharton, 3 How. St. Tr. 1315 (1637). He resisted the oath and declaimed the proceedings, stating:

> Another fundamental right I then contended for, was, that no man's conscience ought to be racked by oaths imposed, to answer to questions concerning himself in matters criminal, or pretended to be so. Haller & Davies, *The Leveller Tracts* 1647–1653, p. 454 (1944).

On account of the Lilburn Trial, Parliament abolished the inquisitorial Court of Star Chamber and went further in giving him generous reparation. The lofty principles to which Lilburn had appealed during his trial gained popular acceptance in England. These sentiments worked their way over to the Colonies and were implanted after great struggle into the Bill of Rights. Those who framed our Constitution and the Bill of Rights were ever aware of subtle encroachments on individual liberty. They knew that "illegitimate and unconstitutional practices get their first footing . . . by silent approaches and slight deviations from legal modes of procedure." *Boyd* v. *United States*, 116 U.S. 616, 635 (1886). The privilege was elevated to constitutional status and has always been "as broad as the mischief against which it seeks to guard." *Counselman* v. *Hitchcock*, 142 U.S. 547, 562 (1892). We cannot depart from this noble heritage.

Thus we may view the historical development of the privilege as one which groped for the proper scope of governmental power over the citizen. As a "noble principle often transcends its origins," the privilege has come rightfully to be recognized in part as an individual's substantive right, a "right to a private enclave where he may lead a private life. That right is the hallmark of our democracy." *United States* v. *Grunewald*, 233 F.2d 556, 579, 581–582 (FRANK, J., dissenting), rev'd, 353 U.S. 391 (1957). We have recently noted that the privilege against self-incrimination—the essential mainstay of our adversary system—is founded on a complex of values. . . . All these policies point to one overriding thought: the constitutional foundation underlying the privilege is the respect a government—state or federal—must accord to the dignity and integrity of its citizens. To maintain a "fair state–individual balance," to require the government "to shoulder the entire load," . . . to respect the inviolability of the human personality, our accusatory system of criminal justice demands that the government seeking to punish an individual produce the evidence against him by its own independent labors, rather than by the cruel, simple expedient of compelling it from his own mouth. *Chambers* v. *Florida*, 309 U.S. 227, 235–238 (1940). In sum, the privilege is fulfilled only when the person is guaranteed the right "to remain silent unless he chooses to speak in the unfettered exercise of his own will." *Malloy* v. *Hogan*, 378 U.S. 1, 8 (1964). . . .

Today, then, there can be no doubt that the Fifth Amendment privilege is available outside of criminal court proceedings and serves to protect persons in all settings in which their freedom of action is curtailed in any significant way from being

compelled to incriminate themselves. We have concluded that without proper safeguards the process of in-custody interrogation of persons suspected or accused of crime contains inherently compelling pressures which work to undermine the individual's will to resist and to compel him to speak where he would not otherwise do so freely. In order to combat these pressures and to permit a full opportunity to exercise the privilege against self-incrimination, the accused must be adequately and effectively apprised of his rights and the exercise of those rights must be fully honored.

It is impossible for us to foresee the potential alternatives for protecting the privilege which might be devised by Congress or the States in the exercise of their creative rule-making capacities. Therefore we cannot say that the Constitution necessarily requires adherence to any particular solution for the inherent compulsions of the interrogation process as it is presently conducted. Our decision in no way creates a constitutional straitjacket which will handicap sound efforts at reform, nor is it intended to have this effect. We encourage Congress and the States to continue their laudable search for increasingly effective ways of protecting the rights of the individual while promoting efficient enforcement of our criminal laws. However, unless we are shown other procedures which are at least as effective in apprising accused persons of their right of silence and in assuring a continuous opportunity to exercise it, the following safeguards must be observed.

At the outset, if a person in custody is to be subjected to interrogation, he must first be informed in clear and unequivocal terms that he has the right to remain silent. For those unaware of the privilege, the warning is needed simply to make them aware of it—the threshold requirement for an intelligent decision as to its exercise. More important, such a warning is an absolute prerequisite in overcoming the inherent pressures of the interrogation atmosphere. It is not just the subnormal or woefully ignorant who succumb to an interrogator's imprecations, whether implied or expressly stated, that the interrogation will continue until a confession is obtained or that silence in the face of accusation is itself damning and will bode ill when presented to a jury. Further, the warning will show the individual that his interrogators are prepared to recognize his privilege should he choose to exercise it.

The Fifth Amendment privilege is so fundamental to our system of constitutional rule and the expedient of giving an adequate warning as to the availability of the privilege so simple, we will not pause to inquire in individual cases whether the defendant was aware of his rights without a warning being given. Assessments of the knowledge the defendant possessed, based on information as to his age, education, intelligence, or prior contact with authorities, can never be more than speculation; a warning is a clearcut fact. More important, whatever the background of the person interrogated, a warning at the time of the interrogation is indispensable to overcome its pressures and to insure that the individual knows he is free to exercise the privilege at that point in time.

The warning of the right to remain silent must be accompanied by the explanation that anything said can and will be used against the individual in court. This warning is needed in order to make him aware not only of the privilege, but also of the consequences of forgoing it. It is only through an awareness of these consequences that there can be any assurance of real understanding and intelligent exercise of the privilege. Moreover, this warning may serve to make the individual more acutely aware that he is faced with a phase of the adversary system—that he is not in the presence of persons acting solely in his interest.

The circumstances surrounding in-custody interrogation can operate very quickly to overbear the will of one merely made aware of his privilege by his in-

terrogators. Therefore, the right to have counsel present at the interrogation is indispensable to the protection of the Fifth Amendment privilege under the system we delineate today. Our aim is to assure that the individual's right to choose between silence and speech remains unfettered throughout the interrogation process. A once-stated warning, delivered by those who will conduct the interrogation, cannot itself suffice to that end among those who most require knowledge of their rights. A mere warning given by the interrogators is not alone sufficient to accomplish that end. Prosecutors themselves claim that the admonishment of the right to remain silent without more "will benefit only the recidivist and the professional." Brief for the National District Attorneys Association as *amicus curiae*, p. 14. Even preliminary advice given to the accused by his own attorney can be swiftly overcome by the secret interrogation process. Cf. *Escobedo* v. *Illinois*, 378 U.S. 478, 485, n. 5. Thus, the need for counsel to protect the Fifth Amendment privilege comprehends not merely a right to consult with counsel prior to questioning, but also to have counsel present during any questioning if the defendant so desires. . . .

In order to fully apprise a person interrogated of the extent of his rights under this system then, it is necessary to warn him not only that he has the right to consult with an attorney, but also that if he is indigent a lawyer will be appointed to represent him. Without this additional warning, the admonition of the right to consult with counsel would often be understood as meaning only that he can consult with a lawyer if he has one or has the funds to obtain one. The warning of a right to counsel would be hollow if not couched in terms that would convey to the indigent—the person most often subjected to interrogation—the knowledge that he too has a right to have counsel present. As with the warnings of the right to remain silent and of the general right to counsel, only by effective and express explanation to the indigent of this right can there be assurance that he was truly in a position to exercise it. . . .

Once warnings have been given, the subsequent procedure is clear. If the individual indicates in any manner, at any time prior to or during questioning, that he wishes to remain silent, the interrogation must cease. At this point he has shown that he intends to exercise his Fifth Amendment privilege; any statement taken after the person invokes his privilege cannot be other than the product of compulsion, subtle or otherwise. Without the right to cut off questioning, the setting of in-custody interrogation operates on the individual to overcome free choice in producing a statement after the privilege has been once invoked. If the individual states that he wants an attorney, the interrogation must cease until an attorney is present. At that time, the individual must have an opportunity to confer with the attorney and to have him present during any subsequent questioning. If the individual cannot obtain an attorney and he indicates that he wants one before speaking to police, they must respect his decision to remain silent.

This does not mean, as some have suggested, that each police station must have a "station house lawyer" present at all times to advise prisoners. It does mean, however, that if police propose to interrogate a person they must make known to him that he is entitled to a lawyer and that if he cannot afford one, a lawyer will be provided for him prior to any interrogation. If authorities conclude that they will not provide counsel during a reasonable period of time in which investigation in the field is carried out, they may refrain from doing so without violating the person's Fifth Amendment privilege so long as they do not question him during that time.

If the interrogation continues without the presence of an attorney and a statement is taken, a heavy burden rests on the government to demonstrate that the

defendant knowingly and intelligently waived his privilege against self-incrimination and his right to retained or appointed counsel. *Escobedo* v. *Illinois*, 378 U.S. 478, 490, n. 14. This Court has always set high standards of proof for the waiver of constitutional rights, *Johnson* v. *Zerbst*, 304 U.S. 458 (1938), and we re-assert these standards as applied to in-custody interrogation. Since the State is responsible for establishing the isolated circumstances under which the interrogation takes place and has the only means of making available corroborated evidence of warnings given during incommunicado interrogation, the burden is rightly on its shoulders.

An express statement that the individual is willing to make a statement and does not want an attorney followed closely by a statement could constitute a waiver. But a valid waiver will not be presumed simply from the silence of the accused after warnings are given or simply from the fact that a confession was in fact eventually obtained. A statement we made in *Carnley* v. *Cochran*, 369 U.S. 506, 516 (1962), is applicable here:

> Presuming waiver from a silent record is impermissible. The record must show, or there must be an allegation and evidence which show, that an accused was offered counsel but intelligently and understandingly rejected the offer. Anything less is not waiver.

The warnings required and the waiver necessary in accordance with our opinion today are, in the absence of a fully effective equivalent, prerequisites to the admissibility of any statement made by a defendant. No distinction can be drawn between statements which are direct confessions and statements which amount to "admissions" of part or all of an offense. The privilege against self-incrimination protects the individual from being compelled to incriminate himself in any manner; it does not distinguish degrees of incrimination. Similarly, for precisely the same reason, no distinction may be drawn between inculpatory statements and statements alleged to be merely "exculpatory." If a statement made were in fact truly exculpatory it would, of course, never be used by the prosecution. In fact, statements merely intended to be exculpatory by the defendant are often used to impeach his testimony at trial or to demonstrate untruths in the statement given under interrogation and thus to prove guilt by implication. These statements are incriminating in any meaningful sense of the word and may not be used without the full warnings and effective waiver required for any other statement. In *Escobedo* itself, the defendant fully intended his accusation of another as the slayer to be exculpatory as to himself.

The principles announced today deal with the protection which must be given to the privilege against self-incrimination when the individual is first subjected to police interrogation while in custody at the station or otherwise deprived of his freedom of action in any significant way. It is at this point that our adversary system of criminal proceedings commences, distinguishing itself at the outset from the inquisitorial system recognized in some countries. Under the system of warnings we delineate today or under any other system which may be devised and found effective, the safeguards to be erected about the privilege must come into play at this point. . . .

In announcing these principles, we are not unmindful of the burdens which law enforcement officials must bear, often under trying circumstances. We also fully recognize the obligation of all citizens to aid in enforcing the criminal laws. This Court, while protecting individual rights, has always given latitude to law enforcement agencies in the legitimate exercise of their duties. The limits we have placed on the interrogation process should not constitute an undue interference with a proper system of law enforcement. As we have noted, our decision does not in any way preclude police from carrying out their traditional investigatory functions. Although confessions may play an important role in some convictions, the cases before us present graphic examples of the overstatement of the "need" for confessions. In each case authorities conducted interrogations ranging up to five days in duration despite the presence, through standard investigating practices, of considerable evidence against each defendant. Further examples are chronicled in our prior cases. See, e.g., *Haynes* v. *Washington*, 373 U.S. 503, 518–519 (1963); *Rogers* v. *Richmond*, 365 U.S. 534, 541 (1961); *Malinski* v. *New York*, 324 U.S. 401, 402 (1945).

. . . We reverse. From the testimony of the officers and by the admission of respondent, it is clear that Miranda was not in any way apprised of his right to consult with an attorney and to have one present during the interrogation, nor was his right not to be compelled to incriminate himself effectively protected in any other manner. Without these warnings the statements were inadmissible. The mere fact that he signed a statement which contained a typed-in clause stating that he had "full knowledge" of his "legal rights" does not approach the knowing and intelligent waiver required to relinquish constitutional rights. Cf. *Haynes* v. *Washington*, 373 U.S. 503, 512–513 (1963); *Haley* v. *Ohio*, 332 U.S. 596, 601 (1948) (opinion of MR. JUSTICE DOUGLAS).

MR. JUSTICE WHITE, with whom MR. JUSTICE HARLAN and MR. JUSTICE STEWART join, dissenting. [Omitted.]

WHAT DO YOU THINK?

1. Do you agree with the Court that custodial interrogation is "inherently" coercive? Explain your answer.
2. What are the criteria for waiving the right against self-incrimination?
3. When is the warning required?

What are the requirements before a person may waive his or her rights against self-incrimination? The Garibay *case discusses this issue.*

UNITED STATES V. GARIBAY
9650606 (9th Cir. May 5, 1998)

PREGERSON, Circuit Judge:

Jose Rosario Garibay, Jr. appeals his convictions by a jury for importing marijuana in violation of 21 U.S.C.SS 952 and 960 and for possession of marijuana with intent to distribute in violation of 21 U.S.C. S 841(a)(1). Garibay asserts that in denying his motion to suppress the district court erred (1) in finding that he had waived his *Miranda* rights before making inculpatory statements to United States Customs Agents; and (2) in denying his request for a downward departure for acceptance of responsibility.

In reviewing the totality of circumstances in which Garibay was interrogated, it is clear that he was not aware of the nature of the constitutional rights he was waiving, and that the district court clearly erred in finding that he knowingly and intelligently waived his *Miranda* rights. Accordingly, we hold that the district court

erred when it failed to suppress Garibay's inculpatory statements and allowed them to go to the jury. We also hold that absent Garibay's incriminating statements obtained in violation of his *Miranda* rights, the evidence before the jury was insufficient to support his convictions. Therefore, we reverse and remand for proceedings consistent with this opinion.

I.

On December 15, 1995, Jose Rosario Garibay, Jr. attempted to drive into the United States across the U.S.–Mexico border at the Calexico Port-of-Entry. A United States Customs Inspector asked Garibay, in Spanish, to open the trunk of the vehicle. Detecting a silicone odor emanating from the trunk, the Inspector directed Garibay to the Second Inspection Lot. A closer inspection of the vehicle revealed a depth-discrepancy in the trunk. The trunk was drilled. The drill bit came out with a green leafy substance that field-tested positive for marijuana. Fifty-five packages of marijuana, weighing approximately 138.65 pounds were removed from beneath the trunk floor. Garibay was arrested and placed in a holding cell.

About an hour later, United States Customs Agents Joseph William Burke and Jennifer Holden questioned Garibay in English. Agent Burke asked Garibay in English if he understood English, to which Garibay responded "yes." Agent Burke then orally read in English Garibay's constitutional rights, pursuant to *Miranda* v. *Arizona*, 384 U.S. 436, 479 (1966). Garibay indicated that he understood. During the interrogation, Garibay made incriminating statements. He moved to suppress those statements on the ground that he did not understand the nature of the rights he was waiving because of his limited-English skills and low mental capacity.

The district court held an evidentiary hearing, and found that the waiver was knowing and intelligent. Garibay proceeded to trial and was convicted on all charges.

II.

A. WAIVER OF MIRANDA RIGHTS

1. *Standard of Review*

We review for clear error a district court's finding that a defendant knowingly and intelligently waived his *Miranda* rights. See *United States* v. *Cazares*, 121 F.3d 1241, 1243 (9th Cir. 1997).

2. *Requirements of a Valid Waiver*

For inculpatory statements made by a defendant during custodial interrogation to be admissible in evidence, the defendant's "waiver of *Miranda* rights must be voluntary, knowing, and intelligent." *United States* v. *Binder*, 769 F.2d 595, 599 (9th Cir. 1985) (citing *Miranda*, 384 U.S. at 479). A valid waiver of *Miranda* rights depends upon the "totality of the circumstances including the background, experience, and conduct of defendant." *United States* v. *Bernard S.*, 795 F.2d 749, 751 (9th Cir. 1986).

There is a presumption against waiver. . . . The prosecution bears the burden of proving by a preponderance of the evidence that a defendant knowingly and intelligently waived his *Miranda* rights. See *Colorado* v. *Connelly*, 479 U.S. 157, 168 (1986). To satisfy this burden, the prosecution must introduce sufficient evidence to establish that under the "totality of the circumstances," the defendant was aware

of "the nature of the right being abandoned and the consequences of the decision to abandon it." *Moran* v. *Burbine*, 475 U.S. 412, 421 (1986). The government's burden to make such a showing "is great," and the court will "indulge every reasonable presumption against waiver of fundamental constitutional rights." . . .

3. *Analysis*

Garibay challenges the finding that he validly waived his *Miranda* rights because he was not aware of the nature of the constitutional rights he was abandoning. Specifically, Garibay contends that he did not understand Agent Burke's recitation of his rights in English because his primary language is Spanish and he has a low verbal IQ. Upon review of the record, we conclude that the prosection did not meet its burden of proving that Garibay knowingly and intelligently waived his *Miranda* rights. . . .

In determining whether a defendant knowingly and intelligently waived his *Miranda* rights, we consider, as one factor, any language difficulties encountered by the defendant during custodial interrogation. . . . In finding that Garibay was proficient in English, the district court relied on the following: (1) Garibay allegedly declined the agents' offer to be questioned in Spanish; and (2) Garibay attended high school in California and opted for an English-only curriculum. But a review of the record reveals that the district court incorrectly stated the facts supporting its conclusion and, as a result, clearly erred in concluding that Garibay's English-language skills were sufficient for him to understand and waive his constitutional rights.

First, contrary to the district court's conclusion, Agent Burke did not offer Garibay the option of conducting the interrogation in Spanish, nor did Garibay decline such an offer. Rather, Agent Burke questioned Garibay in English and assumed that Garibay was sufficiently proficient in English to understand and waive his *Miranda* rights without the assistance of a Spanish-speaking officer. Agent Burke also admitted that he had to rephrase questions when Garibay did not seem to comprehend what was said to him. Although Spanish-speaking agents were available at the time of Garibay's arrest and custodial interrogation, Burke did not enlist those agents to assist him in questioning Garibay.

Second, the record clearly indicates that Garibay's primary language is Spanish and he understands only a few things in English. Garibay attended a U.S. high school where he received English instruction and received D+ grades in eleventh and twelfth grade English. These grades do not support a finding that he is sufficiently proficient in English to have waived his *Miranda* rights. Garibay did not graduate from high school. According to the presentence report, Garibay received the passing grades in English because those classes were taught using Spanish. Moreover, a probation officer reported that several independent sources in the community told him that "they did not believe he[Garibay] could speak English except for a few words." In addition, with the exception of Agent Burke, every witness at the suppression hearing testified that at Garibay's request they would always communicate with him in Spanish. These witnesses include Garibay's former high school counselor, Garibay's former football coach, the clinicall psychologist who examined Garibay, and the probation officer who prepared Garibay's presentence report. . . .

A defendant's mental capacity directly bears upon the question whether he understood the meaning of his Miranda rights and the significance of waiving his constitutional rights. . . . It is undisputed that Garibay's IQ is borderline retarded and that he has difficulty understanding the English language. Additionally, the presentence report confirmed Garibay's inability to understand oral instructions.

Without these skills, Garibay could not have knowingly and intelligently waived his rights. The government presented no evidence to contradict the fact that Garibay, in addition to being limited-English proficient, is borderline retarded with extremely low verbal-English comprehension skills.

In applying the "totality of circumstances" test, we further examine whether other circumstances surrounding Garibay's interrogation indicate that he knowingly and intelligently waived his constitutional rights, despite his English-language difficulties, borderline retarded IQ, and poor verbal comprehension skills. See *Derrick*, 924 F.2d at 817–824. The following considerations guide our inquiry: (1) whether the defendant signed a written waiver . . . (2) whether the defendant was advised of his rights in his native tongue . . . (3) whether the defendant appeared to understand his rights . . . ; (4) whether a defendant had the assistance of a translator . . . ; (5) whether the defendant's rights were individually and repeatedly explained to him . . . ; and (6) whether the defendant had prior experience with the criminal justice system. . . .

Here, none of these considerations are present. Garibay was not given a written waiver to sign in either English or Spanish nor was he advised of his rights in Spanish. Garibay's rights were recited to him only in English. Although translators were available at the time of Garibay's arrest, they were not brought in to help question him. The prosecution offered no evidence that Agent Burke individually explained each constitutional right to Garibay or repeated the explanation.

Moreover, Garibay had no previous experience with the criminal process. Thus, Garibay's personal life experiences do not indicate that he was familiar with his *Miranda* rights and his option to waive those rights. See e.g., *Cooper* v. *Griffin*, 455 F.2d 1142, 1444–45 (5th Cir. 1972) (holding that in view of armed robbery defendants' mental retardation, poor reading comprehension, and no prior experience with the criminal process, confessions obtained after defendants orally waived right to counsel and signed written waiver forms were inadmissable).

The prosecution, however, contends that Garibay indicated to Agent Burke that he understood his rights. Agent Burke, however, also admitted to rephrasing questions when Garibay did not appear to understand him. Also, the testimony of Garibay's football coach clearly shows that Garibay, in the presence of authoritative figures, would indicate he understood what was being said to him in English when he did not.

Thus, the facts surrounding Garibay's interrogation clearly indicate that he did not understand the nature of the rights he was waiving. Moreover, the customs agents took no steps to ensure that Garibay's waiver was knowing and intelligent. Therefore, we conclude that the district court clearly erred in finding that despite Garibay's low IQ and poor English-verbal comprehension, he nonetheless functioned at a level sufficient to have understood and waived the constitutional rights orally read to him in English by Agent Burke. Thus, in the circumstances of this case, the district court erred in not suppressing Garibay's inculpatory statements. . . .

The requirement that a defendant "knowingly and intelligently" waive his *Miranda* rights "implies a rational choice based upon some appreciation of the consequences of the decision." *Cooper*, 455 F.2d at 1145 (citations and internal quotations omitted); see also *Miranda*, 384 U.S. at 464–65. Moreover, the Supreme Court has recognized that "[t]he Fifth Amendment privilege [against self-incrimination] is so fundamental to our system of constitutional rule and the expedient of giving an adequate warning as to the availability of the privilege so simple, we will not pause to inquire in individual cases whether the defendant was aware of his rights without warning being given." *Miranda*, 384 U.S. at 468.

We are troubled by the circumstances surrounding Garibay's alleged waiver. It is hard for us to discern any justification for the agents' failure to ask Garibay whether he preferred Spanish or English and their failure to seek the assistance of bilingual agents in questioning Garibay. The agents' oversight is particularly glaring given that Garibay's primary language is Spanish, that Garibay was arrested at the U.S.–Mexico border, that Agent Burke had to rephrase several questions in English in an attempt to communicate with Garibay, and that bilingual agents were readily available.

Although we have held that an officer need not use a printed waiver form to solicit a valid waiver of *Miranda* rights, *Terrovona* v. *Kincheloe*, 912 F.2d 1176, 1180 (9th Cir. 1990), we are nonetheless troubled with the government's admission at oral argument that a policy exists at the border against using written *Miranda* waivers in either English or Spanish. The right to remain silent and the right to have counsel present during questioning are indispensable to the protection of the Fifth Amendment privilege against self-incrimination. Written waivers coupled with oral recitations help ensure that the necessary procedures are in place to protect such constitutional rights which all officials are sworn to uphold. In the circumstances of Garibay's custodial interrogation, we find that the steps taken to protect these essential rights were deficient.

In light of the foregoing discussion, we reverse and remand for proceedings consistent with this opinion.

REVERSED AND REMANDED.

WHAT DO YOU THINK?

1. Explain the test set forth by the Court by the statement: "For inculpatory statements made by a defendant during custodial interrogation to be admissible in evidence, the defendant's waiver of *Miranda* rights must be voluntary, knowing, and intelligent."

2. What does the "totality of the circumstances" test include?

3. Do you agree that there should be a presumption against waiver and that the prosecution bears the burden of establishing a waiver? Why?

4. The Court noted that there were Spanish-speaking agents available at the time of Garibay's arrest and custodial interrogation, and Burke did not enlist those agents to assist him in questioning Garibay. Should this fact be considered in applying the "totality of circumstances" test?

Is a request by a juvenile being interrogated to talk to his probation officer equivalent to a request to speak to an attorney? The Michael C. *case examines this issue.*

FARE V. MICHAEL C.
442 U.S. 707 (1979)

MR. JUSTICE BLACKMUN delivered the opinion of the Court.

In *Miranda* v. *Arizona*, 384 U.S. 436 (1966), this Court established certain procedural safeguards designed to protect the rights of an accused, under the Fifth and

Justice Harry A. Blackmun was appointed to the Supreme Court by President Nixon and served from 1970 to 1994. (Photograph by Joseph D. Lavenburg, National Geographic Society. Courtesy of the Supreme Court of the United States.)

Fourteenth Amendments, to be free from compelled self-incrimination during custodial interrogation. The Court specified, among other things, that if the accused indicates in any manner that he wishes to remain silent or to consult an attorney, interrogation must cease, and any statement obtained from him during interrogation thereafter may not be admitted against him at his trial....

In this case, the State of California, in the person of its acting chief probation officer, attacks the conclusion of the Supreme Court of California that a juvenile's request, made while undergoing custodial interrogation, to see his probation officer is per se an invocation of the juvenile's Fifth Amendment rights as pronounced in *Miranda.*

I.

Respondent Michael C. was implicated in the murder of Robert Yeager. The murder occurred during a robbery of the victim's home on January 19, 1976. A small truck registered in the name of respondent's mother was identified as having been near the Yeager home at the time of the killing, and a young man answering respondent's description was seen by witnesses near the truck and near the home shortly before Yeager was murdered.

On the basis of this information, Van Nuys, Cal., police took respondent into custody at approximately 6:30 p.m. on February 4. Respondent then was 16-1/2 years old and on probation to the Juvenile Court. He had been on probation since the age of 12. Approximately one year earlier he had served a term in a youth corrections camp under the supervision of the Juvenile Court. He had a record of several previous offenses, including burglary of guns and purse snatching, stretching back over several years.

Upon respondent's arrival at the Van Nuys station house two police officers began to interrogate him. The officers and respondent were the only persons in the room during the interrogation. The conversation was tape-recorded. One of the officers initiated the interview by informing respondent that he had been brought in for questioning in relation to a murder. The officer fully advised respondent of his *Miranda* rights. The following exchange then occurred, as set out in the opinion of the California Supreme Court, *In re Michael C.*, 21 Cal. 3d 471, 473–474, 579 P.2d 7, 8 (1978):

> "Q. . . . Do you understand all of these rights as I have explained them to you?
> "A. Yeah.
> "Q. Okay, do you wish to give up your right to remain silent and talk to us about this murder?
> "A. What murder? I don't know about no murder.
> "Q. I'll explain to you which one it is if you want to talk to us about it.
> "A. Yeah, I might talk to you.
> "Q. Do you want to give up your right to have an attorney present here while we talk about it?
> "A. Can I have my probation officer here?
> "Q. Well I can't get a hold of your probation officer right now. You have the right to an attorney.
> "A. How I know you guys won't pull no police officer in and tell me he's an attorney?
> "Q. Huh?
> "A. [How I know you guys won't pull no police officer in and tell me he's an attorney?]
> "Q. Your probation officer is Mr. Christiansen.
> "A. Yeah.
> "Q. Well I'm not going to call Mr. Christiansen tonight. There's a good chance we can talk to him later, but I'm not going to call him right now. If you want to talk to us without an attorney present, you can. If you don't want to, you don't have to. But if you want to say something, you can, and if you don't want to say something you don't have to. That's your right. You understand that right?
> "A. Yeah.
> "Q. Okay, will you talk to us without an attorney present?
> "A. Yeah I want to talk to you."

Respondent thereupon proceeded to answer questions put to him by the officers. He made statements and drew sketches that incriminated him in the Yeager murder.

Largely on the basis of respondent's incriminating statements, probation authorities filed a petition in Juvenile Court alleging that respondent had murdered Robert Yeager . . . and that respondent therefore should be adjudged a ward of the Juvenile Court . . . Respondent thereupon moved to suppress the statements and sketches he gave the police during the interrogation. He alleged that the statements had been obtained in violation of *Miranda* in that his request to see his probation officer at the outset of the questioning constituted an invocation of his Fifth Amendment right to remain silent, just as if he had requested the assistance of an attorney. Accordingly, respondent argued that since the interrogation did not cease until he had a chance to confer with his probation officer, the statements and sketches could not be admitted against him in the Juvenile Court proceedings. In so arguing, respondent relied by analogy on the decision in *People v. Burton*, 6 Cal.

3d 375, 491 P.2d 793 (1971), where the Supreme Court of California had held that a minor's request, made during custodial interrogation, to see his parents constituted an invocation of the minor's Fifth Amendment rights.

In support of his suppression motion, respondent called his probation officer, Charles P. Christiansen, as a witness. Christiansen testified that he had instructed respondent that if at any time he had "a concern with his family," or ever had "a police contact," App. 27, he should get in touch with his probation officer immediately. The witness stated that, on a previous occasion, when respondent had had a police contact and had failed to communicate with Christiansen, the probation officer had reprimanded him. *Id.*, at 28. This testimony, respondent argued, indicated that when he asked for his probation officer, he was in fact asserting his right to remain silent in the face of further questioning.

In a ruling from the bench, the court denied the motion to suppress. *Id.*, at 41–42. It held that the question whether respondent had waived his right to remain silent was one of fact to be determined on a case-by-case basis, and that the facts of this case showed a "clear waiver" by respondent of that right. *Id.*, at 42. The court observed that the transcript of the interrogation revealed that respondent specifically had told the officers that he would talk with them, and that this waiver had come at the outset of the interrogation and not after prolonged questioning. The court noted that respondent was a "16 and a half year old minor who has been through the court system before, has been to [probation] camp, has a probation officer, [and is not] a young, naive minor with no experience with the courts." *Ibid.* Accordingly, it found that on the facts of the case respondent had waived his Fifth Amendment rights, notwithstanding the request to see his probation officer.

On appeal, the Supreme Court of California took the case by transfer from the California Court of Appeal and, by a divided vote, reversed. *In re Michael C.*, 21 Cal. 3d 471, 579 P.2d 7 (1978). The court held that respondent's "request to see his probation officer at the commencement of interrogation negated any possible willingness on his part to discuss his case with the police [and] thereby invoked his Fifth Amendment privilege." *Id.*, at 474, 579 P.2d, at 8. The court based this conclusion on its view that, because of the juvenile court system's emphasis on the relationship between a probation officer and the probationer, the officer was "a trusted guardian figure who exercises the authority of the state as parens patriae and whose duty it is to implement the protective and rehabilitative powers of the juvenile court." *Id.*, at 476, 579 P.2d, at 10. As a consequence, the court found that a minor's request for his probation officer was the same as a request to see his parents during interrogation, and thus under the rule of Burton constituted an invocation of the minor's Fifth Amendment rights.

The fact that the probation officer also served as a peace officer, and, whenever a proceeding against a juvenile was contemplated, was charged with a duty to file a petition alleging that the minor had committed an offense, did not alter, in the court's view, the fact that the officer in the eyes of the juvenile was a trusted guardian figure to whom the minor normally would turn for help when in trouble with the police. 21 Cal. 3d, at 476, 579 P.2d, at 10. Relying on Burton, the court ruled that it would unduly restrict *Miranda* to limit its reach in a case involving a minor to a request by the minor for an attorney, since it would be " 'fatuous to assume that a minor in custody will be in a position to call an attorney for assistance and it is unrealistic to attribute no significance to his call for help from the only person to whom he normally looks—a parent or guardian.' " 21 Cal. 3d, at 475–476, 579 P.2d, at 9, quoting *People* v. *Burton*, 6 Cal. 3d, at 382, 491 P.2d, at 797–798. The court dismissed the concern expressed by the State that a request

for a probation officer could not be distinguished from a request for one's football coach, music teacher, or clergyman on the ground that the probation officer, unlike those other figures in the juvenile's life, was charged by statute to represent the interests of the juvenile. 21 Cal. 3d, at 477, 579 P.2d, at 10.

The court accordingly held that the probation officer would act to protect the minor's Fifth Amendment rights in precisely the way an attorney would act if called for by the accused. In so holding, the court found the request for a probation officer to be a per se invocation of Fifth Amendment rights in the same way the request for an attorney was found in *Miranda* to be, regardless of what the interrogation otherwise might reveal. In rejecting a totality-of-the-circumstances inquiry, the court stated:

> Here, however, we face conduct which, regardless of considerations of capacity, coercion or voluntariness, per se invokes the privilege against self-incrimination. Thus our question turns not on whether the [respondent] had the ability, capacity or willingness to give a knowledgeable waiver, and hence whether he acted voluntarily, but whether, when he called for his probation officer, he exercised his Fifth Amendment privilege. We hold that in doing so he no less invoked the protection against self-incrimination than if he asked for the presence of an attorney. *Ibid.*, 579 P.2d, at 10–11.

The court went on to conclude that since the State had not met its "burden of proving that a minor who requests to see his probation officer does not intend to assert his Fifth Amendment privilege,"... the trial court should not have admitted the confessions obtained after respondent had requested his probation officer....

II.

... The rule the Court established in *Miranda* is clear. In order to be able to use statements obtained during custodial interrogation of the accused, the State must warn the accused prior to such questioning of his right to remain silent and of his right to have counsel, retained or appointed, present during interrogation. 384 U.S., at 473. "Once [such] warnings have been given, the subsequent procedure is clear." *Ibid.*

> If the individual indicates in any manner, at any time prior to or during questioning, that he wishes to remain silent, the interrogation must cease. At this point he has shown that he intends to exercise his Fifth Amendment privilege; any statement taken after the person invokes his privilege cannot be other than the product of compulsion, subtle or otherwise.... If the individual states that he wants an attorney, the interrogation must cease until an attorney is present. At that time, the individual must have an opportunity to confer with the attorney and to have him present during any subsequent questioning. If the individual cannot obtain an attorney and he indicates that he wants one before speaking to police, they must respect his decision to remain silent. *Id.*, at 473–474 (footnote omitted).

Any statements obtained during custodial interrogation conducted in violation of these rules may not be admitted against the accused, at least during the State's case in chief. *Id.*, at 479. Cf. *Harris* v. *New York*, 401 U.S. 222, 224 (1971).

Whatever the defects, if any, of this relatively rigid requirement that interrogation must cease upon the accused's request for an attorney, *Miranda*'s holding has the virtue of informing police and prosecutors with specificity as to what they may do in conducting custodial interrogation, and of informing courts under what circumstances statements obtained during such interrogation are not admissible.

This gain in specificity, which benefits the accused and the State alike, has been thought to outweigh the burdens that the decision in *Miranda* imposes on law enforcement agencies and the courts by requiring the suppression of trustworthy and highly probative evidence even though the confession might be voluntary under traditional Fifth Amendment analysis. See *Michigan* v. *Tucker*, 417 U.S. 433, 443–446 (1974).

The California court in this case, however, significantly has extended this rule by providing that a request by a juvenile for his probation officer has the same effect as a request for an attorney. Based on the court's belief that the probation officer occupies a position as a trusted guardian figure in the minor's life that would make it normal for the minor to turn to the officer when apprehended by the police, and based as well on the state-law requirement that the officer represent the interest of the juvenile, the California decision found that consultation with a probation officer fulfilled the role for the juvenile that consultation with an attorney does in general, acting as a " 'protective [device] . . . to dispel the compulsion inherent in custodial surroundings.' " 21 Cal. 3d, at 477, 579 P.2d, at 10, quoting *Miranda* v. *Arizona*, 384 U.S., at 458.

The rule in *Miranda*, however, was based on this Court's perception that the lawyer occupies a critical position in our legal system because of his unique ability to protect the Fifth Amendment rights of a client undergoing custodial interrogation. Because of this special ability of the lawyer to help the client preserve his Fifth Amendment rights once the client becomes enmeshed in the adversary process, the Court found that "the right to have counsel present at the interrogation is indispensable to the protection of the Fifth Amendment privilege under the system" established by the Court. *Id.*, at 469. Moreover, the lawyer's presence helps guard against overreaching by the police and ensures that any statements actually obtained are accurately transcribed for presentation into evidence. *Id.*, at 470.

The per se aspect of *Miranda* was thus based on the unique role the lawyer plays in the adversary system of criminal justice in this country. Whether it is a minor or an adult who stands accused, the lawyer is the one person to whom society as a whole looks as the protector of the legal rights of that person in his dealings with the police and the courts. For this reason, the Court fashioned in *Miranda* the rigid rule that an accused's request for an attorney is per se an invocation of his Fifth Amendment rights, requiring that all interrogation cease.

A probation officer is not in the same posture with regard to either the accused or the system of justice as a whole. Often he is not trained in the law, and so is not in a position to advise the accused as to his legal rights. Neither is he a trained advocate, skilled in the representation of the interests of his client before both police and courts. He does not assume the power to act on behalf of his client by virtue of his status as adviser, nor are the communications of the accused to the probation officer shielded by the lawyer–client privilege.

Moreover, the probation officer is the employee of the State which seeks to prosecute the alleged offender. He is a peace officer, and as such is allied, to a greater or lesser extent, with his fellow peace officers. He owes an obligation to the State, notwithstanding the obligation he may also owe the juvenile under his supervision. In most cases, the probation officer is duty bound to report wrongdoing by the juvenile when it comes to his attention even if by communication from the juvenile himself. Indeed, when this case arose, the probation officer had the responsibility for filing the petition alleging wrongdoing by the juvenile and seeking to have him taken into the custody of the Juvenile Court. It was respondent's probation officer who filed the petition against him, and it is the acting chief of pro-

bation for the State of California, a probation officer, who is petitioner in this Court today.

In these circumstances, it cannot be said that the probation officer is able to offer the type of independent advice that an accused would expect from a lawyer retained or assigned to assist him during questioning. Indeed, the probation officer's duty to his employer in many, if not most, cases would conflict sharply with the interests of the juvenile. For where an attorney might well advise his client to remain silent in the face of interrogation by the police, and in doing so would be "exercising [his] good professional judgment . . . to protect to the extent of his ability the rights of his client," *Miranda* v. *Arizona*, 384 U.S., at 480–481, a probation officer would be bound to advise his charge to cooperate with the police. The justices who concurred in the opinion of the California Supreme Court in this case aptly noted: "Where a conflict between the minor and the law arises, the probation officer can be neither neutral nor in the minor's corner." 21 Cal. 3d, at 479, 579 P.2d, at 12. It thus is doubtful that a general rule can be established that a juvenile, in every case, looks to his probation officer as a "trusted guardian figure" rather than as an officer of the court system that imposes punishment.

By the same token, a lawyer is able to protect his client's rights by learning the extent, if any, of the client's involvement in the crime under investigation, and advising his client accordingly. To facilitate this, the law rightly protects the communications between client and attorney from discovery. We doubt, however, that similar protection will be afforded the communications between the probation officer and the minor. Indeed, we doubt that a probation officer, consistent with his responsibilities to the public and his profession, could withhold from the police or the courts facts made known to him by the juvenile implicating the juvenile in the crime under investigation.

We thus believe it clear that the probation officer is not in a position to offer the type of legal assistance necessary to protect the Fifth Amendment rights of an accused undergoing custodial interrogation that a lawyer can offer. The Court in *Miranda* recognized that "the attorney plays a vital role in the administration of criminal justice under our Constitution." 384 U.S., at 481. It is this pivotal role of legal counsel that justifies the per se rule established in *Miranda*, and that distinguishes the request for counsel from the request for a probation officer, a clergyman, or a close friend. A probation officer simply is not necessary, in the way an attorney is, for the protection of the legal rights of the accused, juvenile or adult. He is significantly handicapped by the position he occupies in the juvenile system from serving as an effective protector of the rights of a juvenile suspected of a crime. . . .

. . .The totality-of-the-circumstances approach is adequate to determine whether there has been a waiver even where interrogation of juveniles is involved. We discern no persuasive reasons why any other aproach is required where the question is whether a juvenile has waived his rights, as opposed to whether an adult has done so. The totality approach permits—indeed, it mandates—inquiry into all the circumstances surrounding the interrogation. This includes evaluation of the juvenile's age, experience, education, background, and intelligence, and into whether he has the capacity to understand the warnings given him, the nature of his Fifth Amendment rights, and the consequences of waiving those rights. . . .

In this case, we conclude that the California Supreme Court should have determined the issue of waiver on the basis of all the circumstances surrounding the interrogation of respondent. The Juvenile Court found that under this approach, respondent in fact had waived his Fifth Amendment rights and consented

to interrogation by the police after his request to see his probation officer was denied. Given its view of the case, of course, the California Supreme Court did not consider this issue, thought it did hold that the State had failed to prove that, notwithstanding respondent's request to see his probation officer, respondent had not intended to invoke his Fifth Amendment rights.

We feel that the conclusion of the Juvenile Court was correct. The transcript of the interrogation reveals that the police officers conducting the interrogation took care to ensure that respondent understood his rights. They fully explained to respondent that he was being questioned in connection with a murder. They then informed him of all the rights delineated in *Miranda*, and ascertained that respondent understood those rights. There is no indication in the record that respondent failed to understand what the officers told him. Moreover, after his request to see his probation officer had been denied, and after the police officer once more had explained his rights to him, respondent clearly expressed his willingness to waive his rights and continue the interrogation. . . .

The judgment of the Supreme Court of California is reversed, and the case is remanded for further proceedings not inconsistent with this opinion.

MR. JUSTICE POWELL, dissenting. [Omitted.]

WHAT DO *YOU* THINK?

1. The Court noted that if the accused indicates in any manner that he wishes to remain silent or to consult an attorney, interrogation must cease. Does the request to see his probation officer constitute that the defendant has doubts about his or her conduct in talking to the police?

2. Do you agree with the court's opinion? Why?

3. If the probation officer is considered by the youth as a "trusted guardian figure," should that make a difference in this case?

4. Is the Court stating that the test for waiver by a juvenile is the same as that for an adult when the court made the following statement: "We discern no persuasive reasons why any other approach is required where the question is whether a juvenile has waived his rights, as opposed to whether an adult has done so."?

The next two cases look at the issue of what constitutes "interrogation."

BREWER V. WILLIAMS
430 U.S. 387 (1977)

MR. JUSTICE STEWART delivered the opinion of the Court.

An Iowa trial jury found the respondent, Robert Williams, guilty of murder. The judgment of conviction was affirmed in the Iowa Supreme Court by a closely divided vote. In a subsequent habeas corpus proceeding a Federal District Court ruled that under the United States Constitution Williams is entitled to a new trial, and a divided Court of Appeals for the Eighth Circuit agreed. The question before us is whether the District Court and the Court of Appeals were wrong.

On the afternoon of December 24, 1968, a 10-year-old girl named Pamela Powers went with her family to the YMCA in Des Moines, Iowa, to watch a wrestling tournament in which her brother was participating. When she failed to return from a trip to the washroom, a search for her began. The search was unsuccessful.

Robert Williams, who had recently escaped from a mental hospital, was a resident of the YMCA. Soon after the girl's disappearance Williams was seen in the YMCA lobby carrying some clothing and a large bundle wrapped in a blanket. He obtained help from a 14-year-old boy in opening the street door of the YMCA and the door to his automobile parked outside. When Williams placed the bundle in the front seat of his car the boy "saw two legs in it and they were skinny and white." Before anyone could see what was in the bundle Williams drove away. His abandoned car was found the following day in Davenport, Iowa, roughly 160 miles east of Des Moines. A warrant was then issued in Des Moines for his arrest on a charge of abduction.

On the morning of December 26, a Des Moines lawyer named Henry McKnight went to the Des Moines police station and informed the officers present that he had just received a long-distance call from Williams, and that he had advised Williams to turn himself in to the Davenport police. Williams did surrender that morning to the police in Davenport, and they booked him on the charge specified in the arrest warrant and gave him the warnings required by *Miranda* v. *Arizona*, 384 U.S. 436. The Davenport police then telephoned their counterparts in Des Moines to inform them that Williams had surrendered. McKnight, the lawyer, was still at the Des Moines police headquarters, and Williams conversed with McKnight on the telephone. In the presence of the Des Moines chief of police and a police detective named Leaming, McKnight advised Williams that Des Moines police officers would be driving to Davenport to pick him up, that the officers would not interrogate him or mistreat him, and that Williams was not to talk to the officers about Pamela Powers until after consulting with McKnight upon his return to Des Moines. As a result of these conversations, it was agreed between McKnight and the Des Moines police officials that Detective Leaming and a fellow officer would drive to Davenport to pick up Williams, that they would bring him directly back to Des Moines, and that they would not question him during the trip.

In the meantime, Williams was arraigned before a judge in Davenport on the outstanding arrest warrant. The judge advised him of his *Miranda* rights and committed him to jail. Before leaving the courtroom, Williams conferred with a lawyer named Kelly, who advised him not to make any statements until consulting with McKnight back in Des Moines.

Detective Leaming and his fellow officer arrived in Davenport about noon to pick up Williams and return him to Des Moines. Soon after their arrival they met with Williams and Kelly, who, they understood, was acting as Williams' lawyer. Detective Leaming repeated the *Miranda* warnings, and told Williams:

> [W]e both know that you're being represented here by Mr. Kelly and you're being represented by Mr. McKnight in Des Moines, and . . . I want you to remember this because we'll be visiting between here and Des Moines.

Williams then conferred again with Kelly alone, and after this conference Kelly reiterated to Detective Leaming that Williams was not to be questioned about the disappearance of Pamela Powers until after he had consulted with McKnight back in Des Moines. When Leaming expressed some reservations, Kelly firmly stated that

the agreement with McKnight was to be carried out—that there was to be no interrogation of Williams during the automobile journey to Des Moines. Kelly was denied permission to ride in the police car back to Des Moines with Williams and the two officers.

The two detectives, with Williams in their charge, then set out on the 160-mile drive. At no time during the trip did Williams express a willingness to be interrogated in the absence of an attorney. Instead, he stated several times that "[w]hen I get to Des Moines and see Mr. McKnight, I am going to tell you the whole story." Detective Leaming knew that Williams was a former mental patient, and knew also that he was deeply religious.

The detective and his prisoner soon embarked on a wide ranging conversation covering a variety of topics, including the subject of religion. Then, not long after leaving Davenport and reaching the interstate highway, Detective Leaming delivered what has been referred to in the briefs and oral arguments as the "Christian burial speech." Addressing Williams as "Reverend," the detective said:

> I want to give you something to think about while we're traveling down the road. . . . Number one, I want you to observe the weather conditions, it's raining, it's sleeting, it's freezing, driving is very treacherous, visibility is poor, it's going to be dark early this evening. They are predicting several inches of snow for tonight, and I feel that you yourself are the only person that knows where this little girl's body is, that you yourself have only been there once, and if you get a snow on top of it you yourself may be unable to find it. And, since we will be going right past the area on the way into [430 U.S. 387, 393] Des Moines, I feel that we could stop and locate the body, that the parents of this little girl should be entitled to a Christian burial for the little girl who was snatched away from them on Christmas [E]ve and murdered. And I feel we should stop and locate it on the way in rather than waiting until morning and trying to come back out after a snow storm and possibly not being able to find it at all.

Williams asked Detective Leaming why he thought their route to Des Moines would be taking them past the girl's body, and Leaming responded that he knew the body was in the area of Mitchellville—a town they would be passing on the way to Des Moines. Leaming then stated: "I do not want you to answer me. I don't want to discuss it any further. Just think about it as we're riding down the road."

As the car approached Grinnell, a town approximately 100 miles west of Davenport, Williams asked whether the police had found the victim's shoes. When Detective Leaming replied that he was unsure, Williams directed the officers to a service station where he said he had left the shoes; a search for them proved unsuccessful. As they continued towards Des Moines, Williams asked whether the police had found the blanket, and directed the officers to a rest area where he said he had disposed of the blanket. Nothing was found. The car continued towards Des Moines, and as it approached Mitchellville, Williams said that he would show the officers where the body was. He then directed the police to the body of Pamela Powers.

Williams was indicted for first-degree murder. Before trial, his counsel moved to suppress all evidence relating to or resulting from any statements Williams had made during the automobile ride from Davenport to Des Moines. After an evidentiary hearing the trial judge denied the motion. He found that "an agreement was made between defense counsel and the police officials to the effect that the Defendant was not to be questioned on the return trip to Des Moines," and that the evidence in question had been elicited from Williams during "a critical stage in the proceedings requiring the presence of counsel on his request." The judge ruled, however, that Williams had "waived his right to have an attorney present during the giving of such information."

The evidence in question was introduced over counsel's continuing objection at the subsequent trial. The jury found Williams guilty of murder, and the judgment of conviction was affirmed by the Iowa Supreme Court, a bare majority of whose members agreed with the trial court that Williams had "waived his right to the presence of his counsel" on the automobile ride from Davenport to Des Moines. . . . The four dissenting justices expressed the view that "when counsel and police have agreed defendant is not to be questioned until counsel is present and defendant has been advised not to talk and repeatedly has stated he will tell the whole story after he talks with counsel, the state should be required to make a stronger showing of intentional voluntary waiver than was made here."

. . .There can be no doubt in the present case that judicial proceedings had been initiated against Williams before the start of the automobile ride from Davenport to Des Moines. A warrant had been issued for his arrest, he had been arraigned on that warrant before a judge in a Davenport courtroom, and he had been committed by the court to confinement in jail. The State does not contend otherwise.

There can be no serious doubt, either, that Detective Leaming deliberately and designedly set out to elicit information from Williams just as surely as—and perhaps more effectively than—if he had formally interrogated him. Detective Leaming was fully aware before departing for Des Moines that Williams was being represented in Davenport by Kelly and in Des Moines by McKnight. Yet he purposely sought during Williams' isolation from his lawyers to obtain as much incriminating information as possible. Indeed, Detective Leaming conceded as much when he testified at Williams' trial:

"Q. In fact, Captain, whether he was a mental patient or not, you were trying to get all the information you could before he got to his lawyer, weren't you?

"A. I was sure hoping to find out where that little girl was, yes, sir. . . .

"Q. Well, I'll put it this way: You was [sic] hoping to get all the information you could before Williams got back to McKnight, weren't you?

"A. Yes, sir."

The state courts clearly proceeded upon the hypothesis that Detective Leaming's "Christian burial speech" had been tantamount to interrogation. Both courts recognized that Williams had been entitled to the assistance of counsel at the time he made the incriminating statements. Yet no such constitutional protection would have come into play if there had been no interrogation.

The circumstances of this case are thus constitutionally indistinguishable from those presented in *Massiah* v. *United States, supra.* The petitioner in that case was indicted for violating the federal narcotics law. He retained a lawyer, pleaded not guilty, and was released on bail. While he was free on bail a federal agent succeeded by surreptitious means in listening to incriminating statements made by him. Evidence of these statements was introduced against the petitioner at his trial, and he was convicted. This Court reversed the conviction, holding that "the petitioner was denied the basic protections of that guarantee [the right to counsel] when there was used against him at his trial evidence of his own incriminating words, which federal agents had deliberately elicited from him after he had been indicted and in the absence of his counsel." 377 U.S., at 206.

That the incriminating statements were elicited surreptitiously in the *Massiah* case, and otherwise here, is constitutionally irrelevant. . . . Rather, the clear rule of *Massiah* is that once adversary proceedings have commenced against an individual, he has a right to legal representation when the government interrogates him. It thus

requires no wooden or technical application of the *Massiah* doctrine to conclude that Williams was entitled to the assistance of counsel guaranteed to him by the Sixth and Fourteenth Amendments.

III.

The Iowa courts recognized that Williams had been denied the constitutional right to the assistance of counsel. They held, however, that he had waived that right during the course of the automobile trip from Davenport to Des Moines. The state trial court explained its determination of waiver as follows:

> The time element involved on the trip, the general circumstances of it, and more importantly the absence on the Defendant's part of any assertion of his right or desire not to give information absent the presence of his attorney, are the main foundations for the Court's conclusion that he voluntarily waived such right.

In its lengthy opinion affirming this determination, the Iowa Supreme Court applied "the totality-of-circumstances test for a showing of waiver of constitutionally-protected rights in the absence of an express waiver," and concluded that "evidence of the time element involved on the trip, the general circumstances of it, and the absence of any request or expressed desire for the aid of counsel before or at the time of giving information, were sufficient to sustain a conclusion that defendant did waive his constitutional rights as alleged." 182 N. W. 2d, at 401, 402.

In the federal habeas corpus proceeding the District Court, believing that the issue of waiver was not one of fact but of federal law, held that the Iowa courts had "applied the wrong constitutional standards" in ruling that Williams had waived the protections that were his under the Constitution. 375 F. Supp., at 182. The court held "that it is the government which bears a heavy burden . . . but that is the burden which explicitly was placed on [Williams] by the state courts." *Ibid.* After carefully reviewing the evidence, the District Court concluded:

> [U]nder the proper standards for determining waiver, there simply is no evidence to support a waiver. . . . [T]here is no affirmative indication . . . that [Williams] did waive his rights. . . . [T]he state courts' emphasis on the absence of a demand for counsel was not only legally inappropriate, but factually unsupportable as well, since Detective Leaming himself testified that [Williams], on several occasions during the trip, indicated that he would talk after he saw Mr. McKnight. Both these statements and Mr. Kelly's statement to Detective Leaming that [Williams] would talk only after seeing Mr. McKnight in Des Moines certainly were assertions of [Williams'] "right or desire not to give information absent the presence of his attorney . . . ." Moreover, the statements were obtained only after Detective Leaming's use of psychology on a person whom he knew to be deeply religious and an escapee from a mental hospital—with the specific intent to elicit incriminating statements. In the face of this evidence, the State has produced no affirmative evidence whatsoever to support its claim of waiver, and, a fortiori, it cannot be said that the State has met its "heavy burden" of showing a knowing and intelligent waiver of . . . Sixth Amendment rights. *Id.*, at 182–183 (footnote omitted)

The Court of Appeals approved the reasoning of the District Court:

> A review of the record here . . . discloses no facts to support the conclusion of the state court that [Williams] had waived his constitutional rights other than that [he] had made incriminating statements. . . . The District Court here properly concluded that an incorrect constitutional standard had been applied by the state court in determining the issue of waiver. . . .
>
> [T]his court recently held that an accused can voluntarily, knowingly and intelligently waive his right to have counsel present at an interrogation after counsel has been

appointed. . . . The prosecution, however, has the weighty obligation to show that the waiver was knowingly and intelligently made. We quite agree with Judge Hanson that the state here failed to so show. 509 F.2d, at 233

The District Court and the Court of Appeals were correct in the view that the question of waiver was not a question of historical fact, but one which, in the words of Mr. Justice Frankfurter, requires "application of constitutional principles to the facts as found. . . ." *Brown* v. *Allen*, 344 U.S. 443, 507 (separate opinion). See *Townsend* v. *Sain*, 372 U.S., at 309 n. 6, 318; *Brookhart* v. *Janis*, 384 U.S. 1, 4.

The District Court and the Court of Appeals were also correct in their understanding of the proper standard to be applied in determining the question of waiver as a matter of federal constitutional law—that it was incumbent upon the State to prove "an intentional relinquishment or abandonment of a known right or privilege." *Johnson* v. *Zerbst*, 304 U.S., at 464. That standard has been reiterated in many cases. We have said that the right to counsel does not depend upon a request by the defendant, *Carnley* v. *Cochran*, 369 U.S. 506, 513; *cf. Miranda* v. *Arizona*, 384 U.S., at 471, and that courts indulge in every reasonable presumption against waiver, e.g., *Brookhart* v. *Janis, supra*, at 4; *Glasser* v. *United States*, 315 U.S. 60, 70. This strict standard applies equally to an alleged waiver of the right to counsel whether at trial or at a critical stage of pretrial proceedings. *Schneckloth* v. *Bustamonte*, 412 U.S. 218, 238–240; *United States* v. *Wade*, 388 U.S., at 237.

We conclude, finally, that the Court of Appeals was correct in holding that, judged by these standards, the record in this case falls far short of sustaining petitioner's burden. It is true that Williams had been informed of and appeared to understand his right to counsel. But waiver requires not merely comprehension but relinquishment, and Williams' consistent reliance upon the advice of counsel in dealing with the authorities refutes any suggestion that he waived that right. He consulted McKnight by long-distance telephone before turning himself in. He spoke with McKnight by telephone again shortly after being booked. After he was arraigned, Williams sought out and obtained legal advice from Kelly. Williams again consulted with Kelly after Detective Leaming and his fellow officer arrived in Davenport. Throughout, Williams was advised not to make any statements before seeing McKnight in Des Moines, and was assured that the police had agreed not to question him. His statements while in the car that he would tell the whole story after seeing McKnight in Des Moines were the clearest expressions by Williams himself that he desired the presence of an attorney before any interrogation took place. But even before making these statements, Williams had effectively asserted his right to counsel by having secured attorneys at both ends of the automobile trip, both of whom, acting as his agents, had made clear to the police that no interrogation was to occur during the journey. Williams knew of that agreement and, particularly in view of his consistent reliance on counsel, there is no basis for concluding that he disavowed it.

Despite Williams' express and implicit assertions of his right to counsel, Detective Leaming proceeded to elicit incriminating statements from Williams. Leaming did not preface this effort by telling Williams that he had a right to the presence of a lawyer, and made no effort at all to ascertain whether Williams wished to relinquish that right. The circumstances of record in this case thus provide no reasonable basis for finding that Williams waived his right to the assistance of counsel.

The Court of Appeals did not hold, nor do we, that under the circumstances of this case Williams could not, without notice to counsel, have waived his rights under the Sixth and Fourteenth Amendments. It only held, as do we, that he did not.

The crime of which Williams was convicted was senseless and brutal, calling for swift and energetic action by the police to apprehend the perpetrator and gather evidence with which he could be convicted. No mission of law enforcement officials is more important. Yet "[d]isinterested zeal for the public good does not assure either wisdom or right in the methods it pursues." *Haley* v. *Ohio*, 332 U.S. 596, 605 (Frankfurter, J., concurring in judgment). Although we do not lightly affirm the issuance of a writ of habeas corpus in this case, so clear a violation of the Sixth and Fourteenth Amendments as here occurred cannot be condoned. The pressures on state executive and judicial officers charged with the administration of the criminal law are great, especially when the crime is murder and the victim a small child. But it is precisely the predictability of those pressures that makes imperative a resolute loyalty to the guarantees that the Constitution extends to us all. The judgment of the Court of Appeals is affirmed. [Dissenting opinions omitted.]

WHAT DO *YOU* THINK?

1. Would the detective's statements qualify as interrogation?
2. If the statements were considered as interrogation, was it the type of interrogation that *Miranda* rule was designed to prevent?

RHODE ISLAND V. INNIS
446 U.S. 291 (1980)

MR. JUSTICE STEWART delivered the opinion of the Court.

In *Miranda* v. *Arizona*, 384 U.S. 436, 474, the Court held that, once a defendant in custody asks to speak with a lawyer, all interrogation must cease until a lawyer is present. The issue in this case is whether the respondent was "interrogated" in violation of the standards promulgated in the *Miranda* opinion.

I.

On the night of January 12, 1975, John Mulvaney, a Providence, R.I., taxicab driver, disappeared after being dispatched to pick up a customer. His body was discovered four days later buried in a shallow grave in Coventry, R.I. He had died from a shotgun blast aimed at the back of his head.

On January 17, 1975, shortly after midnight, the Providence police received a telephone call from Gerald Aubin, also a taxicab driver, who reported that he had just been robbed by a man wielding a sawed-off shotgun. Aubin further reported that he had dropped off his assailant near Rhode Island College in a section of Providence known as Mount Pleasant. While at the Providence police station waiting to give a statement, Aubin noticed a picture of his assailant on a bulletin board. Aubin so informed one of the police officers present. The officer prepared a photo array, and again Aubin identified a picture of the same person. That person was the respondent. Shortly thereafter, the Providence police began a search of the Mount Pleasant area.

At approximately 4:30 a.m. on the same date, Patrolman Lovell, while cruising the streets of Mount Pleasant in a patrol car, spotted the respondent standing

in the street facing him. When Patrolman Lovell stopped his car, the respondent walked towards it. Patrolman Lovell then arrested the respondent, who was unarmed, and advised him of his so-called *Miranda* rights. While the two men waited in the patrol car for other police officers to arrive, Patrolman Lovell did not converse with the respondent other than to respond to the latter's request for a cigarette.

Within minutes, Sergeant Sears arrived at the scene of the arrest, and he also gave the respondent the *Miranda* warnings. Immediately thereafter, Captain Leyden and other police officers arrived. Captain Leyden advised the respondent of his *Miranda* rights. The respondent stated that he understood those rights and wanted to speak with a lawyer. Captain Leyden then directed that the respondent be placed in a "caged wagon," a four-door police car with a wire screen mesh between the front and rear seats, and be driven to the central police station. Three officers, Patrolmen Gleckman, Williams, and McKenna, were assigned to accompany the respondent to the central station. They placed the respondent in the vehicle and shut the doors. Captain Leyden then instructed the officers not to question the respondent or intimidate or coerce him in any way. The three officers then entered the vehicle, and it departed.

While en route to the central station, Patrolman Gleckman initiated a conversation with Patrolman McKenna concerning the missing shotgun. As Patrolman Gleckman later testified:

> "At this point, I was talking back and forth with Patrolman McKenna stating that I frequent this area while on patrol and [that because a school for handicapped children is located nearby,] there's a lot of handicapped children running around in this area, and God forbid one of them might find a weapon with shells and they might hurt themselves." App. 43–44.

Patrolman McKenna apparently shared his fellow officer's concern:

> "I more or less concurred with him [Gleckman] that it was a safety factor and that we should, you know, continue to search for the weapon and try to find it." *Id.*, at 53

While Patrolman Williams said nothing, he overheard the conversation between the two officers:

> "He [Gleckman] said it would be too bad if the little—I believe he said a girl—would pick up the gun, maybe kill herself." *Id.*, at 59

The respondent then interrupted the conversation, stating that the officers should turn the car around so he could show them where the gun was located. At this point, Patrolman McKenna radioed back to Captain Leyden that they were returning to the scene of the arrest, and that the respondent would inform them of the location of the gun. At the time the respondent indicated that the officers should turn back, they had traveled no more than a mile, a trip encompassing only a few minutes.

The police vehicle then returned to the scene of the arrest where a search for the shotgun was in progress. There, Captain Leyden again advised the respondent of his *Miranda* rights. The respondent replied that he understood those rights but that he "wanted to get the gun out of the way because of the kids in the area in the school." The respondent then led the police to a nearby field, where he pointed out the shotgun under some rocks by the side of the road.

On March 20, 1975, a grand jury returned an indictment charging the respondent with the kidnaping, robbery, and murder of John Mulvaney. Before trial, the respondent moved to suppress the shotgun and the statements he had made to

the police regarding it. After an evidentiary hearing at which the respondent elected not to testify, the trial judge found that the respondent had been "repeatedly and completely advised of his *Miranda* rights." He further found that it was "entirely understandable that [the officers in the police vehicle] would voice their concern [for the safety of the handicapped children] to each other." The judge then concluded that the respondent's decision to inform the police of the location of the shotgun was "a waiver, clearly, and on the basis of the evidence that I have heard, and [sic] intelligent waiver, of his [*Miranda*] right to remain silent." Thus, without passing on whether the police officers had in fact "interrogated" the respondent, the trial court sustained the admissibility of the shotgun and testimony related to its discovery. That evidence was later introduced at the respondent's trial, and the jury returned a verdict of guilty on all counts.

On appeal, the Rhode Island Supreme Court, in a 3–2 decision, set aside the respondent's conviction. 120 R. I. ___, 391 A. 2d 1158. Relying at least in part on this Court's decision in *Brewer* v. *Williams*, 430 U.S. 387, the court concluded that the respondent had invoked his *Miranda* right to counsel and that, contrary to *Miranda*'s mandate that, in the absence of counsel, all custodial interrogation then cease, the police officers in the vehicle had "interrogated" the respondent without a valid waiver of his right to counsel. It was the view of the state appellate court that, even though the police officers may have been genuinely concerned about the public safety and even though the respondent had not been addressed personally by the police officers, the respondent nonetheless had been subjected to "subtle coercion" that was the equivalent of "interrogation" within the meaning of the *Miranda* opinion. Moreover, contrary to the holding of the trial court, the appellate court concluded that the evidence was insufficient to support a finding of waiver. Having concluded that both the shotgun and testimony relating to its discovery were obtained in violation of the *Miranda* standards and therefore should not have been admitted into evidence, the Rhode Island Supreme Court held that the respondent was entitled to a new trial.

We granted *certiorari* to address for the first time the meaning of "interrogation" under *Miranda* v. *Arizona*. 440 U.S. 934.

II.

In its *Miranda* opinion, the Court concluded that in the context of "custodial interrogation" certain procedural safeguards are necessary to protect a defendant's Fifth and Fourteenth Amendment privilege against compulsory self-incrimination. More specifically, the Court held that "the prosecution may not use statements, whether exculpatory or inculpatory, stemming from custodial interrogation of the defendant unless it demonstrates the use of procedural safeguards effective to secure the privilege against self-incrimination." 384 U.S. at 444. Those safeguards included the now familiar *Miranda* warnings—namely, that the defendant be informed "that he has the right to remain silent, that anything he says can be used against him in a court of law, that he has the right to the presence of an attorney, and that if he cannot afford an attorney one will be appointed for him prior to any questioning if he so desires"—or their equivalent. *Id.*, at 479.

The Court in the *Miranda* opinion also outlined in some detail the consequences that would result if a defendant sought to invoke those procedural safeguards. With regard to the right to the presence of counsel, the Court noted:

Once warnings have been given, the subsequent procedure is clear. . . . If the individual states that he wants an attorney, the interrogation must cease until an attorney is pre-

sent. At that time, the individual must have an opportunity to confer with the attorney and to have him present during any subsequent questioning. If the individual cannot obtain an attorney and he indicates that he wants one before speaking to police, they must respect his decision to remain silent. *Id.*, at 473–474

In the present case, the parties are in agreement that the respondent was fully informed of his *Miranda* rights and that he invoked his *Miranda* right to counsel when he told Captain Leyden that he wished to consult with a lawyer. It is also uncontested that the respondent was "in custody" while being transported to the police station.

The issue, therefore, is whether the respondent was "interrogated" by the police officers in violation of the respondent's undisputed right under *Miranda* to remain silent until he had consulted with a lawyer. In resolving this issue, we first define the term "interrogation" under *Miranda* before turning to a consideration of the facts of this case.

A.

The starting point for defining "interrogation" in this context is, of course, the Court's *Miranda* opinion. There the Court observed that "[b]y custodial interrogation, we mean questioning initiated by law enforcement officers after a person has been taken into custody or otherwise deprived of his freedom of action in any significant way." *Id.*, at 444. This passage and other references throughout the opinion to "questioning" might suggest that the *Miranda* rules were to apply only to those police interrogation practices that involve express questioning of a defendant while in custody.

We do not, however, construe the *Miranda* opinion so narrowly. The concern of the Court in *Miranda* was that the "interrogation environment" created by the interplay of interrogation and custody would "subjugate the individual to the will of his examiner" and thereby undermine the privilege against compulsory self-incrimination. *Id.*, at 457–458. The police practices that evoked this concern included several that did not involve express questioning. For example, one of the practices discussed in *Miranda* was the use of line-ups in which a coached witness would pick the defendant as the perpetrator. This was designed to establish that the defendant was in fact guilty as a predicate for further interrogation. *Id.*, at 453. A variation on this theme discussed in *Miranda* was the so-called "reverse line-up" in which a defendant would be identified by coached witnesses as the perpetrator of a fictitious crime, with the object of inducing him to confess to the actual crime of which he was suspected in order to escape the false prosecution. *Ibid.* The Court in *Miranda* also included in its survey of interrogation practices the use of psychological ploys, such as to "posi[t]" "the guilt of the subject," to "minimize the moral seriousness of the offense," and "to cast blame on the victim or on the society." *Id.*, at 450. It is clear that these techniques of persuasion, no less than express questioning, were thought, in a custodial setting, to amount to interrogation.

This is not to say, however, that all statements obtained by the police after a person has been taken into custody are to be considered the product of interrogation. As the Court in *Miranda* noted:

> Confessions remain a proper element in law enforcement. Any statement given freely and voluntarily without any compelling influences is, of course, admissible in evidence. The fundamental import of the privilege while an individual is in custody is not whether he is allowed to talk to the police without the benefit of warnings and counsel, but whether he can be interrogated. . . . Volunteered statements of any kind are not barred

by the Fifth Amendment and their admissibility is not affected by our holding today."
Id., at 478

It is clear therefore that the special procedural safeguards outlined in *Miranda* are required not where a suspect is simply taken into custody, but rather where a suspect in custody is subjected to interrogation. "Interrogation," as conceptualized in the *Miranda* opinion, must reflect a measure of compulsion above and beyond that inherent in custody itself.

We conclude that the *Miranda* safeguards come into play whenever a person in custody is subjected to either express questioning or its functional equivalent. That is to say, the term "interrogation" under *Miranda* refers not only to express questioning, but also to any words or actions on the part of the police (other than those normally attendant to arrest and custody) that the police should know are reasonably likely to elicit an incriminating response from the suspect. The latter portion of this definition focuses primarily upon the perceptions of the suspect, rather than the intent of the police. This focus reflects the fact that the *Miranda* safeguards were designed to vest a suspect in custody with an added measure of protection against coercive police practices, without regard to objective proof of the underlying intent of the police. A practice that the police should know is reasonably likely to evoke an incriminating response from a suspect thus amounts to interrogation. But, since the police surely cannot be held accountable for the unforeseeable results of their words or actions, the definition of interrogation can extend only to words or actions on the part of police officers that they should have known were reasonably likely to elicit an incriminating response.

B.

Turning to the facts of the present case, we conclude that the respondent was not "interrogated" within the meaning of *Miranda*. It is undisputed that the first prong of the definition of "interrogation" was not satisfied, for the conversation between Patrolmen Gleckman and McKenna included no express questioning of the respondent. Rather, that conversation was, at least in form, nothing more than a dialogue between the two officers to which no response from the respondent was invited.

Moreover, it cannot be fairly concluded that the respondent was subjected to the "functional equivalent" of questioning. It cannot be said, in short, that Patrolmen Gleckman and McKenna should have known that their conversation was reasonably likely to elicit an incriminating response from the respondent. There is nothing in the record to suggest that the officers were aware that the respondent was peculiarly susceptible to an appeal to his conscience concerning the safety of handicapped children. Nor is there anything in the record to suggest that the police knew that the respondent was unusually disoriented or upset at the time of his arrest.

The case thus boils down to whether, in the context of a brief conversation, the officers should have known that the respondent would suddenly be moved to make a self-incriminating response. Given the fact that the entire conversation appears to have consisted of no more than a few offhand remarks, we cannot say that the officers should have known that it was reasonably likely that Innis would so respond. This is not a case where the police carried on a lengthy harangue in the presence of the suspect. Nor does the record support the respondent's contention that, under the circumstances, the officers' comments were particularly "evocative." It is our view, therefore, that the respondent was not subjected by the police to words or actions that the police should have known were reasonably likely to elicit an incriminating response from him. . . .

For the reasons stated, the judgment of the Supreme Court of Rhode Island is vacated, and the case is remanded to that court for further proceedings not inconsistent with this opinion.

It is so ordered.

[Concurring opinions of JUSTICE WHITE and CHIEF JUSTICE BURGER and the dissenting opinions of JUSTICES BRENNAN, MARSHALL, and STEVENS are omitted.]

WHAT DO YOU THINK?

1. How does this case differ from the *Brewer* case?

2. Do you agree with the majority opinion in this case? In the *Brewer* case?

The Byers *case looks at the issue of whether requiring a driver to stop at the accident scene and giving his or her name and address is a violation of the constitutional right against self-incrimination.*

CALIFORNIA V. BYERS
402 U.S. 424 (1971)

MR. CHIEF JUSTICE BURGER announced the judgment of the Court and an opinion in which MR. JUSTICE STEWART, MR. JUSTICE WHITE, and MR. JUSTICE BLACKMUN join.

This case presents the narrow but important question of whether the constitutional privilege against compulsory self-incrimination is infringed by California's so-called "hit and run" statute which requires the driver of a motor vehicle involved in an accident to stop at the scene and give his name and address. Similar "hit and run" or "stop and report" statutes are in effect in all 50 States and the District of Columbia.

On August 22, 1966, respondent Byers was charged in a two-count criminal complaint with two misdemeanor violations of the California Vehicle Code. Count 1 charged that on August 20 Byers passed another vehicle without maintaining the "safe distance". . . . The second count charged that Byers had been involved in an accident but had failed to stop and identify himself. . . .

This statute provides:

The driver of any vehicle involved in an accident resulting in damage to any property including vehicles shall immediately stop the vehicle at the scene of the accident and shall then and there . . . [l]ocate and notify the owner or person in charge of such property of the name and address of the driver and owner of the vehicle involved. . . .

It is stipulated that both charges arose out of the same accident.

Byers demurred to Count 2 on the ground that it violated his privilege against compulsory self-incrimination. His position was ultimately sustained by the California Supreme Court. That court held that the privilege protected a driver who "reasonably believes that compliance with the statute will result in self-incrimination." . . . Here the court found that Byers' apprehensions were reasonable because

compliance with 20002 (a) (1) confronted him with "substantial hazards of self-incrimination." Nevertheless the court upheld the validity of the statute by inserting a judicially created use restriction on the disclosures that it required. The court concluded, however, that it would be "unfair" to punish Byers for his failure to comply with the statute because he could not reasonably have anticipated the judicial promulgation of the use restriction. We granted *certiorari* to assess the validity of the California Supreme Court's premise that without a use restriction 20002 (a) (1) would violate the privilege against compulsory self-incrimination. We conclude that there is no conflict between the statute and the privilege.

(1).

Whenever the Court is confronted with the question of a compelled disclosure that has an incriminating potential, the judicial scrutiny is invariably a close one. Tension between the State's demand for disclosures and the protection of the right against self-incrimination is likely to give rise to serious questions. Inevitably these must be resolved in terms of balancing the public need on the one hand, and the individual claim to constitutional protections on the other; neither interest can be treated lightly.

An organized society imposes many burdens on its constituents. It commands the filing of tax returns for income; it requires producers and distributors of consumer goods to file informational reports on the manufacturing process and the content of products, on the wages, hours, and working conditions of employees. Those who borrow money on the public market or issue securities for sale to the public must file various information reports; industries must report periodically the volume and content of pollutants discharged into our waters and atmosphere. Comparable examples are legion.

In each of these situations there is some possibility of prosecution—often a very real one—for criminal offenses disclosed by or deriving from the information that the law compels a person to supply. Information revealed by these reports could well be "a link in the chain" of evidence leading to prosecution and conviction. But under our holdings the mere possibility of incrimination is insufficient to defeat the strong policies in favor of a disclosure called for by statutes like the one challenged here.

United States v. *Sullivan*, 274 U.S. 259 (1927), shows that an application of the privilege to the California statute is not warranted. There a bootlegger was prosecuted for failure to file an income tax return. He claimed that the privilege against compulsory self-incrimination afforded him a complete defense because filing a return would have tended to incriminate him by revealing the unlawful source of his income. Speaking for the Court, Mr. Justice Holmes rejected this claim on the ground that it amounted to "an extreme if not an extravagant application of the Fifth Amendment." *Id.*, at 263–264. Sullivan's tax return, of course, increased his risk of prosecution and conviction for violation of the National Prohibition Act. But the Court had no difficulty in concluding that an extension of the privilege to cover that kind of mandatory report would have been unjustified. In order to invoke the privilege it is necessary to show that the compelled disclosures will themselves confront the claimant with "substantial hazards of self-incrimination.".

The components of this requirement were articulated in *Albertson* v. *SACB*, 382 U.S. 70 (1965). . . . In *Albertson* the Court held that an order requiring registration by individual members of a Communist organization violated the privilege. There *Sullivan* was distinguished:

> In Sullivan the questions in the income tax return were neutral on their face and directed at the public at large, but here they are directed at a highly selective group in-

herently suspect of criminal activities. Petitioners' claims are not asserted in an essentially noncriminal and regulatory area of inquiry, but against an inquiry in an area permeated with criminal statutes, where response to any of the . . . questions in context might involve the petitioners in the admission of a crucial element of a crime." . . .

Albertson was followed by *Marchetti* and *Grosso* where the Court held that the privilege afforded a complete defense to prosecutions for noncompliance with federal gambling tax and registration requirements. It was also followed in *Haynes* where petitioner had been prosecuted for failure to register a firearm as required by federal statute. In each of these cases the Court found that compliance with the statutory disclosure requirements would confront the petitioner with "substantial hazards of self-incrimination." E.g., *Marchetti* v. *United States*, 390 U.S., at 61.

In all of these cases the disclosures condemned were only those extracted from a "highly selective group inherently suspect of criminal activities" and the privilege was applied only in "an area permeated with criminal statutes"—not in "an essentially noncriminal and regulatory area of inquiry." . . .

Although the California Vehicle Code defines some criminal offenses, the statute is essentially regulatory, not criminal. The California Supreme Court noted that 20002 (a) (1) was not intended to facilitate criminal convictions but to promote the satisfaction of civil liabilities arising from automobile accidents. In *Marchetti* the Court rested on the reality that almost everything connected with gambling is illegal under "comprehensive" state and federal statutory schemes. The Court noted that in almost every conceivable situation compliance with the statutory gambling requirements would have been incriminating. Largely because of these pervasive criminal prohibitions, gamblers were considered by the Court to be "a highly selective group inherently suspect of criminal activities."

In contrast, 20002 (a) (1), like income tax laws, is directed at all persons—here all persons who drive automobiles in California. This group, numbering as it does in the millions, is so large as to render 20002 (a) (1) a statute "directed at the public at large." *Albertson* v. *SACB*, 382 U.S., at 79, construing *United States* v. *Sullivan*, 274 U.S. 259 (1927). It is difficult to consider this group as either "highly selective" or "inherently suspect of criminal activities." Driving an automobile, unlike gambling, is a lawful activity. Moreover, it is not a criminal offense under California law to be a driver "involved in an accident." An accident may be the fault of others; it may occur without any driver having been at fault. No empirical data are suggested in support of the conclusion that there is a relevant correlation between being a driver and criminal prosecution of drivers. So far as any available information instructs us, most accidents occur without creating criminal liability even if one or both of the drivers are guilty of negligence as a matter of tort law.

The disclosure of illegal activity is inherently risky. Our decisions in *Albertson* and the cases following illustrate that truism. But disclosures with respect to automobile accidents simply do not entail the kind of substantial risk of self-incrimination involved in *Marchetti*, *Grosso*, and *Haynes*. Furthermore, the statutory purpose is noncriminal and self-reporting is indispensable to its fulfillment.

. . .Respondent argues that since the statutory duty to stop is imposed only on the "driver of any vehicle involved in an accident," a driver's compliance is testimonial because his action gives rise to an inference that he believes that he was the "driver of [a] vehicle involved in an accident." From this, the respondent tells us, it can be further inferred that he was indeed the operator of an "accident involved" vehicle. In *Wade*, however, the Court rejected the notion that such inferences are communicative or testimonial. There the respondent was placed in a lineup to be

viewed by persons who had witnessed a bank robbery. At one point he was compelled to speak the words alleged to have been used by the perpetrator. Despite the inference that the respondent uttered the words in his normal undisguised voice, the Court held that the utterances were not of a "testimonial" nature in the sense of the Fifth Amendment privilege even though the speaking might well have led to identifying him as the bank robber. *United States* v. *Wade, supra*, at 222–223. Furthermore, the Court noted in *Wade* that no question was presented as to the admissibility in evidence at trial of anything said or done at the lineup. *Id.*, at 223. Similarly no such problem is presented here. Of course, a suspect's normal voice characteristics, like his handwriting, blood, fingerprints, or body may prove to be the crucial link in a chain of evidentiary factors resulting in prosecution and conviction. Yet such evidence may be used against a defendant.

After having stopped, a driver involved in an accident is required by 20002 (a) (1) to notify the driver of the other vehicle of his name and address. A name, linked [402 U.S. 424, 434] with a motor vehicle, is no more incriminating than the tax return, linked with the disclosure of income, in *United States* v. *Sullivan, supra*. It identifies but does not by itself implicate anyone in criminal conduct.

Although identity, when made known, may lead to inquiry that in turn leads to arrest and charge, those developments depend on different factors and independent evidence. Here the compelled disclosure of identity could have led to a charge that might not have been made had the driver fled the scene; but this is true only in the same sense that a taxpayer can be charged on the basis of the contents of a tax return or failure to file an income tax form. There is no constitutional right to refuse to file an income tax return or to flee the scene of an accident in order to avoid the possibility of legal involvement.

The judgment of the California Supreme Court is vacated and the case is remanded for further proceedings not inconsistent with this opinion.

Vacated and remanded.

What Do You Think?

1. Do you agree with the majority opinion that requiring an individual to stop and provide identification is not self-incrimination?

2. The Court states that there is no constitutional right to flee the scene of an accident. How is that relevant to the issue of being required to identify yourself as being involved in the accident?

The next case looks at the issue of whether a defendant's confession is voluntary because "voices" told him to confess.

COLORADO V. CONNELLY
479 U.S. 157 (1986)

CHIEF JUSTICE REHNQUIST delivered the opinion of the Court.

In this case, the Supreme Court of Colorado held that the United States Constitution requires a court to suppress a confession when the mental state of the defendant, at the time he made the confession, interfered with his "rational intel-

lect" and his "free will." Because this decision seemed to conflict with prior holdings of this Court, we granted *certiorari*. 474 U.S. 1050 (1986). We conclude that the admissibility of this kind of statement is governed by state rules of evidence, rather than by our previous decisions regarding coerced confessions and *Miranda* waivers. We therefore reverse.

I.

On August 18, 1983, Officer Patrick Anderson of the Denver Police Department was in uniform, working in an off-duty capacity in downtown Denver. Respondent Francis Connelly approached Officer Anderson and, without any prompting, stated that he had murdered someone and wanted to talk about it. Anderson immediately advised respondent that he had the right to remain silent, that anything he said could be used against him in court, and that he had the right to an attorney prior to any police questioning. See *Miranda* v. *Arizona*, 384 U.S. 436 (1966). Respondent stated that he understood these rights but he still wanted to talk about the murder. Understandably bewildered by this confession, Officer Anderson asked respondent several questions. Connelly denied that he had been drinking, denied that he had been taking any drugs, and stated that, in the past, he had been a patient in several mental hospitals. Officer Anderson again told Connelly that he was under no obligation to say anything. Connelly replied that it was "all right," and that he would talk to Officer Anderson because his conscience had been bothering him. To Officer Anderson, respondent appeared to understand fully the nature of his acts.

Shortly thereafter, Homicide Detective Stephen Antuna arrived. Respondent was again advised of his rights, and Detective Antuna asked him "what he had on his mind." *Id.*, at 24. Respondent answered that he had come all the way from Boston to confess to the murder of Mary Ann Junta, a young girl whom he had killed in Denver sometime during November 1982. Respondent was taken to police headquarters, and a search of police records revealed that the body of an unidentified female had been found in April 1983. Respondent openly detailed his story to Detective Antuna and Sergeant Thomas Haney, and readily agreed to take the officers to the scene of the killing. Under Connelly's sole direction, the two officers and respondent proceeded in a police vehicle to the location of the crime. Respondent pointed out the exact location of the murder. Throughout this episode, Detective Antuna perceived no indication whatsoever that respondent was suffering from any kind of mental illness. *Id.*, at 33–34.

Respondent was held overnight. During an interview with the public defender's office the following morning, he became visibly disoriented. He began giving confused answers to questions, and for the first time, stated that "voices" had told him to come to Denver and that he had followed the directions of these voices in confessing. *Id.*, at 42. Respondent was sent to a state hospital for evaluation. He was initially found incompetent to assist in his own defense. By March 1984, however, the doctors evaluating respondent determined that he was competent to proceed to trial.

At a preliminary hearing, respondent moved to suppress all of his statements. Dr. Jeffrey Metzner, a psychiatrist employed by the state hospital, testified that respondent was suffering from chronic schizophrenia and was in a psychotic state at least as of August 17, 1983, the day before he confessed. Metzner's interviews with respondent revealed that respondent was following the "voice of God." This voice instructed respondent to withdraw money from the bank, to buy an airplane ticket, and to fly from Boston to Denver. When respondent arrived from Boston, God's

voice became stronger and told respondent either to confess to the killing or to commit suicide. Reluctantly following the command of the voices, respondent approached Officer Anderson and confessed.

Dr. Metzner testified that, in his expert opinion, respondent was experiencing "command hallucinations." *Id.*, at 56. This condition interfered with respondent's "volitional abilities; that is, his ability to make free and rational choices." *Ibid.* Dr. Metzner further testified that Connelly's illness did not significantly impair his cognitive abilities. Thus, respondent understood the rights he had when Officer Anderson and Detective Antuna advised him that he need not speak. *Id.*, at 56–57. Dr. Metzner admitted that the "voices" could in reality be Connelly's interpretation of his own guilt, but explained that in his opinion, Connelly's psychosis motivated his confession.

On the basis of this evidence the Colorado trial court decided that respondent's statements must be suppressed because they were "involuntary." Relying on our decisions in *Townsend* v. *Sain*, 372 U.S. 293 (1963), and *Culombe* v. *Connecticut*, 367 U.S. 568 (1961), the court ruled that a confession is admissible only if it is a product of the defendant's rational intellect and "free will." Although the court found that the police had done nothing wrong or coercive in securing respondent's confession, Connelly's illness destroyed his volition and compelled him to confess. *Id.*, at 89. The trial court also found that Conelly's mental state vitiated his attempted waiver of the right to counsel and the privilege against compulsory self-incrimination. Accordingly, respondent's initial statements and his custodial confession were suppressed. *Id.*, at 90.

The Colorado Supreme Court affirmed. 702 P.2d 722 (1985). In that court's view, the proper test for admissibility is whether the statements are "the product of a rational intellect and a free will." *Id.*, at 728. Indeed, "the absence of police coercion or duress does not foreclose a finding of involuntariness. One's capacity for rational judgment and free choice may be overborne as much by certain forms of severe mental illness as by external pressure." *Ibid.* The court found that the very admission of the evidence in a court of law was sufficient state action to implicate the Due Process Clause of the Fourteenth Amendment to the United States Constitution. The evidence fully supported the conclusion that respondent's initial statement was not the product of a rational intellect and a free will. The court then considered respondent's attempted waiver of his constitutional rights and found that respondent's mental condition precluded his [479 U.S. 157, 163] ability to make a valid waiver. *Id.*, at 729. The Colorado Supreme Court thus affirmed the trial court's decision to suppress all of Connelly's statements.

II.

The Due Process Clause of the Fourteenth Amendment provides that no State shall "deprive any person of life, liberty, or property, without due process of law." Just last Term, in *Miller* v. *Fenton*, 474 U.S. 104, 109 (1985), we held that by virtue of the Due Process Clause "certain interrogation techniques, either in isolation or as applied to the unique characteristics of a particular suspect, are so offensive to a civilized system of justice that they must be condemned." See also *Moran* v. *Burbine*, 475 U.S. 412, 432–434 (1986).

Indeed, coercive government misconduct was the catalyst for this Court's seminal confession case, *Brown* v. *Mississippi*, 297 U.S. 278 (1936). In that case, police officers extracted confessions from the accused through brutal torture. The

Court had little difficulty concluding that even though the Fifth Amendment did not at that time apply to the States, the actions of the police were "revolting to the sense of justice." *Id.*, at 286. The Court has retained this due process focus, even after holding, in *Malloy* v. *Hogan*, 378 U.S. 1 (1964), that the Fifth Amendment privilege against compulsory self-incrimination applies to the States. See *Miller* v. *Fenton, supra*, at 109–110.

Thus the cases considered by this Court over the 50 years since *Brown* v. *Mississippi* have focused upon the crucial element of police overreaching. While each confession case has turned on its own set of factors justifying the conclusion that police conduct was oppressive, all have contained a substantial element of coercive police conduct. Absent police conduct causally related to the confession, there is simply no basis for concluding that any state actor has deprived a criminal defendant of due process of law. Respondent correctly notes that as interrogators have turned to more subtle forms of psychological persuasion, courts have found the mental condition of the defendant a more significant factor in the "voluntariness" calculus. See *Spano* v. *New York*, 360 U.S. 315 (1959). But this fact does not justify a conclusion that a defendant's mental condition, by itself and apart from its relation to official coercion, should ever dispose of the inquiry into constitutional "voluntariness."

Respondent relies on *Blackburn* v. *Alabama*, 361 U.S. 199 (1960), and *Townsend* v. *Sain*, 372 U.S. 293 (1963), for the proposition that the "deficient mental condition of the defendants in those cases was sufficient to render their confessions involuntary." Brief for Respondent 20. But respondent's reading of *Blackburn* and *Townsend* ignores the integral element of police overreaching present in both cases. In *Blackburn*, the Court found that the petitioner was probably insane at the time of his confession and the police learned during the interrogation that he had a history of mental problems. The police exploited this weakness with coercive tactics: "the eight- to nine-hour sustained interrogation in a tiny room which was upon occasion literally filled with police officers; the absence of Blackburn's friends, relatives, or legal counsel; [and] the composition of the confession by the Deputy Sheriff rather than by Blackburn." 361 U.S., at 207–208. These tactics supported a finding that the confession was involuntary. Indeed, the Court specifically condemned police activity that "wrings a confession out of an accused against his will." *Id.*, at 206–207. Townsend presented a similar instance of police wrongdoing. In that case, a police physician had given Townsend a drug with truth-serum properties. 372 U.S., at 298–299. The subsequent confession, obtained by officers who knew that Townsend had been given drugs, was held involuntary. These two cases demonstrate that while mental condition is surely relevant to an individual's susceptibility to police coercion, mere examination of the confessant's state of mind can never conclude the due process inquiry.

Our "involuntary confession" jurisprudence is entirely consistent with the settled law requiring some sort of "state action" to support a claim of violation of the Due Process Clause of the Fourteenth Amendment. The Colorado trial court, of course, found that the police committed no wrongful acts, and that finding has been neither challenged by respondent nor disturbed by the Supreme Court of Colorado. The latter court, however, concluded that sufficient state action was present by virtue of the admission of the confession into evidence in a court of the State. 702 P.2d, at 728–729.

The difficulty with the approach of the Supreme Court of Colorado is that it fails to recognize the essential link between coercive activity of the State, on the

one hand, and a resulting confession by a defendant, on the other. The flaw in respondent's constitutional argument is that it would expand our previous line of "voluntariness" cases into a farranging requirement that courts must divine a defendant's motivation for speaking or acting as he did even though there be no claim that governmental conduct coerced his decision.

The most outrageous behavior by a private party seeking to secure evidence against a defendant does not make that evidence inadmissible under the Due Process Clause. See *Walter* v. *United States*, 447 U.S. 649, 656 (1980); *Coolidge* v. *New Hampshire*, 403 U.S. 443, 487–488 (1971); *Burdeau* v. *McDowell*, 256 U.S. 465, 476 (1921). We have also observed that "[j]urists and scholars uniformly have recognized that the exclusionary rule imposes a substantial cost on the societal interest in law enforcement by its proscription of what concededly is relevant evidence." *United States* v. *Janis*, 428 U.S. 433, 448–449 (1976). See also *United States* v. *Havens*, 446 U.S. 620, 627 (1980); *United States* v. *Calandra*, 414 U.S. 338 (1974). Moreover, suppressing respondent's statements would serve absolutely no purpose in enforcing constitutional guarantees. The purpose of excluding evidence seized in violation of the Constitution is to substantially deter future violations of the Constitution. See *United States* v. *Leon*, 468 U.S. 897, 906–913 (1984). Only if we were to establish a brand new constitutional right—the right of a criminal defendant to confess to his crime only when totally rational and properly motivated— could respondent's present claim be sustained.

We have previously cautioned against expanding "currently applicable exclusionary rules by erecting additional barriers to placing truthful and probative evidence before state juries. . . ." *Lego* v. *Twomey*, 404 U.S. 477, 488–489 (1972). We abide by that counsel now. "[T]he central purpose of a criminal trial is to decide the factual question of the defendant's guilt or innocence," *Delaware* v. *Van Arsdall*, 475 U.S. 673, 681 (1986), and while we have previously held that exclusion of evidence may be necessary to protect constitutional guarantees, both the necessity for the collateral inquiry and the exclusion of evidence deflect a criminal trial from its basic purpose. Respondent would now have us require sweeping inquiries into the state of mind of a criminal defendant who has confessed, inquiries quite divorced from any coercion brought to bear on the defendant by the State. We think the Constitution rightly leaves this sort of inquiry to be resolved by state laws governing the admission of evidence and erects no standard of its own in this area. A statement rendered by one in the condition of respondent might be proved to be quite unreliable, but this is a matter to be governed by the evidentiary laws of the forum, see, e.g., Fed. Rule Evid. 601, and not by the Due Process Clause of the Fourteenth Amendment. "The aim of the requirement of due process is not to exclude presumptively false evidence, but to prevent fundamental unfairness in the use of evidence, whether true or false." *Lisenba* v. *California*, 314 U.S. 219, 236 (1941).

We hold that coercive police activity is a necessary predicate to the finding that a confession is not "voluntary" within the meaning of the Due Process Clause of the Fourteenth Amendment. We also conclude that the taking of respondent's statements, and their admission into evidence, constitute no violation of that Clause.

. . .We think that the Supreme Court of Colorado erred in importing into this area of constitutional law notions of "free will" that have no place there. There is obviously no reason to require more in the way of a "voluntariness" inquiry in the *Miranda* waiver context than in the Fourteenth Amendment confession context. The sole concern of the Fifth Amendment, on which *Miranda* was based, is governmental coercion. See *United States* v. *Washington*, 431 U.S. 181, 187 (1977);

Miranda, supra, at 460. Indeed, the Fifth Amendment privilege is not concerned "with moral and psychological pressures to confess emanating from sources other than official coercion." *Oregon* v. *Elstad,* 470 U.S. 298, 305 (1985). The voluntariness of a waiver of this privilege has always depended on the absence of police overreaching, not on "free choice" in any broader sense of the word. See *Moran* v. *Burbine,* 475 U.S., at 421 ("[T]he relinquishment of the right must have been voluntary in the sense that it was the product of a free and deliberate choice rather than intimidation, coercion or deception. . . . [T]he record is devoid of any suggestion that police resorted to physical or psychological pressure to elicit the statements"); *Fare* v. *Michael C.,* 442 U.S. 707, 726–727 (1979) (The defendant was "not worn down by improper interrogation tactics or lengthy questioning or by trickery or deceit. . . . The officers did not intimidate or threaten respondent in any way. Their questioning was restrained and free from the abuses that so concerned the Court in *Miranda*").

Respondent urges this Court to adopt his "free will" rationale, and to find an attempted waiver invalid whenever the defendant feels compelled to waive his rights by reason of any compulsion, even if the compulsion does not flow from the police. But such a treatment of the waiver issue would "cut this Court's holding in [*Miranda*] completely loose from its own explicitly stated rationale." *Beckwith* v. *United States,* 425 U.S. 341, 345 (1976). *Miranda* protects defendants against government coercion leading them to surrender rights protected by the Fifth Amendment; it goes no further than that. Respondent's perception of coercion flowing from the "voice of God," however important or significant such a perception may be in other disciplines, is a matter to which the United States Constitution does not speak.

IV.

The judgment of the Supreme Court of Colorado is accordingly reversed, and the cause is remanded for further proceedings not inconsistent with this opinion.

[Concurring opinions of JUSTICES BLACKMUN and STEVENS and dissenting opinions of BRENNAN and MARSHALL are omitted.]

WHAT DO YOU THINK?

1. Do you agree with the court's opinion? Explain.
2. What does the Court mean by the statement that coercive police activity is a necessary predicate to the finding that a confession is not "voluntary" within the meaning of the Due Process Clause of the Fourteenth Amendment?

The Minnick *case looks at a problem where the accused has invoked his rights and is still interrogated. If a suspect asserts his right to counsel, may the police try again to interrogate? After the defendant is allowed to consult with an attorney, should the police be allowed to reinitiate the interrogation without the counsel being present?*

MINNICK V. MISSISSIPPI
498 U.S. 146 (1990)

JUSTICE KENNEDY delivered the opinion of the Court.

To protect the privilege against self-incrimination guaranteed by the Fifth Amendment, we have held that the police must terminate interrogation of an accused in custody if the accused requests the assistance of counsel. *Miranda* v. *Arizona*, 384 U.S. 436, 474 (1966). We reinforced the protections of *Miranda* in *Edwards* v. *Arizona*, 451 U.S. 477, 484–485 (1981), which held that, once the accused requests counsel, officials may not reinitiate questioning "until counsel has been made available" to him. The issue in the case before us is whether *Edwards'* protection ceases once the suspect has consulted with an attorney.

Petitioner Robert Minnick and fellow prisoner James Dyess escaped from a county jail in Mississippi and, a day later, broke into a mobile home in search of weapons. In the course of the burglary, they were interrupted by the arrival of the trailer's owner, Ellis Thomas, accompanied by Lamar Lafferty and Lafferty's infant son. Dyess and Minnick used the stolen weapons to kill Thomas and the senior Lafferty. Minnick's story is that Dyess murdered one victim and forced Minnick to shoot the other. Before the escapees could get away, two young women arrived at the mobile home. They were held at gunpoint, then bound hand and foot. Dyess and Minnick fled in Thomas' truck, abandoning the vehicle in New Orleans. The fugitives continued to Mexico, where they fought, and Minnick then proceeded alone to California. Minnick was arrested in Lemon Grove, California, on a Mississippi warrant, some four months after the murders.

The confession at issue here resulted from the last interrogation of Minnick while he was held in the San Diego jail, but we first recount the events which preceded it. Minnick was arrested on Friday, August 22, 1986. Petitioner testified that he was mistreated by local police during and after the arrest. The day following the arrest, Saturday, two FBI agents came to the jail to interview him. Petitioner testified that he refused to go to the interview, but was told he would "have to go down or else." App. 45. The FBI report indicates that the agents read petitioner his *Miranda* warnings, and that he acknowledged he understood his rights. He refused to sign a rights waiver form, however, and said he would not answer "very many" questions. Minnick told the agents about the jail break and the flight, and described how Dyess threatened and beat him. Early in the interview, he sobbed "[i]t was my life or theirs," but otherwise he hesitated to tell what happened at the trailer. The agents reminded him he did not have to answer questions without a lawyer present. According to the report, "Minnick stated 'Come back Monday when I have a lawyer,' and stated that he would make a more complete statement then with his lawyer present." App. 16. The FBI interview ended.

After the FBI interview, an appointed attorney met with petitioner. Petitioner spoke with the lawyer on two or three occasions, though it is not clear from the record whether all of these conferences were in person.

On Monday, August 25, Deputy Sheriff J.C. Denham of Clarke County, Mississippi, came to the San Diego jail to question Minnick. Minnick testified that his jailers again told him he would "have to talk" to Denham, and that he "could not refuse." *Id.*, at 45. Denham advised petitioner of his rights, and petitioner again declined to sign a rights waiver form. Petitioner told Denham about the escape, and then proceeded to describe the events at the mobile home. According to petitioner, Dyess jumped out of the mobile home and shot the first of the two victims, once

in the back with a shotgun and once in the head with a pistol. Dyess then handed the pistol to petitioner and ordered him to shoot the other victim, holding the shotgun on petitioner until he did so. Petitioner also said that, when the two girls arrived, he talked Dyess out of raping or otherwise hurting them.

Minnick was tried for murder in Mississippi. He moved to suppress all statements given to the FBI or other police officers, including Denham. The trial court denied the motion with respect to petitioner's statements to Denham, but suppressed his other statements. Petitioner was convicted on two counts of capital murder, and sentenced to death.

On appeal, petitioner argued that the confession to Denham was taken in violation of his rights to counsel under the Fifth and Sixth Amendments. The Mississippi Supreme Court rejected the claims. We granted *certiorari*, 495 U.S. 903 (1990), and, without reaching any Sixth Amendment implications in the case, we decided that the Fifth Amendment protection of *Edwards* is not terminated or suspended by consultation with counsel.

In *Miranda* v. *Arizona, supra*, at 474, we indicated that, once an individual in custody invokes his right to counsel, interrogation "must cease until an attorney is present"; at that point, "the individual must have an opportunity to confer with the attorney and to have him present during any subsequent questioning." *Edwards* gave force to these admonitions, finding it "inconsistent with *Miranda* and its progeny for the authorities, at their instance, to reinterrogate an accused in custody if he has clearly asserted his right to counsel." 451 U.S., at 485. We held that "when an accused has invoked his right to have counsel present during custodial interrogation, a valid waiver of that right cannot be established by showing only that he responded to further police-initiated custodial interrogation even if he has been advised of his rights." *Id.*, at 484. Further, an accused who requests an attorney, having expressed his desire to deal with the police only through counsel, is not subject to further interrogation by the authorities until counsel has been made available to him, unless the accused himself initiates further communication, exchanges, or conversations with the police. *Id.*, at 484–485.

Edwards is "designed to prevent police from badgering a defendant into waiving his previously asserted *Miranda* rights." *Michigan* v. *Harvey*, 494 U.S. 344, 350 (1990). See also *Smith* v. *Illinois*, 469 U.S. 91, 98 (1984). The rule ensures that any statement made in subsequent interrogation is not the result of coercive pressures. *Edwards* conserves judicial resources which would otherwise be expended in making difficult determinations of voluntariness, and implements the protections of *Miranda* in practical and straightforward terms.

The merit of the *Edwards* decision lies in the clarity of its command and the certainty of its application. We have confirmed that the *Edwards* rule provides " 'clear and unequivocal' guidelines to the law enforcement profession." *Arizona* v. *Roberson*, 486 U.S. 675, 682 (1988). Cf. *Moran* v. *Burbine*, 475 U.S. 412, 425–426 (1986). Even before *Edwards*, we noted that *Miranda*'s "relatively rigid requirement that interrogation must cease upon the accused's request for an attorney . . . has the virtue of informing police and prosecutors with specificity as to what they may do in conducting custodial interrogation, and of informing courts under what circumstances statements obtained during such interrogation are not admissible. This gain in specificity, which benefits the accused and the State alike, has been thought to outweigh the burdens that the decision in *Miranda* imposes on law enforcement agencies and the courts by requiring the suppression of trustworthy and highly probative evidence even though the confession might be voluntary under traditional Fifth Amendment analysis." *Fare* v. *Michael C.*, 442 U.S. 707,

718 (1979). This pre-*Edwards* explanation applies as well to *Edwards* and its progeny. *Arizona* v. *Roberson*, *supra*, at 681–682.

The Mississippi Supreme Court relied on our statement in *Edwards* that an accused who invokes his right to counsel "is not subject to further interrogation by the authorities until counsel has been made available to him. . . ." 451 U.S., at 484–485. We do not interpret this language to mean, as the Mississippi court thought, that the protection of *Edwards* terminates once counsel has consulted with the suspect. In context, the requirement that counsel be "made available" to the accused refers to more than an opportunity to consult with an attorney outside the interrogation room.

In *Edwards*, we focused on *Miranda*'s instruction that when the accused invokes his right to counsel, "the interrogation must cease until an attorney is present," 384 U.S., at 474, agreeing with *Edwards*' contention that he had not waived his right "to have counsel present during custodial interrogation." 451 U.S., at 482. In the sentence preceding the language quoted by the Mississippi Supreme Court, we referred to the "right to have counsel present during custodial interrogation," and in the sentence following, we again quoted the phrase " 'interrogation must cease until an attorney is present' " from *Miranda*. 451 U.S., at 484–485. The full sentence relied on by the Mississippi Supreme Court, moreover, says: "We further hold that an accused, such as Edwards, having expressed his desire to deal with the police only through counsel, is not subject to further interrogation by the authorities until counsel has been made available to him, unless the accused himself initiates further communication, exchanges, or conversations with the police." *Ibid.*

Our emphasis on counsel's presence at interrogation is not unique to *Edwards*. It derives from *Miranda*, where we said that, in the cases before us, "[t]he presence of counsel . . . would be the adequate protective device necessary to make the process of police interrogation conform to the dictates of the [Fifth Amendment] privilege. His presence would insure that statements made in the government-established atmosphere are not the product of compulsion." 384 U.S., at 466. See *Fare* v. *Michael C.*, *supra*, at 719. Our cases following *Edwards* have interpreted the decision to mean that the authorities may not initiate questioning of the accused in counsel's absence. Writing for a plurality of the Court, for instance, then-JUSTICE REHNQUIST described the holding of [498 U.S. 146, 153] Edwards to be "that subsequent incriminating statements made without [Edwards'] attorney present violated the rights secured to the defendant by the Fifth and Fourteenth Amendments to the United States Constitution." *Oregon* v. *Bradshaw*, 462 U.S. 1039, 1043 (1983). See also *Arizona* v. *Roberson*, *supra*, at 680 ("The rule of the *Edwards* case came as a corollary to *Miranda*'s admonition that '[i]f the individual states that he wants an attorney, the interrogation must cease until an attorney is present' "); *Shea* v. *Louisiana*, 470 U.S. 51, 52 (1985) ("In *Edwards* v. *Arizona*, . . . this Court ruled that a criminal defendant's rights under the Fifth and Fourteenth Amendments were violated by the use of his confession obtained by police-instigated interrogation—without counsel present—after he requested an attorney"). These descriptions of Edwards' holding are consistent with our statement that "[p]reserving the integrity of an accused's choice to communicate with police only through counsel is the essence of *Edwards* and its progeny." *Patterson* v. *Illinois*, 487 U.S. 285, 291 (1988). In our view, a fair reading of *Edwards* and subsequent cases demonstrates that we have interpreted the rule to bar police-initiated interrogation unless the accused has counsel with him at the time of questioning. Whatever the ambiguities of our ear-

lier cases on this point, we now hold that, when counsel is requested, interrogation must cease, and officials may not reinitiate interrogation without counsel present, whether or not the accused has consulted with his attorney.

We consider our ruling to be an appropriate and necessary application of the *Edwards* rule. A single consultation with an attorney does not remove the suspect from persistent attempts by officials to persuade him to waive his rights, or from the coercive pressures that accompany custody and that may increase as custody is prolonged. The case before us well illustrates the pressures, and abuses, that may be concomitants of custody. Petitioner testified that, though he resisted, he was required to submit to both the FBI and the Denham interviews. In the latter instance, the compulsion to submit to interrogation followed petitioner's unequivocal request during the FBI interview that questioning cease until counsel was present. The case illustrates also that consultation is not always effective in instructing the suspect of his rights. One plausible interpretation of the record is that petitioner thought he could keep his admissions out of evidence by refusing to sign a formal waiver of rights. If the authorities had complied with Minnick's request to have counsel present during interrogation, the attorney could have corrected Minnick's misunderstanding, or indeed counseled him that he need not make a statement at all. We decline to remove protection from police-initiated questioning based on isolated consultations with counsel who is absent when the interrogation resumes.

The exception to *Edwards* here proposed is inconsistent with *Edwards'* purpose to protect the suspect's right to have counsel present at custodial interrogation. It is inconsistent as well with *Miranda*, where we specifically rejected respondent's theory that the opportunity to consult with one's attorney would substantially counteract the compulsion created by custodial interrogation. We noted in *Miranda* that "[e]ven preliminary advice given to the accused by his own attorney can be swiftly overcome by the secret interrogation process. Thus the need for counsel to protect the Fifth Amendment privilege comprehends not merely a right to consult with counsel prior to questioning, but also to have counsel present during any questioning if the defendant so desires." 384 U.S., at 470 (citation omitted).

The exception proposed, furthermore, would undermine the advantages flowing from Edwards' "clear and unequivocal" character. Respondent concedes that, even after consultation with counsel, a second request for counsel should reinstate the *Edwards* protection. We are invited by this formulation to adopt a regime in which *Edwards'* protection could pass in and out of existence multiple times prior to arraignment, at which point the same protection might reattach by virtue of our Sixth Amendment jurisprudence, see *Michigan* v. *Jackson*, 475 U.S. 625 (1986). Vagaries of this sort spread confusion through the justice system and lead to a consequent loss of respect for the underlying constitutional principle. . . .

The judgment is reversed and the case remanded for further proceedings not inconsistent with this opinion. It is so ordered.

[Dissenting opinions of JUSTICE SCALIA is omitted.]

WHAT DO YOU THINK?

1. Do you agree with the majority opinion? Why?
2. What rights are protected by requiring the police to stop interrogation when the defendant requests to consult with an attorney?

Is an undercover officer who is placed in the cell with the defendant required to advise the defendant of his Miranda *rights before asking his cell mate questions? The* Perkins *case looks at that issue.*

ILLINOIS V. PERKINS
496 U.S. 292 (1990)

JUSTICE KENNEDY delivered the opinion of the Court.

An undercover government agent was placed in the cell of respondent Perkins, who was incarcerated on charges unrelated to the subject of the agent's investigation. Respondent made statements that implicated him in the crime that the agent sought to solve. Respondent claims that the statements should be inadmissible because he had not been given *Miranda* warnings by the agent. We hold that the statements are admissible. *Miranda* warnings are not required when the suspect is unaware that he is speaking to a law enforcement officer and gives a voluntary statement.

I.

In November 1984, Richard Stephenson was murdered in a suburb of East St. Louis, Illinois. The murder remained unsolved until March 1986, when one Donald Charlton told police that he had learned about a homicide from a fellow inmate at the Graham Correctional Facility, where Charlton had been serving a sentence for burglary. The fellow inmate was Lloyd Perkins, who is the respondent here. Charlton told police that, while at Graham, he had befriended respondent, who told him in detail about a murder that respondent had committed in East St. Louis. On hearing Charlton's account, the police recognized details of the Stephenson murder that were not well known, and so they treated Charlton's story as a credible one.

By the time the police heard Charlton's account, respondent had been released from Graham, but police traced him to a jail in Montgomery County, Illinois, where he was being held pending trial on a charge of aggravated battery unrelated to the Stephenson murder. The police wanted to investigate further respondent's connection to the Stephenson murder, but feared that the use of an eavesdropping device would prove impracticable and unsafe. They decided instead to place an undercover agent in the cellblock with respondent and Charlton. The plan was for Charlton and undercover agent John Parisi to pose as escapees from a work release program who had been arrested in the course of a burglary. Parisi and Charlton were instructed to engage respondent in casual conversation and report anything he said about the Stephenson murder.

Parisi, using the alias "Vito Bianco," and Charlton, both clothed in jail garb, were placed in the cellblock with respondent at the Montgomery County jail. The cellblock consisted of 12 separate cells that opened onto a common room. Respondent greeted Charlton who, after a brief conversation with respondent, introduced Parisi by his alias. Parisi told respondent that he "wasn't going to do any more time" and suggested that the three of them escape. Respondent replied that the Montgomery County jail was "rinky-dink" and that they could "break out." The trio met in respondent's cell later that evening, after the other inmates were asleep, to refine their plan. Respondent said that his girlfriend could smuggle in a

pistol. Charlton said: "Hey, I'm not a murderer, I'm a burglar. That's your guys' profession." After telling Charlton that he would be responsible for any murder that occurred, Parisi asked respondent if he had ever "done" anybody. Respondent said that he had and proceeded to describe at length the events of the Stephenson murder. Parisi and respondent then engaged in some casual conversation before respondent went to sleep. Parisi did not give respondent *Miranda* warnings before the conversations.

Respondent was charged with the Stephenson murder. Before trial, he moved to suppress the statements made to Parisi in the jail. The trial court granted the motion to suppress, and the State appealed. The Appellate Court of Illinois affirmed, 176 Ill. App. 3d 443, 531 N. E. 2d 141 (1988), holding that *Miranda* v. *Arizona*, 384 U.S. 436 (1966), prohibits all undercover contacts with incarcerated suspects that are reasonably likely to elicit an incriminating response.

We granted *certiorari*, 493 U.S. 808 (1989), to decide whether an undercover law enforcement officer must give *Miranda* warnings to an incarcerated suspect before asking him questions that may elicit an incriminating response. We now reverse.

II.

In *Miranda* v. *Arizona, supra*, the Court held that the Fifth Amendment privilege against self-incrimination prohibits admitting statements given by a suspect during "custodial interrogation" without a prior warning. Custodial interrogation means "questioning initiated by law enforcement officers after a person has been taken into custody. . . ." *Id.*, at 444. The warning mandated by *Miranda* was meant to preserve the privilege during "incommunicado interrogation of individuals in a police-dominated atmosphere." *Id.*, at 445. That atmosphere is said to generate "inherently compelling pressures which work to undermine the individual's will to resist and to compel him to speak where he would not otherwise do so freely." *Id.*, at 467. "Fidelity to the doctrine announced in *Miranda* requires that it be enforced strictly, but only in those types of situations in which the concerns that powered the decision are implicated." *Berkemer* v. *McCarty*, 468 U.S. 420, 437 (1984).

Conversations between suspects and undercover agents do not implicate the concerns underlying *Miranda*. The essential ingredients of a "police-dominated atmosphere" and compulsion are not present when an incarcerated person speaks freely to someone whom he believes to be a fellow inmate. Coercion is determined from the perspective of the suspect. *Rhode Island* v. *Innis*, 446 U.S. 291, 301 (1980); *Berkemer* v. *McCarty, supra*, at 442. When a suspect considers himself in the company of cellmates and not officers, the coercive atmosphere is lacking. *Miranda*, 384 U.S., at 449 ("[T]he 'principal psychological factor contributing to a successful interrogation is privacy—being alone with the person under interrogation' "); *id.*, at 445. There is no empirical basis for the assumption that a suspect speaking to those whom he assumes are not officers will feel compelled to speak by the fear of reprisal for remaining silent or in the hope of more lenient treatment should he confess.

It is the premise of *Miranda* that the danger of coercion results from the interaction of custody and official interrogation. We reject the argument that *Miranda* warnings are required whenever a suspect is in custody in a technical sense and converses with someone who happens to be a government agent. Questioning by captors, who appear to control the suspect's fate, may create mutually reinforcing pressures that the Court has assumed will weaken the suspect's will, but where a suspect does not know that he is conversing with a government agent, these pressures do not exist. The state court here mistakenly assumed that because the suspect was in custody, no undercover questioning could take place. When the suspect has no reason to think that the listeners have official power over him, it should not be assumed that his words are motivated by the reaction he expects from his listeners. "[W]hen the agent carries neither badge nor gun and wears not 'police blue,' but the same prison gray" as the suspect, there is no "interplay between police interrogation and police custody." *Kamisar, Brewer* v. *Williams*, Massiah and *Miranda: What is "Interrogation"? When Does It Matter?*, 67 Geo. L. J. 1, 67, 63 (1978).

Miranda forbids coercion, not mere strategic deception by taking advantage of a suspect's misplaced trust in one he supposes to be a fellow prisoner. As we recognized in *Miranda*: "Confessions remain a proper element in law enforcement. Any statement given freely and voluntarily without any compelling influences is, of course, admissible in evidence." 384 U.S., at 478. Ploys to mislead a suspect or lull him into a false sense of security that do not rise to the level of compulsion or coercion to speak are not within *Miranda*'s concerns. Cf. *Oregon* v. *Mathiason*, 429 U.S. 492, 495–496 (1977) (per curiam); *Moran* v. *Burbine*, 475 U.S. 412 (1986) (where police fail to inform suspect of attorney's efforts to reach him, [496 U.S. 292, 298] neither *Miranda* nor the Fifth Amendment requires suppression of pre-arraignment confession after voluntary waiver).

Miranda was not meant to protect suspects from boasting about their criminal activities in front of persons whom they believe to be their cellmates. This case is illustrative. Respondent had no reason to feel that undercover agent Parisi had any legal authority to force him to answer questions or that Parisi could affect respondent's future treatment. Respondent viewed the cellmate-agent as an equal and showed no hint of being intimidated by the atmosphere of the jail. In recounting the details of the Stephenson murder, respondent was motivated solely by the desire to impress his fellow inmates. He spoke at his own peril.

...We hold that an undercover law enforcement officer posing as a fellow inmate need not give *Miranda* warnings to an incarcerated suspect before asking questions that may elicit an incriminating response. The statements at issue in this case were voluntary, and there is no federal obstacle to their admissibility at trial. We now reverse and remand for proceedings not inconsistent with our opinion.

It is so ordered.

[Concurring opinion of JUSTICE BRENNAN and dissenting opinion of JUSTICE MARSHALL are omitted.]

WHAT DO *YOU* THINK?

1. Should the *Miranda* warnings be required for any in-custody interrogation?
2. Justice Marshall in his dissent stated that "*Miranda* was not, however, concerned solely with police coercion. It deals with any police tactics." Do you agree with his statements? Should the court approve such tactics by the police?

SUMMARY

- The scope of the privilege against self-incrimination includes three basic parts. First, the compulsion to testify must be by the government. Second, the compulsion to testify is prohibited only if it forces a person to be a witness against him or herself. Third, the privilege protects the person from being a witness against him or herself for criminal cases only. Each of these basic parts must be present in order for a person to effectively claim the privilege against self-incrimination.

■ Generally two questions arise when considering the admissibility of a defendant's out-of-court statement: First, was the statement voluntary, i.e., not the result of coercion, and second, have the *Miranda* requirements, if applicable, been complied with.

■ Evidence is not protected by the privilege unless the evidence is testimonial in nature. A defendant may be forced to provide fingerprints, voice exemplars, blood tests, etc. The Fifth Amendment applies only to testimonial evidence, which is evidence that only a witness provides. Any physical evidence is not included in the privilege.

■ The Fifth Amendment protection against self-incrimination does not apply to businesses entities.

■ While the privilege against self-incrimination applies only to criminal cases, it possesses a broader scope than the language applies.

■ The privilege protects individuals from answering any questions in any proceedings if the answers might incriminate them in a future criminal proceeding.

■ Before a confession or admission of an accused may be entered into evidence, it must meet the test of voluntariness and then, if applicable, the requirements of *Miranda*.

■ The *Miranda* rule provides that a confession, admission, or any statement made by a person during custodial interrogation is inadmissible in court unless the person receives the four warnings that describe his or her rights and the person makes a knowing, intelligent, and voluntary waiver of his or her rights. The Court also states that the police must stop questioning when the person invokes his or her rights to remain silent or to speak to an attorney.

DISCUSSION QUESTIONS

1. What rights are protected under the privilege against self-incrimination under the Fourth Amendment?
2. Should we eliminate the privilege against self-incrimination and allow confessions to be admitted only if they are coerced?
3. Under what circumstances should the *Miranda* warnings be given?
4. Do you agree with the *Miranda* holding? Why?

ENDNOTES

1. 1. *Bram* v. *United States*, 168 U.S. 532 (1897).
2. Jerold H. Israel and Wayne R. LaFave, *Criminal Procedure: Constitutional Limitations*, 5th ed. (St. Paul: West, 1993) p. 199
3. Leonard W. Levy, *Origins of the Fifth Amendment Right Against Self-Incrimination* 2d. ed. (1986).
4. 384 U.S. 436 (1966).
5. D. Dolinko, "Is There a Rationale for the Privilege Against Self-Incrimination?" 33 U.C.L.A. L. Rev. 1063 (1986).

6. 410 U.S. 1 (1973).
7. 388 U.S. 218 (1967).
8. 388 U.S. 263 (1967).
9. 496 U.S. 582 (1990).
10. *Doe v. United States*, 487 U.S. 201 (1988).
11. 116 U.S. 616 (1886).
12. 425 U.S. 391 (1976).
13. *In re Doe*, 711 F.2d. 1187 (2d Cir. 1983).
14. *Shapiro v. United States*, 335 U.S. 1 (1948).
15. 402 U.S. 424 (1971).
16. 487 U.S. 99 (1988).
17. 354 U.S. 118 (1957).
18. *In re Grand Jury Subpoena*, 87 F.3d 1198 (11th Cir. 1996).
19. *McCarthy v. Arndstein*, 266 U.S. 34 (1924).
20. 414 U.S. 70 (1973).
21. 99 F 3rd 60 (2nd Cir. 1996).
22. *Malloy v. Hogan*, 378 U.S. 1 (1951).
23. *Fisher v. United States*, 425 U.S. 391 (1976).
24. 925 F.2d 1527 (3rd Cir. 1991).
25. *United States v. Hearst*, 563 F.2d 1331 (9th Cir. 1977).
26. 297 U.S. 278 (1936).
27. *Spano v. New York*, 360 U.S. 315 (1959).
28. 499 U.S. 279 (1991).
29. 479 U.S. 157 (1986).
30. *Haynes v. Washington*, 373 U.S. 503 (1963).
31. *Mincy v. Arizona*, 437 U.S. 385 (1978).
32. *People v. Andersen*, 101 Cal. App. 3rd 563 (1980).
33. *In re Roger G.*, 53 Cal. App. 3d. 198 (1975).
34. 372 U.S. 293 (1963).
35. *Lego v. Twomey*, 404 U.S. 477 (1972).
36. *Lynumn v. Illinois*, 372 U.S. 528 (1963).
37. *Hawkins v. Lynaugh*, 844 F.2d. 1132 (5th Cir. 1988).
38. *United States v. Glasgow*, 451 F.2d. 557 (9th Cir. 1971).
39. *Beckwith v. United States*, 425 U.S. 341 (1976).
40. 168 U.S. 532 (1897).
41. *Hutto v. Ross*, 429 U.S. 28 (1976).
42. 384 U.S. 436 (1966).
43. *Brewer v. Williams*, 430 U.S. 387 (1977).
44. 446 U.S. 291 (1980).
45. 468 U.S. 420 (1984).
46. 394 U.S. 324 (1969).
47. 429 U.S. 492 (1977).
48. 417 U.S. 433 (1974).
49. 470 U.S. 298 (1985).
50. 467 U.S. 649 (1984).
51. 496 U.S. 292 (1990).
52. *Kastigar v. United States*, 406 U.S. 441 (1972).
53. 920 F.2d 940 (D.C. Cir. 1990).
54. 377 U.S. 201 (1964).
55. 430 U.S. 387 (1977).
56. *Johnson v. Zerbst*, 304 U.S. 458 (1938).
57. 487 U.S. 285 (1988).
58. *Maine v. Molton*, 474 U.S. 159 (1985).

7

$\mathcal{R}$EMEDIES

The normal sanction for violation of a defendant's Fourth Amendment rights is to preclude the evidence obtained as the result of the violation from being used against the defendant in his or her criminal trial. It should be noted that the scope of the exclusionary rule is different for each constitutional violation. As noted in chapters 5 and 6, the primary purpose of the exclusionary rule is to deter police misconduct. The "fruit of the poisonous tree" doctrine is also examined in the chapter. As noted by the quotes below, the exclusionary rule is a controversial issue. Many Americans have advocated its demise. Others strongly support the rule.

FOURTH AMENDMENT EXCLUSIONARY RULE

The Fourth Amendment's exclusionary rule can be traced to the 1914 Supreme Court decision in *Weeks* v. *United States*.[1] In *Weeks*, the Court held that evidence obtained by federal officials in violation of the Fourth Amendment would be inadmissible in federal criminal trials. Later, in 1949, the Supreme Court held in *Wolf* v. *Colorado*[2] that the Fourteenth Amendment did not require states to exclude evidence obtained through an illegal search. The Court noted that the exclusionary rule had been rejected by at least 30 states. In 1961, *Mapp* v. *Ohio*[3], the Supreme Court overruled Wolf and held that evidence obtained by illegal searches and seizures should not be admitted in criminal trials against the person whose rights were violated.

JUSTICE BENJAMIN CARDOZO ON THE EXCLUSIONARY RULE

The criminal is to go free because the constable has blundered. . . . The pettiest peace officer would have it in his power, through overzeal or indiscretion, to confer immunity upon an offender for crimes most flagitious. A room is searched against the law, and a body of a murdered man is found. If the place of discovery may not be proved, the other circumstances may be insufficient to connect the defendant with the crime. The privacy of the home has been infringed, and the murderer goes free. . . . [*People* v. *Defore*, 242 N.Y. 13 (1926)]

Justice Benjamin Cardozo was appointed to the Supreme Court by President Hoover and served from 1932 to 1938. (Photograph by Harris & Ewing. Collection of the Supreme Court of the United States.)

YALE KAMISAR ON THE EXCLUSIONARY RULE

A court which admits [evidence illegally obtained] manifests a willingness to tolerate the unconstitutional conduct which produced it. . . . A court which admits the evidence in a case involving a "run of the mill" Fourth Amendment violation demonstrates an insufficient commitment to the guarantee against unreasonable search and seizure. [62 Judicature, pp. 66–84, August, 1978]

THE EXCLUSIONARY RULE REFORM ACT OF 1995

HR 666

Several attempts have been made by Congress to eliminate or modify the exclusionary rule. HR 666, The Exclusionary Rule Reform Act of 1995, stated, *inter alia*, that evidence which is obtained as a result of a search or seizure shall not be excluded in a proceedings in a court of the United States on the ground that the search or seizure was in violation of the fourth amendment to the Constitution of the United States. [This proposed act was defeated by Congress. It is anticipated that future attempts to pass similar legislation will be made.]

In order to object to the admission of evidence obtained as the results of an illegal search, the person must have standing to object. The doctrine of legal standing is a judicially created doctrine. There are two parts to the concept of legal standing. First, the person asserting his or her claim must have suffered an actual injury or invasion of his or her constitutional rights. Second, the rights asserted must be based on that person's legal rights. You cannot assert the rights of a third person. For example, the police illegally arrest Mary and discover evidence that can be used against Steve. Unless Steve's rights were violated, he cannot object that the evidence was discovered as the result of the illegal arrest of Mary. The Supreme Court has held that a person must have standing to assert the exclusionary rule. So in the example, Steve would have to establish that he suffered an injury or an invasion of his own legal rights in order to have the exclusionary rule apply to the evidence against him.

The defendant has the burden of establishing that he or she has legal standing to object to search or seizure in issue.[4] In *United States* v. *Powell*[5], the defendant had someone else drive his car across country to his home. While en route, the car was stopped by the police. The driver consented to a search, and illegal drugs were discovered. The court of appeals held that the owner of the vehicle did not have standing to object even though he owned the car. The court stated that legal standing is generally limited to those who are actually stopped with the car—since it is they who are inconvenienced. If property is being used with the permission of the owner, generally the user will have legal standing. In cases involving overnight guests, the issue of standing generally depends on whether the guests have a reasonable expectation of privacy in the third person's home.[6]

EXCEPTIONS TO THE EXCLUSIONARY RULE

There are at least five exceptions to the exclusionary rule: (1) good-faith exception[7], (2) purged taint exception[8], (3) independent source exception[9], (4) inevitable discovery exception[10], and (5) impeachment of the defendant at trial[11]. The good-faith exception is most popular.

The Good-Faith Exception

The "good-faith" exception is a misnomer. To be a good-faith exception implies that as long as the officer acts in "good faith"—a subjective test—then the evidence should be admissible. The test is, however, an objective, not a subjective, one and thus should be more properly designated as the "reasonable good-faith" exception. The exception is based on the concept that if the police were acting with a reasonable belief in good faith that their actions were legal, then the evidence should not be excluded for constitutional violations.

In *Stone* v. *Powell*[12], Justice White in his dissenting opinion stated that "the Fourth Amendment exclusionary rule should be substantially modified so as to prevent its application in those many circumstances where the evidence at issue was seized by an officer acting in the good-faith belief that his conduct comported with existing law and having reasonable grounds for this belief." Later in *United States* v. *Leon*[13], the Supreme Court, with Justice White then writing for the majority, held that the Fourth Amendment exclusionary rule should be modified so as not to bar its use in the prosecution's case-in-chief of evidence obtained by officers acting in reasonable reliance on a defective search warrant that was issued by a neutral and detached magistrate. The Court noted in *Leon* that the exclusionary rule is designed to deter police misconduct rather than to punish the errors of judges, and there exists no evidence suggesting that the judges and magistrates are inclined to ignore or subvert the Fourth Amendment. The Court noted that there was no basis for believing that exclusion of the evidence seized pursuant to a warrant will have a significant deterrent effect on the issuing judge or magistrate. The Court indicated that exclusion of evidence is inappropriate in those cases where the officer lacks reasonable grounds for believing that the warrant was properly issued.

In *Illinois* v. *Krull*[14], the Supreme Court held that a good-faith exception to the Fourth Amendment exclusionary rule should be recognized in those cases where the officers acted in objectively good faith by relying on a statute which authorized the search in question. The statute was later held unconstitutional.

The Purged Taint Exception

The purged taint exception is based on the concept that the connection has been broken between the unlawful police conduct and the tainted evidence. In *Wong Sun* v. *United States*[15], the defendant was illegally arrested. The police obtained a statement from him in his bedroom within minutes of the illegal arrest. He was then released from custody. While awaiting trial, he returned voluntarily to the police station where he made incriminating statements. The Supreme Court ruled that the statements made after he was released were admissible and that the intervening facts of his release from custody and his voluntary return to talked to the police had purged the taint of his initial illegal arrest.

In *Brown* v. *Illinois*[16], the police arrested Brown without probable cause to question him regarding a murder. He was taken to the police station and advised of his *Miranda* rights. He made an initial incriminating statement within two hours of his arrest and later after being re-advised of his *Miranda* rights made a second incriminating statement. The prosecution argued that by advising the defendant of his *Miranda* rights, the connection between the illegal arrest and the statements had been broken and thus the taint had been purged. The Supreme Court held that both statements were inadmissible because of the illegal arrest. The Court stated that the question in the case was "whether, granting establishment of the primary illegality, the evidence has been come at by exploitation of that illegality or instead by means sufficiently distinguishable to be purged of the primary taint." The Court held that in determining whether the taint had been purged, the temporal proximity of the arrest and the confession, the presence of intervening circumstances and, particularly, the purpose and flagrancy of the official misconduct are all relevant. The mere giving of a *Miranda* warning does not dissipate the taint caused by an illegal arrest.[17]

Independent Source Exception

The independent source exception is based on the concept that even if the police obtained the evidence by a constitutional violation, they could or would have obtained the evidence from a source that was not connected to the illegal action. This exception proceeds from the premise that the source producing the evidence stands apart from the influence of the constitutional violation with no links between the two. In *Murray v. United States*[18], the police made an illegal entry into a warehouse. Later the police obtained a warrant and made a legal entry. The Court held that if the police decision to seek a warrant had not been prompted by what was learned during the earlier unlawful entry, the evidence was admissible. In *Segura v. United States*[19], the police entered an apartment without a warrant and arrested the occupants. The police then remained illegally on the scene for several hours while others obtained a search warrant. The police could have left the apartment and secured the premises from the outside by a "stakeout." The Supreme Court, using the rationale that the police did in fact obtain a valid search warrant and their remaining on the premises had no bearing on the seizure of the evidence, held that the evidence was admissible under the independent source exception.

Inevitable Discovery Exception

In *Nix v. Williams* (also referred to as *Williams II*)[20], the Supreme Court held that even though the evidence was obtained by violating Mr. Williams's *Miranda* rights, it was admissible because the police would have inevitably discovered the evidence in question. In Chapter 6, the *Brewer v. Williams* case (*Williams I*) was discussed involving the "Christian burial speech." In *Williams I*, the Court held that Mr. Williams was interrogated after he had invoked his *Miranda* rights. The *Williams II* case is a continuation of the earlier case. In *Williams II*, the state contended that the evidence discovered as a result of the interrogation of Mr. Williams would have been discovered anyway. The Court reasoned that the body would have been inevitably discovered by the search party. The Court in admitting the evidence ruled that for the inevitable discovery exception to apply, the prosecution must establish by a preponderance of evidence that the information ultimately or inevitably would have been discovered. In *Williams*, the interrogation disclosed the location of the victim's body. At the time of the interrogation, the police and about 200 volunteers were conducting a grid-type search for the body in the area where the body was found. Accordingly, the evidence on the body that linked the killing to Williams was admitted.

Impeachment

A statement taken in violation of the *Miranda* rules may in some situations be used to impeach the defendant when he or she takes the stand in his or her behalf. In *Harris v. New York*[21], the Supreme Court held that a defendant's right to testify in his or her own defense does not include the right to commit perjury. Accordingly, if the defendant has given a voluntary but tainted statement, the statement may be used to impeach his or her testimony at trial. (*Note:* The statement must be voluntary, i.e., it must pass the due process test and it may only be used to impeach the testimony of the defendant.)

LAW IN PRACTICE

*H*OW *E*FFECTIVE IS THE *E*XCLUSIONARY *R*ULE

One researcher concluded that some of the results of the exclusionary rule are as follows:

- Officers now seek warrants, if at all practicable.
- A closer relationship has developed between police officers and prosecutors.
- In most cases where evidence was excluded, the affected officer clearly understood why the evidence was excluded.
- When evidence was excluded, the officer was required to explain to his or her superiors why this happened.
- Officers who repeatedly had evidence suppressed were considered as incompetent by other officers.
- When asked if the exclusionary rule should be scrapped, officers generally stated that the rule should be preserved but with good faith exceptions.

[Orfield, *The Exclusionary Rule and Deterrence: An Empirical Study of Chicago Narcotics Officers,* 54 U. Chi. L.Rev. 1016 (1987).]

FIFTH AMENDMENT EXCLUSIONARY RULE

The Court has been more reluctant to imply the exclusionary rule to *Miranda* violations involving confessions and admissions. Generally the court tries to determine if there is only a *Miranda* violation or if there is also a violation of due process. A violation of due process includes situations where the confession or admission is not a product of the defendant's free and rational choice. For example, in *Mincey* v. *Arizona*[22] the defendant was arrested for murder. He had suffered gunshot wounds and was taken to a hospital. He was advised of his *Miranda* rights and repeatedly interrogated while in a state of pain and shock. In response to the questioning, he gave incriminating statements. The prosecution did not use his statements in the government in its case but used them in rebuttal to impeach the testimony of the accused. The court held that they were inadmissible even for impeachment purposes because they violated the due process test.

As with the Fourth Amendment violations, a person must have a legal standing to object before the exclusionary rule may be applied. For example, the violation of the Fifth Amendment rights of one individual cannot be used to exclude information used to find evidence against a co-defendant.

Sixth Amendment Exclusionary Rule

Unlike Fourth and Fifth Amendment violations, the U.S. Supreme Court has not offered any extensive explanation of why Sixth Amendment violations should invoke the exclusionary rule. In one case, *Massiah* v. *United States*[23], the Supreme Court implied that the evidence taken in violation of the defendant's Sixth Amendment rights must be excluded to prevent trial prejudice from occurring. In *Gilbert* v. *California*[24], the Supreme Court indicated that the exclusionary rule was necessary based on a deterrence rationale similar to that used to support the Fourth Amendment's exclusionary rule. The right to counsel under the Sixth Amendment is only violated if the government "deliberately elicits" information from the accused.

To exclude evidence obtained as the result of a Sixth Amendment violation, the defendant must have legal standing, i.e., a violation of his or her constitutional rights. There does not appear to be a "good faith" exception to Sixth Amendment violations. In *Maine* v. *Moulton*[25], Moulton was under indictment for one crime. The government deliberately elicited information from him regarding another crime for which he had not been indicted. During the conversations, Moulton made statements regarding the crime for which he was under indictment. The Court held that despite the government's good intentions, the statements were inadmissible. (*Note*: The statements may be admissible against the offense for which he had not been indicted, since the right to counsel under the Sixth Amendment is crime specific.)

Limitations to the Exclusionary Rule

The exclusionary rule does not apply to non-criminal trial proceedings. The Supreme Court, holding that the exclusionary rule does not apply to grand jury proceedings, implied that the Fourth Amendment exclusionary rule should apply only in those circumstances in which its remedial objective of deterrence will be most efficaciously served.[26] In *United States* v. *Janis*[27], the Supreme Court held that it did not apply to civil tax proceedings. And in *I.N.S.* v. *Lopez-Mendoza*[28], the court held it did not apply to deportation hearings.

Fruit of the Poisonous Tree Doctrine

Miranda Violations

Is there a "fruit of the poisonous tree" doctrine for *Miranda* violations? Two Supreme Court cases, *Michigan* v. *Tucker*[29] and *Oregon* v. *Elstad*[30] seem to imply that there is no fruit of the poisonous tree doctrine for *Miranda* violations. In the *Tucker* case, the police obtained the name of a witness from a statement made by Tucker in violation of the *Miranda* rules. Although his statement was not admissible, the court allowed the prosecution to call the witness whose name was disclosed in the statement. In the *Elstad* case, the Court noted that there was a difference between the *Miranda* exclusionary rule and the Fourth Amendment exclusionary rule. The Court stated that "the purpose of the Fourth Amendment rule was to deter unreasonable searches, no matter how probative their fruits.", and that the *Miranda* exclusionary rule, however, serves the Fifth Amendment and sweeps more broadly than the Fifth Amendment itself." It may be triggered even in the absence of a Fifth Amendment violation. The Court also stated that "the *Miranda* presumption, though irrebuttable for the purposes of the prosecution's case in chief, does not require that the statements and their fruits be discarded as inherently tainted."

CAPSTONE CASES

Should the prosecutor be allowed to use a statement taken from the defendant in violation of his Miranda rights to impeach the defendant's testimony at trial?

HARRIS V. NEW YORK
401 U.S. 222 (1971)

MR. CHIEF JUSTICE BURGER delivered the opinion of the Court.

We granted the writ in this case to consider petitioner's claim that a statement made by him to police under circumstances rendering it inadmissible to establish the prosecution's case in chief under *Miranda* v. *Arizona*, 384 U.S. 436 (1966), may not be used to impeach his credibility.

The State of New York charged petitioner in a two-count indictment with twice selling heroin to an undercover police officer. At a subsequent jury trial the officer was the State's chief witness, and he testified as to details of the two sales. A second officer verified collateral details of the sales, and a third offered testimony about the chemical analysis of the heroin.

Petitioner took the stand in his own defense. He admitted knowing the undercover police officer but denied a sale on January 4, 1966. He admitted making a sale of contents of a glassine bag to the officer on January 6 but claimed it was baking powder and part of a scheme to defraud the purchaser.

On cross-examination petitioner was asked seriatim whether he had made specified statements to the police immediately following his arrest on January 7—statements that partially contradicted petitioner's direct testimony at trial. In response to the cross-examination, petitioner testified that he could not remember virtually any of the questions or answers recited by the prosecutor. At the request of petitioner's counsel, the written statement from which the prosecutor had read questions and answers in his impeaching process was placed in the record for possible use on appeal; the statement was not shown to the jury.

The trial judge instructed the jury that the statements attributed to petitioner by the prosecution could be considered only in passing on petitioner's credibility and not as evidence of guilt. In closing summations both counsel argued the substance of the impeaching statements. The jury then found petitioner guilty on the second count of the indictment. . . .

At trial the prosecution made no effort in its case in chief to use the statements allegedly made by petitioner, conceding that they were inadmissible under *Miranda* v. *Arizona*, 384 U.S. 436 (1966). The transcript of the interrogation used in the impeachment, but not given to the jury, shows that no warning of a right to appointed counsel was given before questions were put to petitioner when he was taken into custody. Petitioner makes no claim that the statements made to the police were coerced or involuntary.

Some comments in the *Miranda* opinion can indeed be read as indicating a bar to use of an uncounseled statement for any purpose, but discussion of that issue was not at all necessary to the Court's holding and cannot be regarded as controlling. *Miranda* barred the prosecution from making its case with statements of an accused made while in custody prior to having or effectively waiving counsel. It does not follow from *Miranda* that evidence inadmissible against an accused in the prosecution's case in chief is barred for all purposes, provided of course that the trustworthiness of the evidence satisfies legal standards.

In *Walder* v. *United States*, 347 U.S. 62 (1954), the Court permitted physical evidence, inadmissible in the case in chief, to be used for impeachment purposes. It is one thing to say that the Government cannot make an affirmative use of evidence unlawfully obtained. It is quite another to say that the defendant can turn the illegal method by which evidence in the Government's possession was obtained to his own advantage, and provide himself with a shield against contradiction of his untruths. Such an extension of the *Weeks* doctrine would be a perversion of the Fourth Amendment. . . .

Every criminal defendant is privileged to testify in his own defense, or to refuse to do so. But that privilege cannot be construed to include the right to commit perjury. . . . Having voluntarily taken the stand, petitioner was under an obligation to speak truthfully and accurately, and the prosecution here did no more than utilize the traditional truth-testing devices of the adversary process. Had inconsistent statements been made by the accused to some third person, it could hardly be contended that the conflict could not be laid before the jury by way of cross-examination and impeachment.

The shield provided by *Miranda* cannot be perverted into a license to use perjury by way of a defense, free from the risk of confrontation with prior inconsistent utterances. We hold, therefore, that petitioner's credibility was appropriately impeached by use of his earlier conflicting statements.

Affirmed.

MR. JUSTICE BRENNAN, with whom MR. JUSTICE DOUGLAS and MR. JUSTICE MARSHALL join, dissenting. [Omitted.]

WHAT DO YOU THINK?

1. Does a guilty defendant have a right to take the stand and deny that he or she committed the offense in question?
2. Do you agree with the court's opinion? Justify your answer.
3. Would it make any difference to you if the government willfully violated the *Miranda* rule when it took the defendant's statement? Explain your answer.
4. Would it make any difference to you if the accused invoked his rights under *Miranda* to see an attorney and the police continued to interrogate him knowing that the statement could be used only to impeach the defendant if he took the stand? Explain your answer.

The Leon case looks at the good faith exception, which allows the admission of evidence if the police reasonably and honestly rely on a defective search warrant.

UNITED STATES V. LEON
468 U.S. 897 (1984)

JUSTICE WHITE delivered the opinion of the Court.

This case presents the question of whether the Fourth Amendment exclusionary rule should be modified so as not to bar the use in the prosecution's case in chief of evidence obtained by officers acting in reasonable reliance on a search warrant issued by a detached and neutral magistrate but ultimately found to be unsupported by probable cause. To resolve this question, we must consider once again the tension between the sometimes competing goals of, on the one hand, deterring official misconduct and removing inducements to unreasonable invasions of privacy and, on the other, establishing procedures under which criminal defendants are "acquitted or convicted on the basis of all the evidence which exposes the truth." *Alderman* v. *United States*, 394 U.S. 165, 175 (1969).

I.

In August 1981, a confidential informant of unproven reliability informed an officer of the Burbank Police Department that two persons known to him as "Armando" and "Patsy" were selling large quantities of cocaine and methaqualone from their residence at 620 Price Drive in Burbank, Cal. The informant also indicated that he had witnessed a sale of methaqualone by "Patsy" at the residence approximately five months earlier and had observed at that time a shoebox containing a large amount of cash that belonged to "Patsy." He further declared that "Armando" and "Patsy" generally kept only small quantities of drugs at their residence and stored the remainder at another location in Burbank.

On the basis of this information, the Burbank police initiated an extensive investigation focusing first on the Price Drive residence and later on two other residences. Cars parked at the Price Drive residence were determined to belong to respondents Armando Sanchez, who had previously been arrested for possession of marijuana, and Patsy Stewart, who had no criminal record. During the course of the investigation, officers observed an automobile belonging to respondent Ricardo Del Castillo, who had previously been arrested for possession of 50 pounds of marihuana, arrive at the Price Drive residence. The driver of that car entered the house, exited shortly thereafter carrying a small paper sack, and drove away. A check of Del Castillo's probation records led the officers to respondent Alberto Leon, whose telephone number Del Castillo had listed as his employer's. Leon had been arrested in 1980 on drug charges, and a companion had informed the police at that time that Leon was heavily involved in the importation of drugs into this country. Before the current investigation began, the Burbank officers had learned that an informant had told a Glendale police officer that Leon stored a large quantity of methaqualone at his residence in Glendale. During the course of this investigation, the Burbank officers learned that Leon was living at 716 South Sunset Canyon in Burbank.

Subsequently, the officers observed several persons, at least one of whom had prior drug involvement, arriving at the Price Drive residence and leaving with small

packages; observed a variety of other material activity at the two residences as well as at a condominium at 7902 Via Magdalena; and witnessed a variety of relevant activity involving respondents' automobiles. The officers also observed respondents Sanchez and Stewart board separate flights for Miami. The pair later returned to Los Angeles together, consented to a search of their luggage that revealed only a small amount of marihuana, and left the airport. Based on these and other observations . . . Officer Cyril Rombach of the Burbank Police Department, an experienced and well-trained narcotics investigator, prepared an application for a warrant to search 620 Price Drive, 716 South Sunset Canyon, 7902 Via Magdalena, and automobiles registered to each of the respondents for an extensive list of items believed to be related to respondents' drug-trafficking activities. Officer Rombach's extensive application was reviewed by several Deputy District Attorneys.

A facially valid search warrant was issued in September 1981 by a State Superior Court Judge. The ensuing searches produced large quantities of drugs at the Via Magdalena and Sunset Canyon addresses and a small quantity at the Price Drive residence. Other evidence was discovered at each of the residences and in Stewart's and Del Castillo's automobiles. Respondents were indicted . . . and charged with conspiracy to possess and distribute cocaine and a variety of substantive counts.

The respondents then filed motions to suppress the evidence seized pursuant to the warrant. The District Court held an evidentiary hearing and, while recognizing that the case was a close one, granted the motions to suppress in part. It concluded that the affidavit was insufficient to establish probable cause, but did not suppress all of the evidence as to all of the respondents because none of the respondents had standing to challenge all of the searches. In response to a request from the Government, the court made clear that Officer Rombach had acted in good faith, but it rejected the Government's suggestion that the Fourth Amendment exclusionary rule should not apply where evidence is seized in reasonable, good-faith reliance on a search warrant.

The District Court denied the Government's motion for reconsideration and a divided panel of the Court of Appeals for the Ninth Circuit affirmed. . . . The Court of Appeals first concluded that Officer Rombach's affidavit could not establish probable cause to search the Price Drive residence. To the extent that the affidavit set forth facts demonstrating the basis of the informant's knowledge of criminal activity, the information included was fatally stale. The affidavit, moreover, failed to establish the informant's credibility. Accordingly, the Court of Appeals concluded that the information provided by the informant was inadequate. . . . The officers' independent investigation neither cured the staleness nor corroborated the details of the informant's declarations. The Court of Appeals then considered whether the affidavit formed a proper basis for the search of the Sunset Canyon residence. In its view, the affidavit included no facts indicating the basis for the informants' statements concerning respondent Leon's criminal activities and was devoid of information establishing the informants' reliability. Because these deficiencies had not been cured by the police investigation, the District Court properly suppressed the fruits of the search. The Court of Appeals refused the Government's invitation to recognize a good-faith exception to the Fourth Amendment exclusionary rule.

The Government's petition for *certiorari* expressly declined to seek review of the lower courts' determinations that the search warrant was unsupported by probable cause and presented only the question "[w]hether the Fourth Amendment exclusionary rule should be modified so as not to bar the admission of evidence seized in reasonable, good-faith reliance on a search warrant that is subsequently held to be defective." We granted *certiorari* to consider the propriety of such a

modification. Although it undoubtedly is within our power to consider the question whether probable cause existed under the "totality of the circumstances" test announced last Term in *Illinois* v. *Gates*, that question has not been briefed or argued; and it is also within our authority, which we choose to exercise, to take the case as it comes to us, accepting the Court of Appeals' conclusion that probable cause was lacking under the prevailing legal standards.

We have concluded that, in the Fourth Amendment context, the exclusionary rule can be modified somewhat without jeopardizing its ability to perform its intended functions. Accordingly, we reverse the judgment of the Court of Appeals.

II.

Language in opinions of this Court and of individual Justices has sometimes implied that the exclusionary rule is a necessary corollary of the Fourth Amendment ... or that the rule is required by the conjunction of the Fourth and Fifth Amendments. . . . These implications need not detain us long. The Fifth Amendment theory has not withstood critical analysis or the test of time, and the Fourth Amendment "has never been interpreted to proscribe the introduction of illegally seized evidence in all proceedings or against all persons."

A.

The Fourth Amendment contains no provision expressly precluding the use of evidence obtained in violation of its commands, and an examination of its origin and purposes makes clear that the use of fruits of a past unlawful search or seizure "work[s] no new Fourth Amendment wrong." *United States* v. *Calandra*, 414 U.S. 338, 354 (1974). The wrong condemned by the Amendment is "fully accomplished" by the unlawful search or seizure itself, *ibid.*, and the exclusionary rule is neither intended nor able to "cure the invasion of the defendant's rights which he has already suffered." *Stone* v. *Powell*, *supra*, at 540 (WHITE, J., dissenting). The rule thus operates as "a judicially created remedy designed to safeguard Fourth Amendment rights generally through its deterrent effect, rather than a personal constitutional right of the party aggrieved." *United States* v. *Calandra*, *supra*, at 348.

Whether the exclusionary sanction is appropriately imposed in a particular case, our decisions make clear, is "an issue separate from the question whether the Fourth Amendment rights of the party seeking to invoke the rule were violated by police conduct." *Illinois* v. *Gates*, *supra*, at 223. Only the former question is currently before us, and it must be resolved by weighing the costs and benefits of preventing the use in the prosecution's case in chief of inherently trustworthy tangible evidence obtained in reliance on a search warrant issued by a detached and neutral magistrate that ultimately is found to be defective.

The substantial social costs exacted by the exclusionary rule for the vindication of Fourth Amendment rights have long been a source of concern. "Our cases have consistently recognized that unbending application of the exclusionary sanction to enforce ideals of governmental rectitude would impede unacceptably the truth-finding functions of judge and jury." *United States* v. *Payner*, 447 U.S. 727, 734 (1980). An objectionable collateral consequence of this interference with the criminal justice system's truth-finding function is that some guilty defendants may go free or receive reduced sentences as a result of favorable plea bargains. Particularly when law enforcement officers have acted in objective good faith or their transgressions have been minor, the magnitude of the benefit conferred on such guilty defendants offends basic concepts of the criminal justice system. *Stone*

v. *Powell*, 428 U.S., at 490. Indiscriminate application of the exclusionary rule, therefore, may well "generat[e] disrespect for the law and administration of justice." *Id.*, at 491. Accordingly, "[a]s with any remedial device, the application of the rule has been restricted to those areas where its remedial objectives are thought most efficaciously served." . . .

B.

Close attention to those remedial objectives has characterized our recent decisions concerning the scope of the Fourth Amendment exclusionary rule. The Court has, to be sure, not seriously questioned, "in the absence of a more efficacious sanction, the continued application of the rule to suppress evidence from the [prosecution's] case where a Fourth Amendment violation has been substantial and deliberate. . . ." *Franks* v. *Delaware*, 438 U.S. 154, 171 (1978); *Stone* v. *Powell, supra*, at 492. Nevertheless, the balancing approach that has evolved in various contexts—including criminal trials—"forcefully suggest[s] that the exclusionary rule be more generally modified to permit the introduction of evidence obtained in the reasonable good-faith belief that a search or seizure was in accord with the Fourth Amendment." *Illinois* v. *Gates*, 462 U.S., at 255 (WHITE, J., concurring in judgment).

As cases considering the use of unlawfully obtained evidence in criminal trials themselves make clear, it does not follow from the emphasis on the exclusionary rule's deterrent value that "anything which deters illegal searches is thereby commanded by the Fourth Amendment." *Alderman* v. *United States*, 394 U.S., at 174. In determining whether persons aggrieved solely by the introduction of damaging evidence unlawfully obtained from their co-conspirators or codefendants could seek suppression, for example, we found that the additional benefits of such an extension of the exclusionary rule would not outweigh its costs. Standing to invoke the rule has thus been limited to cases in which the prosecution seeks to use the fruits of an illegal search or seizure against the victim of police misconduct. . . .

Even defendants with standing to challenge the introduction in their criminal trials of unlawfully obtained evidence cannot prevent every conceivable use of such evidence. Evidence obtained in violation of the Fourth Amendment and inadmissible in the prosecution's case in chief may be used to impeach a defendant's direct testimony. . . . A similar assessment of the "incremental furthering" of the ends of the exclusionary rule led us to conclude in *United States* v. *Havens*, 446 U.S. 620, 627 (1980), that evidence inadmissible in the prosecution's case in chief or otherwise as substantive evidence of guilt may be used to impeach statements made by a defendant in response to "proper cross-examination reasonably suggested by the defendant's direct examination."

When considering the use of evidence obtained in violation of the Fourth Amendment in the prosecution's case in chief, moreover, we have declined to adopt a per se or "but for" rule that would render inadmissible any evidence that came to light through a chain of causation that began with an illegal arrest. *Brown* v. *Illinois*, 422 U.S. 590 (1975); *Wong Sun* v. *United States, supra*, at 487–488. We also have held that a witness's testimony may be admitted even when his identity was discovered in an unconstitutional search. *United States* v. *Ceccolini*, 435 U.S. 268 (1978). The perception underlying these decisions—that the connection between police misconduct and evidence of crime may be sufficiently attenuated to permit the use of that evidence at trial—is a product of considerations relating to the exclusionary rule and the constitutional principles it is designed to protect. . . . In short, the "dissipation of the taint" concept that the Court has applied in deciding whether exclusion is appropriate in a particular case "attempts to mark the point at which the detrimental consequences of illegal police action become so attenuated that the deterrent effect of the exclusionary rule no longer justifies its cost." . . . Not surprisingly, in view of this purpose an assessment of the flagrancy of the police misconduct constitutes an important step in the calculus. . . .

The same attention to the purposes underlying the exclusionary rule also has characterized decisions not involving the scope of the rule itself. We have not required suppression of the fruits of a search incident to an arrest made in good-faith reliance on a substantive criminal statute that subsequently is declared unconstitutional. *Michigan* v. *DeFillippo*, 443 U.S. 31 (1979). Similarly, although the Court has been unwilling to conclude that new Fourth Amendment principles are always to have only prospective effect, *United States* v. *Johnson*, 457 U.S. 537, 560 (1982), no Fourth Amendment decision marking a "clear break with the past" has been applied retroactively. . . . The propriety of retroactive application of a newly announced Fourth Amendment principle, moreover, has been assessed largely in terms of the contribution retroactivity might make to the deterrence of police misconduct. *United States* v. *Johnson, supra*, at 560–561; *United States* v. *Peltier, supra*, at 536–539, 542.

As yet, we have not recognized any form of good-faith exception to the Fourth Amendment exclusionary rule. But the balancing approach that has evolved during the years of experience with the rule provides strong support for the modification currently urged upon us. As we discuss below, our evaluation of the costs and benefits of suppressing reliable physical evidence seized by officers reasonably relying on a warrant issued by a detached and neutral magistrate leads to the conclusion that such evidence should be admissible in the prosecution's case in chief.

III.

A.

Because a search warrant "provides the detached scrutiny of a neutral magistrate, which is a more reliable safeguard against improper searches than the hurried judgment of a law enforcement officer 'engaged in the often competitive enterprise of ferreting out crime,' " *United States* v. *Chadwick*, 433 U.S. 1, 9 (1977) (quoting *Johnson* v. *United States*, 333 U.S. 10, 14 [1948]), we have expressed a strong preference for warrants and declared that "in a doubtful or marginal case a search under a warrant may be sustainable where without one it would fall." . . . Reasonable minds frequently may differ on the question whether a particular affidavit establishes probable cause, and we have thus concluded that the preference for warrants is most appropriately effectuated by according "great deference" to a magistrate's determination. . . .

Deference to the magistrate, however, is not boundless. It is clear, first, that the deference accorded to a magistrate's finding of probable cause does not preclude inquiry into the knowing or reckless falsity of the affidavit on which that determination was based. *Franks* v. *Delaware*, 438 U.S. 154 (1978). Second, the courts must also insist that the magistrate purport to "perform his 'neutral and detached' function and not serve merely as a rubber stamp for the police." . . . A magistrate failing to "manifest that neutrality and detachment demanded of a judicial officer when presented with a warrant application" and who acts instead as "an adjunct law enforcement officer" cannot provide valid authorization for an otherwise unconstitutional search. . . .

Third, reviewing courts will not defer to a warrant based on an affidavit that does not "provide the magistrate with a substantial basis for determining the existence of probable cause." *Illinois* v. *Gates*, 462 U.S., at 239. "Sufficient information must be presented to the magistrate to allow that official to determine probable cause; his action cannot be a mere ratification of the bare conclusions of others." ... Even if the warrant application was supported by more than a "bare bones" affidavit, a reviewing court may properly conclude that, notwithstanding the deference that magistrates deserve, the warrant was invalid because the magistrate's probable-cause determination reflected an improper analysis of the totality of the circumstances, *Illinois* v. *Gates*, *supra*, at 238–239, or because the form of the warrant was improper in some respect.

Only in the first of these three situations, however, has the Court set forth a rationale for suppressing evidence obtained pursuant to a search warrant; in the other areas, it has simply excluded such evidence without considering whether Fourth Amendment interests will be advanced. To the extent that proponents of exclusion rely on its behavioral effects on judges and magistrates in these areas, their reliance is misplaced. First, the exclusionary rule is designed to deter police misconduct rather than to punish the errors of judges and magistrates. Second, there exists no evidence suggesting that judges and magistrates are inclined to ignore or subvert the Fourth Amendment or that lawlessness among these actors requires application of the extreme sanction of exclusion.

Third, and most important, we discern no basis, and are offered none, for believing that exclusion of evidence seized pursuant to a warrant will have a significant deterrent effect on the issuing judge or magistrate. Many of the factors that indicate that the exclusionary rule cannot provide an effective "special" or "general" deterrent for individual offending law enforcement officers apply as well to judges or magistrates. And, to the extent that the rule is thought to operate as a "systemic" deterrent on a wider audience, it clearly can have no such effect on individuals empowered to issue search warrants. Judges and magistrates are not adjuncts to the law enforcement team; as neutral judicial officers, they have no stake in the outcome of particular criminal prosecutions. The threat of exclusion thus cannot be expected significantly to deter them. Imposition of the exclusionary sanction is not necessary meaningfully to inform judicial officers of their errors, and we cannot conclude that admitting evidence obtained pursuant to a warrant while at the same time declaring that the warrant was somehow defective will in any way reduce judicial officers' professional incentives to comply with the Fourth Amendment, encourage them to repeat their mistakes, or lead to the granting of all colorable warrant requests.

.... Under these circumstances, the officers' reliance on the magistrate's determination of probable cause was objectively reasonable, and application of the extreme sanction of exclusion is inappropriate. Accordingly, the judgment of the Court of Appeals is Reversed.

Justice Blackmun, concurring. [Omitted.]

Justice Brennan, with whom Justice Marshall joins, dissenting. [Omitted.]

What Do *You* Think?

1. What interests does the good-faith exception promote?
2. Write a legal brief on the issue of the "good-faith exception."
3. Several states have refused to except the "good-faith exception." Why is it permissible for those states to refuse to follow this case holding?

If the police acting in reasonable good faith rely on a statute to search property, is the evidence discovered admissible if the statute is determined to be unconstitutional? The case below examines this issue.

ILLINOIS V. KRULL
480 U.S. 340 (1987)

JUSTICE BLACKMUN delivered the opinion of the Court.

In *United States* v. *Leon*, 468 U.S. 897 (1984), this Court ruled that the Fourth Amendment exclusionary rule does not apply to evidence obtained by police officers who acted in objectively reasonable reliance upon a search warrant issued by a neutral magistrate, but where the warrant was ultimately found to be unsupported by probable cause. See also *Massachusetts* v. *Sheppard*, 468 U.S. 981 (1984). The present case presents the question whether a similar exception to the exclusionary rule should be recognized when officers act in objectively reasonable reliance upon a statute authorizing warrantless administrative searches, but where the statute is ultimately found to violate the Fourth Amendment.

. . . We granted *certiorari* . . . to consider whether a good-faith exception to the Fourth Amendment exclusionary rule applies when an officer's reliance on the constitutionality of a statute is objectively reasonable, but the statute is subsequently declared unconstitutional.

. . . When evidence is obtained in violation of the Fourth Amendment, the judicially developed exclusionary rule usually precludes its use in a criminal proceeding against the victim of the illegal search and seizure. *Weeks* v. *United States*, 232 U.S. 383 (1914); *Mapp* v. *Ohio*, 367 U.S. 643 (1961). The Court has stressed that the "prime purpose" of the exclusionary rule "is to deter future unlawful police conduct and thereby effectuate the guarantee of the Fourth Amendment against unreasonable searches and seizures." *United States* v. *Calandra*, 414 U.S. 338, 347 (1974). Application of the exclusionary rule "is neither intended nor able to 'cure the invasion of the defendant's rights which he has already suffered.' " *United States* v. *Leon*, 468 U.S., at 906, quoting *Stone* v. *Powell*, 428 U.S. 465, 540 (1976) (WHITE, J., dissenting). Rather, the rule "operates as 'a judicially created remedy designed to safeguard Fourth Amendment rights generally through its deterrent effect, rather than a personal constitutional right of the party aggrieved.' " 468 U.S., at 906, quoting *United States* v. *Calandra*, 414 U.S., at 348.

As with any remedial device, application of the exclusionary rule properly has been restricted to those situations in which its remedial purpose is effectively advanced. Thus, in various circumstances, the Court has examined whether the rule's deterrent effect will be achieved, and has weighed the likelihood of such deterrence against the costs of withholding reliable information from the truth-seeking process. . . .

In *Leon*, the Court held that the exclusionary rule should not be applied to evidence obtained by a police officer whose reliance on a search warrant issued by a neutral magistrate was objectively reasonable, even though the warrant was ultimately found to be defective. On the basis of three factors, the Court concluded that there was no sound reason to apply the exclusionary rule as a means of deterring misconduct on the part of judicial officers who are responsible for

issuing warrants. First, the exclusionary rule was historically designed "to deter police misconduct rather than to punish the errors of judges and magistrates." 468 U.S., at 916. Second, there was "no evidence suggesting that judges and magistrates are inclined to ignore or subvert the Fourth Amendment or that lawlessness among these actors requires application of the extreme sanction of exclusion." *Ibid.* Third, and of greatest importance to the Court, there was no basis "for believing that exclusion of evidence seized pursuant to a warrant will have a significant deterrent effect on the issuing judge or magistrate." *Ibid.* The Court explained: "Judges and magistrates are not adjuncts to the law enforcement team; as neutral judicial officers, they have no stake in the outcome of particular criminal prosecutions." *Id.*, at 917. Thus, the threat of exclusion of evidence could not be expected to deter such individuals from improperly issuing warrants, and a judicial ruling that a warrant was defective was sufficient to inform the judicial officer of the error made.

The Court then considered whether application of the exclusionary rule in that context could be expected to alter the behavior of law enforcement officers. In prior cases, the Court had observed that, because the purpose of the exclusionary rule is to deter police officers from violating the Fourth Amendment, evidence should be suppressed "only if it can be said that the law enforcement officer had knowledge, or may properly be charged with knowledge, that the search was unconstitutional under the Fourth Amendment." *United States* v. *Peltier*, 422 U.S. 531, 542 (1975); see also *Michigan* v. *Tucker*, 417 U.S. 433, 447 (1974). Where the officer's conduct is objectively reasonable, the Court explained in *Leon*,

> . . . [e]xcluding the evidence will not further the ends of the exclusionary rule in any appreciable way; for it is painfully apparent that. . .the officer is acting as a reasonable officer would and should act in similar circumstances. Excluding the evidence can in no way affect his future conduct unless it is to make him less willing to do his duty.

The Court in *Leon* concluded that a deterrent effect was particularly absent when an officer, acting in objective good faith, obtained a search warrant from a magistrate and acted within its scope. "In most such cases, there is no police illegality and thus nothing to deter," 468 U.S., at 920–921. It is the judicial officer's responsibility to determine whether probable cause exists to issue a warrant, and, in the ordinary case, police officers cannot be expected to question that determination. Because the officer's sole responsibility after obtaining a warrant is to carry out the search pursuant to it, applying the exclusionary rule in these circumstances could have no deterrent effect on a future Fourth Amendment violation by the officer. . . .

Reversed.

[JUSTICES MARSHALL, STEVENS and O'CONNOR dissented.]

WHAT DO *YOU* THINK?

1. Do you agree with the majority opinion? Explain your answer.
2. The majority opinion stated that "Unless a statute is clearly unconstitutional, an officer cannot be expected to question the judgment of the legislature that passed the law." Is a police officer in a position to determine that the legislature has passed a statute that is "clearly unconstitutional?"
3. If a statute is void, shouldn't any decisions based on the unconstitutional statute also be void?

The question presented in the Harvey *case is whether the prosecution may use a statement taken in violation of the* Jackson *prophylactic rule to impeach a defendant's false or inconsistent testimony.*

MICHIGAN V. HARVEY
494 U.S. 344 (1990)

CHIEF JUSTICE REHNQUIST delivered the opinion of the Court.

In *Michigan v. Jackson*, 475 U.S. 625 (1986), the Court established a prophylactic rule that once a criminal defendant invokes his Sixth Amendment right to counsel, a subsequent waiver of that right—even if voluntary, knowing, and intelligent under traditional standards—is presumed invalid if secured pursuant to police-initiated conversation. We held that statements obtained in violation of that rule may not be admitted as substantive evidence in the prosecution's case in chief. The question presented in this case is whether the prosecution may use a statement taken in violation of the *Jackson* prophylactic rule to impeach a defendant's false or inconsistent testimony. We hold that it may do so.

Respondent Tyris Lemont Harvey was convicted of two counts of first-degree criminal sexual conduct in connection with the rape of Audrey Sharp on June 11, 1986. Harvey was taken into custody on July 2, 1986, and on that date, he made a statement to an investigating officer. He was arraigned later on July 2, and counsel was appointed for him. More than two months later, Harvey told another police officer that he wanted to make a second statement, but did not know whether he should talk to his lawyer. Although the entire context of the discussion is not clear from the record, the officer told respondent that he did not need to speak with his attorney, because "his lawyer was going to get a copy of the statement anyway." Respondent then signed a constitutional rights waiver form, on which he initialed the portions advising him of his right to remain silent, his right to have a lawyer present before and during questioning, and his right to have a lawyer appointed for him prior to any questioning. Asked whether he understood his constitutional rights, respondent answered affirmatively. He then gave a statement detailing his version of the events of June 11.

At a bench trial, Sharp testified that Harvey visited her home at 2:30 a.m. on the date in question and asked to use the telephone. After placing a call, Harvey confronted Sharp with a barbecue fork, and a struggle ensued. According to Sharp, respondent struck her in the face, threatened her with the fork and a pair of garden shears, and eventually threw her to the floor of her kitchen. When she ran to the living room to escape, Harvey pursued her with the weapons, demanded that she take off her clothes, and forced her to engage in sexual acts.

Harvey testified in his own defense and presented a conflicting account of the night's events. He claimed that he had gone to Sharp's home at 9 p.m. and invited her to smoke some crack cocaine, which he offered to supply in return for sexual favors. She agreed, but after smoking the cocaine, she refused to perform the favors. When respondent would not leave her house, Sharp allegedly grabbed the barbecue fork and threatened him, triggering a brief fight during which he grabbed the fork and threw it to the floor. The two then moved to the living room, where, according to Harvey, Sharp voluntarily removed her clothes. He testified, however, that the two never engaged in sexual intercourse and that he left shortly thereafter.

On cross-examination, the prosecutor used Harvey's second statement to the police to impeach his testimony. Before doing so, the prosecutor stipulated that the statement "was not subject to proper *Miranda*," and therefore could not have been used in the case in chief. But because the statement was voluntary, the prosecutor argued that it could be used for impeachment under our decision in *Harris* v. *New York*, 401 U.S. 222 (1971). Defense counsel did not object and the trial court permitted the questioning. The prosecutor then impeached certain of Harvey's statements, including his claim that he had thrown the barbecue fork to the floor, by showing that he had omitted that information from his statement to the police. The trial judge believed the victim's testimony and found respondent guilty as charged. The Michigan Court of Appeals reversed the conviction. The court noted that if the second statement had been taken only in violation of the rules announced in *Miranda* v. *Arizona*, 384 U.S. 436 (1966), it could have been used to impeach Harvey's testimony. It held, however, that the statement was inadmissible even for impeachment purposes, because it was taken "in violation of defendant's Sixth Amendment right to counsel." See e.g., *Michigan* v. *Jackson*, 475 U.S. 625. Because the trial "involved a credibility contest between defendant and the victim," the court concluded that the impeachment was not harmless beyond a reasonable doubt. . . . We now reverse.

To understand this case, it is necessary first to review briefly the Court's jurisprudence surrounding the Sixth Amendment. The text of the Amendment provides in pertinent part that "[i]n all criminal prosecutions, the accused shall enjoy the right . . . to have the Assistance of Counsel for his defence." The essence of this right, we recognized in *Powell* v. *Alabama*, 287 U.S. 45 (1932), is the opportunity for a defendant to consult with an attorney and to have him investigate the case and prepare a defense for trial.

More recently, in a line of cases beginning with *Massiah* v. *United States*, 377 U.S. 201 (1964), and extending through *Maine* v. *Moulton*, 474 U.S. 159 (1985), the Court has held that once formal criminal proceedings begin, the Sixth Amendment renders inadmissible in the prosecution's case in chief statements "deliberately elicited" from a defendant without an express waiver of the right to counsel. See also *United States* v. *Henry*, 447 U.S. 264 (1980); *Brewer* v. *Williams*, 430 U.S. 387 (1977). For the fruits of postindictment interrogations to be admissible in a prosecution's case in chief, the State must prove a voluntary, knowing, and intelligent relinquishment of the Sixth Amendment right to counsel. . . . We have recently held that when a suspect waives his right to counsel after receiving warnings equivalent to those prescribed by *Miranda* v. *Arizona*, *supra*, that will generally suffice to establish a knowing and intelligent waiver of the Sixth Amendment right to counsel for purposes of post-indictment questioning. *Patterson* v. *Illinois*, *supra*. In *Michigan* v. *Jackson*, 475 U.S. 625 (1986), the Court created a bright-line rule for deciding whether an accused who has "asserted" his Sixth Amendment right to counsel has subsequently waived that right. Transposing the reasoning of *Edwards* v. *Arizona*, 451 U.S. 477 (1981), which had announced an identical "prophylactic rule" in the Fifth Amendment context, see *Solem* v. *Stumes*, 465 U.S. 638, 644 (1984), we decided that after a defendant requests assistance of counsel, any waiver of Sixth Amendment rights given in a discussion initiated by police is presumed invalid, and evidence obtained pursuant to such a waiver is inadmissible in the prosecution's case in chief. *Jackson*, *supra*, at 636. Thus, to help guarantee that waivers are truly voluntary, Jackson established a presumption which renders invalid some waivers that would be considered voluntary, knowing, and intelligent under the traditional case-by-case inquiry called for by *Brewer* v. *Williams*.

. . . We have already decided that although statements taken in violation of only the prophylactic *Miranda* rules may not be used in the prosecution's case in chief,

they are admissible to impeach conflicting testimony by the defendant. *Harris* v. *New York*, 401 U.S. 222 (1971); *Oregon* v. *Hass*, 420 U.S. 714 (1975). The prosecution must not be allowed to build its case against a criminal defendant with evidence acquired in contravention of constitutional guarantees and their corresponding judicially created protections. But use of statements so obtained for impeachment purposes is a different matter. If a defendant exercises his right to testify on his own behalf, he assumes a reciprocal "obligation to speak truthfully and accurately," *Harris*, 401 U.S., at 225, and we have consistently rejected arguments that would allow a defendant to " 'turn the illegal method by which evidence in the Government's possession was obtained to his own advantage, and provide himself with a shield against contradiction of his untruths.' " *Id.*, at 224 (quoting *Walder* v. *United States*, 347 U.S. 62, 65 [1954]). See also *Hass*, *supra*, at 722; *United States* v. *Havens*, 446 U.S. 620, 626 (1980).

There is no reason for a different result in a *Jackson* case, where the prophylactic rule is designed to ensure voluntary, knowing, and intelligent waivers of the Sixth Amendment right to counsel rather than the Fifth Amendment privilege against self-incrimination or "right to counsel." We have mandated the exclusion of reliable and probative evidence for all purposes only when it is derived from involuntary statements. *New Jersey* v. *Portash*, 440 U.S. 450, 459 (1979) (compelled incriminating statements inadmissible for impeachment purposes); *Mincey* v. *Arizona*, 437 U.S. 385, 398 (1978) (same). We have never prevented use by the prosecution of relevant voluntary statements by a defendant, particularly when the violations alleged by a defendant relate only to procedural safeguards that are "not themselves rights protected by the Constitution," *Tucker*, *supra*, at 444 (*Miranda* rules), but are instead measures designed to ensure that constitutional rights are protected. In such cases, we have decided that the "search for truth in a criminal case" outweighs the "speculative possibility" that exclusion of evidence might deter future violations of rules not compelled directly by the Constitution in the first place. . . .

Respondent argues that there should be a different exclusionary rule for *Jackson* violations than for transgressions of *Edwards* and *Miranda*. The distinction, he suggests, is that the adversarial process has commenced at the time of a *Jackson* violation, and the post-arraignment interrogations thus implicate the constitutional guarantee of the Sixth Amendment itself. But nothing in the Sixth Amendment prevents a suspect charged with a crime and represented by counsel from voluntarily choosing, on his own, to speak with police in the absence of an attorney. We have already held that a defendant whose Sixth Amendment right to counsel has attached by virtue of an indictment may execute a knowing and intelligent waiver of that right in the course of a police-initiated interrogation. *Patterson* v. *Illinois*, 487 U.S. 285 (1988). To be sure, once a defendant obtains or even requests counsel as respondent had here, analysis of the waiver issue changes. But that change is due to the protective rule we created in *Jackson* based on the apparent inconsistency between a request for counsel and a later voluntary decision to proceed without assistance. . . .

The judgment of the Michigan Court of Appeals is reversed, and the case is remanded for further proceedings not inconsistent with this opinion. It is so ordered.

JUSTICE STEVENS, with whom JUSTICE BRENNAN, JUSTICE MARSHALL, and JUSTICE BLACKMUN join, dissenting. [Omitted.]

WHAT DO YOU THINK?

1. Are you satisfied that the Court's opinion answered the contention of the respondent that he was affirmatively misled as to his need for counsel and

that his purported waiver is therefore invalid? Would you have answered his contention in a different manner?

2. Should there be a difference on the admissibility of evidence when there is a *Miranda* violation and when there is a Sixth Amendment violation? How does the Court look at this issue?

The Elstad *case looks at the issue of when is a "taint" disspated.*

OREGON V. ELSTAD
470 U.S. 298 (1985)

JUSTICE O'CONNOR delivered the opinion of the Court.

This case requires us to decide whether an initial failure of law enforcement officers to administer the warnings required by *Miranda* v. *Arizona*, 384 U.S. 436 (1966), without more, "taints" subsequent admissions made after a suspect has been fully advised of and has waived his *Miranda* rights. Respondent, Michael James Elstad, was convicted of burglary by an Oregon trial court. The Oregon Court of Appeals reversed, holding that respondent's signed confession, although voluntary, was rendered inadmissible by a prior remark made in response to questioning without benefit of *Miranda* warnings . . . we now reverse.

I.

In December 1981, the home of Mr. and Mrs. Gilbert Gross, in the town of Salem, Polk Country, Ore., was burglarized. Missing were art objects and furnishings valued at $150,000. A witness to the burglary contacted the Polk County Sheriff's Office, implicating respondent Michael Elstad, an 18-year-old neighbor and friend of the Grosses' teenage son. Thereupon, Officers Burke and McAllister went to the home of respondent Elstad, with a warrant for his arrest. Elstad's mother answered the door. She led the officers to her son's room where he lay on his bed, clad in shorts and listening to his stereo. The officers asked him to get dressed and to accompany them into the living room. Officer McAllister asked respondent's mother to step into the kitchen, where he explained that they had a warrant for her son's arrest for the burglary of a neighbor's residence. Officer Burke remained with Elstad in the living room. He later testified:

> I sat down with Mr. Elstad and I asked him if he was aware of why Detective McAllister and myself were there to talk with him. He stated no, he had no idea why we were there. I then asked him if he knew a person by the name of Gross, and he said yes, he did, and also added that he heard that there was a robbery at the Gross house. And at that point I told Mr. Elstad that I felt he was involved in that, and he looked at me and stated, "Yes, I was there."

The officers then escorted Elstad to the back of the patrol car. As they were about to leave for the Polk County Sheriff's office, Elstad's father arrived home and came to the rear of the patrol car. The officers advised him that his son was a suspect in the burglary. Officer Burke testified that Mr. Elstad became quite agitated, opened the rear door of the car and admonished his son: "I told you that you were going to get into trouble. You wouldn't listen to me. You never learn."

Elstad was transported to the Sheriff's headquarters and approximately one hour later, Officers Burke and McAllister joined him in McAllister's office.

McAllister then advised respondent for the first time of his *Miranda* rights, reading from a standard card. Respondent indicated he understood his rights, and, having these rights in mind, wished to speak with the officers. Elstad gave a full statement, explaining that he had known that the Gross family was out of town and had been paid to lead several acquaintances to the Gross residence and show them how to gain entry through a defective sliding glass door. The statement was typed, reviewed by respondent, read back to him for correction, initialed and signed by Elstad and both officers. As an afterthought, Elstad added and initialed the sentence, "After leaving the house Robby & I went back to [the] van & Robby handed me a small bag of grass." Respondent concedes that the officers made no threats or promises either at his residence or at the Sheriff's office.

Respondent was charged with first-degree burglary. He was represented at trial by retained counsel. Elstad waived his right to a jury, and his case was tried by a Circuit Court Judge. Respondent moved at once to suppress his oral statement and signed confession. He contended that the statement he made in response to questioning at his house "let the cat out of the bag," . . . and tainted the subsequent confession as "fruit of the poisonous tree," . . . The judge ruled that the statement, "I was there," had to be excluded because the defendant had not been advised of his *Miranda* rights. The written confession taken after Elstad's arrival at the Sheriff's office, however, was admitted in evidence. The court found:

> [H]is written statement was given freely, voluntarily and knowingly by the defendant after he had waived his right to remain silent and have counsel present which waiver was evidenced by the card which the defendant had signed. [It] was not tainted in any way by the previous brief statement between the defendant and the Sheriff's Deputies that had arrested him.

Elstad was found guilty of burglary in the first degree. He received a 5-year sentence and was ordered to pay $18,000 in restitution.

Following his conviction, respondent appealed to the Oregon Court of Appeals, relying on *Wong Sun* and *Bayer*. The State conceded that Elstad had been in custody when he made his statement, "I was there," and accordingly agreed that this statement was inadmissible as having been given without the prescribed *Miranda* warnings. But the State maintained that any conceivable "taint" had been dissipated prior to the respondent's written confession by McAllister's careful administration of the requisite warnings. The Court of Appeals reversed respondent's conviction, identifying the crucial constitutional inquiry as "whether there was a sufficient break in the stream of events between [the] inadmissible statement and the written confession to insulate the latter statement from the effect of what went before." The Oregon court concluded:

> Regardless of the absence of actual compulsion, the coercive impact of the unconstitutionally obtained statement remains, because in a defendant's mind it has sealed his fate. It is this impact that must be dissipated in order to make a subsequent confession admissible. In determining whether it has been dissipated, lapse of time and change of place from the original surroundings are the most important considerations.

Because of the brief period separating the two incidents, the "cat was sufficiently out of the bag to exert a coercive impact on [respondent's] later admissions."

. . . The arguments advanced in favor of suppression of respondent's written confession rely heavily on metaphor. One metaphor, familiar from the Fourth Amendment context, would require that respondent's confession, regardless of its integrity, voluntariness, and probative value, be suppressed as the "tainted fruit of the poisonous tree" of the *Miranda* violation. A second metaphor questions whether a confession can be truly voluntary once the "cat is out of the bag." Taken out of context, each of these metaphors can be misleading. They should not be used to obscure fundamental differences between the role of the Fourth Amendment exclusionary rule and the function of *Miranda* in guarding against the prosecutorial use of compelled statements as prohibited by the Fifth Amendment. The Oregon court assumed and respondent here contends that a failure to administer *Miranda* warnings necessarily breeds the same consequences as police infringement of a constitutional right, so that evidence uncovered following an unwarned statement must be suppressed as "fruit of the poisonous tree." We believe this view misconstrues the nature of the protections afforded by *Miranda* warnings and therefore misreads the consequences of police failure to supply them.

. . . Prior to *Miranda*, the admissibility of an accused's in custody statements was judged solely by whether they were "voluntary" within the meaning of the Due Process Clause. . . . If a suspect's statements had been obtained by "techniques and methods offensive to due process," circumstances in which the suspect clearly had no opportunity to exercise "a free and unconstrained will," the statements would not be admitted. The Court in *Miranda* required suppression of many statements that would have been admissible under traditional due process analysis by presuming that statements made while in custody and without adequate warnings were protected by the Fifth Amendment. The Fifth Amendment, of course, is not concerned with nontestimonial evidence. . . . Nor is it concerned with moral and psychological pressures to confess emanating from sources other than official coercion. . . . Voluntary statements "remain a proper element in law enforcement." *Miranda* v. *Arizona*, 384 U.S., at 478. "Indeed, far from being prohibited by the Constitution, admissions of guilt by wrongdoers, if not coerced, are inherently desirable. . . . Absent some officially coerced self-accusation, the Fifth Amendment privilege is not violated by even the most damning admissions."

. . . In *Michigan* v. *Tucker, supra*, the Court was asked to extend the . . . fruits doctrine to suppress the testimony of a witness for the prosecution whose identity was discovered as the result of a statement taken from the accused without benefit of full *Miranda* warnings. As in respondent's case, the breach of the *Miranda* procedures in *Tucker* involved no actual compulsion. The Court concluded that the unwarned questioning "did not abridge respondent's constitutional privilege . . . but departed only from the prophylactic standards later laid down by this Court in *Miranda* to safeguard that privilege." Since there was no actual infringement of the suspect's constitutional rights, the case was not controlled by the doctrine . . . that fruits of a constitutional violation must be suppressed. In deciding "how sweeping the judicially imposed consequences" of a failure to administer *Miranda* warnings should be, the *Tucker* Court noted that neither the general goal of deterring improper police conduct nor the Fifth Amendment goal of assuring trustworthy evidence would be served by suppression of the witness' testimony.

The unwarned confession must, of course, be suppressed, but the Court ruled that introduction of the third-party witness' testimony did not violate *Tucker*'s Fifth Amendment rights.

We believe that this reasoning applies with equal force when the alleged "fruit" of a noncoercive *Miranda* violation is neither a witness nor an article of evidence but the accused's own voluntary testimony. As in *Tucker*, the absence of any coercion or improper tactics undercuts the twin rationales—trust worthiness and deterrence—for a broader rule. Once warned, the suspect is free to exercise his own volition in deciding whether or not to make a statement to the authorities. The Court has often noted: " '[A] living witness is not to be mechanically equated with

the proffer of inanimate evidentiary objects illegally seized. . . . The living witness is an individual human personality whose attributes of will, perception, memory and volition interact to determine what testimony he will give. . . .

Because *Miranda* warnings may inhibit persons from giving information, this Court has determined that they need be administered only after the person is taken into "custody" or his freedom has otherwise been significantly restrained. *Miranda* v. *Arizona*, 384 U.S., at 478. Unfortunately, the task of defining "custody" is a slippery one, and "policemen investigating serious crimes [cannot realistically be expected to] make no errors whatsoever." *Michigan* v. *Tucker, supra,* at 446. If errors are made by law enforcement officers in administering the prophylactic *Miranda* procedures, they should not breed the same irremediable consequences as police infringement of the Fifth Amendment itself. It is an unwarranted extension of *Miranda* to hold that a simple failure to administer the warnings, unaccompanied by any actual coercion or other circumstances calculated to undermine the suspect's ability to exercise his free will, so taints the investigatory process that a subsequent voluntary and informed waiver is ineffective for some indeterminate period. Though *Miranda* requires that the unwarned admission must be suppressed, the admissibility of any subsequent statement should turn in these circumstances solely on whether it is knowingly and voluntarily made.

. . . This Court has never held that the psychological impact of voluntary disclosure of a guilty secret qualifies as state compulsion or compromises the voluntariness of a subsequent informed waiver. The Oregon court, by adopting this expansive view of Fifth Amendment compulsion, effectively immunizes a suspect who responds to pre-*Miranda* warning questions from the consequences of his subsequent informed waiver of the privilege of remaining silent. . . .

There is a vast difference between the direct consequences flowing from coercion of a confession by physical violence or other deliberate means calculated to break the suspect's will and the uncertain consequences of disclosure of a "guilty secret" freely given in response to an unwarned but noncoercive question, as in this case. . . . Reversed.

[JUSTICES BRENNAN, MARSHALL, and STEVENS dissented.]

WHAT DO *YOU* THINK?

1. Do you agree with the majority opinion? Explain your answer.

2. What does the court mean by the metaphor "cat is out of the bag"?

3. What is meant by the "bright-line rule of *Miranda*"?

The Williams II *case looks at the issue of inevitable discovery as an exception to the exclusionary rule.*

NIX V. WILLIAMS (WILLIAMS II)
467 U.S. 431 (1984)

CHIEF JUSTICE BURGER delivered the opinion of the Court.

We granted *certiorari* to consider whether, at respondent Williams' second murder trial in state court, evidence pertaining to the discovery and condition of the

victim's body was properly admitted on the ground that it would ultimately or inevitably have been discovered even if no violation of any constitutional or statutory provision had taken place.

. . . As the police car approached Grinnell, Williams asked Leaming whether the police had found the young girl's shoes. After Leaming replied that he was unsure, Williams directed the police to a point near a service station where he said he had left the shoes; they were not found. As they continued the drive to Des Moines, Williams asked whether the blanket had been found and then directed the officers to a rest area in Grinnell where he said he had disposed of the blanket; they did not find the blanket. At this point Leaming and his party were joined by the officers in charge of the search. As they approached Mitchellville, Williams, without any further conversation, agreed to direct the officers to the child's body.

The officers directing the search had called off the search at 3 P.M., when they left the Grinnell Police Department to join Leaming at the rest area. At that time, one search team near the Jasper County–Polk County line was only two and one-half miles from where Williams soon guided Leaming and his party to the body. The child's body was found next to a culvert in a ditch beside a gravel road in Polk County, about two miles south of Interstate 80, and essentially within the area to be searched.

. . . At Williams' second trial in 1977 in the Iowa court, the prosecution did not offer Williams' statements into evidence, nor did it seek to show that Williams had directed the police to the child's body. However, evidence of the condition of her body as it was found, articles and photographs of her clothing, and the results of post mortem medical and chemical tests on the body were admitted. The trial court concluded that the State had proved by a preponderance of the evidence that, if the search had not been suspended and Williams had not led the police to the victim, her body would have been discovered "within a short time" in essentially the same condition as it was actually found. The trial court also ruled that if the police had not located the body, "the search would clearly have been taken up again where it left off, given the extreme circumstances of this case and the body would [have] been found in short order."

In finding that the body would have been discovered in essentially the same condition as it was actually found, the court noted that freezing temperatures had prevailed and tissue deterioration would have been suspended. The challenged evidence was admitted and the jury again found Williams guilty of first-degree murder; he was sentenced to life in prison. On appeal, the Supreme Court of Iowa again affirmed. . . . That court held that there was in fact a "hypothetical independent source" exception to the exclusionary rule:

> After the defendant has shown unlawful conduct on the part of the police, the State has the burden to show by a preponderance of the evidence that (1) the police did not act in bad faith for the purpose of hastening discovery of the evidence in question, and (2) that the evidence in question would have been discovered by lawful means.

. . . The Iowa Supreme Court correctly stated that the "vast majority" of all courts, both state and federal, recognize an inevitable discovery exception to the exclusionary rule. We are now urged to adopt and apply the so-called ultimate or inevitable discovery exception to the exclusionary rule.

Williams contends that evidence of the body's location and condition is "fruit of the poisonous tree," i.e., the "fruit" or product of Detective Leaming's plea to help the child's parents give her "a Christian burial," which this Court had already held equated to interrogation. He contends that admitting the challenged evidence

violated the Sixth Amendment whether it would have been inevitably discovered or not. . . .

. . . The core rationale consistently advanced by this Court for extending the exclusionary rule to evidence that is the fruit of unlawful police conduct has been that this admittedly drastic and socially costly course is needed to deter police from violations of constitutional and statutory protections. This Court has accepted the argument that the way to ensure such protections is to exclude evidence seized as a result of such violations notwithstanding the high social cost of letting persons obviously guilty go unpunished for their crimes. On this rationale, the prosecution is not to be put in a better position than it would have been in if no illegality had transpired.

By contrast, the derivative evidence analysis ensures that the prosecution is not put in a worse position simply because of some earlier police error or misconduct. The independent source doctrine allows admission of evidence that has been discovered by means wholly independent of any constitutional violation.

That doctrine, although closely related to the inevitable discovery doctrine, does not apply here; Williams' statements to Leaming indeed led police to the child's body, but that is not the whole story. The independent source doctrine teaches us that the interest of society in deterring unlawful police conduct and the public interest in having juries receive all probative evidence of a crime are properly balanced by putting the police in the same, not a worse, position that they would have been in if no police error or misconduct had occurred. See *Murphy* v. *Waterfront Comm'n of New York Harbor*, 378 U.S. 52, 79 (1964); *Kastigar* v. *United States*, 406 U.S. 441, 457, 458–459 (1972). When the challenged evidence has an independent source, exclusion of such evidence would put the police in a worse position than they would have been in absent any error or violation. There is a functional similarity between these two doctrines in that exclusion of evidence that would inevitably have been discovered would also put the government in a worse position, because the police would have obtained that evidence if no misconduct had taken place. Thus, while the independent source exception would not justify admission of evidence in this case, its rationale is wholly consistent with and justifies our adoption of the ultimate or inevitable discovery exception to the exclusionary rule.

It is clear that the cases implementing the exclusionary rule "begin with the premise that the challenged evidence is in some sense the product of illegal governmental activity." *United States* v. *Crews*, 445 U.S. 463, 471 (1980). Of course, this does not end the inquiry. If the prosecution can establish by a preponderance of the evidence that the information ultimately or inevitably would have been discovered by lawful means—here the volunteers' search—then the deterrence rationale has so little basis that the evidence should be received. Anything less would reject logic, experience, and common sense.

The judgment of the Court of Appeals is reversed, and the case is remanded for further proceedings consistent with this opinion. It is so ordered.

[Concurring opinions of JUSTICES WHITE and STEVENS and the dissenting opinions of JUSTICES BRENNAN and MARSHALL are omitted.]

WHAT DO YOU THINK?

1. What is the difference between the "independent source" exception and the "inevitable discovery" exception?

2. What standard of proof does the Court require to establish that the evidence would have been inevitably discovered?

3. Write a brief clearly delineating your reasons for agreement or disagreement with the Court's decision in this case.

Should the exclusionary rule be used in probation revocation proceedings? The Scott *case looks at this issue.*

PENNSYLVANIA BOARD OF PROBATION AND PAROLE V. SCOTT
No. 97-581. Decided June 22, 1998

THOMAS, J., delivered the opinion of the Court, in which REHNQUIST, C. J., and O'CONNOR, SCALIA, and KENNEDY, JJ., joined. STEVENS, J., filed a dissenting opinion. SOUTER, J., filed a dissenting opinion, in which GINSBURG and BREYER, JJ., joined. [Dissenting and concurring opinions omitted.]

JUSTICE THOMAS delivered the opinion of the Court.

This case presents the question whether the exclusionary rule, which generally prohibits the introduction at criminal trial of evidence obtained in violation of a defendant's Fourth Amendment rights, applies in parole revocation hearings. We hold that it does not.

I.

Respondent Keith M. Scott pleaded *nolo contendere* to a charge of third-degree murder and was sentenced to a prison term of 10 to 20 years, beginning on March 31, 1983. On September 1, 1993, just months after completing the minimum sentence, respondent was released on parole. One of the conditions of respondent's parole was that he would refrain from "owning or possessing any firearms or other weapons." The parole agreement, which respondent signed, further provided:

> I expressly consent to the search of my person, property and residence, without a warrant by agents of the Pennsylvania Board of Probation and Parole. Any items, in [sic] the possession of which constitutes a violation of parole/parole shall be subject to seizure, and may be used as evidence in the parole revocation process.

About five months later, after obtaining an arrest warrant based on evidence that respondent had violated several conditions of his parole by possessing firearms, consuming alcohol, and assaulting a co-worker, three parole officers arrested respondent at a local diner. Before being transferred to a correctional facility, respondent gave the officers the keys to his residence. The officers entered the home, which was owned by his mother, but did not perform a search for parole violations until respondent's mother arrived. The officers neither requested nor obtained consent to perform the search, but respondent's mother did direct them to his bedroom. After finding no relevant evidence there, the officers searched an adjacent sitting room in which they found five firearms, a compound bow, and three arrows.

At his parole violation hearing, respondent objected to the introduction of the evidence obtained during the search of his home on the ground that the search was unreasonable under the Fourth Amendment. The hearing examiner, however, rejected the challenge and admitted the evidence. As a result, the Pennsylvania Board

of Probation and Parole found sufficient evidence in the record to support the weapons and alcohol charges and recommitted respondent to serve 36 months' backtime.

The Commonwealth Court of Pennsylvania reversed and remanded, holding, *inter alia*, that the hearing examiner had erred in admitting the evidence obtained during the search of respondent's residence.

The court ruled that the search violated respondent's Fourth Amendment rights because it was conducted without the owner's consent and was not authorized by any state statutory or regulatory framework ensuring the reasonableness of searches by parole officers. The court further held that the exclusionary rule should apply because, in the circumstances of respondent's case, the deterrence benefits of the rule outweighed its costs.

The Pennsylvania Supreme Court affirmed. 698 A. 2d 32, 548 Pa. 418 (1997). The court stated that respondent's Fourth Amendment right against unreasonable searches and seizures was "unaffected" by his signing of the parole agreement giving parole officers permission to conduct warrantless searches. It then held that the search in question was unreasonable because it was supported only by "mere speculation" rather than a "reasonable suspicion" of a parole violation. . . . The court reasoned that, in the absence of the rule, illegal searches would be undeterred when officers know that the subjects of their searches are parolees and that illegally obtained evidence can be introduced at parole hearings.

We granted *certiorari* to determine whether the Fourth Amendment exclusionary rule applies to parole revocation proceedings.

. . . Because the exclusionary rule precludes consideration of reliable, probative evidence, it imposes significant costs: it undeniably detracts from the truthfinding process and allows many who would otherwise be incarcerated to escape the consequences of their actions. See *Stone* v. *Powell, supra*, at 490. Although we have held these costs to be worth bearing in certain circumstances, our cases have repeatedly emphasized that the rule's "costly toll" upon truth-seeking and law enforcement objectives presents a high obstacle for those urging application of the rule. *United States* v. *Payner*, 447 U.S. 727, 734 (1980).

The costs of excluding reliable, probative evidence are particularly high in the context of parole revocation proceedings. Parole is a "variation on imprisonment of convicted criminals," *Morrissey* v. *Brewer*, 408 U.S. 471, 477 (1972), in which the State accords a limited degree of freedom in return for the parolee's assurance that he will comply with the often strict terms and conditions of his release. In most cases, the State is willing to extend parole only because it is able to condition it upon compliance with certain requirements. The State thus has an "overwhelming interest" in ensuring that a parolee complies with those requirements and is returned to prison if he fails to do so. *Id.*, at 483. The exclusion of evidence establishing a parole violation, however, hampers the State's ability to ensure compliance with these conditions by permitting the parolee to avoid the consequences of his noncompliance. The costs of allowing a parolee to avoid the consequences of his violation are compounded by the fact that parolees (particularly those who have already committed parole violations) are more likely to commit future criminal offenses than are average citizens. See *Griffin* v. *Wisconsin*, 483 U.S. 868, 880 (1987). Indeed, this is the very premise behind the system of close parole supervision. *Ibid.*

The exclusionary rule, moreover, is incompatible with the traditionally flexible, administrative procedures of parole revocation. Because parole revocation deprives the parolee not "of the absolute liberty to which every citizen is entitled, but

only of the conditional liberty properly dependent on observance of special parole restrictions," *Morrissey* v. *Brewer*, *supra*, at 480. States have wide latitude under the Constitution to structure parole revocation proceedings. Most States, including Pennsylvania . . . have adopted informal, administrative parole revocation procedures in order to accommodate the large number of parole proceedings. These proceedings generally are not conducted by judges, but instead by parole boards, "members of which need not be judicial officers or lawyers." *Morrisey* v. *Brewer*, 408 U.S., at 489. And traditional rules of evidence generally do not apply. *Ibid.* ("[T]he process should be flexible enough to consider evidence including letters, affidavits, and other material that would not be admissible in an adversary criminal trial.") Nor are these proceedings entirely adversarial, as they are designed to be " 'predictive and discretionary' as well as factfinding." *Gagnon* v. *Scarpelli*, 411 U.S. 778, 787 (1973) (quoting *Morrissey* v. *Brewer*, *supra*, at 480). Application of the exclusionary rule would significantly alter this process.

The exclusionary rule frequently requires extensive litigation to determine whether particular evidence must be excluded. Cf. *United States* v. *Calandra*, 414 U.S., at 349 (noting that application of the exclusionary rule "would delay and disrupt grand jury proceedings" because "[s]uppression hearings would halt the orderly process of an investigation and might necessitate extended litigation of issues only tangentially related to the grand jury's primary objective"); *I.N.S.* v. *Lopez-Mendoza*, 468 U.S., at 1048 (noting that "[t]he prospect of even occasional invocation of the exclusionary rule might significantly change and complicate the character of" the deportation system). Such litigation is inconsistent with the non-adversarial, administrative processes established by the States. Although States could adapt their parole revocation proceedings to accommodate such litigation, such a change would transform those proceedings from a "predictive and discretionary" effort to promote the best interests of both parolees and society into trial-like proceedings "less attuned" to the interests of the parolee. *Gagnon* v. *Scarpelli*, *supra*, at 787–788 (quoting *Morrissey* v. *Brewer*, *supra*, at 480). We are simply unwilling so to intrude into the States' correctional schemes. See *Morrissey* v. *Brewer*, *supra*, at 483 (recognizing that States have an "overwhelming interest" in maintaining informal, administrative parole revocation procedures). Such a transformation ultimately might disadvantage parolees because in an adversarial proceeding, "the hearing body may be less tolerant of marginal deviant behavior and feel more pressure to reincarcerate than to continue nonpunitive rehabilitation." *Gagnon* v. *Scarpelli*, *supra*, at 788. And the financial costs of such a system could reduce the State's incentive to extend parole in the first place, as one of the purposes of parole is to reduce the costs of criminal punishment while maintaining a degree of supervision over the parolee.

The deterrence benefits of the exclusionary rule would not outweigh these costs. As the Supreme Court of Pennsylvania recognized, application of the exclusionary rule to parole revocation proceedings would have little deterrent effect upon an officer who is unaware that the subject of his search is a parolee. 548 Pa., at 431, 698 A. 2d, at 38. In that situation, the officer will likely be searching for evidence of criminal conduct with an eye toward the introduction of the evidence at a criminal trial. The likelihood that illegally obtained evidence will be excluded from trial provides deterrence against Fourth Amendment violations, and the remote possibility that the subject is a parolee and that the evidence may be admitted at a parole revocation proceeding surely has little, if any, effect on the officer's incentives. . . .

WHAT DO *YOU* THINK?

1. Do you agree with the majority opinion? Justify your answer.
2. Do you agree with the statement contained in the majority opinion that the marginal deterrence of unreasonable searches and seizures is insufficient to justify such an intrusion?
3. The Court has said that the primary purpose of the exclusionary rule is "to deter future unlawful police conduct and thereby effectuate the guarantee of the Fourth Amendment against unreasonable searches and seizures." What do you think?

SUMMARY

- The normal sanction for violation of a defendant's Fourth Amendment rights is to preclude the evidence obtained as the result of the violation from being used against the defendant.

- The Fourth Amendment's exclusionary rule can be traced to the 1914 Supreme Court case *Weeks* v. *United States*.

- In order to object to the admission of evidence obtained as the result of an illegal search, the person must have standing to object. The doctrine of legal standing is a judicially created doctrine. There are two parts to the concept of legal standing. First, the person asserting his or her claim must have suffered an actual injury or invasion of constitutional rights. Second, the rights asserted must be based on that person's legal rights.

- There are at least five exceptions to the exclusionary rule: (1) good-faith exception, (2) purged taint exception, (3) independent source exception, (4) inevitable discovery exception, and (5) impeachment of the defendant at trial. The most popular exception is the good-faith exception.

- The Court has been more reluctant to imply the exclusionary rule to *Miranda* violations involving confessions and admissions. Generally the court tries to determine if there is only a *Miranda* violation or if there is also a violation of due process.

- Unlike Fourth and Fifth Amendment violations, the U.S. Supreme Court has not offered any extensive explanation of why Sixth Amendment violations should invoke the exclusionary rule.

- The exclusionary rule does not apply to non-criminal trial proceedings.

- Two Supreme Court cases, *Michigan* v. *Tucker* and *Oregon* v. *Elstad*, seem to imply that there is no "fruit of the poisonous tree" doctrine for *Miranda* violations.

DISCUSSION QUESTIONS

1. The Supreme Court seems to feel that for the Fourth Amendment to work, there must be remedies which deter police misconduct. Do you agree?
2. Does the exclusionary rule actually deter police misconduct?

3. If the exclusionary rule is eliminated, what remedies could be used to protect against unreasonable searches and seizures?

4. What remedies are now available for an individual illegally arrested? Should charges against a defendant be dismissed solely on the grounds that he or she was illegally arrested?

ENDNOTES

1. 232 U.S. 383 (1914).
2. 338 U.S. 25 (1949).
3. 367 U.S. 643 (1961).
4. *Rawlings* v. *Kentucky*, 448 U.S. 98 (1980).
5. 929 F.2d. 1190 (7th Cir. 1991).
6. *Minnesota* v. *Olson*, 495 U.S. 91 (1990).
7. *United States* v. *Leon*, 468 U.S. 897 (1984).
8. *Wong Sun* v. *United States*, 371 U.S. 471 (1963).
9. *United States* v. *Crews*, 445 U.S. 463 (1980).
10. *Nix* v. *Williams*, 467 U.S. 431 (1984).
11. *Harris* v. *New York*, 401 U.S. 222 (1971).
12. 428 U.S. 465 (1967).
13. 468 U.S. 897 (1984).
14. 480 U.S. 340 (1987).
15. 371 U.S. 471 (1963).
16. 422 U.S. 590 (1975).
17. *Dunnaway* v. *New York*, 442 U.S. 200 (1979).
18. 487 U.S. 533 (1988).
19. 468 U.S. 796 (1984).
20. 467 U.S. 157 (1986).
21. 401 U.S. 222 (1971).
22. 437 U.S. 385 (1978).
23. 377 U.S. 201 (1964).
24. 388 U.S. 263 (1967).
25. 474 U.S. 159 (1985).
26. *United States* v. *Calandra*, 414 U.S. 338 (1974).
27. 428 U.S. 433 (1976).
28. 468 U.S. 032 (1984).
29. 417 U.S. 433 (1974).
30. 470 U.S. 298 (1985).

8

/DENTIFICATION

INTRODUCTION

The primary purpose of identification is to obtain evidence to assist in determining whether the defendant is guilty of the charge or charges against him or her. The three major forms of identification are lineup, show-ups, and photographs. Photographs are the most frequently used form. The two legal issues involved with identification evidence are due process rights and right to counsel issues. Only rarely are cases reversed because of unreliable or suggestive identification procedures.

Most researchers in criminal justice contend that mistaken identification has been the single greatest cause of conviction of the innocent.[1] It was not until 1967 that the Supreme Court looked at the issue in depth.[2] One of the most famous cases involved Bernard Pagano, a Roman Catholic priest who was convicted of robbery after being identified by seven eyewitnesses. Later it was established that one Ronald Clouser, not Pagano, had committed the robberies.[3] A similar case involved Randall Dale Adams who was wrongly convicted in 1977 of the capital murder of a Dallas police officer based on eyewitness identification evidence.[4]

IDENTIFICATION PROCEDURES

A person has the right to have counsel present at any out-of-court lineup or show-up after adversary judicial criminal proceeding have commenced.[5] If the government violates the defendant's right to counsel by conducting a lineup after indictment and without affording the defendant the right to have counsel present, the identification evidence of the lineup is probably not admissible. Under the same set of facts, can the government, during the trial and without attempting to introduce the inadmissible identification evidence, have the witness identify the defendant in open court? The general rule is that the prosecution may not obtain an in-court identification of the defendant by the tainted witness unless the prosecution proves by clear and convincing evidence that the in-court identification is not a fruit of the illegal out-of court identification.

Eyewitness Identification

One of the major problems in eyewitness identifications is suggestivity. The U.S. Supreme Court has held that it is a violation of due process if the pretrial identification procedure is "so impermissibly suggestive to give rise to a substantial likelihood of irreparable misidentification."[6] Accordingly, it is a violation of due process to suggest in any way to a witness that any person in a lineup or show-up committed the crime. It also is wrong to tell the victim or witness that he or she has selected the right or wrong person.

LAW IN PRACTICE

*L*INEUPS

The International Association of Chiefs of Police (IACP) recommends the guidelines below for conducting lineups:

- Lineups should have at least five individuals.
- Any suspect placed in a lineup should complete a waiver form if his or her attorney is not present.
- Individuals participating in the lineup should be of comparable age, height, hair and skin color, gender, and race. If this requirement cannot be met, the lineup should be postponed until comparable individuals may be located.
- All individuals participating in the lineup should wear similar types of clothes.
- The suspect should be randomly placed in the lineup.
- Individuals known to the witness should not be in the lineup.
- If juveniles participate in the lineup, they must have permission from their parents.[7]

Show-ups

Show-ups are one-on-one confrontations between the suspect and the witness or victim held shortly after the crime and normally at the crime scene. Show-ups by their very nature tend to be suggestive. The courts have allowed show-ups if held shortly after the crime based on the fact that the offender's looks are fresh in the mind of the victim or witness. Additional rationale for permitting show-ups is that if the suspect is cleared by the victim or witness, the police can go on with their investigation while the trail is still fresh. A suspect does not have the right to have counsel during a lawful "in-field" show-up.[8]

In *Stovall* v. *Denno*[9], the Supreme Court suggested that a court reviewing a show-up should consider all the factors including:

- Did a true emergency justify the show-up?
- Does it appear that the police were acting in good faith?
- Did the police conduct suggest that the individual committed the crime?
- Had a short amount of time elapsed between the crime and the show-up?

In *Stovall*, the Court held that the totality of circumstances test should be used to determine if the witness's identification of a suspect is likely to be reliable. No single factor should be controlling. The Court also noted that a short time lapse between the crime and the show-up does not automatically justify the show-up, but it is an important factor.

Lineups

Under the federal rule, a suspect has no right to an attorney at a physical lineup unless formal charges have been filed.[10] In some states, like California, the accused has the right to have an attorney present at the physical lineup regardless of whether charges have been filed.

The role of a defense attorney at a lineup is that of observer only. The defense counsel cannot rearrange the order of suspects, cross-examine witnesses, or ask any questions. The counsel is present to silently observe and to later recall his observations for purposes of cross-examination at trial.[11] This does not prevent the defense attorney from talking to the police or making suggestions regarding the line-up.

The suspect may waive his or her right to have an attorney present at a physical lineup. In some states, this waiver must be in writing and signed by the suspect. (*Note*: If the suspect already has an attorney, it is improper to ask the person to waive his or her right to counsel without consulting the attorney.)

What if the defendant has been charged with one crime and is placed in a lineup for an unrelated crime? Does he or she have a right to the presence of counsel at the lineup? An appellate court stated that because the defendant was in custody for an unrelated offense at the time of the lineup, no bearing is placed on the right to counsel since the government has not committed itself to prosecuting the defendant for this offense at the time of the lineup.[12]

Photographic Lineups

The suspect has no right to have counsel present at a photographic lineup. A photographic lineup, unlike a physical lineup, can be accurately re-created in court. The Supreme Court in *United States* v. *Ash*[13] distinguished *Wade* by noting that photo displays do not require the presence of the defendant and that they are a mere preparatory step in the gathering of evidence where the defense counsel has an equal ability to seek and interview the witnesses. Several appellate courts have held that the identification of a suspect on videotape is more like a photo display than a lineup and therefore there is no adversarial confrontation with attached right for counsel to attend.[14]

Witness's Testimony

An eyewitness may identify the defendant in court provided that the original identification was not "suggestive." If, however, the original identification was suggestive or the lineup/show-up was illegal, the in-court identification may still be admissible. It is admissible if it can be established that the witness can identify the defendant without relying on the tainted lineup/show-up. In determining whether the courtroom identification was independent of the tainted lineup/show-up, the court looks at the witness's opportunity to view the criminal at the time of the crime, the witness's degree of attention at the time of the crime, the accuracy of any prior descriptions given by the witness, the level of certainty demonstrated by the witness, and the length of time that has passed between the crime and the in-court identification.

Other Identification Procedures

There is no right to counsel at a pretrial confrontation for the purposes of taking handwriting exemplars, blood or other body fluid samples, or fingerprints. In addition, the taking of these items is not a violation of the privilege against self-incrimination since the defendant is not being asked to give "testimonial" or "communicative" evidence. The taking of bodily fluids, however, normally requires a warrant to enter the person's body unless there are exigent circumstances. (*Note*: In most states the police have more latitude in withdrawing a blood sample when the person is suspected of driving under the influence of drugs or alcohol (statutory notice of implied consent by driving on public roads).

The taking of voice recordings (for vocal sound characteristics) and handwriting samples does not violate a person's reasonable expectation of privacy, therefore, no showing of probable cause is required.

Two-Factor Test

The defendant has the burden of proving a violation of his or her due process rights involving the identification evidence. To satisfy this burden, the defendant must first establish that the identification procedures were impermissibly suggestive and, second, that the identification was unreliable under the totality of circumstances test.[15]

If the police procedures are held to be suggestive, then the court will look at several factors in an attempt to determine the reliability of the identification. Those factors include:

- The degree of police suggestiveness
- The opportunity the witness had to view the suspect before the identification, i.e., did the witness get a good look at the scene of the crime
- The degree of attention that the witness focused on the perpetrator during the crime
- The accuracy of any descriptions provided by the witness
- The level of the witness's certainty in the identification

- The length of time that transpired between the pre-identification opportunity to view and the actual identification.
- The character of the witness, i.e., is the witness a person who is easily led?

Trial identifications are subject to the same concerns about reliability. An in-court identification is tantamount to a show-up.

CAPSTONE CASES

In the Wade *case, the Supreme Court looks at the right of the accused to have counsel present at post-indictment lineups.*

UNITED STATES V. WADE
388 U.S. 218 (1967)

MR. JUSTICE BRENNAN delivered the opinion of the Court.

The question here is whether courtroom identifications of an accused at trial are to be excluded from evidence because the accused was exhibited to the witnesses before trial at a post-indictment lineup conducted for identification purposes without notice to and in the absence of the accused's appointed counsel.

A federally insured bank in Eustace, Texas, was robbed on September 21, 1964. A man with a small strip of tape on each side of his face entered the bank, pointed

Justice William J. Brennan, Jr., was appointed to the Supreme Court by President Eisenhower and served from 1957 to 1990. (Photograph by Newark News Photo. Collection of the Supreme Court of the United States.)

a pistol at the female cashier and the vice president, the only persons in the bank at the time, and forced them to fill a pillowcase with the bank's money. The man then drove away with an accomplice who had been waiting in a stolen car outside the bank. On March 23, 1965, an indictment was returned against respondent, Wade, and two others for conspiring to rob the bank, and against Wade and the accomplice for the robbery itself. Wade was arrested on April 2, and counsel was appointed to represent him on April 26. Fifteen days later an FBI agent, without notice to Wade's lawyer, arranged to have the two bank employees observe a lineup made up of Wade and five or six other prisoners and conducted in a courtroom of the local county courthouse. Each person in the line wore strips of tape such as allegedly worn by the robber and upon direction each said something like "put the money in the bag," the words allegedly uttered by the robber. Both bank employees identified Wade in the lineup as the bank robber.

At trial, the two employees, when asked on direct examination if the robber was in the courtroom, pointed to Wade. The prior lineup identification was then elicited from both employees on cross-examination. At the close of testimony, Wade's counsel moved for a judgment of acquittal or, alternatively, to strike the bank officials' courtroom identifications on the ground that conduct of the lineup, without notice to and in the absence of his appointed counsel, violated his Fifth Amendment privilege against self-incrimination and his Sixth Amendment right to the assistance of counsel. The motion was denied, and Wade was convicted. The Court of Appeals for the Fifth Circuit reversed the conviction and ordered a new trial at which the in-court identification evidence was to be excluded, holding that, though the lineup did not violate Wade's Fifth Amendment rights, "the lineup, held as it was, in the absence of counsel, already chosen to represent appellant, was a violation of his Sixth Amendment rights. . . ." . . . We reverse the judgment of the Court of Appeals and remand to that court with direction to enter a new judgment vacating the conviction and remanding the case to the District Court for further proceedings consistent with this opinion.

. . . We have no doubt that compelling the accused merely to exhibit his person for observation by a prosecution witness prior to trial involves no compulsion of the accused to give evidence having testimonial significance. It is compulsion of the accused to exhibit his physical characteristics, not compulsion to disclose any knowledge he might have. It is no different from compelling Schmerber to provide a blood sample or Holt to wear the blouse, and, as in those instances, is not within the cover of the privilege. Similarly, compelling Wade to speak within hearing distance of the witnesses, even to utter words purportedly uttered by the robber, was not compulsion to utter statements of a "testimonial" nature; he was required to use his voice as an identifying physical characteristic, not to speak his guilt. . . .

Moreover, it deserves emphasis that this case presents no question of the admissibility in evidence of anything Wade said or did at the lineup which implicates his privilege. The Government offered no such evidence as part of its case, and what came out about the lineup proceedings on Wade's cross-examination of the bank employees involved no violation of Wade's privilege.

. . . The fact that the lineup involved no violation of Wade's privilege against self-incrimination does not, however, dispose of his contention that the courtroom identifications should have been excluded because the lineup was conducted without notice to and in the absence of his counsel. Our rejection of the right to counsel claim in *Schmerber* rested on our conclusion in that case that "[n]o issue of counsel's ability to assist petitioner in respect of any rights he did possess is presented." 384 U.S., at 766. In contrast, in this case it is urged that the assistance of

counsel at the lineup was indispensable to protect Wade's most basic right as a criminal defendant is his right to a fair trial at which the witnesses against him might be meaningfully cross-examined.

The Framers of the Bill of Rights envisaged a broader role for counsel than under the practice then prevailing in England of merely advising his client in "matters of law," and eschewing any responsibility for "matters of fact." The constitutions in at least 11 of the 13 States expressly or impliedly abolished this distinction. *Powell* v. *Alabama*, 287 U.S. 45, 60–65; Note, 73 Yale L. J. 1000, 1030–1033 (1964). "Though the colonial provisions about counsel were in accord on few things, they agreed on the necessity of abolishing the facts-law distinction; the colonists appreciated that if a defendant were forced to stand alone against the state, his case was foredoomed." 73 Yale L. J., *supra*, at 1033–1034. This background is reflected in the scope given by our decisions to the Sixth Amendment's guarantee to an accused of the assistance of counsel for his defense. . . .

As early as *Powell* v. *Alabama*, *supra*, we recognized that the period from arraignment to trial was "perhaps the most critical period of the proceedings. . . ," *id.*, at 57, during which the accused "requires the guiding hand of counsel. . . ," *id.*, at 69, if the guarantee is not to prove an empty right. That principle has since been applied to require the assistance of counsel at the type of arraignment for example, that provided by Alabama where certain rights might be sacrificed or lost: "What happens there may affect the whole trial. Available defenses may be irretrievably lost, if not then and there asserted. . . ." *Hamilton* v. *Alabama*, 368 U.S. 52, 54. . . .

In sum, the principle of *Powell* v. *Alabama* and succeeding cases requires that we scrutinize any pretrial confrontation of the accused to determine whether the presence of his counsel is necessary to preserve the defendant's basic right to a fair trial as affected by his right meaningfully to cross-examine the witnesses against him and to have effective assistance of counsel at the trial itself. It calls upon us to analyze whether potential substantial prejudice to defendant's rights inheres in the particular confrontation and the ability of counsel to help avoid that prejudice.

. . . The Government characterizes the lineup as a mere preparatory step in the gathering of the prosecution's evidence, not different for Sixth Amendment purposes from various other preparatory steps, such as systematized or scientific analyzing of the accused's fingerprints, blood sample, clothing, hair, and the like. We think there are differences which preclude such stages being characterized as critical stages at which the accused has the right to the presence of his counsel. Knowledge of the techniques of science and technology is sufficiently available, and the variables in techniques few enough, that the accused has the opportunity for a meaningful confrontation of the Government's case at trial through the ordinary processes of cross-examination of the Government's expert witnesses and the presentation of the evidence of his own experts. The denial of a right to have his counsel present at such analyses does not therefore violate the Sixth Amendment; they are not critical stages since there is minimal risk that his counsel's absence at such stages might derogate from his right to a fair trial.

. . . The pretrial confrontation for purpose of identification may take the form of a lineup, also known as an "identification parade" or "showup," as in the present case, or presentation of the suspect alone to the witness, as in *Stovall* v. *Denno*, *supra*. It is obvious that risks of suggestion attend either form of confrontation and increase the dangers inherent in eyewitness identification. But as is the case with secret interrogations, there is serious difficulty in depicting what transpires at lineups and other forms of identification confrontations. "Privacy results in secrecy and

this in turn results in a gap in our knowledge as to what in fact goes on. . . ." *Miranda* v. *Arizona, supra*, at 448. For the same reasons, the defense can seldom reconstruct the manner and mode of lineup identification for judge or jury at trial. Those participating in a lineup with the accused may often be police officers; in any event, the participants' names are rarely recorded or divulged at trial. The impediments to an objective observation are increased when the victim is the witness. Lineups are prevalent in rape and robbery prosecutions and present a particular hazard that a victim's understandable outrage may excite vengeful or spiteful motives. In any event, neither witnesses nor lineup participants are apt to be alert for conditions prejudicial to the suspect. And if they were, it would likely be of scant benefit to the suspect since neither witnesses nor lineup participants are likely to be schooled in the detection of suggestive influences. Improper influences may go undetected by a suspect, guilty or not, who experiences the emotional tension which we might expect in one being confronted with potential accusers. Even when he does observe abuse, if he has a criminal record he may be reluctant to take the stand and open up the admission of prior convictions. Moreover, any protestations by the suspect of the fairness of the lineup made at trial are likely to be in vain; the jury's choice is between the accused's unsupported version and that of the police officers present. In short, the accused's inability effectively to reconstruct at trial any unfairness that occurred at the lineup may deprive him of his only opportunity meaningfully to attack the credibility of the witness' courtroom identification. . . .

WHAT DO *YOU* THINK?

1. If exhibiting the body is not self-incrimination, why does the accused have a right to have counsel present?
2. According to the court, what functions does the defense counsel have at a lineup?
3. Do you agree with the court that a post-indictment pretrial lineup, at which the accused is exhibited to identifying witnesses, is a critical stage of the criminal prosecution? If it is a critical stage, what rights should the defendant have at the proceedings?

The Wade *case held that an accused has a right to presence of counsel at any post-indictment lineups. When does the right to have counsel present begin?*

KIRBY V. ILLINOIS
406 U.S. 682 (1972)

MR. JUSTICE STEWART announced the judgment of the Court and an opinion in which THE CHIEF JUSTICE, MR. JUSTICE BLACKMUN, and MR. JUSTICE REHNQUIST join.

In *United States* v. *Wade*, 388 U.S. 218, and *Gilbert* v. *California*, 388 U.S. 263, this Court held that "a post-indictment pretrial lineup at which the accused is exhibited to identifying witnesses is a critical stage of the criminal prosecution; that police conduct of such a lineup without notice to and in the absence of his counsel denies the accused his Sixth [and Fourteenth] Amendment right to counsel

and calls in question the admissibility at trial of the in-court identifications of the accused by witnesses who attended the lineup." *Gilbert* v. *California, supra*, at 272. Those cases further held that no "in-court identifications" are admissible in evidence if their "source" is a lineup conducted in violation of this constitutional standard. "Only a per se exclusionary rule as to such testimony can be an effective sanction," the Court said, "to assure that law enforcement authorities will respect the accused's constitutional right to the presence of his counsel at the critical lineup." *Id.*, at 273. In the present case we are asked to extend the *Wade-Gilbert* per se exclusionary rule to identification testimony based upon a police station showup that took place before the defendant had been indicted or otherwise formally charged with any criminal offense.

On February 21, 1968, a man named Willie Shard reported to the Chicago police that the previous day two men had robbed him on a Chicago street of a wallet containing, among other things, traveler's checks and a Social Security card. On February 22, two police officers stopped the petitioner and a companion, Ralph Bean, on West Madison Street in Chicago. When asked for identification, the petitioner produced a wallet that contained three traveler's checks and a Social Security card, all bearing the name of Willie Shard. Papers with Shard's name on them were also found in Bean's possession. When asked to explain his possession of Shard's property, the petitioner first said that the traveler's checks were "play money," and then told the officers that he had won them in a crap game. The officers then arrested the petitioner and Bean and took them to a police station.

Only after arriving at the police station, and checking the records there, did the arresting officers learn of the Shard robbery. A police car was then dispatched to Shard's place of employment, where it picked up Shard and brought him to the police station. Immediately upon entering the room in the police station where the petitioner and Bean were seated at a table, Shard positively identified them as the men who had robbed him two days earlier. No lawyer was present in the room, and neither the petitioner nor Bean had asked for legal assistance, or been advised of any right to the presence of counsel.

More than six weeks later, the petitioner and Bean were indicted for the robbery of Willie Shard. Upon arraignment, counsel was appointed to represent them, and they pleaded not guilty. A pretrial motion to suppress Shard's identification testimony was denied, and at the trial Shard testified as a witness for the prosecution. In his testimony he described his identification of the two men at the police station on February 22, and identified them again in the courtroom as the men who had robbed him on February 20. He was cross-examined at length regarding the circumstances of his identification of the two defendants. Cf. *Pointer* v. *Texas*, 380 U.S. 400. The jury found both defendants guilty, and the petitioner's conviction was affirmed on appeal. The Illinois appellate court held that the admission of Shard's testimony was not error, relying upon an earlier decision of the Illinois Supreme Court, *People* v. *Palmer*, 41 Ill. 2d 571, 244 N. E. 2d 173, holding that the *Wade-Gilbert* per se exclusionary rule is not applicable to pre-indictment confrontations. We granted *certiorari*, limited to this question.

The *Wade-Gilbert* exclusionary rule, by contrast, stems from a quite different constitutional guarantee—the guarantee of the right to counsel contained in the Sixth and Fourteenth Amendments. Unless all semblance of principled constitutional adjudication is to be abandoned, therefore, it is to the decisions construing that guarantee that we must look in determining the present controversy.

In a line of constitutional cases in this Court stemming back to the Court's landmark opinion in *Powell* v. *Alabama*, 287 U.S. 45, it has been firmly established that a person's Sixth *and* Fourteenth Amendment rights to counsel attaches only at or after the time that adversary judicial proceedings have been initiated against him. . . .

This is not to say that a defendant in a criminal case has a constitutional right to counsel only at the trial itself. The *Powell* case makes clear that the right attaches at the time of arraignment, and the Court has recently held that it exists also at the time of a preliminary hearing. *Coleman* v. *Alabama, supra.* But the point is that, while members of the Court have differed as to existence of the right to counsel in the contexts of some of the above cases, all of those cases have involved points of time at or after the initiation of adversary judicial criminal proceedings—whether by way of formal charge, preliminary hearing, indictment, information, or arraignment. . . .

The initiation of judicial criminal proceedings is far from a mere formalism. It is the starting point of our whole system of adversary criminal justice. For it is only then that the government has committed itself to prosecute, and only then that the adverse positions of government and defendant have solidified. It is then that a defendant finds himself faced with the prosecutorial forces of organized society, and immersed in the intricacies of substantive and procedural criminal law. It is this point, therefore, that marks the commencement of the "criminal prosecutions" to which alone the explicit guarantees of the Sixth Amendment are applicable. . . .

. . . We decline to depart from that rationale today by imposing a per se exclusionary rule upon testimony concerning an identification that took place long before the commencement of any prosecution whatever.

The judgment is affirmed.

[Chief Justice Burger and Justice Powell concurred. Justices Brennan, Douglas, and Marshall dissented.]

What Do *You* Think?

1. The Court in *Wade* did not emphasize the timing of the lineups. In *Kirby*, the Court drew a line between pre- and post-formal charges. What reasons could the Court have for establishing the new rule?

2. Why should the defendant's rights be less if the lineup is on Monday and she is charged on Tuesday compared to a lineup on Tuesday immediately followed by a lineup?

3. The dissenting justices stated that the "initiation of adversary judicial proceedings was completely irrelevant." Do you agree or disagree? Why?

To determine if a show-up is suggestive, the Supreme Court has adopted the totality of circumstances test. That issue is discussed in the next case.

NEIL V. BIGGERS
409 U.S. 188 (1972)

Mr. Justice Powell delivered the opinion of the Court.

In 1965, after a jury trial in a Tennessee court, respondent was convicted of rape and was sentenced to 20 years' imprisonment. The State's evidence consisted

in part of testimony concerning a station-house identification of respondent by the victim. . . . The District Court held that . . . held in an unreported opinion that the station-house identification procedure was so suggestive as to violate due process. . . .

We proceed, then, to consider respondent's due process claim. As the claim turns upon the facts, we must first review the relevant testimony at the jury trial and at the habeas corpus hearing regarding the rape and the identification. The victim testified at trial that on the evening of January 22, 1965, a youth with a butcher knife grabbed her in the doorway to her kitchen:

"A. [H]e grabbed me from behind, and grappled—twisted me on the floor. Threw me down on the floor.
"Q. And there was no light in that kitchen?
"A. Not in the kitchen.
"Q. So you couldn't have seen him then?
"A. Yes, I could see him, when I looked up in his face.
"Q. In the dark?
"A. He was right in the doorway—it was enough light from the bedroom shining through. Yes, I could see who he was.
"Q. You could see? No light? And you could see him and know him then.
"A. Yes." . . .

When the victim screamed, her 12-year-old daughter came out of her bedroom and also began to scream. The assailant directed the victim to "tell her [the daughter] to shut up, or I'll kill you both." She did so, and was then walked at knifepoint about two blocks along a railroad track, taken into a woods, and raped there. She testified that "the moon was shining brightly, full moon." After the rape, the assailant ran off, and she returned home, the whole incident having taken between 15 minutes and half an hour.

She then gave the police what the Federal District Court characterized as "only a very general description," describing him as "being fat and flabby with smooth skin, bushy hair and a youthful voice." Additionally, though not mentioned by the District Court, she testified at the habeas corpus hearing that she had described her assailant as being between 16 and 18 years old and between five feet ten inches and six feet tall, as weighing between 180 and 200 pounds, and as having a dark brown complexion. This testimony was substantially corroborated by that of a police officer who was testifying from his notes.

On several occasions over the course of the next seven months, she viewed suspects in her home or at the police station, some in lineups and others in showups, and was shown between 30 and 40 photographs. She told the police that a man pictured in one of the photographs had features similar to those of her assailant, but identified none of the suspects. On August 17, the police called her to the station to view respondent, who was being detained on another charge. In an effort to construct a suitable lineup, the police checked the city jail and the city juvenile home. Finding no one at either place fitting respondent's unusual physical description, they conducted a showup instead.

The showup itself consisted of two detectives walking respondent past the victim. At the victim's request, the police directed respondent to say "shut up or I'll kill you." The testimony at trial was not altogether clear as to whether the victim first identified him and then asked that he repeat the words or made her identifi-

cation after he had spoken. In any event, the victim testified that she had "no doubt" about her identification. At the habeas corpus hearing, she elaborated in response to questioning.

> "A. That I have no doubt, I mean that I am sure that when I—see, when I first laid eyes on him, I knew that it was the individual, because his face—well, there was just something that I don't think I could ever forget. I believe _____
> "Q. You say when you first laid eyes on him, which time are you referring to?
> "A. When I identified him—when I seen him in the courthouse when I was took up to view the suspect."

We must decide whether, as the courts below held, this identification and the circumstances surrounding it failed to comport with due process requirements.

. . . The only case to date in which this Court has found identification procedures to be violative of due process is *Foster* v. *California*, 394 U.S. 440, 442 (1969). There, the witness failed to identify Foster the first time he confronted him, despite a suggestive lineup. The police then arranged a showup, at which the witness could make only a tentative identification. Ultimately, at yet another confrontation, this time a lineup, the witness was able to muster a definite identification. We held all of the identifications inadmissible, observing that the identifications were "all but inevitable" under the circumstances. *Id.*, at 443.

In the most recent case of *Coleman* v. *Alabama*, 399 U.S. 1 (1970), we held admissible an in-court identification by a witness who had a fleeting but "real good look" at his assailant in the headlights of a passing car. The witness testified at a pretrial suppression hearing that he identified one of the petitioners among the participants in the lineup before the police placed the participants in a formal line. . . .

Some general guidelines emerge from these cases as to the relationship between suggestiveness and misidentification. It is, first of all, apparent that the primary evil to be avoided is "a very substantial likelihood of irreparable misidentification." *Simmons* v. *United States*, 390 U.S., at 384. While the phrase was coined as a standard for determining whether an in-court identification would be admissible in the wake of a suggestive out-of-court identification, with the deletion of "irreparable" it serves equally well as a standard for the admissibility of testimony concerning the out-of-court identification itself. It is the likelihood of misidentification which violates a defendant's right to due process, and it is this which was the basis of the exclusion of evidence in *Foster*. Suggestive confrontations are disapproved because they increase the likelihood of misidentification, and unnecessarily suggestive ones are condemned for the further reason that the increased chance of misidentification is gratuitous. But as *Stovall* makes clear, the admission of evidence of a showup without more does not violate due process.

. . . We turn, then, to the central question, whether under the "totality of the circumstances" the identification was reliable even though the confrontation procedure was suggestive. As indicated by our cases, the factors to be considered in evaluating the likelihood of misidentification include the opportunity of the witness to view the criminal at the time of the crime, the witness' degree of attention, the accuracy of the witness' prior description of the criminal, the level of certainty demonstrated by the witness at the confrontation, and the length of time between the crime and the confrontation. Applying these factors, we disagree with the District Court's conclusion.

In part, as discussed above, we think the District Court focused unduly on the relative reliability of a lineup as opposed to a showup, the issue on which expert testimony was taken at the evidentiary hearing. It must be kept in mind also that the trial was conducted before *Stovall* and that therefore the incentive was lacking for the parties to make a record at trial of facts corroborating or undermining the identification. The testimony was addressed to the jury, and the jury apparently found the identification reliable. Some of the State's testimony at the federal evidentiary hearing may well have been self-serving in that it too neatly fit the case law, but it surely does nothing to undermine the state record, which itself fully corroborated the identification.

Affirmed in part, reversed in part, and remanded.

Mr. Justice Marshall took no part in the consideration or decision of this case.

Mr. Justice Brennan, with whom Mr. Justice Douglas and Mr. Justice Stewart concur, concurring in part and dissenting in part. [Omitted.]

What Do You Think?

1. Why was the show-up considered to be suggestive?
2. What could the police have done to improve the procedures in this case?
3. The majority opinion indicates that the reliability of the identification is determined by a totality of circumstances test, in which all of the factors involved are relevant and none are dispositive. Do you agree with approach? Why?
4. The Court held that the identification was reliable, despite its suggestiveness. Do you agree? Why?

Does the accused have a right to presence of counsel at a post-indictment photographic lineup? The Ash *case looks at this issue.*

UNITED STATES V. ASH
413 U.S. 300 (1973)

Mr. Justice Blackmun delivered the opinion of the Court.

In this case the Court is called upon to decide whether the Sixth Amendment grants an accused the right to have counsel present whenever the Government conducts a post-indictment photographic display, containing a picture of the accused, for the purpose of allowing a witness to attempt an identification of the offender. . . .

On the morning of August 26, 1965, a man with a stocking mask entered a bank in Washington, D.C., and began waving a pistol. He ordered an employee to hang up the telephone and instructed all others present not to move. Seconds later a second man, also wearing a stocking mask, entered the bank, scooped up money from tellers' drawers into a bag, and left. The gunman followed, and both men escaped through an alley. The robbery lasted three or four minutes.

A government informer, Clarence McFarland, told authorities that he had discussed the robbery with Charles J. Ash, Jr., the respondent here. Acting on this information, an FBI agent, in February 1966, showed five black-and-white mug shots of Negro males of generally the same age, height, and weight, one of which was of Ash, to four witnesses. All four made uncertain identifications of Ash's picture. At this time Ash was not in custody and had not been charged. On April 1, 1966, an indictment was returned charging Ash and a codefendant, John L. Bailey, in five counts related to this bank robbery. . . .

Trial was finally set for May 1968, almost three years after the crime. In preparing for trial, the prosecutor decided to use a photographic display to determine whether the witnesses he planned to call would be able to make in-court identifications. Shortly before the trial, an FBI agent and the prosecutor showed five color photographs to the four witnesses who previously had tentatively identified the black-and-white photograph of Ash. Three of the witnesses selected the picture of Ash, but one was unable to make any selection. None of the witnesses selected the picture of Bailey which was in the group. This post-indictment identification provides the basis for respondent Ash's claim that he was denied the right to counsel at a "critical stage" of the prosecution.

. . . At trial, the three witnesses who had been inside the bank identified Ash as the gunman, but they were unwilling to state that they were certain of their identifications. None of these made an in-court identification of Bailey. The fourth witness, who had been in a car outside the bank and who had seen the fleeing robbers after they had removed their masks, made positive in-court identifications of both Ash and Bailey. Bailey's counsel then sought to impeach this in-court identification by calling the FBI agent who had shown the color photographs to the witnesses immediately before trial. Bailey's counsel demonstrated that the witness who had identified Bailey in court had failed to identify a color photograph of Bailey. During the course of the examination, Bailey's counsel also, before the jury, brought out the fact that this witness had selected another man as one of the robbers. At this point the prosecutor became concerned that the jury might believe that the witness had selected a third person when, in fact, the witness had selected a photograph of Ash. After a conference at the bench, the trial judge ruled that all five color photographs would be admitted into evidence. The Court of Appeals held that this constituted the introduction of a post-indictment identification at the prosecutor's request and over the objection of defense counsel. . . . The five-member majority of the Court of Appeals held that Ash's right to counsel, guaranteed by the Sixth Amendment, was violated when his attorney was not given the opportunity to be present at the photographic displays conducted in May 1968 before the trial.

. . . The function of counsel in rendering "Assistance" continued at the lineup under consideration in *Wade* and its companion cases. Although the accused was not confronted there with legal questions, the lineup offered opportunities for prosecuting authorities to take advantage of the accused. Counsel was seen by the Court as being more sensitive to and aware of suggestive influences than the accused himself, and as better able to reconstruct the events at trial. Counsel present at lineup would be able to remove disabilities of the accused in precisely the same fashion that counsel compensated for the disabilities of the layman at trial. Thus, the Court mentioned that the accused's memory might be dimmed by "emotional tension," that the accused's credibility at trial would be diminished by his status as defendant, and that the accused might be unable to present his version effectively without giving up his privilege against compulsory self-incrimination. *United States* v. *Wade*, 388 U.S., at 230–231. It was in order to compensate for these deficiencies that the Court found the need for the assistance of counsel.

. . . We are not persuaded that the risks inherent in the use of photographic displays are so pernicious that an extraordinary system of safeguards is required.

We hold, then, that the Sixth Amendment does not grant the right to counsel at photographic displays conducted by the Government for the purpose of allowing a witness to attempt an identification of the offender. This holding requires reversal of the judgment of the Court of Appeals. Although respondent Ash has urged us to examine this photographic display under the due process standard enunciated in *Simmons* v. *United States*, 390 U.S., at 384, the Court of Appeals, expressing the view that additional findings would be necessary, refused to decide the issue. 149 U.S. App. D.C., at 7, 461 F.2d, at 98. We decline to consider this question on this record in the first instance. It remains open, of course, on the Court of Appeals' remand to the District Court.

Reversed and remanded.

[JUSTICES STEWART and BRENNAN concurred and JUSTICES DOUGLAS and MARSHALL dissented.]

WHAT DO YOU THINK?

1. Both the majority and the concurring opinion indicate a concern that giving a right to counsel at photographic displays may lead to the extension of the right at all post-indictment pre-trial interviews. The rationale for extending the right to photographic displays is that the identification by eye-witnesses are so damning, they may prematurely decide the guilt or innocence of the defendant. Do you agree with either approach? Explore your feeling on this issue.

2. Do you agree, as the majority opinion implies, that the defendant has a right to counsel only at those stages involving the physical presence of the defendant? Should the rights under the Sixth Amendment be limited in this manner?

3. The three dissenting justices contend that the same "inherent suggestibility" of pre-trial lineups exist in photographic displays, and if counsel is not present there is less likelihood that any irregularities in the procedure will come to light. Do you agree? Is this reason enough to have counsel present at any photographic display?

Should pretrial identification evidence be excluded when a court determines that the examination of a single photograph was unnecessary and suggestive? The next case presents the issue as to whether the Due Process Clause of the Fourteenth Amendment compels the exclusion of reliability, of pretrial identification evidence obtained by a police procedure, that is both suggestive and unnecessary.

MANSON V. BRATHWAITE
432 U.S. 98 (1977)

MR. JUSTICE BLACKMUN delivered the opinion of the Court.

This case presents the issue as to whether the Due Process Clause of the Fourteenth Amendment compels the exclusion, in a state criminal trial, apart from any consideration of reliability, of pretrial identification evidence obtained by a police procedure that was both suggestive and unnecessary. . . .

. . . Jimmy D. Glover, a full-time trooper of the Connecticut State Police, in 1970 was assigned to the Narcotics Division in an undercover capacity. On May 5 of that year, about 7:45 P.M., e. d. t., and while there was still daylight, Glover and Henry Alton Brown, an informant, went to an apartment building at 201 Westland, in Hartford, for the purpose of purchasing narcotics from "Dickie Boy" Cicero, a known narcotics dealer. Cicero, it was thought, lived on the third floor of that apartment building. . . . Glover and Brown entered the building, observed by backup Officers D'Onofrio and Gaffey, and proceeded by stairs to the third floor. Glover knocked at the door of one of the two apartments served by the stairway. The area was illuminated by natural light from a window in the third floor hallway. . .

The door was opened 12 to 18 inches in response to the knock. Glover observed a man standing at the door and, behind him, a woman. Brown identified himself. Glover then asked for "two things" of narcotics. . . . The man at the door held out his hand, and Glover gave him two $10 bills. The door closed. Soon the man returned and handed Glover two glassine bags. While the door was open, Glover stood within two feet of the person from whom he made the purchase and observed his face. Five to seven minutes elapsed from the time the door first opened until it closed the second time. . . .

Glover and Brown then left the building. This was about eight minutes after their arrival. Glover drove to headquarters where he described the seller to D'Onofrio and Gaffey. Glover at that time did not know the identity of the seller. . . . He described him as being "a colored man, approximately five feet eleven inches tall, dark complexion, black hair, short Afro style, and having high cheekbones, and of heavy build. He was wearing at the time blue pants and a plaid shirt." . . . D'Onofrio, suspecting from this description that respondent might be the seller, obtained a photograph of respondent from the Records Division of the Hartford Police Department. He left it at Glover's office. D'Onofrio was not acquainted with respondent personally, but did know him by sight and had seen him "several times" prior to May 5 . . . Glover, when alone, viewed the photograph for the first time upon his return to headquarters on May 7; he identified the person shown as the one from whom he had purchased the narcotics. . . .

The toxicological report on the contents of the glassine bags revealed the presence of heroin. The report was dated July 16, 1970. . . .

Respondent was arrested on July 27 while visiting at the apartment of a Mrs. Ramsey on the third floor of 201 Westland. This was the apartment at which the narcotics sale had taken place on May 5.

Respondent was charged, in a two-count information, with possession and sale of heroin. . . . At his trial in January 1971, the photograph from which Glover had identified respondent was received in evidence without objection on the part of the defense. Glover also testified that, although he had not seen respondent in the eight months that had elapsed since the sale, "there [was] no doubt whatsoever" in his mind that the person shown on the photograph was respondent. Glover also made a positive in-court identification without objection.

No explanation was offered by the prosecution for the failure to utilize a photographic array or to conduct a lineup.

Respondent, who took the stand in his own defense, testified that on May 5, the day in question, he had been ill at his Albany Avenue apartment ("a lot of back pains, muscle spasms . . . a bad heart . . . high blood pressure . . . neuralgia in my face, and sinus," *id.*, at 106), and that at no time on that particular day had he

been at 201 Westland. His wife testified that she recalled, after her husband had refreshed her memory, that he was home all day on May 5. Doctor Wesley M. Vietzke, an internist and assistant professor of medicine at the University of Connecticut, testified that respondent had consulted him on April 15, 1970, and that he took a medical history from him, heard his complaints about his back and facial pain, and discovered that he had high blood pressure. The physician found respondent, subjectively, "in great discomfort." Respondent in fact underwent surgery for a herniated disc at L5 and S1 on August 17.

The jury found respondent guilty on both counts of the information. He received a sentence of not less than six nor more than nine years. His conviction was affirmed per curiam by the Supreme Court of Connecticut. *State* v. *Brathwaite*, 164 Conn. 617, 325 A. 2d 284 (1973). . . .

Fourteen months later, respondent filed a petition for habeas corpus in the United States District Court for the District of Connecticut. He alleged that the admission of the identification testimony at his state trial deprived him of due process of law to which he was entitled under the Fourteenth Amendment. . . .

The District Court, by an unreported written opinion based on the court's review of the state trial transcript, dismissed respondent's petition. On appeal, the United States Court of Appeals for the Second Circuit reversed, with instructions to issue the writ unless the State gave notice of a desire to retry respondent and the new trial occurred within a reasonable time to be fixed by the District Judge. . . .

In brief summary, the court felt that evidence as to the photograph should have been excluded, regardless of reliability, because the examination of the single photograph was unnecessary and suggestive. And, in the court's view, the evidence was unreliable in any event. We granted *certiorari*.

. . . In the present case the District Court observed that the "sole evidence tying Brathwaite to the possession and sale of the heroin consisted in his identifications by the police undercover agent, Jimmy Glover." On the constitutional issue, the court stated that the first inquiry was whether the police used an impermissibly suggestive procedure in obtaining the out-of-court identification. If so, the second inquiry is whether, under all the circumstances, that suggestive procedure gave rise to a substantial likelihood of irreparable misidentification.

. . . The court concluded that there was no substantial likelihood of irreparable misidentification. It referred to the facts: Glover was within two feet of the seller. The duration of the confrontation was at least a "couple of minutes." There was natural light from a window or skylight and there was adequate light to see clearly in the hall. Glover "certainly was paying attention to identify the seller." *Id.*, at 10a. He was a trained police officer who realized that later he would have to find and arrest the person with whom he was dealing. He gave a detailed description to D'Onofrio. The reliability of this description was supported by the fact that it enabled D'Onofrio to pick out a single photograph that was thereafter positively identified by Glover. Only two days elapsed between the crime and the photographic identification. Despite the fact that another eight months passed before the in-court identification, Glover had "no doubt" that Brathwaite was the person who had sold him heroin.

The Court of Appeals confirmed that the exhibition of the single photograph to Glover was "impermissibly suggestive," 527 F.2d, at 366, and felt that, in addition, "it was unnecessarily so." *Id.*, at 367. There was no emergency and little urgency. . . . It was too great a danger that the respondent was convicted because he was a man D'Onofrio had previously observed near the scene, was thought to be a likely offender, and was arrested when he was known to be in Mrs. Ramsey's apartment, rather than because Glover "really remembered him as the seller." *Id.*, at 371–372.

. . . Petitioner at the outset acknowledges that "the procedure in the instant case was suggestive [because only one photograph was used] and unnecessary" [because there was no emergency or exigent circumstance]. Brief for Petitioner 10; Tr. of Oral Arg. 7. The respondent, in agreement with the Court of Appeals, proposes a per se rule of exclusion that he claims is dictated by the demands of the Fourteenth Amendment's guarantee of due process. He rightly observes that this is the first case in which this Court has had occasion to rule upon strictly post-Stovall out-of-court identification evidence of the challenged kind.

. . . There are, of course, several interests to be considered and taken into account. The driving force behind *United States* v. *Wade*, 388 U.S. 218 (1967), *Gilbert* v. *California*, 388 U.S. 263 (1967) (right to counsel at a post-indictment lineup), and *Stovall*, all decided on the same day, was the Court's concern with the problems of eyewitness identification. Usually the witness must testify about an encounter with a total stranger under circumstances of emergency or emotional stress. The witness' recollection of the stranger can be distorted easily by the circumstances or by later actions of the police. Thus, *Wade* and its companion cases reflect the concern that the jury not hear eyewitness testimony unless that evidence has aspects of reliability. It must be observed that both approaches before us are responsive to this concern. The per se rule, however, goes too far since its application automatically and peremptorily, and without consideration of alleviating factors, keeps evidence from the jury that is reliable and relevant.

The second factor is deterrence. Although the per se approach has the more significant deterrent effect, the totality approach also has an influence on police behavior. The police will guard against unnecessarily suggestive procedures under the totality rule, as well as the per se one, for fear that their actions will lead to the exclusion of identifications as unreliable.

The third factor is the effect on the administration of justice. Here the per se approach suffers serious drawbacks. Since it denies the trier reliable evidence, it may result, on occasion, in the guilty going free. Also, because of its rigidity, the per se approach may make error by the trial judge more likely than the totality approach. And in those cases in which the admission of identification evidence is error under the per se approach but not under the totality approach—cases in which the identification is reliable despite an unnecessarily suggestive identification procedure—reversal is a Draconian sanction. Certainly, inflexible rules of exclusion that may frustrate rather than promote justice have not been viewed recently by this Court with unlimited enthusiasm. See, for example, the several opinions in *Brewer* v. *Williams*, 430 U.S. 387 (1977). See also *United States* v. *Janis*, 428 U.S. 433 (1976). . . .

The standard, after all, is that of fairness as required by the Due Process Clause of the Fourteenth Amendment. See *United States* v. *Lovasco*, 431 U.S. 783, 790 (1977); *Rochin* v. *California*, 342 U.S. 165, 170–172 (1952). *Stovall*, with its reference to "the totality of the circumstances," 388 U.S., at 302, and *Biggers*, with its continuing stress on the same totality, 409 U.S., at 199, did not, singly or together, establish a strict exclusionary rule or new standard of due process. . . .

We therefore conclude that reliability is the linchpin in determining the admissibility of identification testimony for both pre- and post-*Stovall* confrontations. The factors to be considered are set out in *Biggers*. 409 U.S., at 199–200. These include the opportunity of the witness to view the criminal at the time of the crime, the witness' degree of attention, the accuracy of his prior description of the criminal, the level of certainty demonstrated at the confrontation, and the time between the crime and the confrontation. Against these factors is to be weighed the corrupting effect of the suggestive identification itself.

V.

We turn, then, to the facts of this case and apply the analysis:

1. *The opportunity to view.* Glover testified that for two to three minutes he stood at the apartment door, within two feet of the respondent. The door opened twice, and each time the man stood at the door. The moments passed, the conversation took place, and payment was made. Glover looked directly at his vendor. It was near sunset, to be sure, but the sun had not yet set, so it was not dark or even dusk or twilight. Natural light from outside entered the hallway through a window. There was natural light, as well, from inside the apartment.

2. *The degree of attention.* Glover was not a casual or passing observer, as is so often the case with eyewitness identification. Trooper Glover was a trained police officer on duty—and specialized in dangerous duty—when he called at the third floor of 201 Westland in Hartford on May 5, 1970. Glover himself was a Negro and unlikely to perceive only general features of "hundreds of Hartford black males," as the Court of Appeals stated. 527 F.2d, at 371. It is true that Glover's duty was that of ferreting out narcotics offenders and that he would be expected in his work to produce results. But it is also true that, as a specially trained, assigned, and experienced officer, he could be expected to pay scrupulous attention to detail, for he knew that subsequently he would have to find and arrest his vendor. In addition, he knew that his claimed observations would be subject later to close scrutiny and examination at any trial.

3. *The accuracy of the description.* Glover's description was given to D'Onofrio within minutes after the transaction. It included the vendor's race, his height, his build, the color and style of his hair, and the high cheekbone facial feature. It also included clothing the vendor wore. No claim has been made that respondent did not possess the physical characteristics so described. D'Onofrio reacted positively at once. Two days later, when Glover was alone, he viewed the photograph D'Onofrio produced and identified its subject as the narcotics seller.

4. *The witness' level of certainty.* There is no dispute that the photograph in question was that of respondent. Glover, in response to a question whether the photograph was that of the person from whom he made the purchase, testified: "There is no question whatsoever." Tr. 38. This positive assurance was repeated. *Id.*, at 41–42.

5. *The time between the crime and the confrontation.* Glover's description of his vendor was given to D'Onofrio within minutes of the crime. The photographic identification took place only two days later. We do not have here the passage of weeks or months between the crime and the viewing of the photograph.

These indicators of Glover's ability to make an accurate identification are hardly outweighed by the corrupting effect of the challenged identification itself. Although identifications arising from single-photograph displays may be viewed in general with suspicion, see *Simmons* v. *United States*, 390 U.S., at 383, we find in the instant case little pressure on the witness to acquiesce in the suggestion that such a display entails. D'Onofrio had left the photograph at Glover's office and was not present when Glover first viewed it two days after the event. There thus was little urgency and Glover could view the photograph at his leisure. And since Glover examined the photograph alone, there was no coercive pressure to make an identification arising from the presence of another. The identification was made in circumstances allowing care and reflection.

Although it plays no part in our analysis, all this assurance as to the reliability of the identification is hardly undermined by the facts that respondent was arrested in the very apartment where the sale had taken place, and that he acknowledged his frequent visits to that apartment.

Surely, we cannot say that under all the circumstances of this case there is "a very substantial likelihood of irreparable misidentification." *Id.*, at 384. Short of that point, such evidence is for the jury to weigh. We are content to rely upon the good sense and judgment of American juries, for evidence with some element of untrustworthiness is customary grist for the jury mill. Juries are not so susceptible that they cannot measure intelligently the weight of identification testimony that has some questionable feature.

Of course, it would have been better had D'Onofrio presented Glover with a photographic array including "so far as practicable . . . a reasonable number of persons similar to any person then suspected whose likeness is included in the array." Model Code 160.2 (2). The use of that procedure would have enhanced the force of the identification at trial and would have avoided the risk that the evidence would be excluded as unreliable. But we are not disposed to view D'Onofrio's failure as one of constitutional dimension to be enforced by a rigorous and unbending exclusionary rule. The defect, if there be one, goes to weight and not to substance.

We conclude that the criteria laid down in *Biggers* are to be applied in determining the admissibility of evidence offered by the prosecution concerning a post-*Stovall* identification, and that those criteria are satisfactorily met and complied with here. The judgment of the Court of Appeals is Reversed.

It is so ordered.

Mr. Justice Stevens, concurring. [Omitted.]

Mr. Justice Marshall, with whom Mr. Justice Brennan joins, dissenting. [Omitted.]

What Do *You* Think?

1. Do you agree with the majority opinion? Explain your answer.
2. Does the majority opinion foster a false sense of security in the public belief that the government has caught the right person? Explain your answer.
3. The dissenting opinion accuses the majority of dismantling the protections of *Wade* and *Gilbert*. Do you agree?

SUMMARY

- The primary purpose of identification is to obtain evidence to assist in determining whether the defendant is guilty of the charge or charges against him or her. The three major forms of identification are lineups, show-ups, and photographs. Photographs are the most frequently used form. The two legal concepts in identification evidence are due process rights and right to counsel issues.

- A person has the right to have counsel present at any out-of-court lineup or show-up after adversary judicial criminal proceedings have commenced.

- One of the major problems in eyewitness identifications is suggestivity. The U.S. Supreme Court has held that it is a violation of due process if the pretrial identification procedure is "so impermissibly suggestive to give rise to a substantial likelihood of irreparable misidentification."

- Show-ups are one-on-one confrontations between the suspect and the witness or victim, held shortly after the crime and normally at the crime scene. Show-ups by their very nature tend to be suggestive. The courts have allowed show-ups if held shortly after the crime based on the fact that the offender's looks are fresh in the mind of the victim or witness.

- Under the federal rule, a suspect has no right to an attorney at a physical lineup unless formal charges have been filed.

- The suspect has no right to have counsel present at a photographic lineup. A photographic lineup, unlike a physical lineup, can be accurately re-created in court.

- An eyewitness may identify the defendant in court provided that the original identification was not suggestive. If, however, the original identification was suggestive or the lineup/show-up was illegal, the in-court identification may still be admissible.

- The defendant has the burden of proving a violation of his or her due process rights involving the identification evidence. To satisfy this burden, the defendant must first establish that the identification procedures were impermissibly suggestive and, second, that the identification was unreliable under the totality of circumstances test.

DISCUSSION QUESTIONS

1. Discuss the dangers of identification procedures.
2. When does the right to counsel apply to identification procedures?
3. What is the role of the defense counsel at a lineup?
4. Explain the two-pronged test used to evaluate due process claims involving identification evidence.
5. What are some of the reasons for misidentifications?

ENDNOTES

1. For an excellent discussion on flaws in identification see: Daniel Goleman, "Studies Point to Flaws in Lineup of Suspects," *New York Times*, January 17, 1995, at B7 and Special Issue on Eyewitness Behavior, 4 L. & Hum. Behav. 237 (1980).
2. *United States* v. *Wade*, 388 U.S. 218 (1967).
3. "Pagano Case Points Finger at Lineups," *National Law Journal* (September 10, 1979), page 1.
4. *Ex Parte Adams*, 768 S.W.2d 280 (Tex.App, 1989).
5. *United States* v. *Wade*, 388 U.S. 218 (1967).
6. *Simmons* v. *United States*, 390 U.S. 377 (1968).
7. "Eyewitness Identification," (Gaithersburg, MD: IACP Police Legal Center, 1975).
8. *People* v. *Danpier*, 159 C.A.3d. 709 (1984).

9. 388 U.S. 293 (1967).
10. *Kirby* v. *Illinois*, 406 U.S. 682 (1972).
11. *People* v. *Bustamante*, 30 Cal.3d 88 (1981).
12. *United States ex rel. Hall* v. *Lane*, 804 F.2d. 79 (7th Cir. 1986).
13. 413 U.S. 300 (1973).
14. *United States* v. *Barker*, 988 F.2d 77 (9th Cir. 1993).
15. *Foster* v. *California*, 394 U.S. 440 (1969).

9

$\mathcal{P}$RETRIAL $\mathcal{P}$ROCEEDINGS

BAIL

The Eighth Amendment prohibits excessive bail. The traditional purpose of bail is to ensure the accused's presence at trial. Bail, for purposes of this chapter, includes the use of bail bonds, property deposits, third-party supervision, or other conditions of release designed to ensure that the accused returns to the court for trial. The Supreme Court has not directly held that the prohibition against excessive bail is incorporated in the due process clause of the Fourteenth Amendment and therefore a prohibition against the states. In *Schilb* v. *Kuebel*[1], however, the Supreme Court stated that it "has been assumed to have application to the States through the Fourteenth Amendment."

It is often stated that the Constitution does not guarantee defendants an absolute right to bail. Most researchers agree that the U.S. Constitution places restrictions on the state's power to deny bail based on the due process clause of the Fourteen Amendment which provides that "No state shall . . . deprive any person of life, liberty, or property, without due process of law."

The amount necessary to secure the defendant's presence at trial varies according to the circumstances of each case. Generally, the following factors are considered by judges in setting bail amounts:

1. Seriousness of the offense charged—some crimes such as capital murder may be assumed as "non-bailable" offenses

2. Weight of the evidence against the defendant

State	Months	Percent of Sentence
Vermont	82	87
Missouri	71	86
Arizona	36	74
Minnesota	35	69
Connecticut	53	68
Alaska	55	67
Rhode Island	46	66
North Dakota	47	64
Oregon	38	63

Source: U.S. Department of Justice, 1998.

3. Defendant's ties with the community, family, and employment
4. Defendant's prior criminal record
5. Any history of failure to appear

Generally the right to be released before trial is conditioned upon the accused's giving adequate assurance to the court that he or she will return to stand trial. The assurance is often in the form of bail. Since the function of bail is the limited purpose of ensuring attendance at trial, the amount of bail varies as to each defendant. Bail set at a figure higher than an amount reasonably calculated to fulfill this purpose is considered to be "excessive" under the Eighth Amendment.[2]

Bail was once limited almost entirely to the posting of cash or a secured bond by a bail-bondsman. Now in many jurisdictions partial bond may be posted with the court and the professional bail-bondsman eliminated. The *Schilb* v. *Kuebel* case, included in this chapter, provides an excellent description of alternate programs in an attempt to eliminate the professional bail-bondsman.

PRETRIAL DETENTION

Pretrial detention impedes the defendant's ability to prepare for trial. He or she cannot help locate witnesses and other evidence. Most importantly, incarceration disrupts an individual's life. Generally an inmate is placed in a cramped jail, is forced to wear distinctive clothes, and cannot maintain responsibility to self and family.

Prior to 1985, it was generally presumed that preclusion of flight was the only constitutionally accepted grounds for setting bail and pretrial detention. The Bail Reform Act of 1984 allowed federal courts to detain an arrestee pending trial if the prosecution could establish by clear and convincing evidence that pretrial detention was necessary for the protection of other persons (witnesses and victims) and the community. Most states soon followed with similar acts. The term *preventive detention* often is used to describe the pretrial detention of a defendant to protect society from the risk of new criminal conduct by the defendant while awaiting trial.

The constitutionality of the Bail Reform Act of 1984 was upheld in *United States* v. *Salerno*[3]. In *Salerno*, the Supreme Court pointed out that the Eighth Amendment addresses pretrial release by providing merely that "excessive bail shall not be required." The amendment says nothing about whether bail shall be available at all. The Court also held that while the primary function of bail is to safeguard the court's role in adjudicating the guilt or innocence of the defendants, the amendment does not prohibit the government from pursuing other admittedly compelling interests through regulation of pretrial release.

What rights do pretrial detainees have? This issue is discussed in the *Bell* v. *Wolfish*[4] case, which is included in this chapter. One of the issues explored in *Wolfish* is whether pretrial detainees are being punished before trial because of the confinement and restrictions on their rights. The Supreme Court held in the *Wolfish* case that not every disability imposed during pretrial detention amounts to punishment in the constitutional sense. The Court stated that once the government has exercised its authority to detain a person pending trial, the government is entitled to employ devices that are calculated to effectuate this detention and that loss of freedom and privacy are inherent incidents of pretrial confinement.

PRETRIAL RELEASE

Most defendants are released prior to trial. Courts rely on a variety of release mechanisms. Some retain a citation release or a summons to appear. Some are released before seeing a judge by posting bond according to a bond schedule that lists amounts required for various offenses. A defendant arrested for an offense that has a bond schedule may generally be released at anytime that the appropriate bond is posted.

Often defendants are released by judges on their own recognizance (O.R. or R.O.R), on the promise of the defendants to appear in court. Many times judges will attach restrictive conditions on the release, such as a promise to reside in the community until trial, to refrain from using drugs or alcohol, or to attend a program for drug or alcohol abuse. Such releases are often termed *supervised releases*. In some cases, the defendants are released to third persons, such as relatives.

The Supreme Court in *Gerstein* v. *Pugh*[5] held that a person arrested and held for trial under a prosecutor's information (in lieu of an indictment) is constitutionally entitled to a judicial determination of probable cause for pretrial restraint of liberty. The majority opinion noted that the consequences of prolonged detention may be more serious than the interference occasioned by arrest and that the Fourth Amendment requires a judicial determination of probable cause as a prerequisite to extended restraint of liberty following an arrest. Later in *County of Riverside* v. *McLaughlin*[6], the Supreme Court attempted to define what is "prompt" under the *Gerstein* rule. The Court stated that their purpose in *Gerstein* was to make clear that the Fourth Amendment requires every State to provide prompt determinations of probable cause, but that the Constitution does not impose on the States a rigid procedural framework. Individual states may choose to comply with *Gerstein* in different ways. The Court then stated that judicial determinations of probable cause within 48 hours of arrest will, as a general matter, comply with the promptness requirements of *Gerstein*.

ARRAIGNMENT

At an arraignment, the defendant is informed of the charges and given an opportunity to enter a plea to the charge or charges alleged in the complaint or indictment. The defendant may enter a plea at that time or request time to consider the plea to be entered. In most jurisdictions the defendant may plea (1) guilty, (2) not guilty, (3) nolo contendere, (4) not guilty by reasons of insanity, or (5) former jeopardy. If the defendant stands mute and refuses to enter a plea, a not guilty plea will be entered by the judge. In most states, unless the defendant raises the issue of insanity by a plea of not guilty by reasons of insanity, the defendant is presumed to have been sane at the time that the crime or crimes were committed.

In some states, there is a first appearance which is different from an arraignment. Generally the first appearance is used to inform the defendant of the charges against him or her, the setting of release conditions or bail, and informing the defendant of his or her rights.

Guilty Plea

In early English common law, a defendant was not permitted to enter a guilty plea since it was thought that the only way justice could be accomplished was by a trial. Now guilty pleas are permitted in almost all situations. Some states do not allow a defendant in a capital trial (death penalty case) to plead guilty on the assumption that such a plea is an attempt to commit suicide. A plea of guilty admits every element of the offense and is considered as equivalent to a conviction.[7]

In most jurisdictions, a plea of guilty in a felony case must be made in open court personally by the defendant. Before a judge may accept a guilty plea, the judge is required to inform the defendant of his or her rights, the elements of the offense, the rights waived by a plea of guilty, and the maximum punishment for the crime to which the accused is pleading. The records of the trial must reflect that the judge advised the accused of the significance of the guilty plea and made a finding that the accused understood the significance of the plea. A guilty plea may be accepted in most jurisdictions even though accompanied by a claim of innocence. A judge may refuse to accept a plea of guilty. The accused does not have a constitutional right to have his or her plea of guilty accepted by the court.[8]

After a plea of guilty is accepted, the next step is to sentence the defendant. If the charge is a misdemeanor, generally the sentence is announced at that time. If the charge is a felony, the judge may set a sentencing date and order a pre-sentence investigation (PSI) to provide the judge with information regarding the appropriate sentence.

Withdrawal of a Plea

If the accused pleads not guilty at the arraignment, generally the court will allow the defendant to change his or her plea to guilty. Often the change in plea is the result of a plea bargain reached between the defendant and the prosecution. Once the change of plea is entered, then the judge proceeds with a guilty plea case.

In most jurisdictions, a defendant may withdraw a guilty plea and enter a not guilty plea on the showing of good cause. Generally this withdrawal must be prior to sentencing. If the withdrawal is permitted, the case then proceeds as a not guilty case. In some cases, the Supreme Court has directed that a guilty plea be withdrawn and a not guilty plea be entered years after the case has been completed. For example, if it can be shown that the defendant did not understand the meaning or significance of a guilty plea, the Supreme Court has directed the lower court to permit the defendant to withdraw the guilty plea and enter a not guilty one.[9] In that case, the defendant had pled guilty to murder in the second degree. Nine years later he claimed that he did not know that an "intent" was a necessary element of second degree murder. The Supreme Court held that his guilty plea was not knowingly made since the records did not indicate that the defendant had been advised of the elements of the offense.

In *Parker* v. *North Carolina*[10], the defendant argued that his guilty plea was entered because of a forced confession. The Supreme Court stated that even if the confession was coerced, the court could not believe that police misconduct during the interrogation period was of such nature or had such enduring effect as to make involuntary a plea of guilty entered over a month later. Accordingly, the decision of the trial judge to refuse his withdrawal of a guilty plea was upheld on review. (*Note:* In this case, the trial judge had held a factual inquiry, and the inquiry indicated that the defendant knew the significance of his plea of guilty at the time it was entered).

Other Pleas

If the defendant refuses to enter a plea or stands mute, the judge may enter a not guilty plea on his or her behalf. A plea of nolo contendere means that "I will not contest it." It is essentially equivalent to a plea of guilty. As with the guilty plea, before the judge can accept such a plea he or she must advise the accused of the significance of the plea. A nolo contendere plea is used generally where the defendant admits committing the act but denies that it is a crime, or where the defendant does not want to admit guilt because of possible civil liability from a civil suit. A defendant does not have a constitutional right to plea nolo contendere. Generally he or she must have consent of the judge to enter this plea.

By entering a plea of not guilty by reason of insanity, the defendant is admitting the commission of the act for which he is charged but alleges that he or she was not sane at the time of the act. In most states the defendant has the burden of going forward in establishing his or her lack of sanity at the time the act was committed. An individual who denies the act and wants to use the defense of insanity must generally plead not guilty and not guilty by reason of insanity. In a few states, the plea of not guilty by reason of insanity is not allowed. In those states, insanity may be raised as an affirmative defense after pleading not guilty.

The plea of once in jeopardy is of ancient origin. It can be traced back to the early Greek and Roman jurisprudence. It was also a part of the common law of England and brought to this country by the colonists. The plea is used to invoke the right against double jeopardy. The right provides that no person may be placed in jeopardy of his or her life or liberty more than once for the same offense. In most jurisdictions, the prohibition against double jeopardy is waived unless pleaded at arraignment. There are exceptions to the prohibition. For example, a defendant who appeals his conviction and wins his appeal generally may be tried again on the same charges. In addition, if there is a mistrial or a hung jury (jury cannot agree on a decision), in most cases the defendant may be tried again on the same charges. In addition, if the defendant is tried in state court for an act that also constitutes a federal crime, he or she may generally be tried in federal court for violation of a federal statute based on the same act. For example, the accused is charged with robbing a federally insured bank. He is tried in state court for robbery. He may also be charged in federal court for violating the federal law against robbing a federally insured bank.

For the prohibition against double jeopardy to apply, the accused must have been placed in jeopardy. The question as to when jeopardy attaches is complicated. As a general rule, once the trial begins, the accused has been placed in jeopardy.

of offenses. A *motion for severance* is commonly made when two or more defendants are being tried jointly. The motion for severance may be based on the fact that allowing the defendant to be tried jointly with another defendant may deprive him or her of the right to a fair trial.

CAPSTONE CASES

The Stack *v.* Boyle *case discusses the purpose of bail.*

STACK V. BOYLE
342 U.S. 1 (1951)

MR. CHIEF JUSTICE VINSON delivered the opinion of the Court.

Indictments have been returned in the Southern District of California charging the twelve petitioners with conspiring to violate the Smith Act, 18 U.S.C. (Supp. IV) 371, 2385. Upon their arrest, bail was fixed for each petitioner in the widely varying amounts of $2,500, $7,500, $75,000 and $100,000. On motion of petitioner Schneiderman following arrest in the Southern District of New York, his bail was reduced to $50,000 before his removal to California. On motion of the Government to increase bail in the case of other petitioners, and after several intermediate procedural steps not material to the issues presented here, bail was fixed in the District Court for the Southern District of California in the uniform amount of $50,000 for each petitioner.

Petitioners moved to reduce bail on the ground that bail as fixed was excessive under the Eighth Amendment. In support of their motion, petitioners submitted statements as to their financial resources, family relationships, health, prior criminal records, and other information. The only evidence offered by the Government was a certified record showing that four persons previously convicted under the Smith Act in the Southern District of New York had forfeited bail. No evidence was produced relating those four persons to the petitioners in this case. At a hearing on the motion, petitioners were examined by the District Judge and cross-examined by an attorney for the Government. Petitioners' factual statements stand uncontroverted.

After their motion to reduce bail was denied, petitioners filed applications for habeas corpus in the same District Court. Upon consideration of the record on the motion to reduce bail, the writs were denied. The Court of Appeals for the Ninth Circuit affirmed. 192 F.2d 56. Prior to filing their petition for *certiorari* in this Court, petitioners filed with MR. JUSTICE DOUGLAS an application for bail and an alternative application for habeas corpus seeking interim relief. Both applications were referred to the Court and the matter was set down for argument on specific questions covering the issues raised by this case.

Relief in this type of case must be speedy if it is to be effective. The petition for *certiorari* and the full record are now before the Court and, since the questions presented by the petition have been fully briefed and argued, we consider it appropriate to dispose of the petition for *certiorari* at this time. Accordingly, the petition for *certiorari* is granted for review of questions important to the administration of criminal justice.

First. From the passage of the Judiciary Act of 1789, 1 Stat. 73, 91, to the present Federal Rules of Criminal Procedure, Rule 46 (a) (1), federal law has

unequivocally provided that a person arrested for a non-capital offense shall be admitted to bail. This traditional right to freedom before conviction permits the unhampered preparation of a defense, and serves to prevent the infliction of punishment prior to conviction. See *Hudson* v. *Parker*, 156 U.S. 277, 285 (1895). Unless this right to bail before trial is preserved, the presumption of innocence, secured only after centuries of struggle, would lose its meaning.

The right to release before trial is conditioned upon the accused's giving adequate assurance that he will stand trial and submit to sentence if found guilty. *Ex* [342 U.S. 1, 5] *parte Milburn*, 9 Pet. 704, 710 (1835). Like the ancient practice of securing the oaths of responsible persons to stand as sureties for the accused, the modern practice of requiring a bail bond or the deposit of a sum of money subject to forfeiture serves as additional assurance of the presence of an accused. Bail set at a figure higher than an amount reasonably calculated to fulfill this purpose is "excessive" under the Eighth Amendment. See *United States* v. *Motlow*, 10 F.2d 657 (1926, opinion by Mr. Justice Butler as Circuit Justice of the Seventh Circuit).

Since the function of bail is limited, the fixing of bail for any individual defendant must be based upon standards relevant to the purpose of assuring the presence of that defendant. The traditional standards as expressed in the Federal Rules of Criminal Procedure are to be applied in each case to each defendant. . . .

If bail in an amount greater than that usually fixed for serious charges of crimes is required in the case of any of the petitioners, that is a matter to which evidence should be directed in a hearing so that the constitutional rights of each petitioner may be preserved. In the absence of such a showing, we are of the opinion that the fixing of bail before trial in these cases cannot be squared with the statutory and constitutional standards for admission to bail.

Second. The proper procedure for challenging bail as unlawfully fixed is by motion for reduction of bail and appeal to the Court of Appeals from an order denying such motion. Petitioners' motion to reduce bail did not merely invoke the discretion of the District Court setting bail within a zone of reasonableness, but challenged the bail as violating statutory and constitutional standards. As there is no discretion to refuse to reduce excessive bail, the order denying the motion to reduce bail is appealable as a "final decision" of the District Court under 28 U.S.C. (Supp. IV) 1291. *Cohen* v. *Beneficial Loan Corp.*, 337 U.S. 541, 545–547 (1949). In this case, however, petitioners did not take an appeal from the order of the District Court denying their motion for reduction of bail. Instead, they presented their claims under the Eighth Amendment in applications for writs of habeas corpus. While habeas corpus is an appropriate remedy for one held in custody in violation of the Constitution, 28 U.S.C. (Supp. IV) 2241 (c) (3), the District Court should withhold relief in this collateral habeas corpus action where an adequate remedy available in the criminal proceeding has not been exhausted. *Ex parte Royall*, 117 U.S. 241 (1886); *Johnson* v. *Hoy*, 227 U.S. 245 (1913).

The Court concludes that bail has not been fixed by proper methods in this case and that petitioners' remedy is by motion to reduce bail, with right of appeal to the Court of Appeals. Accordingly, the judgment of the Court of Appeals is vacated and the case is remanded to the District Court with directions to vacate its order denying petitioners' applications for writs of habeas corpus and to dismiss the applications without prejudice. Petitioners may move for reduction of bail in the criminal proceeding so that a hearing may be held for the purpose of fixing reasonable bail for each petitioner.

It is so ordered.

1. What should be the purpose of bail?
2. Why is it important to individually set bail in each case?
3. Most jurisdictions use bail schedules to establish the presumptive bail amounts. Does this practice violate the *Stack* case? Explain your answer.

Can a state authorize the county to keep of a portion of the bail deposit? The Schilb *case looks at this issue.*

SCHILB V. KUEBEL
404 U.S. 357 (1971)

MR. JUSTICE BLACKMUN delivered the opinion of the Court.

John Schilb, of Belleville, Illinois, was arrested on January 16, 1969, and charged with (a) leaving the scene of an automobile accident and with (b) obstructing traffic. In order to gain his liberty pending trial, and in accord with the Illinois bail statutes hereinafter described, Schilb deposited $75 in cash with the clerk of the court. This amount was 10% of the aggregate bail fixed on the two charges ($500 on the first and $250 on the second). At his ensuing trial Schilb was acquitted of the charge of leaving the scene, but was convicted of traffic obstruction. When he paid his fine, the amount Schilb had deposited was returned to him decreased, however, by $7.50 retained as "bail bond costs" by the court clerk pursuant to the statute. The amount so retained was 1% of the specified bail and 10% of the amount actually deposited. Schilb, by this purported state class action against the court clerk, the country, and the county treasurer, attacks the statutory 1% charge on Fourteenth Amendment due process and equal protection grounds. The Circuit Court of St. Clair County upheld the statute and dismissed the complaint. The Supreme Court of Illinois affirmed, with two justices dissenting. 46 Ill. 2d 538, 264 N. E. 2d 377 (1970). We noted probable jurisdiction.

. . . The parties have stipulated that when bail in a particular case is fixed, the judge's "discretion in such respect is not guided by statute, rule of court or any definite, fixed standard; various and divers judges in fact fix the amount of bail for the same types of offenses at various and divers amounts, without relationship as to guilt or innocence of the particular defendant in a criminal charge, and without relationship of the particular offense charged and the bail fixed." They have also stipulated, "The actual cost of administering the provisions of said Sections 110-7 and 110-8 are substantially the same but there may probably be a slightly greater cost in the administration of Section 110-8."

. . . The Court more than once has said that state legislative reform by way of classification is not to be invalidated merely because the legislature moves one step at a time. "The prohibition of the Equal Protection Clause goes no further than the invidious discrimination." *Williamson* v. *Lee Optical Co.*, 348 U.S. 483, 489 (1955). "Legislatures are presumed to have acted constitutionally. . .and their statutory classifications will be set aside only if no grounds can be conceived to justify them. . . . With this much discretion, a legislature traditionally has been allowed to

take reform 'one step at a time, addressing itself to the phase of the problem which seems most acute to the legislative mind.' " *McDonald* v. *Board of Election Commissioners*, 394 U.S. 802, 809 (1969).

The measure of equal protection has been described variously as whether "the distinctions drawn have some basis in practical experience," *South Carolina* v. *Katzenbach*, 383 U.S. 301, 331 (1966), or whether the legislature's action falls short of "the invidious discrimination," *Williamson* v. *Lee Optical Co.*, 348 U.S., at 489, or whether "any state of facts reasonably may be conceived to justify" the statutory discrimination, *McGowan* v. *Maryland*, 366 U.S. 420, 426 (1961); see *United States* v. *Maryland Savings-Share Ins. Corp.*, 400 U.S. 4, 6 (1970), or whether the classification is "on the basis of criteria wholly unrelated to the objective of [the] statute," *Reed* v. *Reed*, *ante*, p. 71, at 76. But the Court also has refined this traditional test and has said that a statutory classification based upon suspect criteria or affecting "fundamental rights" will encounter equal protection difficulties unless justified by a "compelling governmental interest." *Shapiro* v. *Thompson*, 394 U.S. 618, 634, 638 (1969); *Oregon* v. *Mitchell*, 400 U.S. 112, 247 n. 30 (1970) (opinion of BRENNAN, WHITE, and MARSHALL, JJ.).

. . . But we are not at all concerned here with any fundamental right to bail or with any Eighth Amendment-Fourteenth Amendment question of bail excessiveness. Our concern, instead, is with the 1% cost-retention provision. This smacks of administrative detail and of procedure and is hardly to be classified as a "fundamental" right or as based upon any suspect criterion. The applicable measure, therefore, must be the traditional one: Is the distinction drawn by the statutes invidious and without rational basis? *Dandridge* v. *Williams*, 397 U.S. 471, 483–487 (1970). See *Richardson* v. *Belcher*, *ante*, p. 78, at 81.

. . . With this background, we turn to the appellants' primary argument. It is threefold: (1) that the 1% retention charge under 110-7 (f) is imposed on only one segment of the class gaining pretrial release; (2) that it is imposed on the poor and nonaffluent and not on the rich and affluent; and (3) that its imposition with respect to an accused found innocent amounts to a court cost assessed against the not-guilty person. We are compelled to note preliminary that the attack on the Illinois bail statutes, in a very distinct sense, is paradoxical. The benefits of the new system, as compared with the old, are conceded. And the appellants recognize that under the pre-1964 system Schilb's particular bail bond cost would have been 10% of his bail, or $75; that this premium price for his pretrial freedom, once paid, was irretrievable; and that, if he could not have raised the $75, he would have been consigned to jail until his trial. Thus, under the old system the cost of Schilb's pretrial freedom was $75, but under the new it was only $7.50. While acknowledging this obvious benefit of the statutory reform, Schilb and his coappellants decry the classification the statutes make and present the usual argument that the legislation must be struck down because it does not reform enough.

It is true that no charge is made to the accused who is released on his personal recognizance. We are advised, however, that this was also true under the old (pre-1964) system and that "Illinois has never charged people out on recognizance." Thus, the burden on the State with respect to a personal recognizance is no more under the new system than what the State had assumed under the old. Also, with a recognizance, there is nothing the State holds for safekeeping, with resulting responsibility and additional paperwork. All this provides a rational basis for distinguishing between the personal recognizance and the deposit situations. There is also, however, no retention charge to the accused who deposits the full amount of cash bail or securities or real estate. Yet the administrative cost attendant upon the 10%

deposit and that upon the full deposit are, by the stipulation, "substantially the same" with, indeed, any higher cost incurred with respect to the full deposit.

This perhaps is a more tenuous distinction, but we cannot conclude that it is constitutionally vulnerable. One who deposits securities or encumbers his real estate precludes the use of that property for other purposes. And one who deposits the full amount of his bail in cash is dispossessed of a productive asset throughout the period of the deposit; presumably, at least, its interim possession by the State accrues to the benefit of the State. Further the State's protection against the expenses that inevitably are incurred when bail is jumped is greater when 100% cash or securities or real estate is deposited or obligated than when only 10% of the bail amount is advanced. The Joint Committee's and the State Legislature's decision in balancing these opposing considerations in the way that they did cannot be described as lacking in rationality to the point where equal protection considerations require that they be struck down. . . . Affirmed.

JUSTICE MARSHALL, concurred. [Omitted.]

JUSTICES DOUGLAS, STEWART, and BRENNAN dissented. [Omitted.]

WHAT DO *YOU* THINK?

1. Should the county be allowed to keep a portion of the fee? Explain your answer.

2. If the defendant is acquitted on all charges, should the entire amount be returned to him? Justify your answer.

Traditionally the only purpose of bail was to ensure presence of the accused at trial. Is it unconstitutional to hold a person in pretrial detention for the safety of the community? The next case looks at this issue.

UNITED STATES V. SALERNO
481 U.S. 739 (1987)

CHIEF JUSTICE REHNQUIST delivered the opinion of the Court.

The Bail Reform Act of 1984 (Act) allows a federal court to detain an arrestee pending trial if the Government demonstrates by clear and convincing evidence after an adversary hearing that no release conditions "will reasonably assure . . . the safety of any other person and the community." The United States Court of Appeals for the Second Circuit struck down this provision of the Act as facially unconstitutional, because, in that court's words, this type of pretrial detention violates "substantive due process." We granted *certiorari* because of a conflict among the Courts of Appeals regarding the validity of the Bail Reform Act of 1984. We hold that, as against the facial attack mounted by these respondents, the Act fully comports with constitutional requirements. We therefore reverse.

Responding to "the alarming problem of crimes committed by persons on release," S. Rep. No. 98-225, p. 3 (1983), Congress formulated the Bail Reform Act

of 1984, 18 U.S.C. 3141 et seq. (1982 ed., Supp. III), as the solution to a bail crisis in the federal courts. The Act represents the National Legislature's considered response to numerous perceived deficiencies in the federal bail process. By providing for sweeping changes in both the way federal courts consider bail applications and the circumstances under which bail is granted, Congress hoped to "give the courts adequate authority to make release decisions that give appropriate recognition to the danger a person may pose to others if released." S. Rep. No. 98-225, at 3.

To this end, 3141(a) of the Act requires a judicial officer to determine whether an arrestee shall be detained. Section 3142(e) provides that "[i]f, after a hearing pursuant to the provisions of subsection (f), the judicial officer finds that no condition or combination of conditions will reasonably assure the appearance of the person as required and the safety of any other person and the community, he shall order the detention of the person prior to trial." Section 3142(f) provides the arrestee with a number of procedural safeguards. He may request the presence of counsel at the detention hearing, he may testify and present witnesses in his behalf, as well as proffer evidence, and he may cross-examine other witnesses appearing at the hearing. If the judicial officer finds that no conditions of pretrial release can reasonably assure the safety of other persons and the community, he must state his findings of fact in writing, 3142(i), and support his conclusion with "clear and convincing evidence," 3142(f).

The judicial officer is not given unbridled discretion in making the detention determination. Congress has specified the considerations relevant to that decision. These factors include the nature and seriousness of the charges, the substantiality of the Government's evidence against the arrestee, the arrestee's background and characteristics, and the nature and seriousness of the danger posed by the suspect's release. 3142(g). Should a judicial officer order detention, the detainee is entitled to expedited appellate review of the detention order. 3145(b), (c).

Respondents Anthony Salerno and Vincent Cafaro were arrested on March 21, 1986, after being charged in a 29-count indictment alleging various Racketeer Influenced and Corrupt Organizations Act (RICO) violations, mail and wire fraud offenses, extortion, and various criminal gambling violations. The RICO counts alleged 35 acts of racketeering activity, including fraud, extortion, gambling, and conspiracy to commit murder. At respondents' arraignment, the Government moved to have Salerno and Cafaro detained pursuant to 3142(e), on the ground that no condition of release would assure the safety of the community or any person. The District Court held a hearing at which the Government made a detailed proffer of evidence. The Government's case showed that Salerno was the "boss" of the Genovese crime family of La Cosa Nostra and that Cafaro was a "captain" in the Genovese family. According to the Government's proffer, based in large part on conversations intercepted by a court-ordered wiretap, the two respondents had participated in wide-ranging conspiracies to aid their illegitimate enterprises through violent means. The Government also offered the testimony of two of its trial witnesses, who would assert that Salerno personally participated in two murder conspiracies. Salerno opposed the motion for detention, challenging the credibility of the Government's witnesses. He offered the testimony of several character witnesses as well as a letter from his doctor stating that he was suffering from a serious medical condition. Cafaro presented no evidence at the hearing, but instead characterized the wiretap conversations as merely "tough talk."

The District Court granted the Government's detention motion, concluding that the Government had established by clear and convincing evidence that no condition or combination of conditions of release would ensure the safety of the community or any person:

> "The activities of a criminal organization such as the Genovese Family do not cease with the arrest of its principals and their release on even the most stringent of bail conditions. The illegal businesses, in place for many years, require constant attention and protection, or they will fail. Under these circumstances, this court recognizes a strong incentive on the part of its leadership to continue business as usual. When business as usual involves threats, beatings, and murder, the present danger such people pose in the community is self-evident. 631 F. Supp. 1364, 1375 (SDNY 1986)

Respondents appealed, contending that to the extent that the Bail Reform Act permits pretrial detention on the ground that the arrestee is likely to commit future crimes, it is unconstitutional on its face. Over a dissent, the United States Court of Appeals for the Second Circuit agreed. 794 F.2d 64 (1986). Although the court agreed that pretrial detention could be imposed if the defendants were likely to intimidate witnesses or otherwise jeopardize the trial process, it found "3142(e)'s authorization of pretrial detention [on the ground of future dangerousness] repugnant to the concept of substantive due process, which we believe prohibits the total deprivation of liberty simply as a means of preventing future crimes." *Id.*, at 71–72. The court concluded that the Government could not, consistent with due process, detain persons who had not been accused of any crime merely because they were thought to present a danger to the community.... It reasoned that our criminal law system holds persons accountable for past actions, not anticipated future actions. Although a court could detain an arrestee who threatened to flee before trial, such detention would be permissible because it would serve the basic objective of a criminal system—bringing the accused to trial. The court distinguished our decision in *Gerstein* v. *Pugh*, 420 U.S. 103 (1975), in which we upheld police detention pursuant to arrest. The court construed Gerstein as limiting such detention to the " 'administrative steps incident to arrest.' " 794 F.2d, at 74, quoting *Gerstein, supra*, at 114. The Court of Appeals also found our decision in *Schall* v. *Martin*, 467 U.S. 253 (1984), upholding postarrest, pretrial detention of juveniles, inapposite because juveniles have a lesser interest in liberty than do adults. The dissenting judge concluded that on its face, the Bail Reform Act adequately balanced the Federal Government's compelling interests in public safety against the detainee's liberty interests.

... A facial challenge to a legislative Act is, of course, the most difficult challenge to mount successfully, since the challenger must establish that no set of circumstances exists under which the Act would be valid. The fact that the Bail Reform Act might operate unconstitutionally under some conceivable set of circumstances is insufficient to render it wholly invalid, since we have not recognized an "overbreadth" doctrine outside the limited context of the First Amendment. *Schall* v. *Martin, supra*, at 269, n. 18. We think respondents have failed to shoulder their heavy burden to demonstrate that the Act is "facially" unconstitutional.

Respondents present two grounds for invalidating the Bail Reform Act's provisions permitting pretrial detention on the basis of future dangerousness. First, they rely upon the Court of Appeals' conclusion that the Act exceeds the limitations placed upon the Federal Government by the Due Process Clause of the Fifth Amendment. Second, they contend that the Act contravenes the Eighth Amendment's proscription against excessive bail. We treat these contentions in turn.

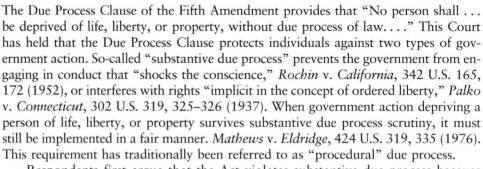

A.

The Due Process Clause of the Fifth Amendment provides that "No person shall . . . be deprived of life, liberty, or property, without due process of law. . . ." This Court has held that the Due Process Clause protects individuals against two types of government action. So-called "substantive due process" prevents the government from engaging in conduct that "shocks the conscience," *Rochin* v. *California*, 342 U.S. 165, 172 (1952), or interferes with rights "implicit in the concept of ordered liberty," *Palko* v. *Connecticut*, 302 U.S. 319, 325–326 (1937). When government action depriving a person of life, liberty, or property survives substantive due process scrutiny, it must still be implemented in a fair manner. *Mathews* v. *Eldridge*, 424 U.S. 319, 335 (1976). This requirement has traditionally been referred to as "procedural" due process.

Respondents first argue that the Act violates substantive due process because the pretrial detention it authorizes constitutes impermissible punishment before trial. See *Bell* v. *Wolfish*, 441 U.S. 520, 535, and n. 16 (1979). The Government, however, has never argued that pretrial detention could be upheld if it were "punishment." The Court of Appeals assumed that pretrial detention under the Bail Reform Act is regulatory, not penal, and we agree that it is. As an initial matter, the mere fact that a person is detained does not inexorably lead to the conclusion that the government has imposed punishment. . . . To determine whether a restriction on liberty constitutes impermissible punishment or permissible regulation, we first look to legislative intent. *Schall* v. *Martin*, 467 U.S., at 269. Unless Congress expressly intended to impose punitive restrictions, the punitive/regulatory distinction turns on " 'whether an alternative purpose to which [the restriction] may rationally be connected is assignable for it, and whether it appears excessive in relation to the alternative purpose assigned [to it].' " *Ibid.*, quoting *Kennedy* v. *Mendoza-Martinez*, 372 U.S. 144, 168–169 (1963).

We conclude that the detention imposed by the Act falls on the regulatory side of the dichotomy. The legislative history of the Bail Reform Act clearly indicates that Congress did not formulate the pretrial detention provisions as punishment for dangerous individuals. See S. Rep. No. 98-225, at 8. Congress instead perceived pretrial detention as a potential solution to a pressing societal problem. *Id.*, at 4–7. There is no doubt that preventing danger to the community is a legitimate regulatory goal. *Schall* v. *Martin*, *supra*. Nor are the incidents of pretrial detention excessive in relation to the regulatory goal Congress sought to achieve. The Bail Reform Act carefully limits the circumstances under which detention may be sought to the most serious of crimes. See 18 U.S.C. 3142(f) (detention hearings available if case involves crimes of violence, offenses for which the sentence is life imprisonment or death, serious drug offenses, or certain repeat offenders). The arrestee is entitled to a prompt detention hearing, *ibid.*, and the maximum length of pretrial detention is limited by the stringent time limitations of the Speedy Trial Act. See 18 U.S.C. 3161 et seq. (1982 ed. and Supp. III). Moreover, as in *Schall* v. *Martin*, the conditions of confinement envisioned by the Act "appear to reflect the regulatory purposes relied upon by the Government." As in *Schall*, the statute at issue here requires that detainees be housed in a "facility separate, to the extent practicable, from persons awaiting or serving sentences or being held in custody pending appeal." 18 U.S.C. 3142(i)(2). We conclude, therefore, that the pretrial detention contemplated by the Bail Reform Act is regulatory in nature, and does not constitute punishment before trial in violation of the Due Process Clause.

The Court of Appeals nevertheless concluded that "the Due Process Clause prohibits pretrial detention on the ground of danger to the community as a regulatory

measure, without regard to the duration of the detention." 794 F.2d, at 71. Respondents characterize the Due Process Clause as erecting an impenetrable "wall" in this area that "no governmental interest—rational, important, compelling or otherwise—may surmount." Brief for Respondents. We do not think the Clause lays down any such categorical imperative. We have repeatedly held that the Government's regulatory interest in community safety can, in appropriate circumstances, outweigh an individual's liberty interest. For example, in times of war or insurrection, when society's interest is at its peak, the Government may detain individuals whom the Government believes to be dangerous. See *Ludecke* v. *Watkins*, 335 U.S. 160 (1948) (approving unreviewable executive power to detain enemy aliens in time of war); *Moyer* v. *Peabody*, 212 U.S. 78, 84–85 (1909) (rejecting due process claim of individual jailed without probable cause by Governor in time of insurrection). Even outside the exigencies of war, we have found that sufficiently compelling governmental interests can justify detention of dangerous persons. Thus, we have found no absolute constitutional barrier to detention of potentially dangerous resident aliens pending deportation proceedings. *Carlson* v. *Landon*, 342 U.S. 524, 537–542 (1952); *Wong Wing* v. *United States*, 163 U.S. 228 (1896). We have also held that the government may detain mentally unstable individuals who present a danger to the public, *Addington* v. *Texas*, 441 U.S. 418 (1979), and dangerous defendants who become incompetent to stand trial, *Jackson* v. *Indiana*, 406 U.S. 715, 731–739 (1972); *Greenwood* v. *United States*, 350 U.S. 366 (1956).

We have approved of postarrest regulatory detention of juveniles when they present a continuing danger to the community. *Schall* v. *Martin*, *supra*. Even competent adults may face substantial liberty restrictions as a result of the operation of our criminal justice system. If the police suspect an individual of a crime, they may arrest and hold him until a neutral magistrate determines whether probable cause exists. *Gerstein* v. *Pugh*, 420 U.S. 103 (1975). Finally, respondents concede and the Court of Appeals noted that an arrestee may be incarcerated until trial if he presents a risk of flight, (see *Bell* v. *Wolfish*, 441 U.S., at 534) or a danger to witnesses.

Respondents characterize all of these cases as exceptions to the "general rule" of substantive due process that the government may not detain a person prior to a judgment of guilt in a criminal trial. Such a "general rule" may freely be conceded, but we think that these cases show a sufficient number of exceptions to the rule that the congressional action challenged here can hardly be characterized as totally novel. Given the well-established authority of the government, in special circumstances, to restrain individuals' liberty prior to or even without criminal trial and conviction, we think that the present statute providing for pretrial detention on the basis of dangerousness must be evaluated in precisely the same manner that we evaluated the laws in the cases discussed above.

The government's interest in preventing crime by arrestees is both legitimate and compelling. *De Veau* v. *Braisted*, 363 U.S. 144, 155 (1960). In *Schall*, *supra*, we recognized the strength of the State's interest in preventing juvenile crime. This general concern with crime prevention is no less compelling when the suspects are adults. Indeed, "[t]he harm suffered by the victim of a crime is not dependent upon the age of the perpetrator." *Schall* v. *Martin*, *supra*, at 264–265. The Bail Reform Act of 1984 responds to an even more particularized governmental interest than the interest we sustained in *Schall*.

The statute we upheld in *Schall* permitted pretrial detention of any juvenile arrested on any charge after a showing that the individual might commit some undefined further crimes. The Bail Reform Act, in contrast, narrowly focuses on a particularly acute problem in which the Government interests are overwhelming.

The Act operates only on individuals who have been arrested for a specific category of extremely serious offenses. 18 U.S.C. 3142(f). Congress specifically found that these individuals are far more likely to be responsible for dangerous acts in the community after arrest. See S. Rep. No. 98-225, at 6–7. Nor is the Act by any means a scattershot attempt to incapacitate those who are merely suspected of these serious crimes. The Government must first of all demonstrate probable cause to believe that the charged crime has been committed by the arrestee, but that is not enough. In a fullblown adversary hearing, the Government must convince a neutral decisionmaker by clear and convincing evidence that no conditions of release can reasonably assure the safety of the community or any person. 18 U.S.C. 3142(f). While the Government's general interest in preventing crime is compelling, even this interest is heightened when the Government musters convincing proof that the arrestee, already indicted or held to answer for a serious crime, presents a demonstrable danger to the community. Under these narrow circumstances, society's interest in crime prevention is at its greatest.

On the other side of the scale, of course, is the individual's strong interest in liberty. We do not minimize the importance and fundamental nature of this right. But, as our cases hold, this right may, in circumstances where the government's interest is sufficiently weighty, be subordinated to the greater needs of society. We think that Congress' careful delineation of the circumstances under which detention will be permitted satisfies this standard. When the Government proves by clear and convincing evidence that an arrestee presents an identified and articulable threat to an individual or the community, we believe that, consistent with the Due Process Clause, a court may disable the arrestee from executing that threat. Under these circumstances, we cannot categorically state that pretrial detention "offends some principle of justice so rooted in the traditions and conscience of our people as to be ranked as fundamental." *Snyder* v. *Massachusetts*, 291 U.S. 97, 105 (1934).

Finally, we may dispose briefly of respondents' facial challenge to the procedures of the Bail Reform Act. To sustain them against such a challenge, we need only find them "adequate to authorize the pretrial detention of at least some [persons] charged with crimes," *Schall*, *supra*, at 264, whether or not they might be insufficient in some particular circumstances. We think they pass that test. As we stated in *Schall*, "there is nothing inherently unattainable about a prediction of future criminal conduct." 467 U.S., at 278; see *Jurek* v. *Texas*, 428 U.S. 262, 274 (1976) (joint opinion of STEWART, POWELL, and STEVENS, JJ.); *id.*, at 279 (WHITE, J., concurring in judgment).

Under the Bail Reform Act, the procedures by which a judicial officer evaluates the likelihood of future dangerousness are specifically designed to further the accuracy of that determination. Detainees have a right to counsel at the detention hearing. 18 U.S.C. 3142(f). They may testify on their own behalf, present information by proffer or otherwise, and cross-examine witnesses who appear at the hearing. *Ibid.* The judicial officer charged with the responsibility of determining the appropriateness of detention is guided by statutorily enumerated factors, which include the nature and the circumstances of the charges, the weight of the evidence, the history and characteristics of the putative offender, and the danger to the community. 3142(g). The Government must prove its case by clear and convincing evidence. 3142(f). Finally, the judicial officer must include written findings of fact and a written statement of reasons for a decision to detain. 3142(i). The Act's review provisions, 3145(c), provide for immediate appellate review of the detention decision.

We think these extensive safeguards suffice to repel a facial challenge. The protections are more exacting than those we found sufficient in the juvenile context, see *Schall, supra*, at 275–281, and they far exceed what we found necessary to effect limited postarrest detention in *Gerstein* v. *Pugh*, 420 U.S. 103 (1975). Given the legitimate and compelling regulatory purpose of the Act and the procedural protections it offers, we conclude that the Act is not facially invalid under the Due Process Clause of the Fifth Amendment.

The judgment of the Court of Appeals is therefore Reversed.

JUSTICE MARSHALL, with whom JUSTICE BRENNAN joins, dissenting. [Omitted.]

WHAT DO *YOU* THINK?

1. Does pretrial detention conflict with the presumption of innocence?
2. What should be the purpose of pretrial detention?
3. Is pretrial detention punishment or a "regulatory device?"

Is a person arrested and held for trial under a prosecutor's information entitled to a judicial determination of probable cause? The Gerstein *case looks at this issue.*

GERSTEIN V. PUGH
420 U.S. 103 (1975)

MR. JUSTICE POWELL delivered the opinion of the Court.

The issue in this case is whether a person arrested and held for trial under a prosecutor's information is constitutionally entitled to a judicial determination of probable cause for pretrial restraint of liberty.

I.

In March 1971 respondents Pugh and Henderson were arrested in Dade County, Fla. Each was charged with several offenses under a prosecutor's information. Pugh was denied bail because one of the charges against him carried a potential life sentence, and Henderson remained in custody because he was unable to post a $4,500 bond.

In Florida, indictments are required only for prosecution of capital offenses. Prosecutors may charge all other crimes by information, without a prior preliminary hearing and without obtaining leave of court. . . . At the time respondents were arrested, a Florida rule seemed to authorize adversary preliminary hearings to test probable cause for detention in all cases. . . . But the Florida courts had held that the filing of an information foreclosed the suspect's right to a preliminary hearing. . . . They had also held that habeas corpus could not be used, except perhaps in exceptional circumstances, to test the probable cause for detention under an information. . . . The only possible methods for obtaining a judicial determination of probable cause were a special statute allowing a preliminary hearing after 30 days . . . and arraignment, which the District Court found was often delayed a month

or more after arrest. . . . As a result, a person charged by information could be detained for a substantial period solely on the decision of a prosecutor.

As framed by the proceedings below, this case presents two issues: whether a person arrested and held for trial on an information is entitled to a judicial determination of probable cause for detention, and if so, whether the adversary hearing ordered by the District Court and approved by the Court of Appeals is required by the Constitution.

A.

Both the standards and procedures for arrest and detention have been derived from the Fourth Amendment and its common-law antecedents. . . . The standard for arrest is probable cause, defined in terms of facts and circumstances "sufficient to warrant a prudent man in believing that the [suspect] had committed or was committing an offense." . . . This standard, like those for searches and seizures, represents a necessary accommodation between the individual's right to liberty and the State's duty to control crime.

"These long-prevailing standards seek to safeguard citizens from rash and unreasonable interferences with privacy and from unfounded charges of crime. They also seek to give fair leeway for enforcing the law in the community's protection. Because many situations which confront officers in the course of executing their duties are more or less ambiguous, room must be allowed for some mistakes on their part. But the mistakes must be those of reasonable men, acting on facts leading sensibly to their conclusions of probability. The rule of probable cause is a practical, nontechnical conception affording the best compromise that has been found for accommodating these often opposing interests. Requiring more would unduly hamper law enforcement. To allow less would be to leave law-abiding citizens at the mercy of the officers' whim or caprice."

To implement the Fourth Amendment's protection against unfounded invasions of liberty and privacy, the Court has required that the existence of probable cause be decided by a neutral and detached magistrate whenever possible. . . .

Maximum protection of individual rights could be assured by requiring a magistrate's review of the factual justification prior to any arrest, but such a requirement would constitute an intolerable handicap for legitimate law enforcement. Thus, while the Court has expressed a preference for the use of arrest warrants when feasible . . . it has never invalidated an arrest supported by probable cause solely because the officers failed to secure a warrant.

Under this practical compromise, a policeman's on-the-scene assessment of probable cause provides legal justification for arresting a person suspected of crime, and for a brief period of detention to take the administrative steps incident to arrest. Once the suspect is in custody, however, the reasons that justify dispensing with the magistrate's neutral judgment evaporate. There no longer is any danger that the suspect will escape or commit further crimes while the police submit their evidence to a magistrate. And, while the State's reasons for taking summary action subside, the suspect's need for a neutral determination of probable cause increases significantly. The consequences of prolonged detention may be more serious than the interference occasioned by arrest. Pretrial confinement may imperil the suspect's job, interrupt his source of income, and impair his family relationships. . . . Even pretrial release may be accompanied by burdensome conditions that effect a significant restraint of liberty. . . . When the stakes are this high, the detached judgment of a neutral magistrate is essential if the Fourth Amendment is to furnish meaningful protection from unfounded interference with liberty. Accordingly, we hold that the Fourth Amendment requires a judicial determination of probable cause as a prerequisite to extended restraint of liberty following arrest.

. . . The sole issue is whether there is probable cause for detaining the arrested person pending further proceedings. This issue can be determined reliably without an adversary hearing. The standard is the same as that for arrest. That standard—probable cause to believe the suspect has committed a crime—traditionally has been decided by a magistrate in a nonadversary proceeding on hearsay and written testimony, and the Court has approved these informal modes of proof.

. . . The use of an informal procedure is justified not only by the lesser consequences of a probable cause determination but also by the nature of the determination itself. It does not require the fine resolution of conflicting evidence that a reasonable-doubt or even a preponderance standard demands, and credibility determinations are seldom crucial in deciding whether the evidence supports a reasonable belief in guilt. See F. Miller, *Prosecution: The Decision to Charge a Suspect with a Crime* 64-109 (1969). This is not to say that confrontation and cross-examination might not enhance the reliability of probable cause determinations in some cases. In most cases, however, their value would be too slight to justify holding, as a matter of constitutional principle, that these formalities and safeguards designed for trial must also be employed in making the Fourth Amendment determination of probable cause.

Because of its limited function and its nonadversary character, the probable cause determination is not a "critical stage" in the prosecution that would require appointed counsel. The Court has identified as "critical stages" those pretrial procedures that would impair defense on the merits if the accused is required to proceed without counsel. . . . The Fourth Amendment probable cause determination is addressed only to pretrial custody. . . .

. . . Although we conclude that the Constitution does not require an adversary determination of probable cause, we recognize that state systems of criminal procedure vary widely. There is no single preferred pretrial procedure and the nature of the probable cause determination usually will be shaped to accord with a State's pretrial procedure viewed as a whole. While we limit our holding to the precise requirement of the Fourth Amendment, we recognize the desirability of flexibility and experimentation by the States.

. . . We agree with the Court of Appeals that the Fourth Amendment requires a timely judicial determination of probable cause as a prerequisite to detention, and we accordingly affirm that much of the judgment. As we do not agree that the Fourth Amendment requires the adversary hearing outlined in the District Court's decree, we reverse in part and remand to the Court of Appeals for further proceedings consistent with this opinion.

It is so ordered.

MR. JUSTICE STEWART, with whom MR. JUSTICE DOUGLAS, MR. JUSTICE BRENNAN, and MR. JUSTICE MARSHALL join concurring. [Omitted.]

WHAT DO YOU THINK?

1. In what situations are *Gerstein*-type hearings required?

2. Why is a state not required to provide for a *Gerstein*-type hearing with a grand jury indictment?

The next case looks at the issue of constitutional rights of pretrial detainees.[11]

BELL V. WOLFISH
441 U.S. 520 (1979)

MR. JUSTICE REHNQUIST delivered the opinion of the Court.

. . . This case requires us to examine the constitutional rights of pretrial detainees—those persons who have been charged with a crime but who have not yet been tried on the charge. The parties concede that to ensure their presence at trial, these persons legitimately may be incarcerated by the Government prior to a determination of their guilt or innocence . . . and it is the scope of their rights during this period of confinement prior to trial that is the primary focus of this case.

This lawsuit was brought as a class action in the United States District Court for the Southern District of New York to challenge numerous conditions of confinement and practices at the Metropolitan Correctional Center (MCC), a federally operated short-term custodial facility in New York City designed primarily to house pretrial detainees. The District Court, in the words of the Court of Appeals for the Second Circuit, "intervened broadly into almost every facet of the institution" and enjoined no fewer than 20 MCC practices on constitutional and statutory grounds. The Court of Appeals largely affirmed the District Court's constitutional rulings and in the process held that under the Due Process Clause of the Fifth Amendment, pretrial detainees may "be subjected to only those 'restrictions and privations' which 'inhere in their confinement itself or which are justified by compelling necessities of jail administration.' " *Wolfish* v. *Levi*, 573 F.2d 118, 124 (1978), quoting *Rhem* v. *Malcolm*, 507 F.2d 333, 336 (CA2 1974). We granted *certiorari* to consider the important constitutional questions raised by these decisions and to resolve an apparent conflict among the Circuits. We now reverse.

I.

The MCC was constructed in 1975 to replace the converted waterfront garage on West Street that had served as New York City's federal jail since 1928. It is located adjacent to the Foley Square federal courthouse and has as its primary objective the housing of persons who are being detained in custody prior to trial for federal criminal offenses in the United States District Courts for the Southern and Eastern Districts of New York and for the District of New Jersey. Under the Bail Reform Act, 18 U.S.C. 3146, a person in the federal system is committed to a detention facility only because no other less drastic means can reasonably ensure his presence at trial. In addition to pretrial detainees, the MCC also houses some convicted inmates who are awaiting sentencing or transportation to federal prison or who are serving generally relatively short sentences in a service capacity at the MCC, convicted prisoners who have been lodged at the facility under writs of habeas corpus ad prosequendum or ad testificandum issued to ensure their presence at upcoming trials, witnesses in protective custody, and persons incarcerated for contempt.

The MCC differs markedly from the familiar image of a jail; there are no barred cells, dank, colorless corridors, or clanging steel gates. It was intended to include the most advanced and innovative features of modern design of detention facilities. As the Court of Appeals stated: "[I]t represented the architectural embodiment of

the best and most progressive penological planning." 573 F.2d, at 121. The key design element of the 12-story structure is the "modular" or "unit" concept, whereby each floor designed to house inmates has one or two largely self-contained residential units that replace the traditional cellblock jail construction. Each unit in turn has several clusters or corridors of private rooms or dormitories radiating from a central 2-story "multipurpose" or common room, to which each inmate has free access approximately 16 hours a day. Because our analysis does not turn on the particulars of the MCC concept or design, we need not discuss them further.

When the MCC opened in August 1975, the planned capacity was 449 inmates, an increase of 50% over the former West Street facility. *Id.*, at 122. Despite some dormitory accommodations, the MCC was designed primarily to house these inmates in 389 rooms, which originally were intended for single occupancy. While the MCC was under construction, however, the number of persons committed to pretrial detention began to rise at an "unprecedented" rate. The Bureau of Prisons took several steps to accommodate this unexpected flow of persons assigned to the facility, but despite these efforts, the inmate population at the MCC rose above its planned capacity within a short time after its opening. To provide sleeping space for this increased population, the MCC replaced the single bunks in many of the individual rooms and dormitories with double bunks. Also, each week some newly arrived inmates had to sleep on cots in the common areas until they could be transferred to residential rooms as space became available.

On November 28, 1975, less than four months after the MCC had opened, the named respondents initiated this action by filing in the District Court a petition for a writ of habeas corpus. The District Court certified the case as a class action on behalf of all persons confined at the MCC, pretrial detainees and sentenced prisoners alike. The petition served up a veritable potpourri of complaints that implicated virtually every facet of the institution's conditions and practices. Respondents charged, *inter alia*, that they had been deprived of their statutory and constitutional rights because of overcrowded conditions, undue length of confinement, improper searches, inadequate recreational, educational, and employment opportunities, insufficient staff, and objectionable restrictions on the purchase and receipt of personal items and books.

In two opinions and a series of orders, the District Court enjoined numerous MCC practices and conditions. With respect to pretrial detainees, the court held that because they are "presumed to be innocent and held only to ensure their presence at trial, 'any deprivation or restriction of . . . rights beyond those which are necessary for confinement alone, must be justified by a compelling necessity.' " *United States ex rel. Wolfish* v. *Levi*, 439 F. Supp. 114, 124 (1977), quoting *Detainees of Brooklyn House of Detention* v. *Malcolm*, 520 F.2d 392, 397 (CA2 1975). And while acknowledging that the rights of sentenced inmates are to be measured by the different standard of the Eighth Amendment, the court declared that to house "an inferior minority of persons . . . in ways found unconstitutional for the rest" would amount to cruel and unusual punishment. *United States ex rel. Wolfish* v. *United States*, 428 F. Supp. 333, 339 (1977).

Applying these standards on cross-motions for partial summary judgment, the District Court enjoined the practice of housing two inmates in the individual rooms and prohibited enforcement of the so-called "publisher-only" rule, which at the time of the court's ruling, prohibited the receipt of all books and magazines mailed from outside the MCC except those sent directly from a publisher or a book club. After a trial on the remaining issues, the District Court enjoined, *inter alia*, the doubling of capacity in the dormitory areas, the use of the common rooms to provide temporary sleeping accommodations, the prohibition against inmates' receipt of packages containing food and items of personal property, and the practice of requiring inmates to expose their body cavities for visual inspection following contact visits. The court also granted relief in favor of pretrial detainees, but not convicted inmates, with respect to the requirement that detainees remain outside their rooms during routine inspections by MCC officials.

The Court of Appeals largely affirmed the District Court's rulings, although it rejected that court's Eighth Amendment analysis of conditions of confinement for convicted prisoners because the "parameters of judicial intervention into . . . conditions . . . for sentenced prisoners are more restrictive than in the case of pretrial detainees." 573 F.2d, at 125. Accordingly, the court remanded the matter to the District Court for it to determine whether the housing for sentenced inmates at the MCC was constitutionally "adequate." But the Court of Appeals approved the due process standard employed by the District Court in enjoining the conditions of pretrial confinement. It therefore held that the MCC had failed to make a showing of "compelling necessity" sufficient to justify housing two pretrial detainees in the individual rooms. *Id.*, at 126–127. And for purposes of our review (since petitioners challenge only some of the Court of Appeals' rulings), the court affirmed the District Court's granting of relief against the "publisher-only" rule, the practice of conducting body-cavity searches after contact visits, the prohibition against receipt of packages of food and personal items from outside the institution, and the requirement that detainees remain outside their rooms during routine searches of the rooms by MCC officials. *Id.*, at 129–132.

II.

As a first step in our decision, we shall address "double-bunking" as it is referred to by the parties, since it is a condition of confinement that is alleged only to deprive pretrial detainees of their liberty without due process of law in contravention of the Fifth Amendment. We will treat in order the Court of Appeals' standard of review, the analysis which we believe the Court of Appeals should have employed, and the conclusions to which our analysis leads us in the case of "double-bunking."

A.

The Court of Appeals did not dispute that the Government may permissibly incarcerate a person charged with a crime but not yet convicted to ensure his presence at trial. However, reasoning from the "premise that an individual is to be treated as innocent until proven guilty," the court concluded that pretrial detainees retain the "rights afforded unincarcerated individuals," and that therefore it is not sufficient that the conditions of confinement for pretrial detainees "merely comport with contemporary standards of decency prescribed by the cruel and unusual punishment clause of the eighth amendment." 573 F.2d, at 124. Rather, the court held, the Due Process Clause requires that pretrial detainees "be subjected to only those 'restrictions and privations' which 'inhere in their confinement itself or which are justified by compelling necessities of jail administration.' " *Ibid.*, quoting *Rhem* v. *Malcolm*, 507 F.2d, at 336. Under the Court of Appeals' "compelling necessity" standard, "deprivation of the rights of detainees cannot be justified by the cries of fiscal necessity, . . . administrative convenience, . . . or by the cold comfort that conditions in other jails are worse." 573 F.2d, at 124. The court acknowledged, however, that it could not "ignore" our admonition in *Procunier* v. *Martinez*, 416 U.S. 396, 405 (1974), that "courts are ill equipped to deal with the increasingly urgent

problems of prison administration," and concluded that it would "not [b]e wise for [it] to second-guess the expert administrators on matters on which they are better informed." 573 F.2d, at 124.

Our fundamental disagreement with the Court of Appeals is that we fail to find a source in the Constitution for its compelling-necessity standard. Both the Court of Appeals and the District Court seem to have relied on the "presumption of innocence" as the source of the detainee's substantive right to be free from conditions of confinement that are not justified by compelling necessity. . . . But the presumption of innocence provides no support for such a rule.

The presumption of innocence is a doctrine that allocates the burden of proof in criminal trials; it also may serve as an admonishment to the jury to judge an accused's guilt or innocence solely on the evidence adduced at trial and not on the basis of suspicions that may arise from the fact of his arrest, indictment, or custody, or from other matters not introduced as proof at trial. . . . It is "an inaccurate, shorthand description of the right of the accused to 'remain inactive and secure, until the prosecution has taken up its burden and produced evidence and effected persuasion; . . .' an 'assumption' that is indulged in the absence of contrary evidence." *Taylor* v. *Kentucky, supra*, at 484 n. 12. Without question, the presumption of innocence plays an important role in our criminal justice system. "The principle that there is a presumption of innocence in favor of the accused is the undoubted law, axiomatic and elementary, and its enforcement lies at the foundation of the administration of our criminal law." *Coffin* v. *United States*, 156 U.S. 432, 453 (1895). But it has no application to a determination of the rights of a pretrial detainee during confinement before his trial has even begun.

The Court of Appeals also relied on what it termed the "indisputable rudiments of due process" in fashioning its compelling-necessity test. We do not doubt that the Due Process Clause protects a detainee from certain conditions and restrictions of pretrial detainment. See *infra*, at 535–540. Nonetheless, that Clause provides no basis for application of a compelling-necessity standard to conditions of pretrial confinement that are not alleged to infringe any other, more specific guarantee of the Constitution.

It is important to focus on what is at issue here. We are not concerned with the initial decision to detain an accused and the curtailment of liberty that such a decision necessarily entails. See *Gerstein* v. *Pugh*, 420 U.S. 103, 114 (1975); *United States* v. *Marion*, 404 U.S. 307, 320 (1971). Neither respondents nor the courts below question that the Government may permissibly detain a person suspected of committing a crime prior to a formal adjudication of guilt. See *Gerstein* v. *Pugh, supra*, at 111–114. Nor do they doubt that the Government has a substantial interest in ensuring that persons accused of crimes are available for trials and, ultimately, for service of their sentences, or that confinement of such persons pending trial is a legitimate means of furthering that interest. Tr. of Oral Arg. 27; see *Stack* v. *Boyle*, 342 U.S. 1, 4 (1951). Instead, what is at issue when an aspect of pretrial detention that is not alleged to violate any express guarantee of the Constitution is challenged, is the detainee's right to be free from punishment, see *infra*, at 535–537, and his understandable desire to be as comfortable as possible during his confinement, both of which may conceivably coalesce at some point. It seems clear that the Court of Appeals did not rely on the detainee's right to be free from punishment, but even if it had that right does not warrant adoption of that court's compelling-necessity test. See *infra*, at 535–540. And to the extent the court relied on the detainee's desire simply does from discomfort, it suffices to say that this desire simply does not rise to the level of those fundamental liberty interests delineated in cases such as *Roe* v. *Wade*, 410 U.S. 113 (1973); *Eisenstadt* v. *Baird*, 405

U.S. 438 (1972); *Stanley* v. *Illinois*, 405 U.S. 645 (1972); *Griswold* v. *Connecticut*, 381 U.S. 479 (1965); *Meyer* v. *Nebraska*, 262 U.S. 390 (1923).

B.

In evaluating the constitutionality of conditions or restrictions of pretrial detention that implicate only the protection against deprivation of liberty without due process of law, we think that the proper inquiry is whether those conditions amount to punishment of the detainee. For under the Due Process Clause, a detainee may not be punished prior to an adjudication of guilt in accordance with due process of law. . . . A person lawfully committed to pretrial detention has not been adjudged guilty of any crime. He has had only a "judicial determination of probable cause as a prerequisite to [the] extended restraint of [his] liberty following arrest." *Gerstein* v. *Pugh*, *supra*, at 114; see *Virginia* v. *Paul*, 148 U.S. 107, 119 (1893). And, if he is detained for a suspected violation of a federal law, he also has had a bail hearing. See 18 U.S.C. 3146, 3148. Under such circumstances, the Government concededly may detain him to ensure his presence at trial and may subject him to the restrictions and conditions of the detention facility so long as those conditions and restrictions do not amount to punishment, or otherwise violate the Constitution.

Not every disability imposed during pretrial detention amounts to "punishment" in the constitutional sense, however. Once the Government has exercised its conceded authority to detain a person pending trial, it obviously is entitled to employ devices that are calculated to effectuate this detention. Traditionally, this has meant confinement in a facility which, no matter how modern or how antiquated, results in restricting the movement of a detainee in a manner in which he would not be restricted if he simply were free to walk the streets pending trial. Whether it be called a jail, a prison, or a custodial center, the purpose of the facility is to detain. Loss of freedom of choice and privacy are inherent incidents of confinement in such a facility. And the fact that such detention interferes with the detainee's understandable desire to live as comfortably as possible and with as little restraint as possible during confinement does not convert the conditions or restrictions of detention into "punishment." . . . [Concurring and dissenting opinions omitted.]

WHAT DO YOU THINK?

1. What are the practical distinctions between pretrial detention and punishment?
2. What interests are at stake in this case?
3. Does the Court overlook the defendants' presumptions of innocence?

In Coleman *v.* Alabama, *the Supreme Court examined the function of a preliminary hearing.*

COLEMAN V. ALABAMA
399 U.S. 1 (1970)

MR. JUSTICE BRENNAN announced the judgment of the Court and delivered the following opinion.

Petitioners were convicted in an Alabama Circuit Court of assault with intent to murder in the shooting of one Reynolds after he and his wife parked their car on an Alabama highway to change a flat tire. The Alabama Court of Appeals affirmed. . . . We vacate and remand.

Petitioners . . . argue that the preliminary hearing prior to their indictment was a "critical stage" of the prosecution and that Alabama's failure to provide them with appointed counsel at the hearing therefore unconstitutionally denied them the assistance of counsel.

. . . At the trial Reynolds testified that at about 11:30 P.M. on July 24, 1966, he was engaged in changing a tire when three men approached from across the highway. One of them shot him from a short distance away. The three then ran up to within three or four feet. Reynolds arose from his stooped position and held on to his wife, who had left the car to watch him as he worked. One of the men put his hand on Mrs. Reynolds' shoulder. Reynolds testified that this was Coleman. Within a few seconds a car with its lights on approached, and the three men turned and "ran across the road. . . ." As they turned to go, Reynolds was shot a second time. He identified petitioner Stephens as the gunman, stating that he saw him "in the car lights" while "looking straight at him." Reynolds repeated on cross-examination his testimony on direct; he said he saw Coleman "face to face"; "I looked into his face," "got a real good look at him."

. . . This Court has held that a person accused of crime "requires the guiding hand of counsel at every step in the proceedings against him," *Powell* v. *Alabama*, 287 U.S. 45, 69 (1932), and that that constitutional principle is not limited to the presence of counsel at trial. "It is central to that principle that in addition to counsel's presence at trial, the accused is guaranteed that he need not stand alone against the State at any stage of the prosecution, formal or informal, in court or out, where counsel's absence might derogate from the accused's right to a fair trial." *United States* v. *Wade*, *supra*, at 226. Accordingly, "the principle of *Powell* v. *Alabama* and succeeding cases requires that we scrutinize any pretrial confrontation of the accused to determine whether the presence of his counsel is necessary to preserve the defendant's basic right to a fair trial as affected by his right meaningfully to cross-examine the witnesses against him and to have effective assistance of counsel at the trial itself. It calls upon us to analyze whether potential substantial prejudice to defendant's rights inheres in the particular confrontation and the ability of counsel to help avoid that prejudice." *Id.*, at 227. Applying this test, the Court has held that "critical stages" include the pretrial type of arraignment where certain rights may be sacrificed or lost. . . .

The preliminary hearing is not a required step in an Alabama prosecution. The prosecutor may seek an indictment directly from the grand jury without a preliminary hearing. . . . The opinion of the Alabama Court of Appeals in this case instructs us that under Alabama law the sole purposes of a preliminary hearing are to determine whether there is sufficient evidence against the accused to warrant presenting his case to the grand jury, and, if so, to fix bail if the offense is bailable. . . . The court continued:

> At the preliminary hearing . . . the accused is not required to advance any defenses, and failure to do so does not preclude him from availing himself of every defense he may have upon the trial of the case . . . bars the admission of testimony given at a pre-trial proceeding where the accused did not have the benefit of cross-examination by and through counsel. Thus, nothing occurring at the preliminary hearing in absence of counsel can substantially prejudice the rights of the accused on trial. . . .

This Court is of course bound by this construction of the governing Alabama law. . . . However, from the fact that in cases where the accused has no lawyer at

the hearing the Alabama courts prohibit the State's use at trial of anything that occurred at the hearing, it does not follow that the Alabama preliminary hearing is not a "critical stage" of the State's criminal process.

The determination whether the hearing is a "critical stage" requiring the provision of counsel depends, as noted, upon an analysis "whether potential substantial prejudice to defendant's rights inheres in the . . . confrontation and the ability of counsel to help avoid that prejudice." *United States* v. *Wade, supra,* at 227. Plainly the guiding hand of counsel at the preliminary hearing is essential to protect the indigent accused against an erroneous or improper prosecution. First, the lawyer's skilled examination and cross-examination of witnesses may expose fatal weaknesses in the State's case that may lead the magistrate to refuse to bind the accused over. Second, in any event, the skilled interrogation of witnesses by an experienced lawyer can fashion a vital impeachment tool for use in cross-examination of the State's witnesses at the trial, or preserve testimony favorable to the accused of a witness who does not appear at the trial. Third, trained counsel can more effectively discover the case the State has against his client and make possible the preparation of a proper defense to meet that case at the trial. Fourth, counsel can also be influential at the preliminary hearing in making effective arguments for the accused on such matters as the necessity for an early psychiatric examination or bail.

The inability of the indigent accused on his own to realize these advantages of a lawyer's assistance compels the conclusion that the Alabama preliminary hearing is a "critical stage" of the State's criminal process at which the accused is "as much entitled to such aid [of counsel] . . . as at the trial itself." *Powell* v. *Alabama, supra,* at 57.

. . . We accordingly vacate the petitioners' convictions and remand the case to the Alabama courts for such proceedings not inconsistent with this opinion as they may deem appropriate to determine whether such denial of counsel was harmless error, see *Gilbert* v. *California, supra,* at 272, and therefore whether the convictions should be reinstated or a new trial ordered.

It is so ordered.

MR. JUSTICE BLACKMUN took no part in the consideration or decision of this case. [Concurring and dissenting opinions omitted.]

WHAT DO YOU THINK?

1. Does the Court in its opinion provide adequate guidelines as to when an attorney is required?
2. What factors did the Court use in determining that the presence of counsel was essential for a fair trial?
3. What does the Court see as the role of counsel at a preliminary hearing?

The Williams *case looks at the requirement to give notice of alibi and the right to a jury of 12 persons.*

WILLIAMS V. FLORIDA
399 U.S. 78 (1970)

MR. JUSTICE WHITE delivered the opinion of the Court.

Prior to his trial for robbery in the State of Florida, petitioner filed a "Motion for a Protective Order," seeking to be excused from the requirements of Rule 1.200 of the Florida Rules of Criminal Procedure. That rule requires a defendant, on written demand of the prosecuting attorney, to give notice in advance of trial if the defendant intends to claim an alibi, and to furnish the prosecuting attorney with information as to the place where he claims to have been and with the names and addresses of the alibi witnesses he intends to use. In his motion petitioner openly declared his intent to claim an alibi, but objected to the further disclosure requirements on the ground that the rule "compels the Defendant in a criminal case to be a witness against himself" in violation of his Fifth and Fourteenth Amendment rights. The motion was denied. Petitioner also filed a pretrial motion to impanel a 12-man jury instead of the six-man jury provided by Florida law in all but capital cases. That motion too was denied. Petitioner was convicted as charged and was sentenced to life imprisonment. The District Court of Appeal affirmed, rejecting petitioner's claims that his Fifth and Sixth Amendment rights had been violated. We granted *certiorari*.

I.

Florida's notice-of-alibi rule is in essence a requirement that a defendant submit to a limited form of pretrial discovery by the State whenever he intends to rely at trial on the defense of alibi. In exchange for the defendant's disclosure of the witnesses he proposes to use to establish that defense, the State in turn is required to notify the defendant of any witnesses it proposes to offer in rebuttal to that defense. Both sides are under a continuing duty promptly to disclose the names and addresses of additional witnesses bearing on the alibi as they become available. The threatened sanction for failure to comply is the exclusion at trial of the defendant's alibi evidence—except for his own testimony—or, in the case of the State, the exclusion of the State's evidence offered in rebuttal of the alibi.

In this case, following the denial of his Motion for a Protective Order, petitioner complied with the alibi rule and gave the State the name and address of one Mary Scotty. Mrs. Scotty was summoned to the office of the State Attorney on the morning of the trial, where she gave pretrial testimony. At the trial itself, Mrs. Scotty, petitioner, and petitioner's wife all testified that the three of them had been in Mrs. Scotty's apartment during the time of the robbery. On two occasions during cross-examination of Mrs. Scotty, the prosecuting attorney confronted her with her earlier deposition in which she had given dates and times that in some respects did not correspond with the dates and times given at trial. Mrs. Scotty adhered to her trial story, insisting that she had been mistaken in her earlier testimony. The State also offered in rebuttal the testimony of one of the officers investigating the robbery who claimed that Mrs. Scotty had asked him for directions on the afternoon in question during the time when she claimed to have been in her apartment with petitioner and his wife.

We need not linger over the suggestion that the discovery permitted the State against petitioner in this case deprived him of "due process" or a "fair trial." Florida law provides for liberal discovery by the defendant against the State, and the notice-of-alibi rule is itself carefully hedged with reciprocal duties requiring state disclosure to the defendant. Given the ease with which an alibi can be fabricated, the State's interest in protecting itself against an eleventh-hour defense is both obvious and legitimate. Reflecting this interest, notice-of-alibi provisions, dating at least from 1927, are now in existence in a substantial number of States. The

adversary system of trial is hardly an end in itself; it is not yet a poker game in which players enjoy an absolute right always to conceal their cards until played. We find ample room in that system, at least as far as "due process" is concerned, for the instant Florida rule, which is designed to enhance the search for truth in the criminal trial by insuring both the defendant and the State ample opportunity to investigate certain facts crucial to the determination of guilt or innocence.

Petitioner's major contention is that he was "compelled . . . to be a witness against himself" contrary to the commands of the Fifth and Fourteenth Amendments because the notice-of-alibi rule required him to give the State the name and address of Mrs. Scotty in advance of trial and thus to furnish the State with information useful in convicting him. No pretrial statement of petitioner was introduced at trial; but armed with Mrs. Scotty's name and address and the knowledge that she was to be petitioner's alibi witness, the State was able to take her deposition in advance of trial and to find rebuttal testimony. Also, requiring him to reveal the elements of his defense is claimed to have interfered with his right to wait until after the State had presented its case to decide how to defend against it. We conclude, however, as has apparently every other court that has considered the issue, that the privilege against self-incrimination is not violated by a requirement that the defendant give notice of an alibi defense and disclose his alibi witnesses.

The defendant in a criminal trial is frequently forced to testify and to call other witnesses in an effort to reduce the risk of conviction. When he presents his witnesses, he must reveal their identity and submit them to cross-examination which in itself may prove incriminating or which may furnish the State with leads to incriminating rebuttal evidence. That the defendant faces such a dilemma demanding a choice between complete silence and presenting a defense has never been thought an invasion of the privilege against compelled self-incrimination. The pressures generated by the State's evidence may be severe but they do not vitiate the defendant's choice to present an alibi defense and witnesses to prove it, even though the attempted defense ends in catastrophe for the defendant. However "testimonial" or "incriminating" the alibi defense proves to be, it cannot be considered "compelled" within the meaning of the Fifth and Fourteenth Amendments.

Very similar constraints operate on the defendant when the State requires pretrial notice of alibi and the naming of alibi witnesses. Nothing in such a rule requires the defendant to rely on an alibi or prevents him from abandoning the defense; these matters are left to his unfettered choice. That choice must be made, but the pressures that bear on his pretrial decision are of the same nature as those that would induce him to call alibi witnesses at the trial: the force of historical fact beyond both his and the State's control and the strength of the State's case built on these facts. Response to that kind of pressure by offering evidence or testimony is not compelled self-incrimination transgressing the Fifth and Fourteenth Amendments.

In the case before us, the notice-of-alibi rule by itself in no way affected petitioner's crucial decision to call alibi witnesses or added to the legitimate pressures leading to that course of action. At most, the rule only compelled petitioner to accelerate the timing of his disclosure, forcing him to divulge at an earlier date information that the petitioner from the beginning planned to divulge at trial. Nothing in the Fifth Amendment privilege entitles a defendant as a matter of constitutional right to await the end of the State's case before announcing the nature of his defense, any more than it entitles him to await the jury's verdict on the State's case-in-chief before deciding whether or not to take the stand himself.

Petitioner concedes that absent the notice-of-alibi rule the Constitution would raise no bar to the court's granting the State a continuance at trial on the ground

of surprise as soon as the alibi witness is called. Nor would there be self-incrimination problems if, during that continuance, the State was permitted to do precisely what it did here prior to trial: take the deposition of the witness and find rebuttal evidence. But if so utilizing a continuance is permissible under the Fifth and Fourteenth Amendments, then surely the same result may be accomplished through pretrial discovery, as it was here, avoiding the necessity of a disrupted trial. We decline to hold that the privilege against compulsory self-incrimination guarantees the defendant the right to surprise the State with an alibi defense.

II.

In *Duncan* v. *Louisiana*, 391 U.S. 145 (1968), we held that the Fourteenth Amendment guarantees a right to trial by jury in all criminal cases that—were they to be tried in a federal court—would come within the Sixth Amendment's guarantee. Petitioner's trial for robbery on July 3, 1968, clearly falls within the scope of that holding. See *Baldwin* v. *New York*, *ante*, p. 66; *DeStefano* v. *Woods*, 392 U.S. 631 (1968). The question in this case then is whether the constitutional guarantee of a trial by "jury" necessarily requires trial by exactly 12 persons, rather than some lesser number—in this case, six. We hold that the 12-man panel is not a necessary ingredient of "trial by jury," and that respondent's refusal to impanel more than the six members provided for by Florida law did not violate petitioner's Sixth Amendment rights as applied to the States through the Fourteenth.

We had occasion in *Duncan* v. *Louisiana, supra*, to review briefly the oft-told history of the development of trial by jury in criminal cases. That history revealed a long tradition attaching great importance to the concept of relying on a body of one's peers to determine guilt or innocence as a safeguard against arbitrary law enforcement. That same history, however, affords little insight into the considerations that gradually led the size of that body to be generally fixed at 12. Some have suggested that the number 12 was fixed upon simply because that was the number of the presentment jury from the hundred, from which the petit jury developed. [399 U.S. 78, 88] Other, less circular but more fanciful reasons for the number 12 have been given, "but they were all brought forward after the number was fixed," and rest on little more than mystical or superstitious insights into the significance of "12." Lord Coke's explanation that the "number of twelve is much respected in holy writ, as 12 apostles, 12 stones, 12 tribes, etc.," is typical. In [399 U.S. 78, 89] short, while sometime in the 14th century the size of the jury at common law came to be fixed generally at 12, that particular feature of the jury system appears to have been a historical accident, unrelated to the great purposes which gave rise to the jury in the first place. The question before us is whether this accidental feature of the jury has been immutably codified into our Constitution.

This Court's earlier decisions have assumed an affirmative answer to this question. The leading case so construing the Sixth Amendment is *Thompson* v. *Utah*, 170 U.S. 343 (1898). There the defendant had been tried and convicted by a 12-man jury for a crime committed in the Territory of Utah. A new trial was granted, but by that time Utah had been admitted as a State. The defendant's new trial proceeded under Utah's Constitution, providing for a jury of only eight members. This Court reversed the resulting conviction, holding that Utah's constitutional provision was an ex post facto law as applied to the defendant. In reaching its conclusion, the Court announced that the Sixth Amendment was applicable to the defendant's trial when Utah was a Territory,

and that the jury referred to in the Amendment was a jury "constituted, as it was at common law, of twelve persons, neither more nor less." 170 U.S., at 349. Arguably unnecessary for the result, this announcement was supported simply by referring to the Magna Carta, and by quoting passages from treatises which noted—what has already been seen—that at common law the jury did indeed consist of 12. Noticeably absent was any discussion of the essential step in the argument: namely, that every feature of the jury as it existed at common law— whether incidental or essential to that institution—was necessarily included in the Constitution wherever that document referred to a "jury." Subsequent decisions have reaffirmed the announcement in *Thompson*, often in dictum and usually by relying—where there was any discussion of the issue at all—solely on the fact that the common-law jury consisted of 12. . . .

MR. JUSTICE BLACKMUN took no part in the consideration or decision of this case.

WHAT DO YOU THINK?

1. Do you agree with the Court's statement that "The adversary system of trial is hardly an end in itself; it is not yet a poker game in which players enjoy an absolute right always to conceal their cards until played"? Justify your answer.
2. Why should the accused be required to disclose an alibi defense prior to trial?

The Boykin *case looks at the duties of the court before accepting a guilty plea.*

BOYKIN V. ALABAMA
395 U.S. 238 (1969)

MR. JUSTICE DOUGLAS delivered the opinion of the Court.

In the spring of 1966, within the period of a fortnight, a series of armed robberies occurred in Mobile, Alabama. The victims, in each case, were local shopkeepers open at night who were forced by a gunman to hand over money. While robbing one grocery store, the assailant fired his gun once, sending a bullet through a door into the ceiling. A few days earlier in a drugstore, the robber had allowed his gun to discharge in such a way that the bullet, on ricochet from the floor, struck a customer in the leg. Shortly thereafter, a local grand jury returned five indictments against petitioner, a 27-year-old Negro, for common-law robbery—an offense punishable in Alabama by death.

Before the matter came to trial, the court determined that petitioner was indigent and appointed counsel to represent him. Three days later, at his arraignment, petitioner pleaded guilty to all five indictments. So far as the record shows, the judge asked no questions of petitioner concerning his plea, and petitioner did not address the court.

Trial strategy may of course make a plea of guilty seem the desirable course. But the record is wholly silent on that point and throws no light on it.

Alabama provides that when a defendant pleads guilty, "the court must cause the punishment to be determined by a jury" (except where it is required to be fixed by the court) and may "cause witnesses to be examined, to ascertain the character of the offense." Ala. Code, Tit. 15, 277 (1958). In the present case, a trial of that dimension was held with the prosecution presenting its case largely through eye-witness testimony. Although counsel for petitioner engaged in cursory cross-examination, petitioner neither testified himself nor presented testimony concerning his character and background. There was nothing to indicate that he had a prior criminal record.

In instructing the jury, the judge stressed that petitioner had pleaded guilty in five cases of robbery, defined as "the felonious taking of money . . . from another against his will . . . by violence or by putting him in fear . . . [carrying] from ten years minimum in the penitentiary to the supreme penalty of death by electrocution." The jury, upon deliberation, found petitioner guilty and sentenced him severally to die on each of the five indictments.

Taking an automatic appeal to the Alabama Supreme Court, petitioner argued that a sentence of death for common-law robbery was cruel and unusual punishment within the meaning of the Federal Constitution, a suggestion which that court unanimously rejected. 281 Ala. 659, 207 So.2d 412. On their own motion, however, four of the seven justices discussed the constitutionality of the process by which the trial judge had accepted petitioner's guilty plea. From the order affirming the trial court, three justices dissented on the ground that the record was inadequate to show that petitioner had intelligently and knowingly pleaded guilty. The fourth member concurred separately, conceding that "a trial judge should not accept a guilty plea unless he has determined that such a plea was voluntarily and knowingly entered by the defendant," but refusing "[f]or aught appearing" "to presume that the trial judge failed to do his duty." 281 Ala., at 662, 663, 207 So.2d, at 414, 415. We granted *certiorari*.

Respondent does not suggest that we lack jurisdiction to review the voluntary character of petitioner's guilty plea because he failed to raise that federal question below and the state court failed to pass upon it. But the question was raised on oral argument and we conclude that it is properly presented. The very Alabama statute (Ala. Code, Tit. 15, 382 [10] [1958]) that provides automatic appeal in capital cases also requires the reviewing court to comb the record for "any error prejudicial to the appellant, even though not called to our attention in brief of counsel." *Lee* v. *State*, 265 Ala. 623, 630, 93 So.2d 757, 763. The automatic appeal statute "is the only provision under the Plain Error doctrine of which we are aware in Alabama criminal appellate review." *Douglas* v. *State*, 42 Ala. App. 314, 331, n. 6, 163 So.2d 477, 494, n. 6. In the words of the Alabama Supreme Court:

> Perhaps it is well to note that in reviewing a death case under the automatic appeal statute, . . .we may consider any testimony that was seriously prejudicial to the rights of the appellant and may reverse thereon, even though no lawful objection or exception was made thereto. [Citations omitted.] Our review is not limited to the matters brought to our attention in brief of counsel. *Duncan* v. *State*, 278 Ala. 145, 157, 176 So.2d 840, 851

It was error, plain on the face of the record, for the trial judge to accept petitioner's guilty plea without an affirmative showing that it was intelligent and voluntary. That error, under Alabama procedure, was properly before the court below and considered explicitly by a majority of the justices and is properly before us on review.

A plea of guilty is more than a confession which admits that the accused did various acts; it is itself a conviction; nothing remains but to give judgment and determine punishment. See *Kercheval* v. *United States*, 274 U.S. 220, 223. Admissibility of a confession must be based on a "reliable determination on the voluntariness issue which satisfies the constitutional rights of the defendant." *Jackson* v. *Denno*, 378 U.S. 368, 387. The requirement that the prosecution spread on the record the prerequisites of a valid waiver is no constitutional innovation. In *Carnley* v. *Cochran*, 369 U.S. 506, 516, we dealt with a problem of waiver of the right to counsel, a Sixth Amendment right. We held: "Presuming waiver from a silent record is impermissible. The record must show, or there must be an allegation and evidence which show, that an accused was offered counsel but intelligently and understandingly rejected the offer. Anything less is not waiver."

We think that the same standard must be applied to determine whether a guilty plea is voluntarily made. For, as we have said, a plea of guilty is more than an admission of conduct; it is a conviction. Ignorance, incomprehension, coercion, terror, inducements, subtle or blatant threats might be a perfect cover-up of unconstitutionality. The question of an effective waiver of a federal constitutional right in a proceeding is of course governed by federal standards. *Douglas* v. *Alabama*, 380 U.S. 415, 422.

Several federal constitutional rights are involved in a waiver that takes place when a plea of guilty is entered in a state criminal trial. First is the privilege against compulsory self-incrimination guaranteed by the Fifth Amendment and applicable to the States by reason of the Fourteenth. *Malloy* v. *Hogan*, 378 U.S. 1. Second is the right to trial by jury. *Duncan* v. *Louisiana*, 391 U.S. 145. Third is the right to confront one's accusers. *Pointer* v. *Texas*, 380 U.S. 400. We cannot presume a waiver of these three important federal rights from a silent record.

What is at stake for an accused facing death or imprisonment demands the utmost solicitude of which courts are capable in canvassing the matter with the accused to make sure he has a full understanding of what the plea connotes and of its consequence. When the judge discharges that function, he leaves a record adequate for any review that may be later sought (*Garner* v. *Louisiana*, 368 U.S. 157, 173; *Specht* v. *Patterson*, 386 U.S. 605, 610), and forestalls the spin-off of collateral proceedings that seek to probe murky memories.

The three dissenting justices in the Alabama Supreme Court stated the law accurately when they concluded that there was reversible error "because the record does not disclose that the defendant voluntarily and understandingly entered his pleas of guilty." 281 Ala., at 663, 207 So.2d, at 415.

Reversed.

MR. JUSTICE HARLAN, whom MR. JUSTICE BLACK joins, dissenting. [Omitted]

WHAT DO YOU THINK?

1. Do you agree that the Court should not accept the defendant's guilty plea without an affirmative showing that it was intelligent and voluntary? Justify your opinion.

2. Why is a plea of guilty more than a confession?

3. Since Boykin never asserted that his plea was involuntary, should the Court have reversed the conviction? Justify your answer.

The Alford *case discusses the issue of whether an accused may plead guilty without admitting his or her guilt.*

NORTH CAROLINA V. ALFORD
400 U.S. 25 (1970)

Mr. Justice White delivered the opinion of the Court.

On December 2, 1963, Alford was indicted for first-degree murder, a capital offense under North Carolina law. The court appointed an attorney to represent him, and this attorney questioned all but one of the various witnesses who appellee said would substantiate his claim of innocence. The witnesses, however, did not support Alford's story but gave statements that strongly indicated his guilt. Faced with strong evidence of guilt and no substantial evidentiary support for the claim of innocence, Alford's attorney recommended that he plead guilty, but left the ultimate decision to Alford himself. The prosecutor agreed to accept a plea of guilty to a charge of second-degree murder, and on December 10, 1963, Alford pleaded guilty to the reduced charge. Before the plea was finally accepted by the trial court, the court heard the sworn testimony of a police officer who summarized the State's case. Two other witnesses besides Alford were also heard. Although there was no eyewitness to the crime, the testimony indicated that shortly before the killing Alford took his gun from his house, stated his intention to kill the victim, and returned home with the declaration that he had carried out the killing. After the summary presentation of the State's case, Alford took the stand and testified that he had not committed the murder but that he was pleading guilty because he faced the threat of the death penalty if he did not do so. In response to the questions of his counsel, he acknowledged that his counsel had informed him of the difference between second- and first-degree murder and of his rights in case he chose to go to trial. The trial court then asked appellee if, in light of his denial of guilt, he still desired to plead guilty to second-degree murder and appellee answered, "Yes, sir. I plead guilty on—from the circumstances that he [Alford's attorney] told me." After eliciting information about Alford's prior criminal record, which was a long one, the trial court sentenced him to 30 years' imprisonment, the maximum penalty for second-degree murder.

Alford sought post-conviction relief in the state court. Among the claims raised was the claim that his plea of guilty was invalid because it was the product of fear and coercion. After a hearing, the state court in 1965 found that the plea was "willingly, knowingly, and understandingly" made on the advice of competent counsel and in the face of a strong prosecution case. Subsequently, Alford petitioned for a writ of habeas corpus, first in the United States District Court for the Middle District of North Carolina, and then in the Court of Appeals for the Fourth Circuit. Both courts denied the writ on the basis of the state court's findings that Alford voluntarily and knowingly agreed to plead guilty. In 1967, Alford again petitioned for a writ of habeas corpus in the District Court for the Middle District of North Carolina. That court, without an evidentiary hearing, again denied relief on the grounds that the guilty plea was voluntary and waived all defenses and nonjurisdictional defects in any prior stage of the proceedings, and that the findings of the state court in 1965 clearly required rejection of Alford's claim that he was denied effective assistance of counsel prior to pleading guilty. On appeal, a divided panel of the Court of Appeals

for the Fourth Circuit reversed on the ground that Alford's guilty plea was made involuntarily. 405 F.2d 340 (1968). In reaching its conclusion, the Court of Appeals relied heavily on *United States* v. *Jackson*, 390 U.S. 570 (1968), which the court read to require invalidation of the North Carolina statutory framework for the imposition of the death penalty because North Carolina statutes encouraged defendants to waive constitutional rights by the promise of no more than life imprisonment if a guilty plea was offered and accepted. Conceding that *Jackson* did not require the automatic invalidation of pleas of guilty entered under the North Carolina statutes, the Court of Appeals ruled that Alford's guilty plea was involuntary because its principal motivation was fear of the death penalty. By this standard, even if both the judge and the jury had possessed the power to impose the death penalty for first-degree murder or if guilty pleas to capital charges had not been permitted, Alford's plea of guilty to second-degree murder should still have been rejected because impermissibly induced by his desire to eliminate the possibility of a death sentence. We noted probable jurisdiction. 394 U.S. 956 (1969). We vacate the judgment of the Court of Appeals and remand the case for further proceedings.

We held in *Brady* v. *United States*, 397 U.S. 742 (1970), that a plea of guilty which would not have been entered except for the defendant's desire to avoid a possible death penalty and to limit the maximum penalty to life imprisonment or a term of years was not for that reason compelled within the meaning of the Fifth Amendment. Jackson established no new test for determining the validity of guilty pleas. The standard was and remains whether the plea represents a voluntary and intelligent choice among the alternative courses of action open to the defendant. . . . That he would not have pleaded except for the opportunity to limit the possible penalty does not necessarily demonstrate that the plea of guilty was not the product of a free and rational choice, especially where the defendant was represented by competent counsel whose advice was that the plea would be to the defendant's advantage. The standard fashioned and applied by the Court of Appeals was therefore erroneous and we would, without more, vacate and remand the case for further proceedings with respect to any other claims of Alford which are properly before that court, if it were not for other circumstances appearing in the record which might seem to warrant an affirmance of the Court of Appeals.

As previously recounted, after Alford's plea of guilty was offered and the State's case was placed before the judge, Alford denied that he had committed the murder but reaffirmed his desire to plead guilty to avoid a possible death sentence and to limit the penalty to the 30-year maximum provided for second-degree murder. Ordinarily, a judgment of conviction resting on a plea of guilty is justified by the defendant's admission that he committed the crime charged against him and his consent that judgment be entered without a trial of any kind. The plea usually subsumes both elements, and justifiably so, even though there is no separate, express admission by the defendant that he committed the particular acts claimed to constitute the crime charged in the indictment. . . . Here Alford entered his plea but accompanied it with the statement that he had not shot the victim.

If Alford's statements were to be credited as sincere assertions of his innocence, there obviously existed a factual and legal dispute between him and the State. Without more, it might be argued that the conviction entered on his guilty plea was invalid, since his assertion of innocence negatived any admission of guilt, which, as we observed last Term in *Brady*, is normally "[c]entral to the plea and the foundation for entering judgment against the defendant. . . ."

In addition to Alford's statement, however, the court had heard an account of the events on the night of the murder, including information from Alford's ac-

quaintances that he had departed from his home with his gun stating his intention to kill and that he had later declared that he had carried out his intention. Nor had Alford wavered in his desire to have the trial court determine his guilt without a jury trial. Although denying the charge against him, he nevertheless preferred the dispute between him and the State to be settled by the judge in the context of a guilty plea proceeding rather than by a formal trial. Thereupon, with the State's telling evidence and Alford's denial before it, the trial court proceeded to convict and sentence Alford for second-degree murder.

State and lower federal courts are divided upon whether a guilty plea can be accepted when it is accompanied by protestations of innocence and hence contains only a waiver of trial but no admission of guilt. Some courts, giving expression to the principle that "[o]ur law only authorizes a conviction where guilt is shown," *Harris* v. *State*, 76 Tex. Cr. R. 126, 131, 172 S. W. 975, 977 (1915), require that trial judges reject such pleas . . . But others have concluded that they should not "force any defense on a defendant in a criminal case," particularly when advancement of the defense might "end in disaster. . . ." *Tremblay* v. *Overholser*, 199 F. Supp. 569, 570 (DC 1961). They have argued that, since "guilt, or the degree of guilt, is at times uncertain and elusive, [a]n accused, though believing in or entertaining doubts respecting his innocence, might reasonably conclude a jury would be convinced of his guilt and that he would fare better in the sentence by pleading guilty. . . ." *McCoy* v. *United States*, 124 U.S. App. D.C. 177, 179, 363 F.2d 306, 308 (1966). As one state court observed nearly a century ago, "[r]easons other than the fact that he is guilty may induce a defendant to so plead, . . . [and] [h]e must be permitted to judge for himself in this respect." *State* v. *Kaufman*, 51 Iowa 578, 580, 2 N. W. 275, 276 (1879) (dictum). . . .

This Court has not confronted this precise issue, but prior decisions do yield relevant principles. In *Lynch* v. *Overholser*, 369 U.S. 705 (1962), Lynch, who had been charged in the Municipal Court of the District of Columbia with drawing and negotiating bad checks, a misdemeanor punishable by a maximum of one year in jail, sought to enter a plea of guilty, but the trial judge refused to accept the plea since a psychiatric report in the judge's possession indicated that Lynch had been suffering from "a manic depressive psychosis, at the time of the crime charged," and hence might have been not guilty by reason of insanity. Although at the subsequent trial Lynch did not rely on the insanity defense, he was found not guilty by reason of insanity and committed for an indeterminate period to a mental institution. On habeas corpus, the Court ordered his release, construing the congressional legislation seemingly authorizing the commitment as not reaching a case where the accused preferred a guilty plea to a plea of insanity. The Court expressly refused to rule that Lynch had an absolute right to have his guilty plea accepted, but implied that there would have been no constitutional error had his plea been accepted even though evidence before the judge indicated that there was a valid defense.

The issue in *Hudson* v. *United States*, 272 U.S. 451 (1926), was whether a federal court has power to impose a prison sentence after accepting a plea of nolo contendere, a plea by which a defendant does not expressly admit his guilt, but nonetheless waives his right to a trial and authorizes the court for purposes of the case to treat him as if he were guilty. The Court held that a trial court does have such power, and, except for the cases which were rejected in *Hudson*, the federal courts have uniformly followed this rule, even in cases involving moral turpitude. *Bruce* v. *United States*, *supra*, at 343 n. 20, 379 F.2d at 120 n. 20 (dictum). . . . Implicit in the nolo contendere cases is a recognition that the Constitution does not bar imposition of a prison

sentence upon an accused who is unwilling expressly to admit his guilt but who, faced with grim alternatives, is willing to waive his trial and accept the sentence.

These cases would be directly in point if Alford had simply insisted on his plea but refused to admit the crime. The fact that his plea was denominated a plea of guilty rather than a plea of nolo contendere is of no constitutional significance with respect to the issue now before us, for the Constitution is concerned with the practical consequences, not the formal categorizations, of state law.... Thus, while most pleas of guilty consist of both a waiver of trial and an express admission of guilt, the latter element is not a constitutional requisite to the imposition of criminal penalty. An individual accused of crime may voluntarily, knowingly, and understandingly consent to the imposition of a prison sentence even if he is unwilling or unable to admit his participation in the acts constituting the crime.

Nor can we perceive any material difference between a plea that refuses to admit commission of the criminal act and a plea containing a protestation of innocence when, as in the instant case, a defendant intelligently concludes that his interests require entry of a guilty plea and the record before the judge contains strong evidence of actual guilt. Here the State had a strong case of first-degree murder against Alford. Whether he realized or disbelieved his guilt, he insisted on his plea because in his view he had absolutely nothing to gain by a trial and much to gain by pleading. Because of the overwhelming evidence against him, a trial was precisely what neither Alford nor his attorney desired. Confronted with the choice between a trial for first-degree murder, on the one hand, and a plea of guilty to second-degree murder, on the other, Alford quite reasonably chose the latter and thereby limited the maximum penalty to a 30-year term. When his plea is viewed in light of the evidence against him, which substantially negated his claim of innocence and which further provided a means by which the judge could test whether the plea was being intelligently entered ... its validity cannot be seriously questioned. In view of the strong factual basis for the plea demonstrated by the State and Alford's clearly expressed desire to enter it despite his professed belief in his innocence, we hold that the trial judge did not commit constitutional error in accepting it.[1]

Relying on *United States* v. *Jackson, supra,* Alford now argues in effect that the State should not have allowed him this choice but should have insisted on proving him guilty of murder in the first degree. The States in their wisdom may take this course by statute or otherwise and may prohibit the practice of accepting pleas to lesser included offenses under any circumstances. But this is not the mandate of the Fourteenth Amendment and the Bill of Rights. The prohibitions against involuntary or unintelligent pleas should not be relaxed, but neither should an exercise in arid logic render those constitutional guarantees counterproductive and put in jeopardy the very human values they were meant to preserve.

The Court of Appeals for the Fourth Circuit was in error to find Alford's plea of guilty invalid because it was made to avoid the possibility of the death penalty.

---

[1][Footnote 11] Our holding does not mean that a trial judge must accept every constitutionally valid guilty plea merely because a defendant wishes so to plead. A criminal defendant does not have an absolute right under the Constitution to have his guilty plea accepted by the court, see *Lynch* v. *Overholser,* 369 U.S., at 719 (by implication), although the States may by statute or otherwise confer such a right. Likewise, the States may bar their courts from accepting guilty pleas from any defendants who assert their innocence. Cf. Fed. Rule Crim. Proc. 11, which gives a trial judge discretion to "refuse to accept a plea of guilty...." We need not now delineate the scope of that discretion.

That court's judgment directing the issuance of the writ of habeas corpus is vacated and the case is remanded to the Court of Appeals for further proceedings consistent with this opinion.

It is so ordered.

MR. JUSTICE BLACK, while adhering to his belief that *United States* v. *Jackson*, 390 U.S. 570, was wrongly decided, concurs in the judgment and in substantially all of the opinion in this case.

MR. JUSTICE BRENNAN, with whom MR. JUSTICE DOUGLAS and MR. JUSTICE MARSHALL join, dissenting. [Omitted.]

WHAT DO YOU THINK?

1. Does an individual have a constitutional right to plead guilty?
2. Should an individual be allowed to plead guilty without admitting his or her guilt?
3. What does a judge need to do before accepting a guilty plea when the accused refuses to admit guilt?

SUMMARY

- The Eighth Amendment prohibits excessive bail. The traditional purpose of bail is to ensure the accused's presence at trial. Bail, for purposes of this chapter, includes the use of bail bonds, property deposits, third-party supervision, or other conditions of release designed to ensure that the accused returns to the court for trial.

- Generally the right to be released before trial is conditioned upon the accused's giving adequate assurance to the court that he or she will return to stand trial. The assurance is often in the form of bail.

- Bail was once limited almost entirely to the posting of cash or a secured bond by a bail-bondsman. Now in many jurisdictions partial bond may be posted with the court and the professional bail-bondsman eliminated.

- Pretrial detention impedes the defendant's ability to prepare for trial. He or she cannot help locate witnesses and other evidence. Most importantly, it disrupts an individual's life.

- Most defendants are released prior to trial. Courts rely on a variety of release mechanisms. Some retain a citation release or a summons to appear. Some are released before seeing a judge by posting bond according to a bond schedule that list amounts required for various offenses. A defendant arrested for an offense that has a bond schedule may generally be released at anytime that the appropriate bond is posted.

- At the arraignment, the defendant is informed of the charges and is given an opportunity to enter a plea to the charge or charges alleged in the complaint or indictment.

- The defendant may enter a plea at that time or request time to consider the plea to be entered. In most jurisdictions the defendant may plea (1) guilty, (2) not guilty, (3) nolo contendere, (4) not guilty by reason of insanity, or (5) former jeopardy.

- In some states, there is a first appearance which is different from an arraignment. Generally the first appearance is used to inform the defendant of the charges against him or her, the setting of release conditions or bail, and to inform the defendant of his or her rights.

- In most jurisdictions, a plea of guilty in a felony case must be made in open court personally by the defendant. Before a judge may accept a guilty plea, the judge is required to inform the defendant of his or her rights, the elements of the offense, the rights waived by a plea of guilty, and the maximum punishment for the crime to which the accused is pleading.

- A defendant may withdraw a guilty plea and enter a not guilty plea on the showing of good cause. Generally this withdrawal must be prior to sentencing.

- About one-half of the states use a preliminary hearing in lieu of a grand jury. It is also referred to as a preliminary examination. At the preliminary hearing, a magistrate decides whether there is adequate cause to require an accused to stand trial for the offense or offenses charged.

- The purpose of pretrial motions is to request that the judge take some action on particular matters. The motions may be made orally in some cases and in others are required to be written. It is not mandatory in most states for the defendant to be present at any hearings on the motions, although it is common practice for many judges to require the presence of the accused at these hearings.

DISCUSSION QUESTIONS

1. What should be the functions of bail?
2. What factors should a judge use in determining whether to release the defendant prior to trial?
3. What rights should individuals in pretrial confinement have?
4. One argument holds that our present system of pretrial confinement or bail punishes the poor defendant. What steps could be taken to ensure that this is not true?
5. What pleas may a defendant enter in your jurisdiction?
6. On what grounds may a defendant withdraw a plea of guilty?
7. What is the purpose of pretrial motions?
8. When would a motion to suppress the evidence be appropriate?

ENDNOTES

1. 404 U.S. 357 (1971).
2. *Stack* v. *Boyle*, 342 U.S. 1 (1951).
3. 481 U.S. 739 (1987).
4. 441 U.S. 520 (1979).
5. 420 U.S. 103 (1975).
6. 500 U.S. 44 (1991).
7. *Boykin* v. *Alabama*, 395 U.S. 238 (1969).
8. *North Carolina* v. *Alford*, 400 U.S. 25 (1970).
9. *Henderson* v. *Morgan*, 426 U.S. 637 (1976).
10. 397 U.S. 790 (1970).
11. The *Bell* v. *Wolfish* case is a comprehensive case involving prisoners' rights. Only a small portion of the decision is reprinted in this chapter.

10

COUNSEL

RIGHT TO COUNSEL

The Sixth Amendment to the U.S. Constitution provides that in all criminal prosecutions, the accused shall enjoy the right to have the assistance of counsel for his defense. The Supreme Court has indicated that the importance of the right to assistance of counsel cannot be overstated. The Court stated in *Gideon* v. *Wainwright*[1] that in our adversarial system of justice, defense counsel are a necessity, not a luxury. While *Gideon* is one of the most popular cases ever decided by the Supreme Court, the constitutional right to counsel was not imposed on the states until two years after the Fourth Amendment exclusionary rule had been imposed on them and eight years after *Griffin* v. *Illinois*.[2] The Court in *Griffin* ruled that indigent defendants must be furnished with trial transcripts at state expense if such transcripts are necessary to effectuate appellate review of the conviction. Most of the Supreme Court decisions on the right to counsel deal with the failure of the state to appoint counsel for an indigent accused and the issue of effective representation.

In our present justice system, the prosecutor acts on behalf of the state and the defense counsel acts on behalf of the accused. It is often pointed out that the only person in the courtroom acting on behalf of the defendant is the defense counsel. I once attended a criminal trial in Leningrad, USSR. At the start of the case, the defense counsel apologized to the judges for "defending an enemy of the people."

There is a difference between when a defendant has the right to assistance of counsel and when the defendant has a right to an appointed counsel. For all practical purposes, the defendant has the right to the assistance of counsel at all stages of a criminal case. The difficult question is, when the defendant cannot afford to retain [hire] an attorney, under what circumstances must the government provide him or her with one? The remedy for the violation of an accused right to counsel is that any subsequent conviction must be reversed.

Right to Appointed Counsel

Appointed counsel refers to counsel appointed by the Court to represent the defendant. *Retained counsel* refers to an attorney hired by the accused. The constitutional right of an indigent defendant to the assistance of court-appointed counsel was first recognized by the Supreme Court in *Powell* v. *Alabama*[3]. The Court based their ruling on the due process clause of the Fourteenth Amendment and carefully limited the decision to situations similar to that before the court—a capital case where the defendants were incapable of making a defense because of ignorance, feeble mindedness, and illiteracy. The Court suggested, however, that even an intelligent and educated defendant lacked the ability to represent himself and that there was a need for the guiding hand of counsel at every stage of the proceedings.

In *Johnson* v. *Zerbst*, the Supreme Court concluded that the average defendant does not have the professional skill to protect himself. The Court in *Zerbst*[4] held that federal courts are required to provide counsel in felony cases tried in federal courts.

In *Betts* v. *Brady*[5], the Court refused to extend *Zerbst* to state courts. The majority opinion in *Betts* held that due process did not necessarily require appointment of counsel in all state cases involving non-capital felonies.[6] The Court concluded that counsel are required to be appointed only in those cases where the particular circumstances indicated that the absence of counsel would result in a trial lacking fundamental fairness. *Betts* was overruled by *Gideon* v. *Wainwright*.[7]

The Supreme Court noted in *Powell* that the right to be heard would be, in many cases, of little avail if it did not comprehend the right to be heard by counsel. The Court in *Gideon* held that the defendant has a Sixth Amendment right to

---

DEFENSE COUNSEL

[Only those cases in which the defendants were convicted and sentenced to prison time were considered.]

Type of Counsel	State Defendants	Federal Defendants
Retained private counsel	22%	43%
Court appointed or public defender	76%	54%
Used both retained and appointed counsel	2%	2%

Information based on a survey of 680,000 state and 53,000 federal inmates.

Source: Bureau of Justice Statistics, 1996.

the assistance of counsel in felony cases and, if the accused could not afford one, he or she is entitled to a court-appointed counsel. For misdemeanor cases, the accused indigent has a right to appointed counsel in any misdemeanor trial in which a sentence of imprisonment could be imposed upon conviction.[8] In summary, the *Gideon*, *Argersinger*, and *Scott* cases may be read as follows: The indigent defendant is entitled to the appointment of counsel in all felony cases and in any misdemeanor case in which the defendant could receive imprisonment.

There is no constitutional right to appointed counsel of choice. Trial judges have broad discretion regarding the appointment of counsel. For example, in *Morris* v. *Slappy*[9], the Supreme Court rejected the concept that a defendant has a Sixth Amendment right to "a meaningful attorney–client relationship. In *Slappy*, the Court upheld a trial judge's refusal to grant a continuance so that the counsel originally appointed could defend him. He was represented over his objection by an appointed replacement counsel.

Right to Appointed Counsel on Appeal

An appeal is different from a trial in several basic areas. The language of the Sixth Amendment provides that the defendant is entitled to counsel for his or her "defense." In an appeal of a conviction the defendant is the moving party, and the government defends the conviction. An additional difference is that at the trial, the defendant is presumed innocent. During an appeal of a conviction, it is assumed that the decision of the trial court is correct.

The Supreme Court used the due process and equal protection clauses of the Fourteenth Amendment to hold that an indigent defendant has the right to appointed counsel on the first appeal of his or her conviction.[10] In the *Douglas* case, the Supreme Court invalidated a California requirement that before an indigent could have an appointed counsel on appeal, the indigent was required to convinced the appellate court that his or her appeal had some merit. The Court held that the requirement of merit was impermissible if persons wealthy enough to hire an attorney do not have to face the same requirement. The Court stated that the discrimination in this area was not between good and bad cases but between people who could afford an attorney and those who could not. The Court stated that this constitutes a violation of the right to due process and equal protection.

The Court noted that a state was not required to have an appellate court system, but if it did the constitution requires equal protection for indigent persons. The Court indicated that the right to appointed counsel applies only to those cases where an individual has a right to have an appellate court to decide his or her appeal. Accordingly, no right to appointed counsel exists on subsequent, discretionary appeals.[11] The Supreme Court in *Ross* reasoned that with the second appeal an indigent has meaningful access to the courts and an adequate opportunity to present his or her appeal without assistance of counsel. The defendant on subsequent appeals has the benefit of the brief filed in the first appellate procedure and many times a written opinion of the lower appellate court explaining the court's decision on the initial appeal.

Technical Support for Indigent Defendants

As noted earlier, an indigent defendant has the right to a trial transcript for his or her initial appeal of a conviction. In *Ake* v. *Oklahoma*[12], the Supreme Court held that the due process clause requires that indigent defendants receive technical

In The Supreme Court of The United States
Washington D.C.

Clarence Earl Gideon }
       Petitioner   Petition for a writ
vs.   of Certiorari Directed
H.G. Cochran, Jr, as   to The Supreme Court
Director, Divisions   State of Florida.
of corrections State
of Florida   No. – 890 Misc.

OCT. TERM 1961
U.S. Supreme Court

To: The Honorable Earl Warren, Chief
    Justice of the United States

    Comes now the petitioner, Clarence
Earl Gideon, a citizen of The United states
of America, in proper person, and appearing
as his own counsel. Who petitions this
Honorable Court for a Writ of Certiorari
directed to The Supreme Court of The State
of Florida. To review the order and Judge-
ment of the court below denying The
petitioner a writ of Habeus Corpus.

    Petitioner submits That The Supreme
Court of the United States has The authority
and jurisdiction to review The final Judge-
ment of The Supreme Court of The State
of Florida the highest court of The State
Under sec. 344 (B) Title 28 U.S.C.A. and
Because The "Due process clause" of the

fourteenth admendment of the constitution and the fifth and sixth articales of the Bill of rights has been violated. ~~For~~ Furthermore, the decision of the court below denying the petitioner a Writ of Habeus Corpus is also inconsistent and adverse to its own previous decisions in parelled cases.

Attached hereto, and made a part of this petition is a true copy of the petition for a Writ of Habeus Corpus as presented to the Florida Supreme Court, Petitioner asks this Honorable Court to cosider the same arguments and authorities cited in the petition for Writ of Habeus Corpus before the Florida Supreme Court, In consideration of this petition for a Writ of Certiorari.

The Supreme Court of Florida did not write any opinion, Order of that court denying petition for Writ of Habeus Corpus dated October 30, 1961, are attached hereto and made a part of this petition.

Petitioner contends that he has been deprived of due process of law Habeus Corpus petition alleging that the lower state court has decided a

DIVISION OF CORRECTIONS

CORRESPONDENCE REGULATIONS

MAIL WILL NOT BE DELIVERED WHICH DOES NOT CONFORM WITH THESE RULES

No. 1 -- Only 2 letters each week, not to exceed 2 sheets letter-size 8 1/2 x 11" and written *on one side only*, and if ruled paper, do not write between lines. *Your complete name* must be signed at the close of your letter. *Clippings, stamps, letters* from other people, *stationery* or *cash must not be enclosed* in your letters.

No. 2 -- All *letters* must be addressed in the *complete prison name* of the inmate. *Cell number*, where applicable, and *prison number* must be placed in lower left corner of envelope, with your complete name and address in the upper left corner.

No. 3 -- *Do not send any packages without a Package Permit.* Unauthorized *packages* will be destroyed.

No. 4 -- *Letters* must be written in English only.

No. 5 -- *Books, magazines, pamphlets,* and *newspapers* of reputable character will be delivered *only if* mailed direct from the publisher.

No. 6 -- *Money* must be sent in the form of *Postal Money Orders* only, in the inmate's complete prison name and prison number.

INSTITUTION _____ CELL NUMBER _____

NAME _____ NUMBER _____

federal question of substance, in a way
not in accord with the applicable
decisions of this Honorable Court. When
at the time of the petitioners trial.
He ask the lower Court for the aid of
counsel. The court refused this aid
Petitioner told the court that this
court had made decision to the effect
that all citizens tried for a felony crime
should have aid of counsel. the lower
court ignored this plea.

Petitioner alleges that prior to
petitioners convictions and sentence
for Breaking and Entering with the intent
to commit petty larceny. he had requested
aid of counsel, that at the time of his
conviction and sentence, petitioner was
without aid of counsel. That the court
refused and did not appoint counsel, and
that he was incapable adequately of
making his own defense. In consequence
of which he was made to stand trial, "Made
a Prime Facia showing of denial of
due process of law. (U.S.C.A. Const.
Amend. 14) William V. Kaiser vs.
State of Missouri 65 c.T. 363
Counsel must be assigned to the
accused if he is unable to employ

Wherefore the premises considered it is respectfully contented that the decision of the court below was in error and the case should be review by this court, accordingly the writ prepared and prayed for should be issue.

It is respectfully submitted

Clarence Earl Gideon
Clarence Earl Gideon
P.O. Box 221
Raiford Florida

State of Florida)
County of Union) ss

Petitioner, Clarence Earl Gideon, personally appearing before me and being duly sworn. Affirms that the foregoing petition and the facts set forth in the petition are correct and true

Sworn and subcribed before me this 5th. day of Jan 1962

Laurence Bunger
Notary Public
Notary Public, State of Florida at Large
My Commission Expires Sept. 19, 1962
Bonded by American Surety Co. of N.Y.

Copy furnished by General William Sutter, formerly Judge Advocate General, U.S. Army, and presently, Clerk, U.S. Supreme Court.

assistance in preparing for and defending the charges during the trial process. The technical assistance generally involves the hiring of expert witnesses and investigators. In most jurisdictions, the defense counsel must move (request to the court) for permission from the court to employ technical or investigative assistance. The court hearing on the motion for technical assistance is referred to as an "Ake" hearing. At the Ake hearing, the defense counsel must establish a need for the technical assistance before any assistance will be authorized. In addition, the judge will set a monetary limit on the hiring of experts.

What Constitutes Indigency?

The Supreme Court has not defined the level of poverty necessary to constitute indigency. It has left this decision to state and federal courts. Accordingly, there are varied standards on what constitutes indigency.

LAW IN
PRACTICE

TEXAS CODE OF CRIMINAL PROCEDURE, ARTICLE 26.05(E)

. . . [i]f the court determines that a defendant has financial resources that enable him to offset in part or in whole the costs of the legal services provided, including any expenses and costs, the court shall order the defendant to pay the amount that it finds the defendant is able to pay.

The below extract from a hearing in Bosque County, Texas, is representative of the problems involved with the appointment of attorneys.

EX PARTE MIRLO LUANA GONZALES, Applicant
Habeas Corpus Application
No. 72,606
from Bosque County

OPINION

Applicant was convicted of burglary of a habitation and sentenced to five years confinement, probated, and given a $3,000 fine. After the trial judge announced her sentence, applicant indicated her desire to appeal and requested a court-appointed attorney. The judge conducted a hearing on applicant's indigency. Applicant testified she did not have any dependents and that she was living with her fiancé. She worked two or three days a week installing sheet rock and rode to work with a neighbor. Applicant stated that looking for a different job with a steady income was difficult because she did not have adequate transportation. Applicant was in the process of repaying her father for money he posted on her trial bond and retaining her trial attorney. Additionally, applicant still owed her trial attorney $1,400. Applicant maintained she could not afford to pay for a statement of facts or hire an attorney for purposes of an appeal.

The trial judge asked applicant how much money she could "come up with on a monthly basis" to which applicant responded, "[p]robably about fifty a week." The trial court made a "limited finding of indigency in regard to statement of facts and in regard to appointed, or in regard to counsel on appeal." The judge appointed applicant appellate counsel and ordered the court reporter to prepare a statement of facts. Applicant was ordered to pay $50.00 per week to the district clerk for the statement of facts and the attorney on appeal until further order of the court.

A few months later, the State filed a Motion to Show Cause alleging applicant failed to make any of the $50.00 weekly payments ordered by the trial court. Appearing pro se at the hearing on the motion, applicant informed the judge she was employed at Taco Bell working eight hours a day, six days a week. She was living by herself and paying rent on a house her father vacated. Applicant was still without transportation and rode to work each day with a neighbor.

Question: *Should the judge hold her in contempt for failing to pay the weekly payments?*

RIGHT OF SELF-REPRESENTATION

Does the accused have a constitutional right of self-representation, or may the court force an attorney on a defendant? This issue was examined in *Faretta* v. *California*.[13] Faretta was charged with grand theft. Before trial, he notified the court that he wished to conduct his own defense. He was a high school graduate and had represented himself in a previous criminal case. The court compelled him to allow an attorney to represent himself, and he was convicted. The Supreme Court held that a criminal defendant has a Sixth Amendment right to conduct his own defense. That the right to counsel is just that—a right to counsel. To thrust a counsel on an unwilling defendant violates his or her rights under the Sixth Amendment. Accordingly, a defendant may waive his or her right to counsel and proceed *pro se* (representing him or herself). The Court also has stated that the right of self-representation "exists to affirm the dignity and autonomy of the accused and to allow the presentation of what may, at least occasionally, be the acucsed's best possible defense."[14]

As long as the waiver of counsel is intelligently made, the state cannot force counsel on the defendant. The requirement that the waiver be intelligently made does not mean that the waiver must be "wise" to be intelligently made. In *Patterson* v. *Illinois*[15], the Supreme Court stated that a trial judge must make a careful inquiry into the defendant's understanding of his or her right to counsel and his or her knowledge of the problems associated with self-representation. The trial judge may ask questions of the defendant designed to test the defendant's awareness of his or her rights, the statutory elements of the crime, and penalties associated with conviction. The trial judge also may attempt to dissuade the defendant from self-representation. If the defendant insists, however, he or she must be permitted to go to trial in *pro per*. (*Note*: There is an old saying in the legal field that an attorney who represents himself has a fool for a client. A similar statement could be made for a defendant who represents him or herself.)

In a case decided after *Faretta*, *McKaskle* v. *Wiggins*[16], the Supreme Court held that a court could force a defendant to have counsel in a consultant role while conducting his or her defense—that a standby counsel does not violate the right of self-representation. In this case, the counsel was at the defense table available for consultations when desired by the defense.

EFFECTIVE REPRESENTATION

The Supreme Court stated in *Strickland* v. *Washington*[17] that the fact that a person who happens to be a lawyer is present at trial alongside the accused is not enough to satisfy the Sixth Amendment. The right to counsel includes the right to effective representation of the client. The Court also held that representation is ineffective if counsel's conduct so undermines the proper functioning of the adversarial process that the trial cannot be relied on as having produced a just result.

Strickland Test

The courts use a two-pronged test (Strickland test) in looking at ineffectiveness of representation claims. To establish that the defendant has been denied the effective assistance of counsel, the defendant must establish (1) that counsel's performance was deficient; and (2) the deficient performance prejudiced the defense.[18]

The proper measurement of an attorney's performance is an objective standard based on prevailing professional norms. There is a strong presumption that the individual received effective assistance of counsel. Any scrutiny of an attorney's performance must be highly deferential. Strategic decisions of an attorney are virtually unchallengeable if they were made after an adequate investigation of the law and facts that relate to the decision.

The Strickland test applies to both retained and appointed counsel.[19] If there is no right to counsel, there is no right to effective assistance of counsel. For example, there is no right to counsel for subsequent discretionary appeals. Accordingly, one may not complain of ineffective assistance of counsel because counsel made an error in a discretionary appeal.

The Supreme Court in Strickland noted that effective assistance of counsel includes both a reasonably thorough investigation and a reasonably competent presentation of the case in court. In order to make informed decisions, the counsel must know the pertinent information concerning the case. Ordinarily this information will be discovered by the counsel in his or her investigation of the facts. For example, a complete failure to interview any witnesses or to conduct any type of investigation will generally be considered as sufficient to find that the representation fell below the objective standards of the profession. The reasonableness of the counsel's investigation is determined by an objective standard. When an accused informed his counsel that he had no prior involvement with the judicial system, it probably would not be error to rely on the accused's presentation of facts, i.e., he had no criminal record.

The presentation of a defense includes the function of decision-making. Those decisions could include which witnesses to call, whether to call the accused to the stand, etc. If counsel makes a decision after an adequate investigation of the facts, seldom will the court find ineffective representation of the defendant. As the Court noted in Strickland, every effort must be made to eliminate the distorting effects of hindsight— counsel's conduct must be evaluated based on the situation at the time the decision in question was made.

To determine if the counsel's errors denied the defendant a fair trial, the court uses the "harmless error" test. That test tries to determine if the error might reasonably have affected the verdict. In applying the harmless error test, the court also looks at the strengths and weaknesses of the government's case. If the government's evidence of guilt was strong, the courts are less likely to find reversible error. If the government's case was weak, reversible error is more likely to be found.

Multiple Representation

The Supreme Court in *Holloway* v. *Arkansas*[20], looked at the issue of multiple representation. Multiple representation involves the representation of more than one client for the same criminal transaction. For example, one attorney is appointed to defend two people charged with jointly committing a crime. In this situation, the counsel cannot explore the opportunity to turn state's evidence and shift the blame from one client to the other since she has a duty to protect each client. Multiple representation also may prevent the attorney from challenging the admission of evidence that is favorable to one of her clients, but unfavorable to the other.

The Strickland two-part test does not apply to those situations where the attorney has a conflict of interest. The standards are different in those cases. The Court in Holloway held that multiple representation is not a *per se* violation of the right to effective assistance of counsel. The Court held, however, that when multiple representation is involved the court must hold a hearing to ensure that the defendants understand the pitfalls of multiple representation. If the trial judge does not hold such a hearing, reversal is required. While the client has a right to conflict-free representation, he or she may waive this right as long as the waiver is made knowingly, intelligently, and voluntarily. A court is not, however, required to accept a waiver. Many judges will not allow a defendant to waive a possible conflict of interest. The courts have traditionally upheld the right of judges to refuse waivers.

Prejudice is presumed if the defendants' counsel have conflicting interests. A defendant may, however, waive his or her right to a conflict-free counsel. The waiver is generally required to be in open court and made a part of the record.

WHEN THE RIGHT TO COUNSEL ATTACHES

While the Sixth Amendment guarantees the right to assistance of counsel in criminal prosecutions, the amendment fails to indicate when the right begins. As noted earlier, a defendant has the right to the presence of counsel at a lineup after formal charges have been filed.[21] Under *Miranda*, a defendant has the right to consult with an attorney during custodial interrogation. In both of those situations the right to counsel is limited. For example, for custodial interrogation the right to counsel exists only if the police wish to continue the interrogation and the defendant fails to waive his or her right to counsel. In most situations involving custodial interrogations, when the defendant requests to consult an attorney the police merely cease the interrogation rather than take the necessary steps to have counsel appointed. For purposes of criminal trial proceedings, when does the right to counsel attach?

The Supreme Court has adopted a two-part test for identifying those events where assistance of counsel is required for criminal trial proceedings. First, the event must occur after formal criminal proceedings have commenced. Next, the event must be a critical stage in the trial process. It is not easy, however, to identify what is a critical stage in the criminal trial proceedings.

As a general rule, the formal commencement of a criminal prosecution begins with the intervention of a prosecutor or a judge in the case. For example, the act of a prosecutor filing a grand jury indictment or an information with the court is the commencement of judicial proceedings. Bringing the defendant before the court for an initial appearance or an arraignment also constitutes a commencement of a criminal prosecution. If the event occurs before the commencement of formal criminal proceedings, it is not part of a criminal prosecution.

A "critical stage" of a criminal trial is a trial-like event, where the defendant is confronted by the procedural system and/or the prosecutor and is a situation where the results, without the presence of counsel, could reduce the trial itself to a mere formality.[22] Some events which the courts have determined to be critical include the preliminary hearing, the post-indictment lineup, plea negotiations, the sentencing hearing, and the deferred sentencing hearing. Some of the events which the court have considered as not critical and thus presence of counsel is not required include photographic lineups, pre-indictment lineups, probation revocation, and administrative detention of inmates.

There are some events that are non-critical or where criminal prosecution has not begun in which the Supreme Court has used the due process clause to require the appointment of counsel to indigent defendants. These events include in-custody interrogation under *Miranda* and in those probation or parole revocation hearings with complex issues.

CAPSTONE CASES

GIDEON V. WAINWRIGHT
372 U.S. 335 (1963)

MR. JUSTICE BLACK delivered the opinion of the Court.

Petitioner was charged in a Florida state court with having broken and entered a poolroom with intent to commit a misdemeanor. This offense is a felony under Florida law. Appearing in court without funds and without a lawyer, petitioner asked the court to appoint counsel for him, whereupon the following colloquy took place:

> "The COURT: Mr. Gideon, I am sorry, but I cannot appoint Counsel to represent you in this case. Under the laws of the State of Florida, the only time the Court can appoint Counsel to represent a Defendant is when that person is charged with a capital offense. I am sorry, but I will have to deny your request to appoint Counsel to defend you in this case.
>
> "The DEFENDANT: The United States Supreme Court says I am entitled to be represented by Counsel."

Put to trial before a jury, Gideon conducted his defense about as well as could be expected from a layman. He made an opening statement to the jury, cross-examined the State's witnesses, presented witnesses in his own defense, declined to testify himself, and made a short argument "emphasizing his innocence to the charge contained in the Information filed in this case." The jury returned a verdict of guilty, and petitioner was sentenced to serve five years in the state prison. Later, petitioner

Justice Hugo Black was appointed to the Supreme Court by President Franklin Roosevelt and served from 1937 to 1971. (Collection of the Supreme Court of the United States.)

filed in the Florida Supreme Court this habeas corpus petition attacking his conviction and sentence on the ground that the trial court's refusal to appoint counsel for him denied him rights "guaranteed by the Constitution and the Bill of Rights by the United States Government." Treating the petition for habeas corpus as properly before it, the State Supreme Court, "upon consideration thereof" but without an opinion, denied all relief. Since 1942, when *Betts* v. *Brady*, 316 U.S. 455, was decided by a divided Court, the problem of a defendant's federal constitutional right to counsel in a state court has been a continuing source of controversy and litigation in both state and federal courts. To give this problem another review here, we granted *certiorari*. . . . Since Gideon was proceeding *in forma pauperis*, we appointed counsel to represent him and requested both sides to discuss in their briefs and oral arguments the following: "Should this Court's holding in *Betts* v. *Brady*, 316 U.S. 455, be reconsidered?". . . .

The Sixth Amendment provides, "In all criminal prosecutions, the accused shall enjoy the right . . . to have the Assistance of Counsel for his defence." We have construed this to mean that in federal courts counsel must be provided for defendants unable to employ counsel unless the right is competently and intelligently waived. Betts argued that this right is extended to indigent defendants in state courts by the Fourteenth Amendment. In response the Court stated that, while the Sixth Amendment laid down "no rule for the conduct of the States, the question recurs

whether the constraint laid by the Amendment upon the national courts expresses a rule so fundamental and essential to a fair trial, and so, to due process of law, that it is made obligatory upon the States by the Fourteenth Amendment." In order to decide whether the Sixth Amendment's guarantee of counsel is of this fundamental nature, the Court in *Betts* set out and considered "[r]elevant data on the subject . . . afforded by constitutional and statutory provisions subsisting in the colonies and the States prior to the inclusion of the Bill of Rights in the national Constitution, and in the constitutional, legislative, and judicial history of the States to the present date." On the basis of this historical data the Court concluded that "appointment of counsel is not a fundamental right, essential to a fair trial." 316 U.S., at 471. It was for this reason the *Betts* Court refused to accept the contention that the Sixth Amendment's guarantee of counsel for indigent federal defendants was extended to or, in the words of that Court, "made obligatory upon the States by the Fourteenth Amendment." Plainly, had the Court concluded that appointment of counsel for an indigent criminal defendant was "a fundamental right, essential to a fair trial." It would have held that the Fourteenth Amendment requires appointment of counsel in a state court, just as the Sixth Amendment requires in a federal court.

. . . We accept *Betts* v. *Brady*'s assumption, based as it was on our prior cases, that a provision of the Bill of Rights which is "fundamental and essential to a fair trial" is made obligatory upon the States by the Fourteenth Amendment. We think the Court in *Betts* was wrong, however, in concluding that the Sixth Amendment's guarantee of counsel is not one of these fundamental rights. Ten years before *Betts* v. *Brady*, this Court, after full consideration of all the historical data examined in *Betts*, had unequivocally declared that "the right to the aid of counsel is of this fundamental character." *Powell* v. *Alabama*, 287 U.S. 45, 68 (1932). While the Court at the close of its *Powell* opinion did by its language, as this Court frequently does, limit its holding to the particular facts and circumstances of that case, its conclusions about the fundamental nature of the right to counsel are unmistakable. Several years later, in 1936, the Court reemphasized what it had said about the fundamental nature of the right to counsel in this language:

> We concluded that certain fundamental rights, safeguarded by the first eight amendments against federal action, were also safeguarded against state action by the due process of law clause of the Fourteenth Amendment, and among them the fundamental right of the accused to the aid of counsel in a criminal prosecution. *Grosjean* v. *American Press Co.*, 297 U.S. 233, 243–244 (1936)

And again in 1938 this Court said:

> [The assistance of counsel] is one of the safeguards of the Sixth Amendment deemed necessary to insure fundamental human rights of life and liberty. . . . The Sixth Amendment stands as a constant admonition that if the constitutional safeguards it provides be lost, justice will not "still be done." . . .

. . . In returning to these old precedents, sounder we believe than the new, we but restore constitutional principles established to achieve a fair system of justice. Not only these precedents but also reason and reflection require us to recognize that in our adversary system of criminal justice, any person haled into court, who is too poor to hire a lawyer, cannot be assured a fair trial unless counsel is provided for him. This seems to us to be an obvious truth. Governments, both state and federal, quite properly spend vast sums of money to establish machinery to try defendants accused of crime. Lawyers to prosecute are everywhere deemed essential to protect the public's interest in an orderly society. Similarly, there are few defendants charged

Justice Hugo Black was appointed to the
Supreme Court by President Franklin Roosevelt
and served from 1937 to 1971. (Collection of
the Supreme Court of the United States.)

filed in the Florida Supreme Court this habeas corpus petition attacking his conviction
and sentence on the ground that the trial court's refusal to appoint counsel for him denied him rights "guaranteed by the Constitution and the Bill of Rights by the United
States Government." Treating the petition for habeas corpus as properly before it, the
State Supreme Court, "upon consideration thereof" but without an opinion, denied all
relief. Since 1942, when *Betts* v. *Brady*, 316 U.S. 455, was decided by a divided Court,
the problem of a defendant's federal constitutional right to counsel in a state court has
been a continuing source of controversy and litigation in both state and federal courts.
To give this problem another review here, we granted *certiorari*. . . . Since Gideon was
proceeding *in forma pauperis*, we appointed counsel to represent him and requested
both sides to discuss in their briefs and oral arguments the following: "Should this
Court's holding in *Betts* v. *Brady*, 316 U.S. 455, be reconsidered?". . . .

    The Sixth Amendment provides, "In all criminal prosecutions, the accused shall
enjoy the right . . . to have the Assistance of Counsel for his defence." We have construed this to mean that in federal courts counsel must be provided for defendants
unable to employ counsel unless the right is competently and intelligently waived.
Betts argued that this right is extended to indigent defendants in state courts by the
Fourteenth Amendment. In response the Court stated that, while the Sixth
Amendment laid down "no rule for the conduct of the States, the question recurs

whether the constraint laid by the Amendment upon the national courts expresses a rule so fundamental and essential to a fair trial, and so, to due process of law, that it is made obligatory upon the States by the Fourteenth Amendment." In order to decide whether the Sixth Amendment's guarantee of counsel is of this fundamental nature, the Court in *Betts* set out and considered "[r]elevant data on the subject . . . afforded by constitutional and statutory provisions subsisting in the colonies and the States prior to the inclusion of the Bill of Rights in the national Constitution, and in the constitutional, legislative, and judicial history of the States to the present date." On the basis of this historical data the Court concluded that "appointment of counsel is not a fundamental right, essential to a fair trial." 316 U.S., at 471. It was for this reason the *Betts* Court refused to accept the contention that the Sixth Amendment's guarantee of counsel for indigent federal defendants was extended to or, in the words of that Court, "made obligatory upon the States by the Fourteenth Amendment." Plainly, had the Court concluded that appointment of counsel for an indigent criminal defendant was "a fundamental right, essential to a fair trial." It would have held that the Fourteenth Amendment requires appointment of counsel in a state court, just as the Sixth Amendment requires in a federal court.

. . . We accept *Betts* v. *Brady*'s assumption, based as it was on our prior cases, that a provision of the Bill of Rights which is "fundamental and essential to a fair trial" is made obligatory upon the States by the Fourteenth Amendment. We think the Court in *Betts* was wrong, however, in concluding that the Sixth Amendment's guarantee of counsel is not one of these fundamental rights. Ten years before *Betts* v. *Brady*, this Court, after full consideration of all the historical data examined in *Betts*, had unequivocally declared that "the right to the aid of counsel is of this fundamental character." *Powell* v. *Alabama*, 287 U.S. 45, 68 (1932). While the Court at the close of its *Powell* opinion did by its language, as this Court frequently does, limit its holding to the particular facts and circumstances of that case, its conclusions about the fundamental nature of the right to counsel are unmistakable. Several years later, in 1936, the Court reemphasized what it had said about the fundamental nature of the right to counsel in this language:

> We concluded that certain fundamental rights, safeguarded by the first eight amendments against federal action, were also safeguarded against state action by the due process of law clause of the Fourteenth Amendment, and among them the fundamental right of the accused to the aid of counsel in a criminal prosecution. *Grosjean* v. *American Press Co.*, 297 U.S. 233, 243–244 (1936)

And again in 1938 this Court said:

> [The assistance of counsel] is one of the safeguards of the Sixth Amendment deemed necessary to insure fundamental human rights of life and liberty. . . . The Sixth Amendment stands as a constant admonition that if the constitutional safeguards it provides be lost, justice will not "still be done.". . .

. . . In returning to these old precedents, sounder we believe than the new, we but restore constitutional principles established to achieve a fair system of justice. Not only these precedents but also reason and reflection require us to recognize that in our adversary system of criminal justice, any person haled into court, who is too poor to hire a lawyer, cannot be assured a fair trial unless counsel is provided for him. This seems to us to be an obvious truth. Governments, both state and federal, quite properly spend vast sums of money to establish machinery to try defendants accused of crime. Lawyers to prosecute are everywhere deemed essential to protect the public's interest in an orderly society. Similarly, there are few defendants charged

with crime, few indeed, who fail to hire the best lawyers they can get to prepare and present their defenses. That government hires lawyers to prosecute and defendants who have the money hire lawyers to defend are the strongest indications of the widespread belief that lawyers in criminal courts are necessities, not luxuries. The right of one charged with crime to counsel may not be deemed fundamental and essential to fair trials in some countries, but it is in ours. From the very beginning, our state and national constitutions and laws have laid great emphasis on procedural and substantive safeguards designed to assure fair trials before impartial tribunals in which every defendant stands equal before the law. This noble ideal cannot be realized if the poor man charged with crime has to face his accusers without a lawyer to assist him. A defendant's need for a lawyer is nowhere better stated than in the moving words of Mr. Justice Sutherland in *Powell* v. *Alabama*:

> The right to be heard would be, in many cases, of little avail if it did not comprehend the right to be heard by counsel. Even the intelligent and educated layman has small and sometimes no skill in the science of law. If charged with crime, he is incapable, generally, of determining for himself whether the indictment is good or bad. He is unfamiliar with the rules of evidence. Left without the aid of counsel he may be put on trial without a proper charge, and convicted upon incompetent evidence, or evidence irrelevant to the issue or otherwise inadmissible. He lacks both the skill and knowledge adequately to prepare his defense, even though he have a perfect one. He requires the guiding hand of counsel at every step in the proceedings against him. Without it, though he be not guilty, he faces the danger of conviction because he does not know how to establish his innocence. 287 U.S., at 68–69

The Court in *Betts* v. *Brady* departed from the sound wisdom upon which the Court's holding in *Powell* v. *Alabama* rested. Florida, supported by two other States, has asked that *Betts* v. *Brady* be left intact. Twenty-two States, as friends of the Court, argue that *Betts* was "an anachronism when handed down" and that it should now be overruled. We agree.

The judgment is reversed and the cause is remanded to the Supreme Court of Florida for further action not inconsistent with this opinion. Reversed.

[Concurring opinions of JUSTICE MARSHALL, HARLAN, and CLARK are omitted.]

WHAT DO YOU THINK?

1. Should the accused have a right to counsel in all criminal cases? Should he or she have a right to state or federally appointed counsel in those cases where the defendant cannot afford an attorney?

2. According to the *Gideon* case, when does the defendant have a right to appointed counsel?

The Gideon *case involved felony charges. Does an indigent defendant have the right to appointment of counsel in non-felony cases? If so, in which cases? The next case looks at these issues.*

ARGERSINGER V. HAMLIN
407 U.S. 25 (1972)

MR. JUSTICE DOUGLAS delivered the opinion of the Court.

Petitioner, an indigent, was charged in Florida with carrying a concealed weapon, an offense punishable by imprisonment up to six months, a $1,000 fine, or both. The trial was to a judge, and petitioner was unrepresented by counsel. He was sentenced to serve 90 days in jail, and brought this habeas corpus action in the Florida Supreme Court, alleging that, being deprived of his right to counsel, he was unable as an indigent layman properly to raise and present to the trial court good and sufficient defenses to the charge for which he stands convicted. The Florida Supreme Court by a four-to-three decision, in ruling on the right to counsel, followed the line we marked out in *Duncan* v. *Louisiana*, 391 U.S. 145, 159, as respects the right to trial by jury and held that the right to court-appointed counsel extends only to trials "for non-petty offenses punishable by more than six months imprisonment." 236 So.2d 442, 443.

The case is here on a petition for *certiorari*, which we granted. . . . We reverse.

The Sixth Amendment, which in enumerated situations has been made applicable to the States by reason of the Fourteenth Amendment. . . . ; and *In re Oliver*, 333 U.S. 257 provides specified standards for "all criminal prosecutions."

One is the requirement of a "public trial." *In re Oliver, supra*, held that the right to a "public trial" was applicable to a state proceeding even though only a 60-day sentence was involved. 333 U.S., at 272.

Another guarantee is the right to be informed of the nature and cause of the accusation. Still another, the right of confrontation. *Pointer* v. *Texas, supra*. And another, compulsory process for obtaining witnesses in one's favor. *Washington* v. *Texas, supra*. We have never limited these rights to felonies or to lesser but serious offenses.

. . . The Sixth Amendment thus extended the right to counsel beyond its common-law dimensions. But there is nothing in the language of the Amendment, its history, or in the decisions of this Court, to indicate that it was intended to embody a retraction of the right in petty offenses wherein the common law previously did require that counsel be provided. . . .

We reject, therefore, the premise that since prosecutions for crimes punishable by imprisonment for less than six months may be tried without a jury, they may also be tried without a lawyer.

. . . The requirement of counsel may well be necessary for a fair trial even in a petty-offense prosecution. We are by no means convinced that legal and constitutional questions involved in a case that actually leads to imprisonment even for a brief period are any less complex than when a person can be sent off for six months or more. See, e.g., *Powell* v. *Texas*, 392 U.S. 514; *Thompson* v. *Louisville*, 362 U.S. 199; *Shuttlesworth* v. *Birmingham*, 382 U.S. 87.

The trial of vagrancy cases is illustrative. While only brief sentences of imprisonment may be imposed, the cases often bristle with thorny constitutional questions. See *Papachristou* v. *Jacksonville*, 405 U.S. 156.

. . . There is evidence of the prejudice which results to misdemeanor defendants from this "assembly-line justice." One study concluded that "[m]isdemeanants represented by attorneys are five times as likely to emerge from police court with all charges dismissed as are defendants who face similar charges without counsel." American Civil Liberties Union, Legal Counsel for Misdemeanants, Preliminary Report 1 (1970).

We must conclude, therefore, that the problems associated with misdemeanor and petty offenses often require the presence of counsel to insure the accused a fair trial. MR. JUSTICE POWELL suggests that these problems are raised even in situations where there is no prospect of imprisonment. *Post*, at 48. We need not consider the requirements of the Sixth Amendment as regards the right to counsel where loss of liberty is not involved, however, for here petitioner was in fact sentenced to jail.

And, as we said in *Baldwin* v. *New York*, 399 U.S., at 73, "the prospect of imprisonment for however short a time will seldom be viewed by the accused as a trivial or 'petty' matter and may well result in quite serious repercussions affecting his career and his reputation."

We hold, therefore, that absent a knowing and intelligent waiver, no person may be imprisoned for any offense, whether classified as petty, misdemeanor, or felony, unless he was represented by counsel at his trial.

The American Bar Association Project on Standards for Criminal Justice states:

> As a matter of sound judicial administration it is preferable to disregard the characterization of the offense as felony, misdemeanor or traffic offense. Nor is it adequate to require the provision of defense services for all offenses which carry a sentence to jail or prison. Often, as a practical matter, such sentences are rarely if ever imposed for certain types of offenses, so that for all intents and purposes the punishment they carry is at most a fine. Thus, the standard seeks to distinguish those classes of cases in which there is real likelihood that incarceration may follow conviction from those types in which there is no such likelihood. It should be noted that the standard does not recommend a determination of the need for counsel in terms of the facts of each particular case; it draws a categorical line at those types of offenses for which incarceration as a punishment is a practical possibility. Providing Defense Services 40 (Approved Draft 1968)

Under the rule we announce today, every judge will know when the trial of a misdemeanor starts that no imprisonment may be imposed, even though local law permits it, unless the accused is represented by counsel. He will have a measure of the seriousness and gravity of the offense and therefore know when to name a lawyer to represent the accused before the trial starts.

The run of misdemeanors will not be affected by today's ruling. But in those that end up in the actual deprivation of a person's liberty, the accused will receive the benefit of "the guiding hand of counsel" so necessary when one's liberty is in jeopardy.

Reversed.

MR. JUSTICE BRENNAN, with whom MR. JUSTICE DOUGLAS and MR. JUSTICE STEWART join, [concurring omitted].

WHAT DO YOU THINK?

1. Do you agree that counsel should be appointed for indigent defendants?
2. Under the rules of this case, when must a state provide counsel for an indigent defendant?
3. If an accused is being prosecuted for an offense that does not involve any possibility of confinement, does he or she still have a right to be represented by counsel at his or her expense?

Does an indigent have the right to an appointed counsel on appeal? The Douglas *case examines this issue.*

DOUGLAS V. CALIFORNIA
372 U.S. 353 (1963)

MR. JUSTICE DOUGLAS delivered the opinion of the Court.

Petitioners, Bennie Will Meyes and William Douglas, were jointly tried and convicted in a California court on an information charging them with 13 felonies. A single public defender was appointed to represent them. At the commencement of the trial, the defender moved for a continuance, stating that the case was very complicated, that he was not as prepared as he felt he should be because he was handling a different defense every day, and that there was a conflict of interest between the petitioners requiring the appointment of separate counsel for each of them. This motion was denied. Thereafter, petitioners dismissed the defender, claiming he was unprepared, and again renewed motions for separate counsel and for a continuance. These motions also were denied, and petitioners were ultimately convicted by a jury of all 13 felonies, which included robbery, assault with a deadly weapon, and assault with intent to commit murder. Both were given prison terms. Both appealed as of right to the California District Court of Appeal. That court affirmed their convictions. 187 Cal. App. 2d 802, 10 Cal. Rptr. 188. Both Meyes and Douglas then petitioned for further discretionary review in the California Supreme Court, but their petitions were denied without a hearing. 187 Cal. App. 2d, at 813, 10 Cal. Rptr., at 195. We granted *certiorari*. 368 U.S. 815.

Although several questions are presented in the petition for *certiorari*, we address ourselves to only one of them. The record shows that petitioners requested, and were denied, the assistance of counsel on appeal, even though it plainly appeared they were indigents. In denying petitioners' requests, the California District Court of Appeal stated that it had "gone through" the record and had come to the conclusion that "no good whatever could be served by appointment of counsel." 187 Cal. App. 2d 802, 812, 10 Cal. Rptr. 188, 195. The District Court of Appeal was acting in accordance with a California rule of criminal procedure which provides that state appellate courts, upon the request of an indigent for counsel, may make "an independent investigation of the record and determine whether it would be of advantage to the defendant or helpful to the appellate court to have counsel appointed. . . .

After such investigation, appellate courts should appoint counsel if, in their opinion, it would be helpful to the defendant or the court, and should deny the appointment of counsel only if in their judgment such appointment would be of no value to either the defendant or the court." *People* v. *Hyde*, 51 Cal. 2d 152, 154, 331 P.2d 42, 43.

We agree, however, with Justice Traynor of the California Supreme Court, who said that the "[d]enial of counsel on appeal [to an indigent] would seem to be a discrimination at least as invidious as that condemned in *Griffin* v. *Illinois*. . . ." *People* v. *Brown*, 55 Cal. 2d 64, 71, 357 P.2d 1072, 1076 (concurring opinion). In *Griffin* v. *Illinois*, 351 U.S. 12, we held that a State may not grant appellate review in such a way as to discriminate against some convicted defendants on account of their poverty. There, as in *Draper* v. *Washington*, post, p. 487, the right to a free transcript on appeal was in issue. Here the issue is whether or not an indigent shall be denied the assistance of counsel on appeal. In either case the evil is the same: discrimination against the indigent. For there can be no equal justice where the kind of an appeal a man enjoys "depends on the amount of money he has." *Griffin* v. *Illinois*, *supra*, at p. 19.

In spite of California's forward treatment of indigents, under its present practice the type of an appeal a person is afforded in the District Court of Appeal hinges upon whether or not he can pay for the assistance of counsel. If he can the appellate court passes on the merits of his case only after having the full benefit of written briefs and oral argument by counsel. If he cannot the appellate court is

forced to prejudge the merits before it can even determine whether counsel should be provided. At this stage in the proceedings only the barren record speaks for the indigent, and, unless the printed pages show that an injustice has been committed, he is forced to go without a champion on appeal. Any real chance he may have had of showing that his appeal has hidden merit is deprived him when the court decides on an *ex parte* examination of the record that the assistance of counsel is not required. We are not here concerned with problems that might arise from the denial of counsel for the preparation of a petition for discretionary or mandatory review beyond the stage in the appellate process at which the claims have once been presented by a lawyer and passed upon by an appellate court. We are dealing only with the first appeal, granted as a matter of right to rich and poor alike (Cal. Penal Code 1235, 1237), from a criminal conviction. We need not now decide whether California would have to provide counsel for an indigent seeking a discretionary hearing from the California Supreme Court after the District Court of Appeal had sustained his conviction (see Cal. Const., Art. VI, 4c; Cal. Rules on Appeal, Rules 28, 29), or whether counsel must be appointed for an indigent seeking review of an appellate affirmance of his conviction in this Court by appeal as of right or by petition for a writ of *certiorari* which lies within the Court's discretion. But it is appropriate to observe that a State can, consistently with the Fourteenth Amendment, provide for differences so long as the result does not amount to a denial of due process or an "invidious discrimination." *Williamson* v. *Lee Optical Co.*, 348 U.S. 483, 489; *Griffin* v. *Illinois, supra*, p. 18. Absolute equality is not required; lines can be and are drawn and we often sustain them. See *Tigner* v. *Texas*, 310 U.S. 141; *Goesaert* v. *Cleary*, 335 U.S. 464. But where the merits of the one and only appeal an indigent has as of right are decided without benefit of counsel, we think an unconstitutional line has been drawn between rich and poor. When an indigent is forced to run this gantlet of a preliminary showing of merit, the right to appeal does not comport with fair procedure. In the federal courts, on the other hand, an indigent must be afforded counsel on appeal whenever he challenges a certification that the appeal is not taken in good faith. *Johnson* v. *United States*, 352 U.S. 565. The federal courts must honor his request for counsel regardless of what they think the merits of the case may be; and "representation in the role of an advocate is required." *Ellis* v. *United States*, 356 U.S. 674, 675. In California, however, once the court has "gone through" the record and denied counsel, the indigent has no recourse but to prosecute his appeal on his own, as best he can, no matter how meritorious his case may turn out to be. The present case, where counsel was denied petitioners on appeal, shows that the discrimination is not between "possibly good and obviously bad cases," but between cases where the rich man can require the court to listen to argument of counsel before deciding on the merits, but a poor man cannot. There is lacking that equality demanded by the Fourteenth Amendment where the rich man, who appeals as of right, enjoys the benefit of counsel's examination into the record, research of the law, and marshalling of arguments on his behalf, while the indigent, already burdened by a preliminary determination that his case is without merit, is forced to shift for himself. The indigent, where the record is unclear or the errors are hidden, has only the right to a meaningless ritual, while the rich man has a meaningful appeal.

We vacate the judgment of the District Court of Appeal and remand the case to that court for further proceedings not inconsistent with this opinion. It is so ordered.

[JUSTICES CLARK, HARLAN and STEWARD dissented.]

1. Under *Douglas*, the Court used both the equal protection and due process concepts to establish the right to counsel on initial appeal. Present an argument using only the Sixth Amendment to establish the right to counsel for an indigent in his or her initial appeal.

2. According to the decision, a state could entirely eliminate its appellate system. Do you feel that approach would be constitutional? Explain your opinion.

The Douglas *case examined the issue of right to appointed counsel on initial appeal. The* Ross *case looks at the right to counsel beyond the initial appeal.*

ROSS V. MOFFITT
417 U.S. 600 (1974)

MR. JUSTICE REHNQUIST delivered the opinion of the Court.

We are asked in this case to decide whether *Douglas* v. *California*, 372 U.S. 353 (1963), which requires appointment of counsel for indigent state defendants on their first appeal as of right, should be extended to require counsel for discretionary state appeals and for applications for review in this Court. . . .

. . . This Court, in the past 20 years, has given extensive consideration to the rights of indigent persons on appeal. In *Griffin* v. *Illinois*, 351 U.S. 12 (1956), the first of the pertinent cases, the Court had before it an Illinois rule allowing a convicted criminal defendant to present claims of trial error to the Supreme Court of Illinois only if he procured a transcript of the testimony adduced at his trial. No exception was made for the indigent defendant, and thus one who was unable to pay the cost of obtaining such a transcript was precluded from obtaining appellate review of asserted trial error. MR. JUSTICE FRANKFURTER, who cast the deciding vote, said in his concurring opinion: ". . . Illinois has decreed that only defendants who can afford to pay for the stenographic minutes of a trial may have trial errors reviewed on appeal by the Illinois Supreme Court." *Id.*, at 22. The Court in *Griffin* held that this discrimination violated the Fourteenth Amendment.

Succeeding cases invalidated similar financial barriers to the appellate process, at the same time reaffirming the traditional principle that a State is not obliged to provide any appeal at all for criminal defendants. *McKane* v. *Durston*, 153 U.S. 684 (1894). The cases encompassed a variety of circumstances but all had a common theme. For example, *Lane* v. *Brown*, 372 U.S. 477 (1963), involved an Indiana provision declaring that only a public defender could obtain a free transcript of a hearing on a *coram nobis* application. If the public defender declined to request one, the indigent prisoner seeking to appeal had no recourse. In *Draper* v. *Washington*, 372 U.S. 487 (1963), the State permitted an indigent to obtain a free transcript of the trial at which he was convicted only if he satisfied the trial judge that his contentions on appeal would not be frivolous. The appealing defendant was in effect bound by the trial court's conclusions in seeking to review the determination of frivolousness, since no transcript or its equivalent was made available to him. In *Smith* v. *Bennett*, 365 U.S. 708 (1961), Iowa had required a filing fee in order to process a state habeas corpus application by a convicted defendant, and in *Burns* v. *Ohio*, 360 U.S. 252 (1959), the State of Ohio required a $20 filing fee in order to move the Supreme Court of Ohio for leave to appeal from a judgment of the Ohio Court of Appeals affirming a criminal conviction. Each of these state-imposed financial barriers to the adjudication of a criminal defendant's appeal was held to violate the Fourteenth Amendment.

The decisions discussed above stand for the proposition that a State cannot arbitrarily cut off appeal rights for indigents while leaving open avenues of appeal for more affluent persons. In *Douglas* v. *California*, 372 U.S. 353 (1963), however, a case decided the same day as *Lane, supra,* and *Draper, supra,* the Court departed somewhat from the limited doctrine of the transcript and fee cases and undertook an examination of whether an indigent's access to the appellate system was adequate. The Court in *Douglas* concluded that a State does not fulfill its responsibility toward indigent defendants merely by waiving its own requirements that a convicted defendant procure a transcript or pay a fee in order to appeal, and held that the State must go further and provide counsel for the indigent on his first appeal as of right. It is this decision we are asked to extend today.

. . . The precise rationale for the *Griffin* and *Douglas* lines of cases has never been explicitly stated, some support being derived from the Equal Protection Clause of the Fourteenth Amendment, and some from the Due Process Clause of that Amendment. Neither Clause by itself provides an entirely satisfactory basis for the result reached, each depending on a different inquiry which emphasizes different factors. "Due process" emphasizes fairness between the State and the individual dealing with the State, regardless of how other individuals in the same situation may be treated. "Equal protection," on the other hand, emphasizes disparity in treatment by a State between classes of individuals whose situations are arguably indistinguishable. . . .

We do not believe that the Due Process Clause requires North Carolina to provide respondent with counsel on his discretionary appeal to the State Supreme Court. At the trial stage of a criminal proceeding, the right of an indigent defendant to counsel is fundamental and binding upon the States by virtue of the Sixth and Fourteenth Amendments. *Gideon* v. *Wainwright*, 372 U.S. 335 (1963). But there are significant differences between the trial and appellate stages of a criminal proceeding. The purpose of the trial stage from the State's point of view is to convert a criminal defendant from a person presumed innocent to one found guilty beyond a reasonable doubt. To accomplish this purpose, the State employs a prosecuting attorney who presents evidence to the court, challenges any witnesses offered by the defendant, argues rulings of the court, and makes direct arguments to the court and jury seeking to persuade them of the defendant's guilt. Under these circumstances "reason and reflection require us to recognize that in our adversary system of criminal justice, any person haled into court, who is too poor to hire a lawyer, cannot be assured a fair trial unless counsel is provided for him." *Id.*, at 344.

By contrast, it is ordinarily the defendant, rather than the State, who initiates the appellate process, seeking not to fend off the efforts of the State's prosecutor but rather to overturn a finding of guilt made by a judge or jury below. The defendant needs an attorney on appeal not as a shield to protect him against being "haled into court" by the State and stripped of his presumption of innocence, but rather as a word to upset the prior determination of guilt. This difference is significant because, while no one would agree that the State may simply dispense with

the trial stage of proceedings without a criminal defendant's consent, it is clear that the State need not provide any appeal at all. *McKane* v. *Durston*, 153 U.S. 684 (1894). The fact that an appeal has been provided does not automatically mean that a State then acts unfairly by refusing to provide counsel to indigent defendants at every stage of the way. *Douglas* v. *California, supra.* Unfairness results only if indigents are singled out by the State and denied meaningful access to the appellate system because of their poverty. That question is more profitably considered under an equal protection analysis.

... Language invoking equal protection notions is prominent both in *Douglas* and in other cases treating the rights of indigents on appeal. The Court in *Douglas*, for example, stated: "[W]here the merits of the one and only appeal an indigent has as of right are decided without benefit of counsel, we think an unconstitutional line has been drawn between rich and poor." 372 U.S., at 357.

The Court in *Burns* v. *Ohio*, stated the issue in the following terms: "[O]nce the State chooses to establish appellate review in criminal cases, it may not foreclose indigents from access to any phase of that procedure because of their poverty." 360 U.S., at 257.

Despite the tendency of all rights "to declare themselves absolute to their logical extreme," there are obviously limits beyond which the equal protection analysis may not be pressed without doing violence to principles recognized in other decisions of this Court. The Fourteenth Amendment "does not require absolute equality or precisely equal advantages," *San Antonio Independent School District* v. *Rodriguez*, 411 U.S. 1, 24 (1973), nor does it require the State to "equalize economic conditions." *Griffin* v. *Illinois*, 351 U.S., at 23 (FRANKFURTER, J., concurring). It does require that the state appellate system be "free of unreasoned distinctions," *Rinaldi* v. *Yeager*, 384 U.S. 305, 310 (1966), and that indigents have an adequate opportunity to present their claims fairly within the adversary system. *Griffin* v. *Illinois, supra*; *Draper* v. *Washington*, 372 U.S. 487 (1963). The State cannot adopt procedures which leave an indigent defendant "entirely cut off from any appeal at all," by virtue of his indigency, *Lane* v. *Brown*, 372 U.S., at 481 or extend to such indigent defendants merely a "meaningless ritual" while others in better economic circumstances have a "meaningful appeal." *Douglas* v. *California, supra*, at 358. The question is not one of absolutes, but one of degrees. In this case we do not believe that the Equal Protection Clause, when interpreted in the context of these cases, requires North Carolina to provide free counsel for indigent defendants seeking to take discretionary appeals to the North Carolina Supreme Court, or to file petitions for *certiorari* in this Court.

... The North Carolina appellate system, as are the appellate systems of almost half the States, is multitiered, providing for both an intermediate Court of Appeals and a Supreme Court. The Court of Appeals was created effective January 1, 1967, and, like other intermediate state appellate courts, was intended to absorb a substantial share of the caseload previously burdening the Supreme Court. In criminal cases, an appeal as of right lies directly to the Supreme Court in all cases which involve a sentence of death or life imprisonment, while an appeal of right in all other criminal cases lies to the Court of Appeals. N.C. Gen. Stat. 7A-27 (1969 and Supp. 1973). A second appeal of right lies to the Supreme Court in any criminal case "(1) (w)hich directly involves a substantial question arising under the Constitution of the United States or of this State, or (2) [i]n which there is a dissent. ..." N.C. Gen. Stat. 7A-30 (1969). All other decisions of the Court of Appeals on direct review of criminal cases may be further reviewed in the Supreme Court on a discretionary basis.

. . . Appointment of counsel for indigents in North Carolina is governed by N.C. Gen. Stat. 7A-450 et seq. (1969 and Supp. 1973). These provisions, although perhaps on their face broad enough to cover appointments such as those respondent sought here, have generally been construed to limit the right to appointed counsel in criminal cases to direct appeals taken as of right. Thus North Carolina has followed the mandate of *Douglas* v. *California, supra,* and authorized appointment of counsel for a convicted defendant appealing to the intermediate Court of Appeals, but has not gone beyond *Douglas* to provide for appointment of counsel for a defendant who seeks either discretionary review in the Supreme Court of North Carolina or a writ of *certiorari* here.

The facts show that respondent, in connection with his Mecklenburg County conviction, received the benefit of counsel in examining the record of his trial and in preparing an appellate brief on his behalf for the state Court of Appeals. Thus, prior to his seeking discretionary review in the State Supreme Court, his claims had "once been presented by a lawyer and passed upon by an appellate court." *Douglas* v. *California,* 372 U.S., at 356.

We do not believe that it can be said, therefore, that a defendant in respondent's circumstances is denied meaningful access to the North Carolina Supreme Court simply because the State does not appoint counsel to aid him in seeking review in that court. At that stage he will have, at the very least, a transcript or other record of trial proceedings, a brief on his behalf in the Court of Appeals setting forth his claims of error, and in many cases an opinion by the Court of Appeals disposing of his case. These materials, supplemented by whatever submission respondent may make *pro se,* would appear to provide the Supreme Court of North Carolina with an adequate basis for its decision to grant or deny review.

We are fortified in this conclusion by our understanding of the function served by discretionary review in the North Carolina Supreme Court. The critical issue in that court, as we perceive it, is not whether there has been "a correct adjudication of guilt" in every individual case, see *Griffin* v. *Illinois,* 351 U.S., at 18, but rather whether "the subject matter of the appeal has significant public interest," whether "the cause involves legal principles of major significance to the jurisprudence of the State," or whether the decision below is in probable conflict with a decision of the Supreme Court. The Supreme Court may deny *certiorari* even though it believes that the decision of the Court of Appeals was incorrect, see *Peaseley* v. *Virginia Iron, Coal & Coke Co.,* 282 N.C. 585, 194 S. E. 2d 133 (1973), since a decision which appears incorrect may nevertheless fail to satisfy any of the criteria discussed above. Once a defendant's claims of error are organized and presented in a lawyer-like fashion to the Court of Appeals, the justices of the Supreme Court of North Carolina who make the decision to grant or deny discretionary review should be able to ascertain whether his case satisfies the standards established by the legislature for such review. . . .

We do not mean by this opinion to in any way discourage those States which have, as a matter of legislative choice, made counsel available to convicted defendants at all stages of judicial review. Some States which might well choose to do so as a matter of legislative policy may conceivably find that other claims for public funds within or without the criminal justice system preclude the implementation of such a policy at the present time. North Carolina, for example, while it does not provide counsel to indigent defendants seeking discretionary review on appeal, does provide counsel for indigent prisoners in several situations where such appointments are not required by any constitutional decision of this Court. Our reading of the Fourteenth Amendment leaves these choices to the State, and respondent was denied no right secured by the Federal Constitution when North Carolina refused to provide counsel to aid him in obtaining discretionary appellate review.

The judgment of the Court of Appeals' holding to the contrary is Reversed.

MR. JUSTICE DOUGLAS, with whom MR. JUSTICE BRENNAN and MR. JUSTICE MARSHALL concur, dissenting. [Omitted.]

WHAT DO YOU THINK?

1. The Court stated that "The question is not one of absolutes, but one of degrees." Explain what the Court meant by that statement.
2. The Court also stated that "In this case we do not believe that the Equal Protection Clause, when interpreted in the context of these cases, requires North Carolina to provide free counsel for indigent defendants seeking to take discretionary appeals to the North Carolina Supreme Court, or to file petitions for *certiorari* in this Court." Do you agree? Justify your answer.
3. The dissenting opinion stated ". . . there can be no equal justice where the kind of an appeal a man enjoys 'depends on the amount of money he has.' " How does the majority opinion answer this contention?
4. Chief Judge Haynsworth could find "no logical basis for differentiation between appeals of right and permissive review procedures in the context of the Constitution and the right to counsel." Do you agree, or do you accept the majority opinion that there is a difference?
5. Chief Judge Haynsworth also observed that the indigent defendant proceeding without counsel is at a substantial disadvantage relative to wealthy defendants represented by counsel when he is forced to fend for himself in seeking discretionary review from the State Supreme Court. How does the majority opinion answer this contention?

The Strickland *case discusses the requirements for determining the lack of effective assistance of counsel.*

STRICKLAND V. WASHINGTON
466 U.S. 668 (1984)

JUSTICE O'CONNOR delivered the opinion of the Court.

This case requires us to consider the proper standards for judging a criminal defendant's contention that the Constitution requires a conviction or death sentence to be set aside because counsel's assistance at the trial or sentencing was ineffective.

I.

A.

During a 10-day period in September 1976, respondent planned and committed three groups of crimes, which included three brutal stabbing murders, torture, kidnaping, severe assaults, attempted murders, attempted extortion, and theft. After his two accomplices were arrested, respondent surrendered to police and voluntar-

ily gave a lengthy statement confessing to the third of the criminal episodes. The State of Florida indicted respondent for kidnaping and murder and appointed an experienced criminal lawyer to represent him.

Counsel actively pursued pretrial motions and discovery. He cut his efforts short, however, and he experienced a sense of hopelessness about the case, when he learned that, against his specific advice, respondent had also confessed to the first two murders. By the date set for trial, respondent was subject to indictment for three counts of first-degree murder and multiple counts of robbery, kidnaping for ransom, breaking and entering and assault, attempted murder, and conspiracy to commit robbery. Respondent waived his right to a jury trial, again acting against counsel's advice, and pleaded guilty to all charges, including the three capital murder charges.

In the plea colloquy, respondent told the trial judge that, although he had committed a string of burglaries, he had no significant prior criminal record and that at the time of his criminal spree he was under extreme stress caused by his inability to support his family. App. 50–53. He also stated, however, that he accepted responsibility for the crimes. E.g., *id.*, at 54, 57. The trial judge told respondent that he had "a great deal of respect for people who are willing to step forward and admit their responsibility" but that he was making no statement at all about his likely sentencing decision. *Id.*, at 62.

Counsel advised respondent to invoke his right under Florida law to an advisory jury at his capital sentencing hearing. Respondent rejected the advice and waived the right. He chose instead to be sentenced by the trial judge without a jury recommendation.

In preparing for the sentencing hearing, counsel spoke with respondent about his background. He also spoke on the telephone with respondent's wife and mother, though he did not follow up on the one unsuccessful effort to meet with them. He did not otherwise seek out character witnesses for respondent. App. to Pet. for Cert. A265. Nor did he request a psychiatric examination, since his conversations with his client gave no indication that respondent had psychological problems. *Id.*, at A266.

Counsel decided not to present and hence not to look further for evidence concerning respondent's character and emotional state. That decision reflected trial counsel's sense of hopelessness about overcoming the evidentiary effect of respondent's confessions to the gruesome crimes. See *id.*, at A282. It also reflected the judgment that it was advisable to rely on the plea colloquy for evidence about respondent's background and about his claim of emotional stress. . . . The plea colloquy communicated sufficient information about these subjects, and by forgoing the opportunity to present new evidence on these subjects, counsel prevented the State from cross-examining respondent on his claim and from putting on psychiatric evidence of its own. *Id.*, at A223–A225.

Counsel also excluded from the sentencing hearing other evidence he thought was potentially damaging. He successfully moved to exclude respondent's "rap sheet." *Id.*, at A227; App. 311. Because he judged that a presentence report might prove more detrimental than helpful, as it would have included respondent's criminal history and thereby would have undermined the claim of no significant history of criminal activity, he did not request that one be prepared. App. to Pet. for Cert. A227–A228, A265–A266.

At the sentencing hearing, counsel's strategy was based primarily on the trial judge's remarks at the plea colloquy as well as on his reputation as a sentencing judge who thought it important for a convicted defendant to own up to his crime. Counsel argued that respondent's remorse and acceptance of responsibility justified

sparing him from the death penalty. *Id.*, at A265–A266. Counsel also argued that respondent had no history of criminal activity and that respondent committed the crimes under extreme mental or emotional disturbance, thus coming within the statutory list of mitigating circumstances. He further argued that respondent should be spared death because he had surrendered, confessed, and offered to testify against a codefendant and because respondent was fundamentally a good person who had briefly gone badly wrong in extremely stressful circumstances. The State put on evidence and witnesses largely for the purpose of describing the details of the crimes. Counsel did not cross-examine the medical experts who testified about the manner of death of respondent's victims.

The trial judge found several aggravating circumstances with respect to each of the three murders. He found that all three murders were especially heinous, atrocious, and cruel, all involving repeated stabbings. All three murders were committed in the course of at least one other dangerous and violent felony, and since all involved robbery, the murders were for pecuniary gain. All three murders were committed to avoid arrest for the accompanying crimes and to hinder law enforcement. In the course of one of the murders, respondent knowingly subjected numerous persons to a grave risk of death by deliberately stabbing and shooting the murder victim's sisters-in-law, who sustained severe—in one case, ultimately fatal—injuries.

With respect to mitigating circumstances, the trial judge made the same findings for all three capital murders. First, although there was no admitted evidence of prior convictions, respondent had stated that he had engaged in a course of stealing. In any case, even if respondent had no significant history of criminal activity, the aggravating circumstances "would still clearly far outweigh" that mitigating factor. Second, the judge found that, during all three crimes, respondent was not suffering from extreme mental or emotional disturbance and could appreciate the criminality of his acts. Third, none of the victims was a participant in, or consented to, respondent's conduct. Fourth, respondent's participation in the crimes was neither minor nor the result of duress or domination by an accomplice. Finally, respondent's age (26) could not be considered a factor in mitigation, especially when viewed in light of respondent's planning of the crimes and disposition of the proceeds of the various accompanying thefts.

In short, the trial judge found numerous aggravating circumstances and no (or a single comparatively insignificant) mitigating circumstance. With respect to each of the three convictions for capital murder, the trial judge concluded: "A careful consideration of all matters presented to the court impels the conclusion that there are insufficient mitigating circumstances . . . to outweigh the aggravating circumstances." See *Washington* v. *State*, 362 So.2d 658, 663–664 (Fla. 1978) (quoting trial court findings), cert. denied, 441 U.S. 937 (1979). He therefore sentenced respondent to death on each of the three counts of murder and to prison terms for the other crimes. The Florida Supreme Court upheld the convictions and sentences on direct appeal.

B.

Respondent subsequently sought collateral relief in state court on numerous grounds, among them that counsel had rendered ineffective assistance at the sentencing proceeding. Respondent challenged counsel's assistance in six respects. He asserted that counsel was ineffective because he failed to move for a continuance to prepare for sentencing, to request a psychiatric report, to investigate and present character witnesses, to seek a presentence investigation report, to present meaningful arguments to the sentencing judge, and to investigate the medical examiner's reports or cross-

examine the medical experts. In support of the claim, respondent submitted 14 affidavits from friends, neighbors, and relatives stating that they would have testified if asked to do so. He also submitted one psychiatric report and one psychological report stating that respondent, though not under the influence of extreme mental or emotional disturbance, was "chronically frustrated and depressed because of his economic dilemma" at the time of his crimes. App. 7; see also *id.*, at 14.

The trial court denied relief without an evidentiary hearing, finding that the record evidence conclusively showed that the ineffectiveness claim was meritless. App. to Pet. for Cert. A206–A243. Four of the assertedly prejudicial errors required little discussion. First, there were no grounds to request a continuance, so there was no error in not requesting one when respondent pleaded guilty. *Id.*, at A218–A220. Second, failure to request a presentence investigation was not a serious error because the trial judge had discretion not to grant such a request and because any presentence investigation would have resulted in admission of respondent's "rap sheet" and thus would have undermined his assertion of no significant history of criminal activity. *Id.*, at A226–A228. Third, the argument and memorandum given to the sentencing judge were "admirable" in light of the overwhelming aggravating circumstances and absence of mitigating circumstances. *Id.*, at A228. Fourth, there was no error in failure to examine the medical examiner's reports or to cross-examine the medical witnesses testifying on the manner of death of respondent's victims, since respondent admitted that the victims died in the ways shown by the unchallenged medical evidence. *Id.*, at A229.

The trial court dealt at greater length with the two other bases for the ineffectiveness claim. The court pointed out that a psychiatric examination of respondent was conducted by state order soon after respondent's initial arraignment. That report states that there was no indication of major mental illness at the time of the crimes. Moreover, both the reports submitted in the collateral proceeding state that, although respondent was "chronically frustrated and depressed because of his economic dilemma," he was not under the influence of extreme mental or emotional disturbance. All three reports thus directly undermine the contention made at the sentencing hearing that respondent was suffering from extreme mental or emotional disturbance during his crime spree. Accordingly, counsel could reasonably decide not to seek psychiatric reports; indeed, by relying solely on the plea colloquy to support the emotional disturbance contention, counsel denied the State an opportunity to rebut his claim with psychiatric testimony. In any event, the aggravating circumstances were so overwhelming that no substantial prejudice resulted from the absence at sentencing of the psychiatric evidence offered in the collateral attack.

The court rejected the challenge to counsel's failure to develop and to present character evidence for much the same reasons. The affidavits submitted in the collateral proceeding showed nothing more than that certain persons would have testified that respondent was basically a good person who was worried about his family's financial problems. Respondent himself had already testified along those lines at the plea colloquy. Moreover, respondent's admission of a course of stealing rebutted many of the factual allegations in the affidavits. For those reasons, and because the sentencing judge had stated that the death sentence would be appropriate even if respondent had no significant prior criminal history, no substantial prejudice resulted from the absence at sentencing of the character evidence offered in the collateral attack. Applying the standard for ineffectiveness claims articulated by the Florida Supreme Court in *Knight* v. *State*, 394 So.2d 997 (1981), the trial court concluded that respondent had not shown that counsel's assistance reflected any substantial and serious deficiency measurably below that of competent

counsel that was likely to have affected the outcome of the sentencing proceeding. The court specifically found: "[A]s a matter of law, the record affirmatively demonstrates beyond any doubt that even if [counsel] had done each of the . . . things [that respondent alleged counsel had failed to do] at the time of sentencing, there is not even the remotest chance that the outcome would have been any different. The plain fact is that the aggravating circumstances proved in this case were completely overwhelming. . . ." App. to Pet. for Cert. A230.

The Florida Supreme Court affirmed the denial of relief. *Washington* v. *State*, 397 So.2d 285 (1981). For essentially the reasons given by the trial court, the State Supreme Court concluded that respondent had failed to make out a *prima facie* case of either "substantial deficiency or possible prejudice" and, indeed, had "failed to such a degree that we believe, to the point of a moral certainty, that he is entitled to no relief. . . ." *Id.*, at 287. Respondent's claims were "shown conclusively to be without merit so as to obviate the need for an evidentiary hearing." *Id.*, at 286.

C.

Respondent next filed a petition for a writ of habeas corpus in the United States District Court for the Southern District of Florida. He advanced numerous grounds for relief, among them ineffective assistance of counsel based on the same errors, except for the failure to move for a continuance, as those he had identified in state court. The District Court held an evidentiary hearing to inquire into trial counsel's efforts to investigate and to present mitigating circumstances. . . .

The District Court disputed none of the state court factual findings concerning trial counsel's assistance and made findings of its own that are consistent with the state court findings. The account of trial counsel's actions and decisions given above reflects the combined findings. On the legal issue of ineffectiveness, the District Court concluded that, although trial counsel made errors in judgment in failing to investigate nonstatutory mitigating evidence further than he did, no prejudice to respondent's sentence resulted from any such error in judgment. . . .

On appeal, a panel of the United States Court of Appeals for the Fifth Circuit affirmed in part, vacated in part, and remanded with instructions to apply to the particular facts the framework for analyzing ineffectiveness claims that it developed in its opinion. . . .

Turning to the merits, the Court of Appeals stated that the Sixth Amendment right to assistance of counsel accorded criminal defendants a right to "counsel reasonably likely to render and rendering reasonably effective assistance given the totality of the circumstances." *Id.*, at 1250. The court remarked in passing that no special standard applies in capital cases such as the one before it: the punishment that a defendant faces is merely one of the circumstances to be considered in determining whether counsel was reasonably effective. *Id.*, at 1250, n. 12. The court then addressed respondent's contention that his trial counsel's assistance was not reasonably effective because counsel breached his duty to investigate nonstatutory mitigating circumstances.

The court agreed that the Sixth Amendment imposes on counsel a duty to investigate, because reasonably effective assistance must be based on professional decisions and informed legal choices can be made only after investigation of options. The court observed that counsel's investigatory decisions must be assessed in light of the information known at the time of the decisions, not in hindsight, and that "[t]he amount of pretrial investigation that is reasonable defies precise measurement." *Id.*, at 1251. Nevertheless, putting guilty-plea cases to one side, the court attempted to classify cases presenting issues concerning the scope of the duty to investigate before proceeding to trial.

If there is only one plausible line of defense, the court concluded, counsel must conduct a "reasonably substantial investigation" into that line of defense, since there can be no strategic choice that renders such an investigation unnecessary. *Id.*, at 1252. The same duty exists if counsel relies at trial on only one line of defense, although others are available. In either case, the investigation need not be exhaustive. It must include " 'an independent examination of the facts, circumstances, pleadings and laws involved.' " *Id.*, at 1253 (quoting *Rummel* v. *Estelle*, 590 F.2d 103, 104 [CA5 1979]). The scope of the duty, however, depends on such facts as the strength of the government's case and the likelihood that pursuing certain leads may prove more harmful than helpful. 693 F.2d, at 1253, n. 16.

If there is more than one plausible line of defense, the court held, counsel should ideally investigate each line substantially before making a strategic choice about which lines to rely on at trial. If counsel conducts such substantial investigations, the strategic choices made as a result "will seldom if ever" be found wanting. Because advocacy is an art and not a science, and because the adversary system requires deference to counsel's informed decisions, strategic choices must be respected in these circumstances if they are based on professional judgment. *Id.*, at 1254.

If counsel does not conduct a substantial investigation into each of several plausible lines of defense, assistance may nonetheless be effective. Counsel may not exclude certain lines of defense for other than strategic reasons. . . .

. . . We granted *certiorari* to consider the standards by which to judge a contention that the Constitution requires that a criminal judgment be overturned because of the actual ineffective assistance of counsel. . . .

In a long line of cases that includes *Powell* v. *Alabama*, 287 U.S. 45 (1932), *Johnson* v. *Zerbst*, 304 U.S. 458 (1938), and *Gideon* v. *Wainwright*, 372 U.S. 335 (1963), this Court has recognized that the Sixth Amendment right to counsel exists, and is needed, in order to protect the fundamental right to a fair trial. . . .

Thus, a fair trial is one in which evidence subject to adversarial testing is presented to an impartial tribunal for resolution of issues defined in advance of the proceeding. The right to counsel plays a crucial role in the adversarial system embodied in the Sixth Amendment, since access to counsel's skill and knowledge is necessary to accord defendants the "ample opportunity to meet the case of the prosecution" to which they are entitled. . . .

Because of the vital importance of counsel's assistance, this Court has held that, with certain exceptions, a person accused of a federal or state crime has the right to have counsel appointed if retained counsel cannot be obtained. See *Argersinger* v. *Hamlin*, 407 U.S. 25 (1972); *Gideon* v. *Wainwright, supra*; *Johnson* v. *Zerbst, supra*. That a person who happens to be a lawyer is present at trial alongside the accused, however, is not enough to satisfy the constitutional command. The Sixth Amendment recognizes the right to the assistance of counsel because it envisions counsel's playing a role that is critical to the ability of the adversarial system to produce just results. An accused is entitled to be assisted by an attorney, whether retained or appointed, who plays the role necessary to ensure that the trial is fair.

For that reason, the Court has recognized that "the right to counsel is the right to the effective assistance of counsel."

. . . The Court has not elaborated on the meaning of the constitutional requirement of effective assistance in the latter class of cases—that is, those presenting claims of "actual ineffectiveness." In giving meaning to the requirement, however, we must take its purpose—to ensure a fair trial—as the guide. The

benchmark for judging any claim of ineffectiveness must be whether counsel's conduct so undermined the proper functioning of the adversarial process that the trial cannot be relied on as having produced a just result.

... As all the Federal Courts of Appeals have now held, the proper standard for attorney performance is that of reasonably effective assistance. When a convicted defendant complains of the ineffectiveness of counsel's assistance, the defendant must show that counsel's representation fell below an objective standard of reasonableness.

... Representation of a criminal defendant entails certain basic duties. Counsel's function is to assist the defendant, and hence counsel owes the client a duty of loyalty, a duty to avoid conflicts of interest. See *Cuyler* v. *Sullivan, supra,* at 346. From counsel's function as assistant to the defendant derive the overarching duty to advocate the defendant's cause and the more particular duties to consult with the defendant on important decisions and to keep the defendant informed of important developments in the course of the prosecution. Counsel also has a duty to bring to bear such skill and knowledge as will render the trial a reliable adversarial testing process....

These basic duties neither exhaustively define the obligations of counsel nor form a checklist for judicial evaluation of attorney performance. In any case presenting an ineffectiveness claim, the performance inquiry must be whether counsel's assistance was reasonable considering all the circumstances.

... Moreover, the purpose of the effective assistance guarantee of the Sixth Amendment is not to improve the quality of legal representation, although that is a goal of considerable importance to the legal system. The purpose is simply to ensure that criminal defendants receive a fair trial.

... Judicial scrutiny of counsel's performance must be highly deferential. It is all too tempting for a defendant to second-guess counsel's assistance after conviction or adverse sentence, and it is all too easy for a court, examining counsel's defense after it has proved unsuccessful, to conclude that a particular act or omission of counsel was unreasonable....

... Thus, a court deciding an actual ineffectiveness claim must judge the reasonableness of counsel's challenged conduct on the facts of the particular case, viewed as of the time of counsel's conduct. A convicted defendant making a claim of ineffective assistance must identify the acts or omissions of counsel that are alleged not to have been the result of reasonable professional judgment. The court must then determine whether, in light of all the circumstances, the identified acts or omissions were outside the wide range of professionally competent assistance. In making that determination, the court should keep in mind that counsel's function, as elaborated in prevailing professional norms, is to make the adversarial testing process work in the particular case. At the same time, the court should recognize that counsel is strongly presumed to have rendered adequate assistance and made all significant decisions in the exercise of reasonable professional judgment.

... An error by counsel, even if professionally unreasonable, does not warrant setting aside the judgment of a criminal proceeding if the error had no effect on the judgment. Cf. *United States* v. *Morrison,* 449 U.S. 361, 364–365 (1981). The purpose of the Sixth Amendment guarantee of counsel is to ensure that a defendant has the assistance necessary to justify reliance on the outcome of the proceeding. Accordingly, any deficiencies in counsel's performance must be prejudicial to the defense in order to constitute ineffective assistance under the Constitution.

... Even if a defendant shows that particular errors of counsel were unreasonable, therefore, the defendant must show that they actually had an adverse effect on the defense.

It is not enough for the defendant to show that the errors had some conceivable effect on the outcome of the proceeding. Virtually every act or omission of counsel would meet that test, *cf. United States* v. *Valenzuela-Bernal*, 458 U.S. 858, 866–867 (1982), and not every error that conceivably could have influenced the outcome undermines the reliability of the result of the proceeding. . . .

On the other hand, we believe that a defendant need not show that counsel's deficient conduct more likely than not altered the outcome in the case. This outcome-determinative standard has several strengths. It defines the relevant inquiry in a way familiar to courts, though the inquiry, as is inevitable, is anything but precise. The standard also reflects the profound importance of finality in criminal proceedings. Moreover, it comports with the widely used standard for assessing motions for new trial based on newly discovered evidence. See Brief for United States as Amicus Curiae 19–20, and nn. 10, 11. Nevertheless, the standard is not quite appropriate.

The defendant must show that there is a reasonable probability that, but for counsel's unprofessional errors, the result of the proceeding would have been different. A reasonable probability is a probability sufficient to undermine confidence in the outcome.

. . . Failure to make the required showing of either deficient performance or sufficient prejudice defeats the ineffectiveness claim. Here there is a double failure. More generally, respondent has made no showing that the justice of his sentence was rendered unreliable by a breakdown in the adversary process caused by deficiencies in counsel's assistance. Respondent's sentencing proceeding was not fundamentally unfair.

We conclude, therefore, that the District Court properly declined to issue a writ of habeas corpus. The judgment of the Court of Appeals is accordingly Reversed.

JUSTICE BRENNAN, concurring in part and dissenting in part. [Omitted.]

JUSTICE MARSHALL, dissenting. [Omitted.]

WHAT DO YOU THINK?

1. What is required before a court should reverse a conviction based on ineffective assistance of counsel?
2. Should the accused be afforded a new trial if he or she establishes a deficient performance on the part of the defense counsel?
3. Is the "ineffectiveness" test clear?
4. Does the presumption of effectiveness impose an almost impossible burden on the accused?
5. Is the majority opinion too deferential to lawyer judgments?

Is the Sixth Amendment right of a criminal defendant to assistance of counsel violated when the attorney refuses to cooperate with the defendant in presenting perjured testimony at his trial? The next case looks at this issue.

NIX V. WHITESIDE
475 U.S. 157 (1986)

CHIEF JUSTICE BURGER delivered the opinion of the Court.

We granted *certiorari* to decide whether the Sixth Amendment right of a criminal defendant to assistance of counsel is violated when an attorney refuses to co-operate with the defendant in presenting perjured testimony at his trial.

. . . Whiteside was convicted of second-degree murder by a jury verdict which was affirmed by the Iowa courts. The killing took place on February 8, 1977, in Cedar Rapids, Iowa. Whiteside and two others went to one Calvin Love's apartment late that night, seeking marijuana. Love was in bed when Whiteside and his companions arrived; an argument between Whiteside and Love over the marijuana ensued. At one point, Love directed his girlfriend to get his "piece," and at another point got up, then returned to his bed. According to Whiteside's testimony, Love then started to reach under his pillow and moved toward Whiteside. Whiteside stabbed Love in the chest, inflicting a fatal wound. Whiteside was charged with murder, and when counsel was appointed he objected to the lawyer initially appointed, claiming that he felt uncomfortable with a lawyer who had formerly been a prosecutor. Gary L. Robinson was then appointed and immediately began an investigation. Whiteside gave him a statement that he had stabbed Love as the latter "was pulling a pistol from underneath the pillow on the bed." Upon questioning by Robinson, however, Whiteside indicated that he had not actually seen a gun, but that he was convinced that Love had a gun. No pistol was found on the premises; shortly after the police search following the stabbing, which had revealed no weapon, the victim's family had removed all of the victim's possessions from the apartment. Robinson interviewed Whiteside's companions who were present during the stabbing, and none had seen a gun during the incident. Robinson advised Whiteside that the existence of a gun was not necessary to establish the claim of self-defense, and that only a reasonable belief that the victim had a gun nearby was necessary even though no gun was actually present.

Until shortly before trial, Whiteside consistently stated to Robinson that he had not actually seen a gun, but that he was convinced that Love had a gun in his hand. About a week before trial, during preparation for direct examination, Whiteside for the first time told Robinson and his associate Donna Paulsen that he had seen something "metallic" in Love's hand. When asked about this, Whiteside responded:

[I]n Howard Cook's case there was a gun. If I don't say I saw a gun, I'm dead.

Robinson told Whiteside that such testimony would be perjury and repeated that it was not necessary to prove that a gun was available but only that Whiteside reasonably believed that he was in danger. On Whiteside's insisting that he would testify that he saw "something metallic" Robinson told him, according to Robinson's testimony:

[W]e could not allow him to [testify falsely] because that would be perjury, and as officers of the court we would be suborning perjury if we allowed him to do it; . . . I advised him that if he did do that it would be my duty to advise the Court of what he was doing and that I felt he was committing perjury; also, that I probably would be allowed to attempt to impeach that particular testimony. App. to Pet. for Cert. A-85

Robinson also indicated he would seek to withdraw from the representation if Whiteside insisted on committing perjury.

Whiteside testified in his own defense at trial and stated that he "knew" that Love had a gun and that he believed Love was reaching for a gun and he had acted swiftly in self-defense. On cross-examination, he admitted that he had not actually seen a gun in Love's hand. Robinson presented evidence that Love had been seen with a sawed-off shotgun on other occasions, that the police search of the apartment may have been careless, and that the victim's family had removed everything from the apartment shortly after the crime. Robinson presented this evidence to show a basis for Whiteside's asserted fear that Love had a gun.

The jury returned a verdict of second-degree murder, and Whiteside moved for a new trial, claiming that he had been deprived of a fair trial by Robinson's admonitions not to state that he saw a gun or "something metallic." The trial court held a hearing, heard testimony by Whiteside and Robinson, and denied the motion. The trial court made specific findings that the facts were as related by Robinson.

. . . The right of an accused to testify in his defense is of relatively recent origin. Until the latter part of the preceding century, criminal defendants in this country, as at common law, were considered to be disqualified from giving sworn testimony at their own trial by reason of their interest as a party to the case. See, e.g., *Ferguson* v. *Georgia*, 365 U.S. 570 (1961); R. Morris, *Studies in the History of American Law* 59–60 (2d ed. 1959). Iowa was among the states that adhered to this rule of disqualification. *State* v. *Laffer*, 38 Iowa 422 (1874).

By the end of the 19th century, however, the disqualification was finally abolished by statute in most states and in the federal courts. Act of Mar. 16, 1878, ch. 37, 20 Stat. 30–31; see Thayer, *A Chapter of Legal History in Massachusetts*, 9 Harv. L. Rev. 1, 12 (1895). Although this Court has never explicitly held that a criminal defendant has a due process right to testify in his own behalf, cases in several Circuits have so held, and the right has long been assumed. See, e.g., *United States* v. *Curtis*, 742 F.2d. 1070, 1076 (CA7 1984); *United States* v. *Bifield*, 702 F.2d 342, 349 (CA2), cert. denied, 461 U.S. 931 (1983). We have also suggested that such a right exists as a corollary to the Fifth Amendment privilege against compelled testimony, see *Harris* v. *New York*, *supra*, at 225. See also *Ferguson*, 365 U.S., at 598–601 (concurring opinion of FRANKFURTER, J.); *id.*, at 601–603 (concurring opinion of CLARK, J.).

B.

In *Strickland* v. *Washington*, we held that to obtain relief by way of federal habeas corpus on a claim of a deprivation of effective assistance of counsel under the Sixth Amendment, the movant must establish both serious attorney error and prejudice. To show such error, it must be established that the assistance rendered by counsel was constitutionally deficient in that "counsel made errors so serious that counsel was not functioning as 'counsel' guaranteed the defendant by the Sixth Amendment." *Strickland*, 466 U.S., at 687.

To show prejudice, it must be established that the claimed lapses in counsel's performance rendered the trial unfair so as to "undermine confidence in the outcome" of the trial. *Id.*, at 694. In *Strickland*, we acknowledged that the Sixth Amendment does not require any particular response by counsel to a problem that may arise. Rather, the Sixth Amendment inquiry is into whether the attorney's conduct was "reasonably effective." To counteract the natural tendency to fault an unsuccessful defense, a court reviewing a claim of ineffective assistance must "indulge a strong presumption that counsel's conduct falls within the wide range of reasonable professional assistance." *Id.*, at 689. In giving shape to the perimeters of this range of reasonable professional assistance, Strickland mandates that

> . . . [p]revailing norms of practice as reflected in American Bar Association Standards and the like, . . . are guides to determining what is reasonable, but they are only guides. *Id.*, at 688

Under the *Strickland* standard, breach of an ethical standard does not necessarily make out a denial of the Sixth Amendment guarantee of assistance of counsel. When examining attorney conduct, a court must be careful not to narrow the wide range of conduct acceptable under the Sixth Amendment so restrictively as to constitutionalize particular standards of professional conduct and thereby intrude into the state's proper authority to define and apply the standards of professional conduct applicable to those it admits to practice in its courts. In some future case challenging attorney conduct in the course of a state-court trial, we may need to define with greater precision the weight to be given to recognized canons of ethics, the standards established by the state in statutes or professional codes, and the Sixth Amendment, in defining the proper scope and limits on that conduct. Here we need not face that question, since virtually all of the sources speak with one voice.

C.

We turn next to the question presented: the definition of the range of "reasonable professional" responses to a criminal defendant client who informs counsel that he will perjure himself on the stand. We must determine whether, in this setting, Robinson's conduct fell within the wide range of professional responses to threatened client perjury acceptable under the Sixth Amendment.

In *Strickland*, we recognized counsel's duty of loyalty and his "overarching duty to advocate the defendant's cause." *Ibid.* Plainly, that duty is limited to legitimate, lawful conduct compatible with the very nature of a trial as a search for truth. Although counsel must take all reasonable lawful means to attain the objectives of the client, counsel is precluded from taking steps or in any way assisting the client in presenting false evidence or otherwise violating the law. This principle has consistently been recognized in most unequivocal terms by expositors of the norms of professional conduct since the first *Canons of Professional Ethics* were adopted by the American Bar Association in 1908. The 1908 Canon 32 provided:

> No client, corporate or individual, however powerful, nor any cause, civil or political, however important, is entitled to receive nor should any lawyer render any service or advice involving disloyalty to the law whose ministers we are, or disrespect of the judicial office, which we are bound to uphold, or corruption of any person or persons exercising a public office or private trust, or deception or betrayal of the public. . . . He must . . . observe and advise his client to observe the statute law. . . .

Of course, this Canon did no more than articulate centuries of accepted standards of conduct. Similarly, Canon 37, adopted in 1928, explicitly acknowledges as an exception to the attorney's duty of confidentiality a client's announced intention to commit a crime:

> The announced intention of a client to commit a crime is not included within the confidences which [the attorney] is bound to respect.

These principles have been carried through to contemporary codifications of an attorney's professional responsibility. Disciplinary Rule 7-102 of the Model Code of Professional Responsibility (1980), entitled "Representing a Client Within the Bounds of the Law," provides:

> (A) In his representation of a client, a lawyer shall not:
> . . . . .
> "(4) Knowingly use perjured testimony or false evidence.
> . . . . .
> "(7) Counsel or assist his client in conduct that the lawyer knows to be illegal or fraudulent.

... These standards confirm that the legal profession has accepted that an attorney's ethical duty to advance the interests of his client is limited by an equally solemn duty to comply with the law and standards of professional conduct; it specifically ensures that the client may not use false evidence. This special duty of an attorney to prevent and disclose frauds upon the court derives from the recognition that perjury is as much a crime as tampering with witnesses or jurors by way of promises and threats, and undermines the administration of justice. See 1 W. Burdick, *Law of Crime* 293, 300, 318–336 (1946).

The offense of perjury was a crime recognized at common law, *id.*, at p. 475, and has been made a felony in most states by statute, including Iowa. Iowa Code 720.2 (1985). See generally 4 C. Torcia, *Wharton's Criminal Law* 631 (14th ed. 1981). An attorney who aids false testimony by questioning a witness when perjurious responses can be anticipated risks prosecution for subornation of perjury under Iowa Code 720.3 (1985).

It is universally agreed that at a minimum the attorney's first duty when confronted with a proposal for perjurious testimony is to attempt to dissuade the client from the unlawful course of conduct. *Model Rules of Professional Conduct*, Rule 3.3, Comment; Wolfram, *Client Perjury*, 50 S. Cal. L. Rev. 809, 846 (1977)....

... The essence of the brief amicus of the American Bar Association reviewing practices long accepted by ethical lawyers is that under no circumstance may a lawyer either advocate or passively tolerate a client's giving false testimony. This, of course, is consistent with the governance of trial conduct in what we have long called "a search for truth." The suggestion sometimes made that "a lawyer must believe his client, not judge him" in no sense means a lawyer can honorably be a party to or in any way give aid to presenting known perjury.

D.

Considering Robinson's representation of respondent in light of these accepted norms of professional conduct, we discern no failure to adhere to reasonable professional standards that would in any sense make out a deprivation of the Sixth Amendment right to counsel. Whether Robinson's conduct is seen as a successful attempt to dissuade his client from committing the crime of perjury, or whether seen as a "threat" to withdraw from representation and disclose the illegal scheme, Robinson's representation of Whiteside falls well within accepted standards of professional conduct and the range of reasonable professional conduct acceptable under *Strickland*....

... Whiteside's attorney treated Whiteside's proposed perjury in accord with professional standards, and since Whiteside's truthful testimony could not have prejudiced the result of his trial, the Court of Appeals was in error to direct the issuance of a writ of habeas corpus and must be reversed. Reversed.

[Concurring opinions of JUSTICES BRENNAN, BLACKMUN, MARSHALL, and STEVENS omitted.]

WHAT DO *YOU* THINK?

1. Do you agree with the opinion? Justify your answer.
2. What would you do as counsel if your client committed perjury [gave false testimony on the witness stand]? Do you have an obligation to inform the court that your client is lying?

Does an accused have a right to represent him or herself? The Faretta
case looks at this issue.

FARETTA V. CALIFORNIA
422 U.S. 806 (1975)

MR. JUSTICE STEWART delivered the opinion of the Court.

The Sixth and Fourteenth Amendments of our Constitution guarantee that a person brought to trial in any state or federal court must be afforded the right to the assistance of counsel before he can be validly convicted and punished by imprisonment. This clear constitutional rule has emerged from a series of cases decided here over the last 50 years. The question before us now is whether a defendant in a state criminal trial has a constitutional right to proceed without counsel when he voluntarily and intelligently elects to do so. Stated another way, the question is whether a State may constitutionally hale a person into its criminal courts and there force a lawyer upon him, even when he insists that he wants to conduct his own defense. It is not an easy question, but we have concluded that a State may not constitutionally do so.

I.

Anthony Faretta was charged with grand theft in an information filed in the Superior Court of Los Angeles County, Cal. At the arraignment, the Superior Court Judge assigned to preside at the trial appointed the public defender to represent Faretta. Well before the date of trial, however, Faretta requested that he be permitted to represent himself. Questioning by the judge revealed that Faretta had once represented himself in a criminal prosecution, that he had a high school education, and that he did not want to be represented by the public defender because he believed that that office was "very loaded down with . . . a heavy case load." The judge responded that he believed Faretta was "making a mistake" and emphasized that in further proceedings Faretta would receive no special favors. Nevertheless, after establishing that Faretta wanted to represent himself and did not want a lawyer, the judge, in a "preliminary ruling," accepted Faretta's waiver of the assistance of counsel. The judge indicated, however, that he might reverse this ruling if it later appeared that Faretta was unable to adequately represent himself.

Several weeks thereafter, but still prior to trial, the judge *sua sponte* held a hearing to inquire into Faretta's ability to conduct his own defense, and questioned him specifically about both the hearsay rule and the state law governing the challenge of potential jurors. After consideration of Faretta's answers, and observation of his demeanor, the judge ruled that Faretta had not made an intelligent and knowing waiver of his right to the assistance of counsel, and also ruled that Faretta had no constitutional right to conduct his own defense. The judge, accordingly, reversed his earlier ruling permitting self-representation and again appointed the public defender to represent Faretta. Faretta's subsequent request for leave to act as cocounsel was rejected, as were his efforts to make certain motions on his own behalf. Throughout the subsequent trial, the judge required that Faretta's defense be conducted only through the appointed lawyer from the public defender's office. At the conclusion of the trial, the jury found Faretta guilty as charged, and the judge sentenced him to prison. . . .

In the federal courts, the right of self-representation has been protected by statute since the beginnings of our Nation. Section 35 of the Judiciary Act of 1789, 1 Stat. 73, 92, enacted by the First Congress and signed by President Washington one day before the Sixth Amendment was proposed, provided that "in all the courts of the United States, the parties may plead and manage their own causes personally or by the assistance of . . . counsel. . . ." The right is currently codified in 28 U.S.C. 1654.

With few exceptions, each of the several States also accords a defendant the right to represent himself in any criminal case. The Constitutions of 36 States explicitly confer that right. Moreover, many state courts have expressed the view that the right is also supported by the Constitution of the United States.

This Court has more than once indicated the same view. In *Adams* v. *United States ex rel. McCann*, 317 U.S. 269, 279, the Court recognized that the Sixth Amendment right to the assistance of counsel implicitly embodies a "correlative right to dispense with a lawyer's help." The defendant in that case, indicted for federal mail fraud violations, insisted on conducting his own defense without benefit of counsel. He also requested a bench trial and signed a waiver of his right to trial by jury. The prosecution consented to the waiver of a jury, and the waiver was accepted by the court. The defendant was convicted, but the Court of Appeals reversed the conviction on the ground that a person accused of a felony could not competently waive his right to trial by jury except upon the advice of a lawyer. This Court reversed and reinstated the conviction, holding that "an accused, in the exercise of a free and intelligent choice, and with the considered approval of the court, may waive trial by jury, and so likewise may he competently and intelligently waive his Constitutional right to assistance of counsel." *Id.*, at 275.

The *Adams* case does not, of course, necessarily resolve the issue before us. It held only that "the Constitution does not force a lawyer upon a defendant." *Id.*, at 279. Whether the Constitution forbids a State from forcing a lawyer upon a defendant is a different question. But the Court in *Adams* did recognize, albeit in dictum, an affirmative right of self-representation:

> The right to assistance of counsel and the correlative right to dispense with a lawyer's help are not legal formalisms. They rest on considerations that go to the substance of an accused's position before the law. . . .
>
> ". . . What were contrived as protections for the accused should not be turned into fetters. . . . To deny an accused a choice of procedure in circumstances in which he, though a layman is as capable as any lawyer of making an intelligent choice, is to impair the worth of great Constitutional safeguards by treating them as empty verbalisms.
>
> ". . . When the administration of the criminal law . . . is hedged about as it is by the Constitutional safeguards for the protection of an accused, to deny him in the exercise of his free choice the right to dispense with some of these safeguards . . . is to imprison a man in his privileges and call it the Constitution." *Id.*, at 279–280

In other settings as well, the Court has indicated that a defendant has a constitutionally protected right to represent himself in a criminal trial. For example, in *Snyder* v. *Massachusetts*, 291 U.S. 97, the Court held that the Confrontation Clause of the Sixth Amendment gives the accused a right to be present at all stages of the proceedings where fundamental fairness might be thwarted by his absence. This right to "presence" was based upon the premise that the "defense may be made easier if the accused is permitted to be present at the examination of jurors or the summing up of counsel, for it will be in his power, if present, to give advice or

suggestion or even to supersede his lawyers altogether and conduct the trial himself." *Id.*, at 106. And in *Price* v. *Johnston*, 334 U.S. 266, the Court, in holding that a convicted person had no absolute right to argue his own appeal, said this holding was in "sharp contrast" to his "recognized privilege of conducting his own defense at the trial." *Id.*, at 285.

The United States Courts of Appeals have repeatedly held that the right of self-representation is protected by the Bill of Rights. In *United States* v. *Plattner*, 330 F.2d 271, the Court of Appeals for the Second Circuit emphasized that the Sixth Amendment grants the accused the rights of confrontation, of compulsory process for witnesses in his favor, and of assistance of counsel as minimum procedural requirements in federal criminal prosecutions. The right to the assistance of counsel, the court concluded, was intended to supplement the other rights of the defendant, and not to impair "the absolute and primary right to conduct one's own defense in propria persona." . . .

. . . The Sixth Amendment does not provide merely that a defense shall be made for the accused; it grants to the accused personally the right to make his defense. It is the accused, not counsel, who must be "informed of the nature and cause of the accusation," who must be "confronted with the witnesses against him," and who must be accorded "compulsory process for obtaining witnesses in his favor." Although not stated in the Amendment in so many words, the right to self-representation—to make one's own defense personally—is thus necessarily implied by the structure of the Amendment. The right to defend is given directly to the accused; for it is he who suffers the consequences if the defense fails. . . .

WHAT DO YOU THINK?

1. Should an accused have a right to represent him or herself? Justify your answer.
2. What could a judge do to prevent a case from being reversed on review when the accused represents him or herself?

SUMMARY

- The Sixth Amendment to the U.S. Constitution provides that in all criminal prosecutions, the accused shall enjoy the right to have the assistance of counsel for his defense.

- The Supreme Court has indicated that the importance of the right to assistance of counsel cannot be overstated.

- Most of the Supreme Court decisions on the right to counsel deal with the failure of the state to appoint counsel for an indigent accused and the issue of effective representation.

- There is a difference between when a defendant has the right to assistance of counsel and when the defendant has a right to an appointed counsel. For all practical purposes, the defendant has the right to the assistance of counsel at all stages in all criminal cases. The difficult question is when the defendant cannot afford to retain (hire) an attorney, under what circumstances must the government provide him or her with one?

- There is no constitutional right to appointed counsel of choice. Trial judges have broad discretion regarding the appointment of counsel.
- The Supreme Court used the due process and equal protection clauses of the Fourteenth Amendment to hold that an indigent defendant has the right to appointed counsel on the first appeal of his or her conviction.
- The Supreme Court held that the due process clause requires that indigent defendants receive technical assistance in addition to an appointed counsel. The technical assistance generally involves the hiring of expert witnesses and investigators. Generally, the defense counsel must move for permission from the court to employ technical or investigative assistance.
- The right to counsel includes the right to effective representation of the client. The Court also held that representation is ineffective if counsel's conduct so undermines the proper functioning of the adversarial process that the trial cannot be relied on as having produced a just result.

DISCUSSION QUESTIONS

1. When does the right to appointed counsel attach?
2. What does prosecution mean under the Sixth Amendment?
3. What is the test used when a question of effective assistance of counsel is raised?
4. What are the rights to counsel on appeal?

ENDNOTES

1. 372 U.S. 335 (1963).
2. 351 U.S. 12 (1956).
3. 287 U.S. 45 (1932).
4. 304 U.S. 458 (1938).
5. 316 U.S. 455 (1942).
6. A capital felony is a felony that has the death penalty as an authorized punishment.
7. 372 U.S. 335 (1963).
8. *Argensinger* v. *Hamlin*, 407 U.S. 25 (1972) and *Scott* v. *Illinois*, 440 U.S. 367 (1979).
9. 461 U.S. 1 (1983).
10. *Douglas* v. *California*, 372 U.S. 353 (1963).
11. *Ross* v. *Moffitt*, 417 600 (1974).
12. 470 U.S. 68 (1985).
13. 422 U.S. 806 (1975).
14. *McKaskle* v. *Wiggins*, 465 U.S. 168 (1984).
15. 487 U.S. 285 (1988).
16. 465 U.S. 168 (1984).
17. 466 U.S. 668 (1984).
18. *Strickland* v. *Washington*, 466 U.S. 668 (1984).
19. *Cuyler* v. *Sullivan*, 446 U.S. 335 (1980).
20. 435 U.S. 475 (1978).
21. *Kirby* v. *Illinois*, 406 U.S. 682 (1972).
22. *United States* v. *Gouveia*, 467 U.S. 180 (1984).

11

GRAND JURY, CHARGING DECISION, AND TRIAL

THE GRAND JURY

A grand jury consists of 16 to 23 persons, appointed to hear certain types of criminal accusations to determine if the individual should be indicted. The Supreme Court in *United States* v. *Williams*[1] stated that the grand jury belongs to no branch of the institutional government and serves as a buffer, or referee, between the government and the people. As stated by the Supreme Court in *Wood* v. *Georgia*[2]:

> Historically, this body [the grand jury] has been regarded as a primary security to the innocent against hasty, malicious and oppressive persecution; it serves the invaluable function in our society of standing between the accuser and the accused, whether the latter be an individual, minority group, or other, to determine whether a charge is founded upon reason or was dictated by an intimidating power or by malice and personal ill will.

The grand jury procedure came into being early in English common law. The Magna Carta provided that no free man was to be seized and imprisoned except by judgment of his peers. Before a person could be held for trial on serious charges, the accusation had to be presented to a council composed of the accused's peers to determine if the charge was well founded. The council later became known as a grand jury, as opposed to a trial or petit jury.

The ideal of the grand jury was brought to this country and was embodied in the Fifth Amendment to the Constitution. The amendment provides that "no person shall be held to answer for a capital or otherwise infamous crime, unless on presentment or indictment of a grand jury." Generally an infamous crime is considered as any felony. While the Fifth Amendment is applicable only to federal charges, states may or may not use the grand jury procedures. Approximately one-half of the states use grand juries. Some states, like California, generally use an information process, but may also use the indictment process. Other states use an information or accusation that is presented to a judge or magistrate at a preliminary hearing in lieu of a grand jury presentation.

The members of a grand jury are generally selected either randomly from a list of qualified voters, or in some states they are appointed by general trial judge from upstanding citizens within the judicial district. While grand juries vary in size, the most standard size is about 19 persons. Generally grand juries serve for terms of six months or one year. After the grand jury is impaneled (sworn-in), one of the jury persons is appointed or elected as the foreperson.

The Indictment

A proposed *indictment* is a document prepared by the prosecuting attorney setting forth a felony charge against the accused. Indictments are not used in misdemeanor cases. The document does not become an indictment until approved by vote of the grand jury. Until then, it is generally considered as a "bill." The *bill* serves several purposes. It informs the grand jury of the charge about which they will receive evidence during the grand jury hearings. If the grand jury votes in favor of holding the accused to answer the charges, also known as endorsing the indictment or true bill, it informs the defendant of the formal charge against him or her. The indictment, when endorsed by the grand jury, becomes the accusatory pleading in trial court. Each crime charged in an indictment is considered as a separate *count*. If the accused is charged with three different crimes in the bill, then there would be three counts to the indictment.

If the accused is not in custody when the indictment is returned, the indictment may be listed as being "sealed" or secret. In this case, no public record will be made of the indictment until the accused has been arrested. Any sealed or secret indictment must be made a public record before the accused is arraigned.

Grand Jury Hearings

Grand juries generally meet at regular times to hear criminal charges presented by a prosecutor. A grand jury also may call a hearing on its own and conduct its own investigations. As noted by the Court in *Williams*, the grand jury is not a judicial body but an investigative body whose historical role is that of an accusatory, not adjudicatory, body.

The grand jury meets in closed sessions, and the procedure remains secret. The accused has no right to be present. In determining whether an accused should be formally charged, jury members will question witnesses and receive evidence. In most cases the prosecuting attorney or an assistant is present during the hearings to assist the grand jury and question witnesses for the grand jury. No one but the jury members may be present during deliberations and voting. In most states a court reporter records the testimony of witnesses during the hearings.

After the evidence is received, the grand jury will deliberate on the facts. If the grand jury decides that the accused should stand trial, they will vote to endorse the

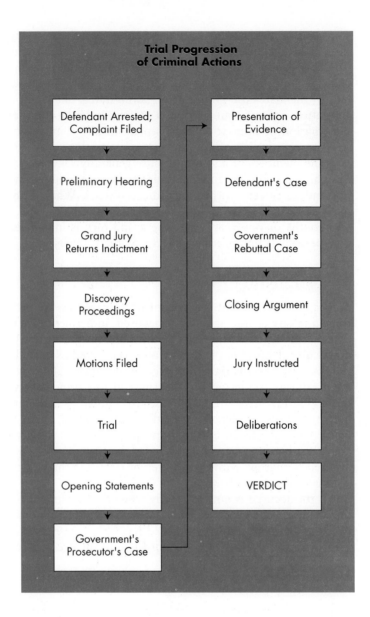

**Trial Progression
of Criminal Actions**

Defendant Arrested;
Complaint Filed

Preliminary Hearing

Grand Jury
Returns Indictment

Discovery
Proceedings

Motions Filed

Trial

Opening Statements

Government's
Prosecutor's Case

Presentation of
Evidence

Defendant's Case

Government's
Rebuttal Case

Closing Argument

Jury Instructed

Deliberations

VERDICT

Source: http://www.uscourts.gov/understanding_courts/gifs/
figure4.gifs

indictment or vote a "true bill." If the grand jury decides that the accused should not stand trial, they refuse to endorse the indictment or vote a "no bill."

With a grand jury of 19 persons, generally 12 votes are required to endorse an indictment. If the grand jury refuses to endorse the indictment, in most states the prosecuting attorney may present the same proposed indictment to the next duly established grand jury. In most states, there is no double jeopardy question in presenting a proposed indictment to a new grand jury. There are a few states that prohibit the prosecuting attorney from presenting the same proposed indictment to a subsequent grand jury.

Grand Jury Indictment

The following grand jury indictment was taken from a case in Texas. The defendant was indicted for capital murder. He was charged with committing murder in a state prison while serving a sentence for another murder.

**The State of Texas vs. Eric Roberto Acosta
Charge: Capital Murder, Penal Code 19.03(a)(6)(A)**

In the Name and by Authority of the State of Texas:

The Grand Jury, for the County of Bee, State of Texas,

duly selected, impaneled, sworn, charged, and organized as such at the July Term A.D., 1996 of the 156th Judicial District Court for said County, upon their oaths present in and to said court at said term that:

ERIC ROBERTO ACOSTA

Count 1

hereinafter styled Defendant, on or about the 13th day of July A.D., 1996, and before the presentment of this indictment, in the County and State aforesaid, Eric Roberto Acosta while in a penal institution to-wit: The Garza East Unit of the Texas Department of Criminal Justice, Institutional Division and serving a sentence for the offense of Murder, did then and there intentionally and knowingly cause the death of another, Daniel Vela, by kicking the said Daniel Vela on or about the head and facial area with Eric Roberto Acosta's shoe clad feet;

Count 2

And hereinafter styled Defendant, on or about the 13th day of July, A.D., 1996, and before the presentment of this indictment, in the County and State aforesaid, Eric Roberto Acosta while in a penal institution to-wit: the Garza East Unit of the Texas Department of Criminal Justice, Institutional Division and serving a sentence for the offense of Murder, did then and there, intending to cause serious bodily injury to an individual, Daniel Vela, commit an act clearly dangerous to human life, to-wit: by kicking the said Daniel Vela on or about the head and facial area with Eric Roberto Acosta's shoe clad feet thereby causing the death of said Daniel Vela.

against the peace and dignity of the state.

[signed by Presiding Grand Juror]

THE DECISION TO PROSECUTE

The Supreme Court in *United States* v. *Goodwin* stated "In our criminal justice system, the government retains "broad discretion" as to whom to prosecute."[3] So long as the prosecutor has probable cause to believe that the accused committed an offense defined by statute, the decision whether or not to prosecute, and what charges to file or bring before a grand jury, generally rests entirely in his or her discretion."[4] According to the Supreme Court:

> This broad discretion rests largely on the recognition that the decision to prosecute is particularly ill-suited to judicial review. Such factors as the strength of the case, the prosecution's general deterrence value, the Government's enforcement priorities, and the case's relationship to the Government's overall enforcement plan are not readily susceptible to the kind of analysis the courts are competent to undertake. Judicial supervision in this area, moreover, entails systemic costs of particular concern. Examining the basis of a prosecution delays the criminal proceeding, threatens to chill law enforcement by subjecting the prosecutor's motives and decisionmaking to outside inquiry, and may undermine prosecutorial effectiveness by revealing the Government's enforcement policy. All these are substantial concerns that make the courts properly hesitant to examine the decision whether to prosecute.[5]

In cases involving selective prosecution claims, the Supreme Court has held that it is appropriate to determine selective prosecution claims according to ordinary equal protection standards. The standards require petitioner to show that the passive enforcement system had a discriminatory effect and that it was motivated by a discriminatory purpose.

RIGHT TO A SPEEDY TRIAL

The U.S. Supreme Court has stated that the right to a speedy trial serves at least three basic demands of criminal justice in the Anglo-American legal system: "1. to prevent undue and oppressive incarceration prior to trial, 2. to minimize anxiety and concern accompanying public accusation, and 3. to limit the possibilities that long delay will impair the ability of an accused to defend himself."[6]

A defendant in a criminal case has a right to a speedy trial. There are two types of speedy trial rights, constitutional and statutory. The constitutional right is based on the Sixth Amendment's right to a speedy trial. The statutory right in federal cases is based on the Speedy Trial Act.[7] Almost all states have speedy trial acts similar to the federal Speedy Trial Act.

Constitutional Right to a Speedy Trial

The Supreme Court has failed to establish a clear rule as to what constitutes a violation of the right to a speedy trial under the Sixth Amendment. In *Barker* v. *Wingo*[8], the Court stated that a balancing test should be used, and the test should be based on the following four factors:

- the length of the delay,
- the reason for the delay,

HISTORY OF THE RIGHT TO A SPEEDY TRIAL

[Excerpt from KLOPFER V. NORTH CAROLINA, 386 U.S. 213 (1967)]

We hold here that the right to a speedy trial is as fundamental as any of the rights secured by the Sixth Amendment. That right has its roots at the very foundation of our English law heritage. Its first articulation in modern jurisprudence appears to have been made in Magna Carta (1215), wherein it was written, "We will sell to no man, we will not deny or defer to any man either justice or right"; but evidence of recognition of the right to speedy justice in even earlier times is found in the Assize of Clarendon (1166). By the late thirteenth century, justices, armed with commissions of gaol delivery and/or oyer and terminer were visiting the countryside three times a year. These justices, Sir Edward Coke wrote in Part II of his *Institutes*, "have not suffered the prisoner to be long detained, but at their next coming have given the prisoner full and speedy justice, . . . without detaining him long in prison." To Coke, prolonged detention without trial would have been contrary to the law and custom of England; but he also believed that the delay in trial, by itself, would be an improper denial of justice. In his explication of Chapter 29 of the Magna Carta, he wrote that the words "We will sell to no man, we will not deny or defer to any man either justice or right" had the following effect:

> And therefore, every subject of this realme, for injury done to him in bonis, terris, vel persona, by any other subject, be he ecclesiasticall, or temporall, free, or bond, man, or woman, old, or young, or be he outlawed, excommunicated, or any other without exception, may take his remedy by the course of the law, and have justice, and right for the injury done to him, freely without sale, fully without any deniall, and speedily without delay.

Coke's *Institutes* were read in the American Colonies by virtually every student of the law. Indeed, Thomas Jefferson wrote that at the time he studied law (1762–1767), "Coke Lyttleton was the universal elementary book of law students." And to John Rutledge of South Carolina, the *Institutes* seemed "to be almost the foundation of our law." To Coke, in turn, Magna Carta was one of the fundamental bases of English liberty. Thus, it is not surprising that when George Mason drafted the first of the colonial bills of rights, he set forth a principle of Magna Carta, using phraseology similar to that of Coke's explication: " [I]n all capital or criminal prosecutions," the Virginia Declaration of Rights of 1776 provided, "a man hath a right . . . to a speedy trial. . . ." That this right was considered fundamental at this early period in our history is evidenced by its guarantee in the constitutions of several of the States of the new nation, as well as by its prominent position in the Sixth Amendment. Today, each of the 50 States guarantees the right to a speedy trial to its citizens.

The history of the right to a speedy trial and its reception in this country clearly establish that it is one of the most basic rights preserved by our Constitution.

- whether the defendant had asserted his or her right to a speedy trial, and
- any prejudice caused the defendant by the delay.

Of the four factors, significant delay must be present or else the motion for a dismissal for lack of speedy trial will have no substance. The presence or lack of presence of the other three factors will be considered by the court in deciding the motion.

The Court in *Barker* stated that the right to a speedy trial is generically different from any of the other rights enshrined in the Constitution for the protection of the accused. There is a strong societal interest in providing a speedy trial which exists separate from, and at times in opposition to, the interest of the accused. In discussing those factors the Court indicated that without a demand for a speedy trial, it could not be assumed that the defendant wanted a speedy trial. Delay, according to the Court, is not an uncommon defense tactic. To raise the issue of lack of speedy trial, there must be a significant time delay between the time a defendant is arrested or indicted and when he or she is tried. If delay is exceedingly long, a court will presume that the delay has prejudiced the defendant.

In *Smith* v. *Hooey*[9], the Court indicated that if there was a lengthy delay following a defense demand for a prompt trial, the primary focus would be on the cause of the delay. In *Smith*, the Court found a speedy trial violation where the state failed to make any effort to respond to the defendant's demand for a prompt trial on pending state charges. In 1960, Smith was indicted in Harris County, Texas, upon a charge of theft. He was then a prisoner in the federal penitentiary at Leavenworth, Kansas. Shortly after the state charge was filed against him, Smith mailed a letter to the Texas trial court requesting a speedy trial. In reply, he was notified that "he would be afforded a trial within two weeks of any date [he] might specify at which he could be present." Thereafter, for the next six years, Smith, "by various letters, and more formal so-called 'motions,' " continued periodically to ask that he be brought to trial. Beyond the response already alluded to, the State took no steps to obtain Smith's appearance in the Harris County trial court. Finally, in 1967, Smith filed in that court a verified motion to dismiss the charge against him for want of prosecution. No action was taken on the motion.

Smith then brought a mandamus proceeding in the Supreme Court of Texas, asking for an order to show cause why the pending charge should not be dismissed. Mandamus was refused in an informal and unreported order of the Texas Supreme Court. Smith then sought *certiorari* in U.S. Supreme Court.

The Court stated:

> There can be no doubt that if the defendant in the present case had been at large for a six-year period following his indictment, and had repeatedly demanded that he be brought to trial, the State would have been under a constitutional duty to try him. And Texas concedes that if during that period he had been confined in a Texas prison for some other state offense, its obligation would have been no less. But the Texas Supreme Court has held that because Smith is, in fact, confined in a federal prison, the State is totally absolved from any duty at all under the constitutional guarantee. We cannot agree.
>
> And while it might be argued that a person already in prison would be less likely than others to be affected by "anxiety and concern accompanying public accusation," there is reason to believe that an outstanding untried charge (of which even a convict may, of course, be innocent) can have fully as depressive an effect upon a prisoner as upon a person who is at large.

There are several reasons used to deny speedy trial motions, including being absent from the jurisdiction or delaying accused's misconduct. If the accused causes the delay, a speedy trial motion will not be granted. For example, a defendant who leaves the country shortly after he is indicted cannot complain regarding the lack of a speedy trial for the period in which he is out of the country. If the government causes the delay in order to obtain a trial advantage, it will be easier for the accused to win a speedy trial motion.

A defendant who has strenuously asserted his or her right to a speedy trial is more likely to be successful. A defendant who has either waived time or has agreed to continuances will not succeed on a speedy trial motion.

While it is generally difficult for the defendant to establish actual prejudice from any delay, the courts may assume prejudice if the delay is unduly long or there is a lengthy period of pretrial incarceration. Prejudice to the defendant includes anxiety, stress, and concern or an adverse impact on the defendant's ability to prepare a defense.

In *Doggett* v. *United States*[10], the lack of affirmative justification for the delay was critical. In *Doggett*, there was no demand by the defendant, but the defendant did not know that charges were pending against him. He was out of the country when he was indicted. The government was negligent in failing to note his return for nearly six years. Based on the unjustified delay, the Court dismissed the charges.

Statutory Right to a Speedy Trial

The Federal Speedy Trial Act requires that not more than 30 days may elapse between the time a suspect is arrested until the time he or she is indicted on or charged with a crime. Once a defendant is formally charged, trial must start within 70 days. The time limits contain many exceptions, and frequently the defense waives time. There are two key differences between the statutory right to a speedy trial and the constitutional right. First, the statutory has definite time limits within which the trial must be held, i.e., seventy days after formal charges are entered. Second, if the constitutional right to a speedy trial is violated, the charges are dismissed with prejudice. A dismissal with prejudice means that the defendant cannot be re-indicted or charged with the offense. Under the statutory right, the judge generally may dismiss the charges for a violation of the statutory right without prejudice, i.e., the government can re-indict or re-charge. Most state speedy trial acts are based on the federal act and contain similar provisions.

THE TRIAL PHASE

The Sixth Amendment to the U.S. Constitution provides that the accused has the right to "a speedy and public trial by an impartial jury of the State and district wherein the crime shall have been committed." The place or geographical location of the trial is the called the *venue*. As noted, the accused has a right to be tried in the district wherein the crime occurred. Often an accused because of pretrial publicly, etc., will move for a change of venue, i.e., to be tried in a different location. The prosecution has no right to a change of venue. As a general rule, the motion for change of venue must be made during pretrial motions and prior to the date set for commencement of the trial.

Right to Trial by Jury

In cases involving serious crimes, the accused has the right to trial by jury. The accused may, however, waive his or her right to a trial by jury and request trial by judge alone, also referred to as a *court trial*. In most jurisdictions a plea of guilty acts as a waiver of the right to trial by jury. In a court trial, the judge makes rulings on all legal issues and all issues of fact. In *Singer* v. *United States*[11], the Supreme Court held that a defendant may waive his or her right to a trial by jury, but the judge may refuse to accept the waiver and set the case for jury trial. In *Singer*, the prosecution objected to the defense request for trial by judge alone. The court stated that the ability to waive a constitutional right does not ordinarily carry with it the right to insist upon the opposite of that right—that a trial by jury has been established by the Constitution as the normal and preferable mode of disposing of issues of fact in a criminal case.

As noted earlier, the right to trial by jury is not an absolute right. The Supreme Court in *Duncan* v. *Louisiana*[12] held that petty offenses may be tried without a jury. The Court also held that a petty offense was one for which the maximum penalty that may be imposed on conviction is imprisonment not to exceed six months.

Size of Jury

At common law, criminal trial juries generally consisted of twelve persons. The Supreme Court in *Williams* v. *Florida*[13] held that in non-capital cases (non-death penalty) a jury composed of less than twelve persons was constitutionally valid. Williams was convicted by a six-person jury and received a sentence of life imprisonment. Later Supreme Court decisions held that six was the minimum number to constitute a jury and that, if the jury size is less than 12, a unanimous verdict is required.

Public Trial

The Sixth Amendment also provides that the accused has the right to a public trial. There is no constitutional definition of what constitutes a "public trial." The general definition of a public trial is one which the public has a right to attend. This right to a public trial does not mean that every person has a right to attend, only that the courtroom be large enough to accommodate a reasonable number of the public to attend. If spectators become disruptive, the judge may clear the courtroom. However, that does not permit the judge to lock the door and prohibit other members of the public from attending.

The Supreme Court in *Richmond Newspapers* v. *Virginia*[14] recognized that the press and the public have a right of access to criminal trials based on the First Amendment. In the *Richmond Newspapers* case, the defense had requested that the public be excluded from his trial. The Court held that the press and the public have a right to attend unless the judge determines that in order to guarantee a fair trial, the public should be excluded from portions of the trial.

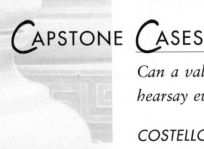

CAPSTONE CASES

Can a valid indictment endorsed by a grand jury be based only on hearsay evidence that is inadmissible at trial?

COSTELLO V. UNITED STATES
350 U.S. 359 (1956)

MR. JUSTICE BLACK delivered the opinion of the Court.

We granted *certiorari* in this case to consider a single question: "May a defendant be required to stand trial and a conviction be sustained where only hearsay evidence was presented to the grand jury which indicted him?"

Petitioner, Frank Costello, was indicated for willfully attempting to evade payment of income taxes due the United States for the years 1947, 1948 and 1949. The charge was that petitioner falsely and fraudulently reported less income than he and his wife actually received during the taxable years in question. Petitioner promptly filed a motion for inspection of the minutes of the grand jury and for a dismissal of the indictment. His motion was based on an affidavit stating that he was firmly convinced there could have been no legal or competent evidence before the grand jury which indicted him since he had reported all his income and paid all taxes due. The motion was denied. At the trial which followed the Government offered evidence designed to show increases in Costello's net worth in an attempt to prove that he had received more income during the years in question than he had reported. To establish its case the Government called and examined 144 witnesses and introduced 368 exhibits. All of the testimony and documents related to business transactions and expenditures by petitioner and his wife. The prosecution concluded its case by calling three government agents. Their investigations had produced the evidence used against petitioner at the trial. They were allowed to summarize the vast amount of evidence already heard and to introduce computations showing, if correct, that petitioner and his wife had received far greater income than they had reported. . . .

Counsel for petitioner asked each government witness at the trial whether he had appeared before the grand jury which returned the indictment. This cross-examination developed the fact that the three investigating officers had been the only witnesses before the grand jury. After the Government concluded its case, petitioner again moved to dismiss the indictment on the ground that the only evidence before the grand jury was "hearsay," since the three officers had no firsthand knowledge of the transactions upon which their computations were based. Nevertheless the trial court again refused to dismiss the indictment, and petitioner was convicted. The Court of Appeals affirmed, holding that the indictment was valid even though the sole evidence before the grand jury was hearsay. Petitioner here urges: (1) that an indictment based solely on hearsay evidence violates that part of the Fifth Amendment providing that "No person shall be held to answer for a capital, or otherwise infamous crime, unless on a presentment or indictment of a Grand Jury. . . ." and (2) that if the Fifth Amendment does not invalidate an indictment based solely on hearsay we should now lay down such a rule for the guidance of federal courts.

The Fifth Amendment provides that federal prosecutions for capital or otherwise infamous crimes must be instituted by presentments or indictments of grand juries. But neither the Fifth Amendment nor any other constitutional provision prescribes the kind of evidence upon which grand juries must act. The grand jury is an English institution, brought to this country by the early colonists and incorporated in the Constitution by the Founders. There is every reason to believe that our constitutional grand jury was intended to operate substantially like its English progenitor. The basic purpose of the English grand jury was to provide a fair method for instituting criminal proceedings against persons believed to have committed crimes. Grand jurors were selected from the body of the people and their work was not hampered by rigid procedural or evidential rules. In fact, grand jurors could act on their own knowledge and were free to make their presentments or indictments on such information as they deemed satisfactory. Despite its broad power to

institute criminal proceedings the grand jury grew in popular favor with the years. It acquired an independence in England free from control by the Crown or judges. Its adoption in our Constitution as the sole method for preferring charges in serious criminal cases shows the high place it held as an instrument of justice. And in this country as in England of old the grand jury has convened as a body of laymen, free from technical rules, acting in secret, pledged to indict no one because of prejudice and to free no one because of special favor. As late as 1927 an English historian could say that English grand juries were still free to act on their own knowledge if they pleased to do so. And in 1852 Mr. Justice Nelson on circuit could say "No case has been cited, nor have we been able to find any, furnishing an authority for looking into and revising the judgment of the grand jury upon the evidence, for the purpose of determining whether or not the finding was founded upon sufficient proof. . . ." *United States* v. *Reed*, 27 Fed. Cas. 727, 738.

In *Holt* v. *United States*, 218 U.S. 245, this Court had to decide whether an indictment should be quashed because it was supported in part by incompetent evidence. Aside from the incompetent evidence, "there was very little evidence against the accused." The Court refused to hold that such an indictment should be quashed, pointing out that "The abuses of criminal practice would be enhanced if indictments could be upset on such a ground." 218 U.S., at 248. The same thing is true where as here all the evidence before the grand jury was in the nature of "hearsay." If indictments were to be held open to challenge on the ground that there was inadequate or incompetent evidence before the grand jury, the resulting delay would be great indeed. The result of such a rule would be that before trial on the merits a defendant could always insist on a kind of preliminary trial to determine the competency and adequacy of the evidence before the grand jury. This is not required by the Fifth Amendment. An indictment returned by a legally constituted and unbiased grand jury, like an information drawn by the prosecutor, if valid on its face, is enough to call for trial of the charge on the merits. The Fifth Amendment requires nothing more.

Petitioner urges that this Court should exercise its power to supervise the administration of justice in federal courts and establish a rule permitting defendants to challenge indictments on the ground that they are not supported by adequate or competent evidence. No persuasive reasons are advanced for establishing such a rule. It would run counter to the whole history of the grand jury institution, in which laymen conduct their inquiries unfettered by technical rules. Neither justice nor the concept of a fair trial requires such a change. In a trial on the merits, defendants are entitled to a strict observance of all the rules designed to bring about a fair verdict. Defendants are not entitled, however, to a rule which would result in interminable delay but add nothing to the assurance of a fair trial.

Affirmed.

MR. JUSTICE CLARK and MR. JUSTICE HARLAN took no part in the consideration or decision of this case.

MR. JUSTICE BURTON, concurring [Omitted.]

WHAT DO *YOU* THINK?

1. Should the prosecutor be required to produce some legally admissible evidence in order to obtain an indictment?
2. Do you see any practical reasons for the Court in refusing to allow the defendant to attack the indictment based solely on lack of admissible evidence?

Is an ordinance that confers a naked and arbitrary power on the board of supervisors to give or withhold consent, not only as to places but as to persons, valid? The Yick Wo *case deals with this issue and the issue of discrimination.*

YICK WO V. HOPKINS
118 U.S. 356 (1886)

MATTHEWS, J.

In the case of the petitioner, brought here by writ of error to the supreme court of California, our jurisdiction is limited to the question whether the plaintiff in error has been denied a right in violation of the constitution, laws, or treaties of the United States. The question whether his imprisonment is illegal, under the constitution and laws of the state, is not open to us. And although that question might have been considered in the circuit court in the application made to it, and by this court on appeal from its order, yet judicial propriety is best consulted by accepting the judgment of the state court upon the points involved in that inquiry. That, however, does not preclude this court from putting upon the ordinances of the supervisors of the county and city of San Francisco an independent construction; for the determination of the question whether the proceedings under these ordinances, and in enforcement of them, are in conflict with the constitution and laws of the United States, necessarily involves the meaning of the ordinances, which, for that purpose, we are required to ascertain and adjudge.

We are consequently constrained, at the outset, to differ from the supreme court of California upon the real meaning of the ordinances in question. That court considered these ordinances as vesting in the board of supervisors a not unusual discretion in granting or withholding their assent to the use of wooden buildings as laundries, to be exercised in reference to the circumstances of each case, with a view to the protection of the public against the dangers of fire. We are not able to concur in that interpretation of the power conferred upon the supervisors. There is nothing in the ordinances which points to such a regulation of the business of keeping and conducting laundries. They seem intended to confer, and actually to confer, not a discretion to be exercised upon a consideration of the circumstances of each case, but a naked and arbitrary power to give or withhold consent, not only as to places, but as to persons; so that, if an applicant for such consent, being in every way a competent and qualified person, and having complied with every reasonable condition demanded by any public interest, should, failing to obtain the requisite consent of the supervisors to the prosecution of his business, apply for redress by the judicial process of mandamus to require the supervisors to consider and act upon his case, it would be a sufficient answer for them to say that the law had conferred upon them authority to withhold their assent, without reason and without responsibility. The power given to them is not confided to their discretion in the legal sense of that term, but is granted to their mere will. It is purely arbitrary, and acknowledges neither guidance nor restraint.

This erroneous view of the ordinances in question led the supreme court of California into the further error of holding that they were justified by the decisions of this court in the cases of *Barbier* v. *Connelly*, 113 U.S. 27, S. C. 5 Sup. Ct. Rep.

357, and *Soon Hing* v. *Crowley*, 113 U.S. 703, S. C. 5 Sup. Ct. Rep. 730. In both of these cases the ordinance involved was simply a prohibition to carry on the washing and ironing of clothes in public laundries and wash houses, within certain prescribed limits of the city and county of San Francisco, from 10 o'clock at night until 6 o'clock in the morning of the following day. This provision was held to be purely a police regulation, within the competency of any municipality possessed of the ordinary powers belonging to such bodies—a necessary measure of precaution in a city composed largely of wooden buildings, like San Francisco, in the application of which there was no invidious discrimination against any one within the prescribed limits; all persons engaged in the same business being treated alike, and subject to the same restrictions, and entitled to the same privileges, under similar conditions. For these reasons that ordinance was adjudged not to be within the prohibitions of the fourteenth amendment to the constitution of the United States, which, it was said in the first case cited, undoubtedly intended, not only that there should be no arbitrary deprivation of life or liberty, or arbitrary spoliation of property, but that equal protection and security should be given to all under like circumstances in the enjoyment of their personal and civil rights; that all persons should be equally entitled to pursue their happiness, and acquire and enjoy property; that they should have like access to the courts of the country for the protection of their persons and property, the prevention and redress of wrongs, and the enforcement of contracts; that no impediment should be interposed to the pursuits of any one, except as applied to the same pursuits by others under like circumstances; that no greater burdens should be laid upon one than are laid upon others in the same calling and condition; and that, in the administration of criminal justice, no different or higher punishment should be imposed upon one than such as is prescribed to all for like offenses. . . . Class legislation, discriminating against some and favoring others, is prohibited; but legislation which, in carrying out a public purpose, is limited in its application, if, within the sphere of its operation, it affects alike all persons similarly situated, is not within the amendment.

The ordinance drawn in question in the present case is of a very different character. It does not prescribe a rule and conditions, for the regulation of the use of property for laundry purposes, to which all similarly situated may conform. It allows, without restriction, the use for such purposes of buildings of brick or stone; but, as to wooden buildings, constituting nearly all those in previous use, it divides the owners or occupiers into two classes, not having respect to their personal character and qualifications for the business, nor the situation and nature and adaptation of the buildings themselves, but merely by an arbitrary line, on one side of which are those who are permitted to pursue their industry by the mere will and consent of the supervisors, and on the other those from whom that consent is withheld, at their mere will and pleasure. And both classes are alike only in this: that they are tenants at will, under the supervisors, of their means of living. The ordinance, therefore, also differs from the not unusual case where discretion is lodged by law in public officers or bodies to grant or withhold licenses to keep taverns, or places for the sale of spirituous liquors, and the like, when one of the conditions is that the applicant shall be a fit person for the exercise of the privilege, because in such cases the fact of fitness is submitted to the judgment of the officer, and calls for the exercise of a discretion of a judicial nature.

The rights of the petitioners, as affected by the proceedings of which they complain, are not less because they are aliens and subjects of the emperor of China. By the third article of the treaty between this government and that of China, concluded November 17, 1880, (22 St. 827), it is stipulated: "If Chinese laborers, or

Chinese of any other class, now either permanently or temporarily residing in the territory of the United States, meet with ill treatment at the hands of any other persons, the government of the United States will exert all its powers to devise measures for their protection, and to secure to them the same rights, privileges, immunities, and exemptions as may be enjoyed by the citizens or subjects of the most favored nation, and to which they are entitled by treaty." The fourteenth amendment to the constitution is not confined to the protection of citizens. It says: "Nor shall any state deprive any person of life, liberty, or property without due process of law; nor deny to any person within its jurisdiction the equal protection of the laws." These provisions are universal in their application, to all persons within the territorial jurisdiction, without regard to any differences of race, of color, or of nationality; and the equal protection of the laws is a pledge of the protection of equal laws. It is accordingly enacted by section 1977 of the Revised Statutes that "all persons within the jurisdiction of the United States shall have the same right, in every state and territory, to make and enforce contracts, to sue, be parties, give evidence, and to the full and equal benefit of all laws and proceedings for the security of persons and property as is enjoyed by white citizens, and shall be subject to like punishment, pains, penalties, taxes, licenses, and exactions of every kind, and to no other." The questions we have to consider and decide in these cases, therefore, are to be treated as involving the rights of every citizen of the United States equally with those of the strangers and aliens who now invoke the jurisdiction of the court.

It is contended on the part of the petitioners that the ordinances for violations of which they are severally sentenced to imprisonment are void on their face, as being within the prohibitions of the fourteenth amendment, and, in the alternative, if not so, that they are void by reason of their administration, operating unequally, so as to punish in the present petitioners what is permitted to others as lawful, without any distinction of circumstances—an unjust and illegal discrimination, it is claimed, which, though not made expressly by the ordinances, is made possible by them.

. . . The present cases, as shown by the facts disclosed in the record, are within this class. It appears that both petitioners have complied with every requisite deemed by the law, or by the public officers charged with its administration, necessary for the protection of neighboring property from fire, or as a precaution against injury to the public health. No reason whatever, except the will of the supervisors, is assigned why they should not be permitted to carry on, in the accustomed manner, their harmless and useful occupation, on which they depend for a livelihood; and while this consent of the supervisors is withheld from them, and from 200 others who have also petitioned, all of whom happen to be Chinese subjects, 80 others, not Chinese subjects, are permitted to carry on the same business under similar conditions. The fact of this discrimination is admitted. No reason for it is shown, and the conclusion cannot be resisted that no reason for it exists except hostility to the race and nationality to which the petitioners belong, and which, in the eye of the law, is not justified. The discrimination is therefore illegal, and the public administration which enforces it is a denial of the equal protection of the laws, and a violation of the fourteenth amendment of the constitution. The imprisonment of the petitioners is therefore illegal, and they must be discharged. To this end the judgment of the supreme court of California in the Case of *Yick Wo*, and that of the circuit court of the United States for the district of California in the Case of *Wo Lee*, are severally reversed, and the cases remanded, each to the proper court, with directions to discharge the petitioners from custody and imprisonment.

1. Do you agree with the decision?
2. The subject regulation was enforced only against Chinese individuals. In cases like this, should the prosecutor be required to justify his or her decisions on whom to prosecute?

May a prosecutor attempt to gain a guilty plea by informing the defendant that if he does not approve a plea bargain, the prosecutor will re-indict under the habitual criminal act? The Bordenkircher *case looks at this issue.*

BORDENKIRCHER V. HAYES
434 U.S. 357 (1978)

MR. JUSTICE STEWART delivered the opinion of the Court.

The question in this case is whether the Due Process Clause of the Fourteenth Amendment is violated when a state prosecutor carries out a threat made during plea negotiations to reindict the accused on more serious charges if he does not plead guilty to the offense with which he was originally charged.

I.

The respondent, Paul Lewis Hayes, was indicted by a Fayette County, Ky., grand jury on a charge of uttering a forged instrument in the amount of $88.30, an offense then punishable by a term of 2 to 10 years in prison. . . . After arraignment, Hayes, his retained counsel, and the Commonwealth's Attorney met in the presence of the Clerk of the Court to discuss a possible plea agreement. During these conferences the prosecutor offered to recommend a sentence of five years in prison if Hayes would plead guilty to the indictment. He also said that if Hayes did not plead guilty and "save the court the inconvenience and necessity of a trial," he would return to the grand jury to seek an indictment under the Kentucky Habitual Criminal Act . . . which would subject Hayes to a mandatory sentence of life imprisonment by reason of his two prior felony convictions. Hayes chose not to plead guilty, and the prosecutor did obtain an indictment charging him under the Habitual Criminal Act. It is not disputed that the recidivist charge was fully justified by the evidence, that the prosecutor was in possession of this evidence at the time of the original indictment, and that Hayes' refusal to plead guilty to the original charge was what led to his indictment under the habitual criminal statute.

A jury found Hayes guilty on the principal charge of uttering a forged instrument and, in a separate proceeding, further found that he had twice before been convicted of felonies. As required by the habitual offender statute, he was sentenced to a life term in the penitentiary. The Kentucky Court of Appeals rejected Hayes' constitutional objections to the enhanced sentence, holding in an unpublished opinion that imprisonment for life with the possibility of parole was constitutionally

permissible in light of the previous felonies of which Hayes had been convicted, and that the prosecutor's decision to indict him as a habitual offender was a legitimate use of available leverage in the plea-bargaining process.

On Hayes' petition for a federal writ of habeas corpus, the United States District Court for the Eastern District of Kentucky agreed that there had been no constitutional violation in the sentence or the indictment procedure, and denied the writ. The Court of Appeals for the Sixth Circuit reversed the District Court's judgment. *Hayes* v. *Cowan*, 547 F.2d 42. While recognizing "that plea bargaining now plays an important role in our criminal justice system," *id.*, at 43, the appellate court thought that the prosecutor's conduct during the bargaining negotiations had violated the principles of *Blackledge* v. *Perry*, 417 U.S. 21, which "protect[ed] defendants from the vindictive exercise of a prosecutor's discretion." 547 F.2d, at 44. Accordingly, the court ordered that Hayes be discharged "except for his confinement under a lawful sentence imposed solely for the crime of uttering a forged instrument." *Id.*, at 45. We granted *certiorari* to consider a constitutional question of importance in the administration of criminal justice. 431 U.S. 953.

II.

It may be helpful to clarify at the outset the nature of the issue in this case. While the prosecutor did not actually obtain the recidivist indictment until after the plea conferences had ended, his intention to do so was clearly expressed at the outset of the plea negotiations. Hayes was thus fully informed of the true terms of the offer when he made his decision to plead not guilty. This is not a situation, therefore, where the prosecutor without notice brought an additional and more serious charge after plea negotiations relating only to the original indictment had ended with the defendant's insistence on pleading not guilty. As a practical matter, in short, this case would be no different if the grand jury had indicted Hayes as a recidivist from the outset, and the prosecutor had offered to drop that charge as part of the plea bargain.

The Court of Appeals nonetheless drew a distinction between "concessions relating to prosecution under an existing indictment," and threats to bring more severe charges not contained in the original indictment—a line it thought necessary in order to establish a prophylactic rule to guard against the evil of prosecutorial vindictiveness. Quite apart from this chronological distinction, however, the Court of Appeals found that the prosecutor had acted vindictively in the present case since he had conceded that the indictment was influenced by his desire to induce a guilty plea. The ultimate conclusion of the Court of Appeals thus seems to have been that a prosecutor acts vindictively and in violation of due process of law whenever his charging decision is influenced by what he hopes to gain in the course of plea bargaining negotiations.

III.

We have recently had occasion to observe: "Whatever might be the situation in an ideal world, the fact is that the guilty plea and the often concomitant plea bargain are important components of this country's criminal justice system. Properly administered, they can benefit all concerned." *Blackledge* v. *Allison*, 431 U.S. 63, 71. The open acknowledgment of this previously clandestine practice has led this Court to recognize the importance of counsel during plea negotiations, *Brady* v. *United*

States, 397 U.S. 742, 758, the need for a public record indicating that a plea was knowingly and voluntarily made, *Boykin* v. *Alabama*, 395 U.S. 238, 242, and the requirement that a prosecutor's plea-bargaining promise must be kept, *Santobello* v. *New York*, 404 U.S. 257, 262. The decision of the Court of Appeals in the present case, however, did not deal with considerations such as these, but held that the substance of the plea offer itself violated the limitations imposed by the Due Process Clause of the Fourteenth Amendment. Cf. *Brady* v. *United States, supra*, at 751 n. 8. For the reasons that follow, we have concluded that the Court of Appeals was mistaken in so ruling.

IV.

This Court held in *North Carolina* v. *Pearce*, 395 U.S. 711, 725, that the Due Process Clause of the Fourteenth Amendment "requires that vindictiveness against a defendant for having successfully attacked his first conviction must play no part in the sentence he receives after a new trial." The same principle was later applied to prohibit a prosecutor from reindicting a convicted misdemeanant on a felony charge after the defendant had invoked an appellate remedy, since in this situation there was also a "realistic likelihood of 'vindictiveness.' " *Blackledge* v. *Perry*, 417 U.S., at 27.

In those cases, the Court was dealing with the State's unilateral imposition of a penalty upon a defendant who had chosen to exercise a legal right to attack his original conviction—a situation "very different from the give-and-take negotiation common in plea bargaining between the prosecution and defense, which arguably possess relatively equal bargaining power." *Parker* v. *North Carolina*, 397 U.S. 790, 809 (opinion of BRENNAN, J.). The Court has emphasized that the due process violation in cases such as *Pearce* and *Perry* lay not in the possibility that a defendant might be deterred from the exercise of a legal right, see *Colten* v. *Kentucky*, 407 U.S. 104; *Chaffin* v. *Stynchcombe*, 412 U.S. 17, but rather in the danger that the State might be retaliating against the accused for lawfully attacking his conviction. See *Blackledge* v. *Perry, supra*, at 26–28.

To punish a person because he has done what the law plainly allows him to do is a due process violation of the most basic sort, see *North Carolina* v. *Pearce, supra*, at 738 (opinion of BLACK, J.), and for an agent of the State to pursue a course of action whose objective is to penalize a person's reliance on his legal rights is "patently unconstitutional." *Chaffin* v. *Stynchcombe, supra*, at 32–33, n. 20. See *United States* v. *Jackson*, 390 U.S. 570. But in the "give-and-take" of plea bargaining, there is no such element of punishment or retaliation so long as the accused is free to accept or reject the prosecution's offer.

Plea bargaining flows from "the mutuality of advantage" to defendants and prosecutors, each with his own reasons for wanting to avoid trial. *Brady* v. *United States, supra*, at 752. Defendants advised by competent counsel and protected by other procedural safeguards are presumptively capable of intelligent choice in response to prosecutorial persuasion, and unlikely to be driven to false self-condemnation. 397 U.S., at 758. Indeed, acceptance of the basic legitimacy of plea bargaining necessarily implies rejection of any notion that a guilty plea is involuntary in a constitutional sense simply because it is the end result of the bargaining process. By hypothesis, the plea may have been induced by promises of a recommendation of a lenient sentence or a reduction of charges, and thus by fear of the possibility of a greater penalty upon conviction after a trial. See ABA *Project on Standards for Criminal Justice, Pleas of Guilty* 3.1 (App. Draft 1968); [434 U.S.

357, 364] Note, Plea Bargaining and the Transformation of the Criminal Process, 90 Harv. L. Rev. 564 (1977). Cf. *Brady* v. *United States*, *supra*, at 751; *North Carolina* v. *Alford*, 400 U.S. 25.

While confronting a defendant with the risk of more severe punishment clearly may have a "discouraging effect on the defendant's assertion of his trial rights, the imposition of these difficult choices [is] an inevitable"—and permissible—"attribute of any legitimate system which tolerates and encourages the negotiation of pleas." *Chaffin* v. *Stynchcombe*, *supra*, at 31. It follows that, by tolerating and encouraging the negotiation of pleas, this Court has necessarily accepted as constitutionally legitimate the simple reality that the prosecutor's interest at the bargaining table is to persuade the defendant to forgo his right to plead not guilty.

It is not disputed here that Hayes was properly chargeable under the recidivist statute, since he had in fact been convicted of two previous felonies. In our system, so long as the prosecutor has probable cause to believe that the accused committed an offense defined by statute, the decision whether or not to prosecute, and what charge to file or bring before a grand jury, generally rests entirely in his discretion. Within the limits set by the legislature's constitutionally valid definition of chargeable offenses, "the conscious exercise of some selectivity in enforcement is not in itself a federal constitutional violation" so long as "the selection was [not] deliberately based upon an unjustifiable standard such as race, religion, or other arbitrary classification." *Oyler* v. *Boles*, 368 U.S. 448, 456. To hold that the prosecutor's desire to induce a guilty plea is an "unjustifiable standard," which, like race or religion, may play no part in his charging decision, would contradict the very premises that underlie the concept of plea bargaining itself. Moreover, a rigid constitutional rule that would prohibit a prosecutor from acting forthrightly in his dealings with the defense could only invite unhealthy subterfuge that would drive the practice of plea bargaining back into the shadows from which it has so recently emerged. See *Blackledge* v. *Allison*, 431 U.S., at 76.

There is no doubt that the breadth of discretion that our country's legal system vests in prosecuting attorneys carries with it the potential for both individual and institutional abuse. And broad though that discretion may be, there are undoubtedly constitutional limits upon its exercise. We hold only that the course of conduct engaged in by the prosecutor in this case, which no more than openly presented the defendant with the unpleasant alternatives of forgoing trial or facing charges on which he was plainly subject to prosecution, did not violate the Due Process Clause of the Fourteenth Amendment.

Accordingly, the judgment of the Court of Appeals is Reversed.

MR. JUSTICE BLACKMUN, with whom MR. JUSTICE BRENNAN and MR. JUSTICE MARSHALL join, dissenting. [Omitted.]

WHAT DO YOU THINK?

1. Should the decision whether or not to prosecute, and what charge to file or bring before a grand jury, generally rest entirely on the prosecutor's discretion?

2. Should the prosecutor be permitted to pressure a defendant to accept a plea bargain by informing him that more severe charges will be brought if the plea bargain is refused?

3. Should the prosecutor be required to provide an explanation on the record for his or her decision to escalate the charges against a defendant?

Does the due process clause of the Fifth Amendment prohibit the government from bringing more serious charges against a defendant after he has invoked his right to a jury trial?

UNITED STATES V. GOODWIN
457 U.S. 368 (1982)

JUSTICE STEVENS delivered the opinion of the Court.

This case involves presumptions. The question presented is whether a presumption that has been used to evaluate a judicial or prosecutorial response to a criminal defendant's exercise of a right to be retried after he has been convicted should also be applied to evaluate a prosecutor's pretrial response to a defendant's demand for a jury trial.

After the respondent requested a trial by jury on pending misdemeanor charges, he was indicted and convicted on a felony charge. Believing that the sequence of events gave rise to an impermissible appearance of prosecutorial retaliation against the defendant's exercise of his right to be tried by jury. . . .

I.

Respondent Goodwin was stopped for speeding by a United States Park Policeman on the Baltimore-Washington Parkway. Goodwin emerged from his car to talk to the policeman. After a brief discussion, the officer noticed a clear plastic bag un-

Justice John Paul Stevens was appointed to the Supreme Court by President Ford and has served from 1975 to the present. (Photograph by Joseph Bailey, National Geographic Society. Courtesy of the Supreme Court of the United States.)

derneath the armrest next to the driver's seat of Goodwin's car. The officer asked Goodwin to return to his car and to raise the armrest. Respondent did so, but as he raised the armrest he placed the car into gear and accelerated rapidly. The car struck the officer, knocking him first onto the back of the car and then onto the highway. The policeman returned to his car, but Goodwin eluded him in a high-speed chase.

The following day, the officer filed a complaint in the District Court charging respondent with several misdemeanor and petty offenses, including assault. Goodwin was arrested and arraigned before a United States Magistrate. The Magistrate set a date for trial, but respondent fled the jurisdiction. Three years later Goodwin was found in custody in Virginia and was returned to Maryland.

Upon his return, respondent's case was assigned to an attorney from the Department of Justice, who was detailed temporarily to try petty crime and misdemeanor cases before the Magistrate. The attorney did not have authority to try felony cases or to seek indictments from the grand jury. Respondent initiated plea negotiations with the prosecutor, but later advised the Government that he did not wish to plead guilty and desired a trial by jury in the District Court.

The case was transferred to the District Court and responsibility for the prosecution was assumed by an Assistant United States Attorney. Approximately six weeks later, after reviewing the case and discussing it with several parties, the prosecutor obtained a four-count indictment charging respondent with one felony count of forcibly assaulting a federal officer and three related counts arising from the same incident. A jury convicted respondent on the felony count and on one misdemeanor count.

Respondent moved to set aside the verdict on the ground of prosecutorial vindictiveness, contending that the indictment on the felony charge gave rise to an impermissible appearance of retaliation. The District Court denied the motion, finding that "the prosecutor in this case has adequately dispelled any appearance of retaliatory intent."

Although the Court of Appeals readily concluded that "the prosecutor did not act with actual vindictiveness in seeking a felony indictment," 637 F.2d, at 252, it nevertheless reversed. Relying on our decisions in *North Carolina* v. *Pearce*, *supra*, and *Blackledge* v. *Perry*, *supra*, the court held that the Due Process Clause of the Fifth Amendment prohibits the Government from bringing more serious charges against a defendant after he has invoked his right to a jury trial, unless the prosecutor comes forward with objective evidence to show that the increased charges could not have been brought before the defendant exercised his rights. Because the court believed that the circumstances surrounding the felony indictment gave rise to a genuine risk of retaliation, it adopted a legal presumption designed to spare courts the "unseemly task" of probing the actual motives of the prosecutor. 637 F.2d, at 255.

II.

To punish a person because he has done what the law plainly allows him to do is a due process violation "of the most basic sort." *Bordenkircher* v. *Hayes*, 434 U.S. 357, 363. In a series of cases beginning with *North Carolina* v. *Pearce* and culminating in *Bordenkircher* v. *Hayes*, the Court has recognized this basic—and itself uncontroversial—principle. For while an individual certainly may be penalized for violating the law, he just as certainly may not be punished for exercising a protected statutory or constitutional right.

The imposition of punishment is the very purpose of virtually all criminal proceedings. The presence of a punitive motivation, therefore, does not provide an

adequate basis for distinguishing governmental action that is fully justified as a legitimate response to perceived criminal conduct from governmental action that is an impermissible response to noncriminal, protected activity. Motives are complex and difficult to prove. As a result, in certain cases in which action detrimental to the defendant has been taken after the exercise of a legal right, the Court has found it necessary to "presume" an improper vindictive motive. Given the severity of such a presumption, however—which may operate in the absence of any proof of an improper motive and thus may block a legitimate response to criminal conduct—the Court has done so only in cases in which a reasonable likelihood of vindictiveness exists.

In *North Carolina* v. *Pearce*, the Court held that neither the Double Jeopardy Clause nor the Equal Protection Clause prohibits a trial judge from imposing a harsher sentence on retrial after a criminal defendant successfully attacks an initial conviction on appeal. The Court stated, however, that "[i]t can hardly be doubted that it would be a flagrant violation [of the Due Process Clause] of the Fourteenth Amendment for a state trial court to follow an announced practice of imposing a heavier sentence upon every reconvicted defendant for the explicit purpose of punishing the defendant for his having succeeded in getting his original conviction set aside." 395 U.S., at 723–724. The Court continued:

> Due process of law, then, requires that vindictiveness against a defendant for having successfully attacked his first conviction must play no part in the sentence he receives after a new trial. And since the fear of such vindictiveness may unconstitutionally deter a defendant's exercise of the right to appeal or collaterally attack his first conviction, due process also requires that a defendant be freed of apprehension of such a retaliatory motivation on the part of the sentencing judge. *Id.*, at 725

In order to assure the absence of such a motivation, the Court concluded:

> [W]henever a judge imposes a more severe sentence upon a defendant after a new trial, the reasons for his doing so must affirmatively appear. Those reasons must be based upon objective information concerning identifiable conduct on the part of the defendant occurring after the time of the original sentencing proceeding. And the factual data upon which the increased sentence is based must be made part of the record, so that the constitutional legitimacy of the increased sentence may be fully reviewed on appeal. *Id.*, at 726

In sum, the Court applied a presumption of vindictiveness, which may be overcome only by objective information in the record justifying the increased sentence.

In *Blackledge* v. *Perry*, 417 U.S. 21, the Court confronted the problem of increased punishment upon retrial after appeal in a setting different from that considered in *Pearce*. Perry was convicted of assault in an inferior court having exclusive jurisdiction for the trial of misdemeanors. The court imposed a 6-month sentence. Under North Carolina law, Perry had an absolute right to a trial *de novo* in the Superior Court, which possessed felony jurisdiction. After Perry filed his notice of appeal, the prosecutor obtained a felony indictment charging him with assault with a deadly weapon. Perry pleaded guilty to the felony and was sentenced to a term of five to seven years in prison.

In reviewing Perry's felony conviction and increased sentence, this Court first stated the essence of the holdings in Pearce and the cases that had followed it:

> The lesson that emerges from *Pearce*, *Colten*, and *Chaffin* is that the Due Process Clause is not offended by all possibilities of increased punishment upon retrial after appeal, but only by those that pose a realistic likelihood of "vindictiveness." 417 U.S., at 27

The Court held that the opportunities for vindictiveness in the situation before it were such "as to impel the conclusion that due process of law requires a rule analogous to that of the Pearce case." *Ibid.* It explained:

> A prosecutor clearly has a considerable stake in discouraging convicted misdemeanants from appealing and thus obtaining a trial de novo in the Superior Court, since such an appeal will clearly require increased expenditures of prosecutorial resources before the defendant's conviction becomes final, and may even result in a formerly convicted defendant's going free. And, if the prosecutor has the means readily at hand to discourage such appeals—by "upping the ante" through a felony indictment whenever a convicted misdemeanant pursues his statutory appellate remedy—the State can insure that only the most hardy defendants will brave the hazards of a de novo trial. *Id.*, at 27–28

The Court emphasized in *Blackledge* that it did not matter that no evidence was present that the prosecutor had acted in bad faith or with malice in seeking the felony indictment. As in *Pearce*, the Court held that the likelihood of vindictiveness justified a presumption that would free defendants of apprehension of such a retaliatory motivation on the part of the prosecutor.

Both *Pearce* and *Blackledge* involved the defendant's exercise of a procedural right that caused a complete retrial after he had been once tried and convicted. The decisions in these cases reflect a recognition by the Court of the institutional bias inherent in the judicial system against the retrial of issues that have already been decided. The doctrines of *stare decisis*, *res judicata*, the law of the case, and double jeopardy all are based, at least in part, on that deep-seated bias. While none of these doctrines barred the retrials in *Pearce* and *Blackledge*, the same institutional pressure that supports them might also subconsciously motivate a vindictive prosecutorial or judicial response to a defendant's exercise of his right to obtain a retrial of a decided question.

In *Bordenkircher v. Hayes*, 434 U.S. 357, the Court for the first time considered an allegation of vindictiveness that arose in a pretrial setting. In that case the Court held that the Due Process Clause of the Fourteenth Amendment did not prohibit a prosecutor from carrying out a threat, made during plea negotiations, to bring additional charges against an accused who refused to plead guilty to the offense with which he was originally charged. The prosecutor in that case had explicitly told the defendant that if he did not plead guilty and "save the court the inconvenience and necessity of a trial" he would return to the grand jury to obtain an additional charge that would significantly increase the defendant's potential punishment. The defendant refused to plead guilty and the prosecutor obtained the indictment. It was not disputed that the additional charge was justified by the evidence, that the prosecutor was in possession of this evidence at the time the original indictment was obtained, and that the prosecutor sought the additional charge because of the accused's refusal to plead guilty to the original charge.

In finding no due process violation, the Court in *Bordenkircher* considered the decisions in *Pearce* and *Blackledge*, and stated:

> In those cases the Court was dealing with the State's unilateral imposition of a penalty upon a defendant who had chosen to exercise a legal right to attack his original conviction— a situation "very different from the give-and-take negotiation common in plea bargaining between the prosecution and defense, which arguably possess relatively equal bargaining power." *Parker* v. *North Carolina*, 397 U.S. 790, 809 (opinion of BRENNAN, J.)." 434 U.S., at 362

The Court stated that the due process violation in *Pearce* and *Blackledge* "lay not in the possibility that a defendant might be deterred from the exercise of a

legal right . . . but rather in the danger that the State might be retaliating against the accused for lawfully attacking his conviction." 434 U.S., at 363

The Court held, however, that there was no such element of punishment in the "give-and-take" of plea negotiation, so long as the accused "is free to accept or reject the prosecution's offer." *Ibid.* The Court noted that, by tolerating and encouraging the negotiation of pleas, this Court had accepted as constitutionally legitimate the simple reality that the prosecutor's interest at the bargaining table is to persuade the defendant to forgo his constitutional right to stand trial. The Court concluded:

> We hold only that the course of conduct engaged in by the prosecutor in this case, which no more than openly presented the defendant with the unpleasant alternatives of forgoing trial or facing charges on which he was plainly subject to prosecution, did not violate the Due Process Clause of the Fourteenth Amendment. *Id.*, at 365.

The outcome in *Bordenkircher* was mandated by this Court's acceptance of plea negotiation as a legitimate process. In declining to apply a presumption of vindictiveness, the Court recognized that "additional" charges obtained by a prosecutor could not necessarily be characterized as an impermissible "penalty." Since charges brought in an original indictment may be abandoned by the prosecutor in the course of plea negotiation—in often what is clearly a "benefit" to the defendant—changes in the charging decision that occur in the context of plea negotiation are an inaccurate measure of improper prosecutorial "vindictiveness." An initial indictment—from which the prosecutor embarks on a course of plea negotiation—does not necessarily define the extent of the legitimate interest in prosecution. For just as a prosecutor may forgo legitimate charges already brought in an effort to save the time and expense of trial, a prosecutor may file additional charges if an initial expectation that a defendant would plead guilty to lesser charges proves unfounded.

III.

This case, like *Bordenkircher*, arises from a pretrial decision to modify the charges against the defendant. Unlike *Bordenkircher*, however, there is no evidence in this case that could give rise to a claim of actual vindictiveness; the prosecutor never suggested that the charge was brought to influence the respondent's conduct. The conviction in this case may be reversed only if a presumption of vindictiveness—applicable in all cases—is warranted.

There is good reason to be cautious before adopting an inflexible presumption of prosecutorial vindictiveness in a pretrial setting. In the course of preparing a case for trial, the prosecutor may uncover additional information that suggests a basis for further prosecution or he simply may come to realize that information possessed by the State has a broader significance. At this stage of the proceedings, the prosecutor's assessment of the proper extent of prosecution may not have crystallized. In contrast, once a trial begins—and certainly by the time a conviction has been obtained—it is much more likely that the State has discovered and assessed all of the information against an accused and has made a determination, on the basis of that information, of the extent to which he should be prosecuted. Thus, a change in the charging decision made after an initial trial is completed is much more likely to be improperly motivated than is a pretrial decision.

In addition, a defendant before trial is expected to invoke procedural rights that inevitably impose some "burden" on the prosecutor. Defense counsel routinely file pretrial motions to suppress evidence; to challenge the sufficiency and form of an indictment; to plead an affirmative defense; to request psychiatric services; to obtain access to government files; to be tried by jury. It is unrealistic to assume that a prosecutor's probable response to such motions is to seek to penalize and to deter. The invocation of procedural rights is an integral part of the adversary process in which our criminal justice system operates.

Thus, the timing of the prosecutor's action in this case suggests that a presumption of vindictiveness is not warranted. A prosecutor should remain free before trial to exercise the broad discretion entrusted to him to determine the extent of the societal interest in prosecution. An initial decision should not freeze future conduct. As we made clear in *Bordenkircher*, the initial charges filed by a prosecutor may not reflect the extent to which an individual is legitimately subject to prosecution.

The nature of the right asserted by the respondent confirms that a presumption of vindictiveness is not warranted in this case. After initially expressing an interest in plea negotiation, respondent decided not to plead guilty and requested a trial by jury in District Court. In doing so, he forced the Government to bear the burdens and uncertainty of a trial. This Court in *Bordenkircher* made clear that the mere fact that a defendant refuses to plead guilty and forces the government to prove its case is insufficient to warrant a presumption that subsequent changes in the charging decision are unjustified. Respondent argues that such a presumption is warranted in this case, however, because he not only requested a trial—he requested a trial by jury.

We cannot agree. The distinction between a bench trial and a jury trial does not compel a special presumption of prosecutorial vindictiveness whenever additional charges are brought after a jury is demanded. To be sure, a jury trial is more burdensome than a bench trial. The defendant may challenge the selection of the venire; the jury itself must be impaneled; witnesses and arguments must be prepared more carefully to avoid the danger of a mistrial. These matters are much less significant, however, than the facts that before either a jury or a judge the State must present its full case against the accused and the defendant is entitled to offer a full defense. As compared to the complete trial de novo at issue in *Blackledge*, a jury trial—as opposed to a bench trial—does not require duplicative expenditures of prosecutorial resources before a final judgment may be obtained. Moreover, unlike the trial judge in *Pearce*, no party is asked "to do over what it thought it had already done correctly." A prosecutor has no "personal stake" in a bench trial and thus no reason to engage in "self-vindication" upon a defendant's request for a jury trial. Perhaps most importantly, the institutional bias against the retrial of a decided question that supported the decisions in *Pearce* and *Blackledge* simply has no counterpart in this case.

There is an opportunity for vindictiveness, as there was in *Colten* and *Chaffin*. Those cases demonstrate, however, that a mere opportunity for vindictiveness is insufficient to justify the imposition of a prophylactic rule. As *Blackledge* makes clear, "the Due Process Clause is not offended by all possibilities of increased punishment . . . but only by those that pose a realistic likelihood of 'vindictiveness.' " 417 U.S., at 27. The possibility that a prosecutor would respond to a defendant's pretrial demand for a jury trial by bringing charges not in the public interest that could be explained only as a penalty imposed on the defendant is so unlikely that a presumption of vindictiveness certainly is not warranted.

IV.

In declining to apply a presumption of vindictiveness, we of course do not foreclose the possibility that a defendant in an appropriate case might prove objectively that the prosecutor's charging decision was motivated by a desire to punish him for doing something that the law plainly allowed him to do. In this case, however, the Court of Appeals stated: "On this record we readily conclude that the prosecutor did not act with actual vindictiveness in seeking a felony indictment." 637 F.2d, at 252. Respondent does not challenge that finding. Absent a presumption of vindictiveness, no due process violation has been established.

The judgment of the Court of Appeals is reversed. The case is remanded for further proceedings consistent with this opinion. It is so ordered.

WHAT DO YOU THINK?

1. Do you agree with the majority opinion that the prosecutor may bring more serious charges against the defendant when the defendant demands a jury trial? Explain your answer.
2. Do you agree that the prosecutor did not act with actual vindictiveness in seeking a felony indictment? Why?
3. Do you agree with the Court's finding that there was no element of punishment in the "give-and-take" of plea negotiation? Explain your answer.

When an act violates more than one criminal statute, does the government need to justify the decision to prosecute under the statute which has the greater penalties?

UNITED STATES V. BATCHELDER
442 U.S. 114 (1979)

MR. JUSTICE MARSHALL delivered the opinion of the Court.

At issue in this case are two overlapping provisions of the Omnibus Crime Control and Safe Streets Act of 1968 (Omnibus Act). Both prohibit convicted felons from receiving firearms, but each authorizes different maximum penalties. We must determine whether a defendant convicted of the offense carrying the greater penalty may be sentenced only under the more lenient provision when his conduct violates both statutes.

I.

Respondent, a previously convicted felon, was found guilty of receiving a firearm that had traveled in interstate commerce, in violation of 18 U.S.C. 922 (h). The District Court sentenced him under 18 U.S.C. 924 (a) to five years' imprisonment, the maximum term authorized for violation of 922 (h).

The Court of Appeals affirmed the conviction but, by a divided vote, remanded for resentencing. 581 F.2d 626 (CA7 1978). The majority recognized that respondent had been indicted and convicted under 922 (h) and that 924 (a) permits five

years' imprisonment for such violations. 581 F.2d, at 629. However, noting that the substantive elements of 922 (h) and 18 U.S.C. App. 1202 (a) are identical as applied to a convicted felon who unlawfully receives a firearm, the court interpreted the Omnibus Act to allow no more than the 2-year maximum sentence provided by 1202 (a). 581 F.2d, at 629. In so holding, the Court of Appeals relied on three principles of statutory construction. Because, in its view, the "arguably contra-dict[ory]" penalty provisions for similar conduct and the "inconclusive" legislative history raised doubt whether Congress had intended the two penalty provisions to co-exist, the court first applied the doctrine that ambiguities in criminal legislation are to be resolved in favor of the defendant. *Id.*, at 630. Second, the court determined that since 1202 (a) was "Congress' last word on the issue of penalty," it may have implicitly repealed the punishment provisions of 924 (a). 581 F.2d, at 630. Acknowledging that the "first two principles cannot be applied to these facts without some difficulty," the majority also invoked the maxim that a court should, if possible, interpret a statute to avoid constitutional questions. *Id.*, at 630–631. Here, the court reasoned, the "prosecutor's power to select one of two statutes that are identical except for their penalty provisions" implicated "important constitutional protections." *Id.*, at 631.

The dissent found no basis in the Omnibus Act or its legislative history for engrafting the penalty provisions of 1202 (a) onto 922 (h) and 924 (a). 581 F.2d, at 638–639. Relying on "the long line of cases . . . which hold that where an act may violate more than one criminal statute, the government may elect to prosecute under either, even if [the] defendant risks the harsher penalty, so long as the prosecutor does not discriminate against any class of defendants," the dissent further concluded that the statutory scheme was constitutional. *Id.*, at 637.

We granted *certiorari*, 439 U.S. 1066 (1979), and now reverse the judgment vacating respondent's 5-year prison sentence.

II.

This Court has previously noted the partial redundancy of 922 (h) and 1202 (a), both as to the conduct they proscribe and the individuals they reach. See *United States* v. *Bass*, 404 U.S. 336, 341–343, and n. 9 (1971). However, we find nothing in the language, structure, or legislative history of the Omnibus Act to suggest that because of this overlap, a defendant convicted under 922 (h) may be imprisoned for no more than the maximum term specified in 1202 (a). As we read the Act, each substantive statute, in conjunction with its own sentencing provision, operates independently of the other.

Section 922 (h), contained in Title IV of the Omnibus Act, prohibits four categories of individuals from receiving "any firearm or ammunition which has been shipped or transported in interstate or foreign commerce." See n. 2, *supra*. Persons who violate Title IV are subject to the penalties provided by 924 (a), which authorizes a maximum fine of $5,000 and imprisonment for up to five years. See n. 3, *supra*. Section 1202 (a), located in Title VII of the Omnibus Act, forbids five categories of individuals from "receiv[ing], possess[ing], or transport[ing] in commerce or affecting commerce . . . any firearm." This same section authorizes a maximum fine of $10,000 and imprisonment for not more than two years.

While 922 and 1202 (a) both prohibit convicted felons such as petitioner from receiving firearms, each Title unambiguously specifies the penalties available to enforce its substantive proscriptions. Section 924 (a) applies without exception to "[w]hoever violates any provision" of Title IV, and 922 (h) is patently such a

provision. See 18 U.S.C., ch. 44; 82 Stat. 226, 234; S. Rep. No. 1097, 90th Cong., 2d Sess., 20–25, 117 (1968). Similarly, because Title VII's substantive prohibitions and penalties are both enumerated in 1202, its penalty scheme encompasses only criminal prosecutions brought under that provision. On their face, these statutes thus establish that 924 (a) alone delimits the appropriate punishment for violations of 922 (h).

That Congress intended to enact two independent gun control statutes, each fully enforceable on its own terms, is confirmed by the legislative history of the Omnibus Act. Section 922 (h) derived from 2 (f) of the Federal Firearms Act of 1938, 52 Stat. 1251, and 5 of that Act, 52 Stat. 1252, authorized the same maximum prison term as 924 (a). Title IV of the Omnibus Act merely recodified with some modification this "carefully constructed package of gun control legislation," which had been in existence for many years. *Scarborough* v. *United States*, 431 U.S. 563, 570 (1977); see *United States* v. *Bass*, *supra*, at 343 n. 10; 15 U.S.C. 902, 905 (1964 ed.).

By contrast, Title VII was a "last-minute" floor amendment, "hastily passed, with little discussion, no hearings, and no report." *United States* v. *Bass*, *supra*, at 344, and n. 11; see *Scarborough* v. *United States*, *supra*, at 569–570, and n. 9. And the meager legislative debates involving that amendment demonstrate no intention to alter the terms of Title IV. Immediately before the Senate passed Title VII, Senator Dodd inquired whether it would substitute for Title IV. 114 Cong. Rec. 14774 (1968). Senator Long, the sponsor of the amendment, replied that 1202 would "take nothing from" but merely "add to" Title IV. 114 Cong. Rec. 14774 (1968). Similarly, although Title VII received only passing mention in House discussions of the bill, Representative Machen made clear that the amendment would "complement . . . the gun-control legislation contained in title IV." *Id.*, at 16286. Had these legislators intended to pre-empt Title IV in cases of overlap, they presumably would not have indicated that the purpose of Title VII was to complement Title IV. See *Scarborough* v. *United States*, *supra*, at 573. These discussions, together with the language and structure of the Omnibus Act, evince Congress' clear understanding that the two Titles would be applied independently.

In construing 1202 (a) to override the penalties authorized by 924 (a), the Court of Appeals relied, we believe erroneously, on three principles of statutory interpretation. First, the court invoked the well-established doctrine that ambiguities in criminal statutes must be resolved in favor of lenity. E.g., *Lewis* v. *United States*, 401 U.S. 808, 812 (1971); *United States* v. *Bass*, 404 U.S., at 347; *United States* v. *Culbert*, 435 U.S. 371, 379 (1978); *United States* v. *Naftalin*, 441 U.S. 768, 778–779 (1979); *Dunn* v. *United States*, *ante*, at 112–113. Although this principle of construction applies to sentencing as well as substantive provisions, see *Simpson* v. *United States*, 435 U.S. 6, 14–15 (1978), in the instant case there is no ambiguity to resolve. Respondent unquestionably violated 922 (h), and 924 (a) unquestionably permits five years' imprisonment for such a violation. That 1202 (a) provides different penalties for essentially the same conduct is no justification for taking liberties with unequivocal statutory language. See *Barrett* v. *United States*, 423 U.S. 212, 217 (1976). By its express terms, 1202 (a) limits its penalty scheme exclusively to convictions obtained under that provision. Where, as here, "Congress has conveyed its purpose clearly, . . . we decline to manufacture ambiguity where none exists." *United States* v. *Culbert*, *supra*, at 379.

Nor can 1202 (a) be interpreted as implicitly repealing 924 (a) whenever a defendant's conduct might violate both Titles. For it is "not enough to show that the two statutes produce differing results when applied to the same factual situation."

Radzanower v. *Touche Ross & Co.*, 426 U.S. 148, 155 (1976). Rather, the legislative intent to repeal must be manifest in the " 'positive repugnancy between the provisions.' " *United States* v. *Borden Co.*, 308 U.S. 188, 199 (1939). In this case, however, the penalty provisions are fully capable of coexisting because they apply to convictions under different statutes.

Finally, the maxim that statutes should be construed to avoid constitutional questions offers no assistance here. This " 'cardinal principle' of statutory construction . . . is appropriate only when [an alternative interpretation] is 'fairly possible' " from the language of the statute. *Swain* v. *Pressley*, 430 U.S. 372, 378 n. 11 (1977); see *Crowell* v. *Benson*, 285 U.S. 22, 62 (1932); *United States* v. *Sullivan*, 332 U.S. 689, 693 (1948); *Shapiro* v. *United States*, 335 U.S. 1, 31 (1948). We simply are unable to discern any basis in the Omnibus Act for reading the term "five" in 924 (a) to mean "two."

III.

In resolving the statutory question, the majority below expressed "serious doubts about the constitutionality of two statutes that provide different penalties for identical conduct." 581 F.2d, at 633–634 (footnote omitted). Specifically, the court suggested that the statutes might (1) be void for vagueness, (2) implicate "due process and equal protection interest[s] in avoiding excessive prosecutorial discretion and in obtaining equal justice," and (3) constitute an impermissible delegation of congressional authority. *Id.*, at 631–633. We find no constitutional infirmities.

A.

It is a fundamental tenet of due process that "[n]o one may be required at peril of life, liberty or property to speculate as to the meaning of penal statutes." *Lanzetta* v. *New Jersey*, 306 U.S. 451, 453 (1939). A criminal statute is therefore invalid if it "fails to give a person of ordinary intelligence fair notice that his contemplated conduct is forbidden." *United States* v. *Harris*, 347 U.S. 612, 617 (1954). See *Connally* v. *General Construction Co.*, 269 U.S. 385, 391–393 (1926); *Papachristou* v. *Jacksonville*, 405 U.S. 156, 162 (1972); *Dunn* v. *United States*, *ante*, at 112–113. So too, vague sentencing provisions may pose constitutional questions if they do not state with sufficient clarity the consequences of violating a given criminal statute. See *United States* v. *Evans*, 333 U.S. 483 (1948); *United States* v. *Brown*, 333 U.S. 18 (1948); *cf. Giaccio* v. *Pennsylvania*, 382 U.S. 399 (1966).

The provisions in issue here, however, unambiguously specify the activity proscribed and the penalties available upon conviction. See *supra*, at 119. That this particular conduct may violate both Titles does not detract from the notice afforded by each. Although the statutes create uncertainty as to which crime may be charged and therefore what penalties may be imposed, they do so to no greater extent than would a single statute authorizing various alternative punishments. So long as overlapping criminal provisions clearly define the conduct prohibited and the punishment authorized, the notice requirements of the Due Process Clause are satisfied.

B.

This Court has long recognized that when an act violates more than one criminal statute, the Government may prosecute under either so long as it does not discriminate against any class of defendants. . . . Whether to prosecute and what charge to file or bring before a grand jury are decisions that generally rest in the prosecutor's discretion. See *Confiscation Cases*, 7 Wall. 454 (1869); *United States* v. *Nixon*, 418 U.S. 683, 693 (1974); *Bordenkircher* v. *Hayes*, 434 U.S. 357, 364 (1978)....

WHAT DO YOU THINK?

1. Do you agree with the majority opinion that the government may prosecute under the statute with the harshest penalty? What about the rule that ambiguities in criminal statutes must be resolved in favor of the defendant?

2. What would be necessary in order to establish that the government was discriminating against any class of defendants?

The next case looks at the issue of speedy trial.

BARKER V. WINGO
407 U.S. 514 (1972)

MR. JUSTICE POWELL delivered the opinion of the Court.

Although a speedy trial is guaranteed the accused by the Sixth Amendment to the Constitution, this Court has dealt with that right on infrequent occasions.... The Court's opinion in *Klopfer* v. *North Carolina*, 386 U.S. 213 (1967), established that the right to a speedy trial is "fundamental" and is imposed by the Due Process Clause of the Fourteenth Amendment on the States....

I.

On July 20, 1958, in Christian County, Kentucky, an elderly couple was beaten to death by intruders wielding an iron tire tool. Two suspects, Silas Manning and Willie Barker, the petitioner, were arrested shortly thereafter. The grand jury indicted them on September 15. Counsel was appointed on September 17, and Barker's trial was set for October 21. The Commonwealth had a stronger case against Manning, and it believed that Barker could not be convicted unless Manning testified against him. Manning was naturally unwilling to incriminate himself. Accordingly, on October 23, the day Silas Manning was brought to trial, the Commonwealth sought and obtained the first of what was to be a series of 16 continuances of Barker's trial. Barker made no objection. By first convicting Manning, the Commonwealth would remove possible problems of self-incrimination and would be able to assure his testimony against Barker.

The Commonwealth encountered more than a few difficulties in its prosecution of Manning. The first trial ended in a hung jury. A second trial resulted in a conviction, but the Kentucky Court of Appeals reversed because of the admission of evidence obtained by an illegal search. *Manning* v. *Commonwealth*, 328 S. W. 2d 421 (1959). At his third trial, Manning was again convicted, and the Court of Appeals again reversed because the trial court had not granted a change of venue. *Manning* v. *Commonwealth*, 346 S. W. 2d 755 (1961). A fourth trial resulted in a hung jury. Finally, after five trials, Manning was convicted, in March 1962, of murdering one victim, and after a sixth trial, in December 1962, he was convicted of murdering the other.

The Christian County Circuit Court holds three terms each year—in February, June, and September. Barker's initial trial was to take place in the September term

of 1958. The first continuance postponed it until the February 1959 term. The second continuance was granted for one month only. Every term thereafter for as long as the *Manning* prosecutions were in process, the Commonwealth routinely moved to continue Barker's case to the next term. When the case was continued from the June 1959 term until the following September, Barker, having spent months in jail, obtained his release by posting a $5,000 bond. He thereafter remained free in the community until his trial. Barker made no objection, through his counsel, to the first continuances.

When on February 12, 1962, the Commonwealth moved for the twelfth time to continue the case until the following term, Barker's counsel filed a motion to dismiss the indictment. The motion to dismiss was denied two weeks later, and the Commonwealth's motion for a continuance was granted. The Commonwealth was granted further continuances in June 1962 and September 1962, to which Barker did not object.

In February 1963, the first term of court following Manning's final conviction, the Commonwealth moved to set Barker's trial for March 19. But on the day scheduled for trial, it again moved for a continuance until the June term. It gave as its reason the illness of the ex-sheriff who was the chief investigating officer in the case. To this continuance, Barker objected unsuccessfully.

The witness was still unable to testify in June, and the trial, which had been set for June 19, was continued again until the September term over Barker's objection. This time the court announced that the case would be dismissed for lack of prosecution if it were not tried during the next term. The final trial date was set for October 9, 1963. On that date, Barker again moved to dismiss the indictment, and this time specified that his right to a speedy trial had been violated. The motion was denied; the trial commenced with Manning as the chief prosecution witness; Barker was convicted and given a life sentence. Barker appealed his conviction to the Kentucky Court of Appeals, relying in part on his speedy trial claim. The court affirmed. *Barker* v. *Commonwealth*, 385 S. W. 2d 671 (1964). In February 1970 Barker petitioned for habeas corpus in the United States District Court for the Western District of Kentucky. Although the District Court rejected the petition without holding a hearing, the court granted petitioner leave to appeal in *forma pauperis* and a certificate of probable cause to appeal. On appeal, the Court of Appeals for the Sixth Circuit affirmed the District Court. 442 F.2d 1141 (1971). It ruled that Barker had waived his speedy trial claim for the entire period before February 1963, the date on which the court believed he had first objected to the delay by filing a motion to dismiss. In this belief the court was mistaken, for the record reveals that the motion was filed in February 1962. The Commonwealth so conceded at oral argument before this Court. The court held further that the remaining period after the date on which Barker first raised his claim and before his trial—which it thought was only eight months but which was actually 20 months—was not unduly long. In addition, the court held that Barker had shown no resulting prejudice, and that the illness of the ex-sheriff was a valid justification for the delay. We granted Barker's petition for *certiorari*. 404 U.S. 1037 (1972).

II.

The right to speedy trial is generically different from any of the other rights enshrined in the Constitution for the protection of the accused. In addition to the general concern that all accused persons be treated according to decent and fair procedures, there is a societal interest in providing a speedy trial which exists separate from, and at

times in opposition to, the interests of the accused. The inability of courts to provide a prompt trial has contributed to a large backlog of cases in urban courts which, among other things, enables defendants to negotiate more effectively for pleas of guilty to lesser offenses and otherwise manipulate the system. In addition, persons released on bond for lengthy periods awaiting trial have an opportunity to commit other crimes. It must be of little comfort to the residents of Christian County, Kentucky, to know that Barker was at large on bail for over four years while accused of a vicious and brutal murder of which he was ultimately convicted. Moreover, the longer an accused is free awaiting trial, the more tempting becomes his opportunity to jump bail and escape. Finally, delay between arrest and punishment may have a detrimental effect on rehabilitation.

If an accused cannot make bail, he is generally confined, as was Barker for 10 months, in a local jail. This contributes to the overcrowding and generally deplorable state of those institutions. Lengthy exposure to these conditions "has a destructive effect on human character and makes the rehabilitation of the individual offender much more difficult." At times the result may even be violent rioting. Finally, lengthy pretrial detention is costly. The cost of maintaining a prisoner in jail varies from $3 to $9 per day, and this amounts to millions across the nation. In addition, society loses wages which might have been earned, and it must often support families of incarcerated breadwinners.

A second difference between the right to speedy trial and the accused's other constitutional rights is that deprivation of the right may work to the accused's advantage. Delay is not an uncommon defense tactic. As the time between the commission of the crime and trial lengthens, witnesses may become unavailable or their memories may fade. If the witnesses support the prosecution, its case will be weakened, sometimes seriously so. And it is the prosecution which carries the burden of proof. Thus, unlike the right to counsel or the right to be free from compelled self-incrimination, deprivation of the right to speedy trial does not per se prejudice the accused's ability to defend himself.

Finally, and perhaps most importantly, the right to speedy trial is a more vague concept than other procedural rights. It is, for example, impossible to determine with precision when the right has been denied. We cannot definitely say how long is too long in a system where justice is supposed to be swift but deliberate. As a consequence, there is no fixed point in the criminal process when the State can put the defendant to the choice of either exercising or waiving the right to a speedy trial. If, for example, the State moves for a 60-day continuance, granting that continuance is not a violation of the right to speedy trial unless the circumstances of the case are such that further delay would endanger the values the right protects. It is impossible to do more than generalize about when those circumstances exist. There is nothing comparable to the point in the process when a defendant exercises or waives his right to counsel or his right to a jury trial. . . .

. . . The amorphous quality of the right also leads to the unsatisfactorily severe remedy of dismissal of the indictment when the right has been deprived. This is indeed a serious consequence because it means that a defendant who may be guilty of a serious crime will go free, without having been tried. Such a remedy is more serious than an exclusionary rule or a reversal for a new trial, but it is the only possible remedy.

. . . In excepting the right to speedy trial from the rule of waiver we have applied to other fundamental rights, courts that have applied the demand-waiver rule have relied on the assumption that delay usually works for the benefit of the accused and on the absence of any readily ascertainable time in the criminal process

for a defendant to be given the choice of exercising or waiving his right. But it is not necessarily true that delay benefits the defendant. There are cases in which delay appreciably harms the defendant's ability to defend himself. Moreover, a defendant confined to jail prior to trial is obviously disadvantaged by delay as is a defendant released on bail but unable to lead a normal life because of community suspicion and his own anxiety.

The nature of the speedy trial right does make it impossible to pinpoint a precise time in the process when the right must be asserted or waived, but that fact does not argue for placing the burden of protecting the right solely on defendants. A defendant has no duty to bring himself to trial; the State has that duty as well as the duty of insuring that the trial is consistent with due process. Moreover, for the reasons earlier expressed, society has a particular interest in bringing swift prosecutions, and society's representatives are the ones who should protect that interest.

It is also noteworthy that such a rigid view of the demand-waiver rule places defense counsel in an awkward position. Unless he demands a trial early and often, he is in danger of frustrating his client's right. If counsel is willing to tolerate some delay because he finds it reasonable and helpful in preparing his own case, he may be unable to obtain a speedy trial for his client at the end of that time. Since under the demand-waiver rule no time runs until the demand is made, the government will have whatever time is otherwise reasonable to bring the defendant to trial after a demand has been made. Thus, if the first demand is made three months after arrest in a jurisdiction which prescribes a six-month rule, the prosecution will have a total of nine months—which may be wholly unreasonable under the circumstances. The result in practice is likely to be either an automatic, pro forma demand made immediately after appointment of counsel or delays which, but for the demand-waiver rule, would not be tolerated. Such a result is not consistent with the interests of defendants, society, or the Constitution.

We reject, therefore, the rule that a defendant who fails to demand a speedy trial forever waives his right. This does not mean, however, that the defendant has no responsibility to assert his right. We think the better rule is that the defendant's assertion of or failure to assert his right to a speedy trial is one of the factors to be considered in an inquiry into the deprivation of the right. Such a formulation avoids the rigidities of the demand-waiver rule and the resulting possible unfairness in its application. It allows the trial court to exercise a judicial discretion based on the circumstances, including due consideration of any applicable formal procedural rule. It would permit, for example, a court to attach a different weight to a situation in which the defendant knowingly fails to object from a situation in which his attorney acquiesces in long delay without adequately informing his client, or from a situation in which no counsel is appointed. It would also allow a court to weigh the frequency and force of the objections as opposed to attaching significant weight to a purely pro forma objection.

In ruling that a defendant has some responsibility to assert a speedy trial claim, we do not depart from our holdings in other cases concerning the waiver of fundamental rights, in which we have placed the entire responsibility on the prosecution to show that the claimed waiver was knowingly and voluntarily made. Such cases have involved rights which must be exercised or waived at a specific time or under clearly identifiable circumstances, such as the rights to plead not guilty, to demand a jury trial, to exercise the privilege against self-incrimination, and to have the assistance of counsel. We have shown above that the right to a speedy trial is unique in its uncertainty as to when and under what circumstances it must be

asserted or may be deemed waived. But the rule we announce today, which comports with constitutional principles, places the primary burden on the courts and the prosecutors to assure that cases are brought to trial. We hardly need add that if delay is attributable to the defendant, then his waiver may be given effect under standard waiver doctrine, the demand rule aside.

We, therefore, reject both of the inflexible approaches—the fixed-time period because it goes further than the Constitution requires; the demand-waiver rule because it is insensitive to a right which we have deemed fundamental. The approach we accept is a balancing test, in which the conduct of both the prosecution and the defendant are weighed.

IV.

A balancing test necessarily compels courts to approach speedy trial cases on an ad hoc basis. We can do little more than identify some of the factors which courts should assess in determining whether a particular defendant has been deprived of his right. Though some might express them in different ways, we identify four such factors: Length of delay, the reason for the delay, the defendant's assertion of his right, and prejudice to the defendant.

The length of the delay is to some extent a triggering mechanism. Until there is some delay which is presumptively prejudicial, there is no necessity for inquiry into the other factors that go into the balance. Nevertheless, because of the imprecision of the right to speedy trial, the length of delay that will provoke such an inquiry is necessarily dependent upon the peculiar circumstances of the case. To take but one example, the delay that can be tolerated for an ordinary street crime is considerably less than for a serious, complex conspiracy charge.

Closely related to length of delay is the reason the government assigns to justify the delay. Here, too, different weights should be assigned to different reasons. A deliberate attempt to delay the trial in order to hamper the defense should be weighted heavily against the government. A more neutral reason such as negligence or overcrowded courts should be weighted less heavily but nevertheless should be considered since the ultimate responsibility for such circumstances must rest with the government rather than with the defendant.

Finally, a valid reason, such as a missing witness, should serve to justify appropriate delay.

We have already discussed the third factor, the defendant's responsibility to assert his right. Whether and how a defendant asserts his right is closely related to the other factors we have mentioned. The strength of his efforts will be affected by the length of the delay, to some extent by the reason for the delay, and most particularly by the personal prejudice, which is not always readily identifiable, that he experiences. The more serious the deprivation, the more likely a defendant is to complain. The defendant's assertion of his speedy trial right, then, is entitled to strong evidentiary weight in determining whether the defendant is being deprived of the right. We emphasize that failure to assert the right will make it difficult for a defendant to prove that he was denied a speedy trial.

A fourth factor is prejudice to the defendant. Prejudice, of course, should be assessed in the light of the interests of defendants which the speedy trial right was designed to protect. This Court has identified three such interests: (i) to prevent oppressive pretrial incarceration; (ii) to minimize anxiety and concern of the accused; and (iii) to limit the possibility that the defense will be impaired. Of these, the most serious is the last, because the inability of a defendant to adequately prepare his

case skews the fairness of the entire system. If witnesses die or disappear during a delay, the prejudice is obvious. There is also prejudice if defense witnesses are unable to recall accurately events of the distant past. Loss of memory, however, is not always reflected in the record because what has been forgotten can rarely be shown.

We have discussed previously the societal disadvantages of lengthy pretrial incarceration, but obviously the disadvantages for the accused who cannot obtain his release are even more serious. The time spent in jail awaiting trial has a detrimental impact on the individual. It often means loss of a job; it disrupts family life; and it enforces idleness. Most jails offer little or no recreational or rehabilitative programs. The time spent in jail is simply dead time. Moreover, if a defendant is locked up, he is hindered in his ability to gather evidence, contact witnesses, or otherwise prepare his defense. Imposing those consequences on anyone who has not yet been convicted is serious. It is especially unfortunate to impose them on those persons who are ultimately found to be innocent. Finally, even if an accused is not incarcerated prior to trial, he is still disadvantaged by restraints on his liberty and by living under a cloud of anxiety, suspicion, and often hostility. . . .

We regard none of the four factors identified above as either a necessary or sufficient condition to the finding of a deprivation of the right of speedy trial. Rather, they are related factors and must be considered together with such other circumstances as may be relevant. In sum, these factors have no talismanic qualities; courts must still engage in a difficult and sensitive balancing process. But, because we are dealing with a fundamental right of the accused, this process must be carried out with full recognition that the accused's interest in a speedy trial is specifically affirmed in the Constitution. . . . The judgment of the Court of Appeals is Affirmed.

Mr. Justice White, with whom Mr. Justice Brennan joins, concurring. [Omitted.]

What Do You Think?

1. The Court stated that the right to speedy trial is a more vague concept than other procedural rights. What did the Court mean by this statement?
2. What is the remedy for denial of the right to speedy trial?
3. What factors are considered in determining if the accused was denied his or her right to speedy trial?

The Doggett *case looks at the issue of whether delay alone is sufficient to deprive the defendant of a right to speedy trial.*

DOGGETT V. UNITED STATES
505 U.S. 647 (1992)

Justice Souter delivered the opinion of the Court.

In this case, we consider whether the delay of 8 1/2 years between petitioner's indictment and arrest violated his Sixth Amendment right to a speedy trial. We hold that it did.

I.

On February 22, 1980, petitioner Marc Doggett was indicted for conspiring with several others to import and distribute cocaine.... Douglas Driver, the Drug Enforcement Administration's (DEA's) principal agent investigating the conspiracy, told the United States Marshal's Service that the DEA would oversee the apprehension of Doggett and his confederates. On March 18, 1980, two police officers set out under Driver's orders to arrest Doggett at his parents' house in Raleigh, North Carolina, only to find that he was not there. His mother told the officers that he had left for Colombia four days earlier.

To catch Doggett on his return to the United States, Driver sent word of his outstanding arrest warrant to all United States Customs stations and to a number of law enforcement organizations. He also placed Doggett's name in the Treasury Enforcement Communication System (TECS), a computer network that helps Customs agents screen people entering the country, and in the National Crime Information Center computer system, which serves similar ends. The TECS entry expired that September, however, and Doggett's name vanished from the system. In September 1981, Driver found out that Doggett was under arrest on drug charges in Panama and, thinking that a formal extradition request would be futile, simply asked Panama to "expel" Doggett to the United States. Although the Panamanian authorities promised to comply when their own proceedings had run their course, they freed Doggett the following July and let him go to Colombia, where he stayed with an aunt for several months. On September 25, 1982, he passed unhindered through Customs in New York City and settled down in Virginia. Since his return to the United States, he has married, earned a college degree, found a steady job as a computer operations manager, lived openly under his own name, and stayed within the law.

Doggett's travels abroad had not wholly escaped the Government's notice, however. In 1982, the American Embassy in Panama told the State Department of his departure to Colombia, but that information, for whatever reason, eluded the DEA, and Agent Driver assumed for several years that his quarry was still serving time in a Panamanian prison. Driver never asked DEA officials in Panama to check into Doggett's status, and only after his own fortuitous assignment to that country in 1985 did he discover Doggett's departure for Colombia. Driver then simply assumed Doggett had settled there, and he made no effort to find out for sure or to track Doggett down, either abroad or in the United States. Thus Doggett remained lost to the American criminal justice system until September, 1988, when the Marshal's Service ran a simple credit check on several thousand people subject to outstanding arrest warrants and, within minutes, found out where Doggett lived and worked. On September 5, 1988, nearly 6 years after his return to the United States and 8 1/2 years after his indictment, Doggett was arrested.

He naturally moved to dismiss the indictment, arguing that the Government's failure to prosecute him earlier violated his Sixth Amendment right to a speedy trial. The Federal Magistrate hearing his motion applied the criteria for assessing speedy trial claims set out in *Barker* v. *Wingo*, 407 U.S. 514 (1972): "[l]ength of delay, the reason for the delay, the defendant's assertion of his right, and prejudice to the defendant." *Id.*, at 530 (footnote omitted). The Magistrate found that the delay between Doggett's indictment and arrest was long enough to be "presumptively prejudicial," Magistrate's Report, reprinted at App. to Pet. for Cert. 27–28, that the

delay "clearly [was] attributable to the negligence of the government," *id.*, at 39, and that Doggett could not be faulted for any delay in asserting his right to a speedy trial, there being no evidence that he had known of the charges against him until his arrest, *id.*, at 42–44.

The Magistrate also found, however, that Doggett had made no affirmative showing that the delay had impaired his ability to mount a successful defense or had otherwise prejudiced him. In his recommendation to the District Court, the Magistrate contended that this failure to demonstrate particular prejudice sufficed to defeat Doggett's speedy trial claim.

The District Court took the recommendation and denied Doggett's motion. Doggett then entered a conditional guilty plea under Federal Rule of Criminal Procedure 11(a)(2), expressly reserving the right to appeal his ensuing conviction on the speedy trial claim. A split panel of the Court of Appeals affirmed . . . the court ruled that Doggett could prevail only by proving "actual prejudice" or by establishing that "the first three Barker factors weigh[ed] heavily in his favor." 906 F.2d, at 582. The majority agreed with the Magistrate that Doggett had not shown actual prejudice, and, attributing the Government's delay to "negligence," rather than "bad faith," *id.*, at 578–579, it concluded that Barker's first three factors did not weigh so heavily against the Government as to make proof of specific prejudice unnecessary. Judge Clark dissented, arguing, among other things, that the majority had placed undue emphasis on Doggett's inability to prove actual prejudice.

We granted Doggett's petition for *certiorari*, 498 U.S. 119 (1991), and now reverse.

II.

The Sixth Amendment guarantees that, "[i]n all criminal prosecutions, the accused shall enjoy the right to a speedy . . . trial. . . ." On its face, the Speedy Trial Clause is written with such breadth that, taken literally, it would forbid the government to delay the trial of an "accused" for any reason at all. Our cases, however, have qualified the literal sweep of the provision by specifically recognizing the relevance of four separate enquiries: whether delay before trial was uncommonly long, whether the government or the criminal defendant is more to blame for that delay, whether, in due course, the defendant asserted his right to a speedy trial, and whether he suffered prejudice as the delay's result. . . .

The first of these is actually a double enquiry. Simply to trigger a speedy trial analysis, an accused must allege that the interval between accusation and trial has crossed the threshold dividing ordinary from "presumptively prejudicial" delay, 407 U.S., at 530–531, since, by definition, he cannot complain that the government has denied him a "speedy" trial if it has, in fact, prosecuted his case with customary promptness. If the accused makes this showing, the court must then consider, as one factor among several, the extent to which the delay sketches beyond the bare minimum needed to trigger judicial examination of the claim. See *id.*, at 533–534. This latter enquiry is significant to the speedy trial analysis because, as we discuss below, the presumption that pretrial delay has prejudiced the accused intensifies over time. In this case, the extraordinary 8 1/2-year lag between Doggett's indictment and arrest clearly suffices to trigger the speedy trial enquiry; its further significance within that enquiry will be dealt with later.

As for Barker's second criterion, the Government claims to have sought Doggett with diligence. The findings of the courts below are to the contrary, however, and

we review trial court determinations of negligence with considerable deference. . . . The Government gives us nothing to gainsay the findings that have come up to us, and we see nothing fatal to them in the record. For six years, the Government's investigators made no serious effort to test their progressively more questionable assumption that Doggett was living abroad, and, had they done so, they could have found him within minutes. While the Government's lethargy may have reflected no more than Doggett's relative unimportance in the world of drug trafficking, it was still findable negligence, and the finding stands.

The Government goes against the record again in suggesting that Doggett knew of his indictment years before he was arrested. Were this true, Barker's third factor, concerning invocation of the right to a speedy trial, would be weighed heavily against him. But here again, the Government is trying to revisit the facts. At the hearing on Doggett's speedy trial motion, it introduced no evidence challenging the testimony of Doggett's wife, who said that she did not know of the charges until his arrest, and of his mother, who claimed not to have told him or anyone else that the police had come looking for him. From this the Magistrate implicitly concluded, Magistrate's Report, reprinted at App. to Pet. for Cert. 42–44, and the Court of Appeals expressly reaffirmed, 906 F.2d, at 579–580, that Doggett had won the evidentiary battle on this point. Not only that, but in the factual basis supporting Doggett's guilty plea, the Government explicitly conceded that it had "no information that Doggett was aware of the indictment before he left the United States in March, 1980, or prior to his arrest. His mother testified at the suppression hearing that she never told him, and Barnes and Riddle [Doggett's confederates] state they did not have contact with him after their arrest [in 1980]." Record, Exh. 63, p. 2.

. . . The Government is left, then, with its principal contention: that Doggett fails to make out a successful speedy trial claim because he has not shown precisely how he was prejudiced by the delay between his indictment and trial.

We have observed in prior cases that unreasonable delay between formal accusation and trial threatens to produce more than one sort of harm, including "oppressive pretrial incarceration," "anxiety and concern of the accused," and "the possibility that the [accused's] defense will be impaired" by dimming memories and loss of exculpatory evidence. . . . Of these forms of prejudice, "the most serious is the last, because the inability of a defendant adequately to prepare his case skews the fairness of the entire system." 407 U.S., at 532. Doggett claims this kind of prejudice, and there is probably no other kind that he can claim, since he was subjected neither to pretrial detention nor, he has successfully contended, to awareness of unresolved charges against him.

. . . We reverse the judgment of the Court of Appeals and remand the case for proceedings consistent with this opinion.

So ordered.

Justice O'Connor, dissenting. [Omitted.]

Justice Thomas, with whom The Chief Justice and Justice Scalia join, dissenting. [Omitted.]

What Do You Think?

1. Since the magistrate found no affirmative showing that the delay had impaired the defendant's ability to mount a successful defense or otherwise prejudiced him, was he deprived of his right to a speedy trial?
2. Do you agree with the majority opinion? Justify your answer.

The Lewis *case explores the issue of when an accused has the right to a trial by jury.*

LEWIS V. UNITED STATES
518 U.S. 322 (1996)
No. 95-6465.

Argued April 23, 1996
  Decided June 24, 1996
JUSTICE O'CONNOR delivered the opinion of the Court.

This case presents the question whether a defendant who is prosecuted in a single proceeding for multiple petty offenses has a constitutional right to a jury trial where the aggregate prison term authorized for the offenses exceeds six months. We are also asked to decide whether a defendant who would otherwise have a constitutional right to a jury trial may be denied that right because the presiding judge has made a pretrial commitment that the aggregate sentence imposed will not exceed six months.

We conclude that no jury-trial right exists where a defendant is prosecuted for multiple petty offenses. The Sixth Amendment's guarantee of the right to a jury trial does not extend to petty offenses, and its scope does not change where a defendant faces a potential aggregate prison term in excess of six months for petty offenses charged. Because we decide that no jury-trial right exists where a defendant is charged with multiple petty offenses, we do not reach the second question.

. . . Petitioner Ray Lewis was a mail handler for the United States Postal Service. One day, postal inspectors saw him open several pieces of mail and pocket the contents. The next day, the inspectors routed "test" mail, containing marked currency, through petitioner's station. After seeing petitioner open the mail and remove the currency, the inspectors arrested him. Petitioner was charged with two counts of obstructing the mail, in violation of 18 U. S. C. Section(s) 1701. Each count carried a maximum authorized prison sentence of six months. Petitioner requested a jury, but the magistrate judge granted the Government's motion for a bench trial. She explained that because she would not, under any circumstances, sentence petitioner to more than six months' imprisonment, he was not entitled to a jury trial.

. . . The Sixth Amendment guarantees that "[i]n all criminal prosecutions, the accused shall enjoy the right to a speedy and public trial, by an impartial jury of the State and district wherein the crime shall have been committed. . . ." It is well-established that the Sixth Amendment, like the common law, reserves this jury-trial right for prosecutions of serious offenses, and that "there is a category of petty crimes or offenses which is not subject to the Sixth Amendment jury trial provision." *Duncan* v. *Louisiana*, 391 U.S. 145, 159 (1968).

To determine whether an offense is properly characterized as "petty," courts at one time looked to the nature of the offense and whether it was triable by a jury at common law. Such determinations became difficult, because many statutory offenses lack common-law antecedents. *Blanton* v. *North Las Vegas*, 489 U.S. 538, (1989). Therefore, more recently, we have instead sought "objective indications of the seriousness with which society regards the offense." *Frank* v. *United States*, 395 U.S. 147, 148 (1969); accord, *District of Columbia* v. *Clawans*, 300 U.S. 617, 628 (1937). Now, to determine whether an offense is petty, we consider the maximum penalty attached to the offense. This criterion is considered the most relevant with

which to assess the character of an offense, because it reveals the legislature's judgment about the offense's severity. "The judiciary should not substitute its judgment as to seriousness for that of a legislature, which is far better equipped to perform the task. . . ." *Blanton*, 489 U.S., at 541 (internal quotation marks omitted). In evaluating the seriousness of the offense, we place primary emphasis on the maximum prison term authorized. While penalties such as probation or a fine may infringe on a defendant's freedom, the deprivation of liberty imposed by imprisonment makes that penalty the best indicator of whether the legislature considered an offense to be "petty" or "serious." *Id.*, at 542. An offense carrying a maximum prison term of six months or less is presumed petty, unless the legislature has authorized additional statutory penalties so severe as to indicate that the legislature considered the offense serious. *Id.*, at 543; *Codispoti* v. *Pennsylvania*, 418 U.S. 506, 512 (1974).

Here, the maximum authorized penalty for obstruction of mail is six months' imprisonment—a penalty that presumptively places the offense in the "petty" category. We face the question whether petitioner is nevertheless entitled to a jury trial, because he was tried in a single proceeding for two counts of the petty offense so that the potential aggregated penalty is 12 months' imprisonment.

Petitioner argues that, where a defendant is charged with multiple petty offenses in a single prosecution, the Sixth Amendment requires that the aggregate potential penalty be the basis for determining whether a jury trial is required. Although each offense charged here was petty, petitioner faced a potential penalty of more than six months' imprisonment; and, of course, if any offense charged had authorized more than six months' imprisonment, he would have been entitled to a jury trial. The Court must look to the aggregate potential prison term to determine the existence of the jury-trial right, petitioner contends, not to the "petty" character of the offenses charged.

We disagree. The Sixth Amendment reserves the jury-trial right to defendants accused of serious crimes. As set forth above, we determine whether an offense is serious by looking to the judgment of the legislature, primarily as expressed in the maximum authorized term of imprisonment. Here, by setting the maximum authorized prison term at six months, the legislature categorized the offense of obstructing the mail as petty. The fact that the petitioner was charged with two counts of a petty offense does not revise the legislative judgment as to the gravity of that particular offense, nor does it transform the petty offense into a serious one, to which the jury-trial right would apply. We note that there is precedent at common law that a jury trial was not provided to a defendant charged with multiple petty offenses. . . .

Petitioner nevertheless insists that a defendant is entitled to a jury trial whenever he faces a deprivation of liberty for a period exceeding six months, a proposition for which he cites our precedent establishing the six-months' prison sentence as the presumptive cut-off for determining whether an offense is "petty" or "serious." To be sure, in the cases in which we sought to determine the line between "petty" and "serious" for Sixth Amendment purposes, we considered the severity of the authorized deprivation of liberty as an indicator of the legislature's appraisal of the offense. . . . But it is now settled that a legislature's determination that an offense carries a maximum prison terms of six months or less indicates its view that an offense is "petty." Where we have a judgment by the legislature that an offense is "petty," we do not look to the potential prison term faced by a particular defendant who is charged with more than one such petty offense. The maximum authorized penalty provides an "objective indicatio[n] of the seriousness with which society regards the offense," *Frank*, 395 U.S., at 148, and it is that indication that

is used to determine whether a jury trial is required, not the particularities of an individual case. Here, the penalty authorized by Congress manifests its judgment that the offense is petty, and the term of imprisonment faced by petitioner by virtue of the second count does not alter that fact.

. . . Because petitioner is not entitled to a jury trial, we need not reach the question whether a judge's self-imposed limitation on sentencing may affect the jury-trial right.

JUSTICE KENNEDY, with whom JUSTICE BREYER joins, concurring in the judgment. [Omitted.]

JUSTICE STEVENS, with whom JUSTICE GINSBURG joins, dissenting. [Omitted.]

WHAT DO YOU THINK?

1. Should the defendant have the right to a trial by jury when the maximum sentence that the defendant may receive is six months confinement? Justify your answer.

2. Under the present rules, if the defendant is tried on one offense that has a maximum sentence of one year confinement, the defendant has the right to a jury trial. If, however, the defendant is charged with 20 offenses and the maximum sentence for each count is six months for a total possible confinement time of ten years, the defendant does not have the right to a jury trial. Is this a due process violation? Explain.

If a defendant is in pretrial custody, is it error to force the defendant to stand trial before a jury in jail uniform? The Williams *case examines this issue.*

ESTELLE V. WILLIAMS
425 U.S. 501 (1976)

MR. CHIEF JUSTICE BURGER delivered the opinion of the Court.

We granted *certiorari* in this case to determine whether an accused who is compelled to wear identifiable prison clothing at his trial by a jury is denied due process or equal protection of the laws.

In November 1970, respondent Williams was convicted in state court in Harris County, Tex., for assault with intent to commit murder with malice. The crime occurred during an altercation between respondent and his former landlord on the latter's property. The evidence showed that respondent returned to the apartment complex where he had formerly resided to visit a female tenant. While there, respondent and his former landlord became involved in a quarrel. Heated words were exchanged, and a fight ensued. Respondent struck the landlord with a knife in the neck, chest, and abdomen, severely wounding him.

Unable to post bond, respondent was held in custody while awaiting trial. When he learned that he was to go on trial, respondent asked an officer at the jail for his civilian clothes. This request was denied. As a result, respondent appeared at trial in clothes that were distinctly marked as prison issue. Neither respondent nor his counsel raised an objection to the prison attire at any time.

A jury returned a verdict of guilty on the charge of assault with intent to murder with malice. The Texas Court of Criminal Appeals affirmed the conviction. *Williams* v. *State*, 477 S. W. 2d 24 (1972). Williams then sought release in the United States District Court on a petition for a writ of habeas corpus. Although holding that requiring a defendant to stand trial in prison garb was inherently unfair, the District Court denied relief on the ground that the error was harmless.

The Court of Appeals reversed . . .

The right to a fair trial is a fundamental liberty secured by the Fourteenth Amendment. *Drope* v. *Missouri*, 420 U.S. 162, 172 (1975). The presumption of innocence, although not articulated in the Constitution, is a basic component of a fair trial under our system of criminal justice. Long ago this Court stated:

> The principle that there is a presumption of innocence in favor of the accused is the undoubted law, axiomatic and elementary, and its enforcement lies at the foundation of the administration of our criminal law. *Coffin* v. *United States*, 156 U.S. 432, 453 (1895)

To implement the presumption, courts must be alert to factors that may undermine the fairness of the factfinding process. In the administration of criminal justice, courts must carefully guard against dilution of the principle that guilt is to be established by probative evidence and beyond a reasonable doubt. *In re Winship*, 397 U.S. 358, 364 (1970).

The actual impact of a particular practice on the judgment of jurors cannot always be fully determined. But this Court has left no doubt that the probability of deleterious effects on fundamental rights calls for close judicial scrutiny. . . . Courts must do the best they can to evaluate the likely effects of a particular procedure, based on reason, principle, and common human experience.

The potential effects of presenting an accused before the jury in prison attire need not, however, be measured in the abstract. Courts have, with few exceptions, determined that an accused should not be compelled to go to trial in prison or jail clothing because of the possible impairment of the presumption so basic to the adversary system.

The American Bar Association's Standards for Criminal Justice also disapprove the practice. ABA Project on Standards for Criminal Justice, Trial by Jury 4.1 (b), p. 91 (App. Draft 1968). This is a recognition that the constant reminder of the accused's condition implicit in such distinctive, identifiable attire may affect a juror's judgment. The defendant's clothing is so likely to be a continuing influence throughout the trial that, not unlike placing a jury in the custody of deputy sheriffs who were also witnesses for the prosecution, an unacceptable risk is presented of impermissible factors coming into play. *Turner* v. *Louisiana*, 379 U.S. 466, 473 (1965).

That such factors cannot always be avoided is manifest in *Illinois* v. *Allen*, 397 U.S. 337 (1970), where we expressly recognized that "the sight of shackles and gags might have a significant effect on the jury's feelings about the defendant . . . ," *id.*, at 344; yet the Court upheld the practice when necessary to control a contumacious defendant. For that reason, the Court authorized removal of a disruptive defendant from the courtroom or, alternatively, binding and gagging of the accused until he agrees to conduct himself properly in the courtroom.

Unlike physical restraints, permitted under *Allen*, *supra*, compelling an accused to wear jail clothing furthers no essential state policy. That it may be more convenient for jail administrators, a factor quite unlike the substantial need to impose physical restraints upon contumacious defendants, provides no justification for the practice. Indeed, the State of Texas asserts no interest whatever in maintaining this procedure.

Similarly troubling is the fact that compelling the accused to stand trial in jail grab operates usually against only those who cannot post bail prior to trial. Persons who can secure release are not subjected to this condition. To impose the condition on one category of defendants, over objection, would be repugnant to the concept of equal justice embodied in the Fourteenth Amendment. . . .

. . . The record is clear that no objection was made to the trial judge concerning the jail attire either before or at any time during the trial. This omission plainly did not result from any lack of appreciation of the issue, for respondent had raised the question with the jail attendant prior to trial. At trial, defense counsel expressly referred to respondent's attire during voir dire. The trial judge was thus informed that respondent's counsel was fully conscious of the situation.

Accordingly, although the State cannot, consistently with the Fourteenth Amendment, compel an accused to stand trial before a jury while dressed in identifiable prison clothes, the failure to make an objection to the court as to being tried in such clothes, for whatever reason, is sufficient to negate the presence of compulsion necessary to establish a constitutional violation.

The judgment of the Court of Appeals is therefore reversed, and the cause is remanded for further proceedings consistent with this opinion.

Reversed and remanded.

MR. JUSTICE STEVENS took no part in the consideration or decision of this case.

MR. JUSTICE POWELL, with whom MR. JUSTICE STEWART joins, concurring. [Omitted.]

MR. JUSTICE BRENNAN, with whom MR. JUSTICE MARSHALL concurs, dissenting. [Omitted.]

WHAT DO YOU THINK?

1. The Court stressed the fact that the defendant's attorney failed to object to the defendant's being forced to wear jail clothes. Why is this factor important to the Court?

2. If the defendant takes the stand and testifies in his or her own defense, should the prosecutor be allowed to asked the defendant if he or she currently is in pretrial custody? Explain your answer.

Under the Sixth Amendment, the accused has the right to confront the witnesses who are against him or her. What does the right of confrontation mean? The Coy case discusses this issue.

COY V. IOWA
487 U.S. 1012 (1988)

JUSTICE SCALIA delivered the opinion of the Court.

Appellant was convicted of two counts of lascivious acts with a child after a jury trial in which a screen placed between him and the two complaining witnesses blocked him from their sight. Appellant contends that this procedure, authorized by state statute, violated his Sixth Amendment right to confront the witnesses against him.

In August 1985, appellant was arrested and charged with sexually assaulting two 13-year-old girls earlier that month while they were camping out in the backyard of the house next door to him. According to the girls, the assailant entered their tent after they were asleep wearing a stocking over his head, shined a flashlight in their eyes, and warned them not to look at him; neither was able to describe his face. In November 1985, at the beginning of appellant's trial, the State made a motion pursuant to a recently enacted statute, Act of May 23, 1985, 6, 1985 Iowa Acts 338, now codified at Iowa Code 910A.14 (1987), to allow the complaining witnesses to testify either via closed-circuit television or behind a screen. The trial court approved the use of a large screen to be placed between appellant and the witness stand during the girls' testimony. After certain lighting adjustments in the courtroom, the screen would enable appellant dimly to perceive the witnesses, but the witnesses to see him not at all.

Appellant objected strenuously to use of the screen, based first of all on his Sixth Amendment confrontation right. He argued that, although the device might succeed in its apparent aim of making the complaining witnesses feel less uneasy in giving their testimony, the Confrontation Clause directly addressed this issue by giving criminal defendants a right to face-to-face confrontation. He also argued that his right to due process was violated, since the procedure would make him appear guilty and thus erode the presumption of innocence. The trial court rejected both constitutional claims, though it instructed the jury to draw no inference of guilt from the screen.

The Iowa Supreme Court affirmed appellant's conviction, 397 N. W. 2d 730 (1986). It rejected appellant's confrontation argument on the ground that, since the ability to cross-examine the witnesses was not impaired by the screen, there was no violation of the Confrontation Clause. It also rejected the due process argument, on the ground that the screening procedure was not inherently prejudicial. We noted probable jurisdiction, 483 U.S. 1019 (1987).

II.

The Sixth Amendment gives a criminal defendant the right "to be confronted with the witnesses against him." This language "comes to us on faded parchment," *California* v. *Green*, 399 U.S. 149, 174 (1970) (HARLAN, J., concurring), with a lineage that traces back to the beginnings of Western legal culture. There are indications that a right of confrontation existed under Roman law. The Roman Governor Festus, discussing the proper treatment of his prisoner, Paul, stated: "It is not the manner of the Romans to deliver any man up to die before the accused has met his accusers face to face, and has been given a chance to defend himself against the charges." Acts 25:16. It has been argued that a form of the right of confrontation was recognized in England well before the right to jury trial. Pollitt, *The Right of Confrontation: Its History and Modern Dress*, 8 J. Pub. L. 381, 384–387 (1959).

Most of this Court's encounters with the Confrontation Clause have involved either the admissibility of out-of-court statements, see, e.g., *Ohio* v. *Roberts*, 448 U.S. 56 (1980); *Dutton* v. *Evans*, 400 U.S. 74 (1970), or restrictions on the scope of cross-examination, *Delaware* v. *Van Arsdall*, 475 U.S. 673 (1986); *Davis* v. *Alaska*, 415 U.S. 308 (1974). Cf. *Delaware* v. *Fensterer*, 474 U.S. 15, 18–19 (1985) (per curiam) (noting these two categories and finding neither applicable). The reason for that is not, as the State suggests, that these elements are the essence of the Clause's protection—but rather, quite to the contrary, that there is at least some room for doubt (and hence litigation) as to the extent to which the Clause includes those elements,

whereas, as Justice Harlan put it, "[s]imply as a matter of English" it confers at least "a right to meet face to face all those who appear and give evidence at trial." *California v. Green*, *supra*, at 175. Simply as a matter of Latin as well, since the word "confront" ultimately derives from the prefix "con-" (from "contra" meaning "against" or "opposed") and the noun "frons" (forehead). Shakespeare was thus describing the root meaning of confrontation when he had Richard the Second say: "Then call them to our presence—face to face, and frowning brow to brow, ourselves will hear the accuser and the accused freely speak. . . ." Richard II, Act 1, sc. 1.

We have never doubted, therefore, that the Confrontation Clause guarantees the defendant a face-to-face meeting with witnesses appearing before the trier of fact. See *Kentucky v. Stincer*, 482 U.S. 730, 748, 749–750 (1987) (MARSHALL, J., dissenting). For example, in *Kirby v. United States*, 174 U.S. 47, 55 (1899), which concerned the admissibility of prior convictions of codefendants to prove an element of the offense of receiving stolen Government property, we described the operation of the Clause as follows: "[A] fact which can be primarily established only by witnesses cannot be proved against an accused . . . except by witnesses who confront him at the trial, upon whom he can look while being tried, whom he is entitled to cross-examine, and whose testimony he may impeach in every mode authorized by the established rules governing the trial or conduct of criminal cases." Similarly, in *Dowdell v. United States*, 221 U.S. 325, 330 (1911), we described a provision of the Philippine Bill of Rights as substantially the same as the Sixth Amendment, and proceeded to interpret it as intended "to secure the accused the right to be tried, so far as facts provable by witnesses are concerned, by only such witnesses as meet him face to face at the trial, who give their testimony in his presence, and give to the accused an opportunity of cross-examination." More recently, we have described the "literal right to 'confront' the witness at the time of trial" as forming "the core of the values furthered by the Confrontation Clause." *California v. Green*, *supra*, at 157. Last Term, the plurality opinion in *Pennsylvania v. Ritchie*, 480 U.S. 39, 51 (1987), stated that "[t]he Confrontation Clause provides two types of protections for a criminal defendant: the right physically to face those who testify against him, and the right to conduct cross-examination."

The Sixth Amendment's guarantee of face-to-face encounter between witness and accused serves ends related both to appearances and to reality. This opinion is embellished with references to and quotations from antiquity in part to convey that there is something deep in human nature that regards face-to-face confrontation between accused and accuser as "essential to a fair trial in a criminal prosecution." *Pointer v. Texas*, 380 U.S. 400, 404 (1965). What was true of old is no less true in modern times. President Eisenhower once described face-to-face confrontation as part of the code of his hometown of Abilene, Kansas. In Abilene, he said, it was necessary to "[m]eet anyone face to face with whom you disagree. You could not sneak up on him from behind, or do any damage to him, without suffering the penalty of an outraged citizenry. . . . In this country, if someone dislikes you, or accuses you, he must come up in front. He cannot hide behind the shadow." Press release of remarks given to the B'nai B'rith Anti-Defamation League, November 23, 1953, quoted in *Pollitt*, *supra*, at 381. The phrase still persists, "Look me in the eye and say that." Given these human feelings of what is necessary for fairness, the right of confrontation "contributes to the establishment of a system of criminal justice in which the perception as well as the reality of fairness prevails." *Lee v. Illinois*, 476 U.S. 530, 540 (1986).

The perception that confrontation is essential to fairness has persisted over the centuries because there is much truth to it. A witness "may feel quite differently

when he has to repeat his story looking at the man whom he will harm greatly by distorting or mistaking the facts. He can now understand what sort of human being that man is." Z. Chafee, *The Blessings of Liberty* 35 (1956), quoted in *Jay v. Boyd*, 351 U.S. 345, 375–376 (1956), (DOUGLAS, J., dissenting). It is always more difficult to tell a lie about a person "to his face" than "behind his back." In the former context, even if the lie is told, it will often be told less convincingly. The Confrontation Clause does not, of course, compel the witness to fix his eyes upon the defendant; he may studiously look elsewhere, but the trier of fact will draw its own conclusions. Thus the right to face-to-face confrontation serves much the same purpose as a less explicit component of the Confrontation Clause that we have had more frequent occasion to discuss—the right to cross-examine the accuser; both "ensur[e] the integrity of the factfinding process." *Kentucky* v. *Stincer*, 482 U.S., at 736. The State can hardly gainsay the profound effect upon a witness of standing in the presence of the person the witness accuses, since that is the very phenomenon it relies upon to establish the potential "trauma" that allegedly justified the extraordinary procedure in the present case. That face-to-face presence may, unfortunately, upset the truthful rape victim or abused child; but by the same token it may confound and undo the false accuser, or reveal the child coached by a malevolent adult. It is a truism that constitutional protections have costs.

III.

The remaining question is whether the right to confrontation was in fact violated in this case. The screen at issue was specifically designed to enable the complaining witnesses to avoid viewing appellant as they gave their testimony, and the record indicates that it was successful in this objective. App. 10-11. It is difficult to imagine a more obvious or damaging violation of the defendant's right to a face-to-face encounter.

The State suggests that the confrontation interest at stake here was outweighed by the necessity of protecting victims of sexual abuse. It is true that we have in the past indicated that rights conferred by the Confrontation Clause are not absolute, and may give way to other important interests. The rights referred to in those cases, however, were not the right narrowly and explicitly set forth in the Clause, but rather rights that are, or were asserted to be, reasonably implicit—namely, the right to cross-examine, see *Chambers* v. *Mississippi*, 410 U.S. 284, 295 (1973); the right to exclude out-of-court statements, see *Ohio* v. *Roberts*, 448 U.S., at 63–65; and the asserted right to face-to-face confrontation at some point in the proceedings other than the trial itself, *Kentucky* v. *Stincer*, *supra*. To hold that our determination of what implications are reasonable must take into account other important interests is not the same as holding that we can identify exceptions, in light of other important interests, to the irreducible literal meaning of the Clause: "a right to meet face to face all those who appear and give evidence at trial." *California* v. *Green*, 399 U.S., at 175 (HARLAN, J., concurring). We leave for another day, however, the question whether any exceptions exist. Whatever they may be, they would surely be allowed only when necessary to further an important public policy. Cf. *Ohio* v. *Roberts*, *supra*, at 64; *Chambers* v. *Mississippi*, *supra*, at 295. The State maintains that such necessity is established here by the statute, which creates a legislatively imposed presumption of trauma. Our cases suggest, however, that even as to exceptions from the normal implications of the Confrontation Clause, as opposed to its most literal application, something more than the type of generalized finding underlying such a statute is needed when the exception is not "firmly . . . rooted in our jurisprudence." *Bourjaily* v. *United States*, 483 U.S. 171, 183 (1987) (citing *Dutton* v. *Evans*, 400 U.S. 74 [1970]). The exception created by the Iowa statute, which was passed in 1985, could hardly be viewed as firmly rooted. Since there have been no individualized findings that these particular witnesses needed special protection, the judgment here could not be sustained by any conceivable exception.

The State also briefly suggests that any Confrontation Clause error was harmless beyond a reasonable doubt under the standard of *Chapman* v. *California*, 386 U.S. 18, 24 (1967). We have recognized that other types of violations of the Confrontation Clause are subject to that harmless-error analysis, see e.g., *Delaware* v. *Van Arsdall*, 475 U.S., at 679, 684, and see no reason why denial of face-to-face confrontation should not be treated the same. An assessment of harmlessness cannot include consideration of whether the witness' testimony would have been unchanged, or the jury's assessment unaltered, had there been confrontation; such an inquiry would obviously involve pure speculation, and harmlessness must therefore be determined on the basis of the remaining evidence. The Iowa Supreme Court had no occasion to address the harmlessness issue, since it found no constitutional violation. In the circumstances of this case, rather than decide whether the error was harmless beyond a reasonable doubt, we leave the issue for the court below.

We find it unnecessary to reach appellant's due process claim. Since his constitutional right to face-to-face confrontation was violated, we reverse the judgment of the Iowa Supreme Court and remand the case for further proceedings not inconsistent with this opinion.

It is so ordered.

JUSTICE KENNEDY took no part in the consideration or decision of this case.

JUSTICE O'CONNOR, with whom JUSTICE WHITE joins, concurring. [Omitted.]

JUSTICE BLACKMUN, with whom THE CHIEF JUSTICE joins, dissenting. [Omitted.]

WHAT DO YOU THINK?

1. Why is the right of confrontation important?

2. What other steps could the judge have taken in this case?

In the Sheppard *case, the Court held that the actions of the press deprived Dr. Sheppard of his right to a fair trial. The movie* The Fugitive *and a popular television series by the same name were based on this case.*

SHEPPARD V. MAXWELL
384 U.S. 333 (1966)

MR. JUSTICE CLARK delivered the opinion of the Court.

This federal habeas corpus application involves the question whether Sheppard was deprived of a fair trial in his state conviction for the second-degree murder of his wife because of the trial judge's failure to protect Sheppard sufficiently from the massive, pervasive and prejudicial publicity that attended his prosecution. The United States District Court held that he was not afforded a fair trial and granted

the writ subject to the State's right to put Sheppard to trial again.... The Court of Appeals for the Sixth Circuit reversed by a divided vote.... We have concluded that Sheppard did not receive a fair trial consistent with the Due Process Clause of the Fourteenth Amendment and, therefore, reverse the judgment.

I.

Marilyn Sheppard, petitioner's pregnant wife, was bludgeoned to death in the upstairs bedroom of their lakeshore home in Bay Village, Ohio, a suburb of Cleveland. On the day of the tragedy, July 4, 1954, Sheppard pieced together for several local officials the following story: He and his wife had entertained neighborhood friends, the Aherns, on the previous evening at their home. After dinner they watched television in the living room. Sheppard became drowsy and dozed off to sleep on a couch. Later, Marilyn partially awoke him saying that she was going to bed. The next thing he remembered was hearing his wife cry out in the early morning hours. He hurried upstairs and in the dim light from the hall saw a "form" standing next to his wife's bed. As he struggled with the "form" he was struck on the back of the neck and rendered unconscious. On regaining his senses he found himself on the floor next to his wife's bed. He rose, looked at her, took her pulse and "felt that she was gone." He then went to his son's room and found him unmolested.

Hearing a noise, he hurried downstairs. He saw a "form" running out the door and pursued it to the lake shore. He grappled with it on the beach and again lost consciousness. Upon his recovery he was lying face down with the lower portion of his body in the water. He returned to his home, checked the pulse on his wife's neck, and "determined or thought that she was gone." He then went downstairs and called a neighbor, Mayor Houk of Bay Village. The Mayor and his wife came over at once, found Sheppard slumped in an easy chair downstairs and asked, "What happened?" Sheppard replied: "I don't know but somebody ought to try to do something for Marilyn." Mrs. Houk immediately went up to the bedroom. The Mayor told Sheppard, "Get hold of yourself. Can you tell me what happened?" Sheppard then related the above-outlined events.

After Mrs. Houk discovered the body, the Mayor called the local police, Dr. Richard Sheppard, petitioner's brother, and the Aherns. The local police were the first to arrive. They in turn notified the Coroner and Cleveland police. Richard Sheppard then arrived, determined that Marilyn was dead, examined his brother's injuries, and removed him to the nearby clinic operated by the Sheppard family. When the Coroner, the Cleveland police and other officials arrived, the house and surrounding area were thoroughly searched, the rooms of the house were photographed, and many persons, including the Houks and the Aherns, were interrogated. The Sheppard home and premises were taken into "protective custody" and remained so until after the trial.

From the outset officials focused suspicion on Sheppard. After a search of the house and premises on the morning of the tragedy, Dr. Gerber, the Coroner, is reported—and it is undenied—to have told his men, "Well, it is evident the doctor did this, so let's go get the confession out of him." He proceeded to interrogate and examine Sheppard while the latter was under sedation in his hospital room. On the same occasion, the Coroner was given the clothes Sheppard wore at the time of the tragedy together with the personal items in them. Later that afternoon Chief Eaton and two Cleveland police officers interrogated Sheppard at some length, confronting him with evidence and demanding explanations. Asked by Officer Shotke to take a lie detector test, Sheppard said he would if it were reliable. Shotke replied that it

was "infallible" and "you might as well tell us all about it now." At the end of the interrogation Shotke told Sheppard: "I think you killed your wife." Still later in the same afternoon a physician sent by the Coroner was permitted to make a detailed examination of Sheppard. Until the Coroner's inquest on July 22, at which time he was subpoenaed, Sheppard made himself available for frequent and extended questioning without the presence of an attorney.

On July 7, the day of Marilyn Sheppard's funeral, a newspaper story appeared in which Assistant County Attorney Mahon—later the chief prosecutor of Sheppard—sharply criticized the refusal of the Sheppard family to permit his immediate questioning. From there on headline stories repeatedly stressed Sheppard's lack of cooperation with the police and other officials. Under the headline "Testify Now In Death, Bay Doctor Is Ordered," one story described a visit by Coroner Gerber and four police officers to the hospital on July 8. When Sheppard insisted that his lawyer be present, the Coroner wrote out a subpoena and served it on him. Sheppard then agreed to submit to questioning without counsel and the subpoena was torn up. The officers questioned him for several hours. On July 9, Sheppard, at the request of the Coroner, re-enacted the tragedy at his home before the Coroner, police officers, and a group of newsmen, who apparently were invited by the Coroner. The home was locked so that Sheppard was obliged to wait outside until the Coroner arrived. Sheppard's performance was reported in detail by the news media along with photographs. The newspapers also played up Sheppard's refusal to take a lie detector test and "the protective ring" thrown up by his family. Front-page newspaper headlines announced on the same day that "Doctor Balks At Lie Test; Retells Story." A column opposite that story contained an "exclusive" interview with Sheppard headlined: " 'Loved My Wife, She Loved Me,' Sheppard Tells News Reporter." The next day, another headline story disclosed that Sheppard had "again late yesterday refused to take a lie detector test" and quoted an Assistant County Attorney as saying that "at the end of a nine-hour questioning of Dr. Sheppard, I felt he was now ruling [a test] out completely." But subsequent newspaper articles reported that the Coroner was still pushing Sheppard for a lie detector test. More stories appeared when Sheppard would not allow authorities to inject him with "truth serum."

On the 20th, the "editorial artillery" opened fire with a front-page charge that somebody is "getting away with murder." The editorial attributed the ineptness of the investigation to "friendships, relationships, hired lawyers, a husband who ought to have been subjected instantly to the same third-degree to which any other person under similar circumstances is subjected. . . ."

The following day, July 21, another page-one editorial was headed: "Why No Inquest? Do It Now, Dr. Gerber." The Coroner called an inquest the same day and subpoenaed Sheppard. It was staged the next day in a school gymnasium; the Coroner presided with the County Prosecutor as his advisor and two detectives as bailiffs. In the front of the room was a long table occupied by reporters, television and radio personnel, and broadcasting equipment. The hearing was broadcast with live microphones placed at the Coroner's seat and the witness stand. A swarm of reporters and photographers attended. Sheppard was brought into the room by police who searched him in full view of several hundred spectators. Sheppard's counsel were present during the three-day inquest but were not permitted to participate. When Sheppard's chief counsel attempted to place some documents in the record, he was forcibly ejected from the room by the Coroner, who received cheers, hugs, and kisses from ladies in the audience. Sheppard was questioned for five and one-half hours about his actions on the night of the murder, his married life, and a love affair with Susan Hayes. At the end of the hearing the Coroner announced that he "could" order Sheppard held for the grand jury, but did not do so.

Throughout this period, the newspapers emphasized evidence that tended to incriminate Sheppard and pointed out discrepancies in his statements to authorities. At the same time, Sheppard made many public statements to the press and wrote feature articles asserting his innocence. During the inquest on July 26, a headline in large type stated: "Kerr [Captain of the Cleveland Police] Urges Sheppard's Arrest." In the story, Detective McArthur "disclosed that scientific tests at the Sheppard home have definitely established that the killer washed off a trail of blood from the murder bedroom to the downstairs section," a circumstance casting doubt on Sheppard's accounts of the murder. No such evidence was produced at trial. The newspapers also delved into Sheppard's personal life. Articles stressed his extramarital love affairs as a motive for the crime. The newspapers portrayed Sheppard as a Lothario, fully explored his relationship with Susan Hayes, and named a number of other women who were allegedly involved with him. The testimony at trial never showed that Sheppard had any illicit relationships besides the one with Susan Hayes.

On July 28, an editorial entitled "Why Don't Police Quiz Top Suspect" demanded that Sheppard be taken to police headquarters. It described him in the following language:

> Now proved under oath to be a liar, still free to go about his business, shielded by his family, protected by a smart lawyer who has made monkeys of the police and authorities, carrying a gun part of the time, left free to do whatever he pleases. . . .

A front-page editorial on July 30 asked: "Why Isn't Sam Sheppard in Jail?" It was later titled "Quit Stalling—Bring Him In." After calling Sheppard "the most unusual murder suspect ever seen around these parts" the article said that "[e]xcept for some superficial questioning during Coroner Sam Gerber's inquest he has been scot-free of any official grilling. . . ." It asserted that he was "surrounded by an iron curtain of protection [and] concealment."

That night at 10 o'clock Sheppard was arrested at his father's home on a charge of murder. He was taken to the Bay Village City Hall where hundreds of people, newscasters, photographers and reporters were awaiting his arrival. He was immediately arraigned—having been denied a temporary delay to secure the presence of counsel—and bound over to the grand jury.

The publicity then grew in intensity until his indictment on August 17. Typical of the coverage during this period is a front-page interview entitled: "DR. SAM: 'I Wish There Was Something I Could Get Off My Chest—but There Isn't.' " Unfavorable publicity included items such as a cartoon of the body of a sphinx with Sheppard's head and the legend below: " 'I Will Do Everything In My Power to Help Solve This Terrible Murder.'—Dr. Sam Sheppard." Headlines announced, inter alia, that: "Doctor Evidence is Ready for Jury," "Corrigan Tactics Stall Quizzing," "Sheppard 'Gay Set' Is Revealed By Houk," "Blood Is Found In Garage," "New Murder Evidence Is Found, Police Claim," "Dr. Sam Faces Quiz At Jail On Marilyn's Fear Of Him." On August 18, an article appeared under the headline "Dr. Sam Writes His Own Story." And reproduced across the entire front page was a portion of the typed statement signed by Sheppard: "I am not guilty of the murder of my wife, Marilyn. How could I, who have been trained to help people and devoted my life to saving life, commit such a terrible and revolting crime?" We do not detail the coverage further. There are five volumes filled with similar clippings from each of the three Cleveland newspapers covering the period from the murder

until Sheppard's conviction in December 1954. The record includes no excerpts from newscasts on radio and television but since space was reserved in the courtroom for these media we assume that their coverage was equally large.

II.

With this background the case came to trial two weeks before the November general election at which the chief prosecutor was a candidate for common pleas judge and the trial judge, Judge Blythin, was a candidate to succeed himself. Twenty-five days before the case was set, 75 veniremen were called as prospective jurors. All three Cleveland newspapers published the names and addresses of the veniremen. As a consequence, anonymous letters and telephone calls, as well as calls from friends, regarding the impending prosecution were received by all of the prospective jurors. The selection of the jury began on October 18, 1954.

The courtroom in which the trial was held measured 26 by 48 feet. A long temporary table was set up inside the bar, in back of the single counsel table. It ran the width of the courtroom, parallel to the bar railing, with one end less than three feet from the jury box. Approximately 20 representatives of newspapers and wire services were assigned seats at this table by the court. Behind the bar railing there were four rows of benches. These seats were likewise assigned by the court for the entire trial. The first row was occupied by representatives of television and radio stations, and the second and third rows by reporters from out-of-town newspapers and magazines. One side of the last row, which accommodated 14 people, was assigned to Sheppard's family and the other to Marilyn's. The public was permitted to fill vacancies in this row on special passes only. Representatives of the news media also used all the rooms on the courtroom floor, including the room where cases were ordinarily called and assigned for trial. Private telephone lines and telegraphic equipment were installed in these rooms so that reports from the trial could be speeded to the papers. Station WSRS was permitted to set up broadcasting facilities on the third floor of the courthouse next door to the jury room, where the jury rested during recesses in the trial and deliberated. Newscasts were made from this room throughout the trial, and while the jury reached its verdict.

On the sidewalk and steps in front of the courthouse, television and newsreel cameras were occasionally used to take motion pictures of the participants in the trial, including the jury and the judge. Indeed, one television broadcast carried a staged interview of the judge as he entered the courthouse. In the corridors outside the courtroom there was a host of photographers and television personnel with flash cameras, portable lights and motion picture cameras. This group photographed the prospective jurors during selection of the jury. After the trial opened, the witnesses, counsel, and jurors were photographed and televised whenever they entered or left the courtroom. Sheppard was brought to the courtroom about 10 minutes before each session began; he was surrounded by reporters and extensively photographed for the newspapers and television. A rule of court prohibited picture-taking in the courtroom during the actual sessions of the court, but no restraints were put on photographers during recesses, which were taken once each morning and afternoon, with a longer period for lunch.

All of these arrangements with the news media and their massive coverage of the trial continued during the entire nine weeks of the trial. The courtroom remained crowded to capacity with representatives of news media. Their movement in and out of the courtroom often caused so much confusion that, despite the loudspeaker system installed in the courtroom, it was difficult for the witnesses and

counsel to be heard. Furthermore, the reporters clustered within the bar of the small courtroom made confidential talk among Sheppard and his counsel almost impossible during the proceedings. They frequently had to leave the courtroom to obtain privacy. And many times when counsel wished to raise a point with the judge out of the hearing of the jury it was necessary to move to the judge's chambers. Even then, news media representatives so packed the judge's anteroom that counsel could hardly return from the chambers to the courtroom. The reporters vied with each other to find out what counsel and the judge had discussed, and often these matters later appeared in newspapers accessible to the jury.

The daily record of the proceedings was made available to the newspapers and the testimony of each witness was printed verbatim in the local editions, along with objections of counsel, and rulings by the judge. Pictures of Sheppard, the judge, counsel, pertinent witnesses, and the jury often accompanied the daily newspaper and television accounts. At times the newspapers published photographs of exhibits introduced at the trial, and the rooms of Sheppard's house were featured along with relevant testimony.

The jurors themselves were constantly exposed to the news media. Every juror, except one, testified at *voir dire* to reading about the case in the Cleveland papers or to having heard broadcasts about it. Seven of the 12 jurors who rendered the verdict had one or more Cleveland papers delivered in their home; the remaining jurors were not interrogated on the point. Nor were there questions as to radios or television sets in the jurors' homes, but we must assume that most of them owned such conveniences. As the selection of the jury progressed, individual pictures of prospective members appeared daily. During the trial, pictures of the jury appeared over 40 times in the Cleveland papers alone. The court permitted photographers to take pictures of the jury in the box, and individual pictures of the members in the jury room. One newspaper ran pictures of the jurors at the Sheppard home when they went there to view the scene of the murder. Another paper featured the home life of an alternate juror. The day before the verdict was rendered—while the jurors were at lunch and sequestered by two bailiffs—the jury was separated into two groups to pose for photographs which appeared in the newspapers.

III.

We now reach the conduct of the trial. While the intense publicity continued unabated, it is sufficient to relate only the more flagrant episodes:

1. On October 9, 1954, nine days before the case went to trial, an editorial in one of the newspapers criticized defense counsel's random poll of people on the streets as to their opinion of Sheppard's guilt or innocence in an effort to use the resulting statistics to show the necessity for change of venue. The article said the survey "smacks of mass jury tampering," called on defense counsel to drop it, and stated that the bar association should do something about it. It characterized the poll as "non-judicial, non-legal, and nonsense." The article was called to the attention of the court but no action was taken.

2. On the second day of voir dire examination a debate was staged and broadcast live over WHK radio. The participants, newspaper reporters, accused Sheppard's counsel of throwing roadblocks in the way of the prosecution and asserted that Sheppard conceded his guilt by hiring a prominent criminal lawyer. Sheppard's counsel objected to this broadcast and requested a continuance, but the judge denied the motion. When counsel asked the court to give some protection from such events, the judge replied that "WHK doesn't have much coverage," and

that "[a]fter all, we are not trying this case by radio or in newspapers or any other means. We confine ourselves seriously to it in this courtroom and do the very best we can."

3. While the jury was being selected, a two-inch headline asked: "But Who Will Speak for Marilyn?" The front-page story spoke of the "perfect face" of the accused. "Study that face as long as you want. Never will you get from it a hint of what might be the answer. . . ." The two brothers of the accused were described as "Prosperous, poised. His two sisters-in law. Smart, chic, well-groomed. His elderly father. Courtly, reserved. A perfect type for the patriarch of a staunch clan." The author then noted Marilyn Sheppard was "still off stage," and that she was an only child whose mother died when she was very young and whose father had no interest in the case. But the author—through quotes from Detective Chief James McArthur—assured readers that the prosecution's exhibits would speak for Marilyn. "Her story," McArthur stated, "will come into this courtroom through our witnesses." The article ends:

> "Then you realize how what and who is missing from the perfect setting will be supplied.
> "How in the Big Case justice will be done.
> "Justice to Sam Sheppard.
> "And to Marilyn Sheppard."

4. As has been mentioned, the jury viewed the scene of the murder on the first day of the trial. Hundreds of reporters, cameramen and onlookers were there, and one representative of the news media was permitted to accompany the jury while it inspected the Sheppard home. The time of the jury's visit was revealed so far in advance that one of the newspapers was able to rent a helicopter and fly over the house taking pictures of the jurors on their tour.

5. On November 19, a Cleveland police officer gave testimony that tended to contradict details in the written statement Sheppard made to the Cleveland police. Two days later, in a broadcast heard over Station WHK in Cleveland, Robert Considine likened Sheppard to a perjurer and compared the episode to Alger Hiss' confrontation with Whittaker Chambers. Though defense counsel asked the judge to question the jury to ascertain how many heard the broadcast, the court refused to do so. The judge also overruled the motion for continuance based on the same ground, saying:

> Well, I don't know, we can't stop people, in any event, listening to it. It is a matter of free speech, and the court can't control everybody. . . . We are not going to harass the jury every morning. . . . It is getting to the point where if we do it every morning, we are suspecting the jury. I have confidence in this jury.

6. On November 24, a story appeared under an eight-column headline: "Sam Called A 'Jekyll-Hyde' By Marilyn, Cousin To Testify." It related that Marilyn had recently told friends that Sheppard was a "Dr. Jekyll and Mr. Hyde" character. No such testimony was ever produced at the trial. The story went on to announce: "The prosecution has a 'bombshell witness' on tap who will testify to Dr. Sam's display of fiery temper—countering the defense claim that the defendant is a gentle physician with an even disposition." Defense counsel made motions for change of venue, continuance and mistrial, but they were denied. No action was taken by the court.

7. When the trial was in its seventh week, Walter Winchell broadcast over WXEL television and WJW radio that Carole Beasley, who was under arrest in

New York City for robbery, had stated that, as Sheppard's mistress, she had borne him a child. The defense asked that the jury be queried on the broadcast. Two jurors admitted in open court that they had heard it. The judge asked each: "Would that have any effect upon your judgment?" Both replied, "No." This was accepted by the judge as sufficient; he merely asked the jury to "pay no attention whatever to that type of scavenging. . . . Let's confine ourselves to this courtroom, if you please." In answer to the motion for mistrial, the judge said:

> "Well, even, so, Mr. Corrigan, how are you ever going to prevent those things, in any event? I don't justify them at all. I think it is outrageous, but in a sense, it is outrageous even if there were no trial here. The trial has nothing to do with it in the Court's mind, as far as its outrage is concerned, but—
>
> "Mr. CORRIGAN: I don't know what effect it had on the mind of any of these jurors, and I can't find out unless inquiry is made.
>
> "The COURT: How would you ever, in any jury, avoid that kind of a thing?"

8. On December 9, while Sheppard was on the witness stand, he testified that he had been mistreated by Cleveland detectives after his arrest. Although he was not at the trial, Captain Kerr of the Homicide Bureau issued a press statement denying Sheppard's allegations which appeared under the headline: " 'Bare-faced Liar,' Kerr Says of Sam." Captain Kerr never appeared as a witness at the trial.

9. After the case was submitted to the jury, it was sequestered for its deliberations, which took five days and four nights. After the verdict, defense counsel ascertained that the jurors had been allowed to make telephone calls to their homes every day while they were sequestered at the hotel. Although the telephones had been removed from the jurors' rooms, the jurors were permitted to use the phones in the bailiffs' rooms. The calls were placed by the jurors themselves; no record was kept of the jurors who made calls, the telephone numbers or the parties called. The bailiffs sat in the room where they could hear only the jurors' end of the conversation. The court had not instructed the bailiffs to prevent such calls. By a subsequent motion, defense counsel urged that this ground alone warranted a new trial, but the motion was overruled and no evidence was taken on the question.

IV.

The principle that justice cannot survive behind walls of silence has long been reflected in the "Anglo-American distrust for secret trials." *In re Oliver*, 333 U.S. 257, 268 (1948). A responsible press has always been regarded as the handmaiden of effective judicial administration, especially in the criminal field. Its function in this regard is documented by an impressive record of service over several centuries. The press does not simply publish information about trials but guards against the miscarriage of justice by subjecting the police, prosecutors, and judicial processes to extensive public scrutiny and criticism. This Court has, therefore, been unwilling to place any direct limitations on the freedom traditionally exercised by the news media for "[w]hat transpires in the court room is public property." *Craig* v. *Harney*, 331 U.S. 367, 374 (1947). The "unqualified prohibitions laid down by the framers were intended to give to liberty of the press . . . the broadest scope that could be countenanced in an orderly society." *Bridges* v. *California*, 314 U.S. 252, 265 (1941). And where there was "no threat or menace to the integrity of the trial," *Craig* v. *Harney*, *supra*, at 377, we have consistently required that the press have a free hand, even though we sometimes deplored its sensationalism.

But the Court has also pointed out that "[l]egal trials are not like elections, to be won through the use of the meeting-hall, the radio, and the newspaper." *Bridges*

v. *California, supra,* at 271. And the Court has insisted that no one be punished for a crime without "a charge fairly made and fairly tried in a public tribunal free of prejudice, passion, excitement, and tyrannical power." *Chambers* v. *Florida,* 309 U.S. 227, 236–237 (1940). "Freedom of discussion should be given the widest range compatible with the essential requirement of the fair and orderly administration of justice." *Pennekamp* v. *Florida,* 328 U.S. 331, 347 (1946). But it must not be allowed to divert the trial from the "very purpose of a court system . . . to adjudicate controversies, both criminal and civil, in the calmness and solemnity of the courtroom according to legal procedures." *Cox* v. *Louisiana,* 379 U.S. 559, 583 (1965) (BLACK, J., dissenting). Among these "legal procedures" is the requirement that the jury's verdict be based on evidence received in open court, not from outside sources. Thus, in *Marshall* v. *United States,* 360 U.S. 310 (1959), we set aside a federal conviction where the jurors were exposed "through news accounts" to information that was not admitted at trial. We held that the prejudice from such material "may indeed be greater" than when it is part of the prosecution's evidence "for it is then not tempered by protective procedures." At 313. At the same time, we did not consider dispositive the statement of each juror "that he would not be influenced by the news articles, that he could decide the case only on the evidence of record, and that he felt no prejudice against petitioner as a result of the articles." At 312. Likewise, in *Irvin* v. *Dowd,* 366 U.S. 717 (1961), even though each juror indicated that he could render an impartial verdict despite exposure to prejudicial newspaper articles, we set aside the conviction holding:

> With his life at stake, it is not requiring too much that petitioner be tried in an atmosphere undisturbed by so huge a wave of public passion. . . . At 728

The undeviating rule of this Court was expressed by Mr. Justice Holmes over half a century ago in *Patterson* v. *Colorado,* 205 U.S. 454, 462 (1907):

> The theory of our system is that the conclusions to be reached in a case will be induced only by evidence and argument in open court, and not by any outside influence, whether of private talk or public print.

Moreover, "the burden of showing essential unfairness . . . as a demonstrable reality," *Adams* v. *United States ex rel. McCann,* 317 U.S. 269, 281 (1942), need not be undertaken when television has exposed the community "repeatedly and in depth to the spectacle of [the accused] personally confessing in detail to the crimes with which he was later to be charged." *Rideau* v. *Louisiana,* 373 U.S. 723, 726 (1963). In *Turner* v. *Louisiana,* 379 U.S. 466 (1965), two key witnesses were deputy sheriffs who doubled as jury shepherds during the trial. The deputies swore that they had not talked to the jurors about the case, but the Court nonetheless held that,

> . . . even if it could be assumed that the deputies never did discuss the case directly with any members of the jury, it would be blinking reality not to recognize the extreme prejudice inherent in this continual association. . . . At 473

Only last Term in *Estes* v. *Texas,* 381 U.S. 532 (1965), we set aside a conviction despite the absence of any showing of prejudice. We said there:

> It is true that in most cases involving claims of due process deprivations we require a showing of identifiable prejudice to the accused. Nevertheless, at times a procedure employed by the State involves such a probability that prejudice will result that it is deemed inherently lacking in due process. At 542–543

And we cited with approval the language of MR. JUSTICE BLACK for the Court in *In re Murchison*, 349 U.S. 133, 136 (1955), that "our system of law has always endeavored to prevent even the probability of unfairness."

V.

It is clear that the totality of circumstances in this case also warrants such an approach. Unlike Estes, Sheppard was not granted a change of venue to a locale away from where the publicity originated; nor was his jury sequestered. The *Estes* jury saw none of the television broadcasts from the courtroom. On the contrary, the *Sheppard* jurors were subjected to newspaper, radio and television coverage of the trial while not taking part in the proceedings. They were allowed to go their separate ways outside of the courtroom, without adequate directions not to read or listen to anything concerning the case. The judge's "admonitions" at the beginning of the trial are representative:

> I would suggest to you and caution you that you do not read any newspapers during the progress of this trial, that you do not listen to radio comments nor watch or listen to television comments, insofar as this case is concerned. You will feel very much better as the trial proceeds. . . . I am sure that we shall all feel very much better if we do not indulge in any newspaper reading or listening to any comments whatever about the matter while the case is in progress. After it is all over, you can read it all to your heart's content. . . .

At intervals during the trial, the judge simply repeated his "suggestions" and "requests" that the jurors not expose themselves to comment upon the case. Moreover, the jurors were thrust into the role of celebrities by the judge's failure to insulate them from reporters and photographers. See *Estes* v. *Texas*, *supra*, at 545–546. The numerous pictures of the jurors, with their addresses, which appeared in the newspapers before and during the trial itself exposed them to expressions of opinion from both cranks and friends. The fact that anonymous letters had been received by prospective jurors should have made the judge aware that this publicity seriously threatened the jurors' privacy.

The press coverage of the *Estes* trial was not nearly as massive and pervasive as the attention given by the Cleveland newspapers and broadcasting stations to Sheppard's prosecution. Sheppard stood indicted for the murder of his wife; the State was demanding the death penalty. For months the virulent publicity about Sheppard and the murder had made the case notorious. Charges and countercharges were aired in the news media besides those for which Sheppard was called to trial. In addition, only three months before trial, Sheppard was examined for more than five hours without counsel during a three-day inquest which ended in a public brawl. The inquest was televised live from a high school gymnasium seating hundreds of people. Furthermore, the trial began two weeks before a hotly contested election at which both Chief Prosecutor Mahon and Judge Blythin were candidates for judgeships.

While we cannot say that Sheppard was denied due process by the judge's refusal to take precautions against the influence of pretrial publicity alone, the court's later rulings must be considered against the setting in which the trial was held. In light of this background, we believe that the arrangements made by the judge with the news media caused Sheppard to be deprived of that "judicial serenity and calm to which [he] was entitled." *Estes* v. *Texas*, *supra*, at 536. The fact is that bedlam reigned at the courthouse during the trial and newsmen took over practically the

entire courtroom, hounding most of the participants in the trial, especially Sheppard. At a temporary table within a few feet of the jury box and counsel table sat some 20 reporters staring at Sheppard and taking notes. The erection of a press table for reporters inside the bar is unprecedented. The bar of the court is reserved for counsel, providing them a safe place in which to keep papers and exhibits, and to confer privately with client and co-counsel. It is designed to protect the witness and the jury from any distractions, intrusions or influences, and to permit bench discussions of the judge's rulings away from the hearing of the public and the jury. Having assigned almost all of the available seats in the courtroom to the news media the judge lost his ability to supervise that environment. The movement of the reporters in and out of the courtroom caused frequent confusion and disruption of the trial. And the record reveals constant commotion within the bar. Moreover, the judge gave the throng of newsmen gathered in the corridors of the courthouse absolute free rein. Participants in the trial, including the jury, were forced to run a gantlet of reporters and photographers each time they entered or left the courtroom. The total lack of consideration for the privacy of the jury was demonstrated by the assignment to a broadcasting station of space next to the jury room on the floor above the courtroom, as well as the fact that jurors were allowed to make telephone calls during their five-day deliberation. . . .

. . . The carnival atmosphere at trial could easily have been avoided since the courtroom and courthouse premises are subject to the control of the court. As we stressed in *Estes*, the presence of the press at judicial proceedings must be limited when it is apparent that the accused might otherwise be prejudiced or disadvantaged. . . . The case is remanded to the District Court with instructions to issue the writ and order that Sheppard be released from custody unless the State puts him to its charges again within a reasonable time.

It is so ordered.

MR. JUSTICE BLACK dissents. [Omitted.]

WHAT DO YOU THINK?

1. What other actions could the judge have taken to ensure a fair trial for the defendant?
2. The trial started in October 1954. The Supreme Court reversed the decision in 1966. Why did the court delay 12 years before reversing the case?
3. Do the newspapers have a right to print their versions of the trial? Explain your answer.

SUMMARY

- Historically, the grand jury has been regarded as a primary security to the innocent against hasty, malicious, and oppressive persecution; it serves the invaluable function in our society of standing between the accuser and the accused—whether the latter be an individual, minority group, or other—to determine whether a charge is founded upon reason or was dictated by an intimidating power or by malice and personal ill will.

- The indictment is a formal document prepared by the prosecuting attorney setting forth the charge against the accused. The indictment serves several purposes. It informs the grand jury of the charge about which they will receive evidence during the grand jury hearings.

- Grand juries generally meet at regular times to hear criminal charges presented by a prosecutor. A grand jury also may call a hearing on its own and conduct its own investigations. The grand jury is not a judicial body but an investigative body, and its historical role is that of an accusatory not adjudicatory body.

- In our criminal justice system, the government retains broad discretion as to whom to prosecute. So long as the prosecutor has probable cause to believe that the accused committed an offense defined by statute, the decision whether or not to prosecute, and what charge to file or bring before a grand jury, generally rests entirely in his discretion.

- The Supreme Court has failed to establish a clear rule as to what constitutes a violation of the right to a speedy trial under the Sixth Amendment. In *Barker* v. *Wingo*, the Court stated that a balancing test should be used and the test should be based on the following four factors: the length of the delay, reason for the delay, whether the defendant had asserted his or her right to a speedy trial, and any prejudice caused the defendant by the delay.

DISCUSSION QUESTIONS

1. What is the purpose and function of the grand jury?
2. Should a defendant have the right to be present when his or her case is presented to the grand jury? Justify your answer.
3. What are the restrictions on a prosecutor's decision to prosecute?
4. How is the right to a speedy trial generically different from any of the other rights in the constitution?

ENDNOTES

1. 504 U.S. 36 (1992).
2. 370 U.S. 375 (1962).
3. 457 U.S. 368 (1982).
4. *Bordenkircher* v. *Hayes*, 434 U.S. 357, 364 (1978).
5. *Wayte* v. *United States*, 470 U.S. 598 (1985).
6. *United States* v. *Ewell*, 383 U.S. 116, 120 (1966).
7. 18 U.S. Code Sections 3161–3174.
8. 407 U.S. 514 (1972).
9. 393 U.S. 374 (1969).
10. 112 S.Ct. 2686 (1992).
11. 380 U.S. 24 (1965).
12. 384 U.S. 373 (1966).
13. 399 U.S. 78 (1970).
14. 448 U.S. 555 (1980).

12

$\mathcal{P}$UNISHMENT

SENTENCING

In no other area of the justice system is there a greater variance between states than in the sentencing phase of justice proceedings. If the defendant is tried for more than one offense, or if he is presently serving a sentence for another crime, it is important to question if the sentences for each offense will be served consecutively or concurrently. A *consecutive sentence* is where one sentence must be served before the other begins. A *concurrent sentence* is where the sentences are served at the same time, i.e., concurrently.

On the conviction of a misdemeanor, the statutes of most states provide that the penalty imposed shall not exceed one year imprisonment in a prison and/or a fine. Generally, for a felony, the defendant may be imprisoned for more than a year. In the majority of states, it is the prerogative of the judge to impose sentence. In some states, like Texas, the defendant may elect to be sentenced by a jury.

To assist judges in attempting to arrive at an equitable sentence and to more nearly make the sentence fit the crime and offender, most states provide for a presentence investigation prior to sentencing in felony cases. The presentence investigation (PSI) is usually conducted by a staff member of the probation department. The investigation generally includes such matters as the offender's family status, educational background, work experience, and prior criminal record. Often the PSI will report the defendant's attitude toward the crime, and whether the offender is remorseful over having committed the crime or is only unhappy about being caught.

The death penalty is a controversial penalty. Heated arguments have taken place over the years concerning the merits of the death penalty. Many contend that there is no place in a civilized society for the penalty. They also argue that the death penalty does not act as a deterrent. Some who oppose the death penalty state that it is in violation of the Eighth Amendment because it is cruel and unusual. An equal number contend that the death penalty *is* a deterrent and as such it should be retained. One major problem with the death penalty is the long delay between the imposition of the penalty and the execution.

The Supreme Court in *Furman* v. *Georgia*[1] stated that the death penalty as such was not cruel and unusual punishment, but the indiscriminatory manner in which it was applied made the death penalty cruel and unusual punishment and thus in violation of the Eighth Amendment. Later, *Woodson* v. *North Carolina*[2] held that a statute made the death penalty mandatory on the conviction of certain offenses and was unconstitutional since it did not allow any consideration to be given to the character and record of the offender. The Supreme Court stated that "Consideration of both the offender and the offense in order to arrive at a just and appropriate sentence has been viewed as progressive and humanizing development."

In *Gregg* v. *Georgia*[3], a Georgia statute which allowed the judge or jury to take into consideration aggravating and mitigating circumstances in imposing the alternate sentence of life imprisonment or death was considered constitutional. As required by *Woodson*, alternate sentencing procedure must be used in death penalty

Justice Thurgood Marshall (shown here in his chambers) was appointed to the Supreme Court by President Lyndon Johnson and served from 1969 to 1991. (Photograph by Deborah L. Rhode. Collection of the Supreme Court of the United States.)

cases. Now in a few states that have the death penalty, a trial is first held to determine the guilt or innocence of the accused. If the accused is found guilty, a second trial is held to determine if the death penalty should be imposed or if the defendant should be given a life imprisonment. In other states with the death penalty, only one trial is held. The jury first deliberates on the guilt or innocence of the defendant. If the defendant is found guilty, then the same jury would deliberate on the penalty to be imposed. Under each method during the sentencing phase, the jury or judge must consider both the aggravating and mitigating circumstances of the case.

The *Gregg* case upheld the death penalty for first degree murder with aggravating circumstances. The Supreme Court in *Coker* v. *Georgia*[4] held that the death penalty for the rape of an adult woman was excessive and disproportionate to the crime. In *Godfrey* v. *Georgia*[5], the Supreme Court held that the death penalty amounted to cruel and unusual punishment when pronounced on the defendant. The Georgia statute in question provided that the death penalty could be imposed where the offense of murder was "outrageously or wantonly vile, horrible, or inhuman." The Court held that while the evidence established that the defendant shot both victims in the head with a shotgun and that they died instantly, there was no evidence of serious suffering by the victims or that the crime was outrageously or wantonly vile, horrible, or inhuman. In *Enmund* v. *Florida*[6], Enmund and two other defendants entered into a conspiracy to rob a victim of money. The three went to the home of the victim. Enmund remained in the car while the other two went into the house to rob the victim. The victim's wife pulled a weapon and shot one of the defendants. The other defendant killed the victim and his wife. All three defendants were convicted of first degree murder and were sentenced to death. Enmund appealed the death sentence on the grounds that under the circumstances of the sentence of death was cruel and unusual. He alleged that he did not participate in the actual killing and had no intent to kill during the robbery. The Supreme Court agreed and set aside the death penalty. Accordingly, it appears that the Supreme Court will approve the death penalty only in those cases involving first degree murder with aggravating circumstances.

FINES

Originally, fines were money and property taken from the offender and paid to the victim of the crime or to relatives of the victim. Eventually, the fines became a source of revenue to the king or the church and the victim and relatives were left to civil remedies. The use of fines as punishment has diminished since the Supreme Court case of *Williams* v. *Illinois*.[7] Williams was convicted of petty theft and received the maximum sentence of one year imprisonment and a $500 fine. Williams was also taxed court costs of $5. The judge directed that if Williams was in default of payment of fines and court costs at the expiration of the one-year sentence, he would be required to remain in jail pursuant to the Illinois Criminal Code to "work off" the monetary obligation at the rate of $5 per day. The Court held that imprisoning one who was indigent and unable to pay the fine beyond the maximum amount of imprisonment prescribed by law was a violation of the equal protection clause of the Fourteenth Amendment. Most jurisdictions have interpreted the *Williams* case as permitting the use of alternate penalties such as thirty days in jail or a $100 fine. A few jurisdictions read the *Williams* case as not permitting an alternate penalty. This question has not to this date been decided by the Supreme Court.

CAPSTONE CASES

In determining a sentence, may a judge give consideration to the defendant's testimony at trial that the judge believes is false? The Grayson *case looks at this issue.*

UNITED STATES V. GRAYSON
438 U.S. 41 (1978)

MR. CHIEF JUSTICE BURGER delivered the opinion of the Court.

We granted *certiorari* to review a holding of the Court of Appeals that it was improper for a sentencing judge, in fixing the sentence within the statutory limits, to give consideration to the defendant's false testimony observed by the judge during the trial.

I.

In August 1975, respondent Grayson was confined in a federal prison camp under a conviction for distributing a controlled substance. In October, he escaped but was apprehended two days later by FBI agents in New York City. He was indicated for prison escape in violation of 18 U.S.C. 751 (a) (1976 ed.).

During its case in chief, the United States proved the essential elements of the crime, including his lawful confinement and the unlawful escape. In addition, it presented the testimony of the arresting FBI agents that Grayson, upon being apprehended, denied his true identity.

Grayson testified in his own defense. He admitted leaving the camp but asserted that he did so out of fear: "I had just been threatened with a large stick with a nail protruding through it by an inmate that was serving time at Allenwood, and I was scared, and I just ran." He testified that the threat was made in the presence of many inmates by prisoner Barnes who sought to enforce collection of a gambling debt and followed other threats and physical assaults made for the same purpose. Grayson called one inmate, who testified: "I heard [Barnes] talk to Grayson in a loud voice one day, but that's all. I never seen no harm, no hands or no shuffling whatsoever."

Grayson's version of the facts was contradicted by the Government's rebuttal evidence and by cross-examination on crucial aspects of his story. For example, Grayson stated that after crossing the prison fence he left his prison jacket by the side of the road. On recross, he stated that he also left his prison shirt but not his trousers. Government testimony showed that on the morning after the escape, a shirt marked with Grayson's number, a jacket, and a pair of prison trousers were found outside a hole in the prison fence. Grayson also testified on cross-examination: "I do believe that I phrased the rhetorical question to Captain Kurd, who was in charge of [the prison], and I think I said something if an inmate

was being threatened by somebody, what would . . . he do? First of all he said he would want to know who it was." On further cross-examination, however, Grayson modified his description of the conversation. Captain Kurd testified that Grayson had never mentioned in any fashion threats from other inmates. Finally, the alleged assailant, Barnes, by then no longer an inmate, testified that Grayson had never owed him any money and that he had never threatened or physically assaulted Grayson.

The jury returned a guilty verdict, whereupon the District Judge ordered the United States Probation Office to prepare a presentence report. At the sentencing hearing, the judge stated:

> I'm going to give my reasons for sentencing in this case with clarity, because one of the reasons may well be considered by a Court of Appeals to be impermissible; and although I could come into this Court Room and sentence this Defendant to a five-year prison term without any explanation at all, I think it is fair that I give the reasons so that if the Court of Appeals feels that one of the reasons which I am about to enunciate is an improper consideration for a trial judge, then the Court will be in a position to reverse this Court and send the case back for re-sentencing.
>
> In my view a prison sentence is indicated, and the sentence that the Court is going to impose is to deter you, Mr. Grayson, and others who are similarly situated. Secondly, it is my view that your defense was a complete fabrication without the slightest merit whatsoever. I feel it is proper for me to consider that fact in the sentencing, and I will do so.

He then sentenced Grayson to a term of two years' imprisonment, consecutive to his unexpired sentence.

On appeal, a divided panel of the Court of Appeals for the Third Circuit directed that Grayson's sentence be vacated and that he be resentenced by the District Court without consideration of false testimony. 550 F.2d 103 (1977). Two judges concluded that this result was mandated by language in a prior decision of the Third Circuit, *Poteet v. Fauver*, 517 F.2d 393, 395 (1975): "[T]he sentencing judge may not add a penalty because he believes the defendant lied." One judge, in a concurring opinion, suggested that the District Court's reliance on Grayson's false testimony in fixing the sentence "trenches upon a defendant's constitutional privilege to testify in his own behalf as well as his right to have criminal charges," such as one for perjury, formally adjudicated "pursuant to procedures required by due process." 550 F.2d, at 108. The dissenting judge challenged both the applicability of *Poteet* and the suggestion that the District Court's approach to Grayson's sentence was constitutionally impermissible.

We granted *certiorari* to resolve conflicts between holdings of the Courts of Appeals. 434 U.S. 816 (1977). We reverse.

II.

In *Williams v. New York*, 337 U.S. 241, 247 (1949), MR. JUSTICE BLACK observed that the "prevalent modern philosophy of penology [is] that the punishment should fit the offender and not merely the crime," and that, accordingly, sentences should be determined with an eye toward the "[r]eformation and rehabilitation of offenders." *Id.*, at 248. But it has not always been so. In the early days of the Republic, when imprisonment had only recently emerged as an alternative to the death penalty, confinement in public stocks, or whipping in the town square, the period of incarceration was generally prescribed with specificity by the legislature. Each crime had its defined punishment. See *Report of Twentieth Century Fund Task Force on Criminal*

Sentencing, Fair and Certain Punishment 83–85 (1976) (Task Force Report). The "excessive rigidity of the [mandatory or fixed sentence] system" soon gave way in some jurisdictions, however, to a scheme permitting the sentencing judge—or jury—to consider aggravating and mitigating circumstances surrounding an offense, and, on that basis, to select a sentence within a range defined by the legislature. Tappan, *Sentencing Under the Model Penal Code, 23 Law & Contemp.* Prob. 528, 529 (1958). Nevertheless, the focus remained on the crime: Each particular offense was to be punished in proportion to the social harm caused by it and according to the offender's culpability. See, e.g., Iowa Code of 1851, Tit. XXIV, ch. 182, 3067, 3068, reprinted in S. Rubin, *Law of Criminal Correction* 131–132 (2d ed. 1973). The purpose of incarceration remained, primarily, retribution and punishment.

Approximately a century ago, a reform movement asserting that the purpose of incarceration, and therefore the guiding consideration in sentencing, should be rehabilitation of the offender, dramatically altered the approach to sentencing. A fundamental proposal of this movement was a flexible sentencing system permitting judges and correctional personnel, particularly the latter, to set the release date of prisoners according to informed judgments concerning their potential for, or actual, rehabilitation and their likely recidivism. Task Force Report 82. Indeed, the most extreme formulations of the emerging rehabilitation model, with its "reformatory sentence," posited that "convicts [regardless of the nature of their crime] can never be rightfully imprisoned except upon proof that it is unsafe for themselves and for society to leave them free, and when confined can never be rightfully released until they show themselves fit for membership in a free community." Lewis, *The Indeterminate Sentence*, 9 Yale L. J. 17, 27 (1899).

This extreme formulation, although influential, was not adopted unmodified by any jurisdiction. See *Tappan, supra*, at 531–533. "The influences of legalism and realism were powerful enough . . . to prevent the enactment of this form of indeterminate sentencing. Concern for personal liberty, skepticism concerning administrative decisions about prisoner reformation and readiness for release, insistence upon the preservation of some measure of deterrent emphasis, and other such factors, undoubtedly, led, instead, to a system—indeed, a complex of systems—in which maximum terms were generally employed." *Id.*, at 530. Thus it is that today the extent of a federal prisoner's confinement is initially determined by the sentencing judge, who selects a term within an often broad, congressionally prescribed range; release on parole is then available on review by the United States Parole Commission, which, as a general rule, may conditionally release a prisoner any time after he serves one-third of the judicially fixed term. See 18 U.S.C. 4205 (1976 ed.). To an unspecified degree, the sentencing judge is obligated to make his decision on the basis, among others, of predictions regarding the convicted defendant's potential, or lack of potential, for rehabilitation.

Indeterminate sentencing under the rehabilitation model presented sentencing judges with a serious practical problem: how rationally to make the required predictions so as to avoid capricious and arbitrary sentences, which the newly conferred and broad discretion placed within the realm of possibility. An obvious, although only partial, solution was to provide the judge with as much information as reasonably practical concerning the defendant's "character and propensities[,] . . . his present purposes and tendencies," *Pennsylvania ex rel. Sullivan* v. *Ashe*, 302 U.S. 51, 55 (1937), and, indeed, "every aspect of [his] life." *Williams* v. *New York*, 337 U.S., at 250. Thus, most jurisdictions provided trained probation officers to conduct presentence investigations of the defendant's life and, on that basis, prepare a presentence report for the sentencing judge.

Constitutional challenges were leveled at judicial reliance on such information, however. In *Williams* v. *New York*, a jury convicted the defendant of murder but recommended a life sentence. The sentencing judge, partly on the basis of information not known to the jury but contained in a presentence report, imposed the death penalty. The defendant argued that this procedure deprived him of his federal constitutional right to confront and cross-examine those supplying information to the probation officer and, through him, to the sentencing judge. The Court rejected this argument. It noted that traditionally "a sentencing judge could exercise a wide discretion in the sources and types of evidence used to assist him in determining the kind and extent of punishment to be imposed within limits fixed by law." *Id.*, at 246. "And modern concepts individualizing punishment have made it all the more necessary that a sentencing judge not be denied an opportunity to obtain pertinent information," *id.*, at 247; indeed, "[t]o deprive sentencing judges of this kind of information would undermine modern penological procedural policies that have been cautiously adopted throughout the nation after careful consideration and experimentation." *Id.*, at 249–250. Accordingly, the sentencing judge was held not to have acted unconstitutionally in considering either the defendant's participation in criminal conduct for which he had not been convicted or information secured by the probation investigator that the defendant was a "menace to society." See *id.*, at 244.

Of course, a sentencing judge is not limited to the often far-ranging material compiled in a presentence report. "[B]efore making [the sentencing] determination, a judge may appropriately conduct an inquiry broad in scope, largely unlimited either as to the kind of information he may consider, or the source from which it may come." *United States* v. *Tucker*, 404 U.S. 443, 446 (1972). Congress recently reaffirmed this fundamental sentencing principle by enacting 18 U.S.C. 3577 (1976 ed.):

> No limitation shall be placed on the information concerning the background, character, and conduct of a person convicted of an offense which a court of the United States may receive and consider for the purpose of imposing an appropriate sentence.

Thus, we have acknowledged that a sentencing authority may legitimately consider the evidence heard during trial, as well as the demeanor of the accused. *Chaffin* v. *Stynchcombe*, 412 U.S. 17, 32 (1973). More to the point presented in this case, one serious study has concluded that the trial judge's "opportunity to observe the defendant, particularly if he chose to take the stand in his defense, can often provide useful insights into an appropriate disposition." ABA *Project on Standards for Criminal Justice, Sentencing Alternatives and Procedures* 5.1, p. 232 (App. Draft 1968).

A defendant's truthfulness or mendacity while testifying on his own behalf, almost without exception, has been deemed probative of his attitudes toward society and prospects for rehabilitation and hence relevant to sentencing. Soon after *Williams* was decided, the Tenth Circuit concluded that "the attitude of a convicted defendant with respect to his willingness to commit a serious crime [perjury] . . . is a proper matter to consider in determining what sentence shall be imposed within the limitations fixed by statute." *Humes* v. *United States*, 186 F.2d 875, 878 (1951). The Second, Fourth, Fifth, Sixth, Seventh, Eighth, and Ninth Circuits have since agreed. See n. 3, *supra*. Judge Marvin Frankel's analysis for the Second Circuit is persuasive:

> The effort to appraise "character" is, to be sure, a parlous one, and not necessarily an enterprise for which judges are notably equipped by prior training. Yet it is in our existing scheme of sentencing one clue to the rational exercise of discretion. If the notion

of "repentance" is out of fashion today, the fact remains that a manipulative defiance of the law is not a cheerful datum for the prognosis a sentencing judge undertakes. . . . Impressions about the individual being sentenced—the likelihood that he will transgress no more, the hope that he may respond to rehabilitative efforts to assist with a lawful future career, the degree to which he does or does not deem himself at war with his society—are, for better or worse, central factors to be appraised under our theory of "individualized" sentencing. The theory has its critics. While it lasts, however, a fact like the defendant's readiness to lie under oath before the judge who will sentence him would seem to be among the more precise and concrete of the available indicia. *United States v. Hendrix*, 505 F.2d 1233, 1236 (1974)

Only one Circuit has directly rejected the probative value of the defendant's false testimony in his own defense. In *Scott v. United States*, 135 U.S. App. D.C. 377, 382, 419 F.2d 264, 269 (1969), the court argued that

... the peculiar pressures placed upon a defendant threatened with jail and the stigma of conviction make his willingness to deny the crime an unpromising test of his prospects for rehabilitation if guilty. It is indeed unlikely that many men who commit serious offenses would balk on principle from lying in their own defense. The guilty man may quite sincerely repent his crime but yet, driven by the urge to remain free, may protest his innocence in a court of law.

See also *United States v. Moore*, 484 F.2d 1284, 1288 (CA4 1973) (CRAVEN, J., concurring). The Scott rationale rests not only on the realism of the psychological pressures on a defendant in the dock—which we can grant—but also on a deterministic view of human conduct that is inconsistent with the underlying precepts of our criminal justice system. A "universal and persistent" foundation stone in our system of law, and particularly in our approach to punishment, sentencing, and incarceration, is the "belief in freedom of the human will and a consequent ability and duty of the normal individual to choose between good and evil." *Morissette v. United States*, 342 U.S. 246, 250 (1952). See also *Blocker v. United States*, 110 U.S. App. D.C. 41, 53, 288 F.2d 853, 865 (1961) (opinion concurring in result). Given that long-accepted view of the "ability and duty of the normal individual to choose," we must conclude that the defendant's readiness to lie under oath—especially when, as here, the trial court finds the lie to be flagrant—may be deemed probative of his prospects for rehabilitation.

III.

Against this background we evaluate Grayson's constitutional argument that the District Court's sentence constitutes punishment for the crime of perjury for which he has not been indicted, tried, or convicted by due process. A second argument is that permitting consideration of perjury will "chill" defendants from exercising their right to testify on their own behalf.

A.

In his due process argument, Grayson does not contend directly that the District Court had an impermissible purpose in considering his perjury and selecting the sentence. Rather, he argues that this Court, in order to preserve due process rights, not only must prohibit the impermissible sentencing practice of incarcerating for the purpose of saving the Government the burden of bringing a separate and subsequent perjury prosecution, but also must prohibit the otherwise permissible practice of considering a defendant's untruthfulness for the purpose of illuminating his

need for rehabilitation and society's need for protection. He presents two interrelated reasons. The effect of both permissible and impermissible sentencing practices may be the same: additional time in prison. Further, it is virtually impossible, he contends, to identify and establish the impermissible practice. We find these reasons insufficient justification for prohibiting what the Court and the Congress have declared appropriate judicial conduct.

First, the evolutionary history of sentencing, set out in Part II, demonstrates that it is proper—indeed, even necessary for the rational exercise of discretion—to consider the defendant's whole person and personality, as manifested by his conduct at trial and his testimony under oath, for whatever light those may shed on the sentencing decision. The "parlous" effort to appraise "character," *United States v. Hendrix, supra,* at 1236, degenerates into a game of chance to the extent that a sentencing judge is deprived of relevant information concerning "every aspect of a defendant's life." *Williams v. New York,* 337 U.S., at 250. The Government's interest, as well as the offender's, in avoiding irrationality is of the highest order. That interest more than justifies the risk that Grayson asserts is present when a sentencing judge considers a defendant's untruthfulness under oath.

Second, in our view, *Williams* fully supports consideration of such conduct in sentencing. There the Court permitted the sentencing judge to consider the offender's history of prior antisocial conduct, including burglaries for which he had not been duly convicted. This it did despite the risk that the judge might use his knowledge of the offender's prior crimes for an improper purpose.

Third, the efficacy of Grayson's suggested "exclusionary rule" is open to serious doubt. No rule of law, even one garbed in constitutional terms, can prevent improper use of firsthand observations of perjury. The integrity of the judges, and their fidelity to their oaths of office, necessarily provide the only and, in our view, adequate assurance against that.

B.

Grayson's argument that judicial consideration of his conduct at trial impermissibly "chills" a defendant's statutory right, 18 U.S.C. 3481 (1976 ed.), and perhaps a constitutional right to testify on his own behalf is without basis. The right guaranteed by law to a defendant is narrowly the right to testify truthfully in accordance with the oath—unless we are to say that the oath is mere ritual without meaning. This view of the right involved is confirmed by the unquestioned constitutionality of perjury statutes, which punish those who willfully give false testimony. See, e.g., 18 U.S.C. 1621 (1976 ed.); *cf. United States v. Wong,* 431 U.S. 174 (1977). Further support for this is found in an important limitation on a defendant's right to the assistance of counsel: Counsel ethically cannot assist his client in presenting what the attorney has reason to believe is false testimony. See *Holloway v. Arkansas,* 435 U.S. 475, 480 n. 4 (1978); *ABA Project on Standards for Criminal Justice, The Defense Function* 7.7 (c), p. 133 (Compilation 1974).

Assuming, arguendo, that the sentencing judge's consideration of defendants' untruthfulness in testifying has any chilling effect on a defendant's decision to testify falsely, that effect is entirely permissible. There is no protected right to commit perjury.

Grayson's further argument that the sentencing practice challenged here will inhibit exercise of the right to testify truthfully is entirely frivolous. That argument misapprehends the nature and scope of the practice we find permissible. Nothing we say today requires a sentencing judge to enhance, in some wooden or reflex

fashion, the sentences of all defendants whose testimony is deemed false. Rather, we are reaffirming the authority of a sentencing judge to evaluate carefully a defendant's testimony on the stand, determine—with a consciousness of the frailty of human judgment—whether that testimony contained willful and material falsehoods, and, if so, assess in light of all the other knowledge gained about the defendant the meaning of that conduct with respect to his prospects for rehabilitation and restoration to a useful place in society. Awareness of such a process realistically cannot be deemed to affect the decision of an accused but unconvicted defendant to testify truthfully in his own behalf.

Accordingly, we reverse the judgment of the Court of Appeals and remand for reinstatement of the sentence of the District Court.

Reversed and remanded.

MR. JUSTICE STEWART, with whom MR. JUSTICE BRENNAN and MR. JUSTICE MARSHALL join, dissenting.

The Court begins its consideration of this case, ante, at 42, with the assumption that the respondent gave false testimony at his trial. But there has been no determination that his testimony was false. This respondent was given a greater sentence than he would otherwise have received—how much greater we have no way of knowing—solely because a single judge thought that he had not testified truthfully. In essence, the Court holds today that whenever a defendant testifies in his own behalf and is found guilty, he opens himself to the possibility of an enhanced sentence. Such a sentence is nothing more or less than a penalty imposed on the defendant's exercise of his constitutional and statutory rights to plead not guilty and to testify in his own behalf. . . .

WHAT DO YOU THINK?

1. What is meant by the statement "the punishment should fit the offender and not merely the crime"?
2. Should a judge be allowed to increase the sentence because the defendant's testimony is not believable?
3. Does the ruling in this case make it more difficult for a defendant to testify on his or her behalf?

The Gregg *case looks at the issue as to whether the sentence of death is cruel and unusual for the crime of murder.*

GREGG V. *GEORGIA*
428 U.S. 153 (1976)

Judgment of the Court, and opinion of MR. JUSTICE STEWART, MR. JUSTICE POWELL, and MR. JUSTICE STEVENS, announced by MR. JUSTICE STEWART.

The issue in this case is whether the imposition of the sentence of death for the crime of murder under the law of Georgia violates the Eighth and Fourteenth Amendments.

. . . We granted the petitioner's application for a writ of *certiorari* limited to his challenge to the imposition of the death sentences in this case as "cruel and unusual" punishment in violation of the Eighth and the Fourteenth Amendments. 423 U.S. 1082 (1976).

. . . We address initially the basic contention that the punishment of death for the crime of murder is, under all circumstances, "cruel and unusual" in violation of the Eighth and Fourteenth Amendments of the Constitution. . . .

The Court on a number of occasions has both assumed and asserted the constitutionality of capital punishment. In several cases that assumption provided a necessary foundation for the decision, as the Court was asked to decide whether a particular method of carrying out a capital sentence would be allowed to stand under the Eighth Amendment. But until *Furman* v. *Georgia*, 408 U.S. 238 (1972), the Court never confronted squarely the fundamental claim that the punishment of death always, regardless of the enormity of the offense or the procedure followed in imposing the sentence, is cruel and unusual punishment in violation of the Constitution. Although this issue was presented and addressed in *Furman*, it was not resolved by the Court. Four Justices would have held that capital punishment is not unconstitutional *per se*; two Justices would have reached the opposite conclusion; and three Justices, while agreeing that the statutes then before the Court were invalid as applied, left open the question whether such punishment may ever be imposed. We now hold that the punishment of death does not invariably violate the Constitution.

A.

The history of the prohibition of "cruel and unusual" punishment already has been reviewed at length. The phrase first appeared in the English Bill of Rights of 1689, which was drafted by Parliament at the accession of William and Mary. See Granucci, "Nor Cruel and Unusual Punishments Inflicted: The Original Meaning," 57 Calif. L. Rev. 839, 852–853 (1969). The English version appears to have been directed against punishments unauthorized by statute and beyond the jurisdiction of the sentencing court, as well as those disproportionate to the offense involved. *Id.*, at 860. The American draftsmen, who adopted the English phrasing in drafting the Eighth Amendment, were primarily concerned, however, with proscribing "tortures" and other "barbarous" methods of punishment." *Id.*, at 842.

In the earliest cases raising Eighth Amendment claims, the Court focused on particular methods of execution to determine whether they were too cruel to pass constitutional muster. The constitutionality of the sentence of death itself was not at issue, and the criterion used to evaluate the mode of execution was its similarity to "torture" and other "barbarous" methods. See *Wilkerson* v. *Utah*, 99 U.S. 130, 136 (1879) ("[I]t is safe to affirm that punishments of torture . . . and all others in the same line of unnecessary cruelty, are forbidden by that amendment. . . ."); *In re Kemmler*, 136 U.S. 436, 447 (1890) ("Punishments are cruel when they involve torture or a lingering death. . . ."). See also *Louisiana ex rel. Francis* v. *Resweber*, 329 U.S. 459, 464 (1947) (second attempt at electrocution found not to violate Eighth Amendment, since failure of initial execution attempt was "an unforeseeable accident" and "[t]here [was] no purpose to inflict unnecessary pain nor any unnecessary pain involved in the proposed execution").

But the Court has not confined the prohibition embodied in the Eighth Amendment to "barbarous" methods that were generally outlawed in the 18th century. Instead, the Amendment has been interpreted in a flexible and dynamic manner. The Court early recognized that "a principle to be vital must be capable of wider application than the mischief which gave it birth." *Weems* v. *United States*,

217 U.S. 349, 373 (1910). Thus, the Clause forbidding "cruel and unusual" punishments "is not fastened to the obsolete but may acquire meaning as public opinion becomes enlightened by a humane justice." *Id.*, at 378. See also *Furman* v. *Georgia*, 408 U.S., at 429–430 (POWELL, J., dissenting); *Trop* v. *Dulles*, 356 U.S. 86, 100–101 (1958) (plurality opinion).

In *Weems* the Court addressed the constitutionality of the Philippine punishment of *cadena temporal* for the crime of falsifying an official document. That punishment included imprisonment for at least 12 years and one day, in chains, at hard and painful labor; the loss of many basic civil rights; and subjection to lifetime surveillance. Although the Court acknowledged the possibility that "the cruelty of pain" may be present in the challenged punishment, 217 U.S., at 366, it did not rely on that factor, for it rejected the proposition that the Eighth Amendment reaches only punishments that are "inhuman and barbarous, torture and the like." *Id.*, at 368. Rather, the Court focused on the lack of proportion between the crime and the offense:

> Such penalties for such offenses amaze those who have formed their conception of the relation of a state to even its offending citizens from the practice of the American commonwealths, and believe that it is a precept of justice that punishment for crime should be graduated and proportioned to offense. *Id.*, at 366–367.

Later, in *Trop* v. *Dulles, supra,* the Court reviewed the constitutionality of the punishment of denationalization imposed upon a soldier who escaped from an Army stockade and became a deserter for one day. Although the concept of proportionality was not the basis of the holding, the plurality observed *in dicta* that "[f]ines, imprisonment and even execution may be imposed depending upon the enormity of the crime." 356 U.S., at 100.

The substantive limits imposed by the Eighth Amendment on what can be made criminal and punished were discussed in *Robinson* v. *California*, 370 U.S. 660 (1962). The Court found unconstitutional a state statute that made the status of being addicted to a narcotic drug a criminal offense. It held, in effect, that it is "cruel and unusual" to impose any punishment at all for the mere status of addiction. The cruelty in the abstract of the actual sentence imposed was irrelevant: "Even one day in prison would be a cruel and unusual punishment for the 'crime' of having a common cold." *Id.*, at 667. Most recently, in *Furman* v. *Georgia, supra,* three Justices in separate concurring opinions found the Eighth Amendment applicable to procedures employed to select convicted defendants for the sentence of death.

It is clear from the foregoing precedents that the Eighth Amendment has not been regarded as a static concept. As MR. CHIEF JUSTICE WARREN said, in an oftquoted phrase, "[t]he Amendment must draw its meaning from the evolving standards of decency that mark the progress of a maturing society." *Trop* v. *Dulles, supra,* at 101. See also *Jackson* v. *Bishop*, 404 F.2d 571, 579 (CA8 1968). Cf. *Robinson* v. *California, supra,* at 666. Thus, an assessment of contemporary values concerning the infliction of a challenged sanction is relevant to the application of the Eighth Amendment. As we develop below more fully, see *infra,* at 175–176, this assessment does not call for a subjective judgment. It requires, rather, that we look to objective indicia that reflect the public attitude toward a given sanction.

But our cases also make clear that public perceptions of standards of decency with respect to criminal sanctions are not conclusive. A penalty also must accord with "the dignity of man," which is the "basic concept underlying the Eighth Amendment." *Trop* v. *Dulles, supra,* at 100 (plurality opinion). This means, at least, that the punishment not be "excessive." When a form of punishment in the ab-

stract (in this case, whether capital punishment may ever be imposed as a sanction for murder) rather than in the particular (the propriety of death as a penalty to be applied to a specific defendant for a specific crime) is under consideration, the inquiry into "excessiveness" has two aspects. First, the punishment must not involve the unnecessary and wanton infliction of pain. *Furman* v. *Georgia, supra*, at 392–393 (BURGER, C. J., dissenting). See *Wilkerson* v. *Utah*, 99 U.S., at 136; *Weems* v. *United States, supra*, at 381. Second, the punishment must not be grossly out of proportion to the severity of the crime. *Trop* v. *Dulles, supra*, at 100 (plurality opinion) (dictum); *Weems* v. *United States, supra*, at 367.

B.

Of course, the requirements of the Eighth Amendment must be applied with an awareness of the limited role to be played by the courts. This does not mean that judges have no role to play, for the Eighth Amendment is a restraint upon the exercise of legislative power.

"Judicial review, by definition, often involves a conflict between judicial and legislative judgment as to what the Constitution means or requires. In this respect, Eighth Amendment cases come to us in no different posture. It seems conceded by all that the Amendment imposes some obligations on the judiciary to judge the constitutionality of punishment and that there are punishments that the Amendment would bar whether legislatively approved or not." *Furman* v. *Georgia*, 408 U.S., at 313–314 (WHITE, J., concurring). But, while we have an obligation to insure that constitutional bounds are not overreached, we may not act as judges as we might as legislators.

"Courts are not representative bodies. They are not designed to be a good reflex of a democratic society. Their judgment is best informed, and therefore most dependable, within narrow limits. Their essential quality is detachment, founded on independence. History teaches that the independence of the judiciary is jeopardized when courts become embroiled in the passions of the day and assume primary responsibility in choosing between competing political, economic and social pressures." *Dennis* v. *United States*, 341 U.S. 494, 525 (1951) (FRANKFURTER, J., concurring in affirmance of judgment).

Therefore, in assessing a punishment selected by a democratically elected legislature against the constitutional measure, we presume its validity. We may not require the legislature to select the least severe penalty possible so long as the penalty selected is not cruelly inhumane or disproportionate to the crime involved. And a heavy burden rests on those who would attack the judgment of the representatives of the people.

This is true in part because the constitutional test is intertwined with an assessment of contemporary standards and the legislative judgment weighs heavily in ascertaining such standards. "[I]n a democratic society legislatures, not courts, are constituted to respond to the will and consequently the moral values of the people." *Furman* v. *Georgia, supra*, at 383 (BURGER, C. J., dissenting). The deference we owe to the decisions of the state legislatures under our federal system, 408 U.S., at 465–470 (REHNQUIST, J., dissenting), is enhanced where the specification of punishments is concerned, for "these are peculiarly questions of legislative policy." *Gore* v. *United States*, 357 U.S. 386, 393 (1958). Cf. *Robinson* v. *California*, 370 U.S., at 664–665; *Trop* v. *Dulles*, 356 U.S., at 103 (plurality opinion); *In re Kemmler*, 136 U.S., at 447. Caution is necessary lest this Court become, "under the aegis of the Cruel and Unusual Punishment Clause, the ultimate arbiter of the standards of

criminal responsibility . . . throughout the country." *Powell* v. *Texas*, 392 U.S. 514, 533 (1968) (plurality opinion). A decision that a given punishment is impermissible under the Eighth Amendment cannot be reversed short of a constitutional amendment. The ability of the people to express their preference through the normal democratic processes, as well as through ballot referenda, is shut off. Revisions cannot be made in the light of further experience. See *Furman* v. *Georgia, supra,* at 461–462 (POWELL, J., dissenting).

C.

In the discussion to this point we have sought to identify the principles and considerations that guide a court in addressing an Eighth Amendment claim. We now consider specifically whether the sentence of death for the crime of murder is a *per se* violation of the Eighth and Fourteenth Amendments to the Constitution. We note first that history and precedent strongly support a negative answer to this question.

The imposition of the death penalty for the crime of murder has a long history of acceptance both in the United States and in England. The common-law rule imposed a mandatory death sentence on all convicted murderers. *McGautha* v. *California,* 402 U.S. 183, 197–198 (1971). And the penalty continued to be used into the 20th century by most American States, although the breadth of the common-law rule was diminished, initially by narrowing the class of murders to be punished by death and subsequently by widespread adoption of laws expressly granting juries the discretion to recommend mercy. *Id.,* at 199–200. See *Woodson* v. *North Carolina, post,* at 289–292.

It is apparent from the text of the Constitution itself that the existence of capital punishment was accepted by the Framers. At the time the Eighth Amendment was ratified, capital punishment was a common sanction in every State. Indeed, the First Congress of the United States enacted legislation providing death as the penalty for specified crimes. C. 9, 1 Stat. 112 (1790). The Fifth Amendment, adopted at the same time as the Eighth, contemplated the continued existence of the capital sanction by imposing certain limits on the prosecution of capital cases:

> No person shall be held to answer for a capital, or otherwise infamous crime, unless on a presentment or indictment of a Grand Jury . . . ; nor shall any person be subject for the same offense to be twice put in jeopardy of life or limb; . . . nor be deprived of life, liberty, or property, without due process of law. . . .

And the Fourteenth Amendment, adopted over three-quarters of a century later, similarly contemplates the existence of the capital sanction in providing that no State shall deprive any person of "life, liberty, or property" without due process of law.

For nearly two centuries, this Court, repeatedly and often expressly, has recognized that capital punishment is not invalid per se. In *Wilkerson* v. *Utah,* 99 U.S., at 134–135, where the Court found no constitutional violation in inflicting death by public shooting, it said:

> Cruel and unusual punishments are forbidden by the Constitution, but the authorities referred to are quite sufficient to show that the punishment of shooting as a mode of executing the death penalty for the crime of murder in the first degree is not included in that category, within the meaning of the eighth amendment.

Rejecting the contention that death by electrocution was "cruel and unusual," the Court in *In re Kemmler, supra,* at 447, reiterated:

[T]he punishment of death is not cruel, within the meaning of that word as used in the Constitution. It implies there something inhuman and barbarous, something more than the mere extinguishment of life.

Again, in *Louisiana ex rel. Francis v. Resweber*, 329 U.S., at 464, the Court remarked: "The cruelty against which the Constitution protects a convicted man is cruelty inherent in the method of punishment, not the necessary suffering involved in any method employed to extinguish life humanely." And in *Trop v. Dulles*, 356 U.S., at 99, MR. CHIEF JUSTICE WARREN, for himself and three other Justices, wrote:

> Whatever the arguments may be against capital punishment, both on moral grounds and in terms of accomplishing the purposes of punishment . . . the death penalty has been employed throughout our history, and, in a day when it is still widely accepted, it cannot be said to violate the constitutional concept of cruelty.

Four years ago, the petitioners in *Furman* and its companion cases predicated their argument primarily upon the asserted proposition that standards of decency had evolved to the point where capital punishment no longer could be tolerated. The petitioners in those cases said, in effect, that the evolutionary process had come to an end, and that standards of decency required that the Eighth Amendment be construed finally as prohibiting capital punishment for any crime regardless of its depravity and impact on society. This view was accepted by two Justices. Three other Justices were unwilling to go so far; focusing on the procedures by which convicted defendants were selected for the death penalty rather than on the actual punishment inflicted, they joined in the conclusion that the statutes before the Court were constitutionally invalid.

The petitioners in the capital cases before the Court today renew the "standards of decency" argument, but developments during the four years since *Furman* have undercut substantially the assumptions upon which their argument rested. Despite the continuing debate, dating back to the 19th century, over the morality and utility of capital punishment, it is now evident that a large proportion of American society continues to regard it as an appropriate and necessary criminal sanction.

The most marked indication of society's endorsement of the death penalty for murder is the legislative response to Furman. The legislatures of at least 35 States have enacted new statutes that provide for the death penalty for at least some crimes that result in the death of another person. And the Congress of the United States, in 1974, enacted a statute providing the death penalty for aircraft piracy that results in death. These recently adopted statutes have attempted to address the concerns expressed by the Court in *Furman* primarily (i) by specifying the factors to be weighed and the procedures to be followed in deciding when to impose a capital sentence, or (ii) by making the death penalty mandatory for specified crimes. But all of the post-*Furman* statutes make clear that capital punishment itself has not been rejected by the elected representatives of the people.

In the only statewide referendum occurring since *Furman* and brought to our attention, the people of California adopted a constitutional amendment that authorized capital punishment, in effect negating a prior ruling by the Supreme Court of California in *People v. Anderson*, 6 Cal. 3d 628, 493 P.2d 880, cert. denied, 406 U.S. 958 (1972), that the death penalty violated the California Constitution.

The jury also is a significant and reliable objective index of contemporary values because it is so directly involved. See *Furman v. Georgia*, 408 U.S., at 439–440 (POWELL, J., dissenting). See generally Powell, *Jury Trial of Crimes*, 23 Wash. & Lee L. Rev. 1 (1966). The Court has said that "one of the most important func-

tions any jury can perform in making . . . a selection [between life imprisonment and death for a defendant convicted in a capital case] is to maintain a link between contemporary community values and the penal system." *Witherspoon* v. *Illinois*, 391 U.S. 510, 519 n. 15 (1968). It may be true that evolving standards have influenced juries in recent decades to be more discriminating in imposing the sentence of death. But the relative infrequency of jury verdicts imposing the death sentence does not indicate rejection of capital punishment per se. Rather, the reluctance of juries in many cases to impose the sentence may well reflect the humane feeling that this most irrevocable of sanctions should be reserved for a small number of extreme cases. See *Furman* v. *Georgia, supra,* at 388 (BURGER, C. J., dissenting). Indeed, the actions of juries in many States since *Furman* are fully compatible with the legislative judgments, reflected in the new statutes, as to the continued utility and necessity of capital punishment in appropriate cases. At the close of 1974 at least 254 persons had been sentenced to death since *Furman,* and by the end of March 1976, more than 460 persons were subject to death sentences.

As we have seen, however, the Eighth Amendment demands more than that a challenged punishment be acceptable to contemporary society. The Court also must ask whether it comports with the basic concept of human dignity at the core of the Amendment. *Trop* v. *Dulles,* 356 U.S., at 100 (plurality opinion). Although we cannot "invalidate a category of penalties because we deem less severe penalties adequate to serve the ends of penology," *Furman* v. *Georgia, supra,* at 451 (POWELL, J., dissenting), the sanction imposed cannot be so totally without penological justification that it results in the gratuitous infliction of suffering. Cf. *Wilkerson* v. *Utah,* 99 U.S., at 135–136; *In re Kemmler,* 136 U.S., at 447. . . .

The death penalty is said to serve two principal social purposes: retribution and deterrence of capital crimes by prospective offenders.

In part, capital punishment is an expression of society's moral outrage at particularly offensive conduct. This function may be unappealing to many, but it is essential in an ordered society that asks its citizens to rely on legal processes rather than self-help to vindicate their wrongs.

> The instinct for retribution is part of the nature of man, and channeling that instinct in the administration of criminal justice serves an important purpose in promoting the stability of a society governed by law. When people begin to believe that organized society is unwilling or unable to impose upon criminal offenders the punishment they "deserve," then there are sown the seeds of anarchy—of self-help, vigilante justice, and lynch law. *Furman* v. *Georgia, supra,* at 308 (STEWART, J., concurring).

"Retribution is no longer the dominant objective of the criminal law," *Williams* v. *New York,* 337 U.S. 241, 248 (1949), but neither is it a forbidden objective nor one inconsistent with our respect for the dignity of men. *Furman* v. *Georgia,* 408 U.S., at 394–395 (BURGER, C. J., dissenting); *id.,* at 452–454 (POWELL, J., dissenting); *Powell* v. *Texas,* 392 U.S., at 531, 535–536 (plurality opinion). Indeed, the decision that capital punishment may be the appropriate sanction in extreme cases is an expression of the community's belief that certain crimes are themselves so grievous an affront to humanity that the only adequate response may be the penalty of death.

Statistical attempts to evaluate the worth of the death penalty as a deterrent to crimes by potential offenders have occasioned a great deal of debate. The results simply have been inconclusive. As one opponent of capital punishment has said:

> [A]fter all possible inquiry, including the probing of all possible methods of inquiry, we do not know, and for systematic and easily visible reasons cannot know, what the truth about this "deterrent" effect may be. . . .

The inescapable flaw is . . . that social conditions in any state are not constant through time, and that social conditions are not the same in any two states. If an effect were observed (and the observed effects, one way or another, are not large) then one could not at all tell whether any of this effect is attributable to the presence or absence of capital punishment. A "scientific"—that is to say, a soundly based—conclusion is simply impossible, and no methodological path out of this tangle suggests itself. C. Black, *Capital Punishment: The Inevitability of Caprice and Mistake* 25–26 (1974)

Although some of the studies suggest that the death penalty may not function as a significantly greater deterrent than lesser penalties, there is no convincing empirical evidence either supporting or refuting this view. We may nevertheless assume safely that there are murderers, such as those who act in passion, for whom the threat of death has little or no deterrent effect. But for many others, the death penalty undoubtedly is a significant deterrent. There are carefully contemplated murders, such as murder for hire, where the possible penalty of death may well enter into the cold calculus that precedes the decision to act. And there are some categories of murder, such as murder by a life prisoner, where other sanctions may not be adequate.

The value of capital punishment as a deterrent of crime is a complex factual issue, the resolution of which properly rests with the legislatures, which can evaluate the results of statistical studies in terms of their own local conditions and with a flexibility of approach that is not available to the courts. *Furman* v. *Georgia, supra,* at 403–405 (BURGER, C. J., dissenting). Indeed, many of the post-*Furman* statutes reflect just such a responsible effort to define those crimes and those criminals for which capital punishment is most probably an effective deterrent.

In sum, we cannot say that the judgment of the Georgia Legislature that capital punishment may be necessary in some cases is clearly wrong. Considerations of federalism, as well as respect for the ability of a legislature to evaluate, in terms of its particular State, the moral consensus concerning the death penalty and its social utility as a sanction, require us to conclude, in the absence of more convincing evidence, that the infliction of death as a punishment for murder is not without justification and thus is not unconstitutionally severe.

Finally, we must consider whether the punishment of death is disproportionate in relation to the crime for which it is imposed. There is no question that death as a punishment is unique in its severity and irrevocability. *Furman* v. *Georgia,* 408 U.S., at 286–291 (BRENNAN, J., concurring); *id.,* at 306 (STEWART, J., concurring). When a defendant's life is at stake, the Court has been particularly sensitive to insure that every safeguard is observed. *Powell* v. *Alabama,* 287 U.S. 45, 71 (1932); *Reid* v. *Covert,* 354 U.S. 1, 77 (1957) (HARLAN, J., concurring in result). But we are concerned here only with the imposition of capital punishment for the crime of murder, and when a life has been taken deliberately by the offender, we cannot say that the punishment is invariably disproportionate to the crime. It is an extreme sanction, suitable to the most extreme of crimes.

We hold that the death penalty is not a form of punishment that may never be imposed, regardless of the circumstances of the offense, regardless of the character of the offender, and regardless of the procedure followed in reaching the decision to impose it.

[Significant portions of this opinion have been omitted.]

IV.

We now consider whether Georgia may impose the death penalty on the petitioner in this case.

A.

While *Furman* did not hold that the infliction of the death penalty per se violates the Constitution's ban on cruel and unusual punishments, it did recognize that the penalty of death is different in kind from any other punishment imposed under our system of criminal justice. Because of the uniqueness of the death penalty, *Furman* held that it could not be imposed under sentencing procedures that created a substantial risk that it would be inflicted in an arbitrary and capricious manner. Mr. Justice White concluded that "the death penalty is exacted with great infrequency even for the most atrocious crimes and . . . there is no meaningful basis for distinguishing the few cases in which it is imposed from the many cases in which it is not." 408 U.S., at 313 (concurring). Indeed, the death sentences examined by the Court in *Furman* were "cruel and unusual in the same way that being struck by lightning is cruel and unusual. For, of all the people convicted of [capital crimes], many just as reprehensible as these, the petitioners [in *Furman* were] among a capriciously selected random handful upon whom the sentence of death has in fact been imposed. . . . [T]he Eighth and Fourteenth Amendments cannot tolerate the infliction of a sentence of death under legal systems that permit this unique penalty to be so wantonly and so freakishly imposed." *Id.*, at 309–310 (Stewart, J., concurring).

Furman mandates that where discretion is afforded a sentencing body on a matter so grave as the determination of whether a human life should be taken or spared, that discretion must be suitably directed and limited so as to minimize the risk of wholly arbitrary and capricious action.

It is certainly not a novel proposition that discretion in the area of sentencing be exercised in an informed manner. We have long recognized that "[f]or the determination of sentences, justice generally requires . . . that there be taken into account the circumstances of the offense together with the character and propensities of the offender." *Pennsylvania ex rel. Sullivan* v. *Ashe*, 302 U.S. 51, 55 (1937). See also *Williams* v. *Oklahoma*, 358 U.S. 576, 585 (1959); *Williams* v. *New York*, 337 U.S., at 247. Otherwise, "the system cannot function in a consistent and a rational manner." American Bar Association *Project on Standards for Criminal Justice, Sentencing Alternatives and Procedures* 4.1 (a), Commentary, p. 201 (App. Draft 1968). See also President's *Commission on Law Enforcement and Administration of Justice*, The Challenge of Crime in a Free Society 144 (1967); ALI, Model Penal Code 7.07, Comment 1, pp. 52–53 (Tent. Draft No. 2, 1954).

The cited studies assumed that the trial judge would be the sentencing authority. If an experienced trial judge, who daily faces the difficult task of imposing sentences, has a vital need for accurate information about a defendant and the crime he committed in order to be able to impose a rational sentence in the typical criminal case, then accurate sentencing information is an indispensable prerequisite to a reasoned determination of whether a defendant shall live or die by a jury of people who may never before have made a sentencing decision.

Jury sentencing has been considered desirable in capital cases in order "to maintain a link between contemporary community values and the penal system—a link without which the determination of punishment could hardly reflect 'the evolving standards of decency that mark the progress of a maturing society.' " But it creates special problems. Much of the information that is relevant to the sentencing decision may have no relevance to the question of guilt, or may even be extremely prejudicial to a fair determination of that question. This problem, however, is scarcely insurmountable. Those who have studied the question suggest that a bifurcated pro-

cedure—one in which the question of sentence is not considered until the determination of guilt has been made—is the best answer. The drafters of the Model Penal Code concluded:

> [If a unitary proceeding is used] the determination of the punishment must be based on less than all the evidence that has a bearing on that issue, such for example as a previous criminal record of the accused, or evidence must be admitted on the ground that it is relevant to sentence, though it would be excluded as irrelevant or prejudicial with respect to guilt or innocence alone. Trial lawyers understandably have little confidence in a solution that admits the evidence and trusts to an instruction to the jury that it should be considered only in determining the penalty and disregarded in assessing guilt.
>
> . . . The obvious solution . . . is to bifurcate the proceeding, abiding strictly by the rules of evidence until and unless there is a conviction, but once guilt has been determined opening the record to the further information that is relevant to sentence. This is the analogue of the procedure in the ordinary case when capital punishment is not in issue; the court conducts a separate inquiry before imposing sentence. ALI, Model Penal Code 201.6, Comment 5, pp. 74–75 (Tent. Draft No. 9, 1959).

See also *Spencer* v. *Texas*, 385 U.S. 554, 567–569 (1967); Report of the Royal Commission on Capital Punishment, 1949–1953, Cmd. 8932, 555, 574; Knowlton, *Problems of Jury Discretion in Capital Cases*, 101 U. Pa. L. Rev. 1099, 1135–1136 (1953). When a human life is at stake and when the jury must have information prejudicial to the question of guilt but relevant to the question of penalty in order to impose a rational sentence, a bifurcated system is more likely to ensure elimination of the constitutional deficiencies identified in *Furman.*

But the provision of relevant information under fair procedural rules is not alone sufficient to guarantee that the information will be properly used in the imposition of punishment, especially if sentencing is performed by a jury. Since the members of a jury will have had little, if any, previous experience in sentencing, they are unlikely to be skilled in dealing with the information they are given. See American Bar Association *Project on Standards for Criminal Justice, Sentencing Alternatives and Procedures*, 1.1 (b), Commentary, pp. 46–47 (Approved Draft 1968); President's Commission on Law Enforcement and Administration of Justice: The Challenge of Crime in a Free Society, Task Force Report: The Courts 26 (1967). To the extent that this problem is inherent in jury sentencing, it may not be totally correctible. It seems clear, however, that the problem will be alleviated if the jury is given guidance regarding the factors about the crime and the defendant that the State, representing organized society, deems particularly relevant to the sentencing decision.

The idea that a jury should be given guidance in its decisionmaking is also hardly a novel proposition. Juries are invariably given careful instructions on the law and how to apply it before they are authorized to decide the merits of a lawsuit. It would be virtually unthinkable to follow any other course in a legal system that has traditionally operated by following prior precedents and fixed rules of law. See *Gasoline Products Co.* v. *Champlin Refining Co.*, 283 U.S. 494, 498 (1931); Fed. Rule Civ. Proc. 51. When erroneous instructions are given, retrial is often required. It is quite simply a hallmark of our legal system that juries be carefully and adequately guided in their deliberations.

While some have suggested that standards to guide a capital jury's sentencing deliberation are impossible to formulate, the fact is that such standards have been developed. When the drafters of the Model Penal Code faced this problem, they concluded "that it is within the realm of possibility to point to the main circumstances of aggravation and of mitigation that should be weighed and weighed against

each other when they are presented in a concrete case." ALI, Model Penal Code 201.6, Comment 3, p. 71 (Tent. Draft No. 9, 1959). While such standards are by necessity somewhat general, they do provide guidance to the sentencing authority and thereby reduce the likelihood that it will impose a sentence that fairly can be called capricious or arbitrary. Where the sentencing authority is required to specify the factors it relied upon in reaching its decision, the further safeguard of meaningful appellate review is available to ensure that death sentences are not imposed capriciously or in a freakish manner.

In summary, the concerns expressed in *Furman* that the penalty of death not be imposed in an arbitrary or capricious manner can be met by a carefully drafted statute that ensures that the sentencing authority is given adequate information and guidance. As a general proposition these concerns are best met by a system that provides for a bifurcated proceeding at which the sentencing authority is apprised of the information relevant to the imposition of sentence and provided with standards to guide its use of the information.

We do not intend to suggest that only the above-described procedures would be permissible under *Furman* or that any sentencing system constructed along these general lines would inevitably satisfy the concerns of *Furman*, for each distinct system must be examined on an individual basis. Rather, we have embarked upon this general exposition to make clear that it is possible to construct capital-sentencing systems capable of meeting *Furman*'s constitutional concerns.

B.

We now turn to consideration of the constitutionality of Georgia's capital-sentencing procedures. In the wake of *Furman*, Georgia amended its capital punishment statute, but chose not to narrow the scope of its murder provisions. See Part II, *supra*. Thus, now as before *Furman*, in Georgia "[a] person commits murder when he unlawfully and with malice aforethought, either express or implied, causes the death of another human being." Ga. Code Ann., 26-1101 (a) (1972). All persons convicted of murder "shall be punished by death or by imprisonment for life." 26-1101 (c) (1972).

Georgia did act, however, to narrow the class of murderers subject to capital punishment by specifying 10 statutory aggravating circumstances, one of which must be found by the jury to exist beyond a reasonable doubt before a death sentence can ever be imposed. In addition, the jury is authorized to consider any other appropriate aggravating or mitigating circumstances. 27-2534.1 (b) (Supp. 1975). The jury is not required to find any mitigating circumstance in order to make a recommendation of mercy that is binding on the trial court, see 27-2302 (Supp. 1975), but it must find a statutory aggravating circumstance before recommending a sentence of death.

These procedures require the jury to consider the circumstances of the crime and the criminal before it recommends sentence. No longer can a Georgia jury do as *Furman*'s jury did: reach a finding of the defendant's guilt and then, without guidance or direction, decide whether he should live or die. Instead, the jury's attention is directed to the specific circumstances of the crime: Was it committed in the course of another capital felony? Was it committed for money? Was it committed upon a peace officer or judicial officer? Was it committed in a particularly heinous way or in a manner that endangered the lives of many persons? In addition, the jury's attention is focused on the characteristics of the person who committed the crime: Does he have a record of prior convictions for capital offenses?

Are there any special facts about this defendant that mitigate against imposing capital punishment (e.g., his youth, the extent of his cooperation with the police, his emotional state at the time of the crime). As a result, while some jury discretion still exists, "the discretion to be exercised is controlled by clear and objective standards so as to produce non-discriminatory application." *Coley* v. *State*, 231 Ga. 829, 834, 204 S. E. 2d 612, 615 (1974).

As an important additional safeguard against arbitrariness and caprice, the Georgia statutory scheme provides for automatic appeal of all death sentences to the State's Supreme Court. That court is required by statute to review each sentence of death and determine whether it was imposed under the influence of passion or prejudice, whether the evidence supports the jury's finding of a statutory aggravating circumstance, and whether the sentence is disproportionate compared to those sentences imposed in similar cases. 27-2537 (c) (Supp. 1975).

In short, Georgia's new sentencing procedures require as a prerequisite to the imposition of the death penalty, specific jury findings as to the circumstances of the crime or the character of the defendant. Moreover, to guard further against a situation comparable to that presented in *Furman*, the Supreme Court of Georgia compares each death sentence with the sentences imposed on similarly situated defendants to ensure that the sentence of death in a particular case is not disproportionate. On their face these procedures seem to satisfy the concerns of *Furman*. No longer should there be "no meaningful basis for distinguishing the few cases in which [the death penalty] is imposed from the many cases in which it is not." 408 U.S., at 313 (WHITE, J., concurring). . . .

. . . For the reasons expressed in this opinion, we hold that the statutory system under which Gregg was sentenced to death does not violate the Constitution. Accordingly, the judgment of the Georgia Supreme Court is affirmed.

It is so ordered.

MR. JUSTICE WHITE, with whom THE CHIEF JUSTICE and MR. JUSTICE REHNQUIST join, concurring in the judgment. [Omitted.]

Statement of THE CHIEF JUSTICE and MR. JUSTICE REHNQUIST:

We concur in the judgment and join the opinion of MR. JUSTICE WHITE, agreeing with its analysis that Georgia's system of capital punishment comports with the Court's holding in *Furman* v. *Georgia*, 408 U.S. 238 (1972).

MR. JUSTICE BLACKMUN, concurring in the judgment.

I concur in the judgment. See *Furman* v. *Georgia*, 408 U.S. 238, 405–414 (1972) (BLACKMUN, J., dissenting), and *id.*, at 375 (BURGER, C. J., dissenting); *id.*, at 414 (POWELL, J., dissenting); *id.*, at 465 (REHNQUIST, J., dissenting).

MR. JUSTICE BRENNAN, dissenting.

The Cruel and Unusual Punishments Clause "must draw its meaning from the evolving standards of decency that mark the progress of a maturing society." The opinions of MR. JUSTICE STEWART, MR. JUSTICE POWELL, and MR. JUSTICE STEVENS today hold that "evolving standards of decency" require focus not on the essence of the death penalty itself but primarily upon the procedures employed by the State to single out persons to suffer the penalty of death. Those opinions hold further that, so viewed, the Clause invalidates the mandatory infliction of the death penalty but not its infliction under sentencing procedures that MR. JUSTICE STEWART, MR. JUSTICE POWELL, and MR. JUSTICE STEVENS conclude adequately safeguard against the risk that the death penalty was imposed in an arbitrary and capricious manner.

In *Furman* v. *Georgia*, 408 U.S. 238, 257 (1972) (concurring opinion), I read "evolving standards of decency" as requiring focus upon the essence of the death

penalty itself and not primarily or solely upon the procedures under which the determination to inflict the penalty upon a particular person was made. I there said:

> From the beginning of our Nation, the punishment of death has stirred acute public controversy. Although pragmatic arguments for and against the punishment have been frequently advanced, this longstanding and heated controversy cannot be explained solely as the result of differences over the practical wisdom of a particular government policy. At bottom, the battle has been waged on moral grounds. The country has debated whether a society for which the dignity of the individual is the supreme value can, without a fundamental inconsistency, follow the practice of deliberately putting some of its members to death. In the United States, as in other nations of the western world, "the struggle about this punishment has been one between ancient and deeply rooted beliefs in retribution, atonement or vengeance on the one hand, and, on the other, beliefs in the personal value and dignity of the common man that were born of the democratic movement of the eighteenth century, as well as beliefs in the scientific approach to an understanding of the motive forces of human conduct, which are the result of the growth of the sciences of behavior during the nineteenth and twentieth centuries." It is this essentially moral conflict that forms the backdrop for the past changes in and the present operation of our system of imposing death as a punishment for crime.

That continues to be my view. For the Clause forbidding cruel and unusual punishments under our constitutional system of government embodies in unique degree moral principles restraining the punishments that our civilized society may impose on those persons who transgress its laws. Thus, I too say: "For myself, I do not hesitate to assert the proposition that the only way the law has progressed from the days of the rack, the screw and the wheel is the development of moral concepts, or, as stated by the Supreme Court ... the application of 'evolving standards of decency'...."

... I therefore would hold, on that ground alone, that death is today a cruel and unusual punishment prohibited by the Clause. "Justice of this kind is obviously no less shocking than the crime itself, and the new 'official' murder, far from offering redress for the offense committed against society, adds instead a second defilement to the first."

Mr. Justice Marshall, dissenting.

In *Furman* v. *Georgia*, 408 U.S. 238, 314 (1972) (concurring opinion), I set forth at some length my views on the basic issue presented to the Court in these cases. The death penalty, I concluded, is a cruel and unusual punishment prohibited by the Eighth and Fourteenth Amendments. That continues to be my view ...

What Do You Think?

1. Are you in favor of the death penalty? Justify your opinion.
2. Is the death penalty effective?
3. Explain the Georgia procedure in capital cases.

SUMMARY

- In no other area of the justice system is there a greater variance between states than in the sentencing phase of justice proceedings.

- The death penalty is a controversial penalty. Heated arguments have taken place over the years concerning the merits of the death penalty.

- Alternate sentencing procedure must be used in death penalty cases. In a few states that have the death penalty, a trial is first held to determine the guilt or innocence of the accused. If the accused is found guilty, a second trial is held to determine if the death penalty should be imposed or the defendant should be given life imprisonment. In other states with the death penalty, only one trial is held. The jury first deliberates on the guilt or innocence of the defendant, then makes a determination as to whether the death penalty should be imposed.

- Originally, fines were money and property taken from the offender and paid to the victim of the crime or to relatives. Eventually, the fines became a source of revenue to the king or the church, and the victim and relatives were left to civil remedies.

DISCUSSION QUESTIONS

1. What should be the purpose of punishment?
2. Does your state use the death penalty? If so, what procedures are used in capital cases?
3. Is punishment effective in deterring crime?

ENDNOTES

1. 408 U.S. 238 (1972).
2. 428 U.S. 280 (1976).
3. 428 U.S. 153 (1976).
4. 433 U.S. 584 (1977).
5. 446 U.S. 420 (1980).
6. 458 U.S. 782 (1982).
7. 399 U.S. 235 (1970).

/NDEX

hearsay, 93
Hearst, Patty, 205
Holmes, Oliver Wendell, 5
hot pursuit, 101
House of Commons, English, 92

identification
eyewitnesses, 295
procedures, 294
immunity, 211
transactional, 211
use and derivative, 212
impeachment, of witnesses, 267
Incorporation Controversy, 59
indictments, 61, 395
indigency, defined, 362
informants, 93, 111
information, gathering, 144
inquisitions, 216
inspections
administrative, 165
health and safety, 141
International Association of Chiefs of
Police, 295
interrogations, 201
covert, 211
in custody, 210
limitations on, 208
psychological, 208
right to counsel, 212
inventory, searches, 143, 149
issue, federal or state, 31

Jefferson, Thomas, 399
Jenkins, Noel, 119
Johnson, Herbert A., 27
Johnson, President Lyndon, 452
judiciary, 64
Judiciary Act of 1789, 323
jurisdiction, 28
jury
grand, 203, 394
right to trial by, 71
size, 342
justices, salaries, 65

Kamisar, Yale, 264
Kansas, court system, 37
King Aethelbert, 9
King George III, 104
King Henry II, 7

King John, 7
Krugman, Dr. Saul, 21

La Cosa Nostra, 328
law
case, 10
common, 8
statutory, 10
lineups, 202, 295
photographic, 296
Los Angeles, court rules, 2
Louisiana, 10
Lyttleton, Coke, 399

Maddox, James, 73
magistrate
neutral and detached, 94
role in charging, 61
Magna Carta, 7, 72, 394
mandamus, 400
Marshall, Chief Justice John, 48, 68, 69
Marshall, Justice Thurgood, 452
material, Brady, 84
materiality, standards of, 85
McWebb, Lawrence, 108
methodology of research, 13
Miranda, exceptions to, 210
misconduct, by police, 292
misdemeanor, sentencing, 451
models
crime control, 12
due process, 12
modus operandi, 113
motions
continuances, 322
discovery, 321
severance, 321
suppress evidence, 322

N.Y. Herald Tribune, 21
Narcotic Control Act of 1956, 102
national community, 90
National Advisory Commission on
Criminal Justice, 4
National Law Journal, 314
National Reporter System, 14
Neuman, Donald, 2, 27
Nevada, 10
New Mexico, 10
New York Medical Society, 21
New York Times, 314
notice
by prosecutor, 84
for searches, 96

Cases Cited